D0759181

The Complete Encyclopedia of *Garden Plants*

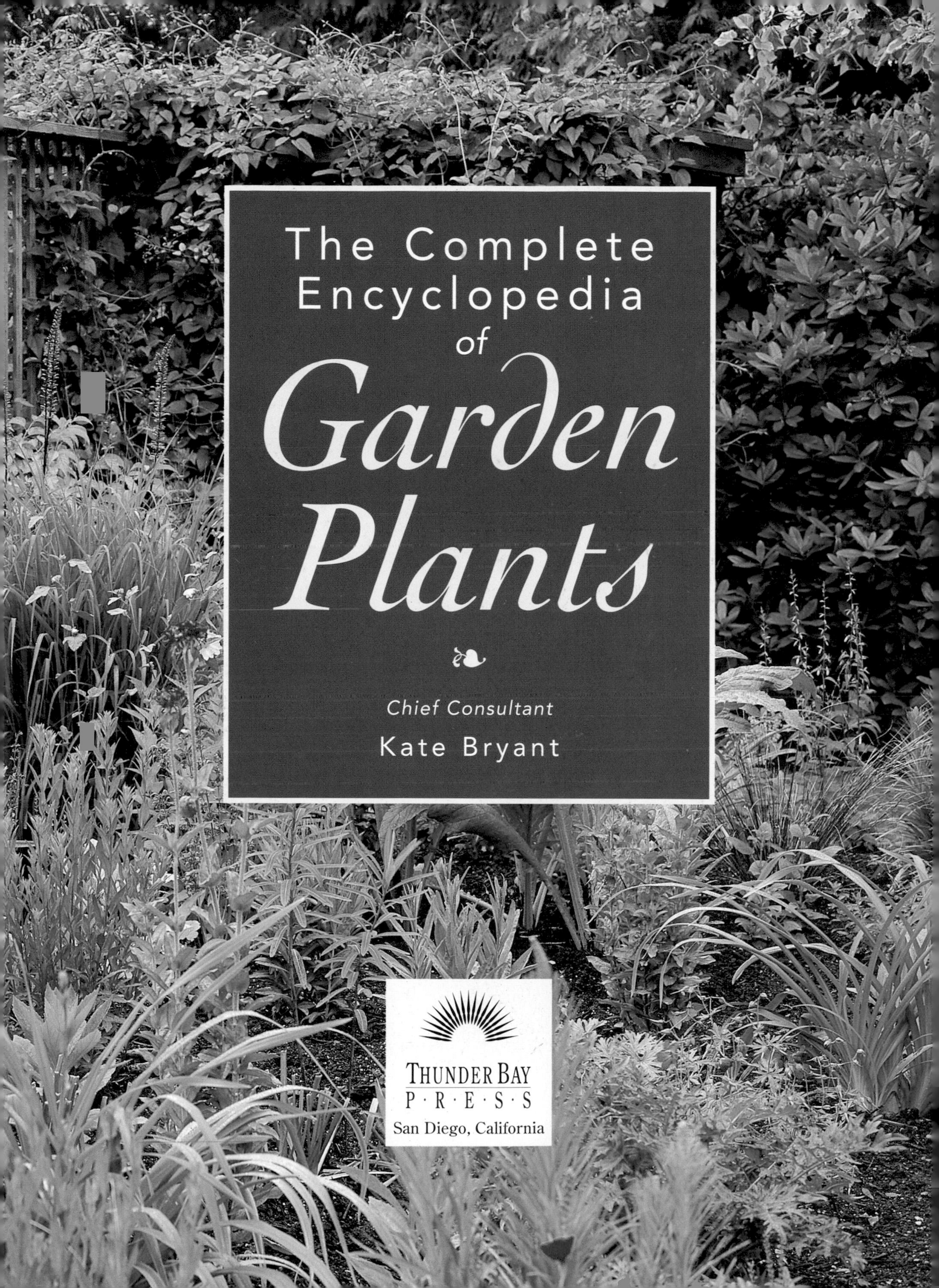
The Complete Encyclopedia of Garden Plants
Chief Consultant
Kate Bryant
THUNDER BAY PRESS
San Diego, California

Contents

A Garden for All Seasons

Growing Plants

As daily existence becomes busier and more complex throughout the industrialized world, plants play an increasingly essential role in our lives. Gardening, whether tending a few house plants on a windowsill or maintaining a large vegetable patch, provides a connection to the earth and the seasons that no other activity can offer. Gardening also provides a rewarding creative outlet, from choosing what plants will go where to deciding what mood or feeling the garden should have.

There are numerous factors to consider, whether renovating a garden or creating a new one from scratch. How much time can be devoted to maintenance? What kinds of plants are a priority, given the available space and local climate? These questions should be kept in mind when contemplating the many different plants that are available and the ways in which they can be used in the garden.

Structure and Screening

The "bones" of a garden are the defining structures upon which everything else is built. This can consist of outbuildings as well as patios, walls, fences, arbors, and paths. It can also include evergreen plants whose consistent year-round presence serves as a solid structure against which deciduous flowering plants can shine. Evergreens can also screen unwanted views and protect understory plants from excessive heat, cold, and wind.

There are evergreen backbone trees for almost every climate in the USA, from the slow-growing cold-tolerant black spruce *(Picea mariana)* to the stately palms of warmer climates. For smaller gardens, evergreens can range from relatively cold-tolerant shrubby hollies such as English holly *(Ilex aquifolium)* to the warm-climate California lilac (*Ceanothus* species). If winter light is desired, deciduous backbone trees and shrubs provide shade during the summer and permit the sun to reach the house and garden in winter.

Using Height and Layers

Many of the best gardens are multilayered and the plants

Above *English holly* (Ilex aquifolium) *brings color to the winter garden with its bright berries and glossy leaves.*
Left *Gardens with mixed plants offer visual interest through the use of different colors, shapes, sizes, and textures.*

occupy various niches, taking advantage of vertical space by growing through one another. This reflects the arrangement of natural woodland and rainforest environments—the canopy protects and supports the understory of low herbaceous or evergreen plants.

Of course, gardens in more open environments without trees grow in layers as well. Tall prairie perennials shade smaller ones, and on a dry Mediterranean hillside a number of tender plants grow through tough evergreens whose leaves offer protection from sun and wind. Even desert plants grow in layers, with small succulents that need shade nestled on the north side of bulkier cacti.

ABOVE *The globe-like heads of mophead hydrangea flowers provide color in summer; some plants have leaves with autumn color.* **LEFT** *Fuchsia flowers give extra value in the color department, as their delightful pendulous flowers are often bicolored.*

Color

Gardeners often create schemes that involve contrasting or harmonious colors, or revolve around single colors. And clever gardeners know that color can be found in more than just flowers. Green leaves can range from chartreuse to almost black-green, and may be variegated with cream, white, yellow, orange, pink, or red. Changing autumn leaf color adds a new dimension to the beauty of many plants like sweet gums (*Liquidambar* species) and oaks (*Quercus* species).

Fruits, stems, and bark can contribute striking color. *Cornus sanguinea* 'Midwinter Fire' offers orange-red branches in winter after its red autumn leaves have dropped. And the coppery red peeling bark of the paperbark maple *(Acer griseum)* seems to bring out the red tones in the garden during any season.

Plant Shapes

Variously shaped plants provide contrast and visual interest when juxtaposed in the garden. *Taxus baccata* 'Fastigiata' and *Berberis thunbergii* 'Helmond Pillar' offer a sense of vertical movement, while horizontal effects are supplied by the flattish flowerheads of yarrow (*Achillea* species) and sedum.

Ornamental grasses, particularly when they flower, create some of the most dramatically beautiful weeping shapes, as do old-fashioned flowering shrubs like hardy fuchsia *(Fuchsia magellanica)*, whose drooping flowers accentuate the plant's delicate weeping habit. Rounded plants include many lavender cultivars and hydrangeas; some have spherical flowerheads that mimic the rounded shape of the shrub itself.

Year-Round Interest

Spring through early autumn is the easy season, with many plants providing a huge range of colors, textures, shapes, forms, and fragrance. From late autumn through winter presents a challenge, and to gardeners in cold climates, the challenge is greater—although the options are surprisingly plentiful.

In most parts of the USA, late autumn bloomers include asters, sedums, Japanese anemone *(Anemone × hybrida)*, and a wide array of ornamental grasses. In warmer climates, schizostylis, toad lily (*Tricyrtis* species), and salvias extend the season even beyond the first light frosts. In the warmest regions, cymbidium orchids, lemon trees (*Citrus* species), and fragrant jasmine *(Jasminum polyanthum)* proffer their flowers in winter. In cold regions, these plants bloom prolifically indoors in a cool bright sunroom while, outdoors, the winterberry *(Ilex verticillata)* displays its bright red or orange berries against the gray sky, and the first forsythia and witch hazel (*Hamamelis* species) buds appear through the snow.

Caring for Your Garden

It is not difficult to create a beautiful and rewarding garden that requires less and less care over time. Choosing appropriate plants for a particular climate and aspect is critical—but equally important is the initial preparation that goes into the site, particularly soil improvement.

Soil Preparation

The most important factor in healthy plant growth rests in the soil. The first step is to determine what there is to work with. County cooperative extension agencies offer valuable information about local soils as well as testing services that evaluate soil structure, pH, and available nutrients.

Since soil composition varies widely, the amendments needed to build healthy soil vary—and most soils can use some improvement. Most garden plants grow best in well-drained, nutrient-rich, moisture-retentive soil. Compost is probably the most valuable tool. It increases the ability of sandy or gravelly soils to hold moisture and nutrients, and also improves the aeration and drainage of heavy clay. Good soil-building composts include aged leaf mold or animal manure, mushroom compost, kitchen waste compost, or aged bark or sawdust, liberally added to a depth of 2 ft (0.6 m).

Watering

Good water practices begin with careful initial design and planning. One good technique is to group plants requiring a lot of water in one area, accessible to a hose or a sprinkler system. Mulch is essential for retaining moisture in the soil while plants are becoming established.

Watering in the morning or evening reduces evaporation. Choose watering methods which reduce the amount of spray released into the atmosphere. Hand watering is the best way to introduce water directly into the soil around plants. But a carefully placed and monitored drip system can also be useful.

Fertilizing

While the best fertilizing practices should focus on building healthy soil that contains readily available nutrients for plants, there are situations where commercial fertilizer is useful. Vegetables, annual flowers, and container plants that need to produce rapid growth respond well to a quick boost. Otherwise, slow-release fertilizers are best, particularly applied early in the growing season.

County cooperative extension agencies often have information on local nutrient deficiencies and their solutions.

Left *Most trees and shrubs only need a layer of organic mulch for nutrition, preferably their own leaves.* **Below left** *Apart from the benefits mulching has for plant growing, the process also keeps gardens neater.* **Below right** *Earthworms aerate the soil as they move, and their waste adds nutrients.*

Mulching

Defined as a material that provides a protective layer over the ground, mulch is excellent for retaining moisture in the soil, keeping roots cool, and suppressing weeds.

Mulch can be non-degradable, such as thick gravel, sometimes used around Mediterranean plants and alpines for its durability and drainage-promoting qualities, or it can consist of organic material such as pine needles, wood chips, shredded bark, chopped leaves, grass clippings, nutshells, and coconut husks. Degradable organic materials improve the nutrition of the soil as they decompose, as well as encourage earthworms and beneficial microbes that, in turn, improve the soil's tilth and aeration. However, it is best to use materials that are well rotted, shredded, or chopped. Quantities of fresh grass clippings or chunky bark, for instance, can draw nitrogen from the soil (and thus from plants' root zones) as they decompose.

Above *The flowering season for these calendulas will be extended if dead flowers are removed daily.*
Left *Pruning the vertically growing plant tips will encourage growth in other directions, giving a bushier plant.*

Weeding

While mulching is perhaps the most important tool when it comes to annual weed suppression, it can only help where perennial weeds have already been almost eradicated.

Where formidable perennial weed problems exist, more serious tactics must be used, beginning with consistent and aggressive hand pulling and digging. Many of the most noxious weeds will respond to little else. Other techniques include the use of landscape fabric, solarizing (a technique in which the heat of the summer sun is harnessed by thick clear plastic to essentially cook weed seeds on the soil's surface), and—as a last resort—herbicide.

Once an area has been cleared of roots, a thick layer of mulch will often suppress any seeds from emerging if the soil's surface is not disturbed. Corn gluten spread on the soil's surface suppresses weed seed germination without harming growing plants.

Pruning

Pruning can be performed to improve a plant's health, to enhance flowering and fruiting, or for aesthetic reasons. While some shrubs take to severe shearing for hedges, screens, and topiary, it is generally best for plants' health to accentuate trees' and shrubs' natural growth habit.

Minor pruning can be done at almost any time of the year. But serious pruning of woody plants and trees is best saved for winter dormancy, or very early spring for evergreens, including conifers. While making correct pruning cuts is not very difficult, it is best to consult a manual, as trees in particular need to be pruned in the correct place if they are to heal properly.

Perennial garden plants are easy to prune in spring, not long after growth resumes, using hedge clippers or hand pruners.

mountains can support European alpines that soon perish in other regions. These, and many other seemingly difficult conditions, can be exploited.

Regional topographical variations will also affect local gardening conditions. These include hills and plateaus, which collect more rain, snow, and wind but, on a cold night, might remain a few degrees warmer than a nearby valley where cold air collects. A forest canopy might provide cover for understory plants while a nearby open field is scoured by frigid wind. Built-up areas with expanses of concrete might retain daytime heat and keep their nearby neighborhood several degrees warmer than outlying areas on a cold night, and stay hotter on summer nights. Large bodies of water can also moderate the temperature of their surrounding areas.

Small variations within a single garden, sometimes known as microclimates, can also be exploited. The quality of the soil can vary from one side of a house to another, as can the exposure to sun and wind, which is affected by the house, trees, downspouts, and neighbors' houses and trees. By taking advantage of a south-facing wall, a nearby evergreen hedge, a shady tree, or a persistently wet area at the base of a downspout, it is possible to grow plants in one section of a garden that would not thrive elsewhere.

The Right Plant for the Right Place

In addition to the more obvious aesthetic considerations, a plant's specific features should be taken into account. For example, its ultimate height and width, shape, growth rate, and type of root system are all part of the picture. Mistakes are less important with herbaceous plants that can be readily moved if they outgrow their space. But these features should be carefully considered prior to planting trees and large shrubs so that they can survive and flourish.

Additionally, any relevant environmental tolerances a plant possesses can be considered, including how it survives winter cold, summer heat, late frosts, humidity, drought, wind, salt spray, insects, and diseases. Plants' varied genetic adaptations have given them different levels of suitability under various conditions and these adaptations can be used to the gardener's advantage.

Observing what thrives in the local area can provide valuable clues as to what kinds of plants to choose. Ideas can be gleaned from the wild, from public gardens, and from neighbors' displays.

Above *South-facing brick walls reflect warmth, creating a microclimate where these* Viola *hybrid cultivars can grow and bloom.*

Left *Coastal areas are always milder than the inland, and even large lakes and dams will moderate temperatures on the land; gardeners enjoy the advantage this gives them.*

Illustrated Guide to

FRUIT TYPES

Fruits are the seed-carrying organs (ovaries) of any of the flowering plants, and may be fleshy or dry, hard or soft, large or tiny. They protect the seed until it has developed and is ready to be dispersed by the wind, animals, birds, or insects, depending on the genus.

Drupe

Berry

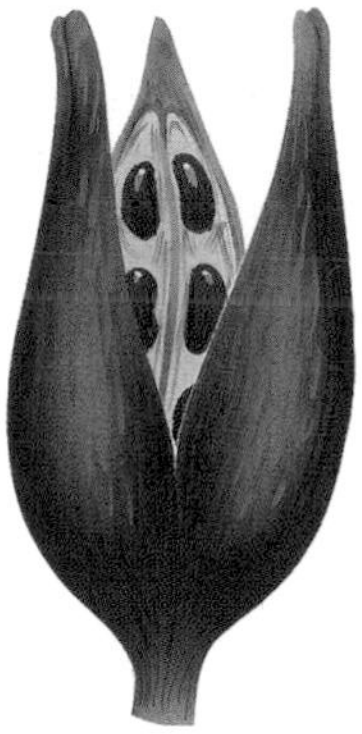

Capsule

Schizocarp

Follicle

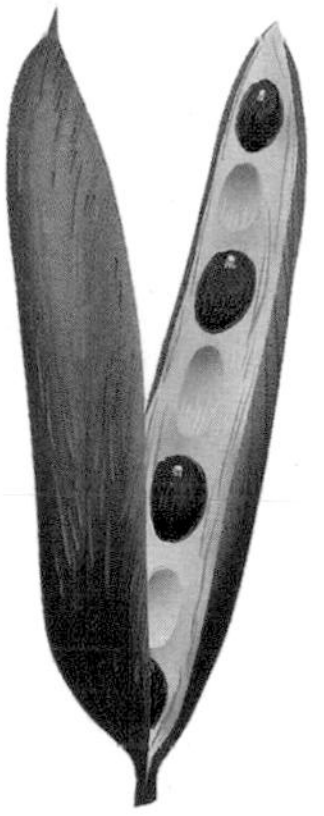

Pod

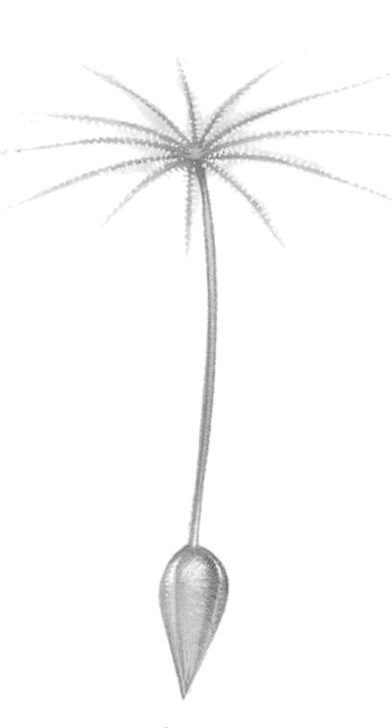

Achene

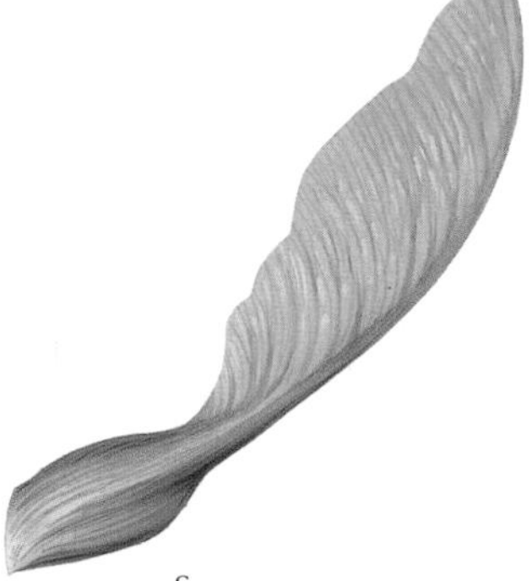

Nut

Samara

Illustrated Guide to

FLOWER TYPES

Flowers are the plant's reproductive center, producing seed in a protected chamber, the ovary, which develops into the fruit. To ensure this, flowers have evolved into a wide range of colors, sizes, and shapes. With cultivation, this diversity has only increased.

STRUCTURE

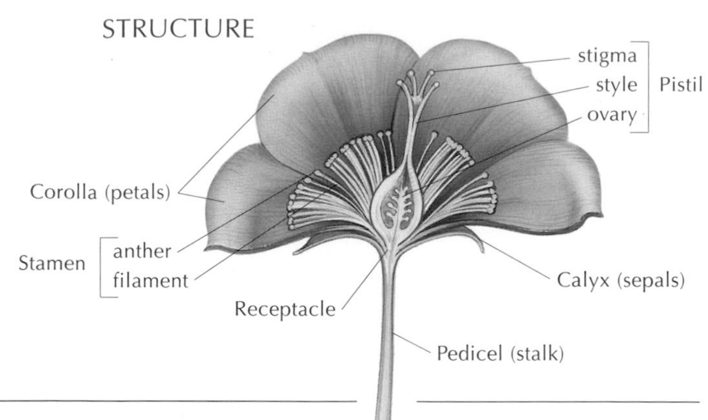

SHAPES

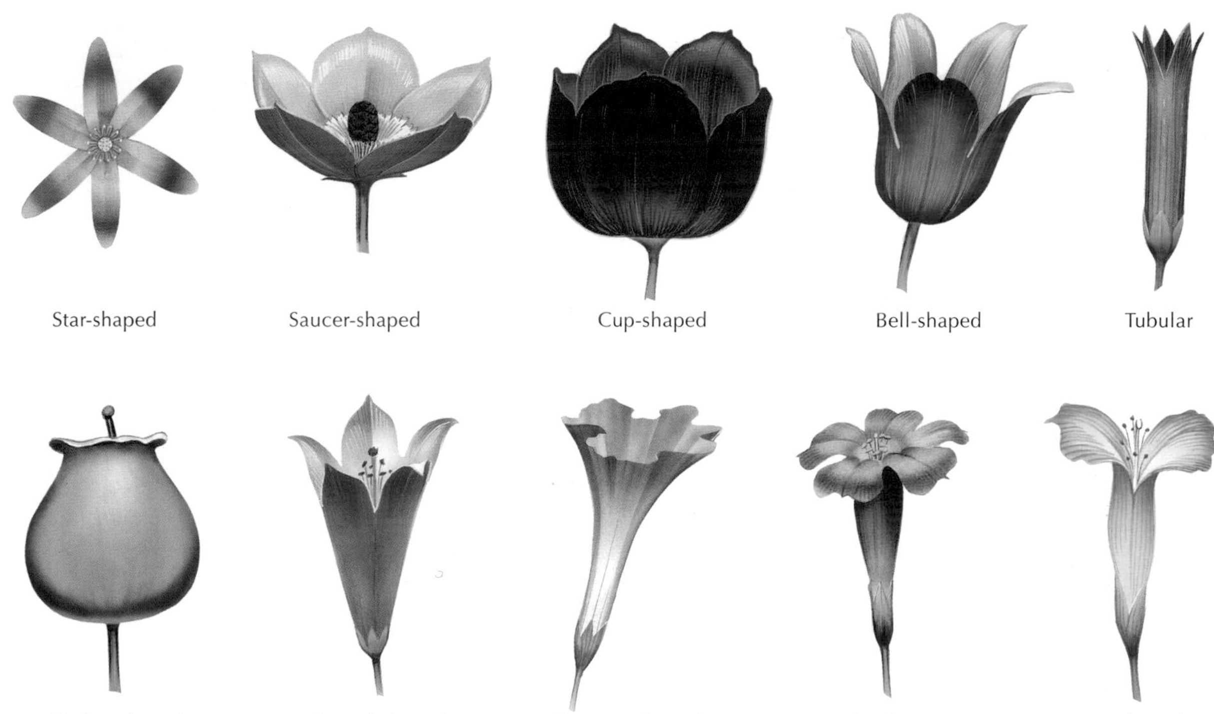

ORIENTATION

INFLORESCENCES

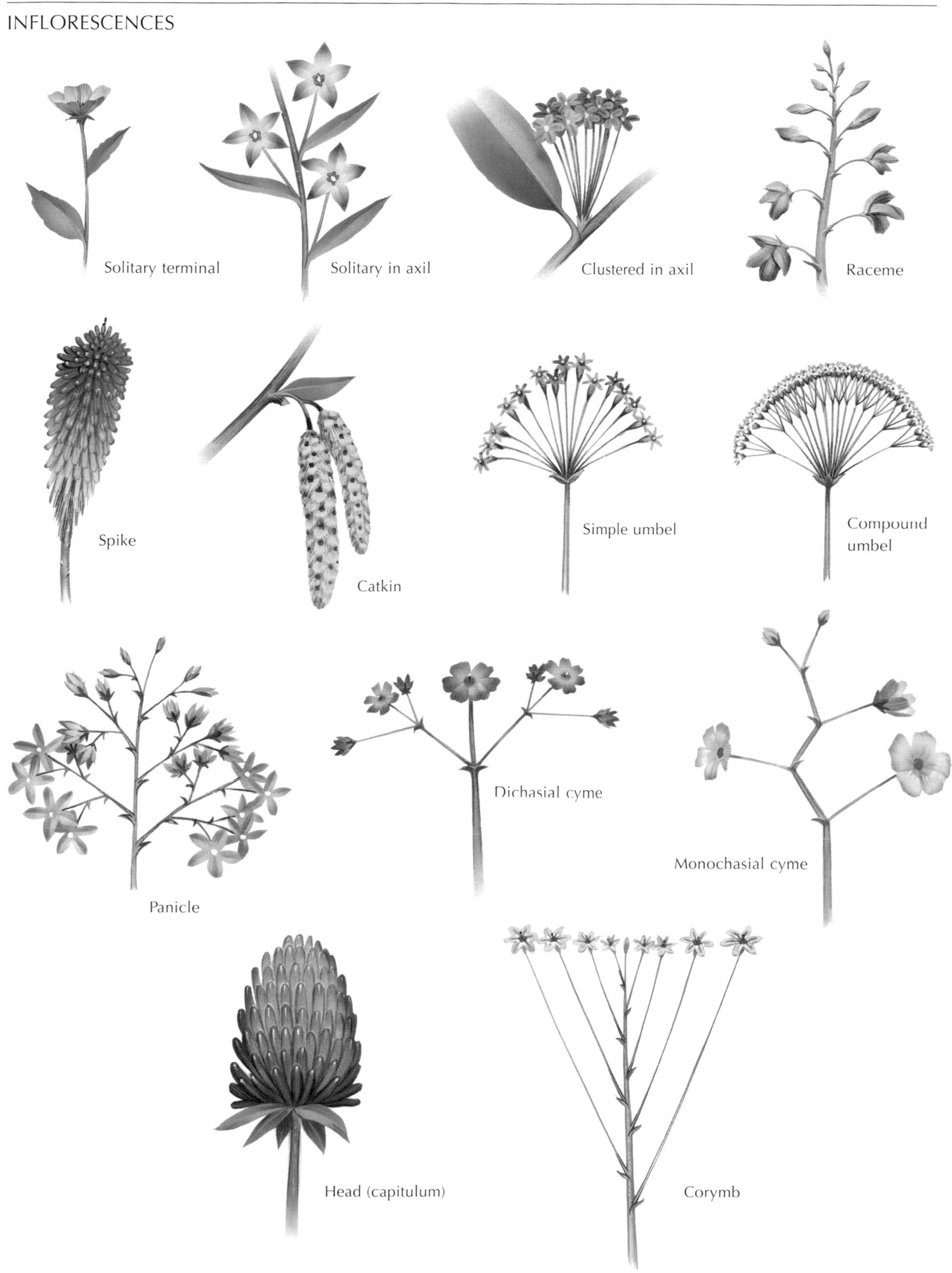

TREES

Trees are more than just the aesthetic backbone of a landscape, although undoubtedly that is an important contribution. Trees also lend dignity to places where they grow, provide shelter for a variety of creatures, and play an essential role in the life of the planet. On a global level, they are major producers of oxygen, without which life on earth would not exist. Forest ecosystems nurture populations of plants, animals, fungi, and microscopic organisms. Regionally, trees help define local character and are used as landmarks to guide us in our travels. And on a more personal level, trees invariably resonate with some of our earliest memories.

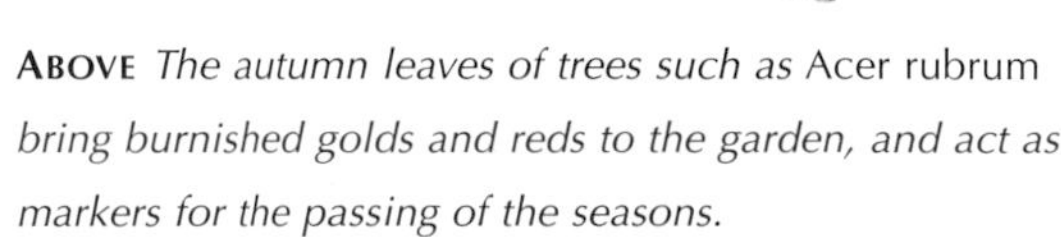

ABOVE *The autumn leaves of trees such as* Acer rubrum *bring burnished golds and reds to the garden, and act as markers for the passing of the seasons.*

LEFT *Some trees, like* Magnolia grandiflora, *bear exquisitely beautiful flowers, while others are valued for their attractive foliage or bark, or their interesting shape.*

THE BACKBONE OF THE GARDEN

Defined as woody perennial plants possessing a dominant trunk, or a few trunks, and a crown of foliage, trees are broadly distinguished from shrubs by exceeding 10–15 ft (3–4.5 m) in height. Most trees are quite long lived: the earth's oldest recorded living entity, at some 4,800 years old, is a bristlecone pine *(Pinus aristata)* growing in California's Sierra Nevada, in the USA. And trees constitute some of the tallest living entities: redwoods *(Sequoia sempervirens),* also native to California, can exceed 360 ft (110 m) in height.

While most garden trees will never attain such an age or height, it is nevertheless important to consider long-term issues when selecting which tree to plant—and where to plant it.

Trees are typically chosen for their ornamental characteristics: showy or fragrant flowers, unique leaf color and texture, colorful bark, autumn foliage, or attractive fruit. These qualities should guide us but not completely drive our decisions. For it is the practical considerations that determine whether the tree will survive in a given position in 5, 10, 20, 40, or 100 years.

Practical issues to consider include the tree's cultural requirements: its cold or heat tolerance, and moisture and sunlight needs. The tree's characteristics should also be examined, including growth rate, eventual height and width, and pest and disease resistance. Features such as canopy density and texture, and whether the tree is deciduous or evergreen are also relevant.

Ultimately, if the right tree is planted where it can mature without interfering with buildings, paving, utilities, and other obstacles, its chances of survival are better and it will only grow increasingly handsome with age. A little planning at the selection stage (and at planting) makes the difference between a tree that creates more problems than it solves and one that becomes an asset and a beloved fixture in the landscape over time.

And there are many beautiful and adaptable trees from which to choose. Trees can be selected for their blossoms—flowering crabapples (*Malus* species), flowering dogwoods (*Cornus* species), and magnolias are perennially popular in cooler climates for their lovely and often fragrant blooms. Others include the Japanese snowbell *(Styrax japonicus),* with fragrant, pendant, white flowers in late spring, or the paperbark maple *(Acer griseum),* with peeling mahogany bark and blazing red autumn foliage. Other trees renowned for their fiery autumn foliage include the sweet gum *(Liquidambar styraciflua),* tulip trees (*Liriodendron* species), and birches (*Betula* species).

ABOVE LEFT *Some trees with decorative bark display a texture that appeals, such as this paperbark maple* (Acer griseum), *while others offer variegated color or intricate patterns.*

LEFT *Flowering deciduous trees bring variety to the garden with every season. This dogwood* (Cornus macrophylla) *is covered with flowers in summer, but in winter it looks very different.*

Above *Apple trees such as* Malus pumila *'Tuscan' are valued for both their wonderful spring blossoms and their delicious fruits.* **Right** *Before deciduous trees like this sweet gum* (Liquidambar styraciflua) *lose their leaves, the foliage changes color. The richness of color can be affected by climatic conditions.*

For those seeking trees of stature and presence that can provide shade, there are beeches (*Fagus* species), oaks (*Quercus* species), maples (*Acer* species), and a range of conifers such as firs (*Abies* species), spruces (*Picea* species), and pine trees (*Pinus* species). Also, in warmer areas can be found jacarandas, crape myrtles (*Lagerstroemia* species), larger magnolias like the southern magnolia *(Magnolia grandiflora),* and strawberry trees (*Arbutus* species).

Trees with large or heavy evergreen leaves provide deep shade, such as the European beech *(Fagus sylvatica),* while others—with smaller and thinner leaves—cast only a light shade, such as the Japanese snowbell *(Styrax japonicus).*

Trees can also be planted to attract wildlife, as they can offer fruits to eat and nesting space to live. Mountain ashes (*Sorbus* species), fruit trees such as apple trees (*Malus* species), and nut trees attract birds and other wildlife to the garden. In warm areas, flowers of wattles (*Acacia* species) and eucalyptus trees attract a variety of different hummingbirds, honeyeaters, and other birds.

And if an accent or screen is desired, there are extremely narrow trees such as the fastigiate maple (*Acer rubrum* 'Columnare'). The range in shape, size, density, and color among trees is astounding.

The joys and pleasures associated with trees are significant, but the civic and cultural values associated with them are considerable as well. Trees buffer noise, help mitigate air pollution and storm-water runoff, shelter wildlife, and lend an ineffable sense of calm and security to urban and rural landscapes alike. But trees are also capable of outliving us. In their growth rings, they capture the history of the earth and put our own existence in perspective.

LEFT Abies koreana *is native to the mountains of South Korea and has striking purple cones. This cultivar, 'Compact Dwarf', is a popular bonsai subject.*
BELOW Abies concolor *grows in western USA down to northern Mexico. 'Masonic Broom' is a dwarf cultivar and grows no more than 30 in (75 cm) in height.*

ABIES

Around 50 species of evergreen conifer trees make up this genus in the pine (Pinaceae) family, which is widely distributed across the northern temperate zones. They usually have an erect conical habit with tiered branches and short, narrow, blunt leaves, often with pale undersides, rather than needles. The cones are very distinctive. The male cones are often brightly colored, usually in purple-pink shades, and the female cones stand erect on top of the branches and may turn a bright purple-blue as they mature. All parts of the trees are very resinous and the cones often exude resin. The Pacific fir *(Abies amabilis)* yields Canada balsam, a clear resin widely used as a cement in optics before modern synthetics.

CULTIVATION

Most species are very hardy and grow better in cool conditions. They do not like hot summers. Plant in full sun or part-shade with moist, humus-rich, well-drained soil, and water well during the growing season. These trees are naturally symmetrical and are best left to develop naturally, untrimmed. Propagation is by grafting or from stratified seed.

Favorites	Cone Color	Cone Shape	Cone Length
Abies alba	red-brown	cylindrical	4–6 in (10–15 cm)
Abies concolor	mid-green to brown	cylindrical	3–5 in (8–12 cm)
Abies koreana	purple	cylindrical	6 in (15 cm)
Abies nordmanniana	green to purple-brown	cylindrical	6 in (15 cm)
***Abies nordmanniana* 'Golden Spreader'**	green to purple-brown	cylindrical	6 in (15 cm)
Abies religiosa	green or purple to brown	cylindrical	6 in (15 cm)

Top Tip

Honey fungus mushrooms can destroy *Abies* trees. Once identified, remove all dead and dying stumps and root systems before the pest spreads further.

ABOVE Abies alba, *European silver fir, produces Europe's tallest tree. Its timber is used for telegraph poles and was used for ship masts in ancient Greece and Rome.*

BELOW *Stands of* Abies religiosa, *known as Mexican fir, provide a winter habitat for the Monarch butterfly. This fir is not as hardy as most others in this genus.*

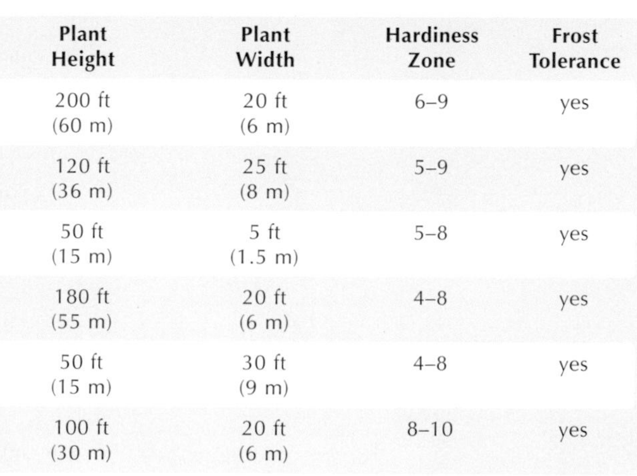

Plant Height	Plant Width	Hardiness Zone	Frost Tolerance
200 ft (60 m)	20 ft (6 m)	6–9	yes
120 ft (36 m)	25 ft (8 m)	5–9	yes
50 ft (15 m)	5 ft (1.5 m)	5–8	yes
180 ft (55 m)	20 ft (6 m)	4–8	yes
50 ft (15 m)	30 ft (9 m)	4–8	yes
100 ft (30 m)	20 ft (6 m)	8–10	yes

ACACIA

Widespread in the southern tropics and subtropics, most of the 1,200 species in this mimosa subfamily of the legume (Fabaceae) family are found in Australia and Africa. Commonly known as wattle or mimosa, they range from small shrubs to large trees and include a few climbers. The African species frequently bear fierce spines. The foliage, often blue-green or silver-gray, is ferny when young and in many species remains that way, but often the leaves change to narrow phyllodes as the plants mature. The flowers are yellow, cream, or white and are densely clustered in rounded heads or short spikes. The flowering season varies with the species, though many bloom from late winter into spring. Acacias yield a resinous gum that has many uses, from medicinal and culinary to use as a cement.

ABOVE *Most often found in eastern Australia,* Acacia crassa *is a tall shrub or small tree up to 40 ft (12 m) high. The golden yellow flower spikes are borne in pairs.*

CULTIVATION

Plant in full sun with light free-draining soil. Although drought tolerant, once established most grow better with reliable summer moisture. Many species are short-lived and some may self-sow too freely, becoming weeds. Propagate from well-soaked seeds.

RIGHT Acacia baileyana *has silver-gray leaves and round yellow flowers. It can be planted as a street tree or as a specimen in any garden to showcase its foliage and add color.*

Favorites	Flower Color	Blooming Season	Flower Fragrance	Plant Height	Plant Width	Hardiness Zone	Frost Tolerance
Acacia baileyana	golden yellow	winter to early spring	yes	6–20 ft (1.8–6 m)	10–20 ft (3–6 m)	8–9	yes
Acacia crassa	golden yellow	late winter to early spring	yes	40 ft (12 m)	35 ft (10 m)	9–11	yes
Acacia dealbata	pale to bright yellow	late winter to spring	yes	80 ft (24 m)	20–35 ft (6–10 m)	8–10	yes
Acacia pravissima	golden yellow	spring	yes	10–25 ft (3–8 m)	10–20 ft (3–6 m)	8–11	yes
Acacia retinoides	lemon yellow	late spring to summer	yes	10–25 ft (3–8 m)	10 ft (3 m)	8–10	yes
Acacia stenophylla	creamy yellow	autumn to winter	yes	15–50 ft (4.5–15 m)	10–20 ft (3–6 m)	8–10	yes

Top Tip

When growing acacias from seed, place them in a cup of boiling water first. Then soak them in cold water for a day before planting.

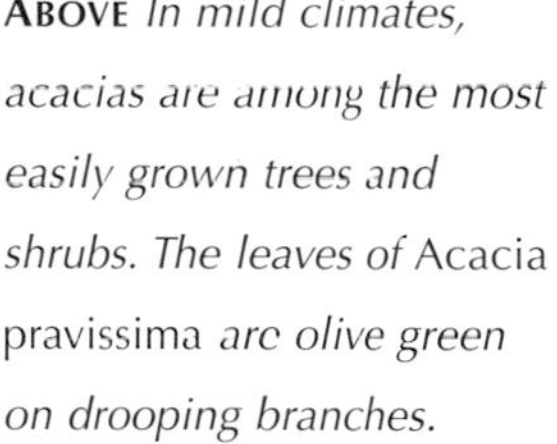

ABOVE *In mild climates, acacias are among the most easily grown trees and shrubs. The leaves of* Acacia pravissima *are olive green on drooping branches.*

BELOW *Known in Europe as mimosa,* Acacia dealbata *can grow as tall as 80 ft (24 m) high in the wild. Generally, it will only reach 60 ft (18 m) in cultivation.*

RIGHT Acer palmatum *'Shishigashira' is known as the lion's head maple. In autumn the foliage turns from deep green to rich red-brown or yellow. It grows well on the coast.*

ACER

Distributed through the northern temperate zone, this largely deciduous genus of 120 species of tree is the type form for the maple (Aceraceae) family. Most are graceful and round-headed trees with broad, often lobed leaves that frequently color brilliantly in autumn. Variegated or colored foliage is common among garden forms. In spring, usually before the foliage develops, they produce small flowers in clusters, upright spikes, or drooping tassels. After flowering, maple trees produce winged fruits, also known as samara or sycamores. Well known as timber trees and for producing maple syrup, these plants can be put to many other practical uses.

Top Tip

The maple tree is very versatile. Use it to add bright autumn color to a garden, or as a shade tree. Some species are popular bonsai specimens.

CULTIVATION

Although a few maples are found in subtropical regions, most generally prefer climates with clearly defined seasons. They grow best in sun or part-shade with a humus-rich well-drained soil that remains moist through the growing season. The species are usually raised from seed, hybrids and cultivars by grafting.

BELOW *Known as fernleaf maple,* Acer japonicum *'Aconitifolium' is native to the dry mountains of Japan. A small tree, the foliage colors crimson in autumn.*

Favorites

Favorites	Flower Color	Blooming Season	Flower Fragrance	Plant Height	Plant Width	Hardiness Zone	Frost Tolerance
Acer campestre	yellowish green	spring	no	30 ft (9 m)	12 ft (3.5 m)	3–8	yes
Acer griseum	green	spring	no	40 ft (12 m)	35 ft (10 m)	4–8	yes
Acer japonicum	purplish red	spring	no	30 ft (9 m)	30 ft (9 m)	6–8	yes
Acer palmatum	purplish red	spring to summer	no	20 ft (6 m)	25 ft (8 m)	6–9	yes
***Acer palmatum* 'Sango-kaku'**	purplish red	spring to summer	no	20 ft (6 m)	25 ft (8 m)	6–9	yes
Acer saccharum	yellowish green	spring	no	100 ft (30 m)	40 ft (12 m)	4–8	yes

LEFT Acer griseum *is a very attractive tree. It features beautifully textured and colored bark which peels to reveal smooth cinnamon red branches.*

BELOW *The state tree of New York, Vermont, West Virginia, and Wisconsin,* Acer saccharum *produces the best sap from which to make maple syrup.*

AESCULUS

The type genus for the horse chestnut (Hippocastanaceae) family, this group of around 15 species of deciduous trees is found in North America—where they are commonly known as buckeye—and Eurasia. They are usually round-headed or pyramidal, with a sturdy trunk and large palmate leaves composed of 5 to 11 smooth-edged to slightly toothed leaflets. In spring, shortly after the leaves have expanded, upright panicles of white to red or yellow flowers develop near the branch tips. A horse chestnut in full flower is among the most colorful of the hardy deciduous trees. Large, sometimes spiny, seed capsules follow the flowers and contain paired nuts. Horse chestnuts are so-called because the fruit is inedible—fit only for horses—unlike that of the edible chestnut *(Castanea sativa).*

LEFT *The crimson flowers of* Aesculus pavia *have earned it the common name of red buckeye. The cultivar 'Atrosanguinea', seen here, has pretty flowers of an even deeper red than the species.*

BELOW *Known as the red horse chestnut,* Aesculus × carnea *is a magnificent sight when in bloom, with masses of deep reddish pink flowers covering the tree.*

Top Tip

Many *Aesculus* species grow to an impressive size. Choose smaller species for the garden and limit pruning to the removal of dead wood.

CULTIVATION

These hardy deciduous trees are most at home in climates with clearly defined seasons and relatively moist summers. Plant in sun with moist humus-rich soil and water well until established. The species are raised from seed, the cultivars by grafting.

RIGHT *The dense foliage of* Aesculus × carnea *'Briottii' offers wonderful shade. At blooming time spectacular deep red-pink blossoms smother the tree.*

Favorites	Flower Color	Blooming Season	Flower Fragrance	Plant Height	Plant Width	Hardiness Zone	Frost Tolerance
Aesculus* × *carnea	reddish pink; yellow blotches	spring	no	30 ft (9 m)	15 ft (4.5 m)	6–9	yes
Aesculus flava	yellow	summer	no	90 ft (27 m)	35 ft (10 m)	4–9	yes
Aesculus hippocastanum	white; yellow to red blotches	late spring	no	100 ft (30 m)	70 ft (21 m)	6–9	yes
Aesculus indica	white	early to mid-summer	no	100 ft (30 m)	70 ft (21 m)	6–9	yes
Aesculus* × *neglecta	yellow	summer	no	50 ft (15 m)	30 ft (9 m)	5–9	yes
Aesculus pavia	crimson	early summer	no	15 ft (4.5 m)	10 ft (3 m)	6–10	yes

RIGHT *Native to central and eastern USA,* Aesculus flava *bears yellow flowers during summer. The flowers are followed by the rounded horse chestnuts.*

ARBUTUS

A genus of around 8 to 10 species of small evergreen trees, it has a scattered distribution in the warmer parts of the northern temperate zone. Members of the heath (Ericaceae) family, they are known as strawberry trees because of their large, fleshy, orange-red to red fruits, which develop from sprays of small, bell-shaped, pink or white flowers. The colorful fruit is edible but not always pleasant tasting. The leaves are usually simple, dark green, leathery ovals, sometimes pointed or toothed. Most species have warm brown bark that flakes or peels to reveal a brighter underbark. Native Americans found medicinal uses for the fruit, bark, and foliage of their local species.

LEFT Arbutus menziesii, *from the North American Pacific coast, is commonly known as madrone. It sheds its outer brick red bark to reveal green underbark.*

BELOW *The white flowers of* Arbutus unedo *are followed by the red fruit that have earned it the common name of strawberry tree.*

CULTIVATION

While not extremely hardy to frost, most of these trees withstand prolonged cold conditions and are easily cultivated in sun or part-shade with cool, moist, humus-rich soil. Like most plants in the heath family, they resent lime. Trim lightly to shape, and propagate from half-hardened cuttings taken in autumn or winter, grafts, or seed.

RIGHT *An eastern Mediterranean native known as the Grecian strawberry tree,* Arbutus andrachne *sheds its warm brown bark to reveal a greenish cream underbark.*

Favorites	Flower Color	Blooming Season	Flower Fragrance	Plant Height	Plant Width	Hardiness Zone	Frost Tolerance
Arbutus andrachne	white	spring	no	20 ft (6 m)	20 ft (6 m)	6–9	yes
Arbutus* × *andrachnoides	white	late winter	no	25 ft (8 m)	25 ft (8 m)	8–10	yes
Arbutus glandulosa	dull pink	winter	no	20 ft (6 m)	40 ft (12 m)	9–10	yes
***Arbutus* 'Marina'**	pink	year-round	no	25–50 ft (8–15 m)	20–40 ft (6–12 m)	8–10	yes
Arbutus menziesii	white	late spring	yes	30 ft (9 m)	30 ft (9 m)	7–9	yes
Arbutus unedo	white	autumn to winter	yes	25 ft (8 m)	20 ft (6 m)	7–10	yes

Top Tip

Arbutus species are low-maintenance trees once established, requiring little in the way of pruning apart from minor trimming to thin out and keep a tidy appearance.

BELOW *Bearing similar characteristics to the species,* Arbutus unedo *'Compacta' is a smaller form, with a maximum height of around 10 ft (3 m).*

Left *Known as the yellow birch,* Betula alleghaniensis *is a North American native. The bright green leaves take on magnificent warm colors in autumn. This tree has commercial value as a timber tree and as a source of wintergreen.*

Top Tip

Prune birches only when essential. Vulnerable to several serious pests and diseases, any open cuts can provide opportunities for attack.

Betula

A genus of some 60 species of deciduous shrubs and trees that are widespread in the cool temperate Northern Hemisphere and the subarctic, *Betula* is the type genus for the birch (Betulaceae) family. While the smaller species can be dense and twiggy, the trees tend to have an open airy growth habit with light branches and fine twigs. Many species have pale, sometimes white, bark that peels in small strips or sheets. The pointed oval leaves have small teeth and often develop vivid yellow autumn tones. Buff catkins appear in spring and shed many tiny seeds. Birch sap can be used as a maple syrup substitute, and the bark was a popular canoe-skinning material among Native Americans.

Cultivation

Very hardy and easily grown in normal garden soils, many birches are natural riverside plants that can tolerate quite damp conditions. Trim lightly to shape but otherwise allow the natural form to develop. Propagate from softwood or half-hardened cuttings, or from seed.

Above *Characterized by gray to red-brown peeling bark and purple-red new growth,* Betula alnoides, *a native of the Himalayas, can reach an immense size.*

Left *The long, drooping, yellow, male catkins of* Betula albosinensis *appear in spring as the glossy green leaves unfurl.*

Favorites	Flower Color	Blooming Season	Flower Fragrance	Plant Height	Plant Width	Hardiness Zone	Frost Tolerance
Betula albosinensis	yellow (male) yellow-brown (female)	spring	no	80 ft (24 m)	30 ft (9 m)	6–9	yes
Betula alleghaniensis	chartreuse (male) green (female)	early spring	no	80 ft (24 m)	30 ft (9 m)	4–9	yes
Betula alnoides	yellow-brown	early spring	no	100 ft (30 m)	20 ft (6 m)	8–10	yes
Betula mandschurica	yellow-brown	early spring	no	70 ft (21 m)	30 ft (9 m)	2–9	yes
Betula nigra	yellow	early spring	no	30 ft (9 m)	15 ft (4.5 m)	4–9	yes
Betula pendula	yellow (male) chartreuse (female)	early spring	no	80 ft (24 m)	35 ft (10 m)	2–8	yes

RIGHT *Native to riversides of eastern USA, the river birch* (Betula nigra) *has smooth white bark initially, which turns to shades of cream, pink, and brown.*

CATALPA

The 11 species of deciduous trees that comprise this genus, a member of the trumpet-vine (Bignoniaceae) family, have an unusual distribution: North America, Cuba, and south-western China. They are large trees that form a broad dome-shaped canopy, with heart-shaped to triangular leaves that taper to a fine point. In summer they carry upright panicles of bell-shaped flowers in white, various pink shades, and soft apricot-orange, followed by clusters of long, pendulous, bean-like seed pods. The bark, leaves, and seeds are used in herbal medicines and one species, *Catalpa speciosa*, is a moderately important timber tree. *Catalpa* was the native North American name for the trees.

CULTIVATION

Mature *Catalpa* trees are frost hardy but young plants and the spring growth are easily damaged. Also, hail and strong winds will tear the large leaves, so young trees are best planted in a sheltered sunny position. The soil should be moist, humus-rich, and well drained. Propagate from softwood summer cuttings or autumn-sown seed.

LEFT *Originating in wooded areas of western China,* Catalpa ovata *features broadly oval leaves that have downy undersides.*
TOP LEFT *From the open mountain terrain of western China,* Catalpa fargesii *produces abundant rosy pink flowers. The leaves are bronze when young.*

ABOVE Catalpa bignonioides *is known as Indian bean tree for the large bean-like seed pods, measuring up to 12 in (30 cm) long, which follow the masses of white summer flowers.*

LEFT Catalpa bungei *makes an ideal shade tree. Pyramidal in habit, it produces lovely rosy pink to white flowers throughout summer. Long seed pods, up to 20 in (50 cm), follow the flowers.*

Top Tip

Catalpa species quite often branch too close to the ground. Train them to a single trunk by carefully removing side branches until the optimal height is achieved.

Favorites	Flower Color	Blooming Season	Flower Fragrance	Plant Height	Plant Width	Hardiness Zone	Frost Tolerance
Catalpa bignonioides	white; marked yellow and purple	summer	no	50 ft (15 m)	40 ft (12 m)	5–10	yes
Catalpa bungei	rosy pink to white	summer	no	30 ft (9 m)	25 ft (8 m)	5–10	yes
Catalpa* × *erubescens	white	summer	no	50 ft (15 m)	50 ft (15 m)	5–10	yes
Catalpa fargesii	rosy pink; marked yellow and purple	summer	no	60 ft (18 m)	40 ft (12 m)	5–10	yes
Catalpa ovata	dull white; marked yellow and red	summer	no	30 ft (9 m)	30 ft (9 m)	5–10	yes
Catalpa speciosa	white	late spring to summer	no	120 ft (36 m)	90 ft (27 m)	5–10	yes

CEDRUS

RIGHT *Sweeping down to the ground, the branches of* Cedrus atlantica *'Glauca Pendula' have a dramatic weeping habit and blue-toned needle-like foliage.*

BELOW Cedrus deodara*, the largest of the cedars, has a graceful growth habit, forming a spire-like crown atop weeping lower branches.*

Found from North Africa through Turkey and the Middle East to the western Himalayas, cedars are large, wide-spreading, evergreen conifers with distinctively tiered branches. Botanists are not entirely in agreement about the species, recognizing from 2 to 4 of these pine (Pinaceae) family trees. The needle-like leaves are usually deep green or blue-green. Both male and female cones stand erect on top of the branches, and the male cones shed huge quantities of pollen that can color the ground around the trees. The female cones eventually break up, releasing papery winged seeds. Cedars are important timber trees with insect-resistant wood. They also yield aromatic, antiseptic, and preservative oils.

CULTIVATION

Cedars are tough adaptable trees and although they prefer a distinctly seasonal climate and are fairly frost hardy, they will not withstand extremely cold or very prolonged winters. Plant in full sun in well-drained soil. They adapt to a range of soil types and become drought tolerant with age. Propagate the species from seed and the cultivars by grafting.

Favorites	Cone Color	Cone Shape	Cone Length	Plant Height	Plant Width	Hardiness Zone	Frost Tolerance
Cedrus atlantica	green	egg-shaped to cylindrical	2–3 in (5–8 cm)	80 ft (24 m)	30 ft (9 m)	6–9	yes
***Cedrus atlantica* 'Glauca Pendula'**	brown	egg-shaped to cylindrical	3–6 in (8–15 cm)	10–15 ft (3–4.5 m)	6–10 ft (1.8–3 m)	6–9	yes
Cedrus deodara	blue-gray to brown	barrel	3–4 in (8–10 cm)	200 ft (60 m)	30 ft (9 m)	7–10	yes
***Cedrus deodara* 'Aurea'**	blue-gray to brown	barrel	5–6 in (12–15 cm)	15–20 ft (4.5–6 m)	10–15 ft (3–4.5 m)	7–10	yes
Cedrus libani	green to brown	barrel	4–6 in (10–15 cm)	150 ft (45 m)	90 ft (27 m)	5–9	yes
***Cedrus libani* 'Sargentii'**	green to brown	barrel	4–6 in (10–15 cm)	5–7 ft (1.5–2 m)	5–7 ft (1.5–2 m)	5–9	yes

Top Tip

Cedars are stately trees, adapted to a range of conditions. The only pruning necessary may be to remove the lower branches if a clear passage beneath the tree is required.

ABOVE *Known as the cedar of Lebanon and a proud feature of the Lebanese flag, the distribution of* Cedrus libani *in its namesake country is now confined to Mt Lebanon alone.*

BELOW *Erect green cones, often with a bluish bloom, are produced close to the branch tips of* Cedrus atlantica, *commonly known as the Atlas cedar.*

CERCIDIPHYLLUM

BELOW *The graceful weeping form of* Cercidiphyllum magnificum *'Pendulum' becomes a cascade of brilliant reds, oranges, and yellows in autumn.*

This genus of just 2 species of deciduous trees is the sole member of its family, the Cercidiphyllaceae. Both species occur in Japan and one is also found in western China. They are erect, with a broad crown and horizontal branches, often down to near ground level. Both species also occur in attractive weeping forms. The leaves are heart-shaped and are bright green when young, mature to blue-green, and then develop yellow, pink, and red autumn tones. The small flowers are largely insignificant. The trees yield a soft, light, fine-grained timber that is widely used for wall linings and small ornamental objects.

CULTIVATION

The trees are hardy but the young growth is prone to damage from late frosts. As the trees often fork low down, they are prone to wind damage. Train young trees to a single trunk to avoid this problem. Plant in sun with a rich, moist, well-drained soil. Propagate from softwood to half-hardened cuttings or sow stratified seed.

Top Tip

Cercidiphyllum species appreciate regular moisture in summer. Gradually reducing watering toward the end of summer will result in improved autumn color.

LEFT *The leaves of* Cercidiphyllum magnificum *are initially purplish red, unfurling to bluish green, before taking on glorious autumn hues.*

Favorites	Flower Color	Blooming Season	Flower Fragrance	Plant Height	Plant Width	Hardiness Zone	Frost Tolerance
Cercidiphyllum japonicum	red	spring	no	60 ft (18 m)	35 ft (10 m)	6–9	yes
Cercidiphyllum japonicum* var. *sinense	red	spring	no	60 ft (18 m)	35 ft (10 m)	6–9	yes
Cercidiphyllum japonicum* f. *pendulum	red	spring	no	20 ft (6 m)	25 ft (8 m)	6–9	yes
***Cercidiphyllum japonicum* 'Rotfuchs'**	red	spring	no	60 ft (18 m)	35 ft (10 m)	6–9	yes
Cercidiphyllum magnificum	red	spring	no	10–25 ft (3–8 m)	10–15 ft (3–4.5 m)	6–9	yes
***Cercidiphyllum magnificum* 'Pendulum'**	red	spring	no	10–25 ft (3–8 m)	10–15 ft (3–4.5 m)	6–9	yes

ABOVE *Taking on wonderful vibrant autumn color, the leaves on the weeping branches of* Cercidiphyllum japonicum *f.* pendulum *change from blue-green to reds, yellows, and pinks.* **LEFT** Cercidiphyllum japonicum *reaches up to 60 ft (18 m) in the wild, but is smaller in cultivation. The blue-green leaves give off an exotic aroma, smelling rather like burnt sugar.*

Top Tip

Make sure a favorable position is selected for planting *Cercis* species. These slow-growing trees resent disturbance and do not transplant well.

CERCIS

A principally North American and temperate East Asian genus, it has around 7 species of deciduous trees and shrubs in the cassia subfamily of the legume (Fabaceae) family. The most widely grown species is, however, an outlier native to the eastern Mediterranean region. The pointed oval leaves are often red- or bronze-tinted when young. Sprays of 5-petalled pea-flowers open in spring and are often a very distinctive light magenta shade that is hard to mistake for any other tree. Bean-like seed pods follow and contain hard dark seeds. The Judas tree *(Cercis siliquastrum)*, the Mediterranean species, was reputed to be the tree from which Judas hanged himself after betraying Christ.

ABOVE *Known as Chinese redbud,* Cercis chinensis *is distinguished from the similar* C. canadensis *by its shorter leaf stalks. It does not do well in cold climates.*

CULTIVATION

Most species are adaptable and quite hardy, preferring a sunny position with light, fertile, free-draining soil that retains some summer moisture. Trim to shape when young, otherwise leave to develop naturally. Propagate by taking half-hardened cuttings or sowing thoroughly soaked seeds.

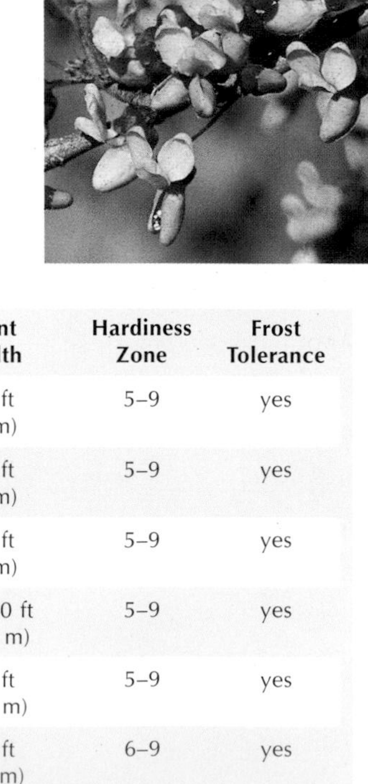

Favorites	Flower Color	Blooming Season	Flower Fragrance	Plant Height	Plant Width	Hardiness Zone	Frost Tolerance
Cercis canadensis	rose pink	late winter to early spring	no	30 ft (9 m)	30 ft (9 m)	5–9	yes
***Cercis canadensis* 'Flame'**	rose pink	late winter to early spring	no	30 ft (9 m)	30 ft (9 m)	5–9	yes
Cercis chinensis	deep rosy purple	late winter to early spring	no	20 ft (6 m)	20 ft (6 m)	5–9	yes
Cercis griffithii	lavender, purple	early spring	no	10–20 ft (3–6 m)	10–20 ft (3–6 m)	5–9	yes
Cercis occidentalis	rose pink	spring	no	15 ft (4.5 m)	12 ft (3.5 m)	5–9	yes
Cercis siliquastrum	rosy purple	early spring	no	35 ft (10 m)	35 ft (10 m)	6–9	yes

LEFT *The rich green leaves of* Cercis siliquastrum *appear after the profusion of rosy purple spring flowers. This species is native to the Mediterranean region.*

ABOVE *The bare branches of* Cercis canadensis*—the state tree of Oklahoma—are filled with rosy pink blooms from late winter to early spring.*
RIGHT *Striking burgundy-colored foliage follows the pink flowers of* Cercis canadensis *'Forest Pansy'. This cultivar needs a shaded position in hotter climates.*

CHAMAECYPARIS

A North American and temperate East Asian genus, it features 8 species of evergreen coniferous trees in the cypress (Cupressaceae) family. They have small scale-like leaves that are tightly pressed to the stems and borne in fan-shaped sprays. The cones are rounded, small, and often very hard. A great number of cultivars have been developed, covering a huge range of foliage colors and growth forms, and these are far more widely grown than the true species. The foliage can cause a type of contact dermatitis in some people. The rapid-growing nature of these trees, particularly the Lawson cypress *(Chamaecyparis lawsoniana),* has made them popular for shelter belts.

CULTIVATION

These hardy adaptable trees are tolerant of a wide range of soil and climatic conditions but generally do best with moist, slightly acidic soil and fairly cool moist summers. Trim to shape when young and thin later. Propagation is usually from half-hardened summer cuttings under mist, or by grafting.

Top Tip

The smaller *Chamaecyparis* species and cultivars can be used for hedging—using types with different colored foliage will add interest.

ABOVE *The golden yellow foliage of* Chamaecyparis lawsoniana *'Minima Aurea', an award-winning tree, will provide interest in the garden throughout the year.*
LEFT *Cultivars of* Chamaecyparis lawsoniana*, such as 'Handcross Park', offer a range of growth habits and foliage color.*

LEFT *The unusual spiraling growth habit of* Chamaecyparis obtusa *'Spiralis' gives a somewhat sculptured look, enhanced by the bright green foliage.* **BELOW** Chamaecyparis pisifera *is most often represented in gardens by cultivars such as 'Plumosa', which has mid-green leaves and red-brown bark.*

Favorites	Cone Color	Cone Shape	Cone Length	Plant Height	Plant Width	Hardiness Zone	Frost Tolerance
Chamaecyparis lawsoniana	gray to rusty brown	round	½ in (12 mm)	100 ft (30 m)	10–15 ft (3–4.5 m)	4–9	yes
***Chamaecyparis lawsoniana* 'Ellwoodii'**	gray to rusty brown	round	½ in (12 mm)	6–8 ft (1.8–2.4 m)	3–4 ft (0.9–1.2 m)	4–9	yes
Chamaecyparis nootkatensis	brown	round	½ in (12 mm)	100 ft (30 m)	25 ft (8 m)	4–9	yes
Chamaecyparis obtusa	orange-brown	round	½ in (12 mm)	60 ft (18 m)	20 ft (6 m)	5–10	yes
Chamaecyparis pisifera	black-brown	round	½ in (12 mm)	75 ft (23 m)	15 ft (4.5 m)	5–10	yes
Chamaecyparis thyoides	purplish black	round to oval	¼ in (6 mm)	50 ft (15 m)	12 ft (3.5 m)	4–9	yes

CHIONANTHUS

BOTTOM *In full bloom,* Chionanthus virginicus *is a glorious sight, its branches laden with panicles of fragrant, fringed, white blossoms.*

BELOW *Native to China and Taiwan, and known as the Chinese fringe tree,* Chionanthus retusus *has fissured, sometimes peeling bark and bright green leaves.*

Belonging to the olive (Oleaceae) family, this principally temperate and subtropical East Asian genus comprises around 100 species of mostly deciduous trees. One well-known and widely grown species, the fringe tree *(Chionanthus virginicus)*, occurs in eastern North America. The leaves are simple, smooth-edged or toothed, and only color slightly in autumn. The main attraction is the fragrant, 4-petalled, white flowers, which are borne in billowing panicles. Single-seeded purple-blue fruits follow. Extracts from the bark of the roots have extensive medicinal uses, and the fruit is sometimes preserved or pickled in the same manner as olives.

Top Tip

Keep soil type in mind when selecting *Chionanthus* species, as soil preferences vary. Some species tolerate alkaline soils, while others prefer neutral or acid soil.

CULTIVATION

Although the cultivated species are generally hardy, they are prone to damage from late frosts and flower best after a long hot summer. Plant in full sun with moist, humus-rich, well-drained soil. Propagate by sowing fresh seed as soon as it is ripe. Germination is slow, and can take up to 18 months.

Favorites	Flower Color	Blooming Season	Flower Fragrance	Plant Height	Plant Width	Hardiness Zone	Frost Tolerance
Chionanthus retusus	white	summer	yes	10 ft (3 m)	10 ft (3 m)	6–10	yes
Chionanthus virginicus	white	summer	yes	10 ft (3 m)	10 ft (3 m)	4–9	yes
***Chionanthus virginicus* 'Angustifolius'**	white	summer	yes	10 ft (3 m)	10 ft (3 m)	4–9	yes

CORNUS

This North American and Eurasian genus of around 40 species of mainly deciduous, spring-flowering shrubs and trees is the type form for the dogwood (Cornaceae) family. The leaves are usually broadly lance-shaped and many of the cultivated plants have variegated leaves that color well in autumn. A few have brightly colored stems that are attractive in winter. The true flowers are tiny but are surrounded by 4 large, decorative, white, cream, or pale green bracts that may become flushed red or pink. Several of the species produce soft edible fruits, the seeds contain a flammable oil, and the young twigs can be used in basketry.

LEFT *Variegated foliage adds to the overall beauty of* Cornus sericea *'Sunshine'. The yellow and green leaves provide a colorful backdrop for the white flowers.*

BELOW *The flowers of* Cornus nuttallii *are small, and are easily hidden by the large white, cream or pale green bracts that surround them.*

CULTIVATION

Dogwoods are hardy adaptable trees, though most need winter cold to flower well and are at home in a climate with distinct seasons. Plant in sun or part-shade with fertile, humus-rich, well-drained soil and water well during the warmer months. Clumping forms may be raised from suckers, otherwise try stratified seed, hardwood cuttings, or grafting.

LEFT *With a vigorous open habit,* Cornus kousa *var.* chinensis *has leaves that are lighter in color and larger than those of the species, and feature smooth edges.*

RIGHT *The dense foliage of* Cornus alternifolia *'Argentea' features mid-green leaves marked with white variegations.*

ABOVE *Lower growing than the species,* Cornus alba *'Sibirica', known as the Siberian dogwood, is admired for its glowing coral red stems and branches.*
RIGHT *Gorgeous rosy pink bracts distinguish* Cornus florida *f.* rubra *from the species. Persistent red berries follow, providing a winter food source for birds.*

Favorites	Flower Color	Blooming Season	Flower Fragrance	Plant Height	Plant Width	Hardiness Zone	Frost Tolerance
Cornus alba	white to creamy white	late spring to early summer	yes	6–10 ft (1.8–3 m)	10 ft (3 m)	4–9	yes
Cornus alternifolia	white to lemon yellow	early summer	no	20–25 ft (6–8 m)	20 ft (6 m)	3–9	yes
Cornus florida	green; white to pinkish bracts	late spring to early summer	no	20–30 ft (6–9 m)	25 ft (8 m)	5–9	yes
Cornus kousa	green; cream bracts	early summer	no	20–25 ft (6–8 m)	15 ft (4.5 m)	5–9	yes
Cornus nuttallii	green; pink-flushed white bracts	late spring and early autumn	no	60 ft (18 m)	40 ft (12 m)	7–8	yes
Cornus sericea	creamy white	summer	no	6–7 ft (1.8–2 m)	7–12 ft (2–3.5 m)	2–10	yes

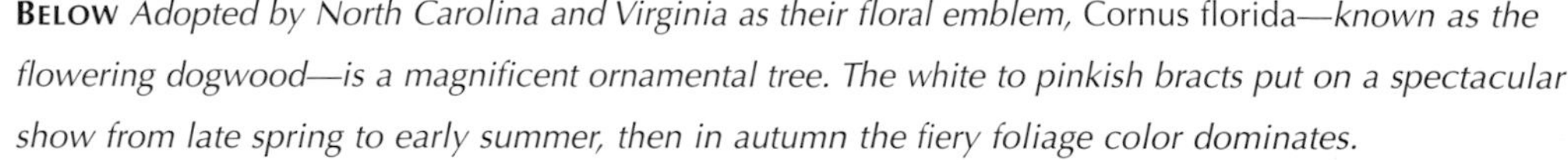

BELOW *Adopted by North Carolina and Virginia as their floral emblem,* Cornus florida*—known as the flowering dogwood—is a magnificent ornamental tree. The white to pinkish bracts put on a spectacular show from late spring to early summer, then in autumn the fiery foliage color dominates.*

LEFT *The oval leaves of* Cornus alba *'Sibirica Variegata' are bright green, distinctively edged in creamy white, with paler undersides.*

Top Tip

The young growth of red-stemmed *Cornus* species is the most vibrant. To encourage colorful new growth, cut back—almost to the ground—in early spring.

EUCALYPTUS

BELOW *Small white summer flowers and circular silvery gray juvenile leaves are distinctive characteristics of the silver dollar tree—*Eucalyptus cinerea.

Although they fuel fierce bushfires and are responsible for increasing soil salinity, eucalypts are the quintessential Australian trees. The genus contains around 800 species of evergreen trees of the myrtle (Myrtaceae) family and is predominantly Australian, with a few stragglers in New Guinea, Indonesia, and the southern Philippines. Usually graceful and open in habit, they are known for their peeling, often multicolored bark and volatile aromatic oils. When young, many species have circular leaves that encircle the stems, but mature trees generally have sickle-shaped leaves. The filamentous flowers appear at varying times and while often insignificant, those of some species are large and colorful. The botanical name is derived from the Greek *eu-kalypto,* meaning "to cover," and refers to the cap of the flower bud.

CULTIVATION

Hardiness varies with the species, though none will tolerate repeated severe frosts or prolonged winters. Plant in light well-drained soil and keep moist when young. They are drought tolerant once established. Propagate from seed.

BELOW *Commonly known as the four-winged mallee,* Eucalyptus tetraptera *features bright green leathery leaves and red flowers with pink stamens.*

Favorites	Flower Color	Blooming Season	Flower Fragrance
Eucalyptus cinerea	creamy white	summer	no
Eucalyptus erythrocorys	bright yellow	summer to autumn	no
Eucalyptus gunnii	creamy white	summer	no
Eucalyptus scoparia	creamy white	spring to summer	no
Eucalyptus tetraptera	red	spring	no
Eucalyptus torquata	pink, red	spring to summer	no

Top Tip

Fast growing and drought tolerant, eucalypts place few demands on gardeners. Pruning is necessary only to enhance shape or to remove old or dead wood.

LEFT *An ornamental species,* Eucalyptus scoparia *is rare in the wild. It is valued for its graceful weeping habit, peeling bark, and glossy green pendulous leaves.*
BELOW Eucalyptus torquata *puts on a floral display of pink and red in spring and summer—year-round in favorable climates. The long leaves are sickle-shaped.*

Plant Height	Plant Width	Hardiness Zone	Frost Tolerance
30–50 ft (9–15 m)	20–30 ft (6–9 m)	8–11	yes
25 ft (8 m)	10 ft (3 m)	9–11	yes
30–80 ft (9–24 m)	20–30 ft (6–9 m)	7–9	yes
40 ft (12 m)	20 ft (6 m)	9–11	yes
10 ft (3 m)	8 ft (2.4 m)	9–11	yes
40 ft (12 m)	15–30 ft (4.5–9 m)	9–11	yes

Top Tip

Take care when siting beech trees. The surface roots will take over the area beneath them, and the dense foliage will plunge underlying plants into deep shade.

FAGUS

The deciduous beech trees, of which there are 10 species spread over the northern temperate zone, make up the type genus for the beech (Fagaceae) family. They are sturdy trees with solid smooth-barked trunks and broad rounded crowns of toothed or wavy-edged, pointed oval leaves. Although the small spring flower clusters are interesting, beeches are grown for their statuesque form and their foliage. Their fresh, translucent green or purple-bronze, spring foliage positively glows at sunset, and their autumn colors should not be underestimated. Beech flowers develop into small bristly seed pods, which when shed form a layer of litter known as beech mast. The oil-rich seeds have some culinary uses, including being roasted to produce a coffee substitute. The wood is also oily and yields creosote.

ABOVE LEFT *The coppery seed pods of* Fagus sylvatica *'Quercina' have a prickly outer coating. They make a striking contrast with the glossy leathery foliage.*

BELOW *The oriental beech,* Fagus orientalis *is a fast-growing tree. It reaches up to 100 ft (30 m) tall in its native habitat, but is much smaller in cultivation.*

CULTIVATION

Beeches grow best in deep, fertile, moist, well-drained soil and prefer climates with distinct seasons. Trim lightly to allow the natural shape to develop. Propagate the species from seed, cultivars by grafting.

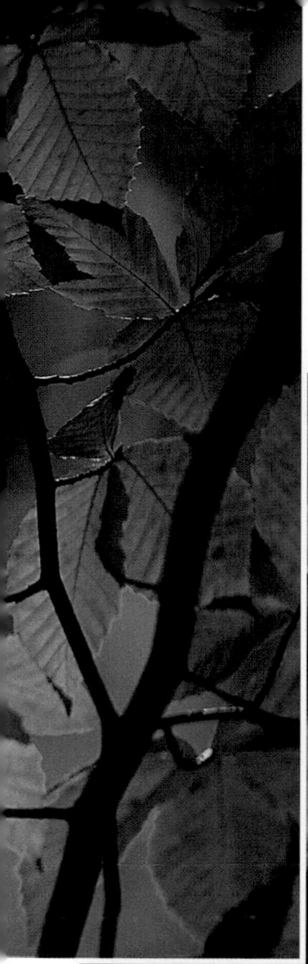

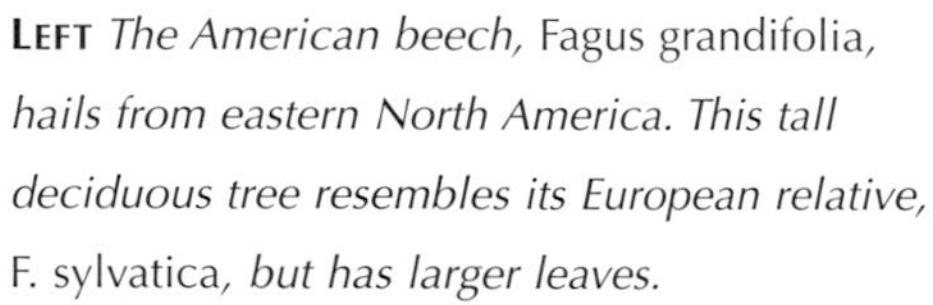

LEFT *The American beech,* Fagus grandifolia, *hails from eastern North America. This tall deciduous tree resembles its European relative,* F. sylvatica, *but has larger leaves.*

BELOW *Twisted branches distinguish* Fagus sylvatica *f.* tortuosa. *These branches carry the glossy green, strongly veined leaves. Prickly greenish seed pods follow the flowers.*

Favorites	Flower Color	Blooming Season	Flower Fragrance	Plant Height	Plant Width	Hardiness Zone	Frost Tolerance
Fagus crenata	yellow-green	spring	no	30 ft (9 m)	20 ft (6 m)	6–8	yes
Fagus grandifolia	yellow-green	spring	no	80 ft (24 m)	35 ft (10 m)	4–8	yes
Fagus orientalis	yellow-green	spring	no	100 ft (30 m)	40 ft (12 m)	6–8	yes
Fagus sylvatica	yellow (male) green (female)	spring	no	100 ft (30 m)	50 ft (15 m)	5–8	yes
***Fagus sylvatica* 'Purpurea'**	yellow-green	spring	no	50–60 ft (15–18 m)	35–50 ft (10–15 m)	5–8	yes
***Fagus sylvatica* 'Riversii'**	yellow-green	spring	no	100 ft (30 m)	50 ft (15 m)	5–8	yes

GINKGO

LEFT *The bright green fan-shaped leaves of* Ginkgo biloba *have earned it the common name of maidenhair tree. This deciduous tree eventually becomes quite large and is an impressive sight year-round.*

There is but one species in this genus, which is the sole member of its family, the Ginkgoaceae. Now unknown in the wild, *Ginkgo biloba* has long been cultivated in China. It is a deciduous, broad-based, conical tree more closely allied to the conifers than the flowering trees. The bark is light and deeply fissured, and the foliage, bright green when young and brilliant yellow in autumn, resembles that of the maidenhair fern. Catkins appear in spring and those of female trees develop into soft, pungent, single-seeded, yellow fruits. Ginkgo extracts are used medicinally and the edible seeds are nutritious, but should be cooked to destroy a mild toxin they contain.

BELOW *The unique* Ginkgo biloba *is an ancient tree that has adapted well to modern times, undeterred by environmental pollutants and extreme conditions.*

Top Tip

Ginkgo biloba needs little maintenance once established. However, regular watering and pruning when young will encourage a pleasing tree shape.

CULTIVATION

The ginkgo is a tough adaptable tree that is planted extensively in parks, but can be too large for small gardens. The fruit is very messy, so avenue specimens should be cutting-grown male trees. Propagate from seed or half-hardened cuttings under mist.

Favorites	Flower Color	Blooming Season	Flower Fragrance	Plant Height	Plant Width	Hardiness Zone	Frost Tolerance
Ginkgo biloba	yellow	spring	no	100 ft (30 m)	25 ft (8 m)	3–10	yes
***Ginkgo biloba* 'Autumn Gold'**	green	spring	no	50 ft (15 m)	30 ft (9 m)	3–10	yes
***Ginkgo biloba* 'Tremonia'**	yellow	spring	no	35 ft (10 m)	10–20 ft (3–6 m)	3–10	yes

Gleditsia

Above Gleditsia japonica *var.* koraiensis *is a native of eastern China. The long leaves—up to 12 in (30 cm) in length—consist of pairs of glossy yellow-green leaflets.*

This genus of 14 species of deciduous trees belongs to the cassia subfamily of the legume (Fabaceae) family. Commonly known as locusts, they are found in the Americas, central Asia, and parts of Africa. Spreading when young, they eventually develop an open crown of slightly pendulous branches clothed in large pinnate or bipinnate leaves. The foliage may color well in autumn and several colored foliage cultivars are available. The branches are often thorny, sometimes fiercely so. The late spring to early summer sprays of largely insignificant flowers are followed by long beanlike pods that contain edible seeds. In some drought-prone areas locusts are cultivated for these pods, which are a nutritious stock food.

Cultivation

Gleditsia species thrive in areas with hot summers and short, sharp, clearly defined winters. Late frosts can cause damage. Plant in a sunny position with well-drained fertile soil. Young trees need irrigation but are drought tolerant once established. Propagate the species from seed, the cultivars by budding or grafting.

Left *A recent introduction from the USA,* Gleditsia triacanthos *'Trueshade' makes an attractive shade tree with its large domed crown and spreading branches.*

Below *Commonly known as the Japanese locust,* Gleditsia japonica *is heavily armed with sharp thorns on its trunk and branches.*

Top Tip

Gleditsia trees are robust, and are ideally suited to street planting or open spaces. For pain-free gardening, choose from the many thornless cultivars available.

Above *An immensely popular cultivar,* Gleditsia triacanthos *f.* inermis *'Sunburst'* (syn. *'Aurea'*) *is fast growing. The attractive new foliage emerges bright yellow in spring, gradually maturing to a fresh lime green color.*

Right *Earning its common name of Caspian locust from its native habitat—the Caspian Sea region of northern Iran—*Gleditsia caspica *is heavily armed with thorns.*

Favorites	Flower Color	Blooming Season	Flower Fragrance	Plant Height	Plant Width	Hardiness Zone	Frost Tolerance
Gleditsia caspica	green	late spring to early summer	no	40 ft (12 m)	30 ft (9 m)	6–10	yes
Gleditsia japonica	whitish green	late spring to early summer	no	70 ft (21 m)	35 ft (10 m)	6–10	yes
Gleditsia triacanthos	whitish green	late spring to early summer	yes	150 ft (45 m)	70 ft (21 m)	3–10	yes
Gleditsia triacanthos* f. *inermis	whitish green	late spring to early summer	yes	50–60 ft (15–18 m)	40–50 ft (12–15 m)	3–10	yes
***Gleditsia triacanthos* f. *inermis* 'Rubylace'**	whitish green	late spring to early summer	yes	50–60 ft (15–18 m)	40–50 ft (12–15 m)	3–10	yes
***Gleditsia triacanthos* f. *inermis* 'Sunburst'**	whitish green	late spring to early summer	yes	30–60 ft (9–18 m)	40–50 ft (12–15 m)	3–10	yes

BELOW *Casting off its bare winter outline, the spring foliage of* Gleditsia triacanthos f. inermis *'Sunburst' (syn. 'Aurea') fills the branches with color. It makes an excellent specimen tree.*

RIGHT *Somewhat heavily armed with thorns,* Gleditsia triacanthos *features bright green ferny foliage that develops glorious color in autumn. Since their introduction, the thornless cultivars are more often seen in cultivation.*

BELOW Gleditsia triacanthos f. inermis *'Moraine' is a tall, elegant, thornless cultivar. Fern-like leaves emerge in spring, densely covering the wide-spreading branches.*

JACARANDA

A member of the trumpet-vine (Bignoniaceae) family, this genus comprises approximately 50 species of evergreen or deciduous trees found in drier areas of central and subtropical South America. The shape and foliage varies but many species develop a broad spreading crown of ferny bipinnate leaves. Deciduous species may develop some foliage color before leaf fall, which is usually brief. Large, brilliantly showy panicles of mauve-blue, rarely pink or white flowers appear from spring to summer, depending on the species. Conspicuous seed pods follow but are not a feature. *Jacaranda* is a Portuguese corruption of the original Brazilian Indian name.

ABOVE *Widely admired for its color,* Jacaranda mimosifolia *is a favorite for avenue planting in tropical and warm-temperate climates.*

CULTIVATION

Though most *Jacaranda* trees will tolerate some frost once established, both warm summers and mild winters are necessary to ensure that the plants flower heavily. Young trees often appear more luxuriant in light shade, and they should be sheltered from wind or staked firmly. Only light trimming is necessary. Propagate from seed in late winter or early spring or from half-hardened cuttings taken during the summer months.

Top Tip

Once established, jacarandas are generally fuss-free, although they will appreciate a regular watering routine throughout the growing season.

Favorites	Flower Color	Blooming Season	Flower Fragrance
Jacaranda caerulea	purple, blue, white	late spring	no
Jacaranda cuspidifolia	bright blue-violet	late spring	no
Jacaranda jasminoides	dark purple	late spring	no
Jacaranda mimosifolia	mauve-blue	late spring to early summer	no
***Jacaranda mimosifolia* 'Variegata'**	mauve-blue	late spring to early summer	no
***Jacaranda mimosifolia* 'White Christmas'**	white	late spring to early summer	no

LEFT *Nature puts on an impressive show when the branches of* Jacaranda mimosifolia *are laden with beautiful mauve-blue blooms.*
BOTTOM *With a spreading canopy, branching habit, and bright green fern-like foliage,* Jacaranda cuspidifolia *makes a fine specimen tree or shade tree.*
BELOW Jacaranda caerulea, *an evergreen tree, is native to the West Indies. In late spring the attractive bell-shaped flowers appear, in shades of purple, blue, or white.*

Plant Height	Plant Width	Hardiness Zone	Frost Tolerance
40–70 ft (12–21 m)	10 ft (3 m)	10–11	yes
15–40 ft (4.5–12 m)	30 ft (9 m)	10–11	yes
12–15 ft (3.5–4.5 m)	4–8 ft (1.2–2.4 m)	10–11	yes
25–50 ft (8–15 m)	20–35 ft (6–10 m)	10–11	yes
25–50 ft (8–15 m)	20–35 ft (6–10 m)	10–11	yes
25–50 ft (8–15 m)	20–35 ft (6–10 m)	10–11	yes

JUNIPERUS

This genus of around 60 species of evergreen coniferous shrubs and trees, widespread in the Northern Hemisphere, is a member of the cypress (Cupressaceae) family. The juvenile foliage is usually very dense, composed of short sharp needles, often with a blue-green tint, while the foliage of mature trees is usually scale-like in the typical cypress fashion. Some species produce fleshy berry-like cones, others have small scaly cones. All parts are very resinous and aromatic. The timber is used to make small objects and is an important fuel source in many remote areas. Juniper berries are edible and perhaps best known for their use in gin distillation.

ABOVE *A Himalayan native,* Juniperus recurva *var.* coxii *has a graceful weeping style. Slow growing, it can reach an ultimate height of 50 ft (15 m) in the wild.*

CULTIVATION

Hardiness varies; all will tolerate repeated frosts but the toughest species can survive subarctic winters and may also prefer correspondingly cool summers. Plant in an open, airy, sunny situation with light but humus-rich well-drained soil. Most junipers are drought tolerant but they respond well to reliable summer moisture. Propagate the species from seed, cultivars from hardwood cuttings, layers, or grafting.

ABOVE *The common juniper,* Juniperus communis *is an extremely variable species. So too are its cultivars, which offer a range of shapes, foliage, and colors, such as 'Pendula', with a classic weeping habit.*

Top Tip

Lightly prune junipers to maintain appearance and enhance shape. Do not prune bare wood as it is unlikely to produce any new growth.

RIGHT Juniperus chinensis *'Pyramidalis' is a perfect plant for borders, rockeries, and containers—its pyramidal form and blue-green foliage provide interest and color.*

Favorites

Favorites	Cone Color	Cone Shape	Cone Length	Plant Height	Plant Width	Hardiness Zone	Frost Tolerance
Juniperus chinensis	blue-green	round	¼–½ in (6–12 mm)	30 ft (9 m)	15 ft (4.5 m)	4–9	yes
Juniperus communis	green to black	round	⅓ in (9 mm)	20 ft (6 m)	3–15 ft (0.9–4.5 m)	2–8	yes
***Juniperus communis* 'Depressa Aurea'**	green to black	round	⅓ in (9 mm)	2–4 ft (0.6–1.2 m)	3 ft (0.9 m)	2–8	yes
Juniperus recurva	blue-black	round	¼–½ in (6–12 mm)	30 ft (9 m)	15 ft (4.5 m)	7–9	yes
Juniperus virginiana	purple	round	¼ in (6 mm)	40 ft (12 m)	12–20 ft (3.5–6 m)	2–8	yes
***Juniperus virginiana* 'Burkii'**	purple	round	¼ in (6 mm)	10 ft (3 m)	6–8 ft (1.8–2.4 m)	2–8	yes

LAGERSTROEMIA

Though commonly known as crape myrtles, *Lagerstroemia* species are not really myrtles, but members of the loosestrife (Lythraceae) family. The 53 species of deciduous and evergreen trees in this genus are found from temperate East Asia through the tropics to northern Australia. They are renowned for their showy summer display of vivid flower panicles. The deciduous species are often also colorful in autumn, when their foliage develops rich red, orange, and bronze tones. The leaves are most often simple pointed ovals in opposite pairs and can be thick and leathery. Their dark green color contrasts well with the attractive, peeling, mostly red-brown bark. The large species are the source of a very hard and dense timber.

CULTIVATION

The commonly cultivated crape myrtle *(Lagerstroemia indica)* is frost hardy but needs a hot summer to flower well. Most other species are far more tender and require a subtropical to tropical climate. Plant in a warm sunny position with fertile well-drained soil. Propagate the species from seed and take half-hardened or hardwood cuttings of the cultivars.

ABOVE *The shiny green leaves of* Lagerstroemia speciosa *are arranged in opposite pairs. Throughout autumn, they delight with a spectacular display of coppery tones.*

Favorites	Flower Color	Blooming Season	Flower Fragrance
Lagerstroemia fauriei	white	summer	no
Lagerstroemia floribunda	lavender-pink	spring to summer	no
Lagerstroemia indica	white, pink to dark red, purple	mid-summer to autumn	no
Lagerstroemia limii	lavender-pink	spring to summer	no
Lagerstroemia speciosa	white, pink, purple	summer to autumn	no
***Lagerstroemia* 'Tuscarora'**	dark coral pink	summer	no

Top Tip

Crape myrtles are known for being adaptable, reliable, easy-to-grow plants. To maximize their flowering potential, prune in winter or early spring.

ABOVE Lagerstroemia floribunda *is native to Myanmar, the Malay Peninsula, and southern Thailand. Its glossy leaves and vibrant spring flowers add a tropical touch to the garden.*
LEFT *Native to China and Japan,* Lagerstroemia indica *has been embraced by gardeners around the world for its rich foliage, attractive peeling bark, and papery-textured flowers.*
BELOW *Known as the pride of India or the queen crape myrtle,* Lagerstroema speciosa *features gray-yellow peeling bark, lustrous green leaves, and showy flowers.*

Plant Height	Plant Width	Hardiness Zone	Frost Tolerance
25 ft (8 m)	15–25 ft (4.5–8 m)	6–10	yes
15–40 ft (4.5–12 m)	15–25 ft (4.5–8 m)	10–12	no
20–25 ft (6–8 m)	20–25 ft (6–8 m)	7–11	yes
17–25 ft (5–8 m)	15–17 ft (4.5–5 m)	7–9	yes
25–50 ft (8–15 m)	15–30 ft (4.5–9 m)	10–12	no
25 ft (8 m)	8–25 ft (2.4–8 m)	7–11	yes

LIQUIDAMBAR

Top Tip

Sweet gums send out surface roots so select a site away from structures and other plants that may be affected by their encroaching root network.

BELOW Liquidambar styraciflua *'Golden Treasure' has stunning variegated foliage. The large mid-green leaves are heavily edged with golden yellow. In autumn the gold coloring gradually changes to rich purple-red.*

A genus of 4 species of deciduous trees of the witchhazel (Hamamelidaceae) family, it has a scattered distribution in the Americas, East Asia, and Turkey. The genus is best known for *Liquidambar styraciflua*, which is one of the most magnificently colored of all autumn foliage trees. The palmately lobed foliage is very reminiscent of maple leaves and variegated cultivars are available, as are selections with reliable autumn tones. Tiny greenish flowers open in spring and are followed by spiky woody seed capsules. Commonly known as sweet gum, *Liquidambar* is the source of a stabilizing gum used in manufactured foods, as well as storax, an aromatic resin used in perfumery and cosmetics.

CULTIVATION

Other than their size, which needs a large garden, sweet gums are hardy and easily grown in a temperate climate. They do best in a bright sunny position with deep, fertile, well-drained soil that remains moist in summer. Propagate the species from seed, cultivars from softwood cuttings.

LEFT *Probably the most commonly cultivated sweet gum, the fresh green spring and summer foliage of* Liquidambar styraciflua *develops wonderful russet tones in autumn.*
BELOW *The curious spiky seed capsules of* Liquidambar orientalis *add a decorative and textural dimension to the tree.*

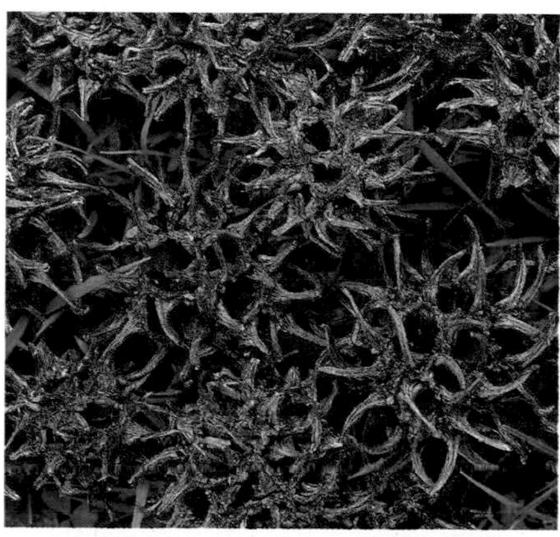

RIGHT *Dramatic autumn coloring is a trademark feature of the sweet gums. Fashioned into stylish tapering lobes, the leaves of* Liquidambar styraciflua *glow with autumn hues.*

Favorites	Flower Color	Blooming Season	Flower Fragrance	Plant Height	Plant Width	Hardiness Zone	Frost Tolerance
Liquidambar formosana	greenish yellow	spring	no	60 ft (18 m)	30 ft (9 m)	7–11	yes
Liquidambar orientalis	yellow-green	spring	no	25 ft (8 m)	15 ft (4.5 m)	8–11	yes
Liquidambar styraciflua	yellow-green	spring	no	70 ft (21 m)	35 ft (10 m)	5–11	yes
***Liquidambar styraciflua* 'Lane Roberts'**	yellow-green	spring	no	15–20 ft (4.5–6 m)	7–10 ft (2–3 m)	5–11	yes
***Liquidambar styraciflua* 'Rotundiloba'**	yellow-green	spring	no	50–70 ft (15–21 m)	35 ft (10 m)	5–11	yes
***Liquidambar styraciflua* 'Worplesdon'**	yellow-green	spring	no	40 ft (12 m)	25 ft (8 m)	5–11	yes

LIRIODENDRON

The 2 species in this genus in the magnolia (Magnoliaceae) family are large, spring-flowering, deciduous trees; one from North America and the other a less widely grown native of southern China, Taiwan, and northern Vietnam. Commonly known as tulip trees, they have distinctive and unusual lobed leaves that color well in autumn, developing yellow and orange tones. The cup-shaped yellow-green flowers are indeed reminiscent of tulips but regretfully they are often too high up in the tree to be properly appreciated. Tulip tree wood is popular with furniture makers for high-grade inlays and for wall linings; at the other end of the scale it is used for plywood.

RIGHT *The solitary, yellow-green, tulip-shaped flowers of* Liriodendron tulipifera *are highlighted with a basal blotch of orange-yellow.*

CULTIVATION

The North American species is hardier than the Asian species, though both will tolerate repeated frosts. Plant in a bright position with fertile, humus-rich, moist, well-drained soil. Shape when young to encourage a high, evenly branched crown. The species are usually raised from seed and the cultivars are grafted.

LEFT *With the ability to reach a height of 100 ft (30 m), the North American tulip tree,* Liriodendron tulipifera, *is well suited to planting in large open landscapes.*

Top Tip

Plant tulip trees in a sheltered spot to prevent damage from strong or drying winds. They also need a reliable supply of moisture, so water regularly during dry periods.

Favorites	Flower Color	Blooming Season	Flower Fragrance	Plant Height	Plant Width	Hardiness Zone	Frost Tolerance
Liriodendron tulipifera	yellow-green	spring	no	100 ft (30 m)	40 ft (12 m)	4–10	yes
***Liriodendron tulipifera* 'Aureomarginatum'**	yellow-green	spring	no	80 ft (24 m)	40 ft (12 m)	4–10	yes
***Liriodendron tulipifera* 'Fastigiatum'**	yellow-green	spring	no	50–60 ft (15–18 m)	20 ft (6 m)	4–10	yes

MAGNOLIA

The type genus for the magnolia (Magnoliaceae) family and among the most ancient of flowering trees, this primarily temperate East Asian and North American genus is composed of over 100 species of deciduous and evergreen trees and shrubs. They have large oval leaves that are sometimes thick and leathery. The flowers may be cup-shaped or more open, have broad or strappy petal-like tepals, and can be quite fragrant. The flowers are usually white, cream, or pink to purple shades and occur mainly in spring, except for the evergreen species, which flower all through the warmer months. Conspicuous, often brightly colored or unusually shaped seed pods follow. *Magnolia grandiflora*—commonly known as the southern magnolia or bull bay—is the state flower of both Louisiana and Mississippi.

ABOVE *The compact form of* Magnolia × loebneri *'Leonard Messel' is covered in bloom during the flowering season. The starry pink and white flowers appear before and after the leaves are produced.*

CULTIVATION

Magnolias are mostly hardy and easily grown in any fertile, moist, humus-rich, well-drained soil in light shade. They have abundant surface roots, so mulch well and avoid cultivating around them. The flowers last longer with wind protection. Propagation is from seed, summer cuttings, or by grafting.

ABOVE RIGHT Magnolia × soulangeana *'Verbanica', one of many cultivars, is a wonderful late-season sight with its stunning pink-tinged white flowers adorning the bare branches.*

RIGHT Magnolia sieboldii *has dark green leaves and graceful, nodding, white flowers. It is perfect for woodland gardens where the heady fragrance of the flowers can fill the air.*

Above *The elegant rich purple-pink flowers of* Magnolia × soulangeana *'Burgundy' sit erect on the branches, appearing ahead of the lustrous, mid- to deep green, oval leaves.*

Top Tip

The surface roots of magnolias can cause problems, lifting pathways and paving in their way. Plant away from any structures to avoid damage and repair work.

Left Magnolia grandiflora *can achieve a substantial height and spread. Plant in woodland gardens or large open landscapes to add color and fragrance.*

Favorites	Flower Color	Blooming Season	Flower Fragrance	Plant Height	Plant Width	Hardiness Zone	Frost Tolerance
***Magnolia* 'Elizabeth'**	pale yellow	mid- to late spring	yes	30 ft (9 m)	20 ft (6 m)	6–9	yes
Magnolia grandiflora	white to creamy white	summer to autumn	yes	30–80 ft (9–24 m)	20–60 ft (6–18 m)	6–11	yes
Magnolia* × *loebneri	white to pink	mid-spring to summer	yes	20–30 ft (6–9 m)	20–25 ft (6–8 m)	4–9	yes
Magnolia sieboldii	white	late spring to late summer	yes	20 ft (6 m)	25 ft (8 m)	6–9	yes
Magnolia* × *soulangeana	white, pink to purple-pink	late winter to mid-spring	yes	20–25 ft (6–8 m)	15–20 ft (4.5–6 m)	4–10	yes
Magnolia virginiana	creamy white	summer	yes	30 ft (9 m)	20 ft (6 m)	5–10	yes

LEFT *The bare branches of* Magnolia × soulangeana *are decorated with pink and white flowers from spring. As the season progresses, the glossy leaves unfurl to add to the display.*

BELOW *Native to swampy areas of coastal USA, and commonly known as swamp laurel,* Magnolia virginiana, *seen here in bud, can be evergreen or deciduous.*

ABOVE *Delicate and fragrant, the flowers of* Magnolia *'Elizabeth' give no indication of the robust nature of this cultivar, which can tolerate cooler temperatures.*

MALUS

RIGHT Malus × purpurea, *a hybrid with an upright open habit, has given rise to many cultivars. Whether in bloom or not, they add a simple charm to garden situations.*

Widespread in the northern temperate zones but centered around Asia, this genus of around 30 species of deciduous trees and shrubs is a member of the rose (Rosaceae) family. Because of the importance of their fruit and the beauty of the flowers, hundreds of cultivars and hybrids have been raised. Apple trees are mainly spreading or broad-crowned, with serrated oval leaves and an abundance of white to deep cerise flowers in spring. The fruit of the wild species is usually small and red or yellow. In addition to being an important part of our diet and a commercially significant crop, apple extracts have some medicinal uses and the wood is popular with turners.

ABOVE *With glossy reddish bark, dark pink buds and flowers, and dark burgundy colored fruit,* Malus ioensis *'Prairifire' is a magnificent sight at any time of year.*

CULTIVATION

Malus thrives in temperate to cool-temperate climates and grows best in deep, fertile, humus-rich soil that remains moist. The plants are very hardy, though late frosts when in bloom can affect the fruit crop. Species may be raised from stratified seed; cultivars are usually grafted.

BELOW *The rich pink buds of* Malus coronaria *var.* dasycalyx *'Charlottae' open to reveal light pink, semi-double to double flowers, which are highly scented.*

Top Tip

Where possible, select apple varieties with disease resistance and be aware that some varieties will only bear fruit every other year.

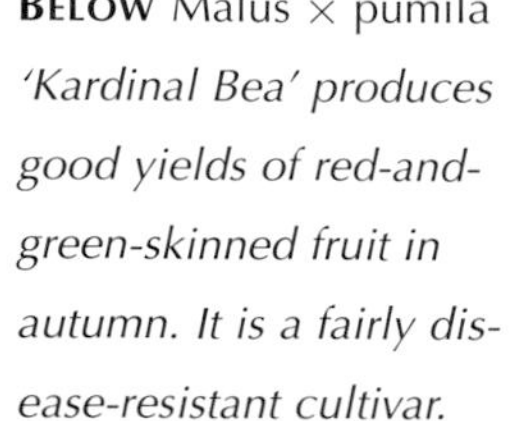

BELOW Malus × pumila *'Kardinal Bea' produces good yields of red-and-green-skinned fruit in autumn. It is a fairly disease-resistant cultivar.*

Favorites	Flower Color	Blooming Season	Flower Fragrance	Plant Height	Plant Width	Hardiness Zone	Frost Tolerance
***Malus* 'Christmas Holly'**	white	spring	no	15 ft (4.5 m)	15 ft (4.5 m)	4–9	yes
Malus coronaria	pink to pink-white	spring	no	30 ft (9 m)	30 ft (9 m)	4–9	yes
Malus ioensis	white, pink on the outside	late spring	yes	20 ft (6 m)	20–25 ft (6–8 m)	2–9	yes
Malus* × *pumila	white, often tinged pink	spring	no	20–50 ft (6–15 m)	15–25 ft (4.5–8 m)	3–9	yes
***Malus* × *pumila* 'Fuji'**	whitish pink	spring	no	15–20 ft (4.5–6 m)	15–20 ft (4.5–6 m)	3–9	yes
Malus* × *purpurea	purple-red	spring	no	20 ft (6 m)	25 ft (8 m)	4–9	yes

NOTHOFAGUS

RIGHT *From Argentina and Chile,* Nothofagus pumilio *can become shrub-like in extreme conditions. It has glossy green leaves that take on fiery hues in autumn.*

The 35-odd species of evergreen and deciduous trees in this genus are found mainly in South America, New Zealand, and southeastern Australia, including Tasmania, where they are among the dominant forest trees. Members of the beech (Fagaceae) family, they are mainly strongly upright, straight-trunked trees with attractive bark and small, dark green leaves in airy open sprays. In spring, small pollen-laden flowers open and are followed by nutlets that eventually break open to shed their very fine seeds. Although southern beeches are still common, they were once far more widely distributed and their fossilized remains have been found in the Antarctic. Several species are important timber trees in their homelands.

ABOVE *The myrtle beech,* Nothofagus cunninghamii *is a fast-growing tree with a conical habit. The lustrous bright green leaves may be red-tinged when young.* **BELOW** *A tall deciduous tree with an upright broad-domed habit,* Nothofagus alessandrii *is best suited to open landscapes.*

CULTIVATION

Mostly too large for small gardens, the southern beeches are otherwise adaptable trees that respond well to cultivation. They will tolerate prolonged cold but not extreme frosts. Plant in sun or part-shade with moist humus-rich soil and water well. Propagate from seed, hardwood cuttings, or layers.

Favorites	Blooming Season	Flower Fragrance	Bark Color
Nothofagus alessandrii	spring	no	purple-brown
Nothofagus antarctica	spring	no	purple-brown
Nothofagus cunninghamii	early summer	no	purple-brown
Nothofagus dombeyi	spring	no	purple-brown
Nothofagus obliqua	spring	no	reddish gray
Nothofagus pumilio	spring	no	purple-brown

Top Tip

Although southern beeches are adaptable trees, they do not tolerate salty coastal winds. Ensure young trees receive regular water until they are well established.

BELOW *With a broad columnar habit,* Nothofagus obliqua *makes a wonderful shade tree in summer. It is fast growing and features attractive reddish gray bark.*

Plant Height	Plant Width	Hardiness Zone	Frost Tolerance
90 ft (27 m)	30 ft (9 m)	8–10	yes
40 ft (12 m)	20 ft (6 m)	8–9	yes
5–100 ft (1.5–30 m)	8–30 ft (2.4–9 m)	8–9	yes
50 ft (15 m)	25 ft (8 m)	8–9	yes
100 ft (30 m)	30 ft (9 m)	8–10	yes
70 ft (21 m)	30 ft (9 m)	8–9	yes

NYSSA

Top Tip

Once the roots of *Nyssa* species have gained a foothold on their position, they are very difficult to transplant. Plant where they are to remain.

The 5 deciduous trees of this North American and Southeast Asian genus are renowned for their autumn foliage color, which develops best after a hot summer with a long warm autumn. Members of the dogwood (Cornaceae) family, they are erect, often rather open trees that in the wild tend to occur in the damp margins of streams, lakes, and swamps. The simple oval leaves can become quite large on mature trees and in the right conditions will develop strong gold and orange tones before falling. Tiny inconspicuous flowers open in spring and are followed by small purple-blue fruits that are edible, though tart. While not particularly strong, the wood has an interesting grain and is occasionally used in veneers.

CULTIVATION

Plant in sun or part-shade with deep, fertile, well-drained soil that remains moist. A sheltered position will help prolong the autumn display. Trim to shape when young, otherwise leave to develop naturally. Propagate from fresh seed or half-hardened cuttings.

ABOVE *Hailing from North America,* Nyssa sylvatica*—known as the black gum—is a rather stately tree with an upright form and horizontal branches.*

LEFT Nyssa sinensis *is known as the Chinese tupelo. It has a spreading habit and in autumn the foliage develops wonderful russet and yellow tones.*

Favorites	Flower Color	Blooming Season	Flower Fragrance	Plant Height	Plant Width	Hardiness Zone	Frost Tolerance
Nyssa sinensis	green	spring	no	40 ft (12 m)	30 ft (9 m)	7–10	yes
Nyssa sylvatica	green	spring	no	50 ft (15 m)	30 ft (9 m)	3–10	yes
***Nyssa sylvatica* 'Wisley Bonfire'**	green	spring	no	50 ft (15 m)	30 ft (9 m)	3–10	yes

PICEA

LEFT Picea orientalis, *the Caucasian spruce, has given rise to a number of cultivars, such as the shorter-growing 'Connecticut Turnpike' with dense glossy green foliage.*

This genus, a member of the pine (Pinaceae) family, contains about 45 species of evergreen coniferous trees, better known to most as spruces. They are found in the temperate to subarctic regions of the northern hemisphere, often in mountainous areas. Mainly conical in shape and superficially similar to the firs (*Abies* species), with rather broad needles, they differ most noticeably in that spruce cones are pendulous, not erect. The foliage often has a strong blue tint that in some of the best forms is an almost metallic silver-blue. Spruces are commercially important trees that are often grown in large plantations. The wood of most species is often weak but the timber is ideal for producing pulp.

CULTIVATION

Hardiness varies, though most tolerate severe frosts and prefer cool summers. Plant in sun with deep, cool, moist, humus-rich, acidic soil. They are best left untrimmed. Propagate species from seed, cultivars from cuttings or by grafting.

ABOVE *Known as the Black Hills spruce,* Picea glauca *'Densata' grows to around 25 ft (8 m) high and features fine, needle-like, green to blue-green foliage.*

LEFT *The spreading branches of* Picea abies *'Nidiformis' form a bowl shape at the apex—hence the common name of bird's nest spruce.*

Favorites	Cone Color	Cone Shape	Cone Length	Plant Height	Plant Width	Hardiness Zone	Frost Tolerance
Picea abies	light brown	cylindrical	8 in (20 cm)	200 ft (60 m)	20 ft (6 m)	2–9	yes
Picea breweriana	light brown	cylindrical	4 in (10 cm)	120 ft (36 m)	15 ft (4.5 m)	2–8	yes
Picea glauca	green to light brown	narrowly cylindrical	2 in (5 cm)	80 ft (24 m)	12–20 ft (3.5–6 m)	1–8	yes
Picea omorika	purple to dark brown	spindle	3 in (8 cm)	100 ft (30 m)	20 ft (6 m)	4–8	yes
Picea orientalis	purple	cylindrical	4 in (10 cm)	100 ft (30 m)	20 ft (6 m)	3–8	yes
Picea pungens	light brown	cylindrical	5 in (12 cm)	100 ft (30 m)	20 ft (6 m)	2–8	yes

ABOVE *Clad with bright green needles, the graceful drooping branches of* Picea omorika *curve upward at the ends, giving the tree an elegant and graceful form.*

RIGHT *Initially purple, and maturing to a rich brown color, the spindle-shaped cones of* Picea omorika *sit among the bright green needle-like foliage.*

BELOW *The long, cylindrical, light brown cones of* Picea abies *'Cranstonii' initially sit erect on the branches, then gradually hang downward.*

RIGHT *A slow-growing form,* Picea abies *'Procumbens' has a spreading habit. The densely layered branches are clothed in bright green needle-like foliage.*

RIGHT *The stunning silvery blue foliage of* Picea pungens *'Glauca Compacta' can be used to good effect for creating contrast when planted in conifer gardens.* Picea pungens *is recognized as the state tree of both Colorado and Utah.*

Top Tip

Though most *Picea* species are too large for suburban gardens, many dwarf cultivars have been raised that are ideal for use as rockery or container plants.

RIGHT Pinus sylvestris, *the Scotch pine, is valuable for timber and Christmas trees. The variety here is* P. s. *var.* lapponica, *which has smaller leaves and cones.*

PINUS

Probably the best known of the large conifers, the genus *Pinus* is the type form for the pine (Pinaceae) family. It is made up of over 100 species that are widely distributed in the Northern Hemisphere, from the near-arctic to the mountains of the tropics. Their long needle-like foliage is instantly recognizable and that of the warm climate species can be particularly luxuriant. Pine bark is thick, deeply furrowed, and often flakes to reveal brighter bark underneath. The cones are often an attractive feature and some yield edible seeds. Pines are extremely resinous and in addition to their commercially important timber, they are sources of turpentine, pine tar, and pine oil.

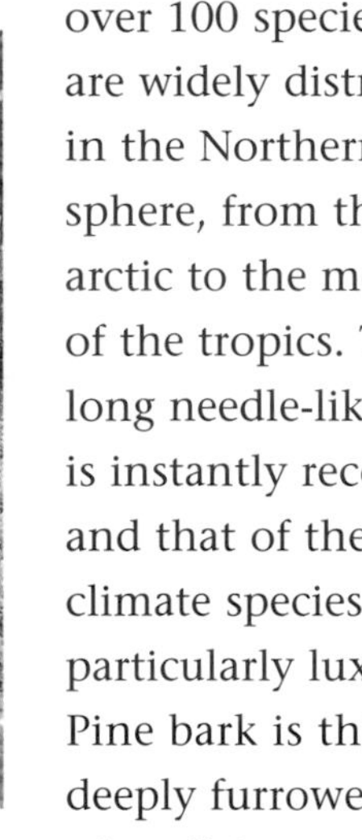

ABOVE Pinus mugo *is one of the few pine species that will tolerate a shaded position. It will grow well in a container or a rock garden and its size and density can be controlled by pruning.*

CULTIVATION

Hardiness varies considerably, so choose species suitable for the climate. Many are too large or too untidy for domestic gardens, shedding needles and cones. Plant in full sun with well-drained soil that can be kept moist until the trees are well established. Trim to shape when young. Propagate the species from seed, cultivars by grafting.

Top Tip

It is usually not necessary to prune pine trees, except to remove dead or broken branches or to cut to achieve a triangular Christmas tree effect.

Favorites	Cone Color	Cone Shape	Cone Length
Pinus densiflora	dull brown	egg-shaped	2 in (5 cm)
Pinus mugo	grayish brown	egg-shaped	1–2 in (2.5–5 cm)
Pinus nigra	light brown	egg-shaped	2–3 in (5–8 cm)
Pinus radiata	yellowish brown	egg-shaped	5 in (12 cm)
Pinus strobus	green to brown	cylindrical	4–7 in (10–18 cm)
Pinus sylvestris	gray-green	conical	2–3 in (5–8 cm)

Above *Generally* Pinus strobus *is a very tall tree that may reach 165 ft (50 m). This cultivar is 'Prostrata' and has a low spreading habit.*
Below Pinus strobus *is more commonly known as the eastern white pine. It is the state tree of Maine and Michigan. This cultivar, 'Pendula', has weeping branches.*

Plant Height	Plant Width	Hardiness Zone	Frost Tolerance
70 ft (21 m)	20 ft (6 m)	4–9	yes
25 ft (8 m)	12 ft (3.5 m)	2–8	yes
120 ft (36 m)	25 ft (8 m)	4–9	yes
100 ft (30 m)	25 ft (8 m)	8–10	yes
165 ft (50 m)	20 ft (6 m)	3–9	yes
100 ft (30 m)	20 ft (6 m)	2–9	yes

PLATANUS

Favorites	Fruit Color	Fruit Shape	Fruit Length
Platanus* × *hispanica	brown	round	1 in (25 mm)
***Platanus* × *hispanica* 'Bloodgood'**	brown	round	1 in (25 mm)
Platanus occidentalis	yellowish brown	round	1–2 in (25–50 mm)
Platanus orientalis	brown	round	1 in (25 mm)
Platanus orientalis* var. *insularis	brown	round	1 in (25 mm)
Platanus racemosa	brown	round	1 in (25 mm)

This genus in the plane (Platanaceae) family consists of 8 species of deciduous trees that are found across the northern temperate zones, including Eurasia, North America, and Mexico. They have large, maple-like, palmate leaves that create a dense, usually high-branching canopy. Their flowers are insignificant but develop into fruits known as achenes that eventually break into a fluffy mass. The most distinctive feature of these trees is their bark, which flakes in small patches, creating a mottled honeycomb of buff, pale green, and ivory. Plane trees are very pollution resistant and were among the few trees to be able to survive the notorious London smogs of the 1940s and 1950s. The timber has limited use for manufacturing furniture.

CULTIVATION

Hardy in all but the coldest areas, plane trees grow quite quickly when young. They prefer an open position with deep moisture-retentive soil. They are superb trees for large home gardens, parklands, and broad avenues. Propagation is from seed, cuttings, or layers.

RIGHT Platanus orientalis *var.* insularis *has bright green leaves with toothed lobes, and hairy fruits. The fruits grow in clusters of 2 to 6.*

Plant Height	Plant Width	Hardiness Zone	Frost Tolerance
100 ft (30 m)	60 ft (18 m)	4–9	yes
100 ft (30 m)	60 ft (18 m)	4–9	yes
150 ft (45 m)	70 ft (21 m)	4–9	yes
100 ft (30 m)	90 ft (27 m)	5–9	yes
100 ft (30 m)	90 ft (27 m)	5–9	yes
100 ft (30 m)	75 ft (23 m)	7–10	yes

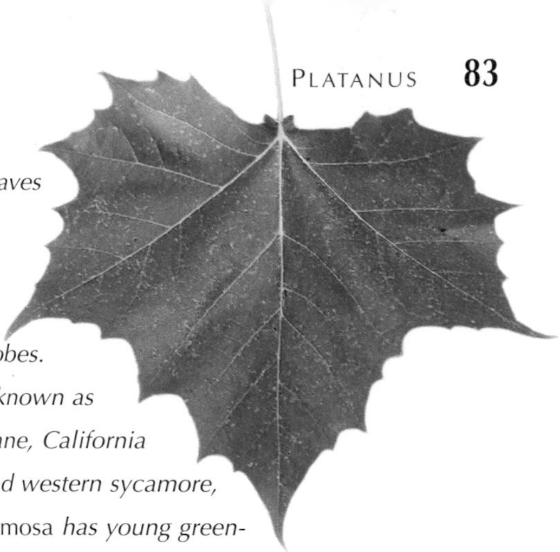

RIGHT *The leaves of* Platanus occidentalis *are simple with 3 to 5 lobes.*

BELOW *Also known as California plane, California sycamore, and western sycamore,* Platanus racemosa *has young green-gray bark that peels to reveal almost pure white inner bark. Older bark is thicker, furrowed, and dark brown.*

BELOW Platanus orientalis *can grow to 100 ft (30 m). It has attractive brown, gray, and greenish white bark.*

Top Tip

Platanus trees are very tolerant of root disturbance. Trees up to around 15 ft (4.5 m) can be transplanted quite easily if the original site is not suitable.

QUERCUS

BELOW Quercus rubra *is also known as the northern red oak. The state tree of New Jersey, its leaves turn bright red before falling in autumn.*

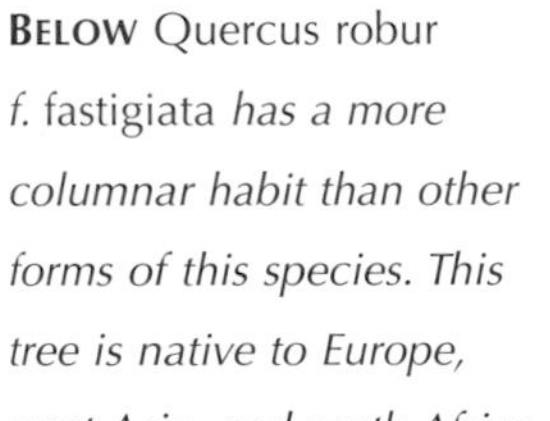

The broad crown of the common or English oak is instantly recognizable in any season, but it is just one of some 600 deciduous and evergreen trees that make up this genus of the beech (Fagaceae) family. While many have the characteristic lobed leaves, others have simpler, toothed foliage. In spring, sprays of tiny green or pale yellow flowers open, followed by the cupped fruits, called acorns, that are such a defining feature of the genus. Oaks have been used for so many things over the years, from hiding kings, to providing timber for furniture and corks, to supplying feed for pigs. They are clearly a most useful tree whose main task is perhaps making our world more beautiful.

BELOW Quercus robur f. fastigiata *has a more columnar habit than other forms of this species. This tree is native to Europe, west Asia, and north Africa.*

CULTIVATION

Hardiness varies, with the evergreens generally less hardy than the deciduous species. Most are too large and ground robbing for small gardens but are magnificent specimen trees for large gardens, arboretums, and parks. Young oaks tolerate shade and prefer deep humus-rich soil that remains moist. Propagation is most often from seed; cultivars are grafted.

Top Tip

When attempting to grow oaks from seed, place the acorn in a bucket of water. Those that sink to the bottom of the bucket are best for planting.

Favorites

Favorites	Flower Color	Blooming Season	Flower Fragrance
Quercus glauca	brown	spring	no
Quercus phillyreoides	greenish brown	spring	no
Quercus robur	yellow-green	spring	no
Quercus rubra	yellow-green	spring	no
Quercus texana	yellow-green	spring	no
Quercus virginiana	yellowish green	spring	no

Plant Height	Plant Width	Hardiness Zone	Frost Tolerance
50 ft (15 m)	15 ft (4.5 m)	7–9	yes
15 ft (4.5 m)	40 ft (12 m)	6–10	yes
100 ft (30 m)	70 ft (21 m)	3–10	yes
100 ft (30 m)	70 ft (21 m)	3–9	yes
50–70 ft (15–21 m)	50–70 ft (15–21 m)	7–10	yes
70 ft (21 m)	35 ft (10 m)	7–11	yes

ABOVE *This acorn is the fruit of the* Quercus texana *species, which is found naturally in Texas and Oklahoma. The acorns ripen in the second year.*

TOP *The state tree of Georgia,* Quercus virginiana *is an evergreen species. It is the only American species that produces valuable timber which is used for ship-building and posts.*

ROBINIA

Found mainly in eastern USA, the 20 or so species of deciduous trees and shrubs that make up this pea-flower subfamily of the legume (Fabaceae) family are cultivated for their graceful pinnate foliage and pendulous floral racemes, which are followed by flat seed pods. The branches tend to be rather thin and brittle and are often armed with fierce thorns. Several cultivars with colored foliage are available, and the species occasionally develop bright yellow autumn tones. The genus name honors Jean Robin (1550–1629) and his son Vespasian (1579–1662), who were herbalists to the Kings of France and the first to cultivate the genus in Europe.

ABOVE Robinia × slavinii *is a shrubby hybrid between* R. kelseyi *and* R. pseudoacacia. *It bears these rose pink flowers in summer, like* R. kelseyi.

CULTIVATION

The brittle branches can be a problem in windy areas and shelter for them may be necessary. Otherwise, these are hardy, easily cultivated trees that thrive in any bright position with moist well-drained soil. Species are raised from seed. While cuttings will strike, the cultivars are usually grafted onto seedling stocks to ensure superior root systems.

Top Tip

Robinias are prone to suckering. Suckers must be controlled otherwise they will grow into large thorny specimens of the original tree.

RIGHT Robinia pseudoacacia *'Frisia' is a thornless cultivar. Its foliage is an attractive yellow-green color but the tree does not bear many flowers.*

ABOVE Robinia hispida *grows dense and bushy to 10 ft (3 m) tall and at least as wide unless it is pruned. Its branches are covered in red bristles that can cause skin irritation.*

TOP Robinia pseudoacacia *is the most widely grown robinia. It is also known as black locust and false acacia. This is the spring growth of cultivar 'Twisted Beauty'.*

Favorites	Flower Color	Blooming Season	Flower Fragrance	Plant Height	Plant Width	Hardiness Zone	Frost Tolerance
Robinia* × *ambigua	pale pink	summer	no	50 ft (15 m)	25 ft (8 m)	3–9	yes
Robinia fertilis	rose pink	spring	no	8 ft (2.4 m)	4 ft (1.2 m)	4–10	yes
Robinia hispida	magenta-pink to purple	late spring	no	10 ft (3 m)	10 ft (3 m)	5–9	yes
Robinia pseudoacacia	white to cream	summer	no	50 ft (15 m)	35 ft (10 m)	3–10	yes
Robinia* × *slavinii	rose pink	spring	no	15 ft (4.5 m)	10 ft (3 m)	5–9	yes
Robinia viscosa	pink with yellow markings	late spring	no	30 ft (9 m)	20 ft (6 m)	3–10	yes

LEFT *Native to mountainous regions of Taiwan,* Sorbus randaiensis *produces small clusters of white to cream flowers, followed by showy tiny red fruits in autumn.*

Top Tip

Grow in a humus-rich, moderately fertile, deep soil with ample summer moisture for best results. Plant in sun or partial shade and prune to shape in autumn or winter.

BELOW *From western China,* Sorbus sargentiana, *also called Sargent's rowan, is known for stunning autumn foliage. Red berries, loved by birds, follow the flowers.*

SORBUS

Spread throughout the northern temperate zones, this genus in the rose (Rosaceae) family is composed of around 100 species of deciduous trees and shrubs. Most have pinnate foliage, though a few species have simple oval leaves with serrated edges. During spring they produce an abundance of flat-topped clusters (corymbs) of small white to cream flowers that can be somewhat unpleasantly scented. These flowers develop into showy clusters of fruit in colors ranging from gold, orange, and red to white, pink, or mauve-purple, depending on the species. In good years bright red autumn foliage tones may develop. In the past, *Sorbus* species were planted beside doors and gates, as they were thought to protect houses and ward off unwelcome visitations.

CULTIVATION

Mostly *Sorbus* species are very hardy and prefer a cool climate, suffering in high summer temperatures. Propagation is from stratified seed or by grafting and sometimes from hardwood cuttings. Prune as necessary after fruiting and be wary of fireblight, which can cause damage.

LEFT *The lobed leaves of* Sorbus hupehensis *turn a strong pink tone, redden, then fall in autumn. Small white berries turn blush pink as they ripen.*
BELOW Sorbus alnifolia *has serrated leaves that turn orange and red in autumn. Masses of showy white flowers are followed by red or yellow fruits.*

Favorites	Flower Color	Blooming Season	Flower Fragrance	Plant Height	Plant Width	Hardiness Zone	Frost Tolerance
Sorbus alnifolia	white	spring	yes	50 ft (15 m)	25 ft (8 m)	6–9	yes
Sorbus americana	white	spring	yes	20–30 ft (6–9 m)	20 ft (6 m)	2–9	yes
Sorbus aria	white	spring	yes	20–40 ft (6–12 m)	25 ft (8 m)	5–9	yes
Sorbus hupehensis	white	spring	yes	30 ft (9 m)	20 ft (6 m)	6–9	yes
Sorbus randaiensis	white to cream	spring	yes	20 ft (6 m)	10 ft (3 m)	7–10	yes
Sorbus sargentiana	white	summer	yes	20–30 ft (6–9 m)	20 ft (6 m)	6–9	yes

STYRAX

A genus of around 100 species of deciduous and evergreen trees and shrubs in the storax (Styraceae) family, it occurs in the northern temperate and tropical zones. Though slow to establish, their size, seldom exceeding 25 ft (8 m) tall, makes them a good option for smaller gardens. The leaves are usually simple, dark green, and have serrated edges, though some species have larger leaves with felted undersides. In spring, showy clusters of small, scented, white to pale pink flowers are borne beneath the branches. Small fleshy fruits then follow. The storax tree *(Styrax officinalis)* is a source of the fragrant resin storax, which is used in perfumery, cosmetics, and sometimes in food. The hard seeds are often made into beads.

Top Tip

The fragrant bell-shaped flowers are best viewed from below, and so site selection needs some thought. A terrace planting is very effective.

ABOVE *Commonly known as the Japanese snowbell,* Styrax japonicus *is native to Korea as well as Japan. Short pendulous clusters of white blooms are borne from late spring to early summer.*
BELOW *The vigorous* Styrax japonicus *'Fargesii' has bigger leaves than the species, and elegant scented blooms.*

CULTIVATION

Styrax prefer deep, fertile, humus-rich soil, and a sheltered position in sun or part-shade. They like regular but not overly abundant watering, and hardy deciduous types grow best in areas with cool moist summers and mild winters. Propagation is from half-hardened cuttings or seed, which may need stratification.

Favorites	Flower Color	Blooming Season	Flower Fragrance	Plant Height	Plant Width	Hardiness Zone	Frost Tolerance
Styrax japonicus	white	spring to summer	yes	20–30 ft (6–9 m)	15 ft (4.5 m)	5–9	yes
Styrax obassia	white	spring to summer	yes	35 ft (10 m)	20 ft (6 m)	6–10	yes
Styrax officinalis	white	summer	yes	20 ft (6 m)	15 ft (4.5 m)	8–10	yes

TILIA

The linden (Tiliaceae) family is based around this genus of 45 species of North American and Eurasian deciduous trees, which are widely cultivated in parks and avenues. Lindens have deep green, heart-shaped to deltoid leaves that often have pale undersides and which often develop attractive yellow tones in autumn. In summer the trees are smothered in fragrant, small, cream flowers backed by pale bracts. To walk under flowering linden trees is to know the hum of bees, which find them irresistible. The flowers are followed by tiny, hard, round seed capsules. This genus is the source of basswood, a soft but easily worked wood that is widely used for interior linings and cheap furniture, as well as for paper pulp.

LEFT Tilia platyphyllos *is a dome-shaped tree found in various forms from western Europe to southwest Asia. It bears clusters of pale yellow flowers in summer.*

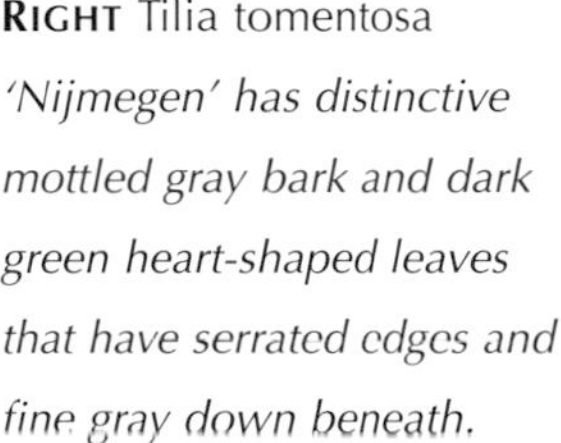

RIGHT Tilia tomentosa *'Nijmegen' has distinctive mottled gray bark and dark green heart-shaped leaves that have serrated edges and fine gray down beneath.*

CULTIVATION

Lindens are hardy adaptable trees that tolerate most soils provided they are deep and moist. They grow best in areas with clearly defined seasons. Trim when young in order to encourage a high-branched even crown. Propagate from stratified seed, cuttings, layers, or by grafting.

RIGHT Tilia tomentosa, *also known as silver linden, is native to areas around the Black Sea and has dull white summer flowers. 'Brabant', seen here, is a broadly conical cultivar.*

Top Tip

Tilia (linden) trees tend to become drought stressed if left without enough water for too long. Give them a deep watering once a week in areas of inadequate rainfall.

ABOVE LEFT Tilia platyphyllos *'Laciniata' has distinctive stems that are hairy when young. It develops a pretty dome shape, and bears yellow flowers from the crown in summer.*
LEFT Tilia cordata *is also known as the little-leaf linden. This cultivar, 'Rancho', has a conical habit, and bears clusters of 5 to 7 fragrant cream flowers in summer.*

Favorites	Flower Color	Blooming Season	Flower Fragrance	Plant Height	Plant Width	Hardiness Zone	Frost Tolerance
Tilia americana	pale yellow	summer	yes	100 ft (30 m)	40 ft (12 m)	3–9	yes
Tilia cordata	cream	summer	yes	80–100 ft (24–30 m)	40 ft (12 m)	3–9	yes
Tilia* × *euchlora	cream	summer	yes	70 ft (21 m)	40 ft (12 m)	4–9	yes
Tilia* × *europaea	cream	summer	yes	100 ft (30 m)	40 ft (12 m)	5–9	yes
Tilia platyphyllos	pale yellow	summer	yes	100 ft (30 m)	50 ft (15 m)	5–9	yes
Tilia tomentosa	dull white	summer	yes	80–100 ft (24–30 m)	50 ft (15 m)	6–9	yes

LEFT *The extremely popular* Tilia americana *'Redmond' is one of the most attractive street or lawn trees in the USA as it has pleasantly scented flowers.*

BELOW *The arched limbs of* Tilia × euchlora *become increasingly pendulous with age. Large cream-colored flowerheads, borne in summer, are attractive to bees.*

ABOVE Tilia cordata *'Chancellor' is tolerant of drought. Its narrow upright habit, to 50 ft (15 m) tall and only 20 ft (6 m) wide, makes it an excellent street tree.*

ULMUS

Some 45 species of deciduous trees and shrubs make up *Ulmus*, the type genus for the elm (Ulmaceae) family. Elms occur naturally in the northern temperate zones and at higher altitudes in the subtropics where at least one rather tender semi-evergreen species can be found. Elms have heavily veined, coarsely serrated, pointed oval leaves of variable size, depending on the species. Clusters of flowers open in spring, usually before the foliage develops. These are largely insignificant but are soon followed by conspicuous, usually pale green, winged seeds (samara). Elm timber is very water-resistant and was extensively used for the keels of large wooden sailing ships.

ABOVE *A disease-resistant tree from Japan, China, and Korea,* Ulmus parvifolia *will keep its small glossy leaves almost all year in mild climates.*

CULTIVATION

Elms are tough adaptable trees that succeed in most well-drained soils. Most species prefer a distinctly seasonal climate. Dutch elm disease, spread by beetle larvae, has in many areas devastated these stately trees. Cultivars are propagated by grafting, which regretfully may help to spread Dutch elm disease. The species may be raised from seed.

RIGHT *The fruit (samara) of* Ulmus × hollandica *'Modolina' consists of a seed surrounded by a thin wing. The fruit ripens in spring as the leaves appear.*

Favorites	Flower Color	Blooming Season	Flower Fragrance	Plant Height	Plant Width	Hardiness Zone	Frost Tolerance
Ulmus glabra	red	spring	no	100 ft (30 m)	70 ft (21 m)	5–9	yes
***Ulmus glabra* 'Camperdownii'**	red	spring	no	25 ft (8 m)	30 ft (9 m)	5–9	yes
Ulmus* × *hollandica	red	spring	no	100 ft (30 m)	80 ft (24 m)	5–9	yes
Ulmus parvifolia	red	summer	no	70 ft (21 m)	30 ft (9 m)	5–10	yes
Ulmus procera	red	spring	no	70–100 ft (21–30 m)	50 ft (15 m)	4–9	yes
***Ulmus* 'Sapporo Autumn Gold'**	red	spring	no	50 ft (15 m)	35 ft (10 m)	4–9	yes

BELOW Ulmus *'Sapporo Autumn Gold' is a cultivar developed with resistance to Dutch elm disease. It requires pruning to achieve the classic elm vase shape.*

BELOW *Commonly known as the tabletop Scotch elm, due to its horizontal spreading branches,* Ulmus glabra *'Pendula' is an excellent shade tree for the garden.*

Top Tip

Elms make good outdoor bonsai subjects, but need protection from frost at temperatures below 23°F (-5°C) to avoid damage to roots.

SHRUBS

With a reputation for being reliable yet somehow dull and old-fashioned, shrubs are too often seen as dense green plants that just grow alongside houses. Many of us remember the traditional clipped boxwood or privet hedges of yesteryear, which—while functional—did little to add to the beauty of the garden. Yet shrubs are a genuinely diverse group of plants, spanning many different genera from virtually all parts of the planet, and they possess a vast array of aesthetic attributes and uses in the garden. Some burst into flower, adding fragrance to the air and encouraging wildlife to the garden; others are simply striking in form.

ABOVE *The rose of Sharon* (Hibiscus syriacus) *has been cultivated in parts of Asia for many centuries. Now there are more than 200 cultivars, such as 'Blue Bird' seen here.*
LEFT *Many shrubs bear colorful flowers, and rhododendrons are among the most spectacular.* Rhododendron *'Madame van Hecke' is an evergreen Indica Azalea Hybrid.*

ADDING DIMENSION TO THE GARDEN

LEFT *Shrubs carry flowers in many different arrangements.* Buddleja davidii *'Dart's Ornamental White' has large eye-catching panicles of fragrant flowers.*
BELOW *Camellias are popular in gardens for their ornamental qualities.* Camellia reticulata *'Change of Day' is one of the pretty Yunnan camellias.*

Defined simply as woody perennials, often with multiple stems arising from a single point, shrubs can range from less than 12 inches (30 cm) to 10–15 ft (3–4.5 m) in height, and their variation in height can add a pleasing visual dimension to the garden. While the distinctions between shrubs and trees can be rather loose, shrubs rarely grow with a solitary trunk unless so pruned. Some, such as the rose of Sharon *(Hibiscus syriacus)*, lead double lives, depending on how they are shaped. Likewise, some vigorous trees such as catalpa can be pruned to the ground each spring, thus stimulating some 10 ft (3 m) of lush multi-stemmed growth each summer that very much resembles a shrub in form.

Those who live in warm- and cool-temperate climates will be familiar with the hardier shrubs: forsythias, hydrangeas, lilacs (*Syringa* species), spiraeas, and viburnums. Most of these bloom in spring or early summer, but many also provide a show of color in autumn before their leaves drop. Warmer climate gardeners have a still greater range of possibilities, with evergreen shrubs such as camellias, azaleas (*Rhododendron* species), daphnes, gardenias, and rock roses (*Cistus* species). Those who garden in the subtropics and tropics enjoy a still different, but often very colorful and sometimes striking palette of shrubs including tropical *Hibiscus* species.

Part of the reason for the diversity of shrub form relates to their habitat of origin. Many shrubs, such as California lilac (*Ceanothus* species), come from fire-prone regions. These plants can survive a fire and resprout from their tough bases. Yews (*Taxus* species) tolerate severe pruning because they have adapted to the damage caused by browsing animals. Still other shrubs, like rock roses (*Cistus* species) and lavender (*Lavandula* species), have very aromatic, sticky, or hairy leaves that repel browsing beasts—but attract humans who enjoy the delicious scent of the volatile oil on the leaves.

The chief reason for the delivery of shrubs from their formerly unexciting reputation is the relatively recent introduction into the West of so many beautiful plants from Asia during the latter part of the twentieth century. Expeditions into China and other previously off-limits regions have expanded Western gardeners' horticultural options with a wealth of new and exciting plant discoveries.

As the options expand, we discover the many creative roles shrubs can play in our gardens. Although they make useful hedges and screens and make great backdrops for other elements in the garden, many are themselves worthy of a featured place in mixed borders and beds.

In terms of flower, fruit, and leaf color, there are shrubs of interest for virtually every season in all but the very coldest regions. Roses (*Rosa* species and hybrid cultivars) feature flowers in every color except blue, while *Deutzia* and *Spiraea* shrubs both become smothered in white to pink flowers during the summer months. Bright red, purple, or orange fruits are a feature of the winterberry *(Ilex verticillata)* and tea viburnum *(Viburnum setigerum). Aucuba* species are grown for the appealing gold speckling on the leathery dark green leaves, while *Nandina* species develop fiery red foliage in winter.

Fragrance is easy to bring into the garden, with a plethora of shrubby choices: *Daphne odora,* a mid-winter bloomer, and the sweet pepper bush *(Clethra alnifolia),* a summer-bloomer, planted near the entrance of a building or alongside a path, provide pleasure to anyone passing by. The delectably scented flowers of mock orange (*Philadelphus* species) may only last for a few weeks in summer, but there is little to match the fragrance.

A whole range of reasonably hardy shrubs flowers in late winter or earliest spring, reminding us that the plant world is still active, even as we bundle up in our cold-weather boots and jackets. Winter- and early spring-blooming shrubs include winter heaths (*Erica* species), the tea camellia *(Camellia sinensis),* and witch hazels (*Hamamelis* species).

Autumn-bloomers such as silverberry *(Elaeagnus pungens)* and the pretty late-blooming *Camellia sasanqua* extend the garden enjoyment still further.

In short, shrubs are coming into their own as plants of beauty as well as mere backdrops, frames, and accents. There is a shrub for virtually every imaginable garden situation, whether the soil is wet, damp, or dry and rocky; acid or alkaline; and whether the position is shady or bright. The difficult part is choosing the best possible shrub from among the seemingly endless options.

ABOVE *Roses are among the most widely grown shrubs.* Rosa, *Modern, English Rose,* Sophy's Rose/ *'Auslot' adds fragrance and color to the garden.*
RIGHT *The fragrant deep purple flower spikes of* Lavandula angustifolia *'Lodden Blue' appear in early summer. This shrub makes a good low hedge.*

ABELIA

A northern temperate to subtropical genus of around 30 species of evergreen and deciduous shrubs, *Abelia* belongs to the woodbine (Caprifoliaceae) family. Most have a densely bushy habit, often with slightly arching branches and small glossy leaves tapering to a fine point. The young foliage has bronze to golden tints that in some cultivars persist to maturity. From late summer, small white to pink flowers smother the bushes. These have darker sepals that continue to provide color after petal-fall. The deciduous species may develop attractive yellow and orange autumn foliage tones. The genus name honors Dr. Clarke Abel (1780–1826), who corresponded with English botanist Sir Joseph Banks and served with the British embassy in China, where he wrote a book of naturalist observations.

Favorites

Favorites	Flower Color	Blooming Season	Flower Fragrance
Abelia biflora	white to pale pink	summer	no
Abelia chinensis	white to pink	late summer to autumn	yes
Abelia engleriana	rose pink	summer	no
Abelia floribunda	pale rose to deep red	summer to autumn	no
Abelia* × *grandiflora	white to mauve-pink	summer	yes
Abelia schumannii	rosy mauve	summer to autumn	yes

CULTIVATION

Although hardiness varies considerably, most are not suitable in areas with severe winters. Plant in sun or part-shade with moist, humus-rich, well-drained soil. Trim to shape in late winter or spring; *Abelia* shrubs may be used for hedging. Propagate from half-hardened or softwood cuttings.

RIGHT *Award-winning* Abelia schumannii, *also known as Schumann's abelia, is a native of China. Its lightly scented flowers are borne in clusters.*

Top Tip

When pruning abelias, cut back some of the older growth to ground level after flowering to maintain an open form and encourage good flower display.

Plant Height	Plant Width	Hardiness Zone	Frost Tolerance
7–10 ft (2–3 m)	3–7 ft (0.9–2 m)	7–8	yes
6 ft (1.8 m)	8 ft (2.4 m)	8–10	yes
4–6 ft (1.2–1.8 m)	4–6 ft (1.2–1.8 m)	3–9	yes
6 ft (1.8 m)	6 ft (1.8 m)	9–11	no
6 ft (1.8 m)	6 ft (1.8 m)	7–10	yes
4 ft (1.2 m)	8 ft (2.4 m)	7–10	yes

BELOW *The striking flowers of* Abelia engleriana *will be produced over a longer period if this evergreen shrub is grown in a sheltered position.*

LEFT Abelia chinensis *is a native of China, as its name implies. Very free flowering, it loses its glossy green leaves in winter.*

BELOW *Flowering profusely over the summer months,* Abelia × grandiflora *is one of the most popular abelias. It has numerous attractive cultivars.*

BELOW *One of the best* Abutilon *hybrids,* Abutilon × hybridum *'Nabob' is a vigorous, free-flowering, upright plant that can reach up to 2–3 ft (0.6–0.9 m).*

ABUTILON

Found in the warm temperate to subtropical regions of Central and South America, Australia, and Africa, this genus in the mallow (Malvaceae) family is made up of around 150 species of perennials, shrubs, and trees. They are often short-lived but grow quickly to become densely foliaged bushes with maple-like palmate leaves and very attractive, pendulous, 5-petalled, bell-shaped flowers that may be borne through most of the year. Because of their quick growth, they are sometimes used as short-term bedding plants. The flowers are edible and quite sweet, as they are nectar-rich. The flower shape is the reason for their common name of Chinese lantern.

ABOVE *The mottled leaves of* Abutilon × hybridum *'Cannington Skies', distinctive red flowers, and dwarf habit make this an ideal plant for containers.*

CULTIVATION

These are most suited to areas with mild winters, because while they are tolerant of moderate frosts, the bark and thin stems will split with repeated freezing. Plant in fertile moist soil in sun or part-shade and water well until established. Trim and thin in late winter, and propagate from half-hardened cuttings.

LEFT Abutilon megapotamicum *has several forms, from an erect shrub with arching branches to an almost prostrate form. All carry the same brightly colored flowers.*

Top Tip

The pendent bell-shaped flowers of *Abutilon* can be appreciated best when seen from below. Use in hanging baskets or train on pillars or over archways.

RIGHT Abutilon ochsenii *is a shrubby Chilean species. Weak-branched and deciduous, it has maple-like leaves, and the inside of the flowers is spotted with dark purple.*

Favorites	Flower Color	Blooming Season	Flower Fragrance	Plant Height	Plant Width	Hardiness Zone	Frost Tolerance
Abutilon* × *hybridum	red, orange, yellow	spring to autumn	no	6–15 ft (1.8–4.5 m)	5–10 ft (1.5–3 m)	8–11	yes
Abutilon megapotamicum	red and yellow	spring to autumn	no	2–8 ft (0.6–2.4 m)	5–8 ft (1.5–2.4 m)	8–10	yes
***Abutilon megapotamicum* 'Variegatum'**	red and yellow	spring to autumn	no	18 in (45 cm)	5 ft (1.5 m)	8–10	yes
Abutilon ochsenii	mauve	summer	no	12 ft (3.5 m)	10 ft (3 m)	8–10	yes
Abutilon* × *suntense	purple, mauve	spring to autumn	no	12–15 ft (3.5–4.5 m)	8 ft (2.4 m)	8–9	yes
Abutilon vitifolium	pink, mauve	spring to summer	no	15 ft (4.5 m)	8 ft (2.4 m)	8–9	yes

Top Tip

Because they prefer at least part-shade, aucubas are useful plants for under the canopy of trees. They also grow well in containers on shady balconies.

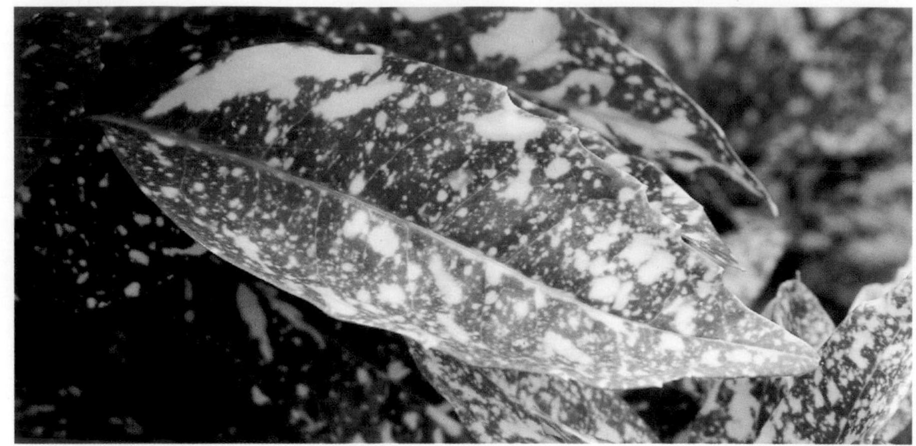

AUCUBA

ABOVE *Slow-growing* Aucuba japonica *'Variegata' is the most popular of the aucubas. The gold-colored speckling on the leaves is quite uneven in size and distribution, and can vary considerably between plants.*

A temperate East Asian genus, this has 3 or 4 species of lushly foliaged evergreen shrubs of the dogwood (Cornaceae) family. Their large, leathery, dark green leaves have coarsely toothed edges and the glossy foliage of the garden cultivars is often flecked and splashed with gold variegations. Sprays of inconspicuous purple or green flowers appear in spring and are followed by slow-ripening red or orange fruits that contain a single nut-like seed. There are separate male and female plants and both are required for fruit to develop. *Aucuba* is a corruption of the Japanese name.

CULTIVATION

Very hardy for such large-leafed evergreens, *Aucuba* adds a semi-tropical touch to the temperate garden. Plant in deep, cool, fertile, humus-enriched soil that remains moist. Plants will fruit more heavily with sun, but the foliage is better in light shade. Propagate from half-hardened summer cuttings. The seed germinates freely, but most seedlings have plain green leaves.

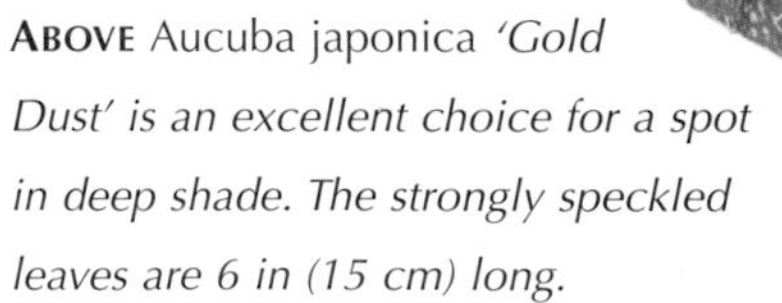

ABOVE Aucuba japonica *'Gold Dust' is an excellent choice for a spot in deep shade. The strongly speckled leaves are 6 in (15 cm) long.*

Favorites	Flower Color	Blooming Season	Flower Fragrance	Plant Height	Plant Width	Hardiness Zone	Frost Tolerance
Aucuba japonica	purple	late spring	no	6 ft (1.8 m)	6 ft (1.8 m)	7–9	yes
***Aucuba japonica* 'Crotonifolia'**	purple	late spring	no	6 ft ft (1.8 m)	6 ft (1.8 m)	7–9	yes
***Aucuba japonica* 'Gold Dust'**	purple	late spring	no	6 ft (1.8 m)	6 ft (1.8 m)	7–9	yes
***Aucuba japonica* 'Golden King'**	purple	late spring	no	6 ft (1.8 m)	6 ft (1.8 m)	7–9	yes
***Aucuba japonica* 'Rozannie'**	purple	late spring	no	3–4 ft (0.9–1.2 m)	4 ft (1.2 m)	7–9	yes
***Aucuba japonica* 'Variegata'**	purple	late spring	no	6 ft (1.8 m)	6 ft (1.8 m)	7–9	yes

ABOVE *The yellow-spotted leaves of* Aucuba japonica *'Marmorata' will look especially striking when set against plants with darker colored leaves.*

LEFT Aucuba japonica *'Salicifolia' (syn. 'Longifolia') is a very fruitful cultivar that copes well with shady positions. The fruits are borne throughout winter.*

BANKSIA

Banksia belongs to the protea (Proteaceae) family and is a genus of around 50 species of evergreen shrubs and trees confined to Australia. Sturdy plants, often with a stout trunk, their leaves tend to be leathery, long, and coarsely toothed, though a few species have finer or more needle-like foliage. Their nectar-rich thread-like flowers are densely packed in cylindrical or globular spikes and are followed by woody long-lasting fruiting cones. Flowering time varies with the species. The name of the genus celebrates Sir Joseph Banks (1743–1820), botanist on James Cook's first expedition to Australia in 1770 and founder of the Royal Horticultural Society.

CULTIVATION

Southwestern Australia is home to the most interesting species, though these can be difficult to cultivate. The eastern species are more adaptable, though they will not withstand hard frosts. The soil should be acidic, very free draining, and preferably be free of phosphorus. Plant in full sun. Propagate from seed, which often germinates better if heated or smoked. Some easy-to-cultivate species will also grow from half-hardened cuttings.

RIGHT *The complex flower spikes of* Banksia ericifolia *are made up of several hundred individual flowers. The plant is commonly known as the heath banksia.*

BELOW *The showy banksia,* Banksia speciosa, *makes a rounded dense shrub that can be used as a feature plant. The flowers are used in floral arrangements.*

Favorites	Flower Color	Blooming Season	Flower Fragrance	Plant Height	Plant Width	Hardiness Zone	Frost Tolerance
Banksia coccinea	scarlet	winter to summer	no	25 ft (8 m)	8 ft (2.4 m)	9–10	no
Banksia ericifolia	yellow to orange-red	autumn to late winter	no	10–20 ft (3–6 m)	6–15 ft (1.8–4.5 m)	9–10	no
***Banksia* 'Giant Candles'**	orange	autumn to winter	no	15 ft (4.5 m)	12 ft (3.5 m)	9–11	no
Banksia prionotes	orange	autumn to winter	no	15–30 ft (4.5–9 m)	10 ft (3 m)	10–11	no
Banksia serrata	cream to yellow-green	summer to winter	no	10–70 ft (3–21 m)	6–25 ft (1.8–8 m)	9–11	no
Banksia speciosa	pale green to light yellow	summer to autumn	no	10–15 ft (3–4.5 m)	10–25 ft (3–8 m)	9–10	no

Top Tip

Usually banksias do not need feeding, as their root system is very efficient, but if fertilizing is required, use only slow-release products low in phosphorus.

ABOVE RIGHT *The soft, woolly, white buds of* Banksia prionotes *open from the bottom of the flowerhead into orange flowers. This ornamental shrub makes a good container plant.*
RIGHT Banksia *'Giant Candles' is grown for its extremely large flower spikes, which reach 15 in (38 cm). Low branching, it can be used as a windbreak or hedge.*

BERBERIS

Widespread in the Northern Hemisphere and also quite common in temperate South America, this group of around 450 species of deciduous and evergreen shrubs is the type genus for the barberry (Berberidaceae) family. They usually form dense thickets of thin whippy branches armed with fierce thorns. The leaves may be thin and dull or thick, glossy, and leathery, and those of the evergreens often have spine-tipped lobes. Clusters of small yellow or orange flowers appear in spring and are followed by showy, variably colored, edible berries. The common name for the genus is barberry. *Berberis* flowers yield a yellow dye and the roots contain berberine, which has antibacterial properties and is used in the treatment of dysentery.

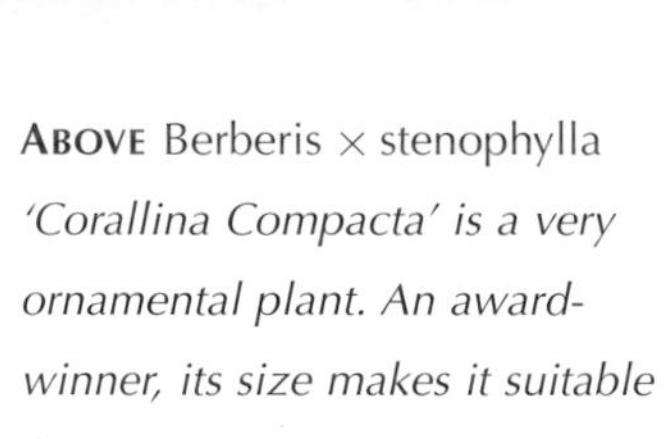

ABOVE Berberis × stenophylla *'Corallina Compacta' is a very ornamental plant. An award-winner, its size makes it suitable for the smaller garden.*

RIGHT *Award-winning* Berberis julianae *is native to China. Very dense and spiny, with bright flower clusters, it can make a decorative and effective barrier.*

BELOW LEFT Berberis darwinii *is a vigorous and free-flowering plant, with the flowers emerging from attractive orange to red buds. It is one of the most popular species.*

CULTIVATION

Mostly very hardy and easily cultivated in sun or part-shade, these like moist well-drained soil. Trim as required; they may be used for hedging. Some species can be invasive, so ensure that barberry is not a weed in your area. Propagation is from seed or soft to half-hardened cuttings.

Favorites	Flower Color	Blooming Season	Flower Fragrance
Berberis* × *bristolensis	yellow	late spring	no
Berberis darwinii	deep yellow, orange	late spring to early summer	no
Berberis* × *gladwynensis	yellow	spring	no
Berberis julianae	yellow-red, yellow	early spring	no
Berberis* × *stenophylla	deep yellow	late spring	no
Berberis thunbergii	pale yellow, yellow-red	mid-spring	no

Top Tip

Some species of *Berberis* have sharp-pointed spines. It is best to place these away from paths so that contact can be avoided. Wear protective gloves when pruning them.

BELOW *In winter some of the leaves of* Berberis × bristolensis *turn bright red, providing a vivid contrast with the white-bloom-covered black fruit.*

Plant Height	Plant Width	Hardiness Zone	Frost Tolerance
5 ft (1.5 m)	6 ft (1.8 m)	6–9	yes
10 ft (3 m)	10 ft (3 m)	7–10	yes
3–6 ft (0.9–1.8 m)	4 ft (1.2 m)	6–9	yes
10 ft (3 m)	10 ft (3 m)	5–9	yes
10 ft (3 m)	15 ft (4.5 m)	6–9	yes
3 ft (0.9 m)	8 ft (2.4 m)	4–9	yes

LEFT Buddleja davidii *'Black Knight' is a deciduous shrub bearing long racemes of fragrant royal purple flowers. It is one of several award-winning cultivars.*

BUDDLEJA

The type genus for the butterfly bush (Buddlejaceae) family is made up of around 100 species of large, sprawling, evergreen to deciduous shrubs renowned for their long nectar-rich flower spikes, which are a favorite with butterflies. They are from the Americas, Asia, and South Africa. Most species have roughly textured, narrow, lance-shaped leaves with pale, sometimes downy undersides. The flowers, while usually in spikes, also occur in globose heads or loose clusters and appear at varying times depending on the species. The genus is named for Adam Buddle (1660–1715), a theologian and early taxonomist. Some species have local medicinal uses, while others yield dyes.

CULTIVATION

The deciduous species are hardier than the evergreens, though none will tolerate prolonged severe winters. Plant in sun or part-shade with moist, fertile, well-drained soil. Regular trimming is necessary to keep the plants tidy. Propagate from half-hardened cuttings in summer.

RIGHT *A semi-deciduous shrub from eastern Asia,* Buddleja lindleyana *bears curved tubular flowers unlike those of most* Buddleja *species.*

Favorites	Flower Color	Blooming Season	Flower Fragrance	Plant Height	Plant Width	Hardiness Zone	Frost Tolerance
Buddleja alternifolia	mauve-pink	late spring to early summer	yes	15 ft (4.5 m)	12–15 ft (3.5–4.5 m)	5–9	yes
Buddleja davidii	purple	summer	yes	10–20 ft (3–6 m)	10–20 ft (3–6 m)	4–10	yes
Buddleja globosa	orange-yellow	late spring to early summer	yes	10–20 ft (3–6 m)	10–20 ft (3–6 m)	7–9	yes
Buddleja lindleyana	purple	summer	no	12 ft (3.5 m)	12 ft (3.5 m)	7–9	yes
***Buddleja* 'Lochinch'**	violet-blue	summer	yes	10–15 ft (3–4.5 m)	8–10 ft (2.4–3 m)	6–9	yes
Buddleja* × *weyeriana	orange-yellow	summer to autumn	yes	15 ft (4.5 m)	10–12 ft (3–3.5 m)	6–9	yes

BELOW Buddleja globosa *is commonly known as the orange ball tree. Its unusual round clusters of flowers have a honey-like fragrance that is very attractive to bees.*

ABOVE Buddleja alternifolia *'Argentea' has a fine growth of silvery hairs on its leaves. Long arching flower stems give plants a pleasing shape like a cascading fountain.*

Top Tip

Buddleja plants are tough, undemanding, fast growing, and salt tolerant, with abundant flowers. In ideal conditions, they will flower in their first year.

CALLISTEMON

BELOW RIGHT *Very free flowering, and one of the most popular bottlebrushes,* Callistemon viminalis *is also known as weeping bottlebrush. There are several attractive cultivars.*

An Australian myrtle (Myrtaceae) family member, this genus has around 30 species of evergreen shrubs and small trees valued for their brightly colored and abundant spikes of thread-like flowers. Most develop into a mass of fine, sometimes arching branches around one or more trunks. They have simple, narrow lance-shaped leaves that are often clustered near the ends of the branches and which are red-tinted when young. Most bloom in spring to early summer and have red, creamy yellow, or purple-pink flowers. The common name, bottlebrush, comes from the shape of the flowers. Long-lasting woody seed capsules follow, encircling the stems. The name *Callistemon* is derived from the Greek *kallos stemon*, and means, appropriately, "beautiful stamens." Several species yield dyes that change color when chemically treated.

ABOVE *The silky new foliage of* Callistemon salignus *is pink, later reverting to mid-green. This spreading evergreen shrub has white papery bark.*

BELOW Callistemon citrinus *'White Anzac'. This cultivar is a sprawling shrub, reaching 40 in (100 cm). The flowers are pure white at first, ageing to creamy white.*

CULTIVATION

Hardiness varies though none will tolerate prolonged frosty winters, and late frosts can devastate the new growth. Plant in a sunny position with light, well-drained, slightly acidic soil. Trim as necessary to keep the plants tidy and propagate from seed or half-hardened cuttings.

RIGHT *Regarded as one of the best* Callistemon *hybrids, 'Harkness' has a profusion of very large brilliant red flowers, up to 10 in (25 cm) long, borne in dense clusters.*

Top Tip

Prune bottlebrushes each year as soon as flowering is over, to encourage more flowers for the next season and to prevent the formation of woody seed capsules.

Favorites	Flower Color	Blooming Season	Flower Fragrance	Plant Height	Plant Width	Hardiness Zone	Frost Tolerance
Callistemon citrinus	bright red to crimson	late spring to autumn	no	10 ft (3 m)	8–10 ft (2.4–3 m)	8–11	no
***Callistemon* 'Harkness'**	bright red	late spring to autumn	no	15 ft (4.5 m)	12 ft (3.5 m)	9–11	no
***Callistemon* 'Little John'**	dark red	late winter to autumn	no	3 ft (0.9 m)	3 ft (0.9 m)	9–10	no
Callistemon salignus	creamy white	spring to early summer	no	15–30 ft (4.5–9 m)	15–20 ft (4.5–6 m)	9–11	no
Callistemon viminalis	bright red	spring to summer	no	25 ft (8 m)	7–10 ft (2–3 m)	9–12	no
***Callistemon* 'Violaceus'**	red-purple	spring	no	10 ft (3 m)	10 ft (3 m)	9–10	no

LEFT Calluna vulgaris *'Rica' makes a broad spreading shrub that produces its pretty little pink flowers in great abundance.*

BELOW *Like most heather cultivars,* Calluna vulgaris *'Robert Chapman' has foliage that changes color over the seasons. Golden in summer, it turns red in winter.*

RIGHT *The tiny buds of* Calluna vulgaris *'Con Brio' open to crimson-red flowers. The yellow-green summer foliage will turn to bronze-red in the winter months.*

CALLUNA

Although there are hundreds of Scotch heather (or ling) cultivars, there is but one species: a small, spreading, mounding, evergreen shrub belonging to the heath (Ericaceae) family. Found in open moorlands through much of the temperate and subarctic Northern Hemisphere, wild Scotch heather has wiry stems, tiny closely overlapping leaves, and produces a haze of small mauve-pink flowers from late summer. Cultivars have been developed in a wide range of sizes and foliage colors, with white, pink, mauve, or purple-red flowers. Scotch heather has a long history of local medicinal use, and extracts of its flowering stems have antiseptic properties.

CULTIVATION

Scotch heather is very cold hardy but has a tendency to be short-lived in areas with hot summers. Plant in a sunny position with cool, moist, humus-rich, acidic soil. Add plenty of peat or leaf mold at planting time to give the bushes a good start. The best time to trim is after flowering or in late winter. Propagation is usually from half-hardened cuttings, though established plants often self-layer.

Favorites	Flower Color	Blooming Season	Flower Fragrance	Plant Height	Plant Width	Hardiness Zone	Frost Tolerance
Calluna vulgaris	mauve-pink	mid-summer to late autumn	no	24 in (60 cm)	30 in (75 cm)	4–9	yes
***Calluna vulgaris* 'Blazeaway'**	lilac	mid-summer to mid-autumn	no	12–18 in (30–45 cm)	18–24 in (45–60 cm)	4–9	yes
***Calluna vulgaris* 'Gold Haze'**	white	mid-summer to mid-autumn	no	10–12 in (25–30 cm)	12–18 in (30–45 cm)	4–9	yes
***Calluna vulgaris* 'Kinlochruel'**	white	mid-summer to mid-autumn	no	8–10 in (20–25 cm)	12–18 in (30–45 cm)	4–9	yes
***Calluna vulgaris* 'Robert Chapman'**	purple	mid-summer to mid-autumn	no	8–10 in (20–25 cm)	24–30 in (60–75 cm)	4–9	yes
***Calluna vulgaris* 'Silver Queen'**	lavender	mid-summer to mid-autumn	no	12–18 in (30–45 cm)	18–24 in (45–60 cm)	4–9	yes

Top Tip

Calluna plants must be grown in well-drained soil, as their roots are highly susceptible to disease in very damp conditions. The soil must also be lime-free.

RIGHT *The double white flowers of* Calluna vulgaris *'Alba Plena' look clean and crisp against the mid-green foliage. The plant makes a dense compact bush.*

CAMELLIA

A genus of around 300 species of evergreen shrubs and small trees, it is part of the tea (Theaceae) family that incorporates the now defunct genus *Thea*. While the large-flowered camellias are so well-known as to hardly need describing, the genus also includes some less easily recognized plants. While all share similar dark green, leathery leaves of varying textures and sizes, not all have large fancy flowers. Indeed many of the wild species have tiny blooms that are somewhat hidden among their foliage. The tea plant *(Camellia sinensis)* is the source of commercially grown tea.

ABOVE Camellia japonica *'Madame Lebois' is one of over 2,000 cultivars of this species, which is native to several islands of China, Korea, Taiwan, and Japan.*

RIGHT Camellia pitardii *is from southern China and has leaves that are lance-shaped and saw-toothed. 'Fairy Bouquet' has dainty pink ruffled petals.*

FAR RIGHT *The Japanese* Camellia sasanqua *blooms in autumn. It is a straggling, woodland, tree-like shrub, and 'Cicada' is a cultivar with snow white flowers.*

BELOW Camellia reticulata *originates in western China and cultivars are sometimes known as Yunnan camellias. 'Suzanne Withers' blooms a delicate light pink.*

CULTIVATION

Camellias can be quite frost hardy, but since many are winter- or early spring-blooming, prolonged winters can damage the flowers. Plant in deep, fertile, humus-rich soil that can be kept moist, but which is well-drained, since waterlogging is deadly. When planting camellias, be mindful that they are long-lived; allow adequate room for their growth. Many are suitable for hedging, edging, topiary, or for training up espaliers. Propagation is from grafts or half-hardened cuttings.

Favorites	Flower Color	Blooming Season	Flower Fragrance	Plant Height	Plant Width	Hardiness Zone	Frost Tolerance
Camellia **'Freedom Bell'**	carmine red	winter to early spring	no	3 ft (0.9 m)	3 ft (0.9 m)	7–10	yes
Camellia hiemalis	white or pale pink	winter to early spring	no	10 ft (3 m)	8 ft (2.4 m)	7–10	yes
Camellia **'Inspiration'**	pink	mid-winter to early spring	no	10 ft (3 m)	8 ft (2.4 m)	7–10	yes
Camellia japonica	red	late autumn to early spring	no	15 ft (4.5 m)	8 ft (2.4 m)	7–10	yes
Camellia japonica **'Doctor Burnside'**	red	winter to early spring	no	15 ft (4.5 m)	8 ft (2.4 m)	7–10	yes
Camellia japonica **'Mrs Tingley'**	pink	winter to early spring	no	15 ft (4.5 m)	8 ft (2.4 m)	7–10	yes
Camellia japonica **'Yours Truly'**	pink with white borders	winter to early spring	no	15 ft (4.5 m)	8 ft (2.4 m)	7–10	yes
Camellia oleifera	white	autumn	yes	20 ft (6 m)	12 ft (3.5 m)	7–9	yes
Camellia pitardii	pink, white	winter to early spring	no	10–20 ft (3–6 m)	8–12 ft (2.4–3.5 m)	8–10	yes
Camellia reticulata	pinkish red	mid-winter to early spring	no	12–20 ft (3.5–6 m)	10 ft (3 m)	8–10	yes
Camellia sasanqua	pink to carmine	early autumn to early winter	yes	15 ft (4.5 m)	10 ft (3 m)	8–11	yes
Camellia sasanqua **'Crimson King'**	deep pink-red	early autumn to early winter	yes	10–17 ft (3–5 m)	5 ft (1.5 m)	8–11	yes
Camellia sasanqua **'Jean May'**	pink	early autumn to early winter	yes	6–10 ft (1.8–3 m)	6–10 ft (1.8–3 m)	8–11	yes
Camellia sinensis	white	winter	no	8–20 ft (2.4–6 m)	8 ft (2.4 m)	9–12	no
Camellia × *williamsii*	white to pink	late winter to spring	no	7–15 ft (2–4.5 m)	4–10 ft (1.2–3 m)	7–10	yes
Camellia × *williamsii* **'Anticipation'**	deep pink	spring	no	15 ft (4.5 m)	7 ft (2 m)	7–10	yes
Camellia × *williamsii* **'Brigadoon'**	pink	early spring	no	17 ft (5 m)	10 ft (3 m)	7–10	yes
Camellia × *williamsii* **'E. G. Waterhouse'**	pink	late winter to spring	no	6 ft (1.8 m)	5 ft (1.5 m)	7–10	yes

BELOW Camellia japonica *'Yours Truly' is quite a striking cultivar that has medium pink petals mapped by darker pink veins, and highlighted with contrasting white borders.*

LEFT Camellia oleifera *has single scented flowers with long, white, lobed, slightly twisted petals, as seen in the attractive cultivar 'Lushan Snow'.*

BOTTOM LEFT Camellia × williamsii hybrids *were first developed in the UK in the 1930s. The very large semi-double blooms of 'Waltz Dream' have rich pink petals.*

BELOW Camellia pitardii *'Our Melissa' is fast growing and has weeping branches. Its anemone-form flowers have soft pink petals that fade somewhat with age.*

Top Tip

A position in part-shade is best, for while sunnier sites yield more flowers, the blooms will not last as long, nor will the foliage be as lush. Trim after flowering is over.

Above Camellia japonica *'Pink Gold' is a slow-growing but vigorous upright form suitable for pots and hedges. Gold-tipped central filaments are suspended above pink petals.*

Above *The attractive* Camellia pitardii *'Snippet' has pale pink notched petals. It is often used as an edging plant, and is particularly suitable for bonsai.*

Right Camellia × williamsii *plants are said to be the most easily grown and free-flowering of all camellias. 'Hari Withers' is tolerant of cooler climates.*

ABOVE Camellia japonica *is also known as the common camellia. 'Anzac' has vivid red petals and a form that is somewhat reminiscent of the blooms of waterlilies.*
BELOW Camellia reticulata *'Damanao' became popular around the world after being imported into the USA in 1948. It has fluted deep pink to red petals, marbled white.*

ABOVE Camellia japonica *'Helena' has white to pale pink petals, spattered and splashed with darker pink—markings similar to those of a Jackson Pollock painting.*
RIGHT *As the pink petals of* Camellia reticulata *'Barbara Clark' move to the center of the bloom they diminish in size, in a symmetry that is very appealing to the eye.*

BELOW Camellia japonica *'Doctor Burnside' is a medium to large semi-double peony form. Gold-tipped stamens peep through scarlet red petals.*

ABOVE Camellia japonica *'C. M. Hovey' has formal double blooms that are deep red in color and borne on a tall upright plant. It dates back to 1850, when it was originally propagated in the USA.*
BELOW Camellia japonica *is the state flower of Alabama. 'Mrs Tingley' has fully double rose pink flowers, which bloom profusely on an upright bush.*

BELOW Camellia reticulata *'Ellie's Girl', a vigorous upright plant, has deep pink, almost red, formal double blooms that grow up to 5 in (12 cm) across.*

ABOVE Camellia reticulata *types are various shades of pink, from very dark to very light. But 'Lady Pamela' is almost entirely white, with only the faintest hint of pink.*

ABOVE *Informal double blooms cover* Camellia pitardii *'Pink Cameo' during the growing season, like many tiny, swirling, Spanish flamenco dancers.*

RIGHT Camellia pitardii *is closely related to* C. reticulata, *but has smaller leaves and flowers. 'Prudence' has petals in a dainty shade of light pink.*

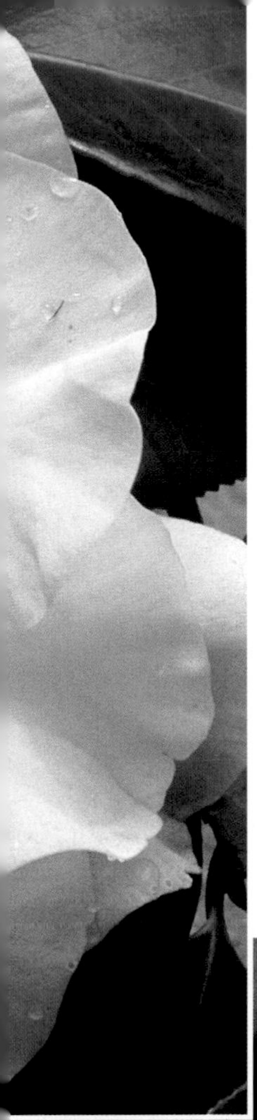

ABOVE *Award-winning* Camellia × williamsii *'E. G. Waterhouse' is a light pink formal double form with numerous rows of overlapping petals, and named for the famous Australian grower.*
BELOW *To Britons and Australians, 'naff' means vulgar, but the showy pink flowers of* Camellia reticulata *'Lila Naff', growing to 5 in (12 cm) across, completely contradict this notion.*

BELOW Camellia sasanqua, *unlike other species, drops its petals singly. 'Paradise Petite' has profuse blooms and is ideal for low hedges or topiaries.*

CEANOTHUS

Although representatives of the 50 species of mainly evergreen shrubs in this genus in the buckthorn (Rhamnaceae) family can be found from northeastern USA to Guatemala, most are Californian natives. They are dense bushy plants with leathery, deeply veined, dark green leaves, often with scalloped or wavy edges. Some species have a spreading habit and can be used as large-scale ground covers. The flowers, usually bright blue but sometimes pink to purple shades or white, are massed in small rounded heads or short spikes with flowering peaking in early summer. Many uses for the genus were found by Native Americans, such as making soap; saponins in the flowers cause them to lather if rubbed vigorously in water.

CULTIVATION

Hardiness varies, but all species tolerate moderate frosts and are easily grown in any sunny position with moist well-drained soil and protection from strong winds. Tip prune young plants; adult plants need little pruning apart from removing dead flowerheads. Propagate from half-hardened or hardwood cuttings.

Favorites	Flower Color	Blooming Season	Flower Fragrance
Ceanothus arboreus	pale blue	spring	yes
Ceanothus gloriosus	lavender-blue	spring	yes
Ceanothus griseus	lilac-blue	spring	yes
***Ceanothus* 'Julia Phelps'**	deep mauve	spring	yes
***Ceanothus* 'Pin Cushion'**	lilac-blue	spring to summer	yes
Ceanothus thyrsiflorus	blue	summer	yes

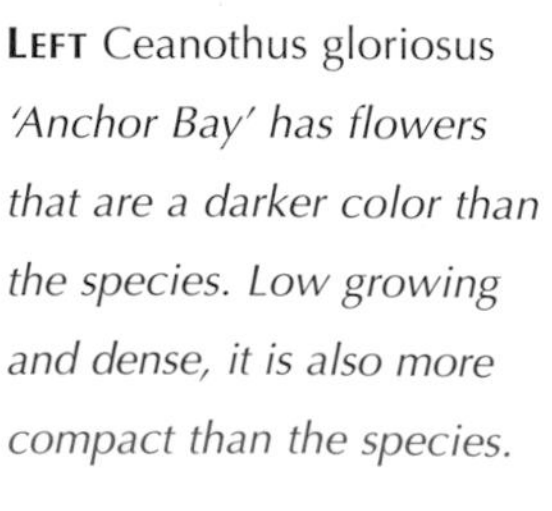

LEFT Ceanothus gloriosus *'Anchor Bay' has flowers that are a darker color than the species. Low growing and dense, it is also more compact than the species.*

Plant Height	Plant Width	Hardiness Zone	Frost Tolerance
20 ft (6 m)	12 ft (3.5 m)	7–9	yes
1 ft (0.3 m)	12 ft (3.5 m)	7–9	yes
10 ft (3 m)	10 ft (3 m)	8–10	yes
7–10 ft (2–3 m)	7–15 ft (2–4.5 m)	7–10	yes
6 ft (1.8 m)	6 ft (1.8 m)	7–10	yes
20 ft (6 m)	20 ft (6 m)	7–9	yes

Above Ceanothus griseus var. horizontalis *'Yankee Point' is a low-growing and spreading form with light blue blooms, which is useful for stabilizing large banks.*
Left *The award-winning hybrid cultivar* Ceanothus *'Julia Phelps' has purple-red buds opening to deep mauve flowers and is quite drought-resistant.*

Top Tip

Although suitable for using as shrub borders, some species are ideal for training up a sunny wall, where they can reach twice the height of prostrate forms.

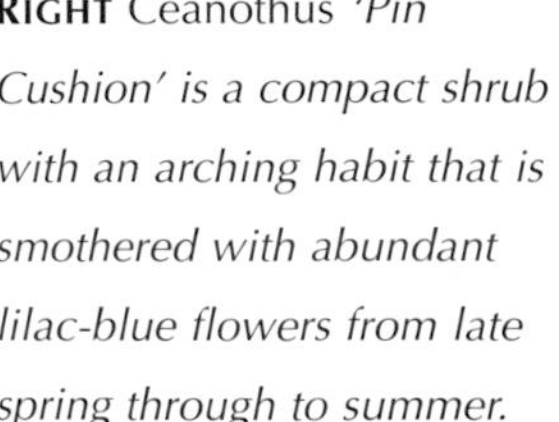

Right Ceanothus *'Pin Cushion' is a compact shrub with an arching habit that is smothered with abundant lilac-blue flowers from late spring through to summer.*

CISTUS

The type genus of the rock-rose (Cistaceae) family, *Cistus* is made up of some 20 species of aromatic resinous shrubs found around the Mediterranean region. Their simple elliptical leaves are often sticky, especially if crushed, and have a covering of very fine hairs. The flowers, borne mostly in spring or early summer, are often large and very showy. They have 5 thin crepe-like petals, in pink shades or white, often with a contrasting basal blotch. Gum can be extracted from several species, and that of *Cistus ladanifer* is used commercially in baking, ice cream, and chewing gum. Of considerably less appeal is the use of the leaves as a tea or marjoram substitute.

Top Tip

Cistus species are drought and heat resistant and even tolerate ocean winds and salt spray. However, they tend to flower better if well fed and watered.

ABOVE *The bright pink to magenta flowers of* Cistus × purpureus *are 2 in (5 cm) wide and set off by dark green leaves with grayish hairs beneath.*

CULTIVATION

Most species will withstand moderate frosts but are less able to tolerate wet winters and cool summers. Plant in full sun with light well-drained soil. Trim lightly to shape after flowering. Propagate from half-hardened cuttings.

RIGHT Cistus creticus *is known as the hairy rock rose, due to its hairy stems and leaves. The appealing flowers are pink-purple to crimson, flushed with yellow at the petal bases.*

Above Cistus creticus *subsp.* incanus *differs from* C. creticus *as it lacks the splash of yellow on the petal bases.*

Left Cistus × pulverulentus *is often sold in nurseries under the name 'Sunset'. It is a hybrid between* C. albidus *and* C. crispus *and flowers bright pink to purple-pink around golden yellow stamens.*

Favorites	Flower Color	Blooming Season	Flower Fragrance	Plant Height	Plant Width	Hardiness Zone	Frost Tolerance
Cistus creticus	pink-purple, deep crimson	summer	no	3 ft (0.9 m)	3 ft (0.9 m)	7–9	yes
Cistus ladanifer	white with crimson blotch	summer	no	5 ft (1.5 m)	5 ft (1.5 m)	8–10	yes
Cistus* × *pulverulentus	rose pink to purple-pink	summer	no	2 ft (0.6 m)	3 ft (0.9 m)	8–10	yes
Cistus* × *purpureus	pink to magenta; dark red blotch	summer	no	4 ft (1.2 m)	4 ft (1.2 m)	7–10	yes
Cistus* × *skanbergii	light pink	summer	no	3 ft (0.9 m)	3 ft (0.9 m)	8–10	yes
***Cistus* 'Victor Reiter'**	medium pink, pales to white at center	spring to summer	no	3 ft (0.9 m)	3 ft (0.9 m)	7–9	yes

CLETHRA

BELOW *The fragrant flowers of* Clethra alnifolia *grow to around 6 in (15 cm) long and bloom in late summer. This plant is also known as summersweet clethra.*

This is a genus of around 60 mainly deciduous shrubs or small trees in the Cyrillaceae family. They are distributed across the Americas and Asia, with a few species native to Madeira. Densely foliaged bushes, they have simple elliptical leaves and some species have peeling red-brown bark. However, they are grown mainly for their racemes of sweetly scented white flowers, which open mainly in summer. Abundant, small, hard seed capsules follow. In its native range, the foliage of *Clethra barbinervis* is used as a flavoring, in much the same way that bay leaves are utilized.

CULTIVATION

The deciduous species are frost hardy but the popular *Clethra arborea* will not tolerate repeated hard frosts or prolonged winters. Plant in sun or part-shade with humus-rich, well-drained, acidic soil that can be kept moist through summer. The very densely foliaged species, such as *Clethra alnifolia*, may be used for hedging. Propagation is from seed, half-hardened and hardwood cuttings, or layers.

BELOW RIGHT *The showy white flowers of* Clethra alnifolia *attract bees and butterflies, and the flowers last for six weeks or more.*

Top Tip

Clethras like acidic soil, so never add lime. They thrive in moist soil and are great to plant by a water feature, natural watercourse, or in boggy soil.

ABOVE Clethra barbinervis *is known as Japanese clethra as it is native to the mountains of Japan. It has peeling rusty brown bark and its foliage is particularly attractive in autumn.*
LEFT *Known as lily-of-the-valley tree due to the resemblance of its blooms to these flowers,* Clethra arborea *is one of the few species from Madeira and needs mild conditions to thrive.*

Favorites	Flower Color	Blooming Season	Flower Fragrance	Plant Height	Plant Width	Hardiness Zone	Frost Tolerance
Clethra acuminata	creamy white	late summer	yes	12 ft (3.5 m)	12 ft (3.5 m)	6–9	yes
Clethra alnifolia	white	late summer	yes	6 ft (1.8 m)	6 ft (1.8 m)	6–9	yes
***Clethra alnifolia* 'Paniculata'**	white	late summer	yes	6 ft (1.8 m)	6 ft (1.8 m)	6–9	yes
***Clethra alnifolia* 'Rosea'**	pale pink	late summer	yes	6 ft (1.8 m)	6 ft (1.8 m)	6–9	yes
Clethra arborea	white	summer	yes	25 ft (8 m)	20 ft (6 m)	9–10	no
Clethra barbinervis	white	summer to autumn	yes	10 ft (3 m)	10 ft (3 m)	8–9	yes

CORYLOPSIS

This is a genus of 10 species of deciduous shrubs and trees in the witchhazel (Hamamelidaceae) family, naturally occurring in temperate areas from the Himalayas to Japan. They have rounded, toothed, dull, mid-green leaves that sometimes taper to a point. The autumn foliage often colors well, but the main feature of the plant is the flowers: masses of small cream to butter yellow blooms in short pendulous racemes. These appear when the plants are leafless, in winter and spring, enhancing their graceful airy effect. Insignificant woody seed capsules follow. The name *Corylopsis* refers to the resemblance between its foliage and that of the hazels *(Corylus)*.

Top Tip

As each plant completes its blooming cycle, prune it back to improve its shape and to keep it compact. Feed it at the same time with a fertilizer that is well balanced.

CULTIVATION

Mostly very hardy, they are easily grown in any moist, well-drained, slightly acidic soil. They are best planted in a position shaded from the hottest summer sunlight. Propagate from freshly ripened seed in autumn or half-hardened early summer cuttings.

ABOVE RIGHT *When in flower,* Corylopsis sinensis *var.* clavescens *f.* veitchiana *bears broad pale lemon flowers with red anthers.*
RIGHT Corylopsis pauciflora *is known as buttercup winter-hazel and is native to Taiwan and Japan. Its foliage is bronze in spring and matures to bright green.*

ABOVE Corylopsis spicata, *spike winter-hazel, eventually grows wider than it is tall. It needs some shelter, especially from winter winds.*
LEFT *The yellow spring flowers of* Corylopsis glabrescens *are not as showy as other species in this genus, but they have an elegant beauty. This species is reported to be the hardiest within the genus and does well in a woodland garden.*

Favorites	Flower Color	Blooming Season	Flower Fragrance	Plant Height	Plant Width	Hardiness Zone	Frost Tolerance
Corylopsis glabrescens	light yellow	spring	yes	15 ft (4.5 m)	15 ft (4.5 m)	6–9	yes
Corylopsis pauciflora	yellow	early spring	yes	8 ft (2.4 m)	8 ft (2.4 m)	7–9	yes
Corylopsis sinensis	yellow	mid-spring to early summer	yes	15 ft (4.5 m)	15 ft (4.5 m)	6–9	yes
Corylopsis sinensis* var. *clavescens* f. *veitchiana	pale lemon	mid-spring to early summer	yes	15 ft (4.5 m)	15 ft (4.5 m)	6–9	yes
***Corylopsis sinensis* 'Spring Purple'**	yellow	mid-spring to early summer	yes	15 ft (4.5 m)	15 ft (4.5 m)	6–9	yes
Corylopsis spicata	bright yellow	spring	yes	6 ft (1.8 m)	10 ft (3 m)	6–9	yes

Top Tip

It is absolutely essential to keep daphnes damp. One of the easiest ways to kill these shrubs is to plant them in soil that dries out too rapidly.

BELOW *These are the fruits of* Daphne bholua. *They ripen to black. This species is known as paper daphne as paper and ropes were once made from its bark.*

DAPHNE

The principal genus of the daphne (Thymelaeaceae) family is made up of around 50 species of evergreen and deciduous shrubs found from Europe to East Asia. They are famed for the scent of their flowers, though not all are fragrant. Most species are evergreen, forming neat compact bushes with leathery lance-shaped leaves. The deciduous plants have less heavy-textured foliage. Their flowers open from mid-winter to late spring, depending on the species, and are usually pale to deep pink or lavender. Small fruits follow and may be brightly colored. Daphnes have been used in herbal medicines and their fragrance is widely used in the cosmetics industry.

CULTIVATION

Hardiness varies with the species, though all will tolerate light frosts. Plant in moist, humus-rich, well-drained, slightly acidic soil in half-sun or dappled shade. Trim lightly to shape. Beware of yellowing associated with iron and magnesium deficiencies. Propagation is usually from cuttings or layers, though species may be raised from seed.

LEFT Daphne laureola *is a tough adaptable plant that tolerates shade. Its fragrant flowers are pale green, and blooms are seen in late winter and early spring.*

Right Spring brings fragrant pink flowers to Daphne × burkwoodii. *This cultivar, 'Carol Mackie', is a variegated foliage form that is perhaps more interesting when not in flower.*

Below Daphne cneorum *'Ruby Glow' will grow well in a rockery or alpine trough, or even in a mixed border alongside plants such as rhododendrons.*

Favorites	Flower Color	Blooming Season	Flower Fragrance	Plant Height	Plant Width	Hardiness Zone	Frost Tolerance
Daphne bholua	white tinged with pink	winter to spring	yes	10 ft (3 m)	4 ft (1.2 m)	7–10	yes
Daphne* × *burkwoodii	light pink	mid- to late spring	yes	5 ft (1.5 m)	5 ft (1.5 m)	5–9	yes
Daphne cneorum	pale to deep pink	spring	yes	8 in (20 cm)	2–7 ft (0.6–2 m)	4–9	yes
***Daphne cneorum* 'Eximia'**	pink to crimson	spring	yes	8 in (20 cm)	2–7 ft (0.6–2 m)	4–9	yes
Daphne laureola	pale green	late winter to spring	yes	5 ft (1.5 m)	5 ft (1.5 m)	7–10	yes
Daphne* × *odora	pale pink	mid-winter	yes	5 ft (1.5 m)	5 ft (1.5 m)	8–10	yes

DEUTZIA

A mainly temperate Asian genus of 60 or so species, *Deutzia* belongs to the hydrangea (Hydrangeaceae) family. Only a few species are evergreen, the rest being fully deciduous and often looking particularly lifeless in winter. Come spring, however, they quickly leaf-up with small lance-shaped leaves and then become a mass of blooms, completely smothering themselves in small, starry, white or pink flowers. Regretfully, despite looking as though they should be fragrant, many species are scentless. The name was originated by Peter Thunberg in honor of his patron Johann van der Deutz (1743–1788).

BELOW *The white star-shaped flowers of* Deutzia setchuenensis *are carried in loose clusters. This profusely flowering deciduous shrub is from China.*

CULTIVATION

Mainly very hardy and easily grown in sun or part-shade in any temperate garden, they prefer moist well-drained soil. Any trimming and thinning should be done immediately after flowering to avoid lessening the next season's show. Remove the thin twigs to promote a sturdy framework of main branches. Propagate the hybrids and cultivars from half-hardened cuttings, the species from seed.

RIGHT *A deciduous native of western China,* Deutzia longifolia *is very free flowering. The buds are deep pink.*

Top Tip

Strong winds can damage the thin leaves of *Deutzia* plants and strip the flowers from the branches, so it is wise to choose a sheltered position for them.

ABOVE *The pink-flushed white flowers of* Deutzia × kalmiiflora *are borne on arching branches. The leaves may turn purple in autumn, before they fall.*
RIGHT Deutzia compacta *is a deciduous species from the Himalayan region. The cascading branches bear an abundance of flowers in small heads.*

Favorites	Flower Color	Blooming Season	Flower Fragrance	Plant Height	Plant Width	Hardiness Zone	Frost Tolerance
Deutzia compacta	white	early to mid-summer	no	6 ft (1.8 m)	7–8 ft (2–2.4 m)	6–9	yes
Deutzia* × *elegantissima	pink	early summer	no	5 ft (1.5 m)	5 ft (1.5 m)	5–9	yes
***Deutzia* × *elegantissima* 'Rosealind'**	white and pink	early summer	no	3–5 ft (0.9–1.5 m)	5 ft (1.5 m)	5–9	yes
Deutzia* × *kalmiiflora	white and pink	early to mid-summer	no	5 ft (1.5 m)	5 ft (1.5 m)	6–9	yes
Deutzia longifolia	pale pink	early summer	no	7 ft (2 m)	6 ft (1.8 m)	6–9	yes
Deutzia setchuenensis	white	summer	no	5–7 ft (1.5–2 m)	6 ft (1.8 m)	6–9	yes

ELAEAGNUS

A diverse genus of up to 40 species of deciduous and evergreen shrubs and trees, this is allied to the olives but placed in a separate family, the oleasters (Elaeagnaceae). They are principally Eurasian, with one North American species, and because of their hardiness and acceptance of trimming, they are mainly used as utility plants for hedging, screens, and shelters. The leaves range from near linear to broad, are silver-gray to deep green, and variegated foliage is common among the cultivars. The leaves are covered in small glands that make them sticky and sometimes aromatic. Clusters of insignificant white to cream or yellow flowers are followed by olive-like green to near-black fruits. The fruits and seeds are edible when fully ripe.

CULTIVATION

Mostly very hardy, these are easily grown in any sunny position with well-drained soil that is not excessively alkaline. Trim to shape as required but do not cut too severely. Propagate the species from seed, and cultivars from softwood or half-hardened cuttings.

LEFT Elaeagnus umbellata *is a strong-growing shrub with small bell-shaped flowers. It is commonly known as the autumn olive because that is when the olive-shaped fruits are ripe.*

Favorites	Flower Color	Blooming Season	Flower Fragrance	Plant Height	Plant Width	Hardiness Zone	Frost Tolerance
Elaeagnus angustifolia	yellow	mid-summer	yes	25 ft (8 m)	20 ft (6 m)	2–9	yes
Elaeagnus commutata	silver and yellow	late spring to early summer	yes	15 ft (4.5 m)	8 ft (2.4 m)	2–9	yes
Elaeagnus* × *ebbingei	creamy white	autumn	yes	10 ft (3 m)	7–10 ft (2–3 m)	8–11	yes
Elaeagnus pungens	creamy white	autumn	yes	15 ft (4.5 m)	20 ft (6 m)	7–10	yes
***Elaeagnus* 'Quicksilver'**	yellow	summer	yes	15 ft (4.5 m)	15 ft (4.5 m)	3–8	yes
Elaeagnus umbellata	yellow to white	late spring to early summer	yes	30 ft (9 m)	30 ft (9 m)	3–9	yes

LEFT *Smaller than the species,* Elaeagnus pungens *'Aurea' has variegated leaves scattered with brown scales underneath. The fruit is attractive to birds.*

RIGHT *Award-winning* Elaeagnus × ebbingei *'Gilt Edge' has strikingly variegated leaves growing to about 4 in (10 cm) long on a dense fast-growing shrub.*

Top Tip

These fast-growing shrubs with sweet-smelling flowers are easy to care for, and are especially useful in coastal gardens, as they cope well with salt-laden winds.

RIGHT *The showy foliage of* Elaeagnus pungens *'Maculata' has made it one of this evergreen species' most popular cultivars.*

ERICA

The type genus for the heath (Ericaceae) family is made up of around 750 species of evergreen shrubs, the majority of which are native to southern Africa. A few species occur in East Africa, Madagascar, and the Atlantic Islands, but the most widely cultivated species are those from Europe and the Mediterranean, because of their greater hardiness. Most species have very narrow needle-like foliage in whorls around fine whippy stems. The flowers are usually clustered at the stem tips. Southern African species tend to have tubular flowers, often in bright colors, while the Europeans have small bell-shaped flowers in muted pink and lavender tones or white. Commonly known as heath or heather, these plants have few practical uses except as fuel and as the source of a yellow dye.

CULTIVATION

Plant in full sun in moist, humus-rich, well-drained soil. Heaths have abundant surface roots, so do not cultivate but use mulch to suppress weeds. Trim lightly after flowering. Propagation is usually from small half-hardened cuttings or seed.

Top Tip

Winter-flowering heathers are lime tolerant and will grow in neutral or alkaline soil, while those that flower in summer prefer either neutral or acid soil.

LEFT Erica carnea *is a low, spreading, eastern European species. 'Pirbright Rose', seen here, grows into a dense mound covered with masses of rose pink flowers.*

LEFT *A low-growing compact shrub that spreads vigorously,* Erica cinerea *'Alice Ann Davies' is one of many cultivars of this western European species.*

ABOVE Erica lusitanica *has pink buds that open to white tubular flowers. This species has naturalized in southern England, New Zealand, and Australia.*

RIGHT *From South Africa's Western Cape region,* Erica ventricosa *bears its clusters of flowers at the branch tips. As the buds open the base swells, making an urn shape.*

Favorites	Flower Color	Blooming Season	Flower Fragrance	Plant Height	Plant Width	Hardiness Zone	Frost Tolerance
Erica bauera	white, pink	all year	no	4 ft (1.2 m)	5 ft (1.5 m)	9–10	no
Erica carnea	purple-pink	winter to spring	no	12 in (30 cm)	22 in (55 cm)	5–9	yes
Erica cinerea	white, purple, pink	summer to early autumn	no	24 in (60 cm)	30 in (75 cm)	5–9	yes
Erica erigena	lilac-pink	winter to spring	yes	8 ft (2.4 m)	3 ft (0.9 m)	7–9	yes
Erica lusitanica	white	winter to spring	yes	5–10 ft (1.5–3 m)	3 ft (0.9 m)	8–10	yes
Erica ventricosa	pinkish red	spring	no	20 in (50 cm)	20 in (50 cm)	9–10	no

FORSYTHIA

This small genus of deciduous shrubs in the olive (Oleaceae) family is made up of just 7 species, 6 from temperate Asia and one from southeastern Europe, but it has given rise to many garden hybrids and cultivars. The plants develop into small thickets of upright cane-like stems with bright to deep green, toothed, lance-shaped leaves that sometimes color well in autumn. From late winter into spring, in most cases while still leafless, they become smothered in 4-petalled golden-yellow flowers. *Forsythia suspensa,* known as lian qiao, has a 4000-year history of primarily antibacterial use in Chinese medicine and is included in the 50 fundamental herbs.

Favorites	Flower Color	Blooming Season	Flower Fragrance
***Forsythia* 'Arnold Dwarf'**	yellow-green	early spring	no
***Forsythia* 'Happy Centennial'**	yellow	early spring	no
Forsythia* × *intermedia	lemon yellow	spring	no
***Forsythia* Maree d'Or/'Courtasol'**	yellow-gold	early spring	no
***Forsythia* 'New Hampshire Gold'**	yellow	early spring	no
Forsythia suspensa	golden yellow	spring	no

CULTIVATION

These hardy and adaptable shrubs thrive in any reasonably bright position with moist well-drained soil. They do, however, need a period of cold to flower well and are best grown in cool-temperate gardens. Thin out unproductive wood after flowering. Propagation is from half-hardened or hardwood cuttings, layers, or seed.

RIGHT *The arching branches of* Forsythia *'New Hampshire Gold' bear masses of deep yellow flowers. The leaves of this fast-growing hybrid cultivar change color in autumn.*

RIGHT *The brilliant yellow flowers of* Forsythia × intermedia *'Goldzauber' appear before the leaves. This is one of the most cold-hardy forsythias.*

Plant Height	Plant Width	Hardiness Zone	Frost Tolerance
18–36 in (45–90 cm)	6 ft (1.8 m)	4–9	yes
12–24 in (30–60 cm)	60 in (150 cm)	3–9	yes
10–15 ft (3–4.5 m)	7–10 ft (2–3 m)	5–9	yes
30 in (75 cm)	60 in (150 cm)	4–9	yes
4–6 ft (1.2–1.8 m)	4–6 ft (1.2–1.8 m)	4–9	yes
10–12 ft (3–3.5 m)	8–10 ft (2.4–3 m)	4–9	yes

ABOVE Forsythia *Maree d'Or/'Courtasol' is a dwarf cultivar that makes an excellent ground cover. Its yellow-gold flowers appear in profusion very early in the season.*

Top Tip

Some *Forsythia* species rapidly grow into a mound the size of a small room. Check the growing information carefully before planting.

ABOVE *An erect spreading bush,* Forsythia × intermedia *'Arnold Giant' has large, nodding, rich yellow flowers and oval-shaped sharply toothed leaves.*

FUCHSIA

This genus belongs to the evening primrose (Onagraceae) family and comprises around 100 species of shrubs and small trees, mostly from Central and South America, with a few from New Zealand and Tahiti. The foliage is deep green, heavily veined, and often lush, and the leaves range from narrow lance-shaped to broad ovals. The flowers have long tubes with flared sepals and a corolla of often contrastingly colored petals. Many of the species have tubular flowers but the garden hybrids usually have rounded flowers with a "skirt" of large sepals around an often double corolla. Fleshy berries follow. In the New Zealand bush *Fuchsia excorticata* is very useful, because its dry papery bark burns when all else is wet.

CULTIVATION

Hardiness varies; the tougher types become deciduous if exposed to frost, the more tender simply die. Plant in part-shade or shade with moist, humus-rich, fertile, well-drained soil. Feed well and deadhead and remove berries to prolong the flowering season. Propagate using softwood or half-hardened cuttings.

LEFT *An erect and vigorous shrub,* Fuchsia magellanica *can be used as a colorful hedge in areas with a mild winter. It is also known as ladies' eardrops.*

ABOVE *The flowers of award-winning* Fuchsia boliviana *var.* alba *have white tubes and sepals with light red marks at bases, and scarlet petals. The shrub is erect.*

LEFT Fuchsia procumbens *is from New Zealand, and makes a prostrate spreading shrub. It has small heart-shaped leaves and small upward-facing flowers.*

BELOW *The very ornamental, double, ruffled flowers of* Fuchsia *'Marcus Graham' appear in abundance. This hybrid cultivar is well suited as a hanging basket plant.*

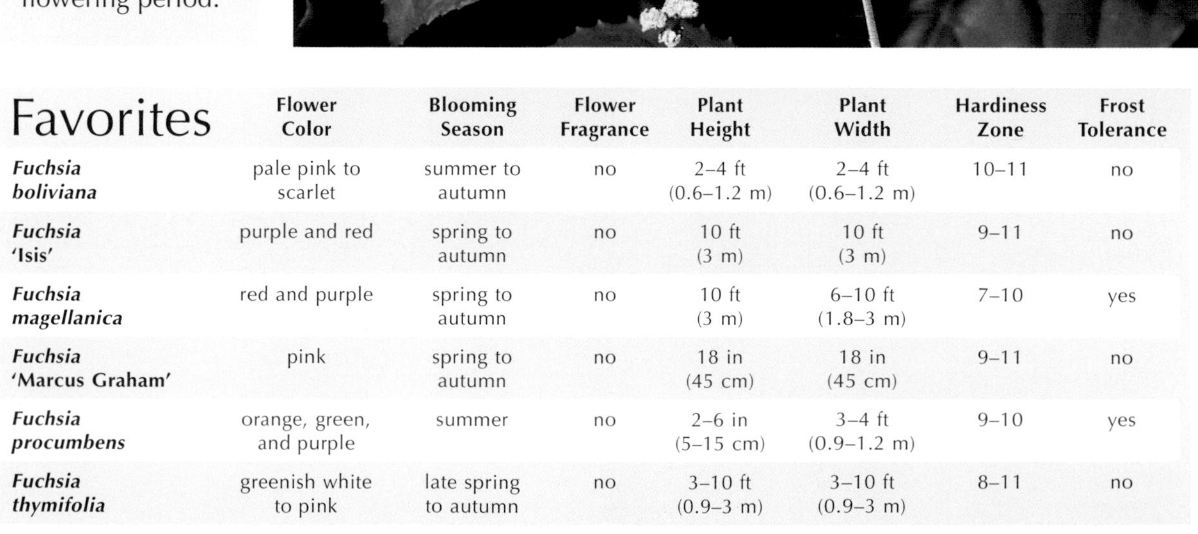

Top Tip

All fuchsias can be grown in containers, doing best in a loam-based compost with added grit. They need regular feeding over the whole flowering period.

Favorites	Flower Color	Blooming Season	Flower Fragrance	Plant Height	Plant Width	Hardiness Zone	Frost Tolerance
Fuchsia boliviana	pale pink to scarlet	summer to autumn	no	2–4 ft (0.6–1.2 m)	2–4 ft (0.6–1.2 m)	10–11	no
***Fuchsia* 'Isis'**	purple and red	spring to autumn	no	10 ft (3 m)	10 ft (3 m)	9–11	no
Fuchsia magellanica	red and purple	spring to autumn	no	10 ft (3 m)	6–10 ft (1.8–3 m)	7–10	yes
***Fuchsia* 'Marcus Graham'**	pink	spring to autumn	no	18 in (45 cm)	18 in (45 cm)	9–11	no
Fuchsia procumbens	orange, green, and purple	summer	no	2–6 in (5–15 cm)	3–4 ft (0.9–1.2 m)	9–10	yes
Fuchsia thymifolia	greenish white to pink	late spring to autumn	no	3–10 ft (0.9–3 m)	3–10 ft (0.9–3 m)	8–11	no

GARDENIA

A mainly African and Asian genus, it has around 250 species of evergreen shrubs or small trees in the madder (Rubiaceae) family. They have luxuriant, often glossy, deep green leaves and fragrant white to creamy yellow flowers. Cultivated forms often have double rose-like flowers, which open from large buds with a distinctive whorl of petals. Fleshy berries then follow. The genus name was given by Linnaeus in honor of Dr. Alexander Garden (1730–1791), a Scottish physician who emigrated to South Carolina and corresponded with the Swedish botanist about American plants.

CULTIVATION

Many gardenias will tolerate light frosts, but they need warm summers, in particular warm evenings, to promote flowering. Plant in sun or part-shade in fertile, moist, humus-rich, acidic soil. Water and feed well to promote lush foliage and heavy flowering. Mulch to control weeds, and avoid surface cultivation or the roots may be damaged. Propagate from half-hardened cuttings in late spring and summer, though the species may also be raised from seed.

LEFT *Native to the humid forests of South Africa,* Gardenia thunbergia *is an upright shrub or small tree that has glossy dark green leaves with wavy margins.*

Favorites	Flower Color	Blooming Season	Flower Fragrance	Plant Height	Plant Width	Hardiness Zone	Frost Tolerance
Gardenia augusta	white, creamy white	summer to autumn	yes	4–7 ft (1.2–2 m)	3–6 ft (0.9–1.8 m)	10–11	no
***Gardenia augusta* 'Chuck Hayes'**	white	summer to autumn	yes	4–7 ft (1.2–2 m)	3–6 ft (0.9–1.8 m)	10–11	no
***Gardenia augusta* 'Florida'**	white	summer to autumn	yes	4–7 ft (1.2–2 m)	3–6 ft (0.9–1.8 m)	10–11	no
***Gardenia augusta* 'Kleim's Hardy'**	white	summer to autumn	yes	24–36 in (60–90 cm)	24–36 in (60–90 cm)	9–11	no
***Gardenia augusta* 'Radicans'**	white	summer to autumn	yes	6–12 in (15–30 cm)	24–36 in (60–90 cm)	10–11	no
Gardenia thunbergia	white, cream	mid-spring to summer	yes	8–15 ft (2.4–4.5 m)	8 ft (2.4 m)	9–11	no

Top Tip

Plant gardenias in spots frequented by people—around decking or patios, paths, windows, or doors—which will allow their sweet fragrance to be best enjoyed by all.

LEFT Gardenia augusta *is a native of southeastern China and Japan with a bushy form and white, wheel-shaped, summer-borne flowers that are strongly fragrant.*

RIGHT Gardenia augusta *'Magnifica' has semi-double creamy white flowers that age to yellow. Also known as Cape jasmine, it needs a protected spot to thrive.*

LEFT Gardenia thunbergia *has fragrant, white or cream, solitary flowers with spoke-like petals at the end of a long tube. The blooms are borne in summer.*

ABOVE Grevillea alpina *has spider-like flowers borne in an almost erect cluster. The flower color can vary; this combination of red and yellow is very striking.*

Favorites	Flower Color	Blooming Season	Flower Fragrance
Grevillea alpina	cream, yellow, pink, red, green	spring to autumn	no
Grevillea juncifolia	golden orange	winter to spring	no
Grevillea juniperina	red, yellow, apricot, orange	winter to spring	no
Grevillea lanigera	pink, red, orange, yellow	winter to spring	no
***Grevillea* 'Robyn Gordon'**	pinkish red	all year	no
Grevillea victoriae	pink, red, orange, yellow	spring to summer	no

GREVILLEA

Mostly confined to Australia except for a few Melanesian natives, the 340-odd species of this genus in the protea (Proteaceae) family range from small shrubs to large trees. They are evergreen, with needle-like to narrow leaves or ferny pinnate foliage, usually in whorls around the stems. Their flowerheads, which open at varying times, are composed of many small flowers, usually in shades of yellow, orange, or red, with long filamentous styles. Some have flowers in rounded heads, others are more spread out, and sometimes they are densely packed and one-sided in the manner of a toothbrush head. The genus is named for Charles Francis Greville (1749–1809), a founder of the Royal Horticultural Society and friend of botanist Sir Joseph Banks.

CULTIVATION

Plant in full sun with light, gritty, free-draining soil low in phosphates. Although drought tolerant once established, they flower more freely and the foliage is healthier for occasional deep watering. Propagation is from half-hardened cuttings; a few cultivars are grafted, and the species may be raised from seed.

Plant Height	Plant Width	Hardiness Zone	Frost Tolerance
2–7 ft (0.6–2 m)	3 ft (0.9 m)	9–11	no
20 ft (6 m)	7 ft (2 m)	8–11	no
8 ft (2.4 m)	7 ft (2 m)	8–10	yes
5 ft (1.5 m)	4 ft (1.2 m)	7–10	yes
3–6 ft (0.9–1.8 m)	5–7 ft (1.5–2 m)	9–11	yes
6 ft (1.8 m)	6 ft (1.8 m)	8–10	yes

Top Tip

Many species of *Grevillea* will encourage birds to visit a garden as the flowers are rich in nectar. The dense and prickly shrubs also give shelter and protection.

ABOVE Grevillea juniperina *flowers make an attractive show against the soft needle-like leaves once all the buds have opened. It is native to southeast Australia.*

BELOW *The fleshy leaves of* Grevillea lanigera *have a soft felting that gives them a silvery appearance in some lights. The flowers are borne in semi-erect clusters.*

ABOVE Grevillea *'Robyn Gordon' shows the bottle-brush-like type of grevillea flower. Compact in shape and very free flowering, it is one of the most popular hybrid cultivars.*

HAMAMELIS

A genus of 5 or 6 species of mainly winter-flowering deciduous shrubs, *Hamamelis* belongs to the witch hazel (Hamamelidaceae) family, and is native to temperate East Asia and eastern North America. They have an upright twiggy growth habit and during the colder months, while leafless, the branches are studded with spidery strappy-petalled flowers in cream, yellow, or orange-bronze that on a still day can scent the garden with their spicy fragrance. Rounded, heavily veined, serrated leaves follow later and often develop gold and orange tones in autumn. The plants are also known as witch hazel; extracts of *Hamamelis virginiana* bark and leaves are used in herbal remedies.

CULTIVATION

Witch hazels grow best in a cool temperate climate with clearly defined seasons and should be planted in sun or light shade with moist well-drained soil. They are naturally rangy plants that cannot really be shaped. Species may be raised from stratified seed; cultivars are usually layered.

RIGHT Hamamelis × intermedia *'Pallida' is an award-winning cultivar with the mop-like flowers that are typical of the genus.*

BELOW LEFT *The 4-petalled yellow flowers with red-brown sepals of* Hamamelis mollis *are borne in clusters, giving the appearance of a much bigger flower.*

Favorites	Flower Color	Blooming Season	Flower Fragrance	Plant Height	Plant Width	Hardiness Zone	Frost Tolerance
***Hamamelis* 'Brevipetala'**	yellow	winter	yes	10–17 ft (3–5 m)	10–15 ft (3–4.5 m)	6–9	yes
Hamamelis* × *intermedia	cream, red, apricot	winter	yes	12 ft (3.5 m)	12 ft (3.5 m)	4–9	yes
***Hamamelis* × *intermedia* 'Arnold Promise'**	dark yellow	winter	yes	12 ft (3.5 m)	12 ft (3.5 m)	4–9	yes
Hamamelis japonica	yellow	winter	yes	15 ft (4.5 m)	12 ft (3.5 m)	4–9	yes
Hamamelis mollis	golden yellow	autumn	yes	15 ft (4.5 m)	12 ft (3.5 m)	4–9	yes
Hamamelis virginiana	yellow	autumn	yes	12–15 ft (3.5–4.5 m)	8–12 ft (2.4–3.5 m)	7–9	yes

LEFT Hamamelis japonica *bears its small to medium flowers from mid- to late winter. They withstand quite severe weather conditions without difficulty.*
BELOW *Award-winning 'Jelena', another of the many cultivars of* Hamamelis × intermedia, *bears flowers suffused with copper red on a large spreading bush.*

Top Tip

The stunning display of autumn foliage is one of the main reasons for growing these shrubs. Shades of purple, orange, red, and yellow vary with the species.

LEFT Hebe macrocarpa *var.* brevifolia *has a stiff upright habit, thick fleshy leaves, and rich pink flowers. This attractive shrub adapts well to coastal conditions.*

RIGHT Hebe × andersonii *'Variegata' bears spikes of purple flowers and attractive leaves in varying shades of green, boldly edged in rich creamy white.*

HEBE

Members of the foxglove (Scrophulariaceae) family, most of the 100 species of evergreen shrubs in this genus are native to New Zealand, with a few from Australia and South America. There are two distinct foliage types: the whipcords, which have scale-like leaves reminiscent of cypress foliage; and the broad-leafed type with fleshy elliptical leaves. The small tubular flowers, in pink, mauve, and purple-red shades or white, are borne in short spikes that develop in the leaf axils. In mild areas flowers may occur year-round, reaching a peak in late spring. The genus is named for Hebe, the Greek goddess of youth, possibly for their ease of propagation.

CULTIVATION

The whipcord types are far hardier than those with large broad leaves. They also prefer to grow in full sun with a cool climate, while broad-leafed hebes will do just as well in part-shade and mild conditions, including coastal environments. Hebes are not fussy about the soil type, provided it is well-drained. Propagate from half-hardened cuttings or seed.

BELOW *Produced in long spikes, the small tubular flowers of* Hebe *'Margret' put on an interesting show throughout the flowering season. Emerging sky blue, they gradually age to white.*

RIGHT *Thick, fleshy, oval leaves of dark green provide a backdrop for the rich imperial purple flowers of* Hebe macrocarpa *var.* latisepala.

Top Tip

Prune hebes after flowering to maintain shape. To achieve this it may be necessary to cut them back quite drastically, but they will respond with strong growth.

Favorites	Flower Color	Blooming Season	Flower Fragrance	Plant Height	Plant Width	Hardiness Zone	Frost Tolerance
Hebe albicans	white	spring to summer	no	18–24 in (45–60 cm)	27 in (70 cm)	8–10	yes
Hebe* × *andersonii	violet	summer to autumn	no	3–7 ft (0.9–2 m)	4 ft (1.2 m)	9–11	yes
Hebe macrocarpa	white	autumn to spring	no	7 ft (2 m)	3 ft (0.9 m)	9–11	no
***Hebe* 'Margret'**	sky blue	spring to early summer	no	16 in (40 cm)	12–24 in (30–60 cm)	8–11	yes
***Hebe* 'Midsummer Beauty'**	lilac-purple	summer	no	6 ft (1.8 m)	4 ft (1.2 m)	8–11	yes
Hebe odora	white	spring to late summer	no	3 ft (0.9 m)	4 ft (1.2 m)	7–10	yes

HIBISCUS

Although there are a few annuals and perennials scattered among them, this widespread genus of about 200 species is better known for its evergreen and deciduous shrubs, and is a member of the mallow (Malvaceae) family. The foliage is variable, ranging from poplar-shaped to the common maple-like palmate leaves to broadly elliptical. The large 5-petalled flowers are characterized by a central staminal column that is often long and protruding, especially in the flamboyant tropical species. For many of us, *Hibiscus* species bring tropical holidays to mind, but in their native regions the leaves and flowers were an everyday food crop. The state flower of Hawaii is *Hibiscus brackenridgei*.

CULTIVATION

Hibiscus vary greatly in hardiness. The deciduous species are usually far tougher than the evergreens and also do not require the same level of summer heat to flower well. Plant in full sun with moist, humus-enriched, well-drained soil. Trim hard after flowering. Propagation is from cuttings, grafts, or seed.

ABOVE RIGHT Hibiscus rosa-sinensis *'Nanette Peach' is a stunning cultivar that displays large, almost double, blooms with frilly pinkish white petals.*

RIGHT *The epitome of tropical charm,* Hibiscus rosa-sinensis *'Chandleri' features flowers of deep pink, shading to deepest red at the petal base.*

Top Tip

Many *Hibiscus* species are suitable for use as hedging and also make effective screens. Pinching off stem tips before flowering will encourage more blooms.

ABOVE Hibiscus arnottianus, *the Hawaiian white hibiscus, has beautiful flowers of pure white, with a long red staminal column in the center. Several cultivars are available, including 'Kona Kai', pictured here.*

RIGHT *There are countless beautiful hybrid cultivars of* Hibiscus rosa-sinensis, *such as 'Moon Beam' with bright yellow reflexed petals highlighted in the center with a bold splash of deep red.*

Favorites	Flower Color	Blooming Season	Flower Fragrance	Plant Height	Plant Width	Hardiness Zone	Frost Tolerance
Hibiscus arnottianus	white	all year	yes	25 ft (8 m)	10 ft (3 m)	10–12	no
Hibiscus brackenridgei	yellow	spring and early summer	no	10 ft (3 m)	5–8 ft (1.5–2.4 m)	10–12	no
Hibiscus moscheutos	white, pink, red	spring to early autumn	no	3–8 ft (0.9–2.4 m)	3 ft (0.9 m)	5–9	yes
Hibiscus rosa-sinensis	red to dark red	mid-summer to early winter	no	5–15 ft (1.5–4.5 m)	4–8 ft (1.2–2.4 m)	9–12	no
***Hibiscus rosa-sinensis* 'Agnes Galt'**	rose pink	mid-summer to early winter	no	8 ft (2.4 m)	5 ft (1.5 m)	9–12	no
Hibiscus syriacus	white, pink, purple; red base	summer to autumn	no	8–12 ft (2.4–3.5 m)	6–10 ft (1.8–3 m)	5–10	yes

HYDRANGEA

Hydrangea is a group of around 100 species of deciduous and evergreen shrubs, small trees, and climbers and is the type genus for the hydrangea (Hydrangeaceae) family. Found mainly in temperate Asia, with a few species in the Americas, hydrangeas have brittle pithy stems and large dark green leaves with serrated edges. Their flowers are borne in heads that usually contain tiny fertile flowers and sterile florets with 4 or 5 conspicuous petals in pink, red, mauve, or blue shades that may vary with soil pH. Dried hydrangea leaves become very sweet and are used to make the "tea of heaven" for Buddhist ceremonies.

CULTIVATION

Most garden hydrangeas are tough plants that thrive in moist, humus-rich, well-drained soil with protection from the hottest sun. Prune hard in late winter to remove any old or dead wood. Propagation is usually from cuttings—softwood in summer or hardwood in winter—though the species may be raised from seed.

ABOVE Hydrangea macrophylla *'Nikko Blue' is a mophead cultivar that produces lovely rounded heads of blue flowers. Mopheads are ideal for coastal situations.*

ABOVE RIGHT *A mophead cultivar,* Hydrangea macrophylla *'Koningin Wilhelmina' bears heads of glowing pinkish red flowers that shade to cream at the center.*

LEFT *With mauve and purplish blue flat-topped lacecap flowers like the species, it is the pinkish veins of the leaves that distinguish* Hydrangea aspera *f.* kawakamii.

Favorites	Flower Color	Blooming Season	Flower Fragrance	Plant Height	Plant Width	Hardiness Zone	Frost Tolerance
Hydrangea arborescens	creamy white	late spring and summer	no	3–12 ft (0.9–3.5 m)	8 ft (2.4 m)	3–10	yes
Hydrangea aspera	pale mauve and purplish blue	summer	no	10 ft (3 m)	10 ft (3 m)	7–10	yes
Hydrangea aspera* subsp. *sargentiana	pinkish white and mauve	summer	no	10 ft (3 m)	10 ft (3 m)	7–10	yes
Hydrangea heteromalla	white	summer	no	10–15 ft (3–4.5 m)	10 ft (3 m)	6–9	yes
Hydrangea macrophylla	pink and blue	summer	no	3–10 ft (0.9–3 m)	8 ft (2.4 m)	5–11	yes
Hydrangea quercifolia	white fading to pink	mid-summer to mid-autumn	no	3–8 ft (0.9–2.4 m)	8 ft (2.4 m)	5–10	yes

Left Hydrangea quercifolia *is known as the oak-leafed hydrangea for its oak-like lobed leaves. The leaves develop wonderful crimson tones in autumn.*

Top Tip

The flower color of *Hydrangea macrophylla* is driven by soil pH. Acid soil will produce blue flowers, alkaline soil will result in pink or red flowers.

HYPERICUM

Top Tip

Most *Hypericum* species are suited to shrub borders, and make useful container plants. To prevent growth becoming too congested, trim and thin as necessary.

This genus, composed of more than 400 species of evergreen and deciduous annuals, perennials, shrubs, and trees, belongs to the St John's wort (Clusiaceae) family and has a near-worldwide distribution. The shrubby species often develop into a congested mass of fine twigs and arching branches, usually with opposite pairs of simple dull green leaves. The flowers are very similar throughout the genus. Except for a few pale pink-flowered forms, all have 5-petalled bright yellow flowers with a prominent central cluster of stamens. Other than the widely used perennial St John's wort *(Hypericum perforatum)*, several species have local medicinal uses and many yield a golden-orange dye.

ABOVE Hypericum *'Hidcote' is an evergreen or semi-evergreen shrub. The dark green foliage is a perfect foil for the large, 5-petalled, cup-shaped, yellow flowers.*

CULTIVATION

Hypericum species are hardy and are easily grown in any free-draining soil in sun or shade. Evergreen species are best sheltered from drying winds. Some species produce runners that can become a nuisance. Propagation is mainly from softwood or half-hardened cuttings.

RIGHT *In dry shade,* Hypericum calycinum *makes a good ground-cover plant. It takes root along its prostrate branches and is a useful plant for stabilizing steep ground.*

Above *A cluster of filamentous stamens protrudes from the center of the starry bright yellow flowers of* Hypericum androsaemum *'Dart's Golden Penny'. Red and black fruits follow the flowers.*
Left Hypericum olympicum *makes an excellent rock-garden plant, but to perform well it needs sharply drained soil. It will reward with a summer display of starry golden yellow flowers.*

Favorites	Flower Color	Blooming Season	Flower Fragrance	Plant Height	Plant Width	Hardiness Zone	Frost Tolerance
Hypericum androsaemum	yellow	mid-summer to autumn	no	36 in (90 cm)	30 in (75 cm)	6–9	yes
Hypericum calycinum	bright yellow	mid-summer to autumn	no	8–24 in (20–60 cm)	60 in (150 cm)	6–9	yes
Hypericum frondosum	golden yellow	summer to autumn	no	2–4 ft (0.6–1.2 m)	2–4 ft (0.6–1.2 m)	5–10	yes
***Hypericum* 'Hidcote'**	deep yellow	summer to autumn	no	4 ft (1.2 m)	4 ft (1.2 m)	7–10	yes
Hypericum olympicum	golden yellow	summer	no	15 in (38 cm)	10 in (25 cm)	6–10	yes
***Hypericum* 'Rowallane'**	golden yellow	late summer to autumn	no	4 ft (1.2 m)	5 ft (1.5 m)	8–10	yes

RIGHT *The glossy green leaves of* Ilex cornuta *'Burfordii' are smooth edged except for a single spine at the tip. This female cultivar makes an excellent hedging plant.*

ILEX

Long associated with mid-winter festivals, particularly Christmas, the holly (Aquifoliaceae) family has as its type genus this group of more than 400 widely distributed species of evergreen and deciduous shrubs, trees, and climbers. While many have the well-known leathery dark green leaves with spine-tipped lobes, others have simple rounded or lance-shaped leaves that look anything but "holly-like." The small white flowers open in spring and are often quite insignificant. However, as male and female flowers occur on separate plants, if one wants the showy crop of berries both sexes are required.

CULTIVATION

Hollies are mostly very hardy and adaptable plants that grow well in sun or shade. They prefer moist well-drained soil and always look better with reliable summer moisture. Propagation is usually from half-hardened cuttings as the seed must be stratified, takes a long time to germinate, and the sex of the seedling remains unknown until flowering.

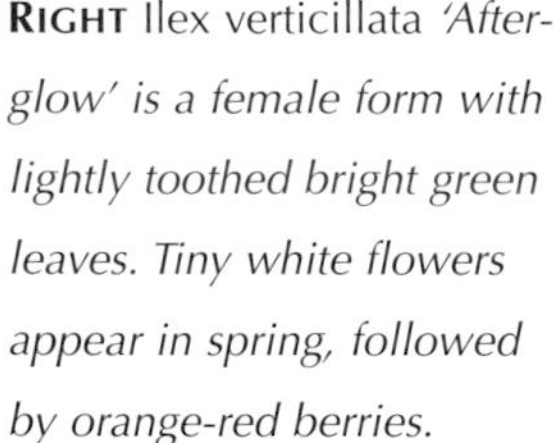

RIGHT Ilex verticillata *'Afterglow' is a female form with lightly toothed bright green leaves. Tiny white flowers appear in spring, followed by orange-red berries.*

Top Tip

Many hollies make excellent hedges, and are easily kept neat with regular pruning. Choose types with smooth-edged leaves for hedges in high foot-traffic areas.

LEFT *A female form,* Ilex aquifolium *'Silver Milkmaid' has spiny mid-green leaves highlighted with silvery white markings.*

BELOW *The highly glossy dark green leaves of* Ilex aquifolium *'Aurea Marginata' are edged in gold, creating a colorful backdrop for the scarlet berries.*

Favorites	Flower Color	Blooming Season	Flower Fragrance	Plant Height	Plant Width	Hardiness Zone	Frost Tolerance
Ilex aquifolium	white	spring	no	40–80 ft (12–24 m)	25 ft (8 m)	6–10	yes
***Ilex aquifolium* 'Silver Queen'**	white	spring	no	10 ft (3 m)	4 ft (1.2 m)	6–10	yes
Ilex cornuta	white	spring	no	6–12 ft (1.8–3.5 m)	6–12 ft (1.8–3.5 m)	6–10	yes
Ilex crenata	white	spring	no	15 ft (4.5 m)	12 ft (3.5 m)	6–10	yes
Ilex verticillata	white	spring	no	15 ft (4.5 m)	15 ft (4.5 m)	3–9	yes
Ilex vomitoria	white	spring	no	20 ft (6 m)	12 ft (3.5 m)	6–10	yes

KALMIA

BELOW *The attractive, fluted, crimson buds of* Kalmia latifolia *'Pink Charm' open to reveal flowers of rich pink, often with darker markings on the interior.*

Found mainly in northeastern USA, this genus contains 7 species of evergreen shrubs, some of which are among the most frost-hardy broad-leafed evergreens. They form neat rounded bushes with lance-shaped leaves. In spring they produce small white, pink, or red flowers that open from buds resembling cake decoration rose-buds. Hard seed capsules follow. *Kalmia* is named for Pehr Kalm (1716–1779), an early student of Linnaeus who spent several years in North America studying the native flora. *Kalmia latifolia* is the state flower of both Connecticut and Pennsylvania.

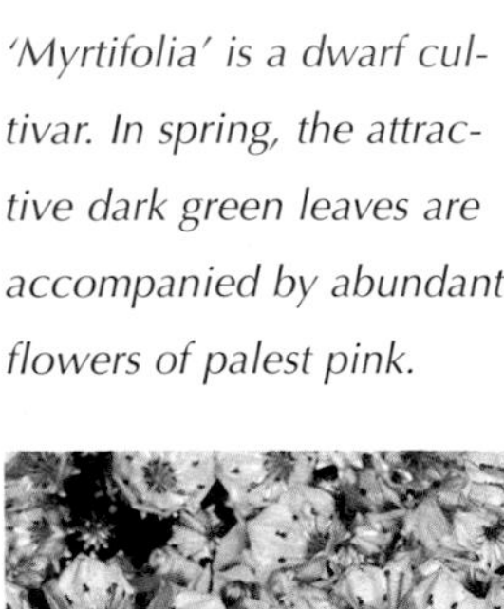

CULTIVATION

As with most heath (Ericaceae) family plants, *Kalmia* resents lime and prefers to grow in moist, humus-rich, well-drained, slightly acid soil. A lightly shaded position is best, or at least one protected from the hottest sun. If necessary, trim lightly after flowering. Because cuttings are slow to strike and seedlings slow to develop, layering is the easiest propagation method.

BELOW Kalmia latifolia *'Myrtifolia' is a dwarf cultivar. In spring, the attractive dark green leaves are accompanied by abundant flowers of palest pink.*

Favorites	Flower Color	Blooming Season	Flower Fragrance
Kalmia angustifolia	reddish pink	early to mid-summer	no
Kalmia latifolia	pale to dark pink	late spring to summer	no
***Kalmia latifolia* 'Olympic Fire'**	pink	late spring	no
***Kalmia latifolia* 'Ostbo Red'**	pink	late spring	no
***Kalmia* 'Pink Charm'**	deep pink	late spring	no
Kalmia polifolia	pinkish purple	spring	no

Top Tip

Most *Kalmia* species are relatively undemanding. However, they do not tolerate heat well, and during dry periods they should receive ample water.

LEFT *In spring, the beautifully crafted red buds of* Kalmia latifolia *'Ostbo Red' open to reveal dainty pink flowers. The flower color intensifies with age.*
BELOW Kalmia latifolia *'Minuet' is a dwarf cultivar. It features pink buds that open to white flowers distinctively marked with bands of maroon within.*

Plant Height	Plant Width	Hardiness Zone	Frost Tolerance
3 ft (0.9 m)	4–5 ft (1.2–1.5 m)	2–9	yes
5–10 ft (1.5–3 m)	6–10 ft (1.8–3 m)	3–9	yes
5–8 ft (1.5–2.4 m)	6 ft (1.8 m)	3–9	yes
6 ft (1.8 m)	6 ft (1.8 m)	3–9	yes
5–8 ft (1.5–2.4 m)	6 ft (1.8 m)	3–9	yes
2 ft (0.6 m)	3 ft (0.9 m)	3–9	yes

Top Tip

A classic fragrance, lavender is a favorite for potpourri blends. Harvest flower spikes before the buds open and dry in a cool, dark, well-ventilated area.

LAVANDULA

RIGHT *Growing to around 24 in (60 cm) high,* Lavandula angustifolia *'Munstead' can be planted as a low hedge, defining areas with its colorful form.*

Famed for its fragrance, this genus in the mint (Lamiaceae) family is composed of 28 species of evergreen aromatic shrubs and subshrubs, mostly originating from around the Mediterranean. The foliage is usually narrow, sometimes with small lobes, and is laden with aromatic oils. While well-known for the haze of purple-mauve blooms associated with commercial lavender fields, the flowers occur in any shade from pink to purple or off-white. Lavenders fall into 3 groups based on flowers and foliage: the Spica Group, with spikes of widely spaced flowers; the Stoechas Group, featuring dense heads terminating in colored bracts; and the Pterostoechas Group, which has pinnate foliage. In addition to being one of the most widely used fragrances, lavender flowers are edible and the oil has strong antiseptic properties.

ABOVE *Throughout the flowering season,* Lavandula stoechas *'Willow Vale' displays large spikes of purplish blue flowers topped with magnificent purple bracts.*

CULTIVATION

Lavender does best in a bright sunny position with light well-drained soil. Hardiness varies with the species and some are quite tender. Trim after flowering. Propagation is usually from half-hardened cuttings, though the species may also be raised from seed.

LEFT *Bred in New Zealand,* Lavandula stoechas *'Helmsdale' is a compact shrub with reddish purple flowers and gray-green foliage.*

BELOW *An ideal edging or rockery plant,* Lavandula angustifolia *'Hidcote' features aromatic silvery foliage and scented purple flowers held on slender stems.*

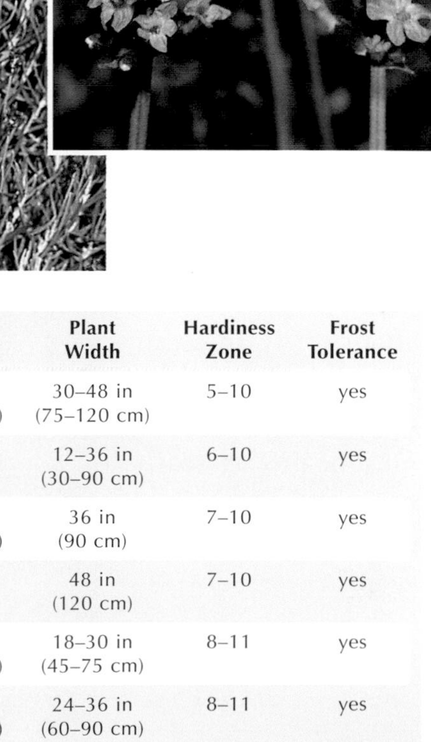

Favorites	Flower Color	Blooming Season	Flower Fragrance	Plant Height	Plant Width	Hardiness Zone	Frost Tolerance
Lavandula angustifolia	purple	summer to early autumn	yes	24–36 in (60–90 cm)	30–48 in (75–120 cm)	5–10	yes
Lavandula* × *intermedia	purple	spring to summer	yes	36 in (90 cm)	12–36 in (30–90 cm)	6–10	yes
Lavandula lanata	purple	mid- to late summer	yes	30–36 in (75–90 cm)	36 in (90 cm)	7–10	yes
Lavandula latifolia	purple	summer	yes	36 in (90 cm)	48 in (120 cm)	7–10	yes
Lavandula stoechas	purple	summer to early autumn	yes	18–30 in (45–75 cm)	18–30 in (45–75 cm)	8–11	yes
***Lavandula stoechas* 'Otto Quast'**	purple	spring to early autumn	yes	24–36 in (60–90 cm)	24–36 in (60–90 cm)	8–11	yes

LONICERA

Known mainly for strongly twining climbers, this Northern Hemisphere genus, which defines the woodbine (Caprifoliaceae) family, also includes several shrubs among its 180 species. Most develop into dense twiggy bushes with somewhat arching stems. The foliage consists of pairs of simple stemless leaves that often partly encircle the stems, and except for the box honeysuckle *(Lonicera nitida)* most of the shrubby species are deciduous. While the vines have long tubular flowers, those of the shrubs are shorter, though often just as fragrant. Small, sometimes colorful berries follow. The genus name honors Adam Lonitzer (1528–1586), a German physician, who like many of his day also wrote about plants.

Top Tip

Plant *Lonicera* species to attract birdlife. The flowers are sought out by nectar-eating birds, while many types of birds will feed on the berries.

CULTIVATION

Honeysuckles are hardy and easily grown in sun or part-shade, provided the soil remains moist. They respond well to trimming and may be trained as hedges. The seed germinates freely if stratified but it is usually simpler to take half-hardened cuttings, or alternatively, they can be grown from layers. Cultivars and hybrids must be propagated from cuttings.

RIGHT *Each panicle on* Lonicera etrusca *'Superba' bears many fragrant flowers that are cream on opening, ageing to yellow-orange.*

Left *A summer-flowering shrub,* Lonicera korolkowii *'Floribunda' features small white flowers and ovate leaves. Red berries follow the flowers.*
Above Lonicera maackii *is a tall deciduous shrub from East Asia. It has a dense bushy habit, purple stemmed leaves, and small, fragrant, white flowers.*
Right *Dainty, tubular, cream to yellow flowers appear on* Lonicera chaetocarpa *during summer. They are followed by attractive red berries.*

Favorites	Flower Color	Blooming Season	Flower Fragrance	Plant Height	Plant Width	Hardiness Zone	Frost Tolerance
Lonicera chaetocarpa	creamy yellow	summer	no	6 ft (1.8 m)	6 ft (1.8 m)	5–9	yes
Lonicera etrusca	cream with red tints	summer to early autumn	yes	12 ft (3.5 m)	10 ft (3 m)	7–10	yes
Lonicera japonica	white to pale yellow	early summer to late autumn	yes	25–30 ft (8–9 m)	25 ft (8 m)	4–11	yes
Lonicera korolkowii	light pink	summer	yes	10 ft (3 m)	12 ft (3.5 m)	5–9	yes
Lonicera maackii	white	spring to summer	yes	15 ft (4.5 m)	15 ft (4.5 m)	2–9	yes
Lonicera xylosteum	cream with red tints	summer	no	6–10 ft (1.8–3 m)	10 ft (3 m)	3–9	yes

RIGHT Nandina domestica *'Nana Purpurea' shares many of the characteristics of the species, but has a more compact habit and shorter leaves made up of wider leaflets.*

NANDINA

The sole species in this genus is an evergreen cane-stemmed shrub found from Himalayan India to Japan. Although commonly known as heavenly or sacred bamboo, it is not a bamboo but a member of the barberry (Berberidaceae) family. It has pinnate foliage that develops intense red tones, especially in winter. Conical heads of mildly scented creamy white flowers open in spring to summer and are followed by showy clusters of red berries that last through winter. The genus name is derived from Nanten, the Japanese name for the plant.

CULTIVATION

Nandina will grow in sun or part-shade with moist well-drained soil. The foliage is often more luxuriant with a little shade but colors better in sun. Planting several together will ensure a better fruit crop. Cut out any old unproductive stems in summer. Propagation is usually from half-hardened cuttings.

Favorites	Flower Color	Blooming Season	Flower Fragrance	Plant Height	Plant Width	Hardiness Zone	Frost Tolerance
Nandina domestica	creamy white	summer	no	7 ft (2 m)	4 ft (1.2 m)	7–10	yes
***Nandina domestica* 'Firepower'**	non-flowering	—	—	2 ft (0.6 m)	2 ft (0.6 m)	7–10	yes
***Nandina domestica* 'Harbor Dwarf'**	white	summer	no	2–3 ft (0.6–0.9 m)	2 ft (0.6 m)	7–10	yes
***Nandina domestica* 'Richmond'**	white	summer	no	4 ft (1.2 m)	2–3 ft (0.6–0.9 m)	7–10	yes
***Nandina* Plum Passion/'Monum'**	white	summer	no	4–5 ft (1.2–1.5 m)	3 ft (0.9 m)	7–10	yes
***Nandina* 'San Gabriel'**	white	summer	no	7 ft (2 m)	4 ft (1.2 m)	7–10	yes

BELOW *Ever-changing, the leaves of* Nandina domestica *transform from their red spring coloring to become green and lustrous before developing beautiful russet tones in autumn.*

ABOVE *Upon the arrival of cooler weather, the blue-green coloring of the summer foliage of* Nandina domestica *'Gulf Stream' is superseded by stunning red hues.*

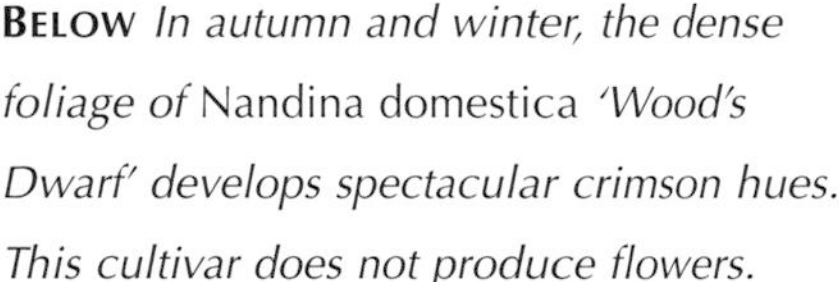

BELOW *In autumn and winter, the dense foliage of* Nandina domestica *'Wood's Dwarf' develops spectacular crimson hues. This cultivar does not produce flowers.*

Top Tip

Generally compact and easy to keep under control, *Nandina* plants are ideal for use in shrub borders and containers, and are effective for hedging and screening.

NERIUM

The sole species in this genus is an evergreen shrub or small tree from North Africa, the Middle East, northern India, and southern China. Commonly known as oleander, it is a member of the dogbane (Apocynaceae) family. It has elongated lance-shaped, dark green leaves and variegated forms are common. Throughout the warmer months, long-tubed 5-petalled flowers are produced. Cultivars are available in many flower colors and forms. Although all parts of oleander are highly poisonous, extracts show considerable promise as cancer treatments; one product is currently available and others are being trialed.

CULTIVATION

Oleander will not tolerate repeated hard frosts or prolonged winters. Plant in a hot sunny position and water while in flower. Oleander thrives near the coast, but its roots may be invasive in sandy soils. Lightly trim to shape after flowering. Take care when pruning as the latex may cause irritation to the skin. Propagate from half-hardened cuttings or seed.

Favorites	Flower Color	Blooming Season	Flower Fragrance
Nerium oleander	white, yellow, pink, red	spring to early autumn	no
Nerium oleander 'Album'	white; creamy white at center	spring to early autumn	no
Nerium oleander 'Hardy Pink'	pink	spring to early autumn	no
Nerium oleander 'Hardy Yellow'	pale yellow	spring to early autumn	no
Nerium oleander 'Petite Salmon'	salmon pink	spring to early autumn	no
Nerium oleander 'Splendens Variegatum'	rosy pink	spring to early autumn	no

ABOVE *An evergreen shrub,* Nerium oleander *'Album' features dark green lance-shaped leaves. The single, white, 5-petalled flowers are produced over a long flowering season.*

LEFT Nerium oleander *has given rise to numerous cultivars. There are single- and double-flowered forms in a wealth of colors, such as this red-flowered cultivar.*

Plant Height	Plant Width	Hardiness Zone	Frost Tolerance
8–15 ft (2.4–4.5 m)	6–12 ft (1.8–3.5 m)	8–11	yes
8–15 ft (2.4–4.5 m)	6–12 ft (1.8–3.5 m)	8–11	yes
6–12 ft (1.8–3.5 m)	10 ft (3 m)	8–11	yes
6–12 ft (1.8–3.5 m)	10 ft (3 m)	8–11	yes
2–4 ft (0.6–1.2 m)	2–4 ft (0.6–1.2 m)	8–11	yes
6–15 ft (1.8–4.5 m)	6–12 ft (1.8–3.5 m)	8–11	yes

BELOW *The double pink flowers of* Nerium oleander *'Splendens Giganteum Variegatum' are accented by the long, narrow, dark green leaves edged in creamy yellow.*

BELOW *The rich pink double blooms of* Nerium oleander *'Splendens' appear from late spring until early autumn, with occasional flowers produced in early winter.*

Top Tip

Due to the toxic nature of oleanders, pruned material should be disposed of with great care. Do not burn or leave within reach of children or pets.

PAEONIA

Known for its many perennial species, the genus *Paeonia*, a member of the peony (Paeoniaceae) family, includes among its 30 species several woody shrubs known as tree peonies. They have rather thin brittle stems and large, matt, mid-green leaves with deeply cut edges. The flowers can be very large and the cultivars are often semi-double, with frilly petals, in a range of brilliant colors. The name *Paeonia* was given in reference to Paeon, mythical Greek physician to the gods, and many of the species have been used in herbal medicine. Indiana has adopted *Paeonia lactiflora* as its state flower.

BELOW Paeonia rockii *is a highly regarded tree peony. The cultivar 'Fen He' has bright green leaves and pink flowers marked with a deep purple central blotch that is a signature of the species.*

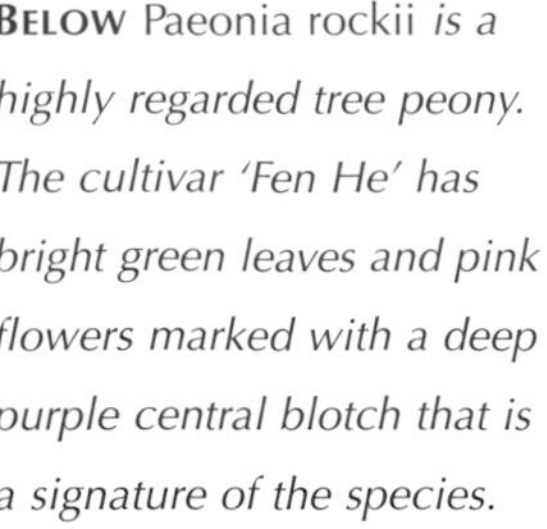

Top Tip

Young growth on peonies can be damaged by frost and strong winds. A temporary shelter can be erected during harsh weather to protect them from the elements.

CULTIVATION

Peonies like a position shaded from the hottest sun and prefer the soil to be as rich as it can be, preferably with ample humus, yet well drained. Incorporate manure before planting. Apply mulch annually, mixed with a dressing of fertilizer. Thin out any old unproductive stems after flowering. Species may be propagated from seed, but the cultivars are root grafted, a difficult process.

BELOW *The huge double flowers of* Paeonia *'Souvenir de Maxime Cornu' are yellow, tinged orange toward the center, with petals glamorously edged in red.*

BELOW Paeonia suffruticosa, *the moutan or tree peony, has given rise to a number of lovely cultivars, such as 'Yellow Heaven' seen here, with clear yellow blooms.*

RIGHT *Classically elegant, the large, semi-double, crisp white flowers of* Paeonia suffruticosa *'Hakuo-Jisi' sometimes feature purple markings at the petal base.*

Favorites	Flower Color	Blooming Season	Flower Fragrance	Plant Height	Plant Width	Hardiness Zone	Frost Tolerance
Paeonia delavayi	dark red	spring to early summer	no	6–7 ft (1.8–2 m)	4–5 ft (1.2–1.5 m)	6–9	yes
Paeonia × lemoinei	yellow with red or orange marks	spring to early summer	no	6 ft (1.8 m)	5–6 ft (1.5–1.8 m)	6–9	yes
Paeonia lutea	bright yellow	spring to early summer	no	5 ft (1.5 m)	5 ft (1.5 m)	6–9	yes
Paeonia rockii	white	spring to summer	no	7 ft (2 m)	3 ft (0.9 m)	7–10	yes
***Paeonia* 'Souvenir de Maxime Cornu'**	yellow-orange	late spring to early summer	yes	30–36 in (75–90 cm)	30–36 in (75–90 cm)	6–9	yes
Paeonia suffruticosa	white, yellow, pink, red	spring	no	3–7 ft (0.9–2 m)	3–7 ft (0.9–2 m)	4–9	yes

PHILADELPHUS

Member of the hydrangea (Hydrangeaceae) family, this genus of around 60 species of spring-flowering deciduous shrubs is widespread in the northern temperate zones. They are densely twiggy bushes, sometimes quite large, with simple lance-shaped leaves and peeling bark. The common names mock orange and syringa refer to the beautiful scent of their white blooms, but the genus is not closely related to oranges or lilacs. Double-flowered and compact-growing cultivars are common. Several species have had local medicinal uses. The flowers are rich in saponins and will lather well if rubbed gently in water. Idaho has claimed *Philadelphus lewisii* as its state flower.

BELOW *A scrambling shrub with drooping branches and rose-scented creamy-white flowers,* Philadelphus mexicanus *is known as the Mexican mock orange.*

CULTIVATION

Philadelphus plants are hardy and easily grown in sun or part-shade in any well-drained soil. Lightly trim after flowering and thin any congested growth. Propagate from softwood cuttings taken in summer, or hardwood cuttings taken in autumn and winter.

Favorites	Flower Color	Blooming Season	Flower Fragrance	Plant Height	Plant Width	Hardiness Zone	Frost Tolerance
***Philadelphus* 'Belle Etoile'**	white; small red blotch	late spring to early summer	yes	6 ft (1.8 m)	6–8 ft (1.8–2.4 m)	5–9	yes
Philadelphus coronarius	white	early summer	yes	10 ft (3 m)	5–8 ft (1.5–2.4 m)	2–9	yes
Philadelphus inodorus	white	summer	no	10 ft (3 m)	4 ft (1.2 m)	5–9	yes
Philadelphus mexicanus	creamy white	summer	yes	10–20 ft (3–6 m)	6–8 ft (1.8–2.4 m)	9–10	no
***Philadelphus* 'Schneesturm'**	white	late spring to early summer	yes	5–10 ft (1.5–3 m)	6 ft (1.8 m)	5–9	yes
Philadelphus subcanus	white	early summer	yes	20 ft (6 m)	6–10 ft (1.8–3 m)	6–9	yes

LEFT *A native of eastern USA,* Philadelphus inodorus *is an ideal plant for woodland gardens and shrub borders. Throughout summer it puts on a display of beautiful white flowers amid rich green leaves.*
BELOW *A small-scale version of the species,* Philadelphus subcanus *var.* magdalenae *is lower growing, with smaller leaves and flowers.*
BOTTOM Philadelphus coronarius *is a classic favorite with gardeners for its vigorous growth, neat dark green leaves, and crisp white blooms that fill the garden with their delightful fragrance.*

Top Tip

To encourage a good floral display, plant *Philadelphus* shrubs in a bright position—they tend to respond to sunlight with a heavier crop of blooms.

RHODODENDRON

Rhododendron is a large genus in the heath (Ericaceae) family. It includes some 800 species, both deciduous and evergreen, ranging from small ground covers to medium-sized trees. While they occur throughout most of the northern temperate regions and into the tropics, temperate East Asia is the center of the genus. The foliage varies greatly, from the rough hairy leaves of the deciduous azaleas to the huge, paddle-sized, leathery leaves of *Rhododendron grande*. The flowers, which open from late winter and occur in all colors except blue, are clustered, sometimes loosely but often crowded into conical heads called trusses. The genus is divided into two main types based on the presence or absence of leaf scales and is further divided into many sections and subsections.

LEFT Rhododendron *'Ethel Stocker' is one of the Hardy Tall Hybrids. Flowering in mid-spring, the rich crimson buds open to reveal beautiful pink flowers with a cluster of long stamens in the center.*

Gardeners can choose from many different types of rhododendrons: alpine rhododendrons, with small leaves, wiry stems, and clusters of tiny flowers; shrub rhododendrons, including those up to 15 ft (4.5 m) tall; tree rhododendrons, with a single trunk and a large head of foliage; evergreen azaleas, which are low to tall bushes with semi-persistent foliage and large light-textured flowers; deciduous azaleas, which are large twiggy bushes with flowers usually in shades of yellow, red, or orange; and vireya rhododendrons, which are tender tropical species with funnel-shaped blooms and no fixed flowering season. Washington and West Virginia claim *Rhododendron macrophylla* and *Rhododendron maximum* respectively as their floral emblem.

CULTIVATION

In common with most heath family plants, rhododendrons need moist, humus-rich, free-draining soil. This is important so that the development of their fine roots is not impeded. Also, to avoid damaging the surface roots, use mulch rather than cultivation for weed control. Species may be raised from seed, or propagate from half-hardened cuttings or layers.

LEFT *Ideal for use as a ground cover,* Rhododendron impeditum *is a compact dwarf form originating from China. From late spring it produces abundant violet to purple flowers.*

LEFT *A Hardy Small Hybrid, usually growing no higher than 3 ft (0.9 m),* Rhododendron *'Chrysomanicum' produces its frilly yellow flowers early in the season.*

Favorites	Flower Color	Blooming Season	Flower Fragrance	Plant Height	Plant Width	Hardiness Zone	Frost Tolerance
Rhododendron augustinii	mauve-blue to purple	mid-spring to summer	no	3–20 ft (0.9–6 m)	2–10 ft (0.6–3 m)	6–9	yes
Rhododendron impeditum	violet to purple	late spring to early summer	no	12 in (30 cm)	12 in (30 cm)	4–8	yes
Rhododendron schlippenbachii	white, pale pink	late spring	no	15 ft (4.5 m)	15 ft (4.5 m)	4–8	yes
***Rhododendron,* Azaleodendron Hybrids**	mauve, pink, yellow, cream	late spring to early summer	yes	2–8 ft (0.6–2.4 m)	2–8 ft (0.6–2.4 m)	5–10	yes
***Rhododendron,* Ghent Azalea Hybrids**	white, pink, red, orange, yellow	late spring to early summer	yes	5–8 ft (1.5–2.4 m)	3–6 ft (0.9–1.8 m)	5–9	yes
***Rhododendron,* Hardy Medium Hybrids**	various	spring	varied	3–6 ft (0.9–1.8 m)	2–8 ft (0.6–2.4 m)	3–9	yes
***Rhododendron,* Hardy Small Hybrids**	various	spring	varied	1–4 ft (0.3–1.2 m)	1–5 ft (0.3–1.5 m)	4–9	yes
***Rhododendron,* Hardy Tall Hybrids**	various	spring	varied	6–35 ft (1.8–10 m)	5–17 ft (1.5–5 m)	4–9	yes
***Rhododendron,* Indica Azalea Hybrids**	various	winter to spring	no	1–10 ft (0.3–3 m)	1–12 ft (0.3–3.5 m)	8–11	yes
***Rhododendron,* Knap Hill and Exbury Azalea Hybrids**	various	mid- to late spring	no	4–10 ft (1.2–3 m)	4–7 ft (1.2–2 m)	5–9	yes
***Rhododendron,* Kurume Azalea Hybrids**	various	spring	no	2–5 ft (0.6–1.5 m)	2–5 ft (0.6–1.5 m)	7–10	yes
***Rhododendron,* Mollis Hybrids**	orange, red, yellow, cream	spring	no	5–8 ft (1.5–2.4 m)	3–7 ft (0.9–2 m)	5–9	yes
***Rhododendron,* Occidentale Azalea Hybrids**	white, pink	mid-spring to summer	yes	6–10 ft (1.8–3 m)	6–10 ft (1.8–3 m)	6–10	yes
***Rhododendron,* Rustica Flore Pleno Azalea Hybrids**	white to red	late spring to early summer	yes	6–10 ft (1.8–3 m)	4–6 ft (1.2–1.8 m)	5–9	yes
***Rhododendron,* Satsuki Azalea Hybrids**	white, pink, purple, red	late spring to early summer	no	1–3 ft (0.3–0.9 m)	2–4 ft (0.6–1.2 m)	7–11	yes
***Rhododendron,* Tender Hybrids**	various	spring	varied	3–17 ft (0.9–5 m)	3–12 ft (0.9–3.5 m)	9–10	yes
***Rhododendron,* Vireya Hybrids**	various	throughout the year	varied	1–6 ft (0.3–1.8 m)	1–5 ft (0.3–1.5 m)	9–12	yes
***Rhododendron,* Yak Hybrids**	white, pink	summer	no	1–6 ft (0.3–1.8 m)	2–6 ft (0.6–1.8 m)	4–9	yes

RIGHT Rhododendron *'Balta' is a Hardy Small Hybrid with an upright habit. The abundant spring flowers are pale pink, almost white, amid glossy green leaves.*
BELOW *Growing up to 5 ft (1.5 m) high,* Rhododendron *'Florence Mann' is a Hardy Medium Hybrid. It is a classic example of the "blue" rhododendrons.*

LEFT *A dark central blotch highlights the pink blooms of* Rhododendron, *Hardy Small Hybrid, 'Chevalier Félix de Sauvage', which are borne in trusses of up to 12 blooms.*

ABOVE *Bred in the USA,* Rhododendron *'Anah Kruschke', a Hardy Medium Hydrid, has lush green foliage that contrasts with the lavender to purple-red spring blooms.*

LEFT *The matt green oval leaves of* Rhododendron *'Wilgen's Surprise', one of the Hardy Medium Hybrids, are the ideal foil for the pretty pink flowers.*

BELOW *With a spreading habit, usually growing wider than it is high,* Rhododendron *'Elsie Watson' is a Hardy Medium Hybrid. The attractive, lavender-pink, funnel-shaped flowers are marked and edged in a rich pink-red.*

Top Tip

Providing their cultural requirements are met, rhododendrons require little maintenance or pruning. Simply removing spent flowers will maintain their beauty.

RIGHT *Suitable for gardens in cooler climates,* Rhododendron *'Donvale Pearl', a Hardy Medium Hybrid, produces large trusses of tubular bell-shaped flowers.*

LEFT Rhododendron *'Coral Flare', a Vireya Hybrid, is a compact shrub that prefers part-shade. The large coral pink flowers are produced throughout the year.*

BELOW *Growing to around 3 ft (0.9 m) in height,* Rhododendron *'Patricia's Day', a Yak Hybrid, produces its dainty pinkish white blooms in mid-season.*

RIGHT *A Yak Hybrid,* Rhododendron *'Fantastica' has a dense compact habit. Rich pink-red at the petal edges, the flowers shade to pale pink at the center.*

BELOW *The* Rhododendron *Vireya Hybrids, such as 'George Bugden' seen here, are typically vividly colored and can be scented.*

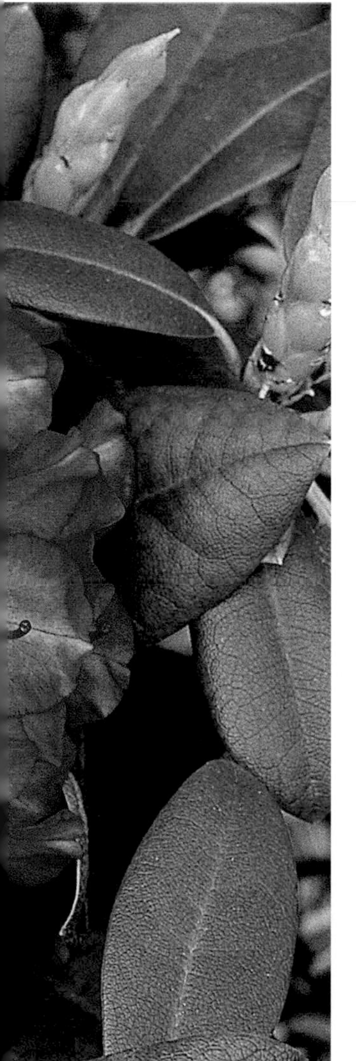

Above *A Knap Hill and Exbury Azalea Hybrid,* Rhododendron *'Berryrose' features dense clusters of funnel-shaped flowers in bright fiery hues.*

Below *Densely packed clusters of yellow flowers bring sunny color to* Rhododendron *'Sun Chariot', one of the Knap Hill and Exbury Azalea Hybrids.*

Above *Occidentale Hybrids, such as* Rhododendron *'Coccinto Speciosa' seen here, are the most drought, heat, and humidity tolerant of all deciduous azaleas.*

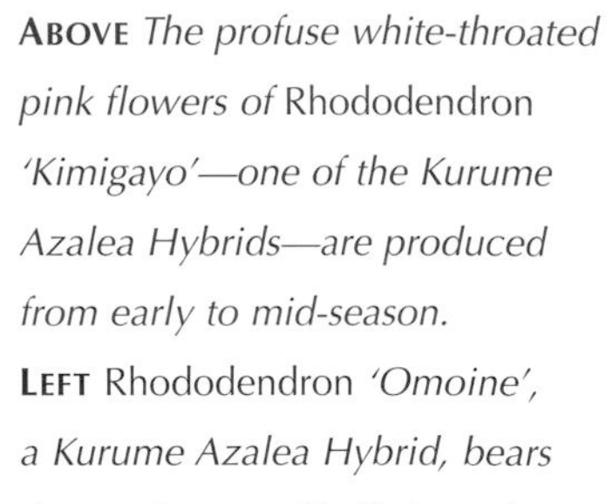

Above *The profuse white-throated pink flowers of* Rhododendron *'Kimigayo'—one of the Kurume Azalea Hybrids—are produced from early to mid-season.*

Left Rhododendron *'Omoine', a Kurume Azalea Hybrid, bears dense clusters of bell-shaped purplish pink flowers, each with long prominent stamens in the center.*

Above *When in bloom, the masses of pink-red flowers of* Rhododendron *'Favorite', one of the Kurume Azalea Hybrids, almost obscure the mid- to dark green foliage.*

Right *Dark spotting, a fine dark edge to the pink petals, and a paler throat are the prime features of* Rhododendron *'Elizabeth Belton', a Kurume Azalea Hybrid.*

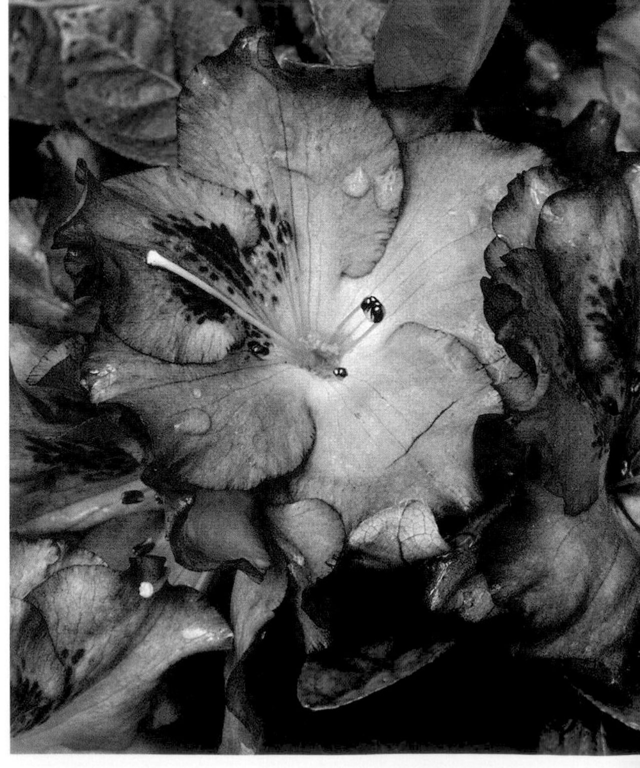

BELOW *One of the Belgian Indica Azalea Hybrids,* Rhododendron *'Eureka' is compact. It bears rich pink-red spring blooms that intensify in color toward the center.*

ABOVE Rhododendron *'Snow Prince', a Southern Indica Azalea Hybrid, is a magnificent sight at bloom time, when it is smothered in masses of white flowers.*

BELOW *The Belgian Indica Azalea Hybrids, such as* Rhododendron *'Eugene Mazel', feature lush foliage and large spring flowers produced in abundance.*

ROSA

LEFT Rosa moyesii *is native to western China and has stout erect stems and scattered thorns.* R. m. fargesii *bears reddish pink single flowers in summer.*

The genus *Rosa*, the type genus for the rose (Rosaceae) family and probably the most widely grown and loved of all plants, includes over 100 species of mainly deciduous shrubs and scrambling climbers found in the northern temperate and subtropical zones. The wild species usually have simple 5-petalled flowers that may or may not be fragrant. Brightly colored, nearly dry fruits follow. These are known as hips or heps and are rich in vitamin C. Rose foliage is generally pinnate, with a few large, toothed leaflets or sometimes many small leaflets. Unlike many genera, *Rosa* species are not usually classified in groups for garden purposes. The garden hybrids, however, are placed in groups based on their parentage and growth form. These include such well-known types as Cluster-flowered (Floribunda), Large-flowered (Hybrid Tea), Gallica, Bourbon, and Miniature, and also less widely cultivated groups such as Portland, Moss, and Noisette. Roses have been in garden use for centuries and now occur in a range of growth forms and all flower colors except blue. Roses have had so many associations, and have been so widely used as symbols, that it is difficult to single one out, but it says something for their popularity that a rose as old as the Apothecary's rose (*Rosa gallica* 'Officinalis'), the original red rose of Lancaster, which dates from before 1450, is still grown today. A much-loved rose thus lasts forever, though that does not seem to prevent the almost continuous introduction of new hybrids, which, by many other names, are "still as sweet."

LEFT Rosa rugosa *is native to Japan and eastern Asia. It bears scented single flowers, light to deep pink, from summer through to autumn and has round red hips.*

Favorites

	Flower Color	Blooming Season	Flower Fragrance	Plant Height	Plant Width	Hardiness Zone	Frost Tolerance
Rosa glauca	pink fading to white in center	summer	yes	6 ft (1.8 m)	6 ft (1.8 m)	3–10	yes
Rosa moyesii	deep red	summer	no	10 ft (3 m)	10 ft (3 m)	5–10	yes
Rosa rugosa	light to deep pink	summer to autumn	yes	5–8 ft (1.5–2.4 m)	5–8 ft (1.5–2.4 m)	2–10	yes
***Rosa*, Modern, Cluster-flowered (Floribunda)**	various	summer to autumn	yes	3–5 ft (0.9–1.5 m)	2–4 ft (0.6–1.2 m)	5–11	yes
***Rosa*, Modern, Hybrid Rugosa**	white, pink, yellow, red	summer to autumn	yes	3–7 ft (0.9–2 m)	3–7 ft (0.9–2 m)	3–10	yes
***Rosa*, Modern, Large-flowered (Hybrid Tea)**	various	summer to autumn	yes	4–7 ft (1.2–2 m)	3–5 ft (0.9–1.5 m)	4–11	yes
***Rosa*, Modern, Miniature**	various	summer to autumn	yes	8–30 in (20–75 cm)	8–18 in (20–45 cm)	5–11	yes
***Rosa*, Modern, Modern Shrub**	various	summer to autumn	yes	4–8 ft (1.2–2.4 m)	4–8 ft (1.2–2.4 m)	4–10	yes
***Rosa*, Modern, Patio (Dwarf Cluster-flowered)**	various	summer to autumn	no	2 ft (0.6 m)	6 ft (1.8 m)	4–11	yes
***Rosa*, Modern, Polyantha**	various	summer to autumn	no	24 in (60 cm)	18 in (45 cm)	3–10	yes
***Rosa*, Old, Alba**	white, pale pink	mid-summer	yes	6–8 ft (1.8–2.4 m)	4–6 ft (1.2–1.8 m)	4–10	yes
***Rosa*, Old, Bourbon**	white, pink, red	summer to early autumn	yes	4–7 ft (1.2–2 m)	3–6 ft (0.9–1.8 m)	6–10	yes
***Rosa*, Old, China**	pink, red	summer to autumn	yes	3–6 ft (0.9–1.8 m)	3–6 ft (0.9–1.8 m)	7–11	yes
***Rosa*, Old, Damask**	white, pale pink	spring or summer	yes	3–7 ft (0.9–2 m)	3–5 ft (0.9–1.5 m)	5–10	yes
***Rosa*, Old, Gallica**	pink, red, pinkish purple	spring or summer	yes	4–6 ft (1.2–1.8 m)	3–5 ft (0.9–1.5 m)	5–10	yes
***Rosa*, Old, Hybrid Perpetual**	white, pink, red	spring to autumn	yes	4–7 ft (1.2–2 m)	3–5 ft (0.9–1.5 m)	5–10	yes
***Rosa*, Old, Moss**	white, pink, red	summer	yes	4–6 ft (1.2–1.8 m)	4–6 ft (1.2–1.8 m)	5–10	yes
***Rosa*, Old, Tea**	cream, yellow, pink, red	summer to autumn	yes	4–7 ft (1.2–2 m)	3–5 ft (0.9–1.5 m)	7–11	yes

CULTIVATION

Most roses are very frost hardy, though only the toughest will survive severe continental winters. They should be planted in a well-ventilated sunny position to lessen the risk of fungal diseases and to promote heavy flowering. A moist, fertile, humus-rich soil is best, and in most areas roses benefit from extra water while in flower. Commercially grown roses are most often budded onto specially grown rootstocks. Budding is quite an easy process but it requires suitable seedlings of cutting-grown stocks. Winter hardwood and summer half-hardened cuttings will strike, but not all types produce good root systems. The seed usually requires stratification, and hybrids will not come true to type from seed.

LEFT *Some species of rose have traditionally been desired as much for their hips as their flowers.* Rosa moyesii *has pendulous, flagon-shaped, orange-red hips.*

ABOVE *Cluster-flowered (Floribunda) roses resulted from crossing the small cluster-flowered Polyantha roses with Large-flowered roses. The elegant 'Allgold' is a golden yellow example.*
BELOW *Sometimes known as 'Fellowship',* Rosa, *Cluster-flowered (Floribunda), 'Livin' Easy' has impressive fiery orange-red blooms.*

ABOVE Rosa, *Cluster-flowered (Floribunda), 'Mariandel' is an award-winning plant with vivid red semi-double flowers that have a mild fragrance. It grows to 2 ft (0.6 m) high.*

Left Rosa, *Cluster-flowered (Floribunda), 'Sexy Rexy' is an award-winning rose that is covered in large clusters of soft salmon pink camellia-like flowers.*

Left Rosa, *Cluster-flowered (Floribunda), 'Shepherd's Delight' is a strong grower with slightly fragrant deep pink blooms that are tinted orange in the center.*
Right Rosa, *Cluster-flowered (Floribunda), 'Betty Boop' has highly fragrant single blooms of creamy white to yellow, shading to red toward the petal edges.*

Top Tip

To maintain strong healthy growth, a simple "tidying up" of dead wood and pruning for size can be just as effective as stricter pruning regimes.

Right *'Kerryman' was bred in 1972 and is a Cluster-flowered (Floribunda) rose with a center of light pink.*

ABOVE *Also known as 'Best Friend' in New Zealand (its highly fragrant flowers have won awards there), 'Caprice de Meilland' is a Large-flowered (Hybrid Tea) rose.*
BELOW *The most popular of all rose groups, thousands of Large-flowered (Hybrid Tea) roses have been bred.* Rosa *'Valencia' is a creamy yellow example.*

ABOVE *'Just Joey' is a Large-flowered (Hybrid Tea) rose, which has coppery red buds that open to large coppery orange flowers paling to soft pink at the petal edges.*
TOP *Large-flowered (Hybrid Tea) rose 'Lagerfeld' has an upright bushy habit to 5 ft (1.5 m) high. Lavender-pink blooms with a silvery sheen are strongly fragrant.*

LEFT Rosa, *Large-flowered (Hybrid Tea), 'Jason' has deep pink petals, lighter on their reverse side. A slightly scented upright plant, it grows to 4 ft (1.2 m) high.*
BELOW *A lovely deep pink, the many single-stemmed blooms borne each year on Rosa 'Peter Frankenfeld', a Large-flowered (Hybrid Tea) rose, make ideal cut flowers.*

LEFT Rosa, *Large-flowered (Hybrid Tea), 'New Zealand' (syn. 'Aotearoa-New Zealand') has soft pink fragrant flowers that open from long pointed buds.*

RIGHT *Also called 'Queen of Denmark',* Rosa, *Alba, 'Königin von Dänemark' is an award-winner, which has smaller double flowers of a deeper pink than other Albas.*
BELOW *Returning from the Middle East, Crusaders took the first Damask roses back to Europe.* Rosa, *Damask, 'Rose de Rescht' has deep pink double flowers.*
BOTTOM *Moss roses are named for the mossy growth that arises on the stems and buds.* Rosa, *Moss, 'William Lobb' has semi-double purplish magenta flowers.*

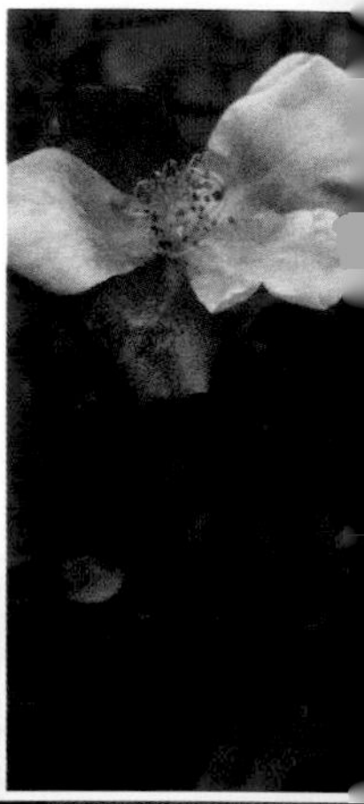

Right Rosa, *Tea, 'Mrs Reynolds Hole' has fragrant, rich purple-pink, double flowers. Tea roses grow better in warmer climates.*
Below Rosa, *China, 'Mutabilis' has buff red-streaked buds opening to single yellow flowers that change in color, moving through shades of pink and soft crimson.*

Above *The fragrant pink blooms of* Rosa, *Bourbon, 'Gros Choux d'Hollande' open from red buds. Humid climates see Bourbon roses prone to fungal diseases.*

Right *Moss roses are large, double, fragrant bloomers, usually flowering only once a year. 'James Veitch' is a vigorous example with mauve-pink blooms.*

SPIRAEA

Found mainly in temperate East Asia and North America, this genus from the rose (Rosaceae) family has around 70 species of deciduous to semi-evergreen spring- and summer-flowering shrubs. Most have fine arching stems and simple alternate leaves, often toothed or lobed. Usually as the new foliage develops, they burst into bloom, bearing masses of tiny 5-petalled white to deep pink flowers. The flowers can occur right along the stems or may be clustered in spikes at the tips. While a few species are used in herbal teas, *Spiraea* plants are grown almost exclusively for their ornamental properties.

CULTIVATION

Spiraea are generally hardy and easily grown in any temperate climate garden with moist well-drained soil. They flower best in sun but in areas with hot summers they may need a little shade. Some flower on the old wood and should be pruned immediately after flowering; others flower on the current season's growth and may be trimmed in winter. Propagate from softwood or half-hardened cuttings.

ABOVE Spiraea thunbergii *is a vase-shaped shrub that is generally as wide as it is tall. It mostly branches from the base and has a yellow-orange autumn color.*

LEFT *The red summer flowers and orange autumn leaves of* Spiraea japonica *'Goldflame' make this cultivar an attractive choice for gardens.*

Top Tip

When positioning a spiraea in your garden, it is best placed in front of green-foliaged plants to provide a backdrop for its beautiful flowers.

ABOVE Spiraea mollifolia *is native to western China. The leaves and young stems of this tall shrub are covered in a silky down. Its branches nod slightly at the tips.*

RIGHT Spiraea japonica *'Dart's Red' has pink-red flowers. Like other* S. japon*ica plants, it is an extremely durable shrub and enhances any mass or group planting.*

Favorites	Flower Color	Blooming Season	Flower Fragrance	Plant Height	Plant Width	Hardiness Zone	Frost Tolerance
Spiraea japonica	rose pink	summer	no	2–6 ft (0.6–1.8 m)	2–6 ft (0.6–1.8 m)	3–10	yes
Spiraea mollifolia	white	summer	no	6–8 ft (1.8–2.4 m)	7 ft (2 m)	6–9	yes
Spiraea nipponica	white	summer	no	3–6 ft (0.9–1.8 m)	3–6 ft (0.9–1.8 m)	5–10	yes
Spiraea thunbergii	white	late spring to summer	no	5 ft (1.5 m)	6 ft (1.8 m)	4–10	yes
Spiraea trichocarpa	white	summer	no	6 ft (1.8 m)	4 ft (1.2 m)	5–9	yes
Spiraea trilobata	white	summer	no	4 ft (1.2 m)	4 ft (1.2 m)	6–9	yes

SYRINGA

Commonly known as lilacs, the 23 species of deciduous shrubs in this genus in the olive (Oleaceae) family flower from spring to early summer and are famed for their fragrance. They are mostly native to temperate Asia, with 2 European species, one of which, the common lilac, *Syringa vulgaris,* is a parent of many garden cultivars and hybrids. Lilac foliage is variably shaped and sometimes colors well in autumn. Most species share similar short-tubed 4-petalled flowers that are more or less densely clustered in heads. The flower colors range from white and soft yellow, through pink and mauve to purple. While lilac is renowned for scent, it also yields dyes: green from the flowers, green and brown from the leaves, and orange-yellow from the stems.

Top Tip

Planted in a mixed border, lilacs are great shrubs that offer color, flowers, fragrance, and golden leaves in autumn. They will appreciate fertilizing each year.

CULTIVATION

Lilacs are hardy and easily grown in sun or light shade with well-drained, preferably slightly alkaline soil. Some sucker freely and may need to be contained. The species may be raised from seed, cultivars from cuttings, layers, or grafts.

Favorites	Flower Color	Blooming Season	Flower Fragrance	Plant Height	Plant Width	Hardiness Zone	Frost Tolerance
Syringa laciniata	pale lavender-pink	late spring	yes	6–12 ft (1.8–3.5 m)	10 ft (3 m)	5–9	yes
Syringa meyeri	purple-mauve	spring to summer	yes	6 ft (1.8 m)	4 ft (1.2 m)	4–9	yes
Syringa pubescens	lilac-purple	spring to early summer	yes	12 ft (3.5 m)	12 ft (3.5 m)	5–9	yes
Syringa vulgaris	blue	late spring to early summer	yes	8–20 ft (2.4–6 m)	6–10 ft (1.8–3 m)	4–9	yes
***Syringa vulgaris* 'Charles Joly'**	reddish purple	spring	yes	8–15 ft (2.4–4.5 m)	6–10 ft (1.8–3 m)	4–9	yes
***Syringa vulgaris* 'Sensation'**	purple with white-edged petals	late spring to early summer	yes	8–15 ft (2.4–4.5 m)	6–10 ft (1.8–3 m)	4–9	yes

ABOVE Syringa vulgaris *is the state flower of New Hampshire. The typical form has blue flowers but cultivars can have pink, purple, or white flowers. This cultivar is 'Magellan'.*

ABOVE RIGHT Syringa meyeri *'Palibin' is the smallest of all lilacs, at around 4 ft (1.2 m) high, and bears pinkish lavender flowers.*

LEFT Syringa vulgaris *'Mrs Edward Harding' bears deep purplish red flowers, shaded pink, which have a delicious scent in early spring. They are attractive to butterflies.*

RIGHT *One of the first of the oriental lilacs to be introduced into the West,* Syringa laciniata, *or cut-leafed lilac, is a tall shrub with pale lavender-pink flowers in spring.*

TAXUS

A genus of 7 species of evergreen conifers, they are mostly from the Northern Hemisphere temperate zone, with a few found in the mountainous areas of the tropics. They are primarily a foliage plant and their short, pointed, narrow, dark green to deep olive leaves are densely crowded in whorls along the stems for most of the year. However, the small floral cones that may have passed unnoticed in spring develop into fleshy red fruit on female plants and can be a feature from late summer. The famed English longbow weapons popular in the Middle Ages were made from yew. Yew also yields an extract that has been promoted as an anti-cancer drug under the name Taxol.

CULTIVATION

Yews are hardy and undemanding plants that grow well in cool areas with deep, moist, well-drained soil. They withstand severe trimming and are popular hedging and topiary subjects. The seeds germinate well but cultivars are propagated from cuttings or grafts.

LEFT Taxus baccata *'Aurea' is a hardy and easy-to-grow plant, and is commonly known as golden English yew. Its golden-yellow young growth ages to green.*

ABOVE Taxus cuspidata, *the Japanese yew, is suitable for hedging and topiary, and is tolerant of pollution. This variety is* T. c. var. nana *and is a low spreading shrub.*

LEFT Taxus baccata *'Standishii' is a slow-growing, upright, female yew that naturally forms a good growing shape without any clipping or trimming.*

FAR LEFT Taxus × media *is a good shrub for hedging or screening. Do not plant them in windswept sites as some discoloration of the foliage can occur.*

Top Tip

Taxus shrubs are a great background for borders, as their dark green foliage sets off both colorful and pale flowers. They are slow growing but long lived.

Favorites	Fruit Color	Fruit Shape	Fruit Length	Plant Height	Plant Width	Hardiness Zone	Frost Tolerance
Taxus baccata	red (on female plants only)	ovoid	¼–½ in (6–12 mm)	50 ft (15 m)	25 ft (8 m)	5–10	yes
***Taxus baccata* 'Aurea'**	red (on female plants only)	ovoid	¼–½ in (6–12 mm)	50 ft (15 m)	25 ft (8 m)	5–10	yes
Taxus chinensis	red (on female plants only)	ovoid	¼–½ in (6–12 mm)	20 ft (6 m)	15 ft (4.5 m)	6–10	yes
Taxus cuspidata	red (on female plants only)	ovoid	¼ in (6 mm)	50 ft (15 m)	20 ft (6 m)	4–9	yes
Taxus* × *media	red (on female plants only)	ovoid	½ in (12 mm)	25 ft (8 m)	20 ft (6 m)	5–9	yes
***Taxus* × *media* 'Hicksii'**	red (on female plants only)	ovoid	¼–½ in (6–12 mm)	6 ft (1.8 m)	5 ft (1.5 m)	5–9	yes

Top Tip

Viburnums are a great addition to an autumn garden. The brightly colored fruits attract birds, and the foliage of some species colors brilliantly.

VIBURNUM

This attractive genus in the woodbine (Caprifoliaceae) family is large and diverse, with over 150 evergreen and deciduous species ranging from ground covers and shrubs to small trees. They are mainly confined to the Northern Hemisphere and generally cultivated for their flowers and colorful fruit, though some are attractive foliage plants and a few are used for hedging. The leaves are oval, sometimes pointed, and may color well in autumn. The flowers are small but densely clustered and can be powerfully fragrant. Clusters of berries follow in various shades, including red, steel blue, and black. The red-fruited species are sometimes called cranberries and their fruits are edible, though the true cranberries are in the genus *Vaccinium*.

CULTIVATION

Mostly very hardy, they are easily grown in any sunny or partly shaded position with moist well-drained soil. Water well in summer. Trim after flowering, thinning out any old, unproductive wood. Propagate from half-hardened cuttings; the species will also grow from seed.

TOP Viburnum plicatum *flowers somewhat resemble those of the the lacecap* Hydrangea. *The blooms of this cultivar 'Summer Snowflake' are long lasting.*

ABOVE *The foliage of* Viburnum × burkwoodii *changes from bronze to dark green to yellow over the seasons. The white flowers open from pink buds.*

Favorites	Flower Color	Blooming Season	Flower Fragrance	Plant Height	Plant Width	Hardiness Zone	Frost Tolerance
Viburnum bitchiuense	pink to white	early summer	yes	10 ft (3 m)	10 ft (3 m)	6–8	yes
Viburnum* × *burkwoodii	white	early spring	yes	8 ft (2.4 m)	8 ft (2.4 m)	6–9	yes
Viburnum plicatum	white	late spring to early summer	no	8–10 ft (2.4–3 m)	10–12 ft (3–3.5 m)	4–9	yes
Viburnum setigerum	white	late spring	no	5–12 ft (1.5–3.5 m)	7 ft (2 m)	5–9	yes
Viburnum tinus	white to pink	autumn to spring	yes	8–12 ft (2.4–3.5 m)	5–10 ft (1.5–3 m)	7–10	yes
***Viburnum tinus* 'Variegatum'**	white to pink	autumn to spring	yes	8–12 ft (2.4–3.5 m)	5–10 ft (1.5–3 m)	7–10	yes

BELOW *The egg-shaped red fruits of* Viburnum bitchiuense *form after the fragrant summer blooms of this attractive deciduous shrub native to Korea.*

RIGHT Viburnum setigerum *is not planted for its flowers, which are insignificant. This species bears gleaming, red and orange, oval fruits, and has great autumn color.*

Annuals and Perennials

Annuals, biennials, and perennials are some of the most beloved and popular garden plants, offering diversity in flower and form and some of the most nuanced colors and textures. They range from diminutive, tiny-leafed, creeping phlox to brash towering daisies, and lend color and beauty to a variety of gardens, from tidy urban planters to voluptuous mixed borders. While often used interchangeably by gardeners, there are significant distinctions between the life cycles of annuals, biennials, and perennials—distinctions that can guide the savvy gardener in creating a satisfying tapestry of texture and color in the garden year after year.

Above Viola *hybrid cultivars like 'Crystal Bowl Orange' are treated as annuals or short-lived garden perennials. Plants like these are valued for their prolific colorful flowers.*

Left Iris, *Tall Bearded, 'Codicil' is a perennial grown from rhizomes. This plant needs to be divided every 5 to 7 years to achieve the best flower production.*

A BURST OF COLOR

Some of the most colorful and brightest flowers are annuals—plants whose life cycle (from seed to flowering) is completed within one year of germinating. The life cycle of annuals—rapid growth and flower production followed by (at least in theory) seed—is designed to take advantage of a short or adverse growing season. The abundance of flowers they produce is a means of ensuring their survival before either summer's heat or winter's cold brings their short life to a close. Although the parent plants die, their progeny can continue the species into the following season, if conditions are suitable.

Some of the most charming traditional garden plants are classified among the annuals, such as nasturtiums (*Tropaeolum* species), pansies (*Viola* species), busy lizzies (*Impatiens* species), and zinnias. For gardeners' purposes, plants generally classified as annuals can be divided into 2 main groups: cool-season and warm-season annuals.

RIGHT *A summer-flowering perennial and a cultivar of common sage,* Salvia officinalis *'Minor' should be divided every 2 or 3 years to maintain vigor.*
BELOW Aquilegia *'Bluebird' is a clump-forming herbaceous perennial that dies down after flowering. One of the Songbird Series, it bears very large flowers.*

Cool-season annuals thrive in moderate temperatures and tolerate light frost, although freezing temperatures will usually fell them. They are also known as half-hardy annuals. In hot summer climates, they are good shoulder-season (spring and autumn) plants and can even grow and flower through the winter in milder climates. In cooler coastal or high-elevation regions, they may flower through the summer too.

Where winters are mild, the seed and young plants of cool-season annuals can be planted in autumn. In cold-winter areas, they should be planted directly in the ground once the soil is workable in spring. Pansies *(Viola × wittrockiana)* and sweet peas *(Lathyrus odoratus)* grow vigorously in cooler weather and flower as long as temperatures remain moderate. If or when temperatures rise, they quickly lose vigor and wither away.

At the other end of the spectrum, warm-season or tender annuals require heat to grow and thrive. Plants such as marigolds (*Tagetes* species) and petunias are best planted indoors in spring or outdoors only after the soil has warmed sufficiently. (Seed packets usually include the soil temperature required for germination.) Originating in tropical or subtropical regions, warm-season annuals flourish in summer's heat but perish soon after the first frost.

Unlike their short-lived annual brethren, perennials are plants which live for more than 2 years, taking a couple of seasons to reach flowering size,

Right Tagetes *'Little Hero Fire' is a very brightly colored warm-season annual. This dwarf hybrid cultivar is extremely heat tolerant.*
Below right *The vivid hues of annuals such as* Zinnia elegans *'Cherry Ruffles' make them good accent plants against a background of deep green foliage.*

then flowering each year henceforth. Biennials, often sold as "short-lived perennials" for simplicity's sake, germinate and grow in their first season, flower and set seed in their second, and then die. Biennials include the common foxglove *(Digitalis purpurea).*

The most common perennial plants (excluding woody perennials such as trees and shrubs) are herbaceous. These are plants that disappear below the ground during part of the growing season, typically winter. This protects them from adverse weather conditions. Perennials such as bee balm (*Monarda* species) fall into this group. Other herbaceous perennials die down directly after flowering in spring or summer, emerging again late in the season with a low overwintering rosette of leaves. Such plants include oriental poppies *(Papaver orientale),* columbines (*Aquilegia* species), and cardinal flowers (*Lobelia* species).

Evergreen and semi-evergreen perennials are sometimes classified as shrubs, but many appear on nursery perennial or annual tables (depending on the climate). Generally originating in warmer areas, these plants include sages (*Salvia* species) and Cape fuchsias (*Phygelius* species). Whether a plant is considered an evergreen or semi-evergreen perennial depends, of course, on the climate in which it is growing and even the severity of a given winter in a particular region. The stunning red-flowering pineapple sage *(Salvia elegans)* may be a hardy evergreen shrub in warm-temperate climates, but in cool-temperate climates, it is a semi-evergreen tender perennial in some areas and an annual in others.

Perennials are among the easiest of plants to grow for beginners. In colder regions, they are best planted out in spring so that their roots can become well established before winter sets in. In milder regions, autumn planting can be beneficial, as it allows time for the plants' roots to become established during a cool moist season.

While earlier gardening trends may have leaned toward the use of showy massed annual bedding plants or the meticulous color schemes of formal perennial borders, today's gardeners take pride in integrating annuals and perennials, as well as shrubs and trees, thereby gaining the best of all available worlds. Trees and shrubs provide structure for the garden, annuals offer color and sizzle, while the perennials provide ever-changing texture and color—and the enjoyment of seeing them develop each year.

Achillea

A Eurasian member of the daisy (Asteraceae) family, *Achillea* has around 100 species of perennials that occur in a wide range of habitats and are mostly very hardy. Their foliage is finely divided, ferny, and often aromatic, usually forming a dense basal clump from which flower stems develop in summer, the height varying considerably with the species. The individual flowers, which occur in many colors, are tiny but are massed in flattened heads at the stem tips to produce a bright display. One common name, milfoil, comes from the French *mille feuille* (thousand leaves). The plants are also known as yarrows.

Above Achillea *'Coronation Gold' is a cross between* A. clypeolata *and* A. filipendulina. *The golden yellow flowerheads measure up to 4 in (10 cm) across. The flowers are long-lasting and the foliage is aromatic.*

Right Achillea millefolium *is known as a herbal anti-inflammatory; the genus is named for Achilles, who is said to have used the plant medicinally. 'Fanal' (syn. 'The Beacon') is one of its most popular cultivars, with crimson-red flowers that fade to orange.*

Cultivation

These plants are best grown in a temperate or cool-temperate climate with a position in full sun. The soil need not be highly fertile but must be well-drained, preferably slightly gritty, and remain moist throughout summer. Some alpine species need protection from winter rain. Propagate by division, though species may be raised from seed.

Right *Although* Achillea millefolium *can be invasive, some of its cultivars are valued for their colorful flowers. 'Heidi' has bright salmon pink flowers with yellow centers.*

Top Tip

The aromatic leaves of many species of these useful border plants repel insects, while the numerous flowers attract bees and butterflies to the garden.

ABOVE *With small flat flowerheads and feathery silver-gray foliage,* Achillea *'King Edward' is a good choice for a rock garden.*

Favorites	Flower Color	Blooming Season	Flower Fragrance	Plant Height	Plant Width	Hardiness Zone	Frost Tolerance
***Achillea* 'Coronation Gold'**	golden yellow	spring to summer	no	36 in (90 cm)	18 in (45 cm)	4–10	yes
Achillea filipendulina	gold	summer	no	24–48 in (60–120 cm)	24–48 in (60–120 cm)	5–10	yes
Achillea* × *kellereri	creamy white	summer	no	6 in (15 cm)	10 in (25 cm)	5–10	yes
***Achillea* 'King Edward'**	pale yellow	summer	no	4 in (10 cm)	10 in (25 cm)	5–10	yes
Achillea millefolium	white to pink	summer to autumn	no	12–30 in (30–75 cm)	18–30 in (45–75 cm)	3–10	yes
Achillea ptarmica	white	summer	no	30 in (75 cm)	30 in (75 cm)	6–10	yes

Top Tip

Agapanthus plants bloom best with congested roots, so resist dividing them. If growing in pots, avoid overly large containers for best flowering.

AGAPANTHUS

The 10 species in this southern African genus are placed in the onion (Alliaceae) family but do not produce true bulbs, though their thickened roots perform much the same function. The leaves are long and strappy and depending on the species may be evergreen or deciduous. Tall stems topped with heads of many tubular to bell-shaped, mauve to purple or white flowers occur throughout the warmer months in mild climates, but elsewhere summer is the main flowering season. *Agapanthus* has been used medicinally for cardiac complaints. Although the various species seem quite distinct, some botanists now believe them to be just one very variable species.

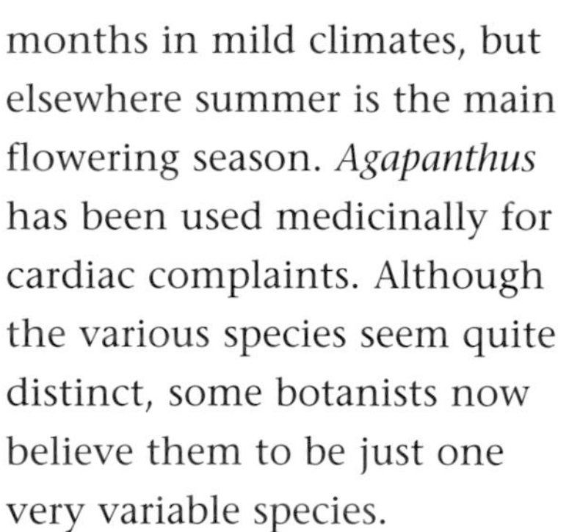

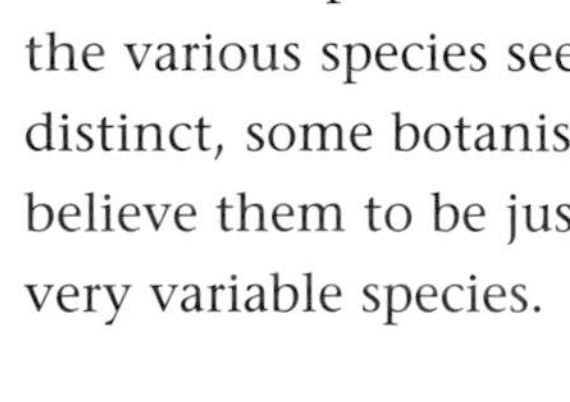

ABOVE LEFT Agapanthus *'Monmid' is a relatively recent cultivar with the trademark name* Midnight Blue. *It has tightly clustered heads of striking dark violet-blue blooms on tall stalks.*

BELOW *Known as "drooping agapanthus" due to its pendulous tubular blue flowers,* Agapanthus inapertus *is also sometimes white. It is native to southeastern South Africa.*

CULTIVATION

Although tolerant of drought and poor soil, both flower and foliage production improves with moisture and feeding. Planting should be in full or half sun in well-drained soil that should be deep enough to accommodate the large rootstock. Deadhead routinely to encourage continuous flowering. Propagate by division when dormant in winter or raise species from seed.

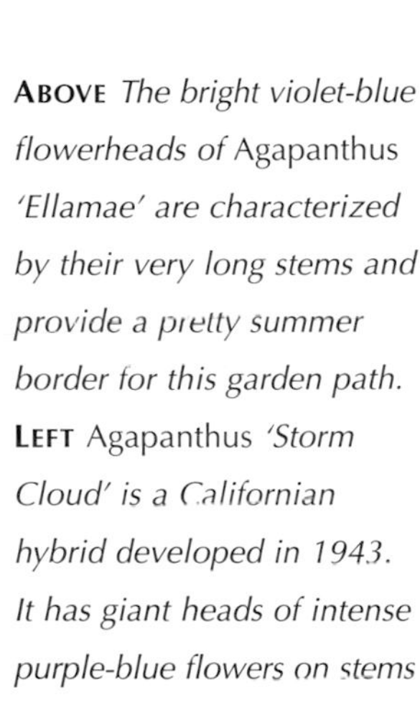

ABOVE *The bright violet-blue flowerheads of* Agapanthus *'Ellamae' are characterized by their very long stems and provide a pretty summer border for this garden path.*
LEFT Agapanthus *'Storm Cloud' is a Californian hybrid developed in 1943. It has giant heads of intense purple-blue flowers on stems up to 6 ft (1.8 m) high.*

Favorites	Flower Color	Blooming Season	Flower Fragrance	Plant Height	Plant Width	Hardiness Zone	Frost Tolerance
Agapanthus africanus	blue-purple	summer to early autumn	no	18–24 in (45–60 cm)	18–36 in (45–90 cm)	8–11	yes
Agapanthus **'Ellamae'**	bright violet-blue	summer to early autumn	no	5–7 ft (1.5–2 m)	2–4 ft (0.6–1.2 m)	7–11	yes
Agapanthus inapertus	deep blue-purple	late summer to autumn	no	4–5 ft (1.2–1.5 m)	2–4 ft (0.6–1.2 m)	7–11	yes
Agapanthus **Midnight Blue/'Monmid'**	deep purple-blue	summer to early autumn	no	3–4 ft (0.9–1.2 m)	2 ft (0.6 m)	7–11	yes
Agapanthus orientalis	lilac-blue	summer to early autumn	no	2–4 ft (0.6–1.2 m)	2 ft (0.6 m)	7–11	yes
Agapanthus **'Storm Cloud'**	intense purple-blue	summer to early autumn	no	4–6 ft (1.2–1.8 m)	2 ft (0.6 m)	7–11	yes

ALSTROEMERIA

Once classified with the lilies, this South American grouping of around 50 species of fleshy- or tuberous-rooted perennials is now considered the type genus for the Alstroemeriaceae family. Although they have very beautifully marked, long-lasting flowers, their roots can be invasive. Modern hybrids generally have a more restrained habit than the wild species. Most form a clump of upright stems bearing slightly twisted, narrow lance-shaped leaves. The flowers are clustered in heads at the stem tips, opening mainly in summer, and are often used as cut blooms. They are commonly known as Peruvian lilies or lilies of the Incas. Be careful when handling the cut stems as the sap can cause dermatitis.

ABOVE Alstroemeria *'Friendship' is an award-winning hybrid. In recent years the range of these* Alstroemeria *hybrids has increased enormously due to the efforts of plant breeders around the world.*

CULTIVATION

Except where the soil freezes, *Alstroemeria* plants are easily cultivated in any sunny position. The soil should be light, well-drained, and remain moist through the flowering season. Propagate hybrids and cultivars by division when dormant or raise the species from seed.

RIGHT *The Little Miss Series of* Alstroemeria *are dwarf plants with large flowers and strong stems. 'Little Miss Olivia' has soft cream flowers with a pale yellow throat and red-brown flecks.*

Favorites	Flower Color	Blooming Season	Flower Fragrance	Plant Height	Plant Width	Hardiness Zone	Frost Tolerance
***Alstroemeria* 'Friendship'**	soft yellow	summer	no	36 in (90 cm)	24 in (60 cm)	7–10	yes
***Alstroemeria* 'Fuego'**	red	summer	no	5–6 ft (1.5–1.8 m)	3–4 ft (0.9–1.2 m)	7–10	yes
Alstroemeria psittacina	red-flushed green	summer	no	27–36 in (70–90 cm)	15–20 in (38–50 cm)	8–10	yes
***Alstroemeria psittacina* 'Royal Star'**	red-flushed green	summer	no	27–36 in (70–90 cm)	15–20 in (38–50 cm)	8–10	yes
***Alstroemeria*, Little Miss Series**	various	summer to autumn	no	6–12 in (15–30 cm)	6–12 in (15–30 cm)	7–10	yes
***Alstroemeria*, Princess Series**	various	spring to autumn	no	12–18 in (30–45 cm)	12–18 in (30–45 cm)	7–10	yes

Below Alstroemeria, *Princess Series, 'Princess Freckles'. The Dutch-raised Princess Series are long flowering and compact, making ideal potted plants.*

Below Alstroemeria *'Little Miss Tara' is one of the most colorful in the Little Miss Series. These hybrids have a long flowering period and do not require staking.*

Top Tip

These easily grown plants are known for their very attractive flowers that are excellent for cutting because they last so well in the vase.

ANEMONE

This genus of about 120 species of perennials is part of the buttercup (Ranunculaceae) family. Widespread in the temperate zones, they are a variable lot, ranging from tiny alpines through small woodland natives to large, spreading, clump-forming species, some with fibrous roots, others forming rhizomes or tubers. In addition to the many species, there are countless hybrids and cultivars. Most form a basal clump of finely divided, sometimes ferny foliage. Flowers appear throughout the warmer months, varying in time, size, and color with the species. *Anemos* was an ancient Greek word for wind (hence the common name, windflower) and is also the origin of the name for the anemometer, the wind-measuring instrument.

ABOVE Anemone blanda *is found from southeastern Europe to the Caucasus region. It features tuberous roots, strong fleshy stems, and ferny base leaves.*
RIGHT *Also known as the anemone of Greece,* Anemone pavonina *is a clump-forming tuberous species. Its foliage is bright green and fern-like.*

CULTIVATION

Anemones vary in their requirements. Alpine species prefer gritty but moisture-retentive soil and full sun; woodland species like humus-rich soil and cool partial shade; and the bedding forms are best grown in a sunny border and should be kept moist when in flower. Propagate by division or from seed.

Favorites	Flower Color	Blooming Season	Flower Fragrance	Plant Height	Plant Width	Hardiness Zone	Frost Tolerance
Anemone blanda	white, blue, pink	spring	no	4–8 in (10–20 cm)	6–12 in (15–30 cm)	6–9	yes
Anemone coronaria	various	spring	no	15–24 in (38–60 cm)	8–15 in (20–38 cm)	8–10	yes
Anemone × hybrida	white to pink	late summer to autumn	no	4–5 ft (1.2–1.5 m)	7 ft (2 m)	6–10	yes
Anemone nemorosa	white-cream	early spring	no	3–6 in (8–15 cm)	12 in (30 cm)	5–9	yes
Anemone pavonina	various	spring	no	12 in (30 cm)	12–15 in (30–38 cm)	8–10	yes
Anemone sylvestris	white	spring and early summer	yes	12 in (30 cm)	12 in (30 cm)	4–9	yes

ABOVE *The white, slightly drooping flowers of the fleshy-stemmed* Anemone sylvestris *are the reason for its common names of snow-drop anemone and snow-drop windflower.*

Top Tip

Their variety means that an anemone can be found for almost any outdoor spot, and some (especially the tuberous ones) make good container plants.

ABOVE Anemone coronaria *bears large flowers in most shades apart from yellow. Also known as the florist's anemone and the wind poppy, it has tuberous roots.*

ANTHURIUM

This tropical American genus includes some 900 species and is a member of the arum (Araceae) family. Quite often seen as indoor plants, they are also very popular in tropical gardens. They develop into a cluster of upright stems bearing large, deep green, lance- to arrowhead-shaped leaves. The flower stems are topped with a leaf-like heart-shaped bract or spathe that often becomes red, cream, or pink as the long flower spike or spadix develops. Anthuriums are also grown as cut flowers. Although some species have been used medicinally where they occur naturally, all parts of the plant are toxic and such use, even externally, is not encouraged.

LEFT *Many cultivars of* Anthurium andraeanum *have been developed, including this attractive pink version. Like those of the species, these flowers are long-lasting when cut.*

CULTIVATION

These tropical plants require constantly warm humid conditions to flower well. They thrive in moist humus-rich soil with part-shade. They will tolerate brief periods of cool weather but should not be exposed to cold drafts. Feed well to encourage lush foliage and continuous flowering. Propagation is usually by division, though the species may be raised from seed.

ABOVE *The dark green arrowhead-shaped leaves of* Anthurium andraeanum *contrast well with the bright red heavily-veined spathes.*
LEFT *Possibly of hybrid origin,* Anthurium andraeanum *'Lady Ruth' has brilliant glossy scarlet spathes and similarly colored spadices.*

Top Tip

As houseplants in non-tropical areas, anthuriums need bright indirect light, moist well-aerated soil, and regular feeding to produce flowers.

Above Anthurium andraeanum *'Small Talk Pink' is a low-growing cultivar with large bright pink spathes and pink-tinted cream spadices.*

Favorites	Flower Color	Blooming Season	Flower Fragrance	Plant Height	Plant Width	Hardiness Zone	Frost Tolerance
Anthurium andraeanum	bright red	all year	no	24 in (60 cm)	8–12 in (20–30 cm)	11–12	no
Anthurium* × *ferrierense	various	all year	no	24–60 in (60–150 cm)	15–30 in (38–75 cm)	11–12	no
Anthurium scandens	green to purple	all year	no	3–10 ft (0.9–3 m)	1–3 ft (0.3–0.9 m)	11–12	no
Anthurium scherzerianum	bright red	all year	no	15–30 in (38–75 cm)	12–20 in (30–50 cm)	11–12	no
Anthurium upalaense	purple-tinted yellow-green	all year	no	18–30 in (45–75 cm)	36–60 in (90–150 cm)	12	no
Anthurium warocqueanum	green	all year	no	2–5 ft (0.6–1.5 m)	8 ft (2.4 m)	12	no

Top Tip

Most *Aquilegia* species are fairly easy to grow, but the plants do not last much beyond 2–3 years. Remove older plants once the bases become very woody.

AQUILEGIA

Found in the northern temperate and sub-arctic zones, the 70 or so mainly perennial species that make up this genus in the buttercup (Ranunculaceae) family are well-known for their dainty long-spurred flowers, which are borne in clusters atop wiry stems. The genus is also known as columbine (the shape of the flowers has been compared to the silhouette of a dove) and granny's bonnet. The foliage is usually blue-green and divided into small fan-shaped leaflets, often resembling maidenhair fern fronds in shape, if not in size. The flowers occur in a wide color range and appear from mid-spring; double-flowered forms are now common. *Aquilegia* flowers are nectar-rich and bumblebees often cut the spurs to reach the nectar at the base. Because of this wealth of nectar the flowers are very sweet and may be added to salads as an unusual edible garnish.

CULTIVATION

Although the genus includes alpine, woodland, and meadow species, they are generally quite adaptable and very hardy, thriving in any cool, well-drained, moist, moderately fertile soil in half-sun. Watch for aphids, which can sometimes smother the plants. Propagate by division when dormant or raise from seed.

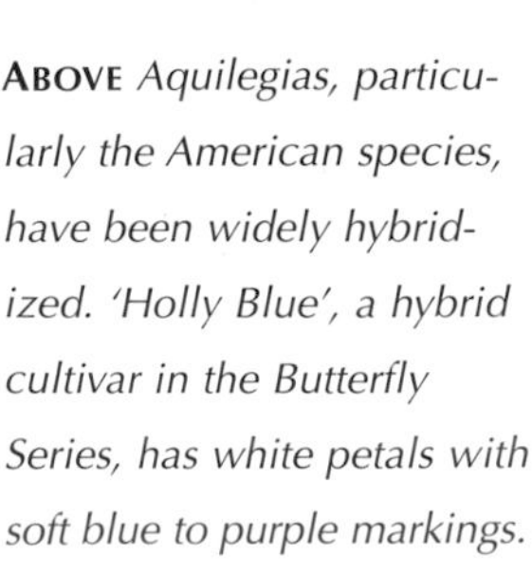

ABOVE *Aquilegias, particularly the American species, have been widely hybridized. 'Holly Blue', a hybrid cultivar in the Butterfly Series, has white petals with soft blue to purple markings.*

Favorites	Flower Color	Blooming Season	Flower Fragrance
Aquilegia alpina	blue, blue and white	summer	no
Aquilegia chrysantha	bright yellow	spring to summer	no
Aquilegia flabellata	blue-purple and white	summer	no
Aquilegia olympica	blue, pink, or purple, and white	spring to summer	no
Aquilegia vulgaris	blue, pink, red, or purple, and white	spring to summer	no
***Aquilegia*, Butterfly Series**	purple, mauve	spring to early summer	no

Right Aquilegia chrysantha, *the golden columbine, is native to southern USA. Its large bright yellow flowers with long curved spurs are very striking.*

Left *'Graeme Iddon Red and White' is a very attractive double-flowered cultivar of* Aquilegia vulgaris, *and belongs to the Flore Pleno Group.*

Below Aquilegia olympica *is an alpine species with pretty nodding flowers and finely divided foliage. Suitable for a rock garden, it grows best in semi-shade.*

Plant Height	Plant Width	Hardiness Zone	Frost Tolerance
8–30 in (20–75 cm)	6–18 in (15–45 cm)	5–9	yes
30–36 in (75–90 cm)	12–30 in (30–75 cm)	3–10	yes
8–18 in (20–45 cm)	6–15 in (15–38 cm)	3–9	yes
12–24 in (30–60 cm)	8–12 in (20–30 cm)	5–9	yes
12–36 in (30–90 cm)	8–18 in (20–45 cm)	3–10	yes
18–36 in (45–90 cm)	12–24 in (30–60 cm)	4–10	yes

Top Tip

When dividing asters, discard the older middle section and replant sections from the outer part of the clump to achieve strong new growth.

Above Aster × frikartii *'Mönch' is an award-winning cultivar of this garden hybrid. Only 15 in (38 cm) tall, 'Mönch' bears lavender-blue flowers.*

Below Aster sedifolius *subsp.* ageratoides *is more compact than the species, with narrower leaves, and its darker purple flowers appear later in the season.*

Aster

This large genus, the type form for the daisy (Asteraceae) family, is made up of over 250 species found mainly in the northern temperate zones, with a toehold in South America. They are mainly herbaceous perennials but also include annuals, biennials, and a few rather shrubby species. While some, usually the alpines, form low clumps, most have erect stems topped with massed compound flowerheads. The leaves are simple, linear, lance- or spatula-shaped, sometimes with toothed edges. Summer to mid-autumn is the main flowering season, with pink, mauve, and purple the predominant colors. Asters are also known as Michaelmas daisies. In recognition of the flowerhead's shape, the name *Aster* is taken from the Latin word for star.

Cultivation

Asters are mostly very frost hardy and prefer a position in full sun with moist well-drained soil. Good air circulation is important to prevent mildew developing. Deadhead routinely to encourage continued flowering. Propagate by division when dormant or from spring basal cuttings.

Favorites	Flower Color	Blooming Season	Flower Fragrance	Plant Height	Plant Width	Hardiness Zone	Frost Tolerance
Aster ericoides	white, blue, pink	summer to autumn	no	30–40 in (75–100 cm)	20–30 in (50–75 cm)	3–9	yes
Aster* × *frikartii	violet-blue	late summer to early autumn	no	20–30 in (50–75 cm)	15–24 in (38–60 cm)	5–9	yes
Aster novae-angliae	violet to purple	late summer to early autumn	no	4–5 ft (1.2–1.5 m)	2–4 ft (0.6–1.2 m)	4–9	yes
***Aster novae-angliae* 'Andenken an Alma Pötschke'**	cerise-pink	late summer to early autumn	no	4 ft (1.2 m)	2 ft (0.6 m)	4–9	yes
Aster novi-belgii	violet to purple	late summer to early autumn	no	4 ft (1.2 m)	3 ft (0.9 m)	4–9	yes
Aster sedifolius	white to pale blue	summer	no	36 in (90 cm)	20 in (50 cm)	7–9	yes

BELOW Aster novae-angliae *'Andenken an Alma Pötschke' is one of this species' most popular cultivars. It is also known by the synonym 'Alma Pötschke'.*

LEFT *This* Aster novi-belgii *cultivar is one of over 400 cultivars belonging to this North American species. Many bloom prolifically, displaying masses of daisy flowers in shades of white, blue, purple, and pink.*

LEFT Astilbe × arendsii *is a hybrid group, involving several parent species. The cultivar 'Bumalda' grows to about 2 ft (0.6 m) and has white flowers with a faint pink blush.*

BELOW Astilbe × crispa *'Perkeo' is the best-known and most popular cultivar in this hybrid group. A very compact plant with dark green leaves, it flowers late in the season.*

ASTILBE

Twelve species of summer-flowering, rhizome-rooted perennials make up this genus from temperate East Asia in the saxifrage (Saxifragaceae) family. The foliage is pinnate, usually finely divided, and often develops bronze or red tints, the intensity of which tends to mirror the depth of flower color. The tiny flowers, in cream, pink, mauve, and red shades, or white, are massed in showy plumes held above the foliage on wiry stems. They are quite similar to *Spiraea* flowers, and so are often known as false spiraea. There are many cultivars and hybrids with flower stems of varying height. In their native range some species are regarded as edible; the young shoots are used as a vegetable and the foliage is made into tea.

CULTIVATION

While full sun and drier conditions are tolerated, these plants prefer woodland conditions: cool moist soil and a position in half-sun. Many astilbes also thrive around pond margins. Propagation is most often by division.

Favorites	Flower Color	Blooming Season	Flower Fragrance
Astilbe* × *arendsii	white, pink, red, purple	summer	no
Astilbe chinensis	pink, purple, red	summer	no
***Astilbe chinensis* 'Pumila'**	pink	summer	no
Astilbe* × *crispa	pink	summer	no
Astilbe japonica	white	summer	no
Astilbe koreana	ivory	summer	no

Top Tip

The spring foliage of some *Astilbe* species is copper-colored, and these young leaves make the plants look good even before the graceful flowers appear in summer.

BELOW *The brightly colored buds of* Astilbe koreana *open to ivory or very pale pink flowers carried on airy arching panicles. This species is native to Korea.*

ABOVE Astilbe japonica *'Laura' is one of many cultivars of this Japanese species. The colorful flowers are borne in pyramidal panicles up to 8 in (20 cm) long.*

Plant Height	Plant Width	Hardiness Zone	Frost Tolerance
2–6 ft (0.6–1.8 m)	2 ft (0.6 m)	6–10	yes
2 ft (0.6 m)	2 ft (0.6 m)	6–10	yes
10 in (25 cm)	10 in (25 cm)	6–10	yes
8–12 in (20–30 cm)	8–12 in (20–30 cm)	6–9	yes
3 ft (0.9 m)	2–3 ft (0.6–0.9 m)	5–10	yes
2 ft (0.6 m)	2 ft (0.6 m)	6–10	yes

BEGONIA

Named after an early French governor of Canada, Michael Bégon (1638–1710), this tropical and subtropical grouping of perennials, shrubs, and a few climbers is made up of some 900 species and is considered the type genus for the family Begoniaceae. Begonias are enormously diverse in growth form, foliage, and flower, with most diversity seen in the Americas. The leaves are often hairy and are frequently lobed and beautifully marked. A distinctive feature is the separate male and female flowers, the males tending to be small, with 2 or more per female bloom. Both the foliage and tubers can be eaten, usually cooked.

ABOVE Begonia gracilis, *also known as the hollyhock begonia, is a tuberous species from Mexico and Guatemala. Its upright succulent stems bear short sprays of pink flowers.*

BELOW *The glossy fan-shaped leaves of* Begonia aconitifolia *are held on cane-like stems. This is a fibrous-rooted species from Brazil.*

CULTIVATION

Although a few species tolerate light frosts, most are tender and will only survive mild winters. In cool climates some are grown as summer annuals, others as house plants, and the tuberous species are lifted and stored over winter. Plant in cool, moist, humus-rich soil in sun to shade depending on the type. Propagate by division, cuttings, or from the dust-like seeds.

Top Tip

Tropical and subtropical begonias (the majority) need humid conditions to perform well. If growing them in pots, place raised pots on pebbles in water trays.

LEFT *The numerous* Begonia *hybrids are divided into 8 main groups. The Shrub-like Group consists of bushy plants with variably sized, colored, and textured leaves. 'Cockatoo', seen here, is easy to grow.*

BELOW Begonia, *Shrub-like Group, 'Richmondensis' bears its 1 in (25 mm) wide blooms throughout the year. The large dark green leaves have red undersides.*

Favorites	Flower Color	Blooming Season	Flower Fragrance	Plant Height	Plant Width	Hardiness Zone	Frost Tolerance
Begonia aconitifolia	white to pale pink	autumn	no	40–48 in (100–120 cm)	24–40 in (60–100 cm)	10–12	no
Begonia crassicaulis	pink	late winter	no	12–36 in (30–90 cm)	12–36 in (30–90 cm)	10–12	no
Begonia gracilis	pink	summer	no	30–36 in (75–90 cm)	20–24 in (50–60 cm)	10–12	no
Begonia grandis	pink	summer to autumn	no	24 in (60 cm)	12–18 in (30–45 cm)	6–9	yes
Begonia grandis* var. *evansiana	pink	summer to autumn	no	18–24 in (45–60 cm)	12–18 in (30–45 cm)	6–9	yes
***Begonia,* Shrub-like Group**	white, cream, pink, red	various times throughout year	no	12–36 in (30–90 cm)	18–48 in (45–120 cm)	9–12	no

CALENDULA

Now widely naturalized, this genus of about 20 species of annuals and perennials in the daisy (Asteraceae) family originates from the Mediterranean and nearby Atlantic Islands. They often colonize waste ground and thrive in poor soils, which doubtless helped them to establish well away from home. Simple lance- to spatula-shaped leaves, often aromatic, make dense clumps that from mid-winter to late autumn, depending on the species, are covered in cream, yellow, or orange flowerheads, often with many ray florets. The genus name *Calendula* reflects this long-flowering habit, as it refers to the first day of the month and indicates that flowers may be found on the plant in almost any month.

Top Tip

Calendulas make great companion plants, discouraging such garden nasties as asparagus beetle, tomato hookworm, and more. Watch out for aphids on cut flowers though!

BELOW Calendula officinalis *'Orange Salad' has petals of a similar color and flavor to saffron and can be used as a substitute in rice, soups, or garnishes.*

CULTIVATION

These undemanding flowers thrive in full sun with light, well-drained soil kept moist through the flowering season. Deadheading frequently will encourage continuous blooming. Mildew can be a problem in autumn. Usually raised from seed, they will self-sow if flowers are left alone.

RIGHT *From southern parts of Europe,* Calendula officinalis *is a bushy annual with slightly downy leaves and orange or yellow daisies to 3 in (8 cm) in diameter.*

Favorites	Flower Color	Blooming Season	Flower Fragrance	Plant Height	Plant Width	Hardiness Zone	Frost Tolerance
Calendula arvensis	yellow, orange	spring to autumn	no	12 in (30 cm)	12 in (30 cm)	6–10	yes
Calendula officinalis	yellow, gold, orange, apricot	spring to autumn	no	12–24 in (30–60 cm)	12–24 in (30–60 cm)	6–10	yes
***Calendula officinalis*, Bon Bon Series**	yellow, orange, apricot	spring to autumn	no	8–12 in (20–30 cm)	12 in (30 cm)	6–10	yes
***Calendula officinalis*, Fiesta Gitana Group**	cream, yellow, gold, orange	spring to autumn	no	8–12 in (20–30 cm)	15 in (38 cm)	6–10	yes
***Calendula officinalis* 'Orange Salad'**	orange	spring to autumn	no	8–12 in (20–30 cm)	12 in (30 cm)	6–10	yes
***Calendula officinalis*, Pacific Beauty Series**	orange, yellow	spring to autumn	no	18–24 in (45–60 cm)	18 in (45 cm)	6–10	yes

LEFT Calendula officinalis *'Needles 'n' Pins' has distinctive spiky quilled petals, which explain the name. Its rich orange color and strong stems make it a great cut-flower choice.*

BELOW Calendula officinalis *'Art Shades' comes in a variety of tones from cream, peach, and apricot to yellow and orange. It is a popular strain of a very hardy annual.*

CAMPANULA

A genus of annuals, biennials, and perennials, *Campanula* is the type form for the bellflower (Campanulaceae) family. Some of the 300 or so species can be found in Asia and North America but most occur in the Balkans, Caucasus, or Mediterranean region. They range from minute crevice dwellers with tiny thimble-like flowers to upright plants with large cup-shaped blooms. The foliage tends to be lance-shaped or rounded, usually toothed or shallowly lobed. The flowers, typically mauve-pink to purple or white, are clustered in heads and can be very abundant. They most often appear from spring to mid-summer. The name *Campanula* comes from the Latin word for bells, *campana*, hence the common name bellflower, and the word campanology (bell-ringing).

BELOW *The tubular bell-shaped cream flowers of* Campanula punctata *f.* rubriflora *are tinged pink-purple, and heavily spotted with red on the inside.*

CULTIVATION

Requirements vary, with some species needing rockery or alpine-house conditions. Most of the larger types, however, thrive with little care if they are given full sun and fertile, moist, well-drained soil. Propagate by division or from small basal cuttings. The species may be raised from seed.

BELOW *A delicate clump-forming perennial from Armenia,* Campanula betulifolia *is an excellent rock-garden plant. It needs protection from winter wet.*

Top Tip

The amazing variety of bellflowers means there is a species suitable for any rock garden, border, woodland, or "wild" garden situation.

LEFT *A vigorous alpine perennial from southern Europe with small heart-shaped leaves,* Campanula portenschlagiana *blooms profusely in summer.*
BELOW Campanula chamissonis *'Superba' is a low-growing fleshy-stemmed perennial with larger flowers than the species. The flowers are carried on individual stems.*

Favorites	Flower Color	Blooming Season	Flower Fragrance	Plant Height	Plant Width	Hardiness Zone	Frost Tolerance
Campanula betulifolia	white, pale pink	summer	no	4–12 in (10–30 cm)	12–15 in (30–38 cm)	4–9	yes
Campanula chamissonis	blue and white	summer	no	2–6 in (5–15 cm)	8–12 in (20–30 cm)	3–9	yes
Campanula portenschlagiana	lavender-blue	summer	no	6 in (15 cm)	18–24 in (45–60 cm)	4–9	yes
Campanula poscharskyana	lavender to violet	summer to autumn	no	6–8 in (15–20 cm)	18–24 in (45–60 cm)	6–9	yes
***Campanula poscharskyana* 'Multiplicity'**	lavender-blue	summer to autumn	no	6–8 in (15–20 cm)	18–24 in (45–60 cm)	6–9	yes
Campanula punctata	creamy white to pale pink	early summer	no	12 in (30 cm)	15–18 in (38–45 cm)	4–8	yes

CANNA

The canna (Cannaceae) family is named after this genus of 9 species found in the New World tropics and subtropics. They are strongly upright rhizome-rooted perennials with strong cane-like stems and large lance-shaped leaves reminiscent of banana foliage. The leaves may be green, purple-tinted, or variegated. Their lily-like flowers (giving them the common name calla lilies) are clustered in heads at the top of tall stems and occur in hot shades of yellow, coral, orange, and red and are frequently strikingly bi- or multi-colored. The starchy rhizomes and the young shoots are a staple food in the plants' native range.

CULTIVATION

Cannas will survive frosts and re-shoot provided the soil does not freeze to any depth. Plant in deep, moist, humus-rich soil with full sun. In cold winter areas the rhizomes may be lifted and stored barely moist until spring. Cannas may be raised from seed, though named hybrids and cultivars are propagated by division.

Favorites	Flower Color	Blooming Season	Flower Fragrance
Canna **'Gran Canaria'**	yellow and orange	summer to autumn	no
Canna **'Lucifer'**	yellow and red	summer to autumn	no
Canna **'Orange Punch'**	orange and yellow	summer to autumn	no
Canna **'Pink Sunburst'**	salmon pink	spring to autumn	no
Canna **'Rosever'**	pink-red	summer to autumn	no
Canna **'Strawberry'**	red	summer to autumn	no

BELOW *The vivid yellow and orange flowers of* Canna *'Gran Canaria' look best when the plants are grown in groups of 3 or more. The blooms do not last in vases.*

LEFT Canna *'Pink Sunburst' is a South African hybrid cultivar. It is most valued for its spectacular variegated foliage, with its salmon pink blooms as a bonus.*

Plant Height	Plant Width	Hardiness Zone	Frost Tolerance
60 in (150 cm)	20–36 in (50–90 cm)	8–12	no
30 in (75 cm)	20–36 in (50–90 cm)	8–12	no
30 in (75 cm)	20–36 in (50–90 cm)	8–12	no
36 in (90 cm)	20–36 in (50–90 cm)	8–12	no
30 in (75 cm)	20–36 in (50–90 cm)	8–12	no
60 in (150 cm)	20–36 in (50–90 cm)	8–12	no

RIGHT *The showy red flowers of* Canna *'Strawberry' add a splash of color to the garden.* Canna *cultivars come in a wide range of sizes and shades; the foliage, too, shows great variety.*

LEFT *One of many dwarf hybrid cultivars,* Canna *'Rosever' has striking rose pink to red flowers. Other* Canna *hybrids can grow up to 7 ft (2 m) tall, more than double the height of this plant.*

Top Tip

Although it is possible to raise cannas from seed, and they may self-seed, such plants may not be of the best quality. Better plants are achieved by dividing clumps.

CHRYSANTHEMUM

Most botanists now consider this genus in the daisy (Asteraceae) family to include just 5 species of European and North African summer-flowering annuals, but the greatly popular florist's chrysanthemum *(Dendranthema × grandiflorum)* is also acceptably classified under this name. These perennials, grouped according to form, begin to bloom as the days shorten. Most are upright plants with lobed leaves, strong stems, and many showy flowerheads at the stem tips. Often a motif in Asian art, the flower is especially significant in Japan where it is a symbol of happiness and longevity, and the royal family has ruled for 2,600 years from the Chrysanthemum Throne.

ABOVE *The Single form is characterized by daisy-like flowers with a flat central "eye."* Chrysanthemum, *Single, 'Harlekijn' has dark pink petals lightening to white tips.*

CULTIVATION

Annual chrysanthemums thrive in bright sunny positions with light, fairly dry soil. The various forms of florist's chrysanthemums are best grown in afternoon shade with a fertile, rather heavy soil, well-drained to protect from diseases. Level any depressions that might collect water. The plants require training and trimming to produce their best flowers. Propagate perennials from cuttings or by division, annuals from seed.

RIGHT *An excellent example of the Spoon-shaped form are the vivid scarlet ray florets and the contrasting rich golden central disc of* Chrysanthemum, *Spoon-shaped, 'Dublin'.*

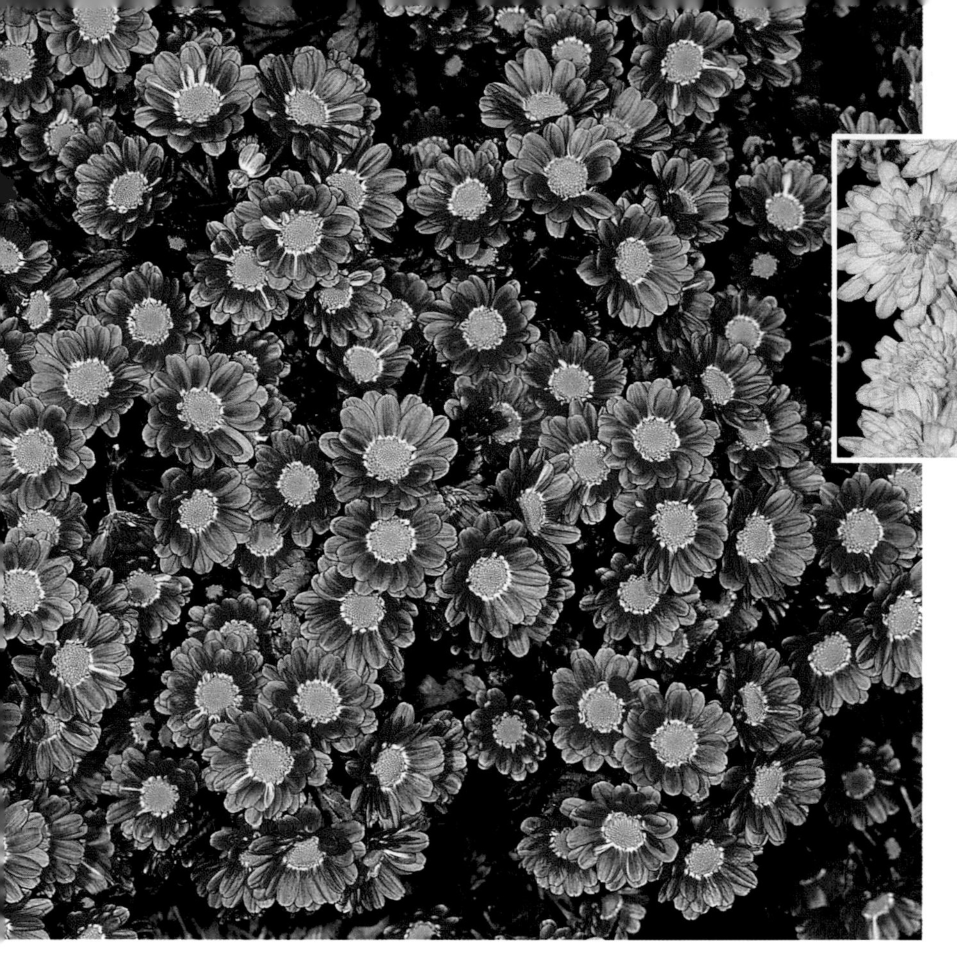

ABOVE *Sprays are noted for having many flowers on a branched stem, rather than just one flower per stem, as seen in the pink blooms of* Chrysanthemum, *Spray, 'Fiji'.*
LEFT Chrysanthemum, *Single, 'Poser' has striking, almost metallic, dark salmon pink petals, contrasting with a green to mustard yellow disc floret.*

Favorites	Flower Color	Blooming Season	Flower Fragrance	Plant Height	Plant Width	Hardiness Zone	Frost Tolerance
Chrysanthemum weyrichii	white to pink	summer to autumn	no	4 in (10 cm)	16–24 in (40–60 cm)	4–9	yes
Chrysanthemum yezoense	white	autumn to early winter	no	12–18 in (30–45 cm)	18–30 in (45–75 cm)	6–9	yes
Chrysanthemum zawadskii	white, pink	late summer to mid-autumn	no	24 in (60 cm)	20–40 in (50–100 cm)	5–9	yes
***Chrysanthemum*, Anemone-centered**	white, pink, red, yellow, orange	late summer to autumn	no	12–60 in (30–150 cm)	18–36 in (45–90 cm)	5–10	yes
***Chrysanthemum*, Incurved**	white, pink, red, yellow, orange	late summer to autumn	no	12–60 in (30–150 cm)	18–36 in (45–90 cm)	5–10	yes
***Chrysanthemum*, Pompon**	white, pink, red, yellow, orange	late summer to autumn	no	12–60 in (30–150 cm)	18–36 in (45–90 cm)	5–10	yes
***Chrysanthemum*, Quill-shaped**	white, pink, red, yellow, orange	late summer to autumn	no	12–60 in (30–150 cm)	18–36 in (45–90 cm)	5–10	yes
***Chrysanthemum*, Reflexed**	white, pink, red, yellow, orange	late summer to autumn	no	12–60 in (30–150 cm)	18–36 in (45–90 cm)	5–10	yes
***Chrysanthemum*, Single**	white, pink, red, yellow, orange	late summer to autumn	no	12–60 in (30–150 cm)	18–36 in (45–90 cm)	5–10	yes
***Chrysanthemum*, Spider-form**	white, pink, red, yellow, orange	late summer to autumn	no	12–60 in (30–150 cm)	18–36 in (45–90 cm)	5–10	yes
***Chrysanthemum*, Spoon-shaped**	white, pink, red, yellow, orange	late summer to autumn	no	12–60 in (30–150 cm)	18–36 in (45–90 cm)	5–10	yes
***Chrysanthemum*, Spray**	white, pink, red, yellow, orange	late summer to autumn	no	12–60 in (30–150 cm)	18–36 in (45–90 cm)	5–10	yes

Top Tip

Chrysanthemums grow best when they receive full sun all day long, so avoid planting in sites where they have to compete with trees for light and water.

Above Chrysanthemum, *Quill-shaped, 'Awesome' (large), and C., Anemone-centered, 'Puma' (small) show how forms can be contrasted to great effect.*
Right Chrysanthemum *comes from the Greek for "golden flower," and C., Anemone-centered, 'Touché' is a classic example of this.*

RIGHT *Pompon forms are typically low bushes, with dense spherical flowerheads such as the green and white blooms of* Chrysanthemum, *Pompon, 'Furore' seen here.*
LEFT Chrysanthemum, *Single, 'Orange Wimbledon' has rich egg-yolk yellow ray florets, surrounding a green central disc floret.*
BELOW *Incurved forms have petals which curve out and upward.* Chrysanthemum, *Incurved, 'Revert' (large) dominates C., Quill-shaped, 'Awesome' (small) here.*

COREOPSIS

This 80-species genus from Mexico and the USA is in the daisy (Asteraceae) family, and includes both annuals and perennials. Species may be sprawling and mounding or upright and shrubby and tend to have fairly simple, often shallowly lobed or linear leaves. Through summer and into autumn they are smothered in bright yellow and/or red, rarely pink flowerheads with ray florets that are often toothed at the tips as if cut by pinking shears. The leaves and flowers of many species were widely used by native North Americans to yield orange to red dyes. The common name tickseed, along with the Greek word *coreopsis* (bug-like), refers to the small black seeds that adhere to clothing and resemble ticks.

Top Tip

Coreopsis blooms are not only great for borders and as cut flowers, but are ideal for attracting butterflies. Deadheading ensures a longer period of attractive blooms.

CULTIVATION

These flowers are quite drought tolerant and are very easily cultivated in any bright sunny position with light well-drained soil. They will flower better with summer moisture, and for longer if deadheaded frequently. Propagate from seed, which may be sown in situ, from cuttings of non-flowering shoots, or by division.

ABOVE RIGHT Coreopsis lanceolata *'Baby Sun' (syn. 'Sonnenkind') is a small cultivar, to 12 in (30 cm) tall, that rewards with masses of all-golden flowers in summer.*
RIGHT Coreopsis verticillata *'Grandiflora' (syn. 'Golden Shower') has large bright yellow flowers. Trimming in midsummer encourages further blooms in autumn.*

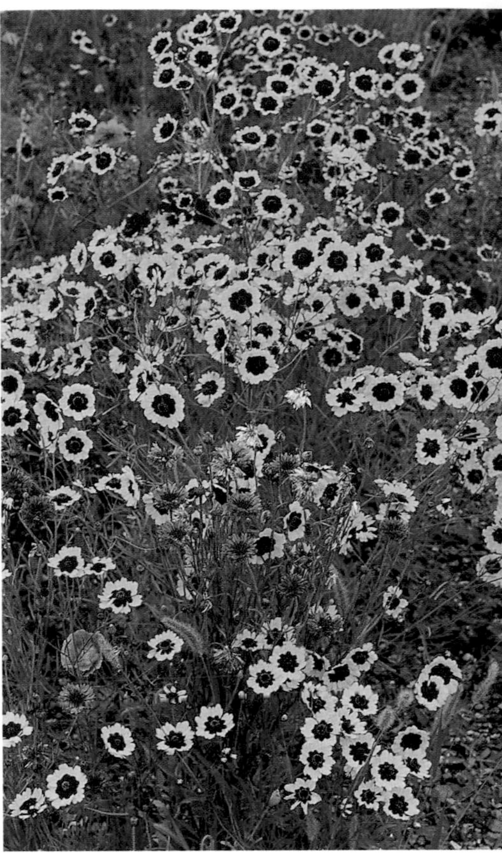

ABOVE *Found across much of North America,* Coreopsis tinctoria *has yellow ray florets, reddening at the base, and red-brown disc florets.*

LEFT Coreopsis lanceolata *'Sterntaler' is a 16 in (40 cm) tall cultivar, with golden ray florets that have a bronze-red blotch next to the yellow central disc.*

Favorites	Flower Color	Blooming Season	Flower Fragrance	Plant Height	Plant Width	Hardiness Zone	Frost Tolerance
Coreopsis gigantea	yellow	spring to summer	no	7–10 ft (2–3 m)	32–48 in (80–120 cm)	8–10	yes
Coreopsis grandiflora	golden yellow	late spring to summer	no	12–24 in (30–60 cm)	12–20 in (30–50 cm)	6–10	yes
Coreopsis lanceolata	golden yellow	late spring to summer	no	24 in (60 cm)	12–16 in (30–40 cm)	3–11	yes
***Coreopsis* 'Sunray'**	deep yellow	spring to summer	no	20 in (50 cm)	12–24 in (30–60 cm)	6–10	yes
Coreopsis tinctoria	yellow with maroon center	summer to autumn	no	36–48 in (90–120 cm)	16–24 in (40–60 cm)	4–10	yes
Coreopsis verticillata	yellow	summer to early autumn	no	36 in (90 cm)	16 in (40 cm)	6–10	yes

COSMOS

A genus of annuals and perennials found from southern USA to northern South America, it belongs to the daisy (Asteraceae) family. Of the 26 species, only 1 perennial and 2 annuals are commonly cultivated. The annuals have fine ferny leaves and produce their large showy flowerheads throughout the warmer months, which in frost-free areas may continue into early winter. The perennials have broader leaflets and smaller, sometimes scented flowers that hint at the relationship between *Cosmos* and *Dahlia*. Appropriately for such a showy and colorful genus, the name is derived from the Greek *kosmos*, meaning "beautiful."

Top Tip

Cosmos love bad conditions. For best results, don't give them any shade, don't over-fertilize the soil, and don't water them unless they are wilting.

RIGHT Cosmos bipinnatus, *Sonata Series, a popular dwarf type, ranges in color from reds and pinks through to the award-winning white.*

CULTIVATION

Cosmos plants thrive in a warm sunny position with light, moist, well-drained soil. The larger annuals produce an abundance of growth, can become top-heavy, especially if overfed, and are easily damaged by the wind. They may need to be staked, and should certainly be frequently deadheaded. Annuals are raised from seed, and perennials are usually propagated from small basal cuttings.

RIGHT Cosmos bipinnatus *'Picotee Double' is, as the name suggests, a double form that has light- to medium pink petals outlined with a contrasting darker pink.*

ABOVE RIGHT *The striking* Cosmos bipinnatus *'Picotee' has petals that are white to pale pink flushed and edged with a deep pinkish red, around a yellow disc floret.*

RIGHT Cosmos bipinnatus *is an annual, native to Mexico and southern USA, and has large long-stemmed flowerheads that are colored pink to lavender in the wild.*

Favorites	Flower Color	Blooming Season	Flower Fragrance	Plant Height	Plant Width	Hardiness Zone	Frost Tolerance
Cosmos atrosanguineus	dark maroon	mid-summer to autumn	yes	12–24 in (30–60 cm)	18–40 in (45–100 cm)	8–10	yes
Cosmos bipinnatus	pink, red, purple, white	summer to autumn	no	4–7 ft (1.2–2 m)	2–4 ft (0.6–1.2 m)	8–11	no
***Cosmos bipinnatus* 'Picotee'**	white to pale pink	summer to autumn	no	30 in (75 cm)	18 in (45 cm)	8–11	no
***Cosmos bipinnatus,* Sensation Series**	pink, white	summer to autumn	no	36 in (90 cm)	18 in (45 cm)	8–11	no
***Cosmos bipinnatus,* Sonata Series**	crimson, pink, white	summer to autumn	no	18–36 in (45–90 cm)	12–18 in (30–45 cm)	8–11	no
Cosmos sulphureus	yellow to red	summer	no	4–7 ft (1.2–2 m)	2–4 ft (0.6–1.2 m)	8–11	no

DAHLIA

RIGHT *Ball dahlias are globular, but may be slightly flattened on top.* Dahlia *'Charles Dickens' has small pink flowers, and is a member of this group.*

BELOW Dahlia *'Vogtland Echo' is a Decorative dahlia, meaning that its pink-tipped creamy white petals form fully double blooms without any central disc.*

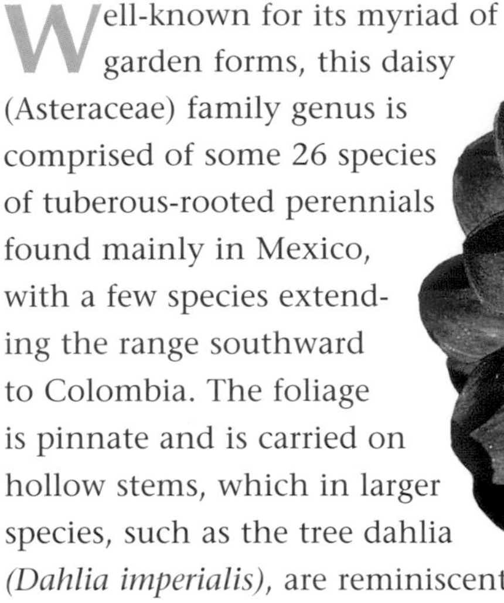

Well-known for its myriad of garden forms, this daisy (Asteraceae) family genus is comprised of some 26 species of tuberous-rooted perennials found mainly in Mexico, with a few species extending the range southward to Colombia. The foliage is pinnate and is carried on hollow stems, which in larger species, such as the tree dahlia *(Dahlia imperialis)*, are reminiscent of bamboo. Flowers of *Dahlia* species can be large and showy but are never as fancy as those of the various garden forms, which occur in a huge range of styles and colors. *Dahlia* tubers were one of the staple foods of the Aztecs and are rich in a starch called inulin, which is used to produce a form of fructose suitable for use by diabetics.

CULTIVATION

Plant in full sun with moist, humus-rich, well-drained soil and ensure good ventilation to lessen the risk of mildew. Remove spent flowers promptly to prevent rotting and encourage continuous blooming. Only if soil does not freeze or become waterlogged can tubers be left in the ground for winter. Propagate by division or from cuttings.

RIGHT *Waterlily dahlias have fully double blooms but are fairly flat, lacking the high center of other forms.* Dahlia *'Vanessa' is an attractive pink example.*

Favorites	Flower Color	Blooming Season	Flower Fragrance	Plant Height	Plant Width	Hardiness Zone	Frost Tolerance
Dahlia coccinea	yellow, orange to dark red	summer to autumn	no	7–10 ft (2–3 m)	2–4 ft (0.6–1.2 m)	8–11	yes
Dahlia imperialis	lavender, pink, white	late autumn to winter	no	12–20 ft (3.5–6 m)	5–10 ft (1.5–3 m)	9–11	yes
Dahlia tenuicaulis	lilac-pink to near magenta	summer to autumn	no	10–15 ft (3–4.5 m)	3–7 ft (0.9–2 m)	9–11	yes
Dahlia, Anemone-flowered	white to pink, red, yellow, orange	summer to autumn	no	2–6 ft (0.6–1.8 m)	12–24 in (30–60 cm)	8–11	yes
Dahlia, Ball	white to pink, red, yellow, orange	summer to autumn	no	1–6 ft (0.3–1.8 m)	12–24 in (30–60 cm)	8–11	yes
Dahlia, Cactus	white to pink, red, yellow, orange	summer to autumn	no	4–6 ft (1.2–1.8 m)	18–30 in (45–75 cm)	8–11	yes
Dahlia, Collarette	white to pink, red, yellow, orange	summer to autumn	no	4 ft (1.2 m)	18 in (45 cm)	9–11	yes
Dahlia, Decorative	white to pink, red, yellow, orange	summer to autumn	no	3–6 ft (0.9–1.8 m)	18–30 in (45–75 cm)	8–11	yes
Dahlia, Pompon	white to pink, red, yellow, orange	summer to autumn	no	12–36 in (30–90 cm)	12–24 in (30–60 cm)	8–11	yes
Dahlia, Semi-cactus	white to pink, red, yellow, orange	summer to autumn	no	4–6 ft (1.2–1.8 m)	18–30 in (45–75 cm)	8–11	yes
Dahlia, Single	white to pink, red, yellow, orange	summer to autumn	no	1–5 ft (0.3–1.5 m)	12–24 in (30–60 cm)	8–11	yes
Dahlia, Waterlily	white to pink, red, yellow, orange	summer to autumn	no	3–5 ft (0.9–1.5 m)	18–30 in (45–75 cm)	8–11	yes

BELOW *Semi-cactus dahlias have broad based ray florets, quilled for less than half their length, as the pink blooms of* Dahlia *'Weston Pinkie' show.*

BELOW Dahlia *'Rot' is a member of the Single-flowered group of dahlias, which means it has the simple wide-open single flowerhead that is typical of this form.*

ABOVE *The slightly inward curving, broad, flat ray florets of the lemon yellow* Dahlia *'Vera Lischke' are typical of a Decorative dahlia, as is the lack of a central disc, as well as the double flower.*

ABOVE Dahlia *'White Aster' is a Pompon dahlia, and has the typical almost-spherical flowerheads of this group. These flowers are smaller than those seen in the Ball group.*

Below Dahlia *'Wagschal's Goldkrone'* is *a Cactus dahlia, as evidenced by the fact that it has fully double flowers with long quilled ray florets and no central disc.*

Above Dahlia *'Fürst Pückler' is a Waterlily dahlia with deep pinkish red, yellow-flushed blooms that resemble the waterlilies for which the group is named.*

Left Dahlia *'Gartenfreude' has striking dark orange-red ray florets with contrasting golden yellow tips, and is a member of the fully double-flowered Semi-cactus group.*

Top Tip

How dahlia tubers are stored prior to planting is crucial. They should be kept in a dark spot with high humidity, and then regularly checked for signs of rotting or mold.

DELPHINIUM

BELOW Delphinium *'Clifford Pink' has pink semi-double flowers. Applying manure every 2–3 weeks over the flowering period enhances bloom quality and quantity.*

RIGHT Delphinium*, Elatum Group, 'Spindrift' is a pretty medium-sized variety. It has lilac petals with a light blue central area, on spikes that grow to 3 ft (0.9 m) long.*

Classified in the buttercup (Ranunculaceae) family, *Delphinium* includes some 250 species of annuals, biennials, and perennials spread throughout the northern temperate zones. The foliage is usually rounded but is often lobed or deeply divided, disguising the basic shape. Delphiniums are mainly spring- and summer-flowering and the cultivated forms are prized for their spectacularly long flower spikes. The genus name comes from the Greek word for a dolphin *(delphis)* and refers to the arched shape of the spur at the back of the flower. Some species of delphiniums have medicinal properties, though care must be taken due to the presence of potent alkaloids.

CULTIVATION

The requirements vary: species from California and Central Asia generally prefer a fairly light, gritty soil, but the commonly cultivated perennials prefer moist, humus-rich, well-drained soil. All are best grown in full sun and the taller forms must be staked to prevent wind damage. The species may be propagated from seed, while the hybrids and cultivars are usually raised from cuttings or by division.

Top Tip

Beware: slugs and snails just love the young shoots of delphiniums! Some builder's lime around the plants, or old sifted ashes among the shoots, keeps them at bay.

RIGHT *The striking electric blue flowers of* Delphinium × belladonna *'Blue Sensation' and the fact that at only 3 ft (0.9 m) high it does not need staking, make this plant a very popular cultivar.*

BELOW *With vivid purple blooms,* Delphinium, *Elatum Group, 'Bruce' grows to a height of 6 ft (1.8 m), and so will need staking.*

Favorites	Flower Color	Blooming Season	Flower Fragrance	Plant Height	Plant Width	Hardiness Zone	Frost Tolerance
Delphinium* × *belladonna	blue	spring to autumn	no	12–40 in (30–100 cm)	6–20 in (15–50 cm)	3–9	yes
***Delphinium* 'Clifford Pink'**	mauve-pink	spring to autumn	no	6 ft (1.8 m)	2 ft (0.6 m)	3–9	yes
***Delphinium* 'Loch Leven'**	mid-blue	spring to summer	no	4–6 ft (1.2–1.8 m)	2 ft (0.6 m)	3–9	yes
***Delphinium,* Elatum Group**	blue, white, purple	summer to autumn	no	3–6 ft (0.9–1.8 m)	2 ft (0.6 m)	3–9	yes
***Delphinium,* Elatum Group, Magic Fountain Series**	various	spring to summer	no	3–6 ft (0.9–1.8 m)	2 ft (0.6 m)	3–9	yes
Delphinium,* Elatum Group, *'Sandpiper'	white	summer to autumn	no	3–6 ft (0.9–1.8 m)	2 ft (0.6 m)	3–9	yes

DIANTHUS

Found mainly in Eurasia, this group of around 300 species of perennials is the type genus for the pink (Caryophyllaceae) family. Most form a small clump or cushion of narrow gray- to blue-green leaves, while a few develop longer, sometimes wiry stems. The flowers, borne singly or in small heads, appear from late spring and occur at the stem tips, and often have a spicy scent. *Dianthus* flowers, particularly those of carnations, are edible and are sometimes candied or used as a garnish. Remove the calyces as they have a bitter taste. *Dianthus caryophyllus* is Ohio's floral emblem.

ABOVE *The fragrant pink flowers of* Dianthus *'Whatfield Can-can', a member of the Pink group of cultivars, have petals with attractive pinked edges, giving a frilly appearance.*

CULTIVATION

These plants are best grown in a bright sunny position with a light, well-drained, yet moist soil. A light annual dressing of dolomite lime is beneficial as is occasional feeding, which helps to prevent the center of the clumps from dying out. Species may be raised from seed and the selected forms from cuttings of non-flowering shoots.

RIGHT Dianthus *'Tempo', one of the many Perpetual-flowering cultivars, provides a year-round display in mild climates, bearing red-edged, pink-flushed, white flowers held aloft on tall stems.*

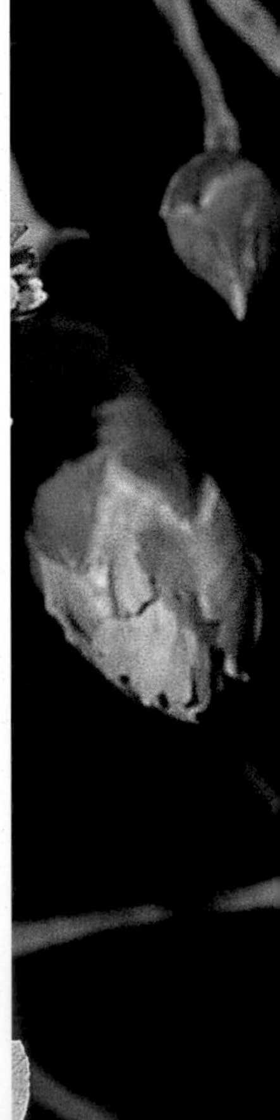

Favorites	Flower Color	Blooming Season	Flower Fragrance	Plant Height	Plant Width	Hardiness Zone	Frost Tolerance
Dianthus arenarius	white to pale pink	late spring	yes	12 in (30 cm)	6–12 in (15–30 cm)	3–9	yes
Dianthus deltoides	white, pink to red	summer	no	6–16 in (15–40 cm)	12 in (30 cm)	3–10	yes
Dianthus gratianopolitanus	pink to crimson	summer	yes	6–8 in (15–20 cm)	15 in (38 cm)	5–9	yes
***Dianthus gratiano-politanus* 'Tiny Rubies'**	red	summer	yes	4 in (10 cm)	4 in (10 cm)	5–9	yes
Dianthus pavonius	pale pink to crimson	summer	no	4 in (10 cm)	6–12 in (15–30 cm)	4–9	yes
Dianthus plumarius	pink, white	summer to early autumn	yes	6–15 in (15–38 cm)	8–16 in (20–40 cm)	3–9	yes
***Dianthus plumarius* 'Essex Witch'**	rose pink	summer to early autumn	yes	5 in (12 cm)	8–16 in (20–40 cm)	3–9	yes
***Dianthus*, Annual Pinks**	white to pink or red, bicolored	late spring to early autumn	no	8–12 in (20–30 cm)	8–12 in (20–30 cm)	8–10	yes
***Dianthus*, Border Carnations**	white, pink, lemon, purple, bicolored	spring to early summer	yes	18–24 in (45–60 cm)	12 in (30 cm)	8–10	yes
***Dianthus*, Malmaison Carnations**	white, pink, red	most of year	yes	18–30 in (45–75 cm)	12–18 in (30–45 cm)	9–11	yes
***Dianthus*, Perpetual-Flowering Carnations**	white, pink, red, yellow, bicolored	all year	yes	36 in (90 cm)	12 in (30 cm)	8–11	yes
***Dianthus*, Pinks**	white, pink to crimson	late spring to early autumn	yes	6–18 in (15–45 cm)	18 in (45 cm)	5–10	yes

LEFT *Delightfully fragrant,* Dianthus *'Letitia Wyatt', a member of the Pink group of cultivars, bears attractive, double, pink flowers.*

BELOW *Known as maiden pink,* Dianthus deltoides *is an attractive perennial with dainty pink flowers and green to blue-green foliage.*

Above *With fragrant, pure white, double blooms, daintily pinked at the petal edges,* Dianthus *'Haytor White', a Perpetual-flowering Carnation, makes an ideal subject for the herbaceous border.*

Above *A small, mat-forming or tufting perennial,* Dianthus pavonius *'Inshriach Dazzler' features lush green foliage and dainty, single, flat-faced, magenta flowers.*

Right *One of the Perpetual-flowering Carnations,* Dianthus *'Prado' will create a focal point in the garden with its stunning blooms of creamy pale green.*

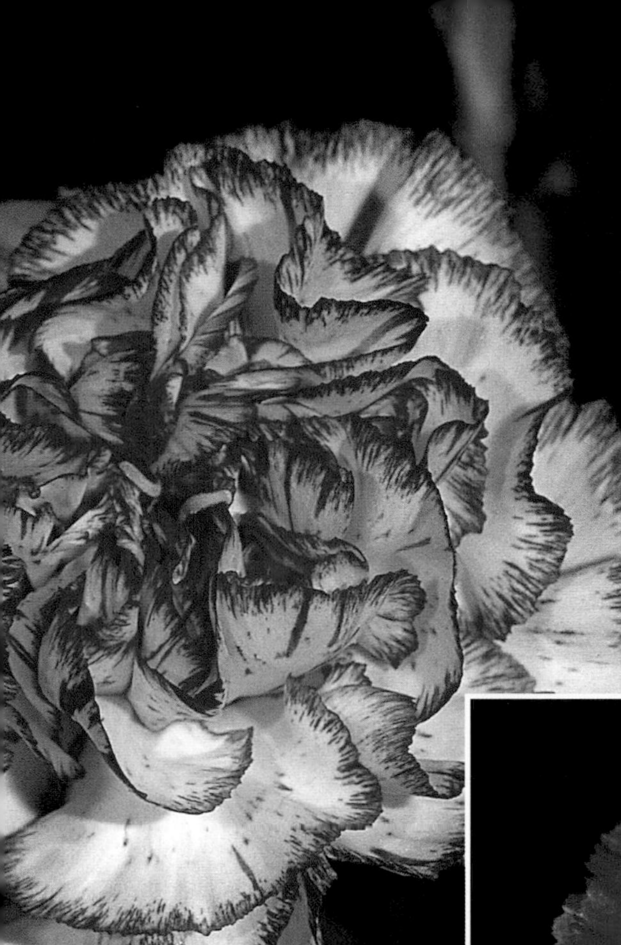

LEFT *The beautiful, tall-stemmed, yellow flowers of the Perpetual-flowering Carnation* Dianthus *'Tundra' are emblazoned with red at the petal edges. It can be enjoyed in the garden for most of the year in favorable climates.*

Top Tip

Taller carnations will need to be staked or tied to a support in order to keep the slender stems upright under the weight of the often fully double blooms.

ABOVE RIGHT *Selfs—blooms of a single color—are more than a match for their glamorous bicolored relatives when they display their full double blooms, such as this boldly colored example,* Dianthus *'Reiko', a Perpetual-flowering Carnation.*
RIGHT *With stunning blooms in shades of orange and apricot, exquisitely frilled at the petal edges,* Dianthus *'Raggio di Sole' is a fine example of the Perpetual-flowering Carnation group.*

Favorites	Flower Color	Blooming Season	Flower Fragrance
Diascia barberae	bright pink	summer	no
Diascia barberae **'Blackthorn Apricot'**	apricot-pink to soft orange	summer	no
Diascia **Coral Belle/'Hecbel'**	coral red	summer	no
Diascia fetcaniensis	pink	summer to early autumn	no
Diascia **Redstart/'Hecstart'**	coral pink to red	summer	no
Diascia vigilis	pink	summer to early winter	no

DIASCIA

In the 30-odd years since this South African genus of around 50 species of annuals and perennials in the foxglove (Scrophulariaceae) family first became better known it has become tremendously popular, primarily because of its heavy flowering and easy cultivation. Consequently, there are now many hybrids and cultivars and they fill an important niche in rockeries, containers, and perennial borders. Commonly known as twinspurs, they are generally low compact plants with small, simple, dark green leaves, and are so-named because of the two short spurs behind the flower. The principal flower colors are apricot, pink, and mauve. *Diascia* means "two sacs" and refers to the nectar sacs at the base of the spurs.

CULTIVATION

Easily grown in a sunny position with light well-drained soil, the perennials require a climate with a fairly mild winter, but the annuals thrive almost anywhere. Routine deadheading will extend the flowering season. The perennials sometimes self-layer or they can be propagated from cuttings. Raise the annual forms from seed.

ABOVE LEFT Diascia *Coral Belle/'Hecbel' has glossy leaves and coral red flowers. It has a semi-trailing habit that makes it an ideal subject for basket culture.*
BELOW *With bright green leaves and rose to salmon pink flowers,* Diascia fetcaniensis *adds a welcome splash of color when used for rockery planting.*

Top Tip

Twinspurs are prolific bloomers, but production can slow if conditions become too hot. To kick-start blooming, keep well-watered and pinch back spent flowers.

Plant Height	Plant Width	Hardiness Zone	Frost Tolerance
12 in (30 cm)	12–16 in (30–40 cm)	8–10	yes
10 in (25 cm)	20 in (50 cm)	8–10	yes
8–18 in (20–45 cm)	12–24 in (30–60 cm)	8–10	yes
12 in (30 cm)	20 in (50 cm)	8–10	yes
8–18 in (20–45 cm)	12–24 in (30–60 cm)	8–10	yes
20 in (50 cm)	24 in (60 cm)	8–10	yes

ABOVE Diascia vigilis *'Jack Elliott' is a reliable fleshy-leafed plant that produces racemes of very large, showy, mid-pink flowers.*

TOP Diascia vigilis *enjoys a longer flowering season than many of its relatives, producing its soft pink flowers, spotted with darker pink at the throat, from summer through to early winter.*

DIGITALIS

Foxgloves, members of the foxglove (Scrophulariaceae) family, occur naturally only in Europe and North Africa, but have naturalized in many temperate climates. The genus comprises some 20 species of biennials and perennials and there are also many hybrids and cultivars. Most form a basal foliage clump of large, heavily veined, sometimes downy leaves. From late spring, tall, strongly erect flower spikes develop. The flowers, which occur mostly in shades of pink to purple-red, less commonly white or yellow, are bell-shaped and usually downward-facing. *Digitalis* species contain potent glycosides that were once used in cardiac medicine, and extracts are still used in some herbal remedies.

LEFT *Rich dark green leaves form a dramatic backdrop for the pretty, bell-shaped, primrose yellow flowers of* Digitalis grandiflora *'Carillon'.*

RIGHT *The tall spires of downward-facing flowers of* Digitalis purpurea, *Excelsior Group, cultivars make an impressive sight as the blooms open progressively up to the apex.*

CULTIVATION

While hardiness varies with the species, most are easily cultivated in temperate areas. They prefer deep, humus-rich, moist, well-drained soil and a position in sun or part-shade. The taller species may need staking. Propagate the perennials by division or from basal offsets; raise annuals from seed.

Top Tip

Foxgloves make excellent border plantings. However, it is best to wear gloves when handling these plants, as contact with the leaves can cause skin irritation.

RIGHT Digitalis × fulva *is a natural hybrid from southern Europe. It features somewhat downy leaves and spires of white to pale yellow-green flowers.*

BELOW *Producing a stunning display when in bloom, the rich red-brown flowers of* Digitalis parviflora *have earned it the common name of chocolate foxglove.*

Favorites	Flower Color	Blooming Season	Flower Fragrance	Plant Height	Plant Width	Hardiness Zone	Frost Tolerance
Digitalis* × *fulva	white to pale yellow-green	late spring to summer	no	40 in (100 cm)	20–24 in (50–60 cm)	7–9	yes
Digitalis grandiflora	lemon yellow	early to mid-summer	no	36 in (90 cm)	18 in (45 cm)	4–9	yes
Digitalis lanata	dull white to buff	late spring to summer	no	40 in (100 cm)	20–24 in (50–60 cm)	6–9	yes
Digitalis* × *mertonensis	pinkish-red to purple-pink	late spring to summer	no	20–30 in (50–75 cm)	16–20 in (40–50 cm)	4–9	yes
Digitalis parviflora	red-brown	early summer	no	24 in (60 cm)	12 in (30 cm)	4–9	yes
Digitalis purpurea	purple, pink, white, yellow	summer	no	3–6 ft (0.9–1.8 m)	2 ft (0.6 m)	5–10	yes

Left Euphorbia schillingii *is a shrubby perennial native to Nepal. Hardy and robust, it has showy yellow-green flowerheads that persist on the plant for a long period of time.*

Euphorbia

This large genus of over 2,000 species of annuals, perennials, shrubs, and trees is the type form for the euphorbia (Euphorbiaceae) family. While the woody species are sometimes thorny and cactus-like in form, the annuals and perennials are usually soft-stemmed and unarmed. Their leaves tend to be narrow to lance-shaped, bright green to blue-green, and the true flowers, which are small and often insignificant, are surrounded by a cup-shaped structure called a cyathia. The flowerheads are sometimes subtended by bracts. All euphorbias exude a potentially irritating milky sap when cut, a feature that has led to some interesting common names, such as caustic plant and mad-woman's milk.

Cultivation

Hardiness varies greatly with the species, though most of the perennials will tolerate some frost. Plant in fairly light well-drained soil and water well during the growing season. Remove the spent flowerheads as they begin to set seed. The annuals are raised from seed and the perennials may be propagated from small cuttings and sometimes by division.

Left *The stunning coloring of* Euphorbia pulcherrima*—or poinsettia, as it is commonly known—is, in fact, provided by the bright red bracts rather than the true flowers. Although this species is often grown as a shrub, dwarf poinsettias are popular indoor pot plants.*

RIGHT Euphorbia characias *subsp.* wulfenii *'Bosahan' is a popular garden cultivar, and is noted for its vigorous growth.*

LEFT Euphorbia polychroma, *known as common spurge, has velvet-textured green leaves and attractive yellow-green flowers that are sometimes highlighted with red.*

Top Tip

Once *Euphorbia* species have completed their floral display, reduce watering, applying just enough to prevent the soil from drying out.

Favorites	Flower Color	Blooming Season	Flower Fragrance	Plant Height	Plant Width	Hardiness Zone	Frost Tolerance
Euphorbia characias	greenish yellow	mid-spring to early summer	no	4–6 ft (1.2–1.8 m)	4 ft (1.2 m)	8–10	yes
Euphorbia griffithii	orange to red	summer	no	36 in (90 cm)	36 in (90 cm)	5–10	yes
***Euphorbia griffithii* 'Dixter'**	orange	summer	no	36 in (90 cm)	36 in (90 cm)	5–10	yes
Euphorbia polychroma	yellow-green	spring to summer	no	24 in (60 cm)	24 in (60 cm)	6–9	yes
Euphorbia pulcherrima	yellow flowers, bright red bracts	winter to early spring	no	10 ft (3 m)	7–10 ft (2–3 m)	10–11	no
Euphorbia schillingii	yellow-green	summer to autumn	no	4 ft (1.2 m)	5 ft (1.5 m)	7–9	yes

GAZANIA

A South African genus of 16 species of annual and perennial daisies in the family Asteraceae, the plants in cultivation are mainly hybrids and there are countless color forms and seedling strains. Most quickly develop into small clumps of narrow lance-shaped leaves that are sometimes downy and lobed near the base, often with pale undersides. The flowers are large and brightly colored with ray florets that tend to be darker at the base, and feature a contrastingly colored central disc. In milder climates gazanias can flower year-round. Early botanists owed much to Theodore of Gaza (1398–1478) who translated into Latin the Greek botanical texts of Theophrastus, and they named *Gazania* in his honor.

Top Tip

Start seeds indoors up to 6 weeks prior to the last spring frost, and transplant outside when all danger of frost has passed. Plant in well-drained soil 12 in (30 cm) apart.

CULTIVATION

Most tolerate very little frost but are otherwise easily grown in any sunny position with light, gritty, well-drained soil. They will thrive in coastal gardens. Deadhead frequently to keep the plants flowering. Propagate annuals from seed; the perennials may also be divided or can be grown from basal cuttings.

ABOVE *Gazanias are also called treasure flowers, and 'Bronze Gnome' seems to explode in vivid tones of orange and yellow that any gardener would treasure.*

Favorites	Flower Color	Blooming Season	Flower Fragrance	Plant Height	Plant Width	Hardiness Zone	Frost Tolerance
***Gazania* 'Bronze Gnome'**	orange-yellow	spring to summer	no	4–6 in (10–15 cm)	20 in (50 cm)	9–11	no
***Gazania* 'Burgundy'**	burgundy	spring to summer	no	6–8 in (15–20 cm)	20 in (50 cm)	9–11	no
Gazania linearis	orange-yellow	summer to autumn	no	6–12 in (15–30 cm)	12–24 in (30–60 cm)	7–11	yes
Gazania rigens	orange-yellow	spring to summer	no	6–8 in (15–20 cm)	24–40 in (60–100 cm)	9–11	no
***Gazania* 'Tiger Mixture'**	various	spring to summer	no	8–10 in (20–25 cm)	20 in (50 cm)	9–11	no
***Gazania,* Chansonette Series**	orange, pink, red, yellow	summer	no	8 in (20 cm)	10 in (25 cm)	9–11	no

LEFT Gazania rigens *is a perennial with fleshy stems that strike root as they spread, forming large leafy clumps. The flowers have yellow or orange ray florets with a dark base.*

BELOW *Although* Gazanias *now come in a wide range of colors, some of the light pinks and creams can look dirty. It is hard to go past a bright orange or yellow for a striking border or rockery.*

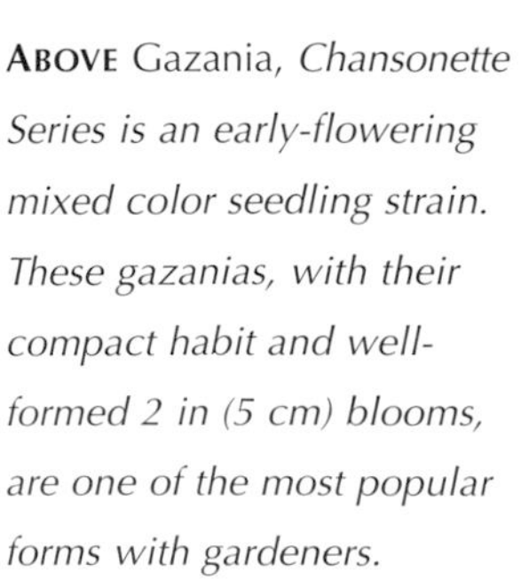

ABOVE Gazania, *Chansonette Series is an early-flowering mixed color seedling strain. These gazanias, with their compact habit and well-formed 2 in (5 cm) blooms, are one of the most popular forms with gardeners.*

Top Tip

Perfect for rockery planting, gentians need a spot with excellent drainage or they can be temperamental and sometimes may not flower.

Left *Ideal for small rock gardens, the leaves of* Gentiana acaulis *'Rannoch' form clumps of wonderful bright green foliage from which emerge the stems of large, dark-centered, deep blue flowers.*

Below *From western and central Asia,* Gentiana septemfida *is an easy-to-grow plant that will reward with arching stems of blue bell-shaped flowers and rich green foliage.*

Gentiana

Below *A native of Japan,* Gentiana makinoi *features mid-green basal leaves. The leafy flower stems produce pretty bell-shaped blue flowers—often spotted on the interior—at the apex and at the leaf axils.*

Around 400 species of annuals, biennials, and perennials make up this genus, the type for the family Gentianaceae. They are widely distributed in temperate zones and many are alpine plants. Gentians typically form a small clump or tuft of simple basal leaves or a cluster of wiry stems with opposite pairs of leaves. The genus is renowned for producing intense blue flowers, but not all gentians are blue, many are white, yellow, or mauve-blue. The flowering season is mainly spring or autumn. Gentians have several herbal uses and the European yellow gentian *(Gentiana lutea)* was once regarded as a virtual "miracle cure."

Cultivation

The usual preference is for a climate with clearly defined seasons, soil that is gritty and free draining yet moisture retentive, and a position in sun or half-shade. Many are superb rockery plants. The species are best raised from seed, while the selected forms may be divided and sometimes strike from layers.

Favorites	Flower Color	Blooming Season	Flower Fragrance	Plant Height	Plant Width	Hardiness Zone	Frost Tolerance
Gentiana acaulis	deep blue, green-spotted interior	spring to early summer	no	4 in (10 cm)	12 in (30 cm)	3–9	yes
Gentiana asclepiadea	violet-blue	late summer to early autumn	no	24 in (60 cm)	18 in (45 cm)	6–9	yes
Gentiana* × *macaulayi	deep blue	summer to autumn	no	4 in (10 cm)	16 in (40 cm)	4–9	yes
Gentiana makinoi	pale blue to violet-blue	summer	no	24 in (60 cm)	16 in (40 cm)	6–9	yes
Gentiana septemfida	dark blue to blue-purple	late summer	no	6–12 in (15–30 cm)	12–16 in (30–40 cm)	3–9	yes
Gentiana sino-ornata	blue	autumn	no	6 in (15 cm)	12 in (30 cm)	6–9	yes

RIGHT *A native of southern Europe, found from Spain to the Balkans,* Gentiana acaulis *features a basal rosette of glossy leaves and green-spotted, dark blue, bell-shaped flowers.*

GERANIUM

RIGHT *Vibrant yellow-green leaves and gorgeous, dark-centered, magenta flowers are the trademark features of the popular cultivar* Geranium *'Ann Folkard'.*

Among the gardening public there is a great deal of confusion over geraniums and pelargoniums. Most of the plants commonly called geraniums are actually pelargoniums, though both belong in the geranium (Geraniaceae) family. True geraniums make up a genus of around 300 species of perennials and subshrubs spread throughout the temperate zones. Many are low, spreading plants with simple purple-pink flowers, but a few, such as *Geranium maderense*, are larger and have semi-woody stems and large sprays of blooms. Garden forms widen the flower color range to include white, pink, and purple-blue. Geraniums have a long history of use in herbal medicines and some species yield aromatic oils used in fragrances.

ABOVE *Semi-trailing to bushy in habit,* Geranium *'Johnson's Blue' bears dainty, pale purple-blue, 5-petalled flowers over a lengthy flowering season from spring to autumn.*

CULTIVATION

Requirements vary, as does hardiness. Many are drought tolerant but some prefer damp ground, and while most are very frost tolerant a few are rather tender. A sunny airy position with moist well-drained soil is usually suitable. Propagate from seed or by division.

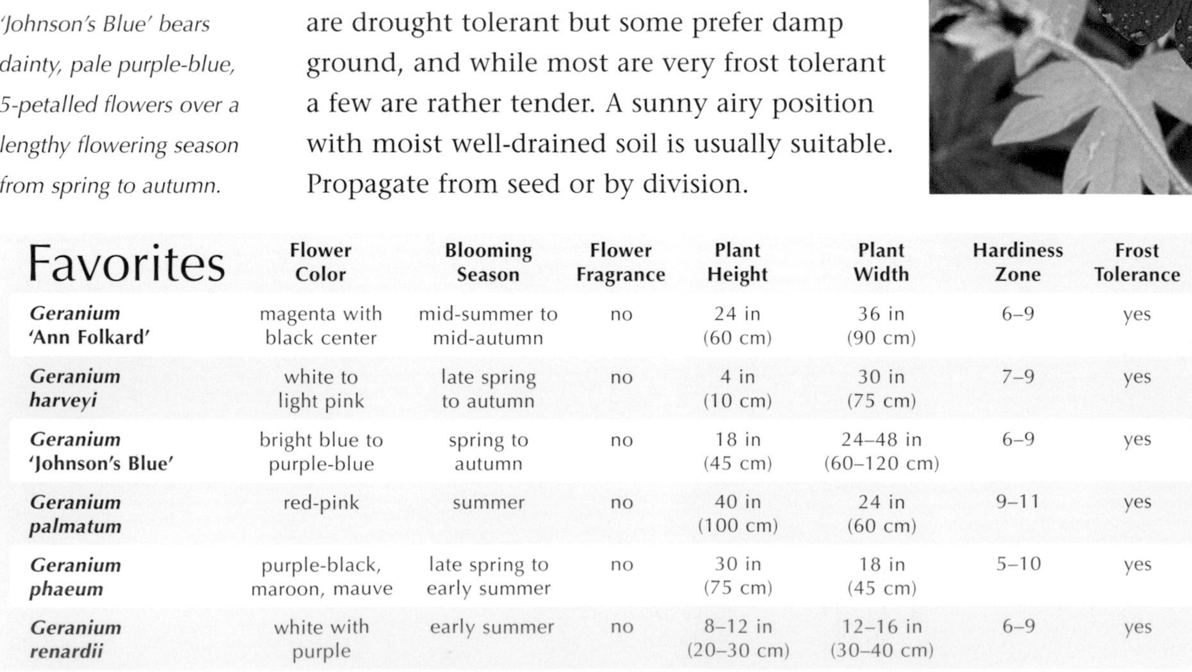

Favorites	Flower Color	Blooming Season	Flower Fragrance	Plant Height	Plant Width	Hardiness Zone	Frost Tolerance
***Geranium* 'Ann Folkard'**	magenta with black center	mid-summer to mid-autumn	no	24 in (60 cm)	36 in (90 cm)	6–9	yes
Geranium harveyi	white to light pink	late spring to autumn	no	4 in (10 cm)	30 in (75 cm)	7–9	yes
***Geranium* 'Johnson's Blue'**	bright blue to purple-blue	spring to autumn	no	18 in (45 cm)	24–48 in (60–120 cm)	6–9	yes
Geranium palmatum	red-pink	summer	no	40 in (100 cm)	24 in (60 cm)	9–11	yes
Geranium phaeum	purple-black, maroon, mauve	late spring to early summer	no	30 in (75 cm)	18 in (45 cm)	5–10	yes
Geranium renardii	white with purple	early summer	no	8–12 in (20–30 cm)	12–16 in (30–40 cm)	6–9	yes

Above *With the rather sinister common name of black widow,* Geranium phaeum *features clusters of richly colored flowers that range in hue from maroon and mauve to almost black.*

Below *Producing heads of attractive reddish pink flowers,* Geranium palmatum *is a charming evergreen perennial that is native to Madeira.*

Top Tip

Geraniums are happy left to themselves until overcrowding becomes a problem. Dividing the clump in spring should rectify the problem.

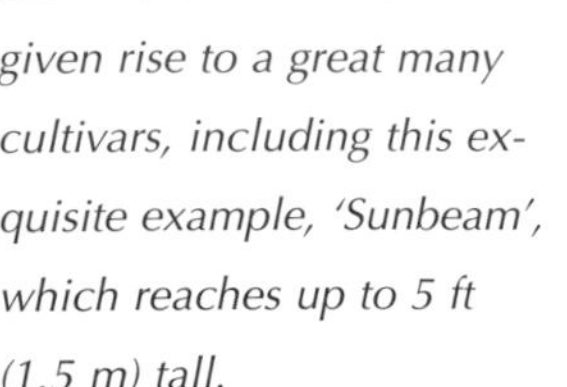

LEFT Helianthus annuus *has given rise to a great many cultivars, including this exquisite example, 'Sunbeam', which reaches up to 5 ft (1.5 m) tall.*

BELOW *Ringed with gold at the petal bases,* Helianthus annuus *'Italian White' has ray florets of palest yellow, almost white, which radiate around the greenish disc.*

HELIANTHUS

This genus of some 70 species of annual and perennial daisies (family Asteraceae) from the Americas is best known for the common or giant sunflower *(Helianthus annuus),* which in addition to being a very impressive plant is the source of sunflower seeds and sunflower oil, and has been adopted by Kansas as its state flower. Most species develop into a clump of erect bristly stems with simple lance- to heart-shaped leaves. Species almost always have yellow flowerheads, but garden forms occur in a range of warm colors and with double flowerheads. Flowering starts around mid-summer and continues well into autumn. Sunflowers are so-called because their flowerheads turn to follow the sun.

CULTIVATION

Plant in full sun with light free-draining soil. Water and feed well during the summer months. Taller forms may need staking. While annual sunflowers can be left to produce their interesting seed heads, the perennials should be deadheaded frequently to keep them flowering. Propagate from seed; the perennials can sometimes be divided or struck from basal cuttings.

Favorites	Flower Color	Blooming Season	Flower Fragrance	Plant Height	Plant Width	Hardiness Zone	Frost Tolerance
Helianthus annuus	yellow	summer to early autumn	no	8–15 ft (2.4–4.5 m)	2 ft (0.6 m)	4–11	yes
Helianthus debilis	yellow	summer	no	7 ft (2 m)	2 ft (0.6 m)	7–11	yes
Helianthus giganteus	yellow	mid-summer	no	15 ft (4.5 m)	3 ft (0.9 m)	4–9	yes
Helianthus* × *multiflorus	golden yellow	late summer to mid-autumn	no	3–6 ft (0.9–1.8 m)	3 ft (0.9 m)	5–9	yes
***Helianthus* 'Sunny'**	bright yellow	autumn	no	4–7 ft (1.2–2 m)	3–4 ft (0.9–1.2 m)	5–10	yes
Helianthus tuberosus	yellow	autumn	no	10 ft (3 m)	5 ft (1.5 m)	4–9	yes

Top Tip

Sunflowers can often overshadow their neighbors, so plant at the rear of borders or around shrubs to ensure a share of the sunshine for all.

Above *The epitome of its name,* Helianthus *'Sunny' presents a sunny face to the world with its double rows of bright yellow petals around a bronze disc.*

Right *Growing up to 5 ft (1.5 m) tall,* Helianthus × multiflorus *'Loddon Gold' bears large, double, golden yellow flowerheads from late summer to mid-autumn.*

HELLEBORUS

RIGHT *Contrasting dark spotting peppers the creamy white flowers of* Helleborus orientalis *subsp.* guttatus, *a semi-evergreen plant from the Caucasus region.*

BELOW *From Corsica and Sardinia,* Helleborus argutifolius *features leathery, mid-green to gray-green, toothed leaves, accompanied by clusters of green flowers from winter to spring.*

A member of the buttercup (Ranunculaceae) family, this genus contains some 15 species of rhizome-rooted perennials found in the northern temperate zone from Europe to western China. Commonly known as lenten rose or winter rose, most are low-growing compact plants with pinnate or palmate leaves. The flowers are simple but are backed by long-lasting petal-like sepals that persist well after the flower has died and which often continue to intensify in color. A range of species will provide a succession of flowers from late autumn to early summer. *Helleborus niger* is sometimes used in herbal medicines, though the plants mentioned in herbalist literature are often the unrelated false hellebores (*Veratrum* species).

CULTIVATION

These plants are best grown in deciduous woodland conditions to provide light in winter and shade in summer. The soil should be cool, humus-rich, moist, and well-drained. Smaller species do well in cool rockeries. Tidy up the foliage once the flowers are spent. These plants are usually propagated by division as the seed may require two periods of stratification.

RIGHT *The lovely greenish purple flowers of* Helleborus orientalis *subsp.* abchasicus *'Early Purple' will brighten the winter garden with their cheerful rosy color.*

Favorites	Flower Color	Blooming Season	Flower Fragrance	Plant Height	Plant Width	Hardiness Zone	Frost Tolerance
Helleborus argutifolius	pale green	late winter to early spring	no	40–48 in (100–120 cm)	24 in (60 cm)	6–9	yes
Helleborus cyclophyllus	yellow-green	winter	no	12–16 in (30–40 cm)	16 in (40 cm)	5–9	yes
Helleborus foetidus	green with red margins	mid-winter to mid-spring	no	30 in (75 cm)	18–40 in (45–100 cm)	6–10	yes
Helleborus lividus	greenish with pink-purple tint	mid-winter to early spring	no	18 in (45 cm)	12–24 in (30–60 cm)	7–9	yes
Helleborus niger	white, pink; greenish center	early winter to early spring	no	12 in (30 cm)	12–18 in (30–45 cm)	3–9	yes
Helleborus orientalis	white, cream, green, purple	mid-winter to mid-spring	no	12–24 in (30–60 cm)	18–24 in (45–60 cm)	6–10	yes

RIGHT Helleborus cyclophyllus, *a deciduous species, features bright green, noticeably veined leaves that are downy beneath, and yellow-green winter flowers.*

Top Tip

Hellebores are valued as much for their lush verdant foliage as for their winter flowers. Plant where they are to remain, as they resent any disturbance.

HEMEROCALLIS

Daylilies are so-named because each flower lasts just one day. The botanical name, derived from Greek, also reflects this trait, as it means "day-beauty." The type genus for the daylily (Hemerocallidaceae) family, *Hemerocallis* is a temperate East Asian genus made up of 15 species of rhizome-rooted perennials. They develop into clumps of grassy to strappy leaves from which emerge wiry flower stems bearing large lily-like flowers, most often in warm tones of pink, yellow, orange, red, or purple. The flowers, which appear throughout the warmer months, are edible and make an interesting and colorful addition to salads, or can be used as a garnish.

Top Tip

The short lifespan of daylilies does not preclude their use as cut flowers. Select stems with plenty of buds—each will open over several days.

BELOW Hemerocallis *'Red Precious' bears vivid coral red flowers, each petal marked with a bold central stripe of bright yellow.*

CULTIVATION

Apart from the need to control slug and snail damage, and rust fungus in some climates, daylilies are easily grown in any sunny or partly shaded position with moist humus-rich soil. The flowers always face the sun, so take care to site your plants where the flowers can be seen. Propagation is most often by division, though the seed germinates freely.

LEFT *Though each individual flower lasts just a single day,* Hemerocallis *'Many Happy Returns' bears its delicately colored blooms over a long flowering period.*

Favorites	Flower Color	Blooming Season	Flower Fragrance
***Hemerocallis* 'Corky'**	yellow	summer	no
***Hemerocallis* 'Many Happy Returns'**	pale yellow	summer	no
***Hemerocallis* 'Red Precious'**	coral red	summer	no
***Hemerocallis* 'Stafford'**	bright red	summer	no
***Hemerocallis* 'Stella d'Oro'**	bright yellow	summer	no
***Hemerocallis* 'Stoke Poges'**	lilac-pink	summer	no

Above *Slender wiry stems carry the spectacular blooms of* Hemerocallis *'Stafford'—each bloom has brilliant red petals that are a rich yellow color at the center.*

Plant Height	Plant Width	Hardiness Zone	Frost Tolerance
24 in (60 cm)	24–36 in (60–90 cm)	4–9	yes
16 in (40 cm)	12–24 in (30–60 cm)	4–9	yes
22 in (55 cm)	12–24 in (30–60 cm)	4–9	yes
24 in (60 cm)	24–36 in (60–90 cm)	4–9	yes
12 in (30 cm)	18 in (45 cm)	5–11	yes
24 in (60 cm)	24–36 in (60–90 cm)	4–9	yes

Below *Striking crimson markings, lilac-pink petals, and a golden center make* Hemerocallis *'Stoke Poges' a stunning choice for the garden or as a cut flower.*

RIGHT *Heart-shaped leaves and dainty bell-shaped flowers in reds, pinks, or whites are the trademark features of the Bressingham Hybrids, popular forms of* Heuchera × brizoides.

HEUCHERA

A North American genus of about 55 species of perennials in the saxifrage (Saxifragaceae) family, it is commonly known as alum root or coral bells. Many are near-evergreen and are grown as much for their foliage as for the flowers. The basic leaf shape is rounded, but the small pointed lobes create a maple-leaf effect. Modern hybrids often have unusually marked foliage. From late spring to autumn they bear erect wiry stems with sprays of sometimes petal-less tiny flowers, usually in shades of white, cream, or pink. The genus name honors Johann Heinrich von Heucher (1677–1747), who was professor of medicine at Wittenburg University, and perhaps refers to the plant's use in herbal medicines, as Heucher specialized in medicinal plants.

CULTIVATION

Suitable for rockeries, perennial borders, and containers, as well as being hardy and adaptable, *Heuchera* plants should be placed in full or part-sun with fertile, moist, humus-rich, well-drained soil. Deadhead regularly to keep tidy and to encourage continued blooming. Propagate by division or from fresh seed.

Favorites	Flower Color	Blooming Season	Flower Fragrance
Heuchera* × *brizoides	pink, red, white	late spring to autumn	no
***Heuchera* 'Chocolate Ruffles'**	white	late spring to autumn	no
***Heuchera* 'Fireglow'**	red	late spring to autumn	no
***Heuchera* 'Mint Frost'**	cream	late spring to autumn	no
***Heuchera* 'Petite Marble Burgundy'**	pink	late spring to autumn	no
***Heuchera* 'Wendy'**	pink	late spring to autumn	no

LEFT *Held on elegant tall stems, the fiery red bell-flowers of* Heuchera *'Fireglow' tower high above the dense clumps of heart-shaped leaves.*

Top Tip

Although generally rugged and reliable plants, *Heuchera* species will appreciate a regular watering regime during dry periods to keep the foliage looking at its best.

ABOVE *A shimmering silver sheen on the rich green leaves gives a frosted appearance to this aptly named cultivar—* Heuchera *'Mint Frost'.*

BELOW Heuchera *'Petite Marble Burgundy' is grown as much for its impressive foliage of silver-dusted leaves as it is for its attractive, pink, bell-shaped flowers.*

Plant Height	Plant Width	Hardiness Zone	Frost Tolerance
12–30 in (30–75 cm)	12–18 in (30–45 cm)	4–10	yes
12–24 in (30–60 cm)	12–24 in (30–60 cm)	5–10	yes
24 in (60 cm)	12–18 in (30–45 cm)	5–10	yes
24 in (60 cm)	12–18 in (30–45 cm)	5–10	yes
8–10 in (20–25 cm)	12–18 in (30–45 cm)	5–10	yes
24 in (60 cm)	36–48 in (90–120 cm)	5–10	yes

HOSTA

Made up of around 40 species of temperate East Asian herbaceous perennials, commonly known as plantain lilies, *Hosta* is a member of the agave (Agavaceae) family. They are grown mainly for their bold heart-shaped foliage, which forms a dense basal clump, though their small, funnel-shaped, lily-like flowers are also attractive. Modern hosta cultivars come in a vast array of foliage colors, sizes, and textures, and are indispensable plants for shade. The flowers, usually in mauve and purple shades or white, appear from mid-summer. Although it may be difficult for western gardeners to imagine, hostas were a staple leaf vegetable in their homelands and are still widely used as such.

LEFT *The green to blue-green leaves of* Hosta *'Shade Fanfare' are edged in a rich creamy white. Pretty pale mauve flowers are borne from mid-summer.*

Top Tip

Hostas are ideal plants for beginners. Adaptable and reliable, they do particularly well in shady spots, flourishing where other plants falter.

CULTIVATION

Hostas prefer deep, cool, moist, humus-rich, well-drained soil and light shade. Although hybridizers have tried hard to produce sun-tolerant forms, hostas are woodlanders at heart. Water and feed well to produce lush foliage and use baits and a dry surface mulch to lessen slug and snail damage. Propagation is most often by division in late winter.

RIGHT *Adding textural interest to the garden, the large blue-green leaves of* Hosta sieboldiana *'Blue Angel' are etched with veins and have a distinctly puckered surface.*

LEFT Hosta plantaginea, *commonly known as august lily or maruba, has lush bright green leaves that are a perfect foil for the crisp white fragrant flowers.*

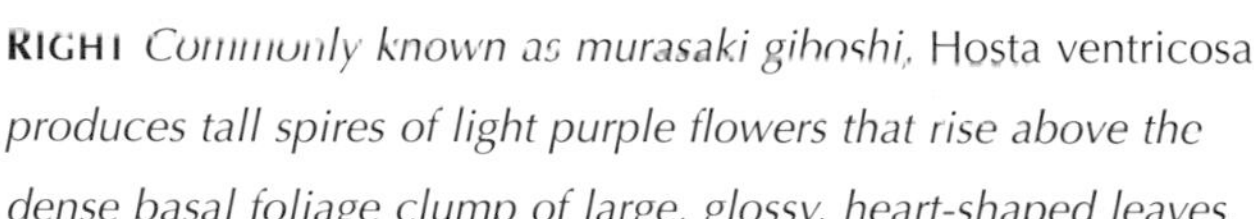

RIGHT *Commonly known as murasaki giboshi,* Hosta ventricosa *produces tall spires of light purple flowers that rise above the dense basal foliage clump of large, glossy, heart-shaped leaves.*

Favorites	Flower Color	Blooming Season	Flower Fragrance	Plant Height	Plant Width	Hardiness Zone	Frost Tolerance
***Hosta* 'Frances Williams'**	lavender	mid-summer	no	24 in (60 cm)	36 in (90 cm)	6–10	yes
***Hosta* 'Krossa Regal'**	white to pale mauve	mid-summer	no	30–60 in (75–150 cm)	30 in (75 cm)	6–10	yes
Hosta plantaginea	white	mid-summer to autumn	yes	26 in (65 cm)	32 in (80 cm)	8–10	yes
***Hosta* 'Shade Fanfare'**	pale mauve	mid-summer	no	24 in (60 cm)	24 in (60 cm)	6–10	yes
Hosta sieboldiana	white to mauve	mid-summer to early autumn	no	20–24 in (50–60 cm)	36–60 in (90–150 cm)	6–10	yes
Hosta ventricosa	light purple	mid-summer to autumn	no	40 in (100 cm)	24–32 in (60–80 cm)	6–10	yes

Impatiens

Top Tip

The fast-growing nature of busy lizzies means that their appearance can become a little untidy. Pinch back unruly stems to keep plants looking neat and tidy.

This widespread type genus of the balsam (Balsaminaceae) family includes some 850 species of annuals, perennials, and subshrubs that are known by various common names, such as balsam, busy lizzie, and water fuchsia. They are erect plants with soft fleshy stems and elongated lance-shaped toothed leaves. Modern garden forms range from 6 in (15 cm) to over 6 ft (1.8 m) high, and can feature brightly colored foliage. The spurred 5-petalled flowers occur in many colors and appear in the warmer months. Conspicuous seed pods follow and often eject their contents explosively, spreading the seeds over a wide area—hence the name *Impatiens*, from the Latin for impatient.

Above *The brilliant red blooms of* Impatiens, *New Guinea Group, 'Improved Quepos' are matched by equally striking dark green leaves.*

Cultivation

Impatiens will not tolerate frost, but as they are easily propagated and develop quickly, they may be grown as summer annuals. Some species can establish so freely that they become weeds. Plant in deep, cool, moist, humus-rich soil with shade from the hottest sun. Water and feed well to encourage strong growth. Raise bedding forms from seed and the rest from softwood cuttings.

Below *This stunning variegated form of* Impatiens walleriana *features gorgeous pink-red flowers nestled among the white-edged dark green leaves.*

Favorites

Favorites	Flower Color	Blooming Season	Flower Fragrance	Plant Height	Plant Width	Hardiness Zone	Frost Tolerance
Impatiens balsamina	pink, red, purple, white	summer to early autumn	no	12–30 in (30–75 cm)	12–18 in (30–45 cm)	9–12	no
Impatiens omeiana	yellow	early autumn	no	12 in (30 cm)	36 in (90 cm)	8–10	no
Impatiens pseudoviola	white to bright pink	summer	no	12 in (30 cm)	24–48 in (60–120 cm)	10–12	no
Impatiens walleriana	red, pink, white, orange, purple	most of year	no	8–24 in (20–60 cm)	8–24 in (20–60 cm)	9–12	no
***Impatiens*, New Guinea Group**	pink, cerise, red, orange, white	summer	no	8–24 in (20–60 cm)	16–36 in (40–90 cm)	10–12	no
***Impatiens*, New Guinea Group, 'Tango'**	bright orange	summer	no	24 in (60 cm)	16–24 in (40–60 cm)	10–12	no

RIGHT *Mid- to dark green leaves provide a backdrop for the lavender-pink flowers of* Impatiens *'Celebration Light Lavender', one of the New Guinea Group.*

LEFT Impatiens walleriana, *Garden Leader Series comes in a wide range of colors, such as this coral pink-flowered example—aptly named 'Coral'.*

IRIS

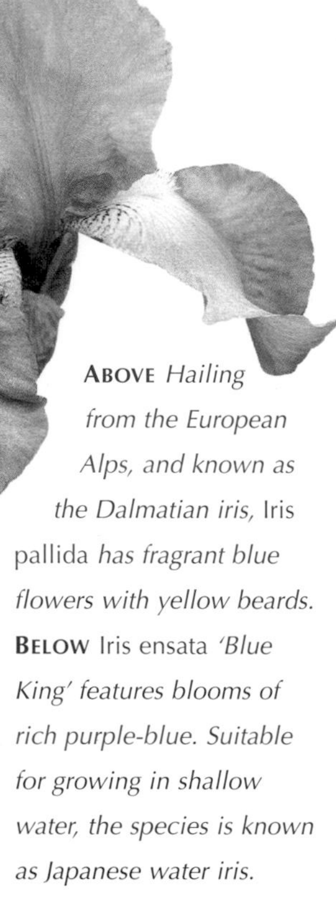

Iris, the type genus for the family Iridaceae, comprises some 300 species of bulbous, fibrous, and rhizome-rooted perennials widely distributed throughout the northern temperate regions. Most develop into dense foliage clumps with fans of grassy to sword-shaped leaves. Their flowers, the model for the fleur-de-lis, have 6 petals: 3 erect petals known as standards and 3 that droop, the falls. As befits a genus named for Iris, the Greek goddess of the rainbow, the flowers occur in all colors and often incorporate brilliant combinations of colors. The flowers appear from late winter to late summer, depending on the species. The state flower of Tennessee is *Iris germanica*.

ABOVE *Hailing from the European Alps, and known as the Dalmatian iris,* Iris pallida *has fragrant blue flowers with yellow beards.*
BELOW Iris ensata *'Blue King' features blooms of rich purple-blue. Suitable for growing in shallow water, the species is known as Japanese water iris.*

CULTIVATION

All irises prefer sun or partial shade but soil requirements vary with the growth form. Bog irises need permanently damp soil; woodland irises prefer moist well-drained soil; bearded irises should be kept moist when actively growing and flowering but should then be kept dry; and rockery irises need moist but perfectly drained gritty soil. Propagation is usually by division when dormant.

ABOVE Iris *'Broadleigh Nancy' is a beautiful representative of the Californian Hybrids, with an eye-catching color combination of white, purple, and yellow on the petals.*
LEFT *Flowering well if placed in a sunny spot,* Iris *'Barocco', one of the Intermediate Bearded irises, produces stunning deep pink to maroon blooms.*

Favorites	Flower Color	Blooming Season	Flower Fragrance	Plant Height	Plant Width	Hardiness Zone	Frost Tolerance
Iris ensata	white, purple, lavender	late spring to early summer	no	36 in (90 cm)	12–40 in (30–100 cm)	4–10	yes
Iris laevigata	purple, mauve, white	summer	no	24–60 in (60–150 cm)	60 in (150 cm)	3–9	yes
Iris pallida	blue; yellow beards	early summer	yes	36–48 in (90–120 cm)	12 in (30 cm)	5–9	yes
Iris sibirica	blue, purple, white	late spring to early summer	no	24–48 in (60–120 cm)	8–24 in (20–60 cm)	4–10	yes
***Iris,* Arilbred Hybrids**	white, blue, red, yellow, brown	mid-spring to early summer	no	12–30 in (30–75 cm)	8–18 in (20–45 cm)	5–9	yes
***Iris,* Californian Hybrids**	yellow to pink, purple	spring to summer	no	10–20 in (25–50 cm)	12 in (30 cm)	5–9	yes
***Iris,* Dutch Hybrids**	blue to violet, yellow, orange	spring to early summer	no	10–36 in (25–90 cm)	6–18 in (15–45 cm)	5–9	yes
***Iris,* Dwarf Bearded**	various	late spring	no	8–15 in (20–38 cm)	12–24 in (30–60 cm)	3–10	yes
***Iris,* Intermediate Bearded**	various	late spring	no	10–27 in (25–70 cm)	12–24 in (30–60 cm)	3–10	yes
***Iris,* Louisiana Hybrids**	various	mid-spring to early summer	no	18–60 in (45–150 cm)	3–7 ft (0.9–2 m)	6–11	yes
***Iris,* Spuria Hybrids**	various	late spring to early summer	no	24–48 in (60–120 cm)	18–24 in (45–60 cm)	4–9	yes
***Iris,* Tall Bearded**	various	late spring	no	30–36 in (75–90 cm)	12–24 in (30–60 cm)	3–10	yes

LEFT *A testament to the vast color range of the genus,* Iris *'Buisson de Roses', a Tall Bearded iris, bears delicate salmon pink blooms, marked with a darker beard.*
BELOW *The Louisiana Hybrids, such as the violet-blue-flowered* Iris *'Marie Caillet', are well suited to waterside planting. In garden situations provide ample water.*

LEFT *The ruffled petals of* Iris *'Bal Masque', a Tall Bearded iris, comprise pure white standards and rich purple-blue falls marked with white at the beard.*
BELOW *The creamy flowers of* Iris *'Happy Mood', an Intermediate Bearded iris, feature a delicate lavender edging to the ruffled petals.*

Top Tip

Irises may become overcrowded after several years. They can be divided when dormant, at which time any spent plants should be discarded.

LEFT *Beautiful ruffled petals of softest lemon, slightly deeper colored at the center and at the petal edges, are the outstanding features of* Iris, *Tall Bearded, 'Samsara'.*

BELOW *The brilliant yellow-orange flowers of* Iris *'Pirate's Quest', one of the Tall Bearded irises, will certainly prove a prized treasure in the garden.*

BELOW *With rich blue flowers held on tall slender stems high above the lush dark green foliage,* Iris sibirica *'Marcus Perry' makes an impact in the garden.*

KNIPHOFIA

Mostly South African in origin, the 70 species of clump-forming perennials that make up this aloe (Aloeaceae) family genus are grown mainly for their tall flower stems that are topped with vivid bottle-brush-shaped heads of red, orange, yellow, cream, and sometimes green flowers. They develop from rhizomes and form clumps of grassy to sword-shaped leaves from which emerge the long sturdy flower stems. Flowering starts from mid- to late summer, varying with the species, and the blooms last well when cut. The genus name honors German professor Johann Hieronymus Kniphof (1704–1763), who developed an extensive herbal collection and was among the first physicians to use St John's Wort *(Hypericum perfoliatum)* to treat depression.

ABOVE Kniphofia pumila *is a compact plant, native to Ethiopia, with grassy foliage and dense cylindrical heads of yellow to red flowers on short stems, from summer.*

LEFT Kniphofia linearifolia *is an evergreen perennial, which has narrow deep green leaves, red buds, and large, ovoid, yellow-green to orange flowerheads.*

CULTIVATION

A position in full sun with moist, humus-rich, well-drained soil is best, and they should be watered well during the flowering season. Most species tolerate light to moderate frosts, but not repeated freezing; they tolerate salt winds and will thrive near the coast. Propagation is usually by division after flower, or from seed.

Favorites	Flower Color	Blooming Season	Flower Fragrance	Plant Height	Plant Width	Hardiness Zone	Frost Tolerance
Kniphofia caulescens	coral red, fading to yellow	late summer to mid-autumn	no	4 ft (1.2 m)	20–24 in (50–60 cm)	7–10	yes
Kniphofia ensifolia	greenish yellow, dull pink buds	late summer to winter	no	2–7 ft (0.6–2 m)	24–40 in (60–100 cm)	8–10	yes
Kniphofia linearifolia	yellow-green to orange	late summer to mid-autumn	no	4 ft (1.2 m)	32 in (80 cm)	8–10	yes
Kniphofia northiae	pale yellow	summer	no	4–6 ft (1.2–1.8 m)	36–40 in (90–100 cm)	6–10	yes
Kniphofia pumila	yellow to red	late summer to mid-autumn	no	20–32 in (50–80 cm)	12–20 in (30–50 cm)	9–11	no
Kniphofia triangularis	yellow to soft red	late summer to mid-autumn	no	36 in (90 cm)	16–24 in (40–60 cm)	8–10	yes

Top Tip

Avoid dividing until the flowers visibly decline or weaken from overcrowding. Kniphofias resent disturbance, so be prepared to wait for any new blooms after division.

LEFT Kniphofia ensifolia *has broad green leaves and tall spikes with cylindrical heads of often green-tinted white to soft yellow flowers.*

ABOVE Kniphofia caulescens *is a tough alpine species with coppery stems and dense heads of coral red flowers, which open from red buds.*

LEFT Lathyrus cyaneus *is a low spreading perennial from the Caucasus region. From late spring to early summer it bears racemes of deep lavender-blue flowers.*

Top Tip

Climbing sweet peas make equally good spillover plants for walls and banks, trailing their stems over the surface and providing a mass of color when in bloom.

LATHYRUS

Commonly known as sweet peas, vetchling, or wild peas, this genus of 110 species of annuals and perennials—distributed mainly through Eurasia, North America, and temperate South America—is the type grouping for the pea-flower subfamily of the legume (Fabaceae) family. While best known for its climbers, the genus also includes low spreaders and shrubby plants. Most species have blue-green pinnate leaves, often with a grasping tendril where the terminal leaflet would normally be located. The flowers may be solitary or clustered in racemes. Pink and purple flowers are common in the wild, though garden forms occur in a wealth of shades. Between 1850–1950, British horticulturalists were fascinated by sweet peas and introduced hundreds of cultivars.

CULTIVATION

Garden varieties are usually best grown in a sunny position with moist well-drained soil and good ventilation to reduce the risk of mildew and botrytis. Climbers need to be trained on stakes or wires. Raise the annuals from seed and the perennials from seed or by division when dormant.

Favorites	Flower Color	Blooming Season	Flower Fragrance	Plant Height	Plant Width	Hardiness Zone	Frost Tolerance
Lathyrus cyaneus	deep lavender-blue	late spring to early summer	no	12 in (30 cm)	24–40 in (60–100 cm)	6–9	yes
Lathyrus latifolius	red-purple, pink, white	summer	no	6 ft (1.8 m)	6–12 ft (1.8–3.5 m)	5–10	yes
Lathyrus odoratus	various	late winter to early summer	yes	6–8 ft (1.8–2.4 m)	2–3 ft (0.6–0.9 m)	6–11	yes
***Lathyrus odoratus* 'Anniversary'**	pink-edged white	late winter to early summer	yes	6–8 ft (1.8–2.4 m)	2–3 ft (0.6–0.9 m)	6–11	yes
***Lathyrus odoratus* 'Jilly'**	cream	late winter to early summer	yes	6–8 ft (1.8–2.4 m)	2–3 ft (0.6–0.9 m)	6–11	yes
Lathyrus vernus	purple-blue to blue-green	winter to spring	no	24 in (60 cm)	18–40 in (45–100 m)	5–9	yes

RIGHT *Heavier flowering than the species,* Lathyrus odoratus *'Jilly' is a beautiful cultivar with large, rich cream, fragrant flowers that age to creamy white.*

BELOW LEFT *The blue-green foliage of* Lathyrus odoratus *'Anniversary' is almost completely hidden when the pink-edged white flowers abound.*

BELOW *Vibrant, fragrant, and abundant—this sums up the floral component of the spectacular cultivar* Lathyrus odoratus *'Eclipse'.*

LOBELIA

LEFT Lobelia erinus *is commonly known as bedding or edging lobelia. The cultivar pictured here displays the typical mounding habit and dark green foliage.*

A member of the bellflower (Campanulaceae) family, *Lobelia* is an incredibly diverse and widespread genus of some 350 species annuals, perennials, and shrubs. Perhaps best known for the small mounding bedding annuals, with their masses of blue, purple, or white flowers, *Lobelia* also contributes to the perennial border with a large range of upright clump-forming plants that have a basal clump of simple leaves and showy terminal flower spikes—these perennial lobelias offer a wider color range than the annuals. *Lobelia* flowers have 5 lobes, the lower 3 of which are enlarged to create a lip. Often, dark-flowered forms have purple- or red-tinted foliage. Found throughout the Americas, lobelias were used extensively by Native Americans in herbal medicines and are now found in homeopathic remedies.

CULTIVATION

Lobelias generally prefer a sunny position. The hardy North American perennials will grow in fairly heavy soil; a light free-draining soil is preferable for the annuals. Tall types may need staking. Propagate annuals from seed and perennials by division or from basal cuttings.

Top Tip

As soon as the flowering spikes of lobelias have finished blooming, they should be cut back to the base—this will encourage further flowering.

RIGHT *Shrubby in habit,* Lobelia laxiflora *is a variable species, commonly known as torch lobelia for the flame-like appearance of its yellow-tipped red flowers.*

Below *The glossy leaves of* Lobelia aberdarica *cluster around a central point from which the tall flowering panicle emerges, bearing blue to white flowers.*

Right *A Chilean native,* Lobelia tupa *features gray-green leaves with a lightly felted surface. Red flowers are borne on tall flowering spikes to 6 ft (1.8 m) high.*

Favorites	Flower Color	Blooming Season	Flower Fragrance	Plant Height	Plant Width	Hardiness Zone	Frost Tolerance
Lobelia aberdarica	blue to white	summer	no	8 ft (2.4 m)	10 ft (3 m)	9–11	yes
Lobelia erinus	blue, purple, red, pink, white	spring to early autumn	no	3–8 in (8–20 cm)	12–18 in (30–45 cm)	7–11	no
Lobelia* × *gerardii	pink or violet to purple	summer	no	60 in (150 cm)	20–24 in (50–60 cm)	7–10	yes
Lobelia laxiflora	red and yellow	summer	no	3 ft (0.9 m)	3–6 ft (0.9–1.8 m)	9–11	yes
Lobelia* × *speciosa	scarlet to purple	summer to autumn	no	60 in (150 cm)	12 in (30 cm)	4–10	yes
Lobelia tupa	scarlet to red-purple	late summer to autumn	no	3–8 ft (0.9–2.4 m)	3 ft (0.9 m)	8–10	yes

MONARDA

Commonly known as bee balm, bergamot, or horsemint, the genus *Monarda* contains 16 species of annuals and perennials from North and Central America and belongs to the mint (Lamiaceae) family. The perennials disappear entirely over winter but from spring quickly develop into large dense clumps of upright angled stems. The lance-shaped leaves often have serrated edges and can be red-tinted. By early summer each stem is topped with red, pink, or purple tubular flowers backed by similarly colored leafy bracts. The genus name honors Nicholas Monardes (1493–1588), Spanish botanist and physician to Phillip II, who traveled in the Americas, and was among the first to describe tobacco use and who wrote *Joyfull Newes out of the Newe Founde Worlde*.

ABOVE *Hybridizing naturally,* Monarda didyma *and* M. fistulosa *have given rise to such lovely cultivars as the red-flowered* Monarda *'Ruby Glow'.*

RIGHT Monarda *'Cambridge Scarlet' has long been a favorite in gardens for its large, feathery, scarlet flowers that are produced over a lengthy flowering season.*

CULTIVATION

Fully hardy, these plants prefer an open sunny position in moist well-drained soil. Do not crowd the plants or mildew may be a problem in late summer. Propagate by division in late winter or from basal cuttings.

Favorites	Flower Color	Blooming Season	Flower Fragrance	Plant Height	Plant Width	Hardiness Zone	Frost Tolerance
***Monarda* 'Beauty of Cobham'**	lavender-pink	summer	no	50 in (130 cm)	20–32 in (50–80 cm)	4–9	yes
***Monarda* 'Cambridge Scarlet'**	scarlet	mid-summer to early autumn	no	36 in (90 cm)	18 in (45 cm)	4–9	yes
***Monarda* 'Croftway Pink'**	bright mid-pink	summer	no	40 in (100 cm)	20–32 in (50–80 cm)	4–9	yes
Monarda didyma	white, pink, red	mid- to late summer	no	36 in (90 cm)	18–40 in (45–100 cm)	4–9	yes
***Monarda* 'Fire Beacon'**	orange-red	summer	no	20–60 in (50–150 cm)	20–32 in (50–80 cm)	4–9	yes
***Monarda* 'Ruby Glow'**	pinkish red	summer	no	24–30 in (60–75 cm)	20–32 in (50–80 cm)	4–9	yes

RIGHT *A North American perennial,* Monarda didyma *is commonly known as bee balm or Oswego tea. A collar of red-tinted bracts surrounds the red flowers that rise on tall stems above the large leaves.*

Top Tip

Planting bee balm will encourage these winged visitors to the garden. Birds will also be attracted by the plants, as they like to feed on the nectar-rich flowers.

ABOVE *The tubular orange-red flowers of* Monarda *'Fire Beacon' bring a blaze of fiery color to the garden. The dark green leaves, up to 6 in (15 cm) long, are pleasantly aromatic.*

PAPAVER

Principally from Eurasia and North America, with a few more scattered representatives, the genus *Papaver* includes 50 species of annuals and perennials and is the type form for the poppy (Papaveraceae) family. Although diverse, poppies are usually instantly recognizable, forming a basal rosette of toothed, often hairy, light green to gray-green leaves. Their showy, long-stemmed, 4-petalled flowers open from nodding buds and are typically yellow, orange, or red, though garden forms occur in a huge color range. The blooming season ranges from late winter to mid-summer. The best known poppy is probably *Papaver rhoeas*, which we associate with war remembrance days. Formerly called the corn poppy, since World War I it has been better known as the Flanders poppy.

ABOVE *The large flowers of* Papaver orientale *'Mrs Perry' feature crape-like petals of delicate salmon pink, each marked with a distinct dark blotch near the base.*

CULTIVATION

Poppies are mostly very hardy and easily grown, preferring a position in full sun with light, moist, and well-drained soil. With the exception of fancy-flowered perennial cultivars, which are propagated by root cuttings, poppies are raised from seed.

Top Tip

Poppies die down to a papery brown mound once the flowering season is over. Trim back to improve appearance until plants are ready to resurface again.

RIGHT *Nestled among the bristly leaves, the large blooms of* Papaver orientale *'Orangeade Maison' have papery textured petals of shimmering rich orange.*

Favorites	Flower Color	Blooming Season	Flower Fragrance	Plant Height	Plant Width	Hardiness Zone	Frost Tolerance
Papaver nudicaule	white, yellow, orange, pink	winter to spring	yes	12–24 in (30–60 cm)	6–12 in (15–30 cm)	2–10	yes
Papaver orientale	pink to red; black spot at petal base	summer	no	18–36 in (45–90 cm)	12–36 in (30–90 cm)	3–9	yes
***Papaver orientale* 'Cedric Morris'**	soft pink; dark spot at petal base	summer	no	18–36 in (45–90 cm)	12–36 in (30–90 cm)	3–9	yes
Papaver rhaeticum	yellow, orange	summer	no	4 in (10 cm)	6 in (15 cm)	5–9	yes
Papaver rhoeas	bright red	summer	no	36–48 in (90–120 cm)	12–16 in (30–40 cm)	5–9	yes
Papaver somniferum	white, pink, red, purple	summer	no	24–48 in (60–120 cm)	12–24 in (30–60 cm)	7–10	yes

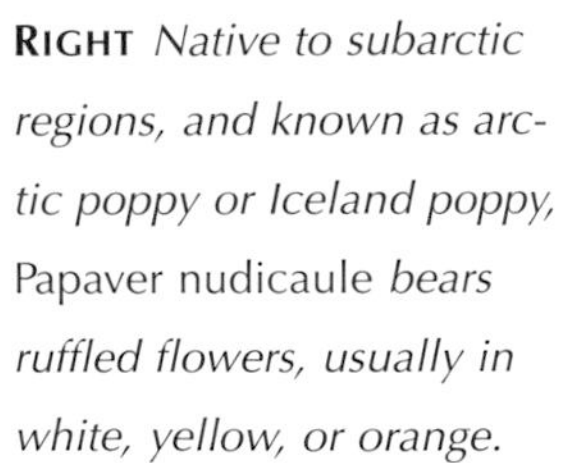

Right *Native to subarctic regions, and known as arctic poppy or Iceland poppy,* Papaver nudicaule *bears ruffled flowers, usually in white, yellow, or orange.*

Left Papaver *flowers are followed by unusual seed pods, such as these of* Papaver orientale *'Splendissimum', which can be used in fresh or dried floral arrangements.*

PELARGONIUM

Although a few occur naturally in Australia, the Middle East, and other parts of Africa, the majority of the 250 species of annuals, perennials, and subshrubs in this genus come from South Africa. Commonly known as storksbill, they belong to the geranium (Geraniaceae) family, and are a diverse lot—particularly in regard to the foliage, which is frequently lobed, often aromatic, sometimes hairy, and occasionally interestingly marked. More consistent in form are the flowers, being simple 5-petalled structures. Wild species tend to flower rather sparsely, but the garden plants often bloom profusely and are brightly colored. Aromatic types, such as the rose-scented geranium *(Pelargonium graveolens)*, yield oils used in perfumery, aromatherapy, and confectionary.

CULTIVATION

Pelargoniums are rather tender and in cool climates are treated as annuals. They need a bright sunny position with light well-drained soil and thrive in coastal gardens. Water when in growth and flower but otherwise keep dry. The annuals are propagated from seed; the perennials are propagated from cuttings.

BELOW *Growing to 16 in (40 cm) tall,* Pelargonium, *Angel, 'Black Night' has rich purple-red flowers, with a fine pale pink edge and a light-colored center.*

LEFT *Zonal pelargonium hybrids have a low bushy habit and rounded to kidney-shaped leaves. Tall stems hold the flowers above the foliage, such as in this pink- to red-flowered example, 'Gemini'.*

Top Tip

In cooler climates pelargoniums grown in containers can be enjoyed in the garden during the warmer months and then brought indoors once the weather cools.

ABOVE *Regal pelargonium hybrids feature large single or double flowers that resemble those of evergreen azaleas. 'Lord Bute' has single flowers, the pink-edged rich maroon coloring creating a velvety effect.*

LEFT *One of the Angel hybrids,* Pelargonium *'Oldbury Duet' produces flowers with upper petals colored rich deep red contrasting with the lower petals of bright pink and white.*

Favorites	Flower Color	Blooming Season	Flower Fragrance	Plant Height	Plant Width	Hardiness Zone	Frost Tolerance
Pelargonium cordifolium	purple	spring to summer	no	40 in (100 cm)	40 in (100 cm)	9–11	no
Pelargonium fruticosum	white to pink	spring to autumn	no	12–16 in (30–40 cm)	16–20 in (40–50 cm)	9–11	no
***Pelargonium*, Angel**	pink, purple, red, white	spring to summer	no	10–18 in (25–45 cm)	12–18 in (30–45 cm)	9–11	no
***Pelargonium*, Dwarf**	white, pink, orange, red	spring to summer	no	8 in (20 cm)	8 in (20 cm)	9–11	no
***Pelargonium*, Ivy-leafed**	white, pink, red, purple	spring to autumn	no	8–36 in (20–90 cm)	12–36 in (30–90 cm)	9–11	no
***Pelargonium*, Miniature**	white, pink, orange, red	spring to autumn	no	6 in (15 cm)	6 in (15 cm)	9–11	no
***Pelargonium*, Regal**	white, purple, pink to red	late spring to summer	no	24 in (60 cm)	36–60 in (90–150 cm)	9–11	no
Pelargonium*, Regal, *'Rembrandt'	purple; mauve-pink edged	late spring to summer	no	24 in (60 cm)	36–60 in (90–150 cm)	9–11	no
***Pelargonium*, Scented-leafed**	white, pink, purple	spring to early summer	no	12–36 in (30–90 cm)	12–36 in (30–90 cm)	9–11	no
***Pelargonium*, Stellar**	white, pink, orange, red	spring to summer	no	12–30 in (30–75 cm)	12–24 in (30–60 cm)	9–11	no
***Pelargonium*, Unique**	white, pink, red, purple, orange	spring to early summer	no	18 in (45 cm)	18 in (45 cm)	9–11	no
***Pelargonium*, Zonal**	red, pink, white, orange, cream	spring to autumn	no	24–48 in (60–120 cm)	18–36 in (45–90 cm)	9–11	no

Left *Prized as much for its aromatic foliage as it is for its superb pink flowers with dramatic dark markings,* Pelargonium *'Orsett' is a Scented-leafed hybrid.*
Below right *With large single flowers of vivid pink, intensifying in color toward the petal base, and rich green fragrant foliage,* Pelargonium *'Bolero' is one of the Unique hybrids.*

Right *Small in stature, big on impact, the Dwarf hybrid* Pelargonium *'Beryl Read' bears pink flowers, marked with red near the petal base.*
Below Pelargonium *'Delli', a Regal hybrid, has lovely, large, heavily ruffled, pink-and-white flowers.*

Above Pelargonium fruticosum, *a low-spreading South African perennial, produces dainty starry flowers of white to pink, often with red basal markings.*

LEFT *One of the Scented-leafed hybrids,* Pelargonium *'Sweet Mimosa' not only bears aromatic foliage, but also features dainty flowers of soft pink.*

BELOW *With large heads of ruffled double flowers in light to dark shades of rose amid a backdrop of light green lobed leaves,* Pelargonium *'Melody' is one of the Zonal hybrids.*

PENSTEMON

ABOVE *A Californian native,* Penstemon heterophyllus *is known as foothills penstemon. It features slender leaves and lavender-pink to bright blue flowers.*
BELOW *Growing up to 3 ft (0.9 m) tall, compact in habit, and bearing large, white-throated, purple-red flowers,* Penstemon *'Maurice Gibbs' is an ideal plant for the perennial border.*

Found mainly in the Americas from Alaska to Guatemala, the 250 species of perennials and subshrubs in this genus—a member of the foxglove (Scrophulariaceae) family—range from tiny carpeting plants to rapid growers that can exceed 4 ft (1.2 m) tall. Most develop into a mounding clump of erect stems with simple linear to lance-shaped leaves. Spikes of 5-lobed, foxglove-like flowers open at the stem tips in summer. In recent years many new garden varieties have become available, generally with increased hardiness. Several species were used by Native Americans, primarily for their analgesic and styptic properties but also to control stomach disorders.

CULTIVATION

Penstemons are best grown in full or half-sun with moist well-drained soil. Alpine species and those from southwestern USA often prefer gritty soil. Gardeners in cold areas should try the new hardy types. While the species may be raised from seed, garden penstemons are usually propagated by division or from cuttings of non-flowering stems.

Top Tip

Penstemon cultivars are mostly good all-round performers, but are particularly suited to border planting, rock gardens, or "wild" gardens.

Left *A perennial from Arizona and New Mexico in the USA, and neighboring parts of Mexico,* Penstemon pinifolius *produces orange-red flowers.*
Below *With pretty purple-red flowers during summer,* Penstemon *'Rich Ruby' was bred for hardiness—like many hybrid cultivars, it is frost tolerant.*

Favorites	Flower Color	Blooming Season	Flower Fragrance	Plant Height	Plant Width	Hardiness Zone	Frost Tolerance
***Penstemon* 'Blackbird'**	dark purple	summer	no	36 in (90 cm)	36 in (90 cm)	6–10	yes
Penstemon eatonii	scarlet	spring to summer	no	12–36 in (30–90 cm)	8–24 in (20–60 cm)	4–9	yes
Penstemon heterophyllus	lavender-pink to bright blue	summer	no	12–20 in (30–50 cm)	8–12 in (20–30 cm)	8–10	yes
***Penstemon* 'Maurice Gibbs'**	purple-red	spring to autumn	no	36 in (90 cm)	8–16 in (20–40 cm)	6–10	yes
Penstemon pinifolius	orange-red	late spring to mid-summer	no	6–16 in (15–40 cm)	18 in (45 cm)	8–10	yes
***Penstemon* 'Rich Ruby'**	purple-red	summer	no	36 in (90 cm)	8–16 in (20–40 cm)	6–10	yes

Top Tip

Planted in full sun, petunias put on a superb floral display. If planted in shade, the lush foliage will flourish but fewer flowers will be produced.

ABOVE *The Storm Series cultivars of* Petunia × hybrida, *such as the pink-flowered 'Storm Pink Morn', have been bred for improved weather resistance.*

BELOW Petunia × hybrida, *Mirage Series, 'Mirage Red' features large single flowers of lipstick red. Many of the flowers in this series feature dark veining on the petals.*

PETUNIA

Think of the fancy garden petunias and it may be difficult to imagine them as members of the nightshade (Solanaceae) family, but they are, though more closely allied to tobacco *(Nicotiana)*. There are some 35 species in this tropical South American genus, and most are low spreading plants with simple, rounded, downy leaves and large 5-lobed flowers. The wild species are often aromatic, with scented flowers, but as is often the case the fancy garden forms have lost these charms. However, they compensate with an abundance of blooms and a wealth of color. Modern petunias are remarkably tough plants—their flowers are weather resistant and in mild climates many will flower year-round.

CULTIVATION

Plant in full sun with moist well-drained soil and deadhead frequently to keep the plants flowering. The very fancy double- and large-flowered forms are seed-raised, but the perennial forms will grow from cuttings.

Favorites	Flower Color	Blooming Season	Flower Fragrance	Plant Height	Plant Width	Hardiness Zone	Frost Tolerance
Petunia × *hybrida*	various	summer	no	4–16 in (10–40 cm)	8–40 in (20–100 cm)	9–11	no
Petunia × *hybrida*, Fantasy Series	various	spring to summer	no	10–12 in (25–30 cm)	10–12 in (25–30 cm)	9–11	no
Petunia × *hybrida*, Mirage Series	various	summer	no	4–16 in (10–40 cm)	8–40 cm (20–100 cm)	9–11	no
Petunia × *hybrida*, Storm Series	purple, pink	summer	no	12 in (30 cm)	12–15 in (30–38 cm)	9–11	no
Petunia × *hybrida*, Surfinia Series	purple, pink, mauve, blue	summer	no	4–6 in (10–15 cm)	8–48 in (20–120 cm)	9–11	no
Petunia integrifolia	violet; purple-pink interior	late spring to late autumn	no	12–24 in (30–60 cm)	24 in (60 cm)	9–11	no

RIGHT *An Argentinian species,* Petunia integrifolia *is often treated as an annual. Throughout summer it produces dainty violet flowers that are purple-pink within.*
BELOW *Throughout the flowering season,* Petunia × hybrida, *Surfinia Series, Surfinia Blue Vein/'Sunsolos' produces abundant mauve flowers, attractively marked with darker veins.*

Phlox

Top Tip

After flowering, phlox plants should be trimmed back to remove all spent flowers. Thin out overcrowded plants at the same time to encourage healthy vigorous growth next season.

This North American genus containing 67 species of annuals and perennials belongs to the phlox (Polemoniaceae) family. They are a variable group, ranging from carpeting rockery ground covers through wiry-stemmed trailers to large bushy perennials with strongly erect stems. Their foliage differs markedly too: from tiny linear leaves to lance-shaped dark green foliage over 4 in (10 cm) long. All, however, produce showy heads of small long-tubed flowers with 5 widely flared lobes. Pink to purple and white are the predominant flower colors, and the blooming season ranges from spring to autumn depending on the species.

Cultivation

Plant *Phlox* species in full sun or half-shade. Rockery phloxes and those grown in hanging baskets prefer a fairly light soil. Border phloxes need a heavier, more humus-rich soil and may need staking. They also need good ventilation to prevent late-season mildew. Depending on the growth form, *Phlox* species are propagated from seed or cuttings, or by division.

Top *With a mat-forming growth habit, colorful pink flowers, and downy leaves,* Phlox douglasii *'Crackerjack' will add color and texture to the rock garden.*

Above right Phlox subulata, *commonly known as moss phlox or mountain phlox, has given rise to many cultivars. 'Bonita', seen here, is a splendid example, with small glossy leaves and abundant pale lavender flowers.*

Favorites	Flower Color	Blooming Season	Flower Fragrance
Phlox carolina	pink, purple	spring to early summer	no
Phlox divaricata	blue, lavender, white	spring	yes
Phlox douglasii	pink, red, mauve, purple	spring to early summer	yes
Phlox drummondii	pink, red, purple, cream	summer to autumn	yes
Phlox paniculata	pink to red, purple, white	summer to autumn	yes
Phlox subulata	pink, lavender-blue, white	late spring to early summer	no

ABOVE Phlox carolina *'Bill Baker' reaches a height of 18 in (45 cm). This compact plant features glossy leathery leaves and attractive, large, pink to mauve flowers.*

Plant Height	Plant Width	Hardiness Zone	Frost Tolerance
48 in (120 cm)	16–24 in (40–60 cm)	5–10	yes
15 in (38 cm)	20–40 in (50–100 cm)	4–9	yes
2–6 in (5–15 cm)	12–20 in (30–50 cm)	5–10	yes
6–15 in (15–38 cm)	8–16 in (20–40 cm)	6–10	yes
24–48 in (60–120 cm)	16–36 in (40–90 cm)	4–9	yes
2–4 in (5–10 cm)	12–30 in (30–75 cm)	3–9	yes

ABOVE *A perennial from eastern USA,* Phlox paniculata *is known as annual or summer phlox. 'Tenor', with its eye-catching reddish pink flowers, is just one of many cultivars.*

PHYGELIUS

BELOW *Slender sturdy stems, often towering up to 3 ft (0.9 m) in height, carry the soft green leaves and pendent pale yellow flowers of* Phygelius aequalis *'Yellow Trumpet'.*

RIGHT Phygelius × rectus *is a cross of garden origin. 'Moonraker', with dark green foliage, displays clusters of tubular, creamy yellow flowers in late summer.*

This South African genus of evergreen perennials or subshrubs is a member of the foxglove (Scrophulariaceae) family. Although there are just 2 species, they have been hybridized and extensively developed to produce a range of garden forms. They are upright to slightly sprawling plants with serrated, lance-shaped to pointed oval leaves. Throughout the warmer months they bear open heads of pendent tubular flowers in shades of yellow, pink, orange, or red. The name *Phygelius* is derived from Greek and means "to flee the sun," which is not all that appropriate for plants such as these that often need a little extra warmth in cool climates.

RIGHT *With flowers that resemble those of fuchsias,* Phygelius aequalis *sends up tall stems of dusky pink blooms, accompanied by soft bright green leaves.*

CULTIVATION

These plants are tolerant of occasional moderate frosts but likely to suffer in cool wet winters, though they can re-shoot if cut to the ground by frost. Plant in half-sun with humus-rich, fertile, well-drained soil. Water and feed well when in active growth and during flowering. They are propagated from cuttings of non-flowering stems.

Top Tip

In favorable conditions, *Phygelius* plants are ideal for border planting, adding height and color to the landscape. Trim after flowering to maintain appearance.

ABOVE *The clusters of pendent, tubular, flesh pink flowers of* Phygelius aequalis *'Trewidden Pink' top the 3 ft (0.9 m) tall leafy stems during late summer.*

Favorites	Flower Color	Blooming Season	Flower Fragrance	Plant Height	Plant Width	Hardiness Zone	Frost Tolerance
Phygelius aequalis	dusky pink	late summer	no	3 ft (0.9 m)	3 ft (0.9 m)	8–10	yes
***Phygelius aequalis* 'Yellow Trumpet'**	pale yellow	late summer	no	3 ft (0.9 m)	3 ft (0.9 m)	8–11	yes
Phygelius capensis	orange	summer to autumn	no	6 ft (1.8 m)	2 ft (0.6 m)	8–10	yes
Phygelius* × *rectus	red, orange, yellow	late summer	no	4 ft (1.2 m)	4 ft (1.2 m)	8–10	yes
***Phygelius* × *rectus* 'African Queen'**	orange	late summer	no	4 ft (1.2 m)	4 ft (1.2 m)	8–10	yes
***Phygelius* × *rectus* 'Devil's Tears'**	red	late summer	no	4 ft (1.2 m)	4 ft (1.2 m)	8–10	yes

PRIMULA

Encompassing around 400 species of perennials with a mainly Northern Hemisphere temperate zone distribution, *Primula* is the type genus for the primrose (Primulaceae) family and takes its name from the Italian for spring, *primavera*. The name is appropriate for these harbingers of spring that can be found brightening woodlands, rockeries, and annual beds in winter and early spring. Most primulas develop a basal foliage rosette of sometimes downy or heavily veined leaves. The flower stems, from 1–2 in (2.5–5 cm) to over 3 ft (0.9 m) tall depending on the species, emerge from the center of the rosette and carry 5-petalled flowers in a wide array of colors. Primulas have a minor role in herbal medicines but should not be confused with evening primrose (*Oenothera* species).

CULTIVATION

Primulas are usually most at home in deciduous woodland with dappled light and cool, moist, humus-rich, well-drained soil. Bog or candelabra primroses prefer wetter conditions. Propagate from seed or by division of well-established clumps when dormant.

RIGHT *Glamorous heads of creamy-centered purple-red flowers, with lighter coloring at the petal edges, top the stems of* Primula auricula *'Jeannie Telford'.*

ABOVE *A rosette-forming species from China,* Primula forrestii *has leaves with hairy upper surfaces. The dainty lobed flowers are bright yellow with a collar of leafy bracts.*

BELOW *One of the Pruhonicensis Hybrids,* Primula *'Ken Dearman' features fragrant double flowers in stunning shades of apricot and orange.*

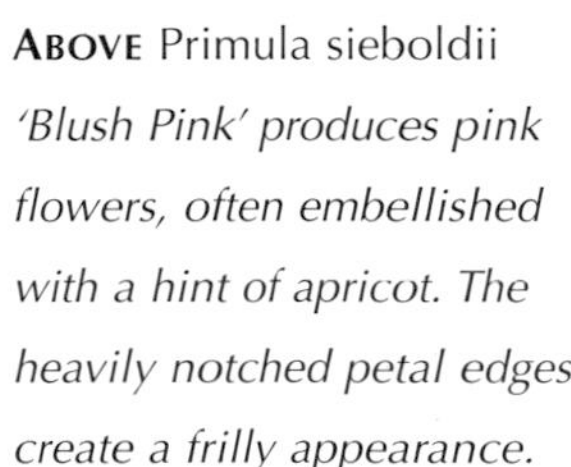

ABOVE Primula sieboldii *'Blush Pink' produces pink flowers, often embellished with a hint of apricot. The heavily notched petal edges create a frilly appearance.*

Top Tip

While there are primroses suited to many different applications and garden conditions, they all appreciate the establishment of a regular watering routine.

Favorites	Flower Color	Blooming Season	Flower Fragrance	Plant Height	Plant Width	Hardiness Zone	Frost Tolerance
Primula auricula	various	spring to mid-summer	yes	3–8 in (8–20 cm)	6–16 in (15–40 cm)	3–9	yes
Primula denticulata	pink to purple	early to mid-spring	no	12 in (30 cm)	10–18 in (25–45 cm)	6–9	yes
Primula forrestii	bright yellow	spring to summer	no	24 in (60 cm)	18 in (45 cm)	6–9	yes
***Primula* 'Inverewe'**	bright orange-red	spring to summer	no	24–36 in (60–90 cm)	12–20 in (30–50 cm)	6–9	yes
Primula sieboldii	white, pink, purple	spring to early summer	no	12 in (30 cm)	12–24 in (30–60 cm)	5–9	yes
***Primula,* Pruhonicensis Hybrids**	various	spring to summer	no	4–12 in (10–30 cm)	6–16 in (15–40 cm)	7–9	yes

RIGHT Salvia microphylla *'Huntington Red' is very easy to grow. Its bright scarlet flowers are borne on a bushy perennial plant with mid-green leaves.*

SALVIA

At around 900 species, *Salvia* is the largest genus in the mint (Lamiaceae) family. Though more than half the species are native to the Americas, the genus has a distribution that is almost worldwide. The plants range from small annuals to large shrubby perennials and encompass a wide variety of foliage types, including several species with heavily felted silver-gray leaves. All bear their flowers in upright spikes, often with whorls of blooms around the stem. The flowers are usually small but abundant and often downy, with conspicuous lips, and although best-known for the red- and blue-flowered bedders, *Salvia* includes most flower colors. The common name for the genus is sage, and while the use of the herb sage *(Salvia officinalis)* hardly needs describing, other species also have culinary and medicinal applications.

Top Tip

For the best results at flowering time, prune shrubby perennial *Salvia* plants in late winter or early spring to remove straggly, bare, and frost-damaged stems.

CULTIVATION

With such a diverse genus it is difficult to give general guidelines. Most species, however, prefer a sunny position with moist, humus-rich, well-drained soil. Hardiness varies considerably and many are tender. Propagate from seed or softwood cuttings.

RIGHT *The tall flower spikes of* Salvia indica *rise in spring from a mound of gray leaves with scalloped margins. The plant may die down during the warmer months.*

LEFT *Also known as common or garden sage,* Salvia officinalis *has aromatic leaves that have been used for centuries for medicinal and culinary purposes.*

ABOVE Salvia microphylla *is a variable species, and flowers can appear in pink, red, or deep purple shades. The species is native to southern USA and Mexico.*

Favorites	Flower Color	Blooming Season	Flower Fragrance	Plant Height	Plant Width	Hardiness Zone	Frost Tolerance
Salvia buchananii	magenta	summer to autumn	no	12–20 in (30–50 cm)	12 in (30 cm)	10–11	no
Salvia elegans	bright red	late summer to autumn	no	4–6 ft (1.2–1.8 m)	3–6 ft (0.9–1.8 m)	9–11	no
Salvia guaranitica	blue	early summer to autumn	no	4–5 ft (1.2–1.5 m)	16–27 in (40–70 cm)	8–11	yes
Salvia indica	purple and white	spring	no	24–36 in (60–90 cm)	24 in (60 cm)	9–11	no
Salvia microphylla	pink, red, deep purple	summer to autumn	no	4 ft (1.2 m)	3 ft (0.9 m)	8–11	yes
Salvia officinalis	white to pink and purple	summer	no	18–30 in (45–75 cm)	24–36 in (60–90 cm)	5–10	yes

SOLENOSTEMON

This genus of around 60 species of shrubby, sometimes succulent perennials from the tropics of Asia and Africa is known in cultivation through just a few of its members, of which only the coleus or painted nettle *(Solenostemon scutellarioides)* is common. A member of the mint (Lamiaceae) family, *Solenostemon* includes several other species with interestingly colored foliage, although they have never become popular with gardeners. The flowers are usually small and white, cream, or blue in color, and would be easily overlooked except that they are borne in short spikes.

ABOVE Solenostemon scutellarioides *'Display' is just one of the many cultivars developed from this tropical species, which was formerly known as* Coleus scutellarioides.

CULTIVATION

Solenostemon species are generally tender and need winter protection outside the subtropics. They are grown outdoors in cooler climates, but only as summer annuals. Plant in sun or half-shade with moist well-drained soil. To keep the foliage lush, pinch out flower spikes as they develop. The plants may be propagated from seed, though cuttings strike so easily that this is not usually necessary.

BELOW *The ornamental foliage of* Solenostemon scutellarioides *has been popular since Victorian times. 'Winsley Tapestry' looks at its best when grown en masse.*

Top Tip

Coleus perennials can be used as accent plants in garden beds, borders, baskets, and pots, as massed displays, and as colorful house plants.

Favorites	Flower Color	Blooming Season	Flower Fragrance	Plant Height	Plant Width	Hardiness Zone	Frost Tolerance
Solenostemon scutellarioides	white, blue	summer to autumn	no	12–36 in (30–90 cm)	12–24 in (30–60 cm)	10–12	no
***Solenostemon scutellarioides* 'Black Dragon'**	white, blue	late spring to early autumn	no	12–18 in (30–45 cm)	6–8 in (15–20 cm)	10–12	no
***Solenostemon scutellarioides* 'Crimson Ruffles'**	white, blue	summer to autumn	no	12–36 in (30–90 cm)	12–24 in (30–60 cm)	10–12	no
***Solenostemon scutellarioides* 'Display'**	white, blue	summer to autumn	no	12–36 in (30–90 cm)	12–24 in (30–60 cm)	10–12	no
***Solenostemon scutellarioides* 'Walter Turner'**	white, blue	summer to autumn	no	12–36 in (30–90 cm)	12–24 in (30–60 cm)	10–12	no
***Solenostemon scutellarioides* 'Winsley Tapestry'**	white, blue	summer to autumn	no	12–36 in (30–90 cm)	12–24 in (30–60 cm)	10–12	no

LEFT *A lower-growing cultivar,* Solenostemon scutellarioides *'Black Dragon' has very striking markings, and does best in partial shade.*

ABOVE *A number of cultivars of* Solenostemon scutellarioides *have ruffled leaves. 'Crimson Ruffles' has bright markings along the main leaf veins.*

LEFT Tagetes, *Safari Series, 'Safari Scarlet' has 3 in (8 cm) wide anemone-type flowers. This series of French marigolds is mainly derived from* Tagetes patula.
BELOW *The Little Hero Series of* Tagetes, *such as 'Little Hero Yellow', are small-growing types. The flowers are 2 in (5 cm) wide and come in a variety of colors.*

TAGETES

A genus of some 50 species of annuals and perennials, it belongs to the daisy (Asteraceae) family. Almost all are found naturally in the American tropics and subtropics, which may seem a little strange when the garden forms are commonly known as African or French marigolds, but such are the mysteries of common names. Marigolds have aromatic, dark green, pinnate leaves and, apart from the very compact single-flowered forms, they tend to be upright plants with sturdy stems. Although the flowers may be typically daisy-like, they are often so fully double that the disc florets are hidden. Yellow, orange, and brownish red are the usual colors. Marigolds are edible and the flowers yield a yellow dye that is sometimes used as a saffron substitute.

CULTIVATION

Plant in a sunny position with light well-drained soil. Water and feed well for lush foliage and abundant flowers. Also, deadhead frequently to keep the plants blooming. Propagate from seed, either sown in situ in warm soil or started indoors in cooler climates.

Favorites	Flower Color	Blooming Season	Flower Fragrance
Tagetes 'Jolly Jester'	red and yellow	late spring to autumn	no
Tagetes 'Naughty Marietta'	yellow and red	summer to autumn	no
Tagetes tenuifolia	yellow	summer to autumn	no
Tagetes, Antigua Series	yellow, gold, orange	late spring to autumn	no
Tagetes, Little Hero Series	yellow, red, orange	late spring to autumn	no
Tagetes, Safari Series	yellow, red, orange	late spring to early autumn	no

Top Tip

Planting marigolds is thought to repel both aboveground insects and nematodes attacking plant roots. This has not yet been verified, but may be worth a try.

ABOVE *The pompon-like flowers of* Tagetes, *Antigua Series, 'Antigua Gold' are 3 in (8 cm) wide, and are carried above the leaves in a spectacular display.*

Plant Height	Plant Width	Hardiness Zone	Frost Tolerance
24 in (60 cm)	24 in (60 cm)	9–12	no
10 in (25 cm)	8 in (20 cm)	9–12	no
12–24 in (30–60 cm)	8–12 in (20–30 cm)	9–12	no
10–12 in (25–30 cm)	12–18 in (30–45 cm)	9–12	no
6–8 in (15–20 cm)	6 in (15 cm)	9–12	no
8–12 in (20–30 cm)	8 in (20 cm)	9–12	no

ABOVE *The harlequin-like yellow stripes on red petals give* Tagetes *'Jolly Jester' its name. The bushy plants bear an abundance of flowers which last well in the vase.*

TRICYRTIS

BELOW *The orchid-like flowers of* Tricyrtis formosana *open from maroon or brown buds and are borne in terminal clusters. This species is native to Taiwan.*

Found from the eastern Himalayas to Japan, Taiwan, and the Philippine Islands, the 16 species of herbaceous perennials in this genus belong in the lily-of-the-valley (Convallariaceae) family. They are mainly woodland perennials but may also be sometimes found in mountainous areas and on cliffsides. They form clumps of arching stems clothed with often glossy, pointed lance-shaped leaves. The waxy, widely flared bell- or trumpet-shaped flowers are often attractively marked, despite the common name of toad lily. They appear from late summer to late autumn, depending on the species. In Japan, the young leaves and shoots of the native species were cooked and eaten.

RIGHT *Easy to grow and fast growing,* Tricyrtis affinis *has large, broadly oval leaves and unusually colored flowers. It does best in full to part-shade.*

BELOW Tricyrtis macropoda *has small flowers (seen here in bud), but its elegant clumps of erect stems and slightly heart-shaped leaves are very attractive.*

CULTIVATION

These hardy plants are usually best grown in woodland conditions with cool, moist, well-drained, humus-rich soil and dappled shade. Plants may be divided when dormant, though rather than disturb well-established clumps it is often best just to remove a few offsets from the side. They may also be raised from seed.

Top Tip

Tricyrtis species are useful plants for a shady border where their flowers are very welcome late in the growing season. Some cultivars have variegated foliage.

Favorites	Flower Color	Blooming Season	Flower Fragrance	Plant Height	Plant Width	Hardiness Zone	Frost Tolerance
Tricyrtis affinis	white and purple-pink	mid-summer to autumn	no	36 in (90 cm)	24 in (60 cm)	5–9	yes
Tricyrtis formosana	white, pale lilac, and purple-pink	mid-summer to autumn	no	36 in (90 cm)	18 in (45 cm)	5–9	yes
Tricyrtis hirta	white and dark purple	autumn	no	36 in (90 cm)	24 in (60 cm)	4–9	yes
Tricyrtis macropoda	lavender and purple	summer	no	30 in (75 cm)	24 in (60 cm)	5–9	yes
Tricyrtis ohsumiensis	yellow	early autumn	no	20 in (50 cm)	10 in (25 cm)	5–9	yes
***Tricyrtis* 'Tojen'**	white and pale lilac to pink	autumn	no	36 in (90 cm)	20 in (50 cm)	5–9	yes

RIGHT *The striking appearance of* Tricyrtis hirta *makes it one of the most popular* Tricyrtis *species. It spreads slowly, and is known as the hairy toad lily because the stems are slightly hairy.*

TROPAEOLUM

Found from southern Mexico to Tierra del Fuego in South America's far south, this genus has over 80 species of annuals and perennials. Known as canary bird vine, flame creeper, and nasturtium, it belongs to the nasturtium (Tropaeolaceae) family. Some climb using their twining leaf stalks, others, especially the small cultivars of *Tropaeolum majus*, are used as bedding plants. Their foliage, which is often blue-green, is variable and may be many-lobed, trifoliate, or shield-shaped. The long-spurred flowers occur mainly in shades of yellow, orange, and red and have 5 petals. Many of the species with large tubers were cultivated like potatoes in South America, and nasturtium flowers are widely used as a colorful garnish.

CULTIVATION

While hardiness varies, most species are easily cultivated—sometimes too easily, as they may become invasive. Plant in full or half-sun with moist well-drained soil and trim occasionally. Propagate by division when dormant, from basal cuttings, or from seed.

LEFT Tropaeolum majus *'Whirlibird Cherry Rose' is a very free-flowering dwarf cultivar. The vividly colored semi-double flowers contrast well with the green foliage.*
BELOW *The edible bright lemon yellow flowers and the leaves of* Tropaeolum majus *'Gleaming Lemons' can add color and peppery flavor to a summer salad.*

Top Tip

Nasturtiums are excellent plants for young gardeners. The large seeds are easy to handle, and the plants develop rapidly after sowing, producing big bright flowers.

ABOVE LEFT Tropaeolum majus *'Peach Schnapps' has pinkish orange flowers with dark orange veining, and delightfully marbled leaves. It can be used as a ground cover and in containers.*
LEFT Tropaeolum tricolor *is a colorful trailer or climber from Bolivia and Chile. The flowers have short yellow or cream petals and long, upturned, black-tipped spurs.*

Favorites	Flower Color	Blooming Season	Flower Fragrance	Plant Height	Plant Width	Hardiness Zone	Frost Tolerance
Tropaeolum ciliatum	golden yellow	summer	no	20 ft (6 m)	20 ft (6 m)	8–10	yes
Tropaeolum majus	yellow, orange, red	summer to autumn	no	8–24 in (20–60 cm)	36 in (90 cm)	8–11	no
***Tropaeolum majus*, Alaska Series**	cream, red, orange yellow	summer to autumn	no	12 in (30 cm)	18 in (45 cm)	8–11	no
***Tropaeolum majus*, Jewel Series**	red and yellow	spring to autumn	no	12 in (30 cm)	18 in (45 cm)	8–11	no
Tropaeolum polyphyllum	yellow to orange	summer	no	2–3 in (5–8 cm)	36 in (90 cm)	8–11	yes
Tropaeolum tricolor	cream to yellow and red and black	spring to autumn	no	7 ft (2 m)	7 ft (2 m)	8–11	no

VERBENA

This genus in the vervain (Verbenaceae) family contains 250 species of annuals, perennials, and subshrubs native to tropical and subtropical America. Bringing a welcome splash of color to the garden, these plants feature clusters of sometimes fragrant, tubular, lobed flowers in vibrant shades of purple, pink, red, and white. With a sprawling to erect habit, they make ideal candidates for hanging baskets, ground covers, or for use in borders. The small bright green to dark green leaves are variously divided. The genus is commonly known as vervain, derived from the Celtic *ferfaen* meaning "to drive away a stone"—a reference to the use of *Verbena officinalis* as a cure for bladder infections. It was also a supposed aphrodisiac and cure-all for problems ranging from snakebites to heart disease.

CULTIVATION

These colorful additions to the garden do best in full sun in moderately fertile, moist, but well-drained soil. Annuals can be propagated from seed, while perennials can be propagated from seed, cuttings, or by division.

Favorites	Flower Color	Blooming Season	Flower Fragrance
Verbena bonariensis	purple	mid-summer to autumn	no
***Verbena* 'Homestead Purple'**	purple	summer to autumn	no
Verbena rigida	purple to magenta	spring to autumn	no
***Verbena* 'Sissinghurst'**	magenta-pink	spring to autumn	no
***Verbena* 'Temari Bright Pink'**	bright pink	summer to autumn	no
Verbena tenuisecta	lilac, mauve, purple, blue, white	spring	no

ABOVE LEFT Verbena *'Temari Bright Pink' produces large, brightly colored flowerheads over a long period, as well as dense mats of dark green, fern-like foliage.*

BELOW *The tiny flowers of* Verbena bonariensis *appear in flat-topped clusters above sparse, lance-shaped, serrated leaves. This plant is native to South America.*

Plant Height	Plant Width	Hardiness Zone	Frost Tolerance
3–5 ft (0.9–1.5 m)	2 ft (0.6 m)	7–10	yes
8 in (20 cm)	36 in (90 cm)	7–10	yes
24–36 in (60–90 cm)	12 in (30 cm)	8–10	yes
8 in (20 cm)	36 in (90 cm)	7–10	yes
8 in (20 cm)	36 in (90 cm)	7–10	yes
12 in (30 cm)	12–20 in (30–50 cm)	9–11	no

ABOVE RIGHT *Sprawling* Verbena tenuisecta *is also known as moss verbena. Its stems are aromatic, and the flower spikes can be white, mauve, purple, or blue.*

RIGHT Verbena *'Homestead Purple' is a very vigorous grower and flowers prolifically over a long season. This hybrid is thought to have occurred by chance.*

Top Tip

Most prostrate *Verbena* species are fast growing, so they are an excellent choice as a colorful ground cover for an unsightly bare patch in the garden.

VIOLA

LEFT Viola *'Ultima Baron Red' has abundant, red, medium-sized flowers, about $2\frac{1}{2}$ in (6 cm) wide, and a compact habit. This hybrid cultivar is part of the Ultima Series, which comes in a wide range of colors.*

Viola belongs to the violet (Violaceae) family, and encompasses around 500 species of annuals, perennials, and subshrubs with an almost worldwide temperate distribution. Also known as violets, pansies, and heartsease, most form small clumps of lobed, elliptical, kidney- or heart-shaped leaves with sometimes sweetly scented 5-petalled flowers, the lower petal of which often bears darker markings. Among the species, white, yellow, and purple are the predominant flower colors, but cultivated violets can be found in every shade. Violet fragrance has long been a favorite with the perfume industry, but at over 100 lb (45 kg) of flowers per fluid ounce (30 ml) of essence it is no surprise that synthetics have now largely replaced natural oil.

CULTIVATION

Tough and adaptable, most violets are natural woodland plants, preferring semi-shade and moist humus-rich soil, though the alpines need a little more grit, and the bedding hybrids flower best in brighter positions. Depending on the growth form, propagation is from seed, by division, or from basal cuttings.

LEFT *Banner Series violas are vigorous plants giving a massed display of mainly bright clear colors.* Viola *'Banner Violet with Blotch' is an attractive representative of the series.*

Top Tip

Violas are very useful in the garden, making excellent accent plants, ground covers, mass plantings, borders, and container plants.

Favorites	Flower Color	Blooming Season	Flower Fragrance	Plant Height	Plant Width	Hardiness Zone	Frost Tolerance
Viola **'Banner Violet with Blotch'**	purple and black	summer	no	6–12 in (15–30 cm)	8–16 in (20–40 cm)	7–10	yes
Viola cornuta	violet	late spring to summer	no	6–12 in (15–30 cm)	8–15 in (20–38 cm)	7–10	yes
Viola **'Crystal Bowl True Blue'**	violet-blue	late spring to summer	no	5–12 in (12–30 cm)	8–12 in (20–30 cm)	7–10	yes
Viola **'Joker Poker Face'**	orange, purple, and black	spring to autumn	no	6–8 in (15–20 cm)	8 in (20 cm)	7–10	yes
Viola pedata	orange	early spring to early summer	no	2–6 in (5–15 cm)	4–8 in (10–20 cm)	7–10	yes
Viola **'Ultima Baron Red'**	deep red and yellow	spring	no	6–8 in (15–20 cm)	8 in (20 cm)	7–10	yes

LEFT *Poker Series cultivars of* Viola *bear boldly patterned mid-sized flowers. 'Joker Poker Face' is orange with black blotch and purple edges.*

BELOW Viola *'Crystal Bowl True Blue' is a compact hybrid plant that tolerates heat well. The small clear violet-blue flowers are about 2 in (5 cm) wide.*

ZINNIA

Centered around Mexico but native to the area from south-central USA to Argentina, the genus *Zinnia* includes some 20 species of annuals, perennials, and small shrubs belonging to the daisy (Asteraceae) family. Most species have soft, downy, light green leaves and simple daisy-like flowers, often in yellow, orange, red, or pink shades. Modern garden zinnias are an example of the plant breeders's art, extending the color range of the species enormously and turning those simple daisies into very fancy flowers. The genus name honors Johann Gottfried Zinn (1727–1759), who first described the genus. He was also a physician, and the "ligament of Zinn" was first noted in his 1755 monograph on the eye.

BELOW Zinnia angustifolia *'Coral Beauty' bears its vivid flowers on a 3 ft (0.9 m) tall plant. The profusion of blooms looks stunning in a massed planting.*

CULTIVATION

Zinnias prefer full sun, long warm summers, and freedom from cold drafts and sudden weather changes. In suitable conditions few other flowers can make such a prolonged display. The soil should be light and well-drained. Deadhead frequently and use liquid fertilizers to ensure continued blooming and steady growth.

ABOVE *Excellent for cutting, the flowers of* Zinnia elegans, *Oklahoma Series, 'Oklahoma Pink' are semi-double, $1\frac{1}{2}$ in (35 mm) wide, and are borne on sturdy stems.*

LEFT Zinnia peruviana *'Yellow Peruvian' (syn. 'Bonita Yellow') grows to about 2 ft (0.6 m) tall, and bears single, 1 in (25 mm) wide flowers that fade to a soft gold color.*

Top Tip

Cutting zinnias regularly will not only prolong the blooming time and encourage branching, but also supply brightly colored cut flowers that last well in the vase.

RIGHT *The award-winning* Zinnia elegans *'Profusion Orange' is very easy to grow, and bears abundant 2–3 in (5–8 cm) wide flowers.*

Favorites	Flower Color	Blooming Season	Flower Fragrance	Plant Height	Plant Width	Hardiness Zone	Frost Tolerance
Zinnia angustifolia	orange	summer	no	8–16 in (20–40 cm)	12–20 in (30–50 cm)	9–11	no
Zinnia elegans	various	summer to autumn	no	10–30 in (25–75 cm)	12–18 in (30–45 cm)	8–11	no
***Zinnia elegans*, Ruffles Series**	various	summer to autumn	no	24–36 in (60–90 cm)	12–24 in (30–60 cm)	8–11	no
Zinnia grandiflora	yellow	summer	no	12 in (30 cm)	24–32 in (60–80 cm)	9–11	no
Zinnia haageana	orange, yellow, bronze	summer to early autumn	no	24 in (60 cm)	8–12 in (20–30 cm)	8–11	no
Zinnia peruviana	yellow, red, tangerine	summer to early autumn	no	24–36 in (60–90 cm)	12–16 in (30–40 cm)	8–11	no

Grasses, Sedges, and Bamboos

Comprising some of the most adaptable and widespread plants on earth, grasses, sedges, and bamboos can be found in virtually every part of the planet from the Arctic to the Antarctic. They are of tremendous economic importance: all of our cereals and grains have been derived from grasses, including barley, maize, oats, rice, rye, and wheat—all foodstuffs upon which civilizations and trade have been built. For many years, the use of grass for lawns and sports fields around the world has overshadowed the ornamental use of grasses, sedges, and bamboos in the garden. But their adaptability, beauty, subtlety, and unique qualities of movement are now attracting well-deserved attention.

RIGHT *Bamboos are giant grasses, though their size and woody hollow stems distinguish them from most grasses. The* Bambusa *genus features many decorative cultivars.*

LEFT *The distinctively colored blue-green foliage of* Festuca glauca *adds interest to any garden. 'Elijah Blue', seen here, is one of several popular cultivars of this species.*

MORE THAN JUST LAWNS

LEFT *When the delicate soft reddish purple flower plumes of* Pennisetum setaceum *'Atrosanguineum' move in the breeze, their pollen is spread far and wide. The foliage is burgundy colored.* **BELOW** Miscanthus sinensis *'Yaku jima' produces masses of tall flowerheads in late summer through autumn. These often remain on the plant for several months, giving winter appeal.*

Grasses actually consist of some 635 genera and 9,000 species, including the bamboos. There are also a number of grass-like plants often lumped together with the grasses—these include sedges, rushes, and a number of lily relatives.

True grasses are herbs that have solid or hollow stems and clumping, tussock-forming, or rhizomatous root systems. Their long narrow leaves grow in 2 rows within a sheath, and flowers are produced in spikelets on stalks that can be hefty or delicate, depending on the species.

There is a surprising degree of variety among grasses. Some, such as blue fescue *(Festuca glauca),* are small and form neat tufts. Others, such as giant silver grass (*Miscanthus* 'Giganteus'), form large clumps and can reach over 15 ft (4.5 m) tall. Grasses can be thin- or thick-leafed, stiff and upright or wispy and graceful. Some are dense and suitable for screening, and others have an airy see-through quality.

Herbaceous grasses, which put up fresh growth each spring (as opposed to evergreens), often retain their dried leaves through the winter, providing warm tawny color and structure. A number of grasses are prized for their winter color and stature, including silver grass (*Miscanthus* species) and feather reed grass (*Calamagrostis* species). But evergreen grasses also have their virtues: not only do they provide structure, warm living color, and texture in winter, but their maintenance needs are few, requiring only a quick springtime trim of any winter-burned foliage. A particularly attractive evergreen grass is pink muhly *(Muhlenbergia capillaris)* from the USA.

Foliage color is generally subtle and includes silvery and steely blue, purple-blue, blue-green, yellow-green, yellow, rust, reddish brown, copper, and blood red. Grasses, with their rich tones and variable shapes, work beautifully with other plants in the garden, both as foil and as feature.

Bamboos are members of the grass family, and the diversity among them is amazing. Encompassing some 100 genera and 1,500 species, along with a multitude of cultivated varieties, bamboos range from hip-high ground covers to timber bamboos reaching over 70 ft (21 m) in height. There are also lesser-known climbing bamboos and even herbaceous species. Bamboo roots can be clumping or running. Clumping types gradually increase in size, while running types are sometimes feared for their vigorous spreading root systems. However, they can be contained by various planting techniques, including the use of bamboo barriers and annual pruning or by planting in containers, to which they are well suited.

There are a number of exceptionally cold-hardy bamboos, including *Phyllostachys bissettii,* one of only a small handful of bamboos hardy to –20°F (–29°C). Numerous tropical and subtropical bamboos make elegant garden subjects, including members of the beautiful and diverse genus *Bambusa.* In between the cold-hardy and tropical types is a world of options, including bamboos used for hedges and borders, screens, bonsai, house plants, edible shoots, and wood for building. Others tolerate deep shade, waterlogged soil, alkaline soil, and salt air.

And then there are grass look-alikes that are actually not members of the grass family, including sedges (*Carex* species), a genus of grass-like clumping plants found worldwide and grown for their long, often evergreen leaves and unusual colors and markings. Examples include *Carex testacea* from New Zealand, with narrow arching leaves varying from green to yellow-brown with orange tips, or *Carex morrowii* 'Variegata', a cultivar of a Japanese sedge, with crisp white-striped leaves. Another attractive sedge is the bright yellow Bowles golden grass (*Carex elata* 'Aurea'), a plant that thrives in standing water. For warm climates, the umbrella plant *(Cyperus alternifolius)* is an attractive sedge for damp to wet areas, while its close relative, the historic papyrus of paper-making fame *(C. papyrus)* is suited to tropical regions. Both plants make excellent additions to ponds and outdoor water features and thrive in bright conditions indoors, particularly when their roots are partially submerged in water.

Grasses, sedges, and bamboos are especially good at lending a natural relaxed air to landscapes. Even though some possess substantial architectural presence, strong lines, and even imposing height, they still somehow suggest something appealingly casual. Whether true grasses or look-alikes, the ornamentals we call "grasses" are coming into their own. Planted in containers, integrated into perennial beds, or used in swathes, grasses, sedges, and bamboos bring welcome life and movement into the landscape.

ABOVE *The dense tufts of the sedge* Carex testacea *appear to best effect when grown in groups, cascading over pots, or with dark-foliage plants.*
RIGHT *The dramatic black canes of* Phyllostachys nigra *make it a popular bamboo species. However, it spreads very aggressively and must be contained.*

BAMBUSA

Found through most of the tropics and extending into the subtropics of Asia, this is a genus of around 120 species of giant grasses—commonly known as bamboo—belonging to the family Poaceae. Non-suckering, they form clumps of smooth, strongly erect stems called culms that can be over 80 ft (24 m) tall. Feathery flowerheads appear sporadically, and some species die after flowering. The stems are hollow, except at the nodes where small branching sprays of narrow leaves appear, and are remarkably strong yet flexible. In the west we think of bamboo as being used for small ornamental objects and garden furniture, but until one visits East Asia, it is difficult to appreciate bamboo's importance as a construction material. Even today, it is used not only in country areas as it always has been, but in scaffolding and screening in cities.

Favorites	Plant Height	Plant Width	Hardiness Zone	Frost Tolerance
Bambusa multiplex	35 ft (10 m)	10 ft (3 m)	9–12	no
***Bambusa multiplex* 'Alphonse Karr'**	25–35 ft (8–10 m)	10 ft (3 m)	9–12	no
***Bambusa multiplex* 'Fernleaf'**	20 ft (6 m)	5–10 ft (1.5–3 m)	9–12	no
Bambusa oldhamii	60 ft (18 m)	20–40 ft (6–12 m)	9–12	no
Bambusa vulgaris	50 ft (15 m)	15–30 ft (4.5–9 m)	9–12	no
***Bambusa vulgaris* 'Striata'**	5–6 ft (1.5–1.8 m)	2–3 ft (0.6–0.9 m)	9–12	no

CULTIVATION

Hardiness varies, though few species can tolerate repeated frosts and most prefer to grow in warm humid conditions with humus-rich well-drained soil and a steady supply of moisture. Plant in a sheltered but sunny position. Bamboo is most often propagated by division.

BELOW Bambusa vulgaris *'Striata' (syn. 'Vittata') is distinguished from the species by its golden yellow culms that are randomly striped with dark green.*

Top Tip

Bambusa species are generally less invasive than many other bamboos, so they can be put to use in the garden for screening, informal hedges, or windbreaks.

CALAMAGROSTIS

The 250 species of grasses that make up this genus in the family Poaceae are widespread in the northern temperate zones. Commonly known as reed grass, many are too large or invasive for domestic gardens but a few species and their cultivars are grown for the foliage, which is often variegated, and for their fluffy flower spikes that are usually held clear of the foliage. The flowerheads remain attractive as they dry and set seed. Reed grasses are known for the wave-like movement of the flowerheads and foliage when touched by the slightest breeze.

BELOW *When young, the leaves of* Calamagrostis foliosa *'Zebrina' are light green with horizontal bands of green and yellow. In summer, plumes of light green flowers are produced.*

CULTIVATION

Reed grasses are very hardy and easily grown in full or half-sun with moist well-drained soil. Some species are moderately drought tolerant once established. Cut back the dried foliage in early winter. As most of the cultivated plants are selected forms, propagation is usually by division in late winter. A few species are considered local weeds.

Favorites	Plant Height	Plant Width	Hardiness Zone	Frost Tolerance
Calamagrostis* × *acutiflora	5–7 ft (1.5–2 m)	3–4 ft (0.9–1.2 m)	4–10	yes
***Calamagrostis* × *acutiflora* 'Karl Foerster'**	5–6 ft (1.5–1.8 m)	2–3 ft (0.6–0.9 m)	4–10	yes
***Calamagrostis* × *acutiflora* 'Overdam'**	2–3 ft (0.6–0.9 m)	2–3 ft (0.6–0.9 m)	4–10	yes
Calamagrostis brachytricha	40 in (100 cm)	20–40 in (50–100 cm)	7–9	yes
Calamagrostis foliosa	6–16 in (15–40 cm)	8–20 in (20–50 cm)	7–9	yes
***Calamagrostis foliosa* 'Zebrina'**	6–16 in (15–40 cm)	8–20 in (20–50 cm)	7–9	yes

BELOW *Growing slightly taller than the species,* Calamagrostis × acutiflora *'Stricta' produces fluffy, pinkish bronze-tinged, summer flowerheads that age to a buff color.*

Top Tip

Many *Carex* species are ornamental, and are perfect candidates for waterside planting. Smaller types can become a focal point when planted in pots.

CAREX

This worldwide genus of grass-like sedges belonging to the family Cyperaceae is usually found growing in permanently moist or seasonally boggy conditions. Their leaves may be green, red, or brown and range from fine and hair-like, sometimes with curled tips, to quite broad with a noticeable midrib and sometimes razor sharp edges. Short flowerheads develop in the warmer months, and although these are held clear of the foliage, they are seldom much of a feature, the plants being grown for their form and color of the foliage. In New Zealand, *Carex* sedges or tussocks are among the dominant plants in grassland areas, and have produced several popular cultivars.

BELOW Carex pendula *is a native of Europe. Throughout the flowering season, arching stems hold catkin-like spikes of flowers above the bright green foliage.*

CULTIVATION

Plant *Carex* species in full sun with moist well-drained soil. Despite their natural preference for damp conditions, some species will tolerate drought and can be extremely effective at binding thin soils. Sedges are easy-care plants, though some species can be invasive. New plants can be raised from seed but as most species quickly reach divisible size, it is seldom necessary.

TOP RIGHT Carex comans *'Frosted Curls' is so-named for the curling light-colored tips of the pale green- to buff-colored grassy leaves.*

RIGHT Carex elata *is a European species, known as the tufted sedge. 'Aurea', pictured here, has golden leaves edged in green and is usually seen in cultivation more often than the true species.*

Favorites	Plant Height	Plant Width	Hardiness Zone	Frost Tolerance
Carex buchananii	24–30 in (60–75 cm)	18–24 in (45–60 cm)	7–10	yes
Carex comans	12–16 in (30–40 cm)	24–30 in (60–75 cm)	7–10	yes
Carex elata	3 ft (0.9 m)	3 ft (0.9 m)	7–10	yes
Carex grayi	30 in (75 cm)	30 in (75 cm)	7–10	yes
Carex oshimensis	12 in (30 cm)	18 in (45 cm)	5–10	yes
Carex pendula	3 ft (0.9 m)	3–6 ft (0.9–1.8 m)	5–10	yes

BELOW *The dried seed heads of* Carex *species are popular for use in floral arrangements. In particular, the spiky seed heads of* Carex grayi *are valued for their unusual structure.*

CYPERUS

Widespread throughout tropical and warm-temperate regions, *Cyperus* is the type genus for the sedge (Cyperaceae) family and includes some 600-odd annual and perennial species. Some species, such as nut grass *(Cyperus rotundus)*, are extremely serious weeds. Others, however, are ornamental and sometimes useful. Many are marginal plants found around lakes and streams or in boggy areas. They have strongly upright grassy stems and very prominent, umbrella-like, green to brown flowerheads on thickened stalks up to 5 ft (1.5 m) high or more. The earliest form of paper, the papyrus of the Egyptians, was made from the pith of the stems of *Cyperus papyrus*.

CULTIVATION

Most *Cyperus* species prefer a bright sunny position and will grow in ordinary well-drained garden soil, though many species can tolerate up to 2 in (5 cm) of water over the roots. Hardiness varies greatly, and some of the best ornamentals need mild winters and hot summers. Propagate from seed or by division.

Favorites

Favorites	Plant Height	Plant Width	Hardiness Zone	Frost Tolerance
Cyperus albostriatus	24 in (60 cm)	12 in (30 cm)	9–12	no
Cyperus involucratus	3–7 ft (0.9–2 m)	2–3 ft (0.6–0.9 m)	9–12	no
***Cyperus involucratus* 'Variegatus'**	3–7 ft (0.9–2 m)	2–3 ft (0.6–0.9 m)	9–12	no
Cyperus longus	3–5 ft (0.9–1.5 m)	1–3 ft (0.3–0.9 m)	6–9	yes
Cyperus papyrus	7–17 ft (2–5 m)	5–10 ft (1.5–3 m)	9–12	no
***Cyperus papyrus* 'Nanus'**	4–6 ft (1.2–1.8 m)	2–3 ft (0.6–0.9 m)	9–12	no

Top Tip

Despite their natural affinity with watery locations, *Cyperus* species make attractive indoor plants, and can overwinter safely indoors in cooler climates.

ABOVE RIGHT Cyperus longus *is commonly known as galingale. Quite at home growing in shallow water, the erect bright green stems bear spoke-like bracts around tiny brownish flowers.*
RIGHT *Long bright green bracts radiate out around the cluster of tiny flowers of* Cyperus involucratus. *Regarded as a weed in some areas, this species hails from Africa.*

DESCHAMPSIA

A charming genus of about 50 species in the grass (Poaceae) family, *Deschampsia* are clump-forming perennial plants that can be evergreen or herbaceous. They are widely distributed throughout temperate to cold regions, preferring habitats such as woodlands, moors, and mountainous areas. Commonly known as hair grass, they are grown for their thin graceful foliage and airy flowerheads, which are popular in floral arrangements. Many interesting clones have been selected by growers, especially in Germany.

CULTIVATION

Deschampsia plants will grow in any good garden soil in sun or light shade, but prefer moist humus-rich soil and part-shade. Remove spent flower stems in early spring to allow for new growth. Propagate the species from seed, but named clones must be divided in spring.

ABOVE *Commonly known as tufted hair grass or tussock grass,* Deschampsia cespitosa *forms a clump of wispy leaves. Tall plumes carry abun dant small flowers in summer.*

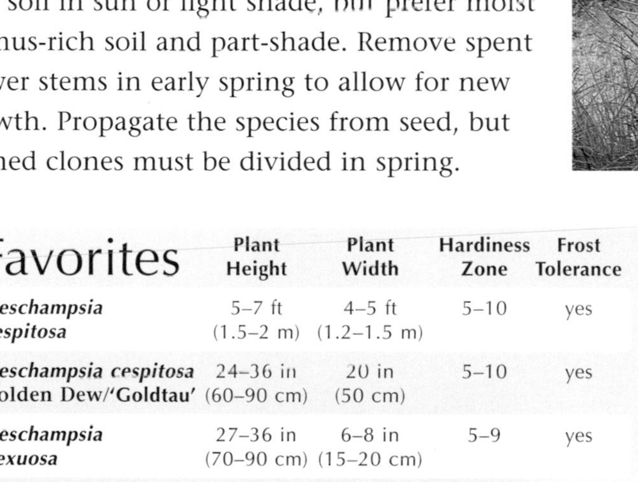

Favorites	Plant Height	Plant Width	Hardiness Zone	Frost Tolerance
Deschampsia cespitosa	5–7 ft (1.5–2 m)	4–5 ft (1.2–1.5 m)	5–10	yes
Deschampsia cespitosa **Golden Dew/'Goldtau'**	24–36 in (60–90 cm)	20 in (50 cm)	5–10	yes
Deschampsia flexuosa	27–36 in (70–90 cm)	6–8 in (15–20 cm)	5–9	yes

LEFT *In summer, the flowers of* Deschampsia cespitosa *Golden Dew/'Goldtau' create a billowy golden green haze high above the clump of fine narrow leaf blades.*

Top Tip

Using ornamental grasses adds interest to the landscape. Hair grass can be a useful accent plant, but provision should be made for the tall summer flower spikes.

FESTUCA

A genus of some 300 species belonging to the grass (Poaceae) family, it has a global distribution. Often better known by their common name of fescue, the plants in this genus are mostly small and unassuming, though they have tremendous ornamental value, and are also considered some of the finest lawn grasses available, especially for high-quality low-traffic lawns. The leaves, often distinctively colored, are usually folded around the midrib, making the foliage very fine and hair-like in some species. Usually standing taller than the foliage, the showy flower plumes are feathery and open.

CULTIVATION

While hardiness varies, most fescues are at home in temperate zones and thrive in most soils with minimal attention, though few will tolerate prolonged poor drainage. Plant in full sun or partial shade. As lawn grasses, they appreciate annual dethatching and aeration. In favorable conditions they will remain green year-round. Propagate by dividing established clumps, or raise from seed.

Favorites

Favorites	Plant Height	Plant Width	Hardiness Zone	Frost Tolerance
Festuca californica	24–36 in (60–90 cm)	24 in (60 cm)	5–9	yes
Festuca californica 'Serpentine Blue'	24–36 in (60–90 cm)	24 in (60 cm)	5–9	yes
Festuca glauca	12 in (30 cm)	10 in (25 cm)	4–10	yes
Festuca glauca 'Blaufuchs'	6–10 in (15–25 cm)	10 in (25 cm)	4–10	yes
Festuca valesiaca	6 in (15 cm)	6 in (15 cm)	5–9	yes
Festuca varia	22 in (55 cm)	15 in (38 cm)	5–9	yes

Top Tip

Fescues are able to withstand many extremes of nature, such as dry, frosty, or salty conditions. Their salt tolerance makes them ideal subjects for gardens near the sea.

LEFT *The fine, grassy, silvery blue-toned foliage of* Festuca glauca *'Blauglut' (syn. Blue Glow) makes a dramatic contrast when situated near green-leafed plants.*

RIGHT *Found in mountain areas of southern Europe,* Festuca varia *subsp.* scoparia *forms a clump of wispy blue-tipped leaves.*

GLYCERIA

A genus of 16 species of perennial marsh grasses, *Glyceria* is a member of the family Poaceae. Commonly known as manna grass, meadow grass, or sweet grass, they are widely distributed throughout the northern temperate zones and temperate regions of South America, Australia, and New Zealand. They spread by rhizomes, from which develop reed-like stems bearing long, strappy, succulent leaves. Large flower plumes, often purple-tinted, develop in summer, followed by edible small seeds. *Glyceria* plants will grow in shallow water, and are useful as pond plants.

CULTIVATION

Glyceria plants are mostly frost hardy and easily grown in any temperate climate. Plant in full sun with moist humus-rich soil. Although naturally adapted to damp conditions, they will grow well enough in regular garden soils if they are kept moist. Propagate from seed or by division.

ABOVE *A North American species found growing in moist woodland and swampy areas,* Glyceria striata *is commonly known as fowl manna grass. The narrow leaves are pale to bright green.*

Favorites	Plant Height	Plant Width	Hardiness Zone	Frost Tolerance
Glyceria maxima	3–8 ft (0.9–2.4 m)	5–10 ft (1.5–3 m)	3–9	yes
Glyceria maxima* var. *variegata	3–5 ft (0.9–1.5 m)	5–10 ft (1.5–3 m)	3–9	yes
Glyceria striata	12–36 in (30–90 cm)	12–36 in (30–90 cm)	3–9	yes

Top Tip

Glyceria species are useful for waterside planting, however, they have the potential to become invasive and their spread should be closely monitored and controlled.

LEFT *The cream-edged green leaves of* Glyceria maxima *var.* variegata *(striped manna grass) form a mound of arching foliage. Tall plumes of ivory flowers are borne in summer.*

LOMANDRA

This largely Australian genus is made up of around 50 species of clump-forming perennials, belonging to the grass-tree (Xanthorrhoeaceae) family. Rush- or sedge-like, they have rather coarse grassy foliage and their flower panicles are largely hidden among the foliage. While not among the most attractive plants, mat-rushes are very drought tolerant and useful for binding together light soils that would otherwise easily erode. In its native Australia, the genus was once despised by farmers as a destroyer of pastures but is now recognized as important in maintaining a habitat for ground-nesting birds, lizards, and other easily threatened species.

Favorites

Favorites	Plant Height	Plant Width	Hardiness Zone	Frost Tolerance
Lomandra banksii	3–5 ft (0.9–1.5 m)	2–4 ft (0.6–1.2 m)	10–12	no
Lomandra glauca	8 in (20 cm)	15 in (38 cm)	10–11	no
Lomandra longifolia	20–40 in (50–100 cm)	30–36 in (75–90 cm)	8–12	no

CULTIVATION

Hardiness varies, though none of the grass-trees will tolerate repeated hard frosts or prolonged wet winters. Plant in full sun with light well-drained soil. A thatch of dead foliage tends to build up around the base of the plants, and can be removed by cutting back hard or raking the clump, though burning off the tops encourages a lush thicket of new growth. They are easily propagated from seed or by division.

ABOVE *Often used in gardens for its ornamental qualities,* Lomandra longifolia *is a tussock-forming evergreen perennial from eastern Australia.*

LEFT *Commonly known as clumping mat-rush or May rush,* Lomandra banksii *features above-ground stems with strap-like bright green leaves.*

Top Tip

Lomandra species are easily cultivated and can serve as background foliage in border plantings. They appreciate regular watering throughout the growing season.

MISCANTHUS

This genus, belonging to the grass (Poaceae) family, contains about 20 deciduous or evergreen species, used widely in ornamental gardens as a feature and for screening. Their natural distribution ranges from Africa to East Asia. Tufted spreading plants, they have showy, green, silver, white, and mottled foliage. Commonly referred to as reeds, they have clumps of leaves that cascade from rounded upright stems. They bear masses of tall flowerheads in late summer to autumn, sometimes taking on autumnal colors of orange, yellow, red, or purple, and often remaining on plants right through winter. Fresh or dried, the flowerheads are ideal subjects for floral arrangements.

Top Tip

The unique ornamental qualities of *Miscanthus* species can add a touch of simple elegance to borders. They are also well suited to waterside planting.

CULTIVATION

Miscanthus species do best in moist open soils with a sunny aspect. Propagate by dividing into small clumps in autumn. They can also be propagated from seed, though it is often slow to germinate. Seed should be sown in containers in spring after the risk of frost has passed.

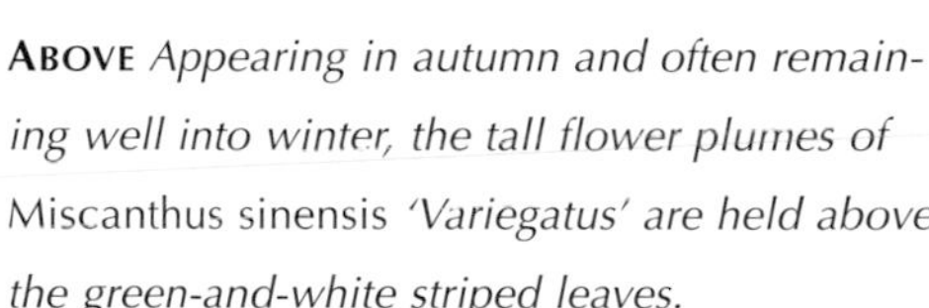

ABOVE *Appearing in autumn and often remaining well into winter, the tall flower plumes of* Miscanthus sinensis *'Variegatus' are held above the green-and-white striped leaves.*

BELOW Miscanthus sinensis *var.* condensatus *is a clump-forming grass that grows taller than the species. A fine ornamental grass, it features wide leaves accented by a central cream stripe.*

Favorites

Favorites	Plant Height	Plant Width	Hardiness Zone	Frost Tolerance
Miscanthus oligostachyus	40 in (100 cm)	32 in (80 cm)	5–9	yes
Miscanthus sacchariflorus	5 ft (1.5 m)	5 ft (1.5 m)	5–9	yes
Miscanthus sinensis	15 ft (4.5 m)	4 ft (1.2 m)	5–9	yes
***Miscanthus sinensis* 'Gracillimus'**	4–6 ft (1.2–1.8 m)	6–8 ft (1.8–2.4 m)	5–9	yes
***Miscanthus sinensis* 'Morning Light'**	5–6 ft (1.5–1.8 m)	3–4 ft (0.9–1.2 m)	5–9	yes
Miscanthus transmorrisonensis	40 in (100 cm)	36 in (90 cm)	7–10	yes

MUHLENBERGIA

Commonly known as muhly grass, this genus of 125 species of often spectacular grasses in the family Poaceae is native to the Americas and temperate East Asia. They form large clumps of fine foliage and during the summer months produce billowing plumes of flowers, often in soft pink to purple-red shades. Some species are grown for their foliage, which can be blue-gray, others for their flowerheads, and a few for both. Strangely, for such showy plants, these grasses have only recently become appreciated as garden plants. Some species are useful for sand dune stabilization.

Favorites	Plant Height	Plant Width	Hardiness Zone	Frost Tolerance
Muhlenbergia capillaris	3 ft (0.9 m)	6 ft (1.8 m)	9–11	yes
Muhlenbergia emersleyi	18 in (45 cm)	3–4 ft (0.9–1.2 m)	9–11	yes
Muhlenbergia japonica	12–20 in (30–50 cm)	24 in (60 cm)	9–11	yes
Muhlenbergia japonica 'Cream Delight'	12–20 in (30–50 cm)	24 in (60 cm)	9–11	yes
Muhlenbergia lindheimeri	5 ft (1.5 m)	5 ft (1.5 m)	9–11	yes
Muhlenbergia rigens	5 ft (1.5 m)	4 ft (1.2 m)	9–11	yes

CULTIVATION

Hardiness varies considerably, but the tougher muhly grasses are easily grown in any sunny position with moist well-drained soil. The tender species are often worth cultivating as annuals in colder areas, or they may be potted and moved under cover for winter. They may be raised from seed but the best forms must be propagated by division, usually in late winter.

BELOW LEFT *An ideal accent plant,* Muhlenbergia capillaris *(syn.* M. filipes*) forms a neat mound of foliage. In summer, towering plumes of flowers are produced.*
BELOW RIGHT *Native to southern North America and Mexico,* Muhlenbergia rigens *is a clump-forming species that is commonly known as deer grass.*

Top Tip

Drought tolerant, muhly grasses are able to survive on minimal water. However, they will perform to their full potential if extra water is provided in dry times.

LEFT *Commonly known as fountain grass for its cascading form,* Pennisetum setaceum *bears pink to purple summer flowerheads that often last into autumn.*

ABOVE *The fine bristles that cover the flowerheads of* Pennisetum villosum *give a feathery effect, earning this perennial grass the common name of feathertop.*

PENNISETUM

A genus of about 80 species of grasses in the family Poaceae, it includes some very ornamental species and others that are among the worst weeds. Widespread in warm-temperate to tropical areas, they spread by rhizomes or stolons to form clumps of overarching, short-stemmed, narrow to quite broad leaves that often have a prominent midrib. The flower stems usually extend above the foliage clump and carry plume-like heads of flowers that are often strongly pink-tinted. Many gardeners have been put off this genus by kikuyu grass *(Pennisetum flaccidum)*, which can be extremely difficult to control. Pearl millet *(Pennisetum americanum)* is a minor pasture, fodder, and grain crop.

CULTIVATION

The commonly cultivated species will tolerate light to moderate frosts but prefer mild winters. They are otherwise easily grown in any sunny or lightly shaded position with moist well-drained soil. The species may be raised from seed, the cultivars by division in late winter.

Top Tip

Trim off the fluffy flower plumes of *Pennisetum* species before the seeds mature to prevent seed dispersal. The dried plumes can be used in floral arrangements.

Favorites

Favorites	Plant Height	Plant Width	Hardiness Zone	Frost Tolerance
Pennisetum alopecuroides	48–60 in (120–150 cm)	18–24 in (45–60 cm)	5–9	yes
***Pennisetum alopecuroides* 'Little Bunny'**	12–18 in (30–45 cm)	18–24 in (45–60 cm)	5–9	yes
Pennisetum orientale	5–6 ft (1.5–1.8 m)	3–4 ft (0.9–1.2 m)	8–10	yes
Pennisetum setaceum	3–5 ft (0.9–1.5 m)	2–3 ft (0.6–0.9 m)	9–10	no
***Pennisetum setaceum* 'Atrosanguineum'**	3–5 ft (0.9–1.5 m)	2–3 ft (0.6–0.9 m)	9–10	no
Pennisetum villosum	24–48 in (60–120 cm)	18–24 in (45–60 cm)	8–10	no

Phyllostachys

Found from the Himalayas to Japan, with most native to China, the 50-odd species of bamboos in this genus belong to the family Poaceae. Their vigorous spreading rhizomes sprout widely spaced culms that usually have a flattened side, sometimes with a shallow longitudinal groove.

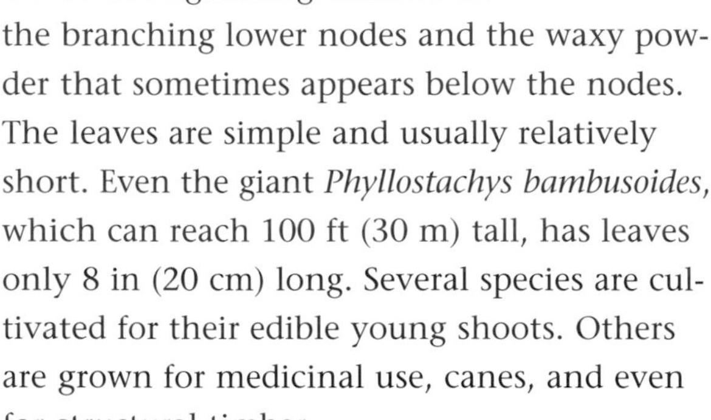

Other distinguishing features are the branching lower nodes and the waxy powder that sometimes appears below the nodes. The leaves are simple and usually relatively short. Even the giant *Phyllostachys bambusoides*, which can reach 100 ft (30 m) tall, has leaves only 8 in (20 cm) long. Several species are cultivated for their edible young shoots. Others are grown for medicinal use, canes, and even for structural timber.

Above *A native of China,* Phyllostachys flexuosa *is commonly known as zig-zag bamboo. This fast-growing bamboo develops an elegant arching form.*

Top Tip

These bamboos are unsuitable for small gardens and can be difficult to control unless contained. To combat spread, insert a solid barrier at least 24 in (60 cm) deep.

Below Phyllostachys aureosulcata, *a vigorous spreading bamboo, hails from northeastern China. The culms are etched with a distinctive yellow groove.*

Cultivation

Most *Phyllostachys* species are surprisingly frost hardy, though they do need warm humid summers to grow well. Smaller species are suitable for planting in tubs or planter boxes, but need to be kept well watered. These bamboos are easily propagated by division.

Favorites	Plant Height	Plant Width	Hardiness Zone	Frost Tolerance
Phyllostachys aurea	25 ft (8 m)	20–40 ft (6–12 m)	7–11	yes
Phyllostachys aureosulcata	25 ft (8 m)	25–50 ft (8–15 m)	6–11	yes
Phyllostachys bambusoides	40–100 ft (12–30 m)	20–60 ft (6–18 m)	7–11	yes
Phyllostachys edulis	40–75 ft (12–23 m)	30–100 ft (9–30 m)	6–10	yes
Phyllostachys flexuosa	8–15 ft (2.4–4.5 m)	10–20 ft (3–6 m)	6–10	yes
Phyllostachys nigra	25–50 ft (8–15 m)	20–50 ft (6–15 m)	7–10	yes

PLEIOBLASTUS

A genus of some 20 species of mostly low-growing bamboos that have running rhizomes, they are largely confined to Japan and China, and are in the grass (Poaceae) family. They form clumps of fine canes with variably sized dark green leaves, sometimes with narrow longitudinal stripes of lighter coloration. Japanese gardeners have produced many variegated cultivars but due to difficulties in classification some are listed as species when they are most likely to be of garden origin. Several species produce edible shoots or canes that can be used as plant stakes or tool handles.

CULTIVATION

Though mostly very hardy and not too tall, in mild areas they will quickly fill a fairly large area. Their running habit means that they should be contained with solid underground barriers. The foliage can be kept lush by cutting the clumps back to the ground in late winter. Propagation is by division.

Favorites

Favorites	Plant Height	Plant Width	Hardiness Zone	Frost Tolerance
Pleioblastus auricomus	3–6 ft (0.9–1.8 m)	3–5 ft (0.9–1.5 m)	6–10	yes
Pleioblastus chino	6–12 ft (1.8–3.5 m)	6 ft (1.8 m)	7–11	yes
Pleioblastus gramineus	6–15 ft (1.8–4.5 m)	6 ft (1.8 m)	7–11	yes
Pleioblastus humilis	4 ft (1.2 m)	5 ft (1.5 m)	7–11	yes
Pleioblastus pygmaeus	16 in (40 cm)	5 ft (1.5 m)	6–10	yes
Pleioblastus variegatus	27–40 in (70–100 cm)	3–5 ft (0.9–1.5 m)	5–10	yes

LEFT Pleioblastus variegatus, *an upright form from Japan also known as dwarf white-striped bamboo, has leaves to 6 in (15 cm) long, boldly striped with white.*

BELOW *With distinct nodes that divide stem segments,* Pleioblastus auricomus *has attractive green and gold variegated leaves to 10 in (25 cm) long.*

Top Tip

Division is best in early spring, before new shoots appear. The larger the transplant, the better the chance of success. Lightly fertilize, and water heavily for 2 weeks afterward.

SASA

Top Tip

Because of their invasive nature, a root barrier is advisable for some sasas, extending down 3 ft (0.9 m) for taller species. Alternatively, grow in a container.

A grass (Poaceae) family genus, it has 60 species of bamboos found in temperate East Asia from southeastern Russia to southern China, Korea, and Japan. They have running rhizomes and quickly form dense thickets of fairly fine, arching canes that are seldom over 7 ft (2 m) tall. Foliage is often dense and the leaves can be broad. The leaves of some species tend to dry off along the edges, but rather than appearing damaged or dying, they can benefit from an interesting variegated effect. *Sasa* or *Zasa* is the Japanese name for bamboo and is used in the common names of several types, not just those found in this genus, for example *Pleioblastus auricomus* is known as kamuro-zasa.

ABOVE Sasa veitchii *has 10 in (25 cm) long leaves that turn white at the edges. Its purple stems branch from each node, with a whitish powder beneath each node.*

CULTIVATION

Mostly very hardy with a greater preference for cooler summer conditions than other bamboos, plant them in half-sun or dappled sunlight with moist, humus-rich, well-drained soil. They have strong running rhizomes that need to be contained. Propagation is by division.

BELOW *A Japanese cultivar,* Sasa palmata *'Nebulosa' has stems with distinctive brown to black markings and large oblong palm-like leaves, as the species name indicates.*

Favorites	Plant Height	Plant Width	Hardiness Zone	Frost Tolerance
Sasa kurilensis	3–10 ft (0.9–3 m)	10–20 ft (3–6 m)	7–11	yes
Sasa palmata	7 ft (2 m)	10–20 ft (3–6 m)	7–11	yes
***Sasa palmata* 'Nebulosa'**	6–8 ft (1.8–2.4 m)	10–20 ft (3–6 m)	7–11	yes
Sasa tsuboiana	4–6 ft (1.2–1.8 m)	10–20 ft (3–6 m)	8–10	yes
Sasa veitchii	3–5 ft (0.9–1.5 m)	10–20 ft (3–6 m)	6–11	yes
Sasa veitchii* f. *minor	2 ft (0.6 m)	5–10 ft (1.5–3 m)	8–10	yes

Typha

Top Tip

Outdoors, bulrushes usually demand plenty of space. To enjoy them on a smaller scale, plant them in pots where they can be a focal point when in flower.

The type genus for the bulrush (Typhaceae) family, *Typha* contains up to 12 species of marginal aquatic perennials with a near-worldwide distribution outside the polar regions. Most have tall, strongly erect stems that are very light and have pithy centers. Conspicuous sheaths cover the young stems, peeling away and dying as the stems mature. The leaves are long, flat, narrow, and deep green to blue green when young. Dense cylindrical flower spikes appear near the top of pointed spear-like flower stems and eventually disintegrate, dispersing their seeds on the wind. The small species tend to be more grass-like. Bulrush clumps aid in their own demise, as their roots and debris help fill and drain the ponds in which they grow.

Cultivation

Bulrushes will grow in up to 12 in (30 cm) of water and should be planted in full sun. They are too large for small ponds, but where they can run wild they need little or no maintenance. Propagate from seed or by division.

Below left *The striking foliage of* Typha latifolia *'Variegata' makes it popular for aquatic and waterside plantings. The slender blades are striped with cream.*

Above Typha shuttleworthii *is a bulrush from southern Europe. Throughout summer it produces brown to silvery gray flowers that are followed by tiny fruit.*

Favorites	Plant Height	Plant Width	Hardiness Zone	Frost Tolerance
Typha angustifolia	7 ft (2 m)	3–5 ft (0.9–1.5 m)	3–9	yes
Typha latifolia	3–10 ft (0.9–3 m)	3–5 ft (0.9–1.5 m)	3–10	yes
***Typha latifolia* 'Variegata'**	3–5 ft (0.9–1.5 m)	3–5 ft (0.9–1.5 m)	3–10	yes
Typha minima	2½–3 in (6–8 cm)	1¼–2 in (3–5 cm)	3–11	yes
Typha orientalis	3–8 ft (0.9–2.4 m)	1–2 ft (0.3–0.6 m)	9–11	yes
Typha shuttleworthii	3–5 ft (0.9–1.5 m)	1–3 ft (0.3–0.9 m)	5–8	yes

Fruit Trees, Nut Trees, and Other Fruits

Harvesting food from the garden is one of the most rewarding aspects of gardening. In addition to the satisfaction of polishing the bloom off a sun-warmed apple and crunching into it or tasting the difference between store-bought and fresh walnuts, there are many practical reasons for growing fruits and nuts. Home-grown fruits and nuts can be raised with minimal to no pesticides, particularly if attention is paid at the outset to choosing suitable varieties for the region. Home-grown fruit is less expensive and more accessible than store-bought fruit. And garden varieties may be chosen for flavor rather than for the qualities commercial growers seek.

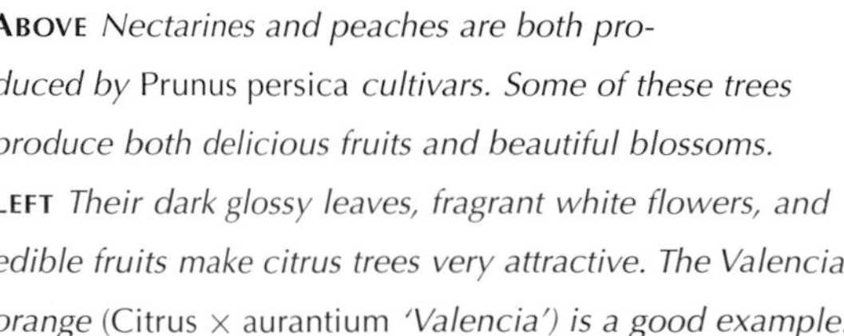

Above *Nectarines and peaches are both produced by* Prunus persica *cultivars. Some of these trees produce both delicious fruits and beautiful blossoms.*
Left *Their dark glossy leaves, fragrant white flowers, and edible fruits make citrus trees very attractive. The Valencia orange* (Citrus × aurantium *'Valencia') is a good example.*

A Fruitful Garden Harvest

Fruit, whether on a tree, bush, or vine, is essentially a mature ovary enclosing and protecting a plant's seed. In order to guard the seed, most fruit is distinctly bitter and unpalatable until the seed is ripe and ready for dispersal—at which point the fruit becomes sweet and delicious, attracting potential foragers. Nuts, while internally organized somewhat differently (the ovary becomes a hard shell protecting the nut), essentially function the same way: foraging creatures are kept at bay by the unpalatable flavor and impossibly hard shell until the seed is developed sufficiently and ready for dispersal.

Over the centuries, humans have manipulated the flavor of various wild fruits and nuts to satisfy our tastes and preferences. As well as selecting for flavor, we have selected for qualities such as size, color, skin or rind thickness, seedlessness, storage quality, and ripening time. In terms of the plants themselves, we have sought larger or smaller trees, heavier cropping, disease and insect resistance, and other qualities that improve crops.

Only since the rise of mass production in the past century has the flavor of fruit been so sacrificed for the sake of storage and shipping convenience.

Perhaps for no reason other than this, backyard fruit production is tremendously gratifying, for it allows the gardener to seek out the most delicious varieties, old and new, without having to take into account commercial concerns. If the varieties chosen are appropriate to the climate and are planted and cultivated with some attention, it is not difficult to enjoy some of the finest fresh food the earth has to offer.

The first matter to consider is climate. Many temperate-climate fruits such as apples (*Malus* species) require a certain number of hours of cool weather (chill time) between 32° and 45°F (0° and 7°C). Raspberries (*Rubus* species) also require some winter chill to produce well. Tropical fruits such as mangoes (*Mangifera* species), on the other hand, grow and fruit best where winter temperatures remain above 45°F (7°C). *Prunus* species such as peaches, apricots, and almonds tolerate considerable cold in winter, but flower early in the season and can lose their buds—and consequently the entire season's fruit—in areas prone to late frosts. In addition, many fruits require warmth to ripen. These include *Citrus* species and mangoes. Within the *Citrus* genus, lemons, limes, and other sour types generally need less heat to ripen than oranges and other sweet forms.

Most fruits and nuts require full sun in all but the hottest

ABOVE LEFT Prunus persica *'Jerseyglo' is a freestone peach with sweet firm flesh that ripens late in the season. The tree is spreading and strong growing.*

LEFT *The wineberry or wine raspberry* (Rubus phoenicolasius) *bears juicy fruits in summer on arching canes. Like blackberries, these can become invasive.*

Above *Although blueberries* (Vaccinium corymbosum) *are best known for their flavorful fruits, these attractive plants also make interesting informal hedges.*
Right *Colorful cowberries* (Vaccinium vitis-idaea) *appear on a low-growing evergreen bush. They have a slightly sour taste.*

climates. Moist but well-drained and reasonably fertile soil that is slightly acidic is best. Exceptions include blueberries and other *Vaccinium* species, which prefer very acidic soil with lower fertility and plenty of humus.

Many, but not all, fruits require a pollinator. Cane fruits such as raspberries and blackberries (*Rubus* species) do not need pollination, but Chinese gooseberries (*Actinidia* species) will not produce fruit without a pollinator. For apples and pears (*Pyrus* species), good pollinators are often, but not always, varieties whose flowering times overlap. Blueberries do not require cross-pollination, but their production is much improved by it. When planting a new fruit, it is important to find out whether more than one plant is needed to produce fruit and, if so, which kind is needed for pollination.

Most fruiting plants need annual pruning to balance the amount of new and old wood, prevent disease, and improve photosynthesis. Some are best pruned directly after harvest, such as cane fruits; others, like pears and apples, are pruned in early spring, before buds break their winter dormancy.

Although most fruit is produced on trees and shrubs, there are a number of desirable fruiting vines such as grapes (*Vitis* species) and kiwi or Chinese gooseberry (*Actinidia* species). Both of these are highly ornamental and can produce large quantities of delicious fruit.

Fruiting plants encompass a tremendously varied group of many genera, and span climates from the frigid to the tropical. Most regions of the world are known for their local fruits, and in many cases there are locally adapted and commonly grown varieties that have proven their suitability over many years. While it is always good to try new varieties and test boundaries, it is also worth knowing which varieties have a track record in an area and making use of local expertise when choosing which varieties to grow.

Actinidia

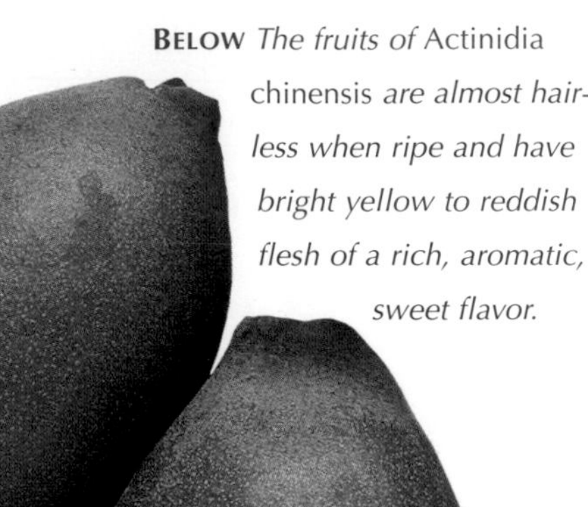

Below *The fruits of* Actinidia chinensis *are almost hairless when ripe and have bright yellow to reddish flesh of a rich, aromatic, sweet flavor.*

A genus of around 60 species of vigorous evergreen and deciduous twining East Asian vines, it is part of the Actinidiaceae family. Some species are grown just for their ornamental foliage but the 2 best-known species, *Actinidia deliciosa* and *Actinidia arguta*, are cultivated for their fruit. Most parts of the plant are bristly, except the cream flowers, which open from late spring and can pose pollination difficulties. The fruits develop during summer to be ripe by early winter. That kiwi fruit is synonymous with New Zealand shows the power of marketing; it is really a Chinese native.

Cultivation

Both male and female vines are required for fruit production. Plant where the roots will be cool and the tops will receive plenty of sunlight. The soil should be deep, fertile, humus-rich, and well-drained. Strong supports are necessary for these heavy vines. Water well when in flower and as the fruits ripen. Prune after harvesting. So that their sex is known, vines are usually propagated vegetatively from cuttings, or by layering or grafting.

Actinidia kolomikta is a good choice for those in cooler climates. It survives freezing conditions and also produces grape-sized fruits that taste similar to regular kiwi fruit.

Favorites	Flower Color	Blooming Season	Produce Season	Plant Height	Plant Width	Hardiness Zone	Frost Tolerance
Actinidia arguta	white, tinged green	mid- to late summer	late summer to autumn	20–30 ft (6–9 m)	20–30 ft (6–9 m)	4–9	yes
***Actinidia arguta* 'Issai'**	white, tinged green	mid- to late summer	late summer to autumn	20–30 ft (6–9 m)	20–30 ft (6–9 m)	4–9	yes
Actinidia chinensis	cream	spring	late summer to autumn	10–20 ft (3–6 m)	15–30 ft (4.5–9 m)	7–10	yes
Actinidia deliciosa	cream	spring	late autumn to winter	35 ft (10 m)	35 ft (10 m)	7–10	yes
***Actinidia deliciosa* Zespri Green/'Hayward'**	cream	spring	late autumn to winter	35 ft (10 m)	35 ft (10 m)	7–10	yes
Actinidia kolomikta	white	late spring to summer	late autumn to winter	20–35 ft (6–10 m)	17–20 ft (5–6 m)	4–9	yes

Above *Zespri Green is the trademarked name of* Actinidia deliciosa *'Hayward', the commercial form most commonly seen on shelves, and best known as kiwi fruit.*
Left *A climber native to East Asia,* Actinidia kolomikta *has handsome leaves, tipped white or pink, and variegated after 1 or 2 years. It is not produced commercially.*
Above left Actinidia arguta *is a vigorous twining vine of variable habit that comes from Japan, Korea, and northeastern China. It has oval serrated leaves to 6 in (15 cm) long.*

CITRUS

The genus *Citrus* is part of the rue (Rutaceae) family and is made up of around 20 species of evergreen aromatic trees and shrubs found naturally in Southeast Asia and the Pacific Islands. They are usually neat rounded plants with lustrous mid- to deep green leaves and fragrant, waxy, white flowers. The fruits that follow, such as oranges, lemons, limes, grapefruit, and mandarins, vary in size and flavor but share a similar segmented structure and slow-ripening habit. The first recorded use of the word "orange" is in a poem dated around A.D. 1044, but the fruit did not arrive in Europe until at least A.D. 1200. The word "orange" was derived from the Sanskrit *na rangi*.

CULTIVATION

Citrus need sunlight, warmth, water, and feeding to develop. Plant in a sheltered sunny position with moist, humus-rich, well-drained, slightly acidic soil. Trim lightly at harvesting time. *Citrus* tolerate only light frost and can make attractive pot plants in colder areas. Fruiting varieties are propagated from cuttings or grafts.

Top Tip

During the growing season, citrus trees need plenty of water and regular feeding of nitrogen-based fertilizer to promote fruit size and growth.

BELOW LEFT Citrus × aurantium *'Washington Navel' (syn.* C. sinensis *'Washington Navel') belongs to the Sweet Orange Group. This group's fruit is delicious.*
BELOW *The fruit of* Citrus japonica, *the cumquat tree, has a unique flavor and the peel is eaten with the flesh.*

LEFT Citrus × meyeri *'Meyer' is a lemon/orange hybrid. It is usually treated as a lemon, due perhaps to its shape, but it is not as acidic as a true lemon.*

ABOVE Citrus × microcarpa *is a popular ornamental shrub that is a hybrid of the cumquat and the mandarin. It can be successfully grown in pots, indoors and out.*

Favorites	Flower Color	Blooming Season	Produce Season	Plant Height	Plant Width	Hardiness Zone	Frost Tolerance
Citrus* × *aurantiifolia	white	spring to summer	summer to winter	8–15 ft (2.4–4.5 m)	10 ft (3 m)	11–12	no
Citrus* × *aurantium	white	spring to summer	autumn to spring	15–35 ft (4.5–10 m)	10–20 ft (3–6 m)	9–11	no
Citrus japonica	white	spring to summer	autumn to spring	6 ft (1.8 m)	3 ft (0.9 m)	9–10	no
Citrus maxima	white	spring to summer	autumn to spring	20–40 ft (6–12 m)	10 ft (3 m)	10–12	no
***Citrus* × *meyeri* 'Meyer'**	cream	most of year	most of year	7–10 ft (2–3 m)	5–8 ft (1.5–2.4 m)	9–11	no
Citrus* × *microcarpa	white	most of year	most of year	8 ft (2.4 m)	4 ft (1.2 m)	9–11	no

CORYLUS

Corylus is a genus in the birch (Betulaceae) family that has about 15 species of deciduous shrubs and trees native to the northern temperate zones. They have heavily veined, mid-green, rounded leaves, and from mid- to late winter they bear yellowish male flower catkins that persist until the new leaves form in the spring. The female flowers are inconspicuous but develop into the nuts, which are ripe when they fall in late summer or early autumn.

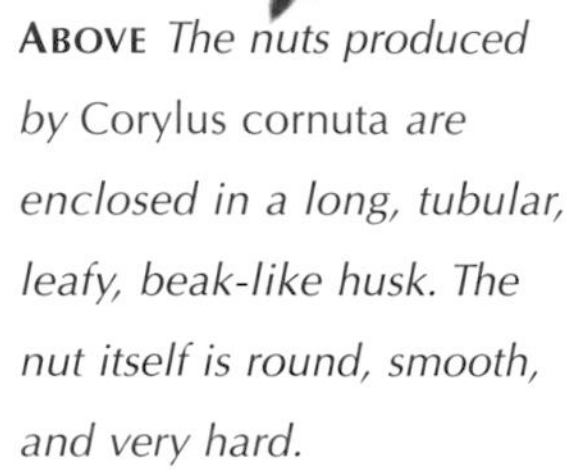

ABOVE *The nuts produced by* Corylus cornuta *are enclosed in a long, tubular, leafy, beak-like husk. The nut itself is round, smooth, and very hard.*

CULTIVATION

Hazels are very hardy and grow well in a sunny position with fertile well-drained soil. Although flowers of both sexes occur on the same plant, if grown for their fruit, pollinators are required to ensure a good yield. Special varieties, such as 'Daviana', can pollinate at least 20 trees in the near vicinity. Removing suckers is the simplest propagation method, or use half-hardened summer cuttings, treated with hormone powder. The seed germinates if stratified but the nuts will be of variable quality.

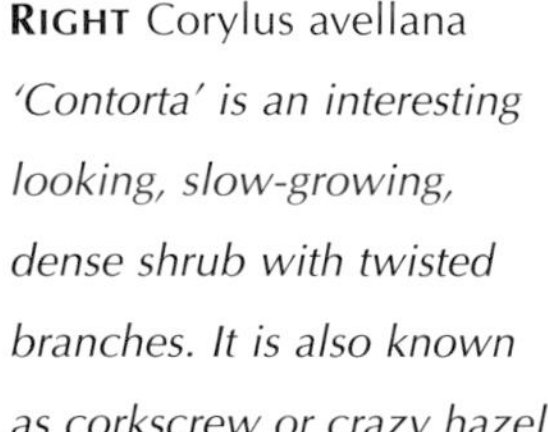

RIGHT Corylus avellana *'Contorta' is an interesting looking, slow-growing, dense shrub with twisted branches. It is also known as corkscrew or crazy hazel.*

Favorites	Flower Color	Blooming Season	Produce Season	Plant Height	Plant Width	Hardiness Zone	Frost Tolerance
Corylus americana	light brown and red	autumn to spring	late summer to autumn	10 ft (3 m)	10 ft (3 m)	4–8	yes
Corylus avellana	yellow and red	winter to early spring	late summer	15 ft (4.5 m)	15 ft (4.5 m)	4–8	yes
Corylus colurna	yellow and red	winter to early spring	early autumn	80 ft (24 m)	25 ft (8 m)	4–8	yes
Corylus cornuta	light brown and red	autumn to spring	late summer	10 ft (3 m)	10 ft (3 m)	4–8	yes
Corylus maxima	reddish purple and red	late winter to spring	mid- to late autumn	15–30 ft (4.5–9 m)	15 ft (4.5 m)	5–9	yes
***Corylus maxima* 'Purpurea'**	reddish purple and red	late winter to spring	mid- to late autumn	15–30 ft (4.5–9 m)	15 ft (4.5 m)	5–9	yes

ABOVE *Purple-leaf hazelnut,* Corylus maxima, *is widely grown in gardens for the coppery purple tint in its young leaves. This cultivar is 'Purpurea'.*

BELOW Corylus colurna *thrives in continental climates—hot summers and cold winters. It is unusual to the genus, growing with one straight trunk.*

Top Tip

Corylus species can be used as hedging plants. Leave untrimmed or trimmed only very lightly if you wish the shrubs to bear a crop of nuts.

Fragaria

Fragaria is a genus of 12 species of perennials in the rose (Rosaceae) family. Found in the northern temperate zones and Chile, they are tough adaptable plants that spread by runners. Commonly known as strawberries, their foliage is usually trifoliate, with broad toothed leaflets. From spring, clusters of small white flowers appear, which are followed by the luscious fruits. Strawberries bear their seeds on the outside and if one were to be fussy, this means that they are not really a fruit.

Cultivation

Strawberries are very hardy and grow well in full sun on broad mounds of moist well-drained soil, or with a surrounding of dry mulch, such as straw, to prevent the fruits rotting before they ripen. Cultivars vary in their fruiting period, the earliest flower in winter and their fruits may need frost protection. Often the entire crop will need to be covered with netting to prevent bird damage. Propagate by layering the stolons or by using them as cuttings.

Top right Fragaria × ananassa *'Eros' is a very hardy cultivar that has been bred to be resistant to the disease red stele. It bears large, glossy, red fruits.*
Right Fragaria × ananassa *'Tribute' is one of the most successful varieties of strawberries for commerical plantings. It produces medium to large, flavorful fruit.*

Favorites	Flower Color	Blooming Season	Produce Season	Plant Height	Plant Width	Hardiness Zone	Frost Tolerance
Fragaria* × *ananassa	white	late spring to autumn	summer to autumn	6 in (15 cm)	40 in (100 cm)	3–10	yes
***Fragaria* × *ananassa* 'Benton'**	white	late spring to autumn	summer to autumn	6 in (15 cm)	40 in (100 cm)	3–10	yes
***Fragaria* × *ananassa* 'Fort Laramie'**	white	late spring to autumn	summer to autumn	6 in (15 cm)	40 in (100 cm)	3–10	yes
***Fragaria* × *ananassa* 'Rainier'**	white	late spring to autumn	summer to autumn	6 in (15 cm)	40 in (100 cm)	3–10	yes
Fragaria chiloensis	white	spring to summer	autumn	6 in (15 cm)	20 in (50 cm)	4–10	yes
***Fragaria* 'Rosie'**	red	spring to autumn	summer to autumn	2–6 in (5–15 cm)	8–60 in (20–150 cm)	5–9	yes

Top Tip

During the first growing season of a strawberry plant, remove the flowers for the first month. The plant will grow stronger, producing a larger fruit crop the following year.

ABOVE *As well as producing a good yield of fruits, the hybrid cultivar 'Rosie' has red blooms instead of white. This plant makes a pretty and practical ground cover.*

RIGHT *When selecting a strawberry variety, consider season of ripening and disease resistance.* Fragaria × ananassa *'Symphony' produces late-season fruits.*

JUGLANS

The type genus for the walnut (Juglandaceae) family, *Juglans* is composed of some 20 species of deciduous trees found in southern Europe and the temperate regions of the Americas and East Asia. They have large pinnate leaves and grow very quickly when young. The flowers, small and often well hidden among the foliage, develop into large fruits that mature from late summer around hard cases that contain the nuts. In addition to the fruits, walnuts have wonderfully grained timber that is prized for the finest furniture, ornamental items, and veneers. Some species produce juglose, which can poison apple trees.

ABOVE *Commonly known as the butternut,* Juglans cinerea *is found from New Brunswick, Canada to Georgia, USA. It is particularly cultivated in New England where its nuts are used to make maple-butternut candy.*

RIGHT Juglans regia, *the English or Persian walnut, produces the largest and most easily cracked nuts. Cultivars of the Carpathian Group are cold hardy and popular throughout USA, particularly as commercial crops.*

CULTIVATION

Mature trees are very hardy but the soft spring growth is easily damaged by late frosts and strong winds. Grow in a bright position with moist, deep, well-drained soil, and water well as the fruits mature. The nuts may be subject to fungal problems in areas with high summer humidity. Sow ripe seeds in early spring from cool storage. Prune to shape when young.

Top Tip

Prune walnut trees when the plant is either fully dormant or fully in leaf. Otherwise any cuts will bleed profusely and severely weaken the tree.

RIGHT *Be sure to plant this species,* Juglans cathayensis, *in its permanent position. This tree produces a deep tap root and does not tolerate root disturbance. It will bear nuts after 4 or 5 years.*

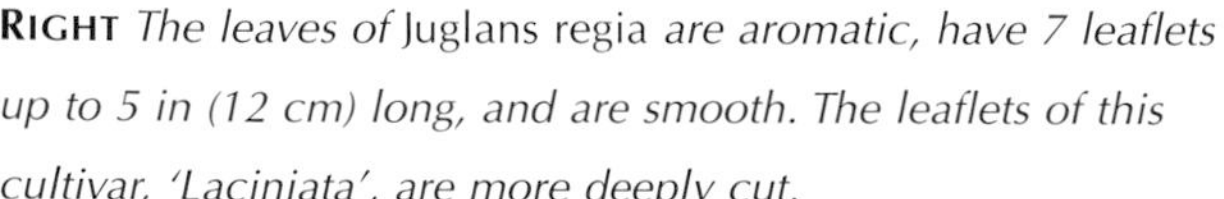

RIGHT *The leaves of* Juglans regia *are aromatic, have 7 leaflets up to 5 in (12 cm) long, and are smooth. The leaflets of this cultivar, 'Laciniata', are more deeply cut.*

Favorites	Flower Color	Blooming Season	Produce Season	Plant Height	Plant Width	Hardiness Zone	Frost Tolerance
Juglans ailanthifolia	brown and red	summer	autumn	50 ft (15 m)	40 ft (12 m)	4–9	yes
Juglans cathayensis	brown and greenish	spring to summer	autumn	50–70 ft (15–21 m)	50 ft (15 m)	5–10	yes
Juglans cinerea	yellowish green	spring to summer	autumn	60 ft (18 m)	50 ft (15 m)	4–9	yes
Juglans major	yellowish green	late spring to early summer	autumn to winter	50 ft (15 m)	30 ft (9 m)	9–11	yes
Juglans nigra	yellowish green	late spring to early summer	autumn	100 ft (30 m)	70 ft (21 m)	4–10	yes
Juglans regia	yellowish green	summer	autumn	40–60 ft (12–18 m)	35 ft (10 m)	4–10	yes

RIGHT Mangifera indica *is from Southeast Asia, especially Myanmar and eastern India. It has leaves that are red when young, but which age to a shiny dark green over time.*
FAR RIGHT *There are many cultivars of the mango species* Mangifera indica. *'Campeche' is a cultivar that has bright green leaves and deep yellow fruits with a reddish pink tinge.*

Top Tip

Give plenty of water through late spring and summer, less in autumn, and none from winter to early spring. Fertilize trees 2 or 3 times each summer, once established.

MANGIFERA

Although this cashew (Anacardiaceae) family genus contains around 50 species of evergreen shrubs and trees found from India to the Solomon Islands, only one, *Mangifera indica,* is widely cultivated. Commonly known as the mango, it is an Indian native that develops quickly to form a large, many-branched, spreading tree. Panicles of small yellow to red flowers develop into clusters of oval greenish yellow fruits with a red blush. The fruits have quite a distinctive odor and flavor and contain 1 large seed. The timber is hard and durable but needs careful handling as the sap and sawdust can cause dermatitis and eye irritations.

CULTIVATION

Mangoes prefer a warm frost-free climate to crop well. Plant them in full or half-sun in a well-drained humus-rich soil. Mangoes occur naturally in areas with seasonal rainfall and so they prefer dry conditions at flowering and fruit set but need more moisture thereafter. They may be raised from seed but superior cultivars are grafted.

RIGHT Mangifera indica *has fruits that are fleshy and irregularly egg-shaped. They may be "alternate-bearing," fruiting heavily only every 2 to 4 years.*

ABOVE Mangifera caesia *can grow up to 120 ft (36 m) in the wild. Also known as jack or binjai, its fruit flavor is said to resemble a mix of mango and pineapple.*

Favorites	Flower Color	Blooming Season	Produce Season	Plant Height	Plant Width	Hardiness Zone	Frost Tolerance
Mangifera caesia	lavender-blue	spring	mid-spring to summer	120 ft (36 m)	30 ft (9 m)	11–12	no
Mangifera indica	yellowish or reddish	spring	mid-spring to summer	80 ft (24 m)	25 ft (8 m)	11–12	no
***Mangifera indica* 'Campeche'**	yellowish or reddish	spring	mid-spring to summer	50 ft (15 m)	20 ft (6 m)	11–12	no
***Mangifera indica* 'Edward'**	yellowish or reddish	spring	mid-spring to summer	50 ft (15 m)	20 ft (6 m)	11–12	no
***Mangifera indica* 'Kensington Pride'**	yellowish or reddish	spring	mid-spring to summer	50 ft (15 m)	20 ft (6 m)	11–12	no
***Mangifera indica* 'Kent'**	yellowish or reddish	spring	mid-spring to summer	50 ft (15 m)	20 ft (6 m)	11–12	no

PRUNUS

Among the most beloved of flowering trees and also extremely useful for the wide range of fruits they produce, the 430 species of the genus *Prunus* are members of the rose (Rosaceae) family. Those grown for their fruit are medium-sized deciduous trees with simple, serrated, elliptical leaves. Their brilliant spring show of white, pink, crimson, or soft orange flowers soon gives way to a heavy crop of fleshy fruits with a hard pit or stone at the center. The fruit matures quite quickly and may be ripe by mid-summer. The foliage often develops fiery autumn tones. Cherry wood is dark and beautifully grained, and is often used for inlays and small objects.

CULTIVATION

Mostly very hardy, but prone to flower damage through late frosts, *Prunus* are reliable trees that, with the exceptions of apricots, peaches, and nectarines, will fruit well even in areas with cool summers. Plant in a bright position with moist, humus-rich, well-drained soil. Keep the trees evenly moist but do not use overhead irrigation or the fruits may split. Superior fruiting forms are grafted.

RIGHT Prunus *'Shirofugen' is one of the Sato-zakura Group of hybrids mostly grown as ornamentals for their flower display. The white flowers age to pink.*

LEFT Prunus persica *is the state flower of Delaware, and the state fruit of South Carolina. There are many ornamental and fruiting cultivars available.*

ABOVE *The fragrant white flowers of* Prunus tomentosa *are followed by downy red fruits. This species is also known as the Manchu, or Nanking, cherry.*

Favorites	Flower Color	Blooming Season	Produce Season	Plant Height	Plant Width	Hardiness Zone	Frost Tolerance
Prunus* × *domestica	white	spring	summer to autumn	30 ft (9 m)	15 ft (4.5 m)	5–9	yes
Prunus maackii	creamy white	mid-spring	summer	30–50 ft (9–15 m)	25 ft (8 m)	2–9	yes
Prunus mume	rose pink	mid-winter to early spring	early summer	20–30 ft (6–9 m)	25 ft (8 m)	6–10	yes
Prunus* × *persica	white, pink	late winter to early spring	summer to early autumn	8–20 ft (2.4–6 m)	6–20 ft (1.8–6 m)	5–10	yes
Prunus salicina	white	spring	summer to early autumn	30 ft (9 m)	25 ft (8 m)	6–10	yes
***Prunus salicina* 'Satsuma'**	white	spring	summer	25 ft (8 m)	25 ft (8 m)	6–10	yes
Prunus serrula	white	mid-spring	summer	30 ft (9 m)	30 ft (9 m)	6–8	yes
Prunus* × *subhirtella	white, pink	autumn, spring	summer	50 ft (15 m)	25 ft (8 m)	5–9	yes
***Prunus* × *subhirtella* 'Autumnalis'**	pink and white	late autumn, spring	summer	25 ft (8 m)	25 ft (8 m)	5–9	yes
Prunus tomentosa	white to pale pink	early spring	summer	8 ft (2.4 m)	8 ft (2.4 m)	2–8	yes
Prunus triloba	pink	spring	summer	6–12 ft (1.8–3.5 m)	8–12 ft (2.4–3.5 m)	5–9	yes
***Prunus*, Sato-zakura Group**	white, pink	spring	no fruit	30 ft (9 m)	30 ft (9 m)	5–9	yes

ABOVE Prunus maackii *(the Amur choke cherry) has very attractive peeling or flaking bark, varying in color from brownish yellow to cinnamon brown.*

BELOW RIGHT *Produced early to mid-season,* Prunus persica *'Texstar' peaches have yellow flesh. The best-quality fruits are fully ripened on the tree.*

Top Tip

Most *Prunus* cultivars need to be grown with another different cultivar for cross-pollination and fruit production to occur. Not all cultivars are compatible.

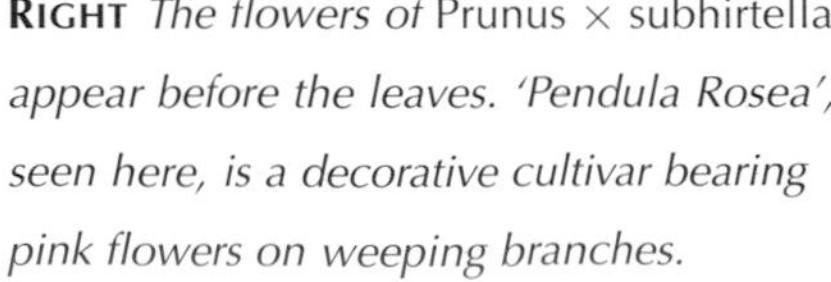

RIGHT *The flowers of* Prunus × subhirtella *appear before the leaves. 'Pendula Rosea', seen here, is a decorative cultivar bearing pink flowers on weeping branches.*

LEFT Prunus × domestica, *the European plum, has yellow- or red-skinned fruit. 'Beühlerfrühwetsch' is a purple-skinned cultivar from Germany.*

FAR LEFT *The fruits of* Prunus mume *are known as umeboshi plums, a Japanese delicacy. This cultivar, 'Geisha', is grown for its fragrant, pink, semi-double flowers.*

BELOW Prunus triloba *'Multiplex' is a double-flowered dwarf flowering almond. This decorative small tree makes an excellent accent plant.*

Above Pyrus communis *'Doyenné du Comice' (syn. 'Comice') is regarded as one of the best cultivars. The fruit has sweet, creamy, juicy flesh.*

Right *The thorny branches of* Pyrus communis *are covered with blossoms in spring. This species has been cultivated for centuries for its large sweet-tasting fruit.*

Pyrus

A genus in the rose (Rosaceae) family, *Pyrus* is closely related to the apples *(Malus)*. There are around 20 species of pears, but the cultivated fruiting forms are all cultivars of the common pear *(Pyrus communis)* of Eurasia or the China pear *(Pyrus pyrifolia)* from Japan and China. They have leathery deep green leaves with shallowly serrated edges and in spring are smothered in white flowers. These soon fall and the fruits develop. They ripen slowly and may not become really sweet until they have been in storage for a while. Pear wood is heavy, fine-grained, and durable. It is used mainly in musical instruments.

Cultivation

Pyrus plants tolerate a wide range of soil types and climatic conditions but can be difficult to grow in very mild areas or those with late frosts. Plant in a sunny position with moist well-drained soil and shelter from strong winds. Prune to shape when young and trim annually. Dwarf varieties are grafted onto quince stocks and can be espaliered. The best forms are propagated by grafting.

Top Tip

Thin out the developing fruit if necessary. Leave only one pear in each cluster, with about 6 in (15 cm) between pears. This will increase the size of the remaining fruit.

RIGHT *The fruits of* Pyrus pyrifolia *are known as Asian pears or nashi, and are sweet, crisp, and juicy. 'Hosui' is a popular cultivar with particularly good flavor.*

LEFT Pyrus salicifolia *makes a small graceful tree and is known as the willow-leafed pear or the silver pear, as its narrow willow-like leaves are silvery when young.*

Favorites	Flower Color	Blooming Season	Produce Season	Plant Height	Plant Width	Hardiness Zone	Frost Tolerance
Pyrus calleryana	white	spring	autumn	40 ft (12 m)	40 ft (12 m)	5–9	yes
Pyrus communis	white	spring	summer to autumn	50 ft (15 m)	20 ft (6 m)	2–9	yes
***Pyrus communis* 'Doyenné du Comice'**	white	spring	summer to autumn	12–20 ft (3.5–6 m)	7–15 ft (2–4.5 m)	2–9	yes
Pyrus pyrifolia	white	spring	summer to autumn	50 ft (15 m)	30 ft (9 m)	4–9	yes
***Pyrus pyrifolia* 'Nijisseiki'**	white	spring	summer to autumn	12–20 ft (3.5–6 m)	7–15 ft (2–4.5 m)	4–9	yes
Pyrus salicifolia	white	spring	summer to autumn	25 ft (8 m)	15 ft (4.5 m)	4–9	yes

RIGHT Ribes aureum *is known as the golden currant and is mainly grown as an ornamental. The flowers are strongly scented. The berries ripen to blue-black.*

RIBES

A genus of the gooseberry (Grossulariaceae) family, this has over 150 species of deciduous and evergreen shrubs from the northern temperate zones with a few in South America. Those grown for fruit are deciduous bushes with lobed, often bristly leaves and sometimes thorny stems. Sprays of small cream, yellow, green, or pink flowers open in spring and may be inconspicuous. Berries (generally known as currants) in varying colors follow and are a rich source of vitamin C. The name *Ribes* is derived from the Persian, *ribas*, meaning "acid-tasting," which describes the unripe fruit.

CULTIVATION

Currant bushes do not require much winter chilling but often crop better with cold winters. They will grow in most soils but they must be well-drained. Prune to shape when young and thin out old wood annually. Fruit forms on short lateral branches. The main branches should be cut back to allow lateral fruiting spurs to develop. Feed annually with a balanced general fertilizer. Propagate good fruiting forms from cuttings or layers.

RIGHT Ribes nigrum *'Ben Connan' is a very high-yielding cultivar with a compact growth habit. It produces a delicious fresh fruit that can also be used for jam-making.*

Favorites	Flower Color	Blooming Season	Produce Season	Plant Height	Plant Width	Hardiness Zone	Frost Tolerance
Ribes aureum	yellow	spring	summer	6 ft (1.8 m)	6 ft (1.8 m)	2–9	yes
Ribes malvaceum	pink	mid-winter to spring	late spring to summer	6 ft (1.8 m)	6 ft (1.8 m)	7–10	yes
Ribes nigrum	yellow-green	spring	summer	7 ft (2 m)	6 ft (1.8 m)	5–9	yes
Ribes rubrum	red and green	late spring to early summer	summer	3–5 ft (0.9–1.5 m)	5–7 ft (1.5–2 m)	3–9	yes
Ribes uva-crispa	green	late winter to early spring	late spring to summer	3 ft (0.9 m)	3 ft (0.9 m)	5–9	yes
***Ribes uva-crispa* 'Leveller'**	green	spring	summer	3 ft (0.9 m)	3 ft (0.9 m)	5–9	yes

LEFT *Commonly known as the gooseberry, the fruit of* Ribes uva-crispa *is cooked to make excellent tarts, pies, and jams. The taste ranges from sweet to acid.*

Top Tip

The newer cultivars of currants and gooseberries have larger fruits and better resistance to a range of diseases than the selections available earlier.

RIGHT *The red currant,* Ribes rubrum, *is a deciduous shrub which produces translucent red berries. It makes a good garden ornamental, and the berries taste good too.*

RUBUS

A near-worldwide genus belonging to the rose (Rosaceae) family, *Rubus* has 250 species of often thorny deciduous and evergreen shrubs, scramblers, and vines. Those grown for their fruit are deciduous shrubs that form clumps of erect or arching canes that are fiercely thorny. The foliage is lobed and usually bristly. Simple 4- or 5-petalled white or pale pink flowers open in spring and are soon followed by soft multi-celled fruits, usually red or purple-black. Native Americans used the roots medicinally and made dyes from the fruits.

CULTIVATION

While the canes need training and support for maximum production, *Rubus* plants are easily cultivated. Add plenty of compost to the soil before planting, grow in full sun, and water well as the fruits ripen. The canes fruit in their second year and are best trained along wires or against a fence. Remove any spent canes after harvest. Bird damage and fungal diseases are the main risks. Propagate from cuttings or layers, or by division.

ABOVE *A late-bearing cultivar,* Rubus idaeus *'Heritage' produces heavily into early autumn and requires fewer hours of winter chilling than other raspberries.*

LEFT Rubus *'Tayberry' is the result of a cross between a raspberry and a blackberry. The freely produced berries ripen to purple, and have a delightful sweet flavor.*

Favorites	Flower Color	Blooming Season	Produce Season	Plant Height	Plant Width	Hardiness Zone	Frost Tolerance
Rubus idaeus	white	late spring to early summer	summer	5 ft (1.5 m)	4 ft (1.2 m)	3–9	yes
***Rubus idaeus* 'Autumn Bliss'**	white	summer	autumn	5 ft (1.5 m)	18 in (45 cm)	3–9	yes
***Rubus idaeus* 'Tulameen'**	white	spring to summer	summer	5 ft (1.5 m)	18 in (45 cm)	3–9	yes
Rubus parviflorus	white	summer	summer	15 ft (4.5 m)	10 ft (3 m)	3–9	yes
Rubus spectabilis	pink-purple	spring	summer to autumn	6 ft (1.8 m)	5 ft (1.5 m)	5–9	yes
***Rubus* 'Tayberry'**	white	summer	late summer to autumn	6 ft (1.8 m)	6 ft (1.8 m)	5–9	yes

BELOW *Although the flowers of* Rubus parviflorus *are small, they are still quite attractive. They are followed by even smaller fruits, hence the common name of thimbleberry.*

Top Tip

Trellising *Rubus* plants makes access to the fruit easier, and allows more sunlight to reach the leaves and branches. This will increase the amount of fruit produced.

ABOVE *The pink to purple flowers of* Rubus spectabilis *are carried on thorny stems. Native to western North America, these plants often form dense thickets.*

VACCINIUM

This primarily northern temperate to sub-arctic genus in the heath (Ericaceae) family contains around 450 species of evergreen and deciduous shrubs, small trees, and vines, and includes several species cultivated for their edible fruits and many others from which the fruits are gathered in the wild. The cultivated species are deciduous bushes with dark green lance-shaped leaves and wiry stems. Clusters of cream to pale pink, downward-facing, urn-shaped flowers open in spring and are followed by red, purple-blue, or black berries, sometimes with a powdery bloom. In recent years the antioxidant properties of blueberries have seen them promoted as something of a wonder drug, but regardless of how true that proves to be, they taste very good.

CULTIVATION

These hardy deciduous bushes prefer moist, well-drained, humus-rich, acid soil and may take a few years before producing regular crops. The fruits develop on one-year-old wood and once cropping well the bushes should be pruned and thinned annually. Propagate from half-hardened cuttings or layers.

ABOVE *A northern highbush blueberry (the most widely planted group),* Vaccinium corymbosum *'Earliblue' bears medium-sized sweet fruits on an erect bush.*

LEFT Vaccinium vitis-idaea *is a creeping evergreen shrub. The tiny oval leaves develop bronze tones in winter, and bright red edible but tart berries known as cowberries follow the flower clusters.*

RIGHT *In mild areas* Vaccinium *'Sharpeblue' (syn. 'Sharpblue') will flower and fruit for most of the year. Plants are fast growing and high yielding.*

Favorites	Flower Color	Blooming Season	Produce Season	Plant Height	Plant Width	Hardiness Zone	Frost Tolerance
Vaccinium corymbosum	white, white and red	spring	summer	3–6 ft (0.9–1.8 m)	5 ft (1.5 m)	2–9	yes
***Vaccinium corymbosum* 'Bluecrop'**	white	spring	summer	6–8 ft (1.8–2.4 m)	6–8 ft (1.8–2.4 m)	3–9	yes
***Vaccinium corymbosum* 'Patriot'**	white	early spring	early to mid-summer	6–8 ft (1.8–2.4 m)	6–8 ft (1.8–2.4 m)	2–9	yes
Vaccinium nummularia	pink	late spring	summer	12–15 in (30–38 cm)	12–15 in (30–38 cm)	7–10	yes
***Vaccinium* 'Sharpeblue'**	white	early spring	late spring to summer	6 ft (1.8 m)	6 ft (1.8 m)	7–10	yes
Vaccinium vitis-idaea	white to pink	late spring	autumn	6 in (15 cm)	24–48 in (60–120 cm)	2–8	yes

BELOW *An attractive ground cover or rock-garden plant,* Vaccinium nummularia *makes a small evergreen shrub. Edible blue-black berries follow the flowers.*

Top Tip

A thick layer of mulch will reduce the risk of damage to the very shallow roots of blueberries. Mulching will also help keep the soil cool and moist, especially in pots.

VITIS

As befits one of the longest cultivated plants, *Vitis* is the type genus for the grape (Vitaceae) family, and is composed of around 60 species of woody deciduous vines from the temperate Northern Hemisphere. Most of the cultivated grape varieties are derived from one species, *Vitis vinifera*, though others, such as the North American native *Vitis labrusca*, are grown in small quantities. Grapes have large, lobed, or occasionally toothed leaves, and in spring produce small clusters of green flowers that soon start to develop into the familiar bunches of round berries. No plant has a more colorful history than the grape, which probably features in more legends than all other plants combined.

CULTIVATION

Grape varieties differ most obviously in fruit color: white, red, or black. Some are table grapes, others wine grapes, and a few are dual purpose. Plant in full sun with light well-drained soil. Table grapes will benefit from additional humus and summer moisture for producing the plumpest fruit. In winter, prune back to within two buds of the main stem to encourage the strong new growth on which the flowers and fruit will form. Grapes are best trained along wires or against fences. Propagate from cuttings, or by layering or grafting.

ABOVE Vitis vinifera *'Merlot' grapes ripen to medium-sized blue-black fruits that are used to produce smooth red wines. These plants need some protection from wind.*

LEFT *An Austrian cultivar,* Vitis vinifera *'Gelber Muskateller' is grown for white wine-making. It has aromatic qualities, and is a member of the muscat group of grapes.*

Top Tip

Grapes change color well before reaching their best size and sweetness, so taste-test before picking. Flavor does not improve after harvesting.

Left *The small round fruits of* Vitis vinifera *'Chardonnay' are used to make white wine. This vigorous vine usually produces a reliable crop of grapes.*

Above *Another wine-making cultivar,* Vitis vinifera *'Pinot Noir' produces small to medium-sized grapes. These vines can be slow to establish, but are reliable producers.*

Favorites	Flower Color	Blooming Season	Produce Season	Plant Height	Plant Width	Hardiness Zone	Frost Tolerance
Vitis **'Concord'**	green	spring	summer to autumn	15–20 ft (4.5–6 m)	15–20 ft (4.5–6 m)	5–8	yes
Vitis vinifera	green	late spring to early summer	late summer to autumn	35 ft (10 m)	15–30 ft (4.5–9 m)	6–9	yes
Vitis vinifera **'Cabernet Sauvignon'**	green	late spring to early summer	late summer to autumn	35 ft (10 m)	15–30 ft (4.5–9 m)	6–9	yes
Vitis vinifera **'Chardonnay'**	green	late spring to early summer	late summer to autumn	35 ft (10 m)	15–30 ft (4.5–9 m)	6–9	yes
Vitis vinifera **'Pinot Gris'**	green	late spring to early summer	late summer to autumn	35 ft (10 m)	15–30 ft (4.5–9 m)	6–9	yes
Vitis vinifera **'Thompson Seedless'**	green,	spring	summer to autumn	35 ft (10 m)	15–30 ft (4.5–9 m)	6–9	yes

Bulbs, Corms, and Tubers

Bulbs, corms, and tubers produce some of the most exciting plants in the garden. Half the thrill comes from the speed at which they can grow from embryonic bud to voluptuous flower. The other half comes from the many ways they contribute to our garden. They offer paintbox-colorful blossoms, as with Persian ranunculus; distinctive shapes such as the curiously backward-curving blossoms of cyclamen; huge architectural flowers like the larger flowering onions (*Allium* species) and calla lilies (*Zantedeschia* species); and flowers from the earliest inkling of spring (*Crocus* species) to its end (*Schizostylis* species).

Above *Whether used as potted specimen plants or in massed plantings, tulips add beauty and color.* Tulipa *'Jacqueline' belongs to the Lily-flowered Group.*
Left Hyacinthus *cultivars are grown in an amazing variety of colors. The fragrance of these showy blooms is another attractive feature, and they are popular cut flowers.*

SURPRISE PACKETS OF THE GARDEN

Plants possessing underground storage systems of different types, including bulbs, corms, and tubers, are known scientifically as geophytes, but are generally all called bulbs. The seasonal dormancy they employ is a strategy to survive periods of adverse weather: usually cold winter temperatures or summer droughts.

True bulbs are perhaps the best known of these types of plants. A true bulb is a modified bud comprised of compressed leaf scales that emerge from a basal plate. Some bulbs consist of fleshy scaly leaves surrounding an embryonic central stem, such as lilies (*Lilium* species). Others, such as daffodils (*Narcissus* species), tulips (*Tulipa* species), and onions (*Allium* species), are covered with a thin papery tunic.

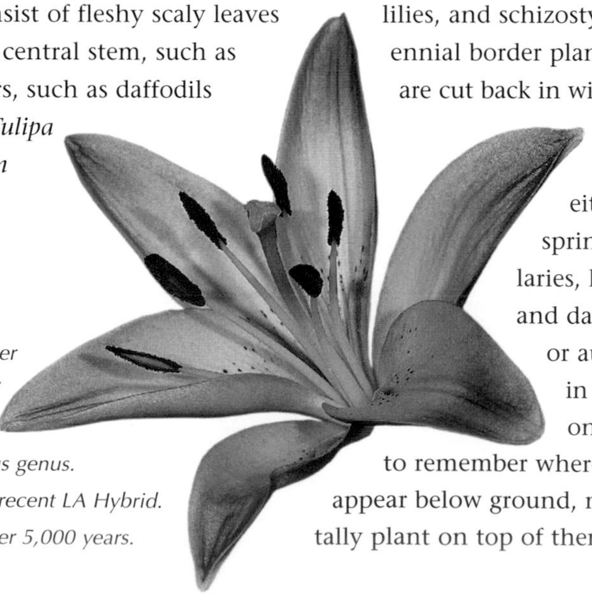

ABOVE *The white calla lily is better known, but* Zantedeschia *'Flame' is a more compact and colorful hybrid cultivar of this rhizomatous genus.*
RIGHT Lilium *'Royal Sunset' is a recent LA Hybrid. Lilies have been cultivated for over 5,000 years.*

Corms consist of a swollen underground stem, replaced annually, that does not contain leaves packed inside. Corms include colchicums, crocuses, and dogtooth violets (*Erythronium* species). Although some corms such as colchicums are covered with a papery tunic, most—such as crocuses and gladioli (*Gladiolus* species)—have a more fibrous tunic.

Tubers are specialized underground stems with a fleshy non-scaly structure. The potato is perhaps the most renowned tuber; other examples include dahlias, cyclamen, and many anemones. Some plants, such as *Schizostylis coccinea* and its cultivars, have a slightly different underground stem called a rhizome. Many iris family plants are rhizomatous.

Most bulbous plants from regions with a pronounced wet-dry period evolved in response to seasonal drought. Some require a dry baking rest period in summer and can rot if they receive excessive water at this time. These include many tulip species, daffodils, crocus species, and fritillaries (*Fritillaria* species). Some bulbs, such as certain dogtooth violets and wake robins (*Trillium* species), come from moister environments. They grow well in shady woodland garden conditions. Still others, such as the common calla lily *(Zantedeschia aethiopica),* thrive in very moist soil.

Many types of bulbous plants, such as crocosmia, lilies, and schizostylis, behave as regular perennial border plants that arise in spring and are cut back in winter. But many others completely disappear into the ground after flowering, either in late spring for early spring bloomers (crocus, fritillaries, hyacinths, muscari, tulips, and daffodils) or in late summer or autumn for plants blooming in summer (summer-flowering onions). While it can be hard to remember where bulbs are when they disappear below ground, making it easy to accidentally plant on top of them, many gardeners make an art of combining bulbs with perennials and shrubs by planting successive waves of color and timing them to take maximum advantage of space.

For that reason, bulbs make a wonderful addition to the border. Bulbs that are integrated into a border should be smaller, such as the more diminutive daffodils and flowering onions. Larger daffodils, with their vigorous spreading habit, can occupy too much space, both in the soil and with their coarse leaves that take a month or more to die back. Larger daffodils and tulips are some of the best bulbs for solo mass plantings, creating wonderful seasonal displays—and then being removed so that something new may be planted. Other good border mixers include *Crocosmia* species, *Gladiolus* species, and lilies.

Bulbs from the Mediterranean and the steppes of central Asia are well suited to sunny dry areas with well-drained soil. These include fritillaries, crocus, smaller daffodils, and tulip species. They look good planted in gravel with lavender (*Lavandula* species), *Agave* species, *Yucca* species, *Penstemon* species, as well as other drought-adapted plants.

Taller daffodils make fine naturalized wild-meadow plants, flowering in spring, then dying back in time for the first mowing of the season.

Bulbs are some of the most dramatic container plants, either by themselves or in combination with herbs and other perennials. A pot thickly planted with the simplest red tulips or packed with spidery pink nerines makes a gorgeous display, inside or out. Perhaps the most famous indoor flowering bulbs are amaryllis (*Hippeastrum* plants), which brighten cold-climate winters with their huge colorful blossoms. In warm climates, mass plantings of amaryllis make a spectacular display.

Containers may also be layered with crocus, early daffodils, and later-blooming flowering onions for a long-lasting display. Crocus and other smaller bulbs are lovely peeking through ground covers, or with perennials such as euphorbias, whose growing leaves obscure the bulbs' foliage as it dries. With so many different bulbs hailing from such diverse climates worldwide, the possibilities are limitless.

ABOVE *One of the grape hyacinths,* Muscari aucheri *is a summer-flowering bulb. It makes a good bedding display.* **RIGHT** *Tulips are perhaps the best-known bulbs.* Tulipa *'Golden Parade' is a stunning Darwin Hybrid Group tulip.*

Top Tip

The ornamental species of *Allium* make excellent long-lasting cut flowers. Alternatively they can be cut and dried for use in floral arrangements.

ALLIUM

Unlike the ornamental onions, the edible species among the 700 members of this genus are not grown for their flowers but for their bulbs or foliage. The type genus for the onion (Alliaceae) family, they typically have blue-green foliage that may be grassy, as with chives, strappy like that of leeks, or broad-based and hollow, as with onion leaves. With the exception of chives, which are perennial, the edible alliums tend to be biennial and if the flowers appear they are said to have "run to seed" and the bulbs will be of poor quality or useless. The genus features widely in myths and legends, of which the use of garlic to ward off vampires is probably the best known.

ABOVE *Exquisitely dainty, the heads of pure white nodding flowers of* Allium paradoxum *var.* normale *can each contain up to 10 blooms. Unlike the species, it does not produce bulbils (small bulb-like shoots that develop from the base of the parent bulb).*

CULTIVATION

Onions fall into two basic categories: those to be used immediately and those that will keep for several months. They are either raised from seed sown in situ or from transplants. Shallots and garlic are grown from offsets (cloves) planted in well-drained soil in full sun, usually around mid-winter. They are ready when the tops die back, which is usually in mid-summer. Leeks demand a rich soil with plenty of organic matter. The seed may be sown from spring to early autumn. Bought seedlings are a common method of establishing a crop and can be planted out from spring until early winter. Modern varieties are largely self-blanching but better results are still obtained by mounding soil around the stems as they mature.

BELOW *Slender yet strong upright stems hold aloft the rich purple flowers of* Allium rosenbachianum *'Purple King'. The contrasting foliage is blue-green.*

BELOW Allium howellii *is a Californian native. In late spring it bears rounded heads of starry white, sometimes cream, flowers with prominent stamens.*

RIGHT *Best known for its aromatic grass-like leaves,* Allium schoenoprasum, *or chives, can make a wonderful addition to the herb garden. The pretty pink summer flowers are an added bonus.*

Favorites	Flower Color	Blooming Season	Flower Fragrance	Plant Height	Plant Width	Hardiness Zone	Frost Tolerance
Allium howellii	white to cream	late spring	no	12–20 in (30–50 cm)	6–8 in (15–20 cm)	8–10	yes
Allium moly	golden yellow	late spring	no	8–15 in (20–38 cm)	8–12 in (20–30 cm)	4–9	yes
Allium paradoxum	white	spring	no	6–12 in (15–30 cm)	4–8 in (10–20 cm)	5–9	yes
Allium rosenbachianum	purple, white	spring	no	24–40 in (60–100 cm)	12–20 in (30–50 cm)	7–10	yes
Allium schoenoprasum	pink	summer	no	6–20 in (15–50 cm)	4–12 in (10–30 cm)	5–10	yes
Allium tuberosum	white	late summer	yes	20 in (50 cm)	8–12 in (20–30 cm)	7–10	yes

Top Tip

The leaves of these plants must be allowed to die back in summer and can be unsightly, so plant *Colchicum* among other low-growing plants.

LEFT *The striking double flowers of* Colchicum *'Waterlily' do indeed resemble a waterlily. They bloom in autumn, before the spring foliage appears.*

COLCHICUM

Although superficially similar to the true crocuses (*Crocus* species) and known as autumn crocuses, the 45 species of this Eurasian genus belong in their own family, the Colchicaceae. They have variable foliage, from grassy to broad and strappy, which may or may not be present when in flower. The flowers, usually white, pink, or light magenta, are cup-shaped, with 2 whorls of 3 petals, and open in autumn or spring, depending on the species. Autumn-flowering species often carry their foliage through winter. *Colchicum* is well-known as the source of the mutagenic drug colchicine and also has other medicinal uses.

CULTIVATION

These are mostly very hardy and grow best in climates with well-defined seasons. Autumn crocuses are at home in herbaceous borders, rockeries, and containers, and generally prefer a sunny or partly shaded position with moist well-drained soil. They may be raised from seed, but often multiply naturally from offsets.

Favorites	Flower Color	Blooming Season	Flower Fragrance	Plant Height	Plant Width	Hardiness Zone	Frost Tolerance
Colchicum agrippinum	lilac-pink	early autumn	no	3–6 in (8–15 cm)	2–4 in (5–10 cm)	5–9	yes
Colchicum cilicium	pinkish purple	autumn	no	4–8 in (10–20 cm)	3–6 in (8–15 cm)	5–9	yes
Colchicum parnassicum	lilac-pink	autumn	no	4–6 in (10–15 cm)	3–6 in (8–15 cm)	8–10	yes
***Colchicum* 'Rosy Dawn'**	pink and white	autumn	yes	8 in (20 cm)	3–6 in (8–15 cm)	5–9	yes
Colchicum speciosum	lilac-pink	autumn	no	4–8 in (10–20 cm)	4–6 in (10–15 cm)	6–9	yes
***Colchicum* 'Waterlily'**	lavender-pink	autumn	no	8 in (20 cm)	6 in (15 cm)	6–9	yes

RIGHT Colchicum *'Rosy Dawn' produces large well-scented blooms. Like most plants in this genus, it is easy to grow in the garden or in containers.*

LEFT Colchicum speciosum *cultivars are available with pink- or white-colored flowers. They bear their flowers in autumn and their broad green leaves in spring.*

BELOW *The pale-centered bright lilac-pink flowers of* Colchicum speciosum *are carried on pale green stems. This species is often used as a parent of hybrid cultivars.*

CROCOSMIA

This genus of some 7 species of corms is native to the grasslands of South Africa, and is a member of the iris (Iridaceae) family. Variously known as montbretia or falling stars, they are popular garden plants for their ornamental value, ease of cultivation, and vibrant colors. The handsome leaves, which often feature a veined or pleated surface, stand erect, and in some species can reach up to 40 in (100 cm) tall. Throughout mid- to late summer, tall, wiry, arching stems rise above the clump of leaves to display the attractive sprays of brightly colored funnel-shaped flowers.

CULTIVATION

These plants will thrive when planted in full sun in moist well-drained soil. Once established, corms multiply easily and should be divided when they become very overcrowded. This easy growth has resulted in some species now being regarded as weeds in some parts of the world. Propagate from offsets.

Top Tip

Crocosmia plants seem to flower best when they are a little crowded, but it is a good idea if they are divided every 3 years or so and the older rhizomes discarded.

BELOW LEFT Crocosmia masoniorum *'Rowallane Yellow' bears graceful sprays of upward-facing yellow flowers on arching stems in summer.*

Below *The arching stems of* Crocosmia *'Citronella' (syn. 'Golden Fleece') bear an abundance of attractive yellow flowers. This hybrid is easy to grow.*

Left *The spectacular intensely red flowers of* Crocosmia *'Lucifer' appear early in the season. This hybrid is also valued for its striking pleated leaves and decorative seed heads.*

Above *Groups of* Crocosmia × crocosmiiflora *make an eye-catching garden feature. The showy funnel-shaped flowers are about 2 in (5 cm) across, and are good for cutting.*

Favorites	Flower Color	Blooming Season	Flower Fragrance	Plant Height	Plant Width	Hardiness Zone	Frost Tolerance
***Crocosmia* 'Citronella'**	yellow; red-brown markings	summer	no	30 in (75 cm)	24 in (60 cm)	7–10	yes
Crocosmia* × *crocosmiiflora	yellow to orange-red	summer	no	20–30 in (50–75 cm)	24 in (60 cm)	6–9	yes
***Crocosmia* × *crocosmiiflora* 'Solfaterre'**	yellow	summer	no	20–24 in (50–60 cm)	24 in (60 cm)	6–9	yes
***Crocosmia* 'Lucifer'**	red	summer	no	3–4 ft (0.9–1.2 m)	2 ft (0.6 m)	7–10	yes
Crocosmia masoniorum	orange to flame red	late summer	no	3–4 ft (0.9–1.2 m)	2–3 ft (0.6–0.9 m)	7–10	yes
Crocosmia pottsii	red-tinged orange	late summer	no	32–36 in (80–90 cm)	32–36 in (80–90 cm)	7–10	yes

Crocus

Known as a harbinger of spring, *Crocus* is a member of the iris (Iridaceae) family. This Eurasian genus includes a few autumn-flowering species, though it should not be confused with autumn crocus (*Colchicum* species). *Crocus* is made up of around 80 species of corms that usually have fine grassy foliage and short-stemmed, long-tubed, 6-petalled flowers with a conspicuous divided style at the center. The flowers may be white, yellow, or any shade from lavender to purple. The brightly colored styles of *Crocus sativus* are the source of saffron, the cost of which is understandable when one considers that it takes 4,000 hand-picked crocuses to produce 1 ounce (28 g) of saffron.

Top Tip

Crocus bulbs can be left undisturbed in the garden for years if winters are not too wet. Established bulbs will bloom earlier in the season than newly planted ones.

Cultivation

Mostly very hardy and easily grown in any sunny or partly shaded position, crocuses do well in rockeries or may be naturalized in lawns or deciduous woodlands. While their seeds germinate freely, established clumps multiply naturally and can be broken up every few years.

Favorites	Flower Color	Blooming Season	Flower Fragrance	Plant Height	Plant Width	Hardiness Zone	Frost Tolerance
Crocus chrysanthus	pale yellow to orange-yellow	spring	yes	3–4 in (8–10 cm)	4 in (10 cm)	4–9	yes
***Crocus* 'Jeanne d'Arc'**	white	spring	no	4 in (10 cm)	4 in (10 cm)	4–9	yes
Crocus sativus	lilac-purple, white	autumn	yes	2–4 in (5–10 cm)	4 in (10 cm)	6–8	yes
Crocus serotinus	white to mauve	autumn	yes	2–4 in (5–10 cm)	4 in (10 cm)	5–9	yes
Crocus sieberi	white, lilac-blue; yellow throat	spring to summer	yes	3–4 in (8–10 cm)	3 in (8 cm)	7–9	yes
Crocus tommasinianus	lavender-blue; silver highlights	late winter to spring	no	6 in (15 cm)	3 in (8 cm)	5–9	yes

LEFT *The grass-like leaves of* Crocus serotinus *may emerge with the flowers in autumn. The flowers of strong-growing* C. s. *subsp.* salzmannii, *seen here, are larger than the species.*
BELOW *The source of saffron,* Crocus sativus *is a low-growing plant with decorative flowers. The red style is harvested by hand, then dried before being used as a flavoring.*

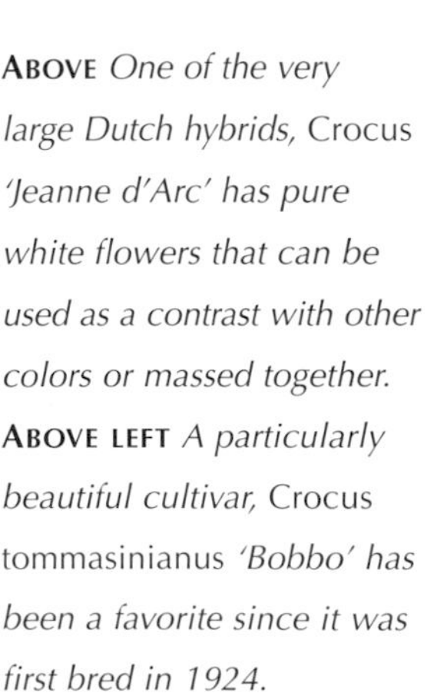

ABOVE *One of the very large Dutch hybrids,* Crocus *'Jeanne d'Arc'* has pure *white flowers that can be used as a contrast with other colors or massed together.*
ABOVE LEFT *A particularly beautiful cultivar,* Crocus tommasinianus *'Bobbo'* has *been a favorite since it was first bred in 1924.*

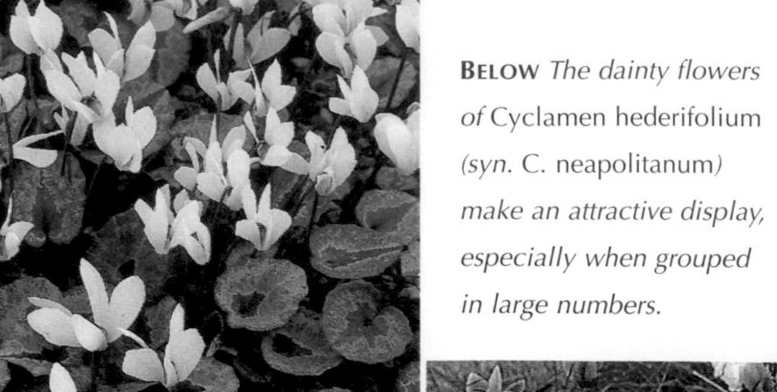

Right Cyclamen cilicium *'Album' bears masses of snow white flowers displaying the slightly twisted petals of the species. This vigorous plant has rounded heart-shaped leaves.*

Below *The dainty flowers of* Cyclamen hederifolium *(syn.* C. neapolitanum*) make an attractive display, especially when grouped in large numbers.*

Cyclamen

Instantly recognizable because of the popularity of the potted florists' cyclamen (cultivars of *Cyclamen persicum*), this genus in the primrose (Primulaceae) family has 19 species of tuberous perennials that in their wild forms are far daintier than those usually seen. They occur naturally around the Mediterranean and in western Asia, and most species have heart-shaped leaves, often with marbled patterning. The foliage may be evergreen or briefly deciduous. At varying times depending on the species, long-stemmed, nodding, white, pink, red, or purple flowers develop from the center of the tuber. *Cyclamen* is known as sow-bread, as pigs relish the tubers. Don't be tempted to try them though, as they apparently have drastic purgative effects on people.

Cultivation

Cyclamen vary in hardiness but few will tolerate prolonged cold wet conditions. They need perfect drainage, preferably with the tuber planted on or near the soil surface. Dappled shade is best and a cool rockery is ideal. Some do well in deciduous woodlands. Propagate from seed or by division.

Top Tip

Whether growing florists' cyclamens indoors or wild species in the garden, the right amount of water is the key to success. Never over-water.

Favorites

Favorites	Flower Color	Blooming Season	Flower Fragrance
Cyclamen africanum	pale to deep pink	autumn	no
Cyclamen cilicium	soft pink, darker at petal base	autumn to early spring	yes
Cyclamen coum	white, pink, purple-pink	winter to early spring	no
Cyclamen hederifolium	pink, darker at petal base	autumn	yes
Cyclamen persicum	white, mauve, pink	winter	yes
Cyclamen purpurascens	pale to dark purple-red	summer	yes

RIGHT *The large silver-marked leaves of* Cyclamen purpurascens *appear with the vibrantly colored strongly scented flowers during summer.*

BELOW Cyclamen persicum *flowers occur naturally in shades of white, pink, and mauve, with darker centers. The leaves, too, are variably colored and marked.*

Plant Height	Plant Width	Hardiness Zone	Frost Tolerance
6 in (15 cm)	8–12 in (20–30 cm)	9–10	no
3–5 in (8–12 cm)	4–6 in (10–15 cm)	7–10	yes
2–4 in (5–10 cm)	6–12 in (15–30 cm)	6–10	yes
4–6 in (10–15 cm)	6–12 in (15–30 cm)	6–9	yes
8–12 in (20–30 cm)	6–12 in (15–30 cm)	9–10	no
4–6 in (10–15 cm)	6–12 in (15–30 cm)	5–9	yes

BELOW *Creamy white petals, deepening to rich yellow toward the base, and leaves mottled with brown are the signature characteristics of* Erythronium helenae.

ERYTHRONIUM

Belonging to the lily (Liliaceae) family, this genus of spring-flowering bulbs contains around 20 species. Commonly known as trout lily or dogtooth violet, many species are North American, while a few are found from Europe to temperate East Asia. The leaves may be matt to quite glossy and in some cases are marbled, mottled, or spotted with silver, brown, maroon, or bronze. The white, cream, soft yellow, or pink flowers often face downward and are starry, with 6 reflexed petals. The seed pods and bulbs were popular foods with Native Americans, though as some are known to be emetic it seems unlikely that they were eaten in large quantities.

CULTIVATION

Natural woodlanders, *Erythronium* species are most at home under deciduous trees or in shaded rockeries. They prefer dappled shade with gritty yet humus-rich well-drained soil. They do not tolerate humid heat. Most prefer cool climates. Most species multiply quickly, sometimes by stolons, and may be divided after a few years. Otherwise, raise from seed, which should be sown as soon as it ripens.

RIGHT *As the pink buds of* Erythronium revolutum *open, the petals gradually recurve to display a beautiful coloring of cyclamen pink, centered with yellow.*

ABOVE *A Californian native,* Erythronium tuolumnense *bears yellow lily-like flowers on tall stems. Otherwise unadorned, the leaves are slightly wavy at the edges.*

LEFT *With mottled leaves and nodding creamy white flowers marked with yellow and maroon,* Erythronium californicum *'White Beauty' is a popular cultivar.*

Top Tip

Once established, *Erythronium* species resent disturbance to their roots. Plant them where they are to remain, and divide them only when they become too crowded.

Favorites	Flower Color	Blooming Season	Flower Fragrance	Plant Height	Plant Width	Hardiness Zone	Frost Tolerance
Erythronium californicum	creamy white, yellow center	spring	no	10 in (25 cm)	6 in (15 cm)	4–9	yes
Erythronium dens-canis	white, pink, lilac	spring to early summer	no	6–8 in (15–20 cm)	6 in (15 cm)	3–9	yes
Erythronium helenae	white to cream, yellow center	spring	no	6–15 in (15–38 cm)	4 in (10 cm)	4–9	yes
***Erythronium* 'Pagoda'**	sulfur yellow	spring	no	6–12 in (15–30 cm)	8 in (20 cm)	4–9	yes
Erythronium revolutum	cyclamen pink, yellow center	spring	no	6–8 in (15–20 cm)	6 in (15 cm)	4–9	yes
Erythronium tuolumnense	bright yellow	spring	no	8–15 in (20–38 cm)	8 in (20 cm)	4–9	yes

FRITILLARIA

Widespread in the temperate Northern Hemisphere, with many species from southwest Asia, this genus contains around 100 species of spring- to early summer-flowering bulbs and belongs to the lily (Liliaceae) family. They usually have simple grassy or strappy leaves and heads of nodding bell-shaped flowers that have 6 petals (more correctly tepals) and occur in a range of most unusual colors, such as purple and green, mustard yellow or near-black, often with checkered markings. Many botanists and gardeners have become hooked on fritillaries and it is easy to understand the fascination. A fritillus was a Roman dice box, of which the patterned flowers are reminiscent.

LEFT *The golden yellow petals of* Fritillaria glauca *'Goldilocks' are often dappled with darker markings. This low-growing cultivar is an ideal plant for borders.* **RIGHT** *The beauty of the pristine white flowers of* Fritillaria meleagris *'Aphrodite', with their delicate green veining and graceful nodding stance, belies their rather pungent odor.* **BELOW** Fritillaria tuntasia *is native to the Greek Islands. This species features striking flowers that are dark purple, almost black.*

CULTIVATION

Although most *Fritillaria* species are very hardy, they can be difficult to cultivate. Some simply want a well-drained position in a rockery, others, such as the crown imperial *(Fritillaria imperialis)*, are better suited to perennial borders. The alpine and scree species require more specialist care and often need to be kept dry over winter. Propagation is from natural offsets or seed.

Favorites	Flower Color	Blooming Season	Flower Fragrance	Plant Height	Plant Width	Hardiness Zone	Frost Tolerance
Fritillaria biflora	dark brown	early to mid-spring	no	10–16 in (25–40 cm)	1¾–2 in (4–5 cm)	7–9	yes
Fritillaria camschatcensis	purple-black, maroon, green	summer	no	8–18 in (10–45 cm)	1¾–4 in (4–10 cm)	4–9	yes
Fritillaria glauca	yellow	spring to early summer	no	4–6 in (10–15 cm)	1¾–2 in (4–5 cm)	6–8	yes
Fritillaria meleagris	white, green, pink to purple	spring	no	7–12 in (18–30 cm)	1¾–6 in (4–15 cm)	4–9	yes
Fritillaria olivieri	rusty brown and green	early summer	no	12–15 in (30–38 cm)	3 in (8 cm)	5–9	yes
Fritillaria tuntasia	purple to purple-black	late spring	no	4–15 in (10–38 cm)	2½ in (6 cm)	8–10	yes

RIGHT *The dainty bell-shaped flowers of* Fritillaria olivieri *are purplish brown, each petal with a wide green central stripe. This species is native to mountain regions of Iran.*

Top Tip

Fritillaria plants can be exacting in their cultivation requirements. Consider the native habitat of each species to pinpoint those that are best suited to local conditions.

GLADIOLUS

A member of the iris (Iridaceae) family, this genus comprises some 180 species of cormous perennials found from Europe to western Asia and southern Africa. The leaves range from grassy to sword-like, and the flowers, which are funnel-shaped and borne in a spike, usually open in summer. The large-flowered garden hybrids are mainly derived from South African species, and while their showy flowers will always make them the most popular plants, the less flamboyant species have their own charms, such as the evening scent of *Gladiolus tristis*. A *gladius*—also the origin of the word gladiator—was a Roman sword and the name reflects the sword-shaped foliage.

CULTIVATION

Plant *Gladiolus* species in a sunny position with moist well-drained soil. The corms are best planted fairly deeply as this ensures that the stems are well-anchored, sturdy, and less susceptible to wind damage. Keep well watered while flowering then allow to dry. In cold areas the corms may be lifted and stored dry. Propagate from natural offsets.

ABOVE *Commonly known as the Abyssinian sword lily, each stem of* Gladiolus callianthus *carries up to 10 fragrant white flowers, marked with red or purple.*

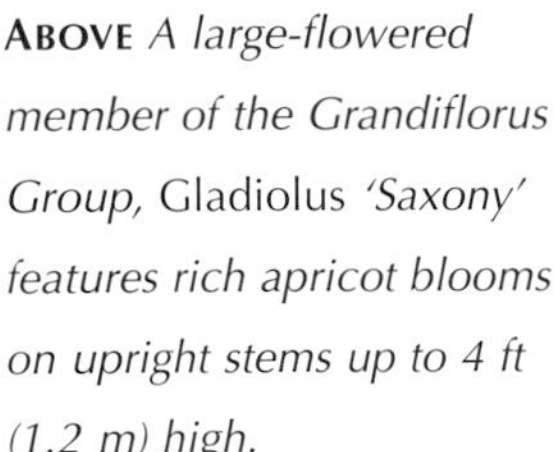

ABOVE *A large-flowered member of the Grandiflorus Group,* Gladiolus *'Saxony' features rich apricot blooms on upright stems up to 4 ft (1.2 m) high.*

RIGHT *Available in a wide range of colors, the small flowers of* Gladiolus, *Primulinus Group hybrid cultivars have a hooded upper petal, as seen in this deep pink-flowered form.*

Top Tip

Use the height of taller *Gladiolus* species to advantage in border plantings. Smaller-growing types make excellent container plants.

RIGHT *Magnificent 6 in (15 cm) wide flowers are the signature of* Gladiolus, *Grandiflorus Group. 'Blue Bird' is a fine example with large purple-blue flowers.*

Favorites	Flower Color	Blooming Season	Flower Fragrance	Plant Height	Plant Width	Hardiness Zone	Frost Tolerance
Gladiolus callianthus	white with purple or red markings	late summer to early autumn	yes	36–40 in (90–100 cm)	2–12 in (5–30 cm)	9–11	no
Gladiolus communis	pink with red or white markings	spring to summer	no	36–40 in (90–100 cm)	10–12 in (25–30 cm)	6–10	yes
Gladiolus tristis	creamy yellow	spring	yes	24–60 in (60–150 cm)	8–12 in (20–30 cm)	7–10	no
Gladiolus viridiflorus	yellow-green and dull pink	late autumn to winter	no	6–12 in (15–30 cm)	6 in (15 cm)	7–10	yes
***Gladiolus*, Grandiflorus Group**	various	late spring to summer	no	24–60 in (60–150 cm)	12 in (30 cm)	9–11	yes
***Gladiolus*, Primulinus Group**	various	summer	no	24 in (60 cm)	12 in (30 cm)	9–11	yes

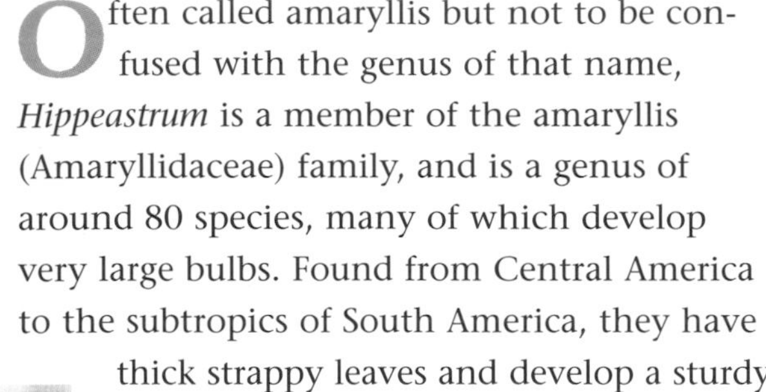

HIPPEASTRUM

BELOW *Known as the butterfly amaryllis,* Hippeastrum papilio *creates a striking impression with its green and cream flowers heavily marked with maroon.*

Often called amaryllis but not to be confused with the genus of that name, *Hippeastrum* is a member of the amaryllis (Amaryllidaceae) family, and is a genus of around 80 species, many of which develop very large bulbs. Found from Central America to the subtropics of South America, they have thick strappy leaves and develop a sturdy flower stem topped with a head of often very large trumpet-shaped flowers. Red, white, and pink are the principal flower colors, though modern hybrids occur in a wealth of patterns and include other colors. The genus name means "horse flower" and comes from a fancied resemblance of the flower to a horse's head.

CULTIVATION

Hippeastrum species are suitable for outdoor cultivation only in mild frost-free areas. They are otherwise grown as greenhouse or conservatory plants. Plant in moist well-drained soil with the neck of the bulb protruding above soil level. A bright but not overly sunny position is best. Keep dry in winter and propagate from natural offsets or seed.

ABOVE Hippeastrum *hybrid cultivars, such as 'Royal Velvet', are warmth-loving plants, needing temperatures above 55°F (13°C) for optimum growth and flowering.*

Favorites	Flower Color	Blooming Season	Flower Fragrance	Plant Height	Plant Width	Hardiness Zone	Frost Tolerance
***Hippeastrum* 'Flamingo'**	red	late winter to mid-summer	no	18–24 in (45–60 cm)	12–16 in (30–40 cm)	9–12	no
***Hippeastrum* 'Las Vegas'**	bright red; central white stripe	late winter to mid-summer	no	18–24 in (45–60 cm)	12–16 in (30–40 cm)	9–12	no
***Hippeastrum* 'Pamela'**	scarlet	late winter to mid-summer	no	18–24 in (45–60 cm)	12–16 in (30–40 cm)	9–12	no
Hippeastrum papilio	greenish cream, maroon markings	mid-winter to spring	no	18–30 in (45–75 cm)	12–16 in (30–40 cm)	9–12	no
Hippeastrum reticulatum	crimson-pink	late summer	no	10–15 in (25–38 cm)	15–18 in (38–45 cm)	9–10	no
***Hippeastrum* 'Royal Velvet'**	deep red	late winter to mid-summer	no	18–24 in (45–60 cm)	12–16 in (30–40 cm)	9–12	no

Top Tip

Hippeastrum species and cultivars have high nutrition and water requirements during the growing season. Reduce watering when flowering is over.

BELOW *Bold and bright, like the city for which it is named,* Hippeastrum *'Las Vegas' prefers warmth and is suitable for indoor culture in cooler climates.*

ABOVE *Flamboyant flowers of vivid red, centered with prominent red stamens, are the hallmark characteristics of the hybrid cultivar* Hippeastrum *'Flamingo'.*

Hyacinthus

A genus of 3 spring-flowering bulbs, found from western to central Asia, *Hyacinthus* is the type genus for the family Hyacinthaceae. One species, *Hyacinthus orientalis*, has given rise to countless cultivars and is commercially grown because it can be forced into bloom in any season. Dutch hyacinths, the most widely grown style, have strappy but not overly long leaves and short sturdy flower stems topped with dense cylindrical heads of small fragrant flowers with 6 reflexed petals. Less common forms, the Roman and Multiflora types, produce several rather open heads per bulb. The flowers yield a blue dye and a fragrant oil used in perfumery. It takes over 1¼ tons (1250 kg) of flowers to produce a pound (450 g) of oil.

Above *One of the Multiflora Group,* Hyacinthus orientalis *'Multiflora Blue' produces heads of purple-blue flowers that carry a delightful fragrance.*

Cultivation

Hyacinths thrive in cool areas with clearly defined seasons. They flower best when they can develop slowly rather than rushing into growth with the sudden arrival of spring. Plant in sun or dappled shade with fertile, humus-rich, well-drained soil. Propagate from natural offsets, seed, or by bulb scoring.

Top Tip

Contact with hyacinths may cause an allergic reaction in some people. To avoid this risk, it is advisable to wear gloves when handling these plants.

Favorites	Flower Color	Blooming Season	Flower Fragrance	Plant Height	Plant Width	Hardiness Zone	Frost Tolerance
Hyacinthus orientalis	white, pink, blue to purple	early to mid-spring	yes	8–12 in (20–30 cm)	3 in (8 cm)	5–9	yes
***Hyacinthus orientalis* 'Bismarck'**	lilac-blue	spring	yes	8–12 in (20–30 cm)	3 in (8 cm)	5–9	yes
***Hyacinthus orientalis* 'Carnegie'**	white	spring	yes	8–12 in (20–30 cm)	3 in (8 cm)	5–9	yes
***Hyacinthus orientalis* 'King of the Blues'**	dark blue	spring	yes	8–12 in (20–30 cm)	3 in (8 cm)	5–9	yes
***Hyacinthus orientalis* 'Multiflora Blue'**	dark lilac-blue	summer	yes	8–12 in (20–30 cm)	3 in (8 cm)	5–9	yes
***Hyacinthus orientalis* 'Violet Pearl'**	carmine pink	spring	yes	8–12 in (20–30 cm)	3 in (8 cm)	5–9	yes

LEFT *A Dutch hyacinth,* Hyacinthus orientalis *'Bismarck' has waxy petals in shades of lilac-blue. The densely packed flower spikes are accompanied by mid-green leaves.*

BELOW Hyacinthus orientalis *'Violet Pearl' is a lovely single-flowered form. Erect stout stems carry the waxy bell-shaped flowers colored in shades of carmine pink.*

BELOW *The white blooms of* Hyacinthus orientalis *'Carnegie' are crowded on erect stems. Appearing late in the season, they emit a heady fragrance.*

LILIUM

The type genus for the lily (Liliaceae) family, *Lilium* is a group of 100 species of mainly summer-flowering scaly bulbs found through most of the northern temperate zones, especially in East Asia. They are narrow erect plants, usually with one leafy stem per bulb. Large, sometimes fragrant, trumpet-shaped flowers with widely flared or recurved petals form at the top of the stems. The flowers occur in all colors except blue and are often beautifully marked with contrasting colors. Ernest Wilson (1876–1930), who introduced *Lilium regale*, broke his leg during the expedition in which he discovered this plant and thereafter walked with what he referred to as his "lily limp."

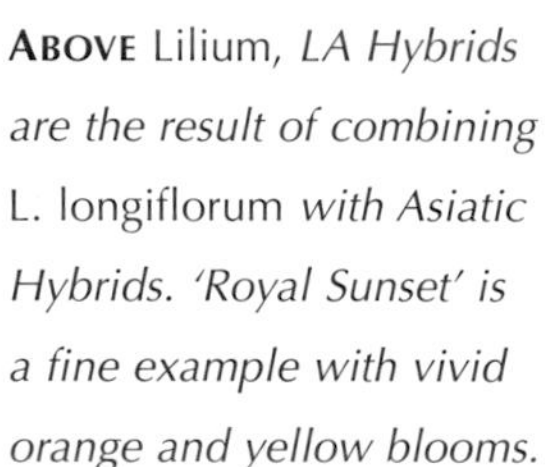

RIGHT *The upward-facing blooms of* Lilium, *Asiatic Hybrid, 'Hup Holland' feature glowing orange petals that become paler in color and spotted at the base.*

ABOVE Lilium, *LA Hybrids are the result of combining* L. longiflorum *with Asiatic Hybrids. 'Royal Sunset' is a fine example with vivid orange and yellow blooms.*

Top Tip

Apply mulch around lily plants. This will provide an insulating layer and will also minimize weeding, thus preventing damage to the roots caused by garden tools.

CULTIVATION

Lilies will grow in sun or part-shade and prefer a deep, cool, humus-rich soil, preferably made fertile with well-rotted manure. They need good drainage but must not be allowed to dry out. Lilies are easily propagated from natural offsets, bulb scales, seeds, and sometimes from bulbils that form in the leaf axils.

RIGHT *One of the Asiatic Hybrids, with trumpet flowers characteristic of the group,* Lilium *'Her Grace' has gorgeous golden yellow blooms that face outward.*

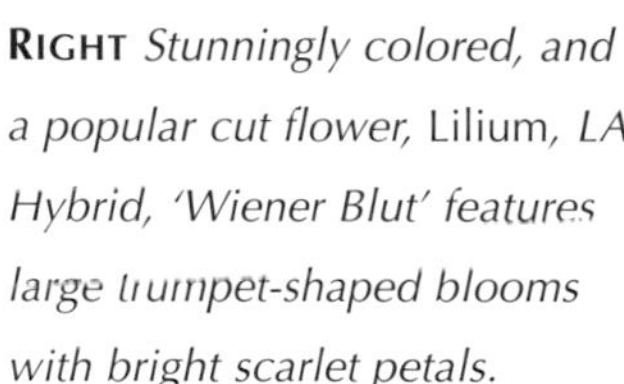

RIGHT *Stunningly colored, and a popular cut flower,* Lilium, *LA Hybrid, 'Wiener Blut' features large trumpet-shaped blooms with bright scarlet petals.*

Favorites

Favorites	Flower Color	Blooming Season	Flower Fragrance	Plant Height	Plant Width	Hardiness Zone	Frost Tolerance
Lilium candidum	white	summer to early autumn	yes	3–7 ft (0.9–2 m)	12–18 in (30–45 cm)	6–9	yes
Lilium martagon	dull pink	early summer to early autumn	no	3–8 ft (0.9–2.4 m)	12–18 in (30–45 cm)	4–9	yes
Lilium nepalense	yellow-green; maroon markings	summer	no	24–40 in (60–100 cm)	12–18 in (30–45 cm)	5–9	yes
Lilium pumilum	bright scarlet	summer to early autumn	yes	15–18 in (38–45 cm)	12–18 in (30–45 cm)	5–9	yes
***Lilium,* American Hybrids**	pink, yellow, red, darker spotted	summer	no	4–6 ft (1.2–1.8 m)	12 in (30 cm)	5–10	yes
***Lilium,* Asiatic Hybrids**	various	summer	no	18–48 in (45–120 cm)	12–18 in (30–45 cm)	5–10	yes
***Lilium,* Candidum Hybrids**	white, pink to orange-red	summer	no	24–48 in (60–120 cm)	12–18 in (30–45 cm)	6–9	yes
***Lilium,* LA Hybrids**	various	early to mid-summer	yes	18–36 in (45–90 cm)	12–24 in (30–60 cm)	5–9	yes
***Lilium,* Longiflorum Hybrids**	white	late spring to summer	yes	36 in (90 cm)	24 in (60 cm)	5–10	yes
***Lilium,* Martagon Hybrids**	cream, pink, gold, dull red	mid-summer	yes	5–6 ft (1.5–1.8 m)	12–18 in (30–45 cm)	5–9	yes
***Lilium,* Oriental Hybrids**	white, pink, red, yellow stripe	summer to ealry autumn	yes	4–7 ft (1.2–2 m)	15–24 in (38–60 cm)	6–9	yes
***Lilium,* Trumpet and Aurelian Hybrids**	white, gold, pink, deep red, greenish	summer	no	3–6 ft (0.9–1.8 m)	12–18 in (30–45 cm)	5–9	yes

LEFT *One of the Oriental Hybrids,* Lilium *'Expression' features large glowing white blooms with recurved petals, centered with prominent stamens.*

BELOW Lilium *'Salmon Classic' is a member of the LA Hybrids. Beautifully scented, the attractive apricot flowers feature light spotting at the petal base and a slightly deeper colored midrib.*

ABOVE Lilium*, Oriental Hybrid, 'Esperanto' is a glamorous lily. The white petals have an overlay of soft pink and a midrib of soft yellow, all with a spattering of maroon spots.*

ABOVE *A flamboyant lily,* Lilium, *Oriental Hybrid, 'Black Tie' catches the eye with the vibrant coloring of the upward-facing red and white flowers.*

BELOW Lilium *'Monte Negro', one of the Asiatic Hybrids, bears abundant blooms of bold orange to dark red that carry the characteristic spotting at the petal base.*

ABOVE *The cyclamen pink petals of* Lilium, *Oriental Hybrid, 'Sissi' have a dusting of dark pink spots and gently ruffled edges that are trimmed with white.*

LEFT *The strawberries-and-cream coloring of* Lilium, *Oriental Hybrid, 'Sorbonne' has made it popular for both garden cultivation and as a cut flower.*

MUSCARI

This Mediterranean and western Asian genus of 30 species of spring-flowering bulbs in the hyacinth (Hyacinthaceae) family is commonly known as grape hyacinth. The grassy to strap-like foliage may be evergreen or deciduous, depending on species and climate. Spikes of tiny, downward-facing, bell-shaped flowers open from late winter and range in color from white and soft yellow through blue shades to deepest purple. Small seed pods follow. The closely related genus *Bellevalia* is often mistaken for *Muscari*. The genus name is derived from the Turkish name for these bulbs.

CULTIVATION

Grape hyacinths are very easily cultivated, often far too easily, though there are much worse weeds than these pretty bulbs. Plant in sun or part-shade with moist well-drained soil. Clumps can be divided every few years. The seed germinates freely and often self-sows.

ABOVE *Borne on sturdy stems, the dark purplish buds of* Muscari macrocarpum *open to reveal delicately scented greenish yellow flowers.*

Top Tip

Grape hyacinths are versatile plants that are suitable for woodland gardens, for planting beneath trees, using in rockeries, or as pot plants.

LEFT *Densely packed on stiff stems, the lavender flowers of* Muscari armeniacum *'Valerie Finnis' resemble bunches of grapes.*

Favorites	Flower Color	Blooming Season	Flower Fragrance	Plant Height	Plant Width	Hardiness Zone	Frost Tolerance
Muscari armeniacum	bright blue	summer	yes	8 in (20 cm)	2 in (5 cm)	6–9	yes
Muscari aucheri	bright blue	early summer	no	4–6 in (10–15 cm)	2 in (5 cm)	6–9	yes
Muscari azureum	bright blue	early summer	yes	4–6 in (10–15 cm)	2 in (5 cm)	6–9	yes
Muscari botryoides	bright blue	early summer	yes	4–6 in (10–15 cm)	2 in (5 cm)	6–9	yes
Muscari latifolium	violet-black	early summer	no	8 in (20 cm)	2 in (5 cm)	6–9	yes
Muscari macrocarpum	greenish yellow	spring	yes	4–6 in (10–15 cm)	4 in (10 cm)	8–9	yes

LEFT *Held above the single mid-green leaves, the flower spikes of* Muscari latifolium *have a two-tone appearance, with violet-black fertile flowers topped by violet-blue sterile flowers.*

RIGHT *The crowded spikes of* Muscari armeniacum *'Blue Spike' are laden with dainty, double, urn-shaped flowers of soft blue, finely rimmed with white.*

RIGHT *With its head gracefully bowed,* Narcissus *'W. P. Milner', a Trumpet daffodil, bears lemon yellow flowers that age to white.*

NARCISSUS

Is any spring-flowering bulb better known than the daffodil? However, there is not just one daffodil but over 50 species and countless hybrids and cultivars. They are members of the amaryllis (Amaryllidaceae) family and occur naturally from southern Europe to North Africa and Japan. Many have the typical strappy blue-green leaves but some have fine grassy foliage. The flowers have a cup- or trumpet-shaped corona backed by 6 petals that are sometimes very much reduced in size. Daffodils, including the species, are divided into 10 groups based on their flower shape and form. All parts are poisonous and can cause a form of hyperactive seizure that leads to depression and possibly coma.

ABOVE *A Large-cupped daffodil,* Narcissus *'Salomé' is an attractive hybrid cultivar that features a prominent golden corona surrounded by 6 white petals.*

BELOW *The Small-cupped daffodils have outer petals three times as long as the corona.* Narcissus *'Verger' has white petals and a yellow corona edged in orange.*

CULTIVATION

Daffodils have varying soil preferences. The traditional large-cupped forms do best in a fairly heavy loam, while the southern Mediterranean and North African species like a drier grittier soil—but they all need good drainage. Leave the foliage to die off naturally before lifting. While seed can be sown, propagation is normally from natural offsets.

Right *Native to France, Spain, and Portugal, the yellow petals of* Narcissus bulbocodium *look like narrow rays behind the matching colored flaring trumpet.*

Favorites	Flower Color	Blooming Season	Flower Fragrance	Plant Height	Plant Width	Hardiness Zone	Frost Tolerance
Narcissus bulbocodium	soft lemon to bright yellow	early spring	no	4–6 in (10–15 cm)	12 in (30 cm)	6–10	yes
Narcissus pseudonarcissus	yellow	early spring	yes	8–15 in (20–38 cm)	12 in (30 cm)	4–10	yes
***Narcissus,* Cyclamineus**	pale to deep yellow, orange	early to mid-spring	no	6–12 in (15–30 cm)	3–8 in (8–20 cm)	5 10	yes
***Narcissus,* Double-flowered**	white to deep yellow	mid-spring	no	10–18 in (25–45 cm)	6–12 in (15–30 cm)	4–10	yes
***Narcissus,* Jonquilla**	pale to deep yellow	mid- to late spring	yes	8–18 in (20–45 cm)	6–12 in (15–30 cm)	4–10	yes
***Narcissus,* Large-cupped**	white, yellow, orange, pink	mid-spring	no	12–18 in (30–45 cm)	6–12 in (15–30 cm)	4–10	yes
***Narcissus,* Poeticus**	white with orange-scarlet center	late spring to early summer	yes	6–18 in (15–45 cm)	6–10 in (15–25 cm)	4–10	yes
***Narcissus,* Small-cupped**	white, yellow, orange, pink	early to mid-spring	no	12–18 in (30–45 cm)	6–12 in (15–30 cm)	4–10	yes
***Narcissus,* Split-corona**	white, yellow, orange, pink	spring	no	12–18 in (30–45 cm)	6–12 in (15–30 cm)	4–10	yes
***Narcissus,* Tazetta**	white to yellow, orange center	autumn to spring	yes	12–18 in (30–45 cm)	8–18 in (20–45 cm)	5–10	yes
***Narcissus,* Triandrus**	white to deep yellow	mid- to late spring	no	6–12 in (15–30 cm)	4–8 in (10–20 cm)	4–10	yes
***Narcissus,* Trumpet**	white, yellow, orange, pink	spring	no	12–18 in (30–45 cm)	6–12 in (15–30 cm)	4–10	yes

RIGHT *Petals of softest yellow frame the clear yellow cup of* Narcissus, *Tazetta, 'Minnow'. Tazetta daffodils are small-flowered, with up to 20 flowers per stem.*

BELOW *Typical of the Poeticus daffodils,* Narcissus *'Felindre' has a bold bright corona rimmed with red. Gleaming white petals complete the effect.*

Top Tip

The delicate beauty of daffodils belies their robust nature. Although they are almost maintenance-free, they will appreciate supplemental water during dry periods.

LEFT *The yellow and orange corona of this Double daffodil,* Narcissus *'Tahiti', is comprised of many parts rather than the single unit of other daffodil groups.*

RIGHT *A large flaring trumpet backed by soft yellow petals are the distinguishing features of* Narcissus *'Spellbinder', a Trumpet daffodil.*

LEFT *One of the Jonquilla daffodils,* Narcissus *'Quail' has petals and a corona of rich buttercup yellow. Typical of the group, it carries a delightful fragrance.*

BELOW *A brilliant orange cup that appears almost flat surrounded by pale yellow petals are the signature of* Narcissus *'Charles Sturt', a Large-cupped daffodil.*

LEFT Nerine bowdenii *'Marnie Rogerson' is one of the hardiest of the nerines and is easily grown against a sunny wall. It blooms a pleasant pale pink.*

NERINE

From southern Africa, this genus in the amaryllis (Amaryllidaceae) family has around 30 species of autumn- to early winter-flowering bulbs. Mostly dormant during the warm dry months, the leaves or flower buds on this plant do not appear until late summer when the days shorten noticeably. Depending on the species, the flower stems may develop with or after the grassy or narrow strappy leaves appear. The flower stems exceed the foliage height and carry heads of many 6-petalled flowers, with stamens that protrude from the flowers. Pink, orange-red, or white are the common flower colors. The common name Guernsey lily and the genus name *Nerine* (from the sea nymph Nereis) recall how bulbs were found growing wild on the island of Guernsey, possibly having floated in from a shipwreck.

CULTIVATION

Plant in sun or part-shade with light gritty soil. They are hardy to moderate frosts, but not suitable for areas where the soil freezes. In cold areas, container cultivation is the best option. Water when in flower and allow to dry when dormant. Propagation is usually by division, though the seed germinates freely.

ABOVE Nerine bowdenii *bears clusters of up to seven bright pink flowers in autumn. The pale to dark green glossy foliage comes up in early winter, when flowering is over.*

ABOVE RIGHT Nerine masoniorum *is a dainty species from the eastern Cape region of South Africa. Its soft pink flowers are up to $^{3}/_{4}$ in (18 mm) across, with narrow wavy petals.*

FAR RIGHT *Nerines look great against dark or evergreen foliage.* Nerine bowdenii *'Mark Fenwick' has large deep pink flowers, more richly colored than other cultivars.*

Favorites

	Flower Color	Blooming Season	Flower Fragrance	Plant Height	Plant Width	Hardiness Zone	Frost Tolerance
Nerine bowdenii	pink with darker central rib	autumn	yes	16–24 in (40–60 cm)	12 in (30 cm)	8–11	yes
***Nerine bowdenii* 'Marnie Rogerson'**	pale pink	late autumn	no	16–24 in (40–60 cm)	12 in (30 cm)	8–11	yes
Nerine filifolia	white, rosy pink to red	autumn	no	10 in (25 cm)	6 in (15 cm)	9–10	no
Nerine masoniorum	pink with darker central rib	autumn	no	8–18 in (20–45 cm)	4–6 in (10–15 cm)	8–11	yes
Nerine sarniensis	bright red to orange-red	early autumn	no	16–24 in (40–60 cm)	3–6 in (8–15 cm)	8–10	yes
Nerine undulata	mid-pink	autumn	no	16–20 in (40–50 cm)	6 in (15 cm)	9–11	no

Top Tip

Nerines have a dramatic impact in autumn and winter. Their spectacular blooms give an injection of color after the vibrancy of summer planting has all but faded.

RANUNCULUS

This large cosmopolitan genus of the buttercup (Ranunculaceae) family includes among its 400 members several species with thickened rhizomes that were once considered a type of corm. The foliage is usually pinnate and often deeply cut and divided. The wild species usually have simple, 5-petalled, yellow or red flowers, but garden forms often have fully double flowers in a wide color range. Spring is the main flowering season, but the blooming may be extended with staggered planting. A seed head tightly packed with feathered seeds, technically an achene, follows but is best removed to prolong flowering. The commonly grown turban buttercup *(Ranunculus asiaticus)* is sometimes known as the Persian crowsfoot because of the shape of the "corms."

ABOVE Ranunculus asiaticus, *Bloomingdale Series, 'Pure Yellow' has fully double flowers with flounced petals of rich buttercup yellow.*

CULTIVATION

Plant *Ranunculus* species in a sunny or partly shaded position with moist well-drained soil. They are hardy where the soil does not freeze, but in colder climates the "corms" should be lifted and stored dry. They can be propagated either from seed or by division.

Top Tip

Once the leaves appear, *Ranunculus asiaticus* and its many attractive hybrids and cultivars appreciate extra water during the growing and blooming season.

LEFT *The Tecolote Hybrids of* Ranunculus asiaticus *have a compact growth habit and large double blooms. They are sold in single colors or mixed color strains.*

LEFT *The pure white flowers of* Ranunculus asiaticus, *Bloomingdale Series, 'White' bring a touch of stylish elegance to the garden in spring and summer.*

RIGHT *Lower growing than the species,* Ranunculus asiaticus, *Bloomingdale Series offers large, fully double, ruffled blooms in a wide range of colors.*

Favorites	Flower Color	Blooming Season	Flower Fragrance	Plant Height	Plant Width	Hardiness Zone	Frost Tolerance
Ranunculus asiaticus	white, pink, red, yellow, orange	spring to summer	no	8–18 in (20–45 cm)	8–12 in (20–30 cm)	8–10	yes
***Ranunculus asiaticus*, Bloomingdale Series**	various	spring to summer	no	8–10 in (20–25 cm)	8–16 in (20–40 cm)	8–10	yes
***Ranunculus asiaticus* 'Cappucino'**	white; pink edges	spring to summer	no	10–15 in (25–38 cm)	8–12 in (20–30 cm)	8–10	yes
***Ranunculus asiaticus* 'Double Mixed'**	various	spring to summer	no	8–18 in (20–45 cm)	8–12 in (20–30 cm)	8–10	yes
***Ranunculus asiaticus*, Tecolote Hybrids**	various	spring to summer	no	12–16 in (30–40 cm)	12–16 in (30–40 cm)	8–10	yes
***Ranunculus asiaticus*, Victoria Series**	various	spring to summer	no	8–18 in (20–45 cm)	8–12 in (20–30 cm)	8–10	yes

Schizostylis

The sole species in this genus in the iris (Iridaceae) family is a variable bulbous-rooted perennial from South Africa, though it may soon be reclassified into the genus *Hesperantha*. It has grassy near-evergreen foliage and its flowers, which appear from mid-autumn, are clustered in heads at the top of wiry stems that often well exceed the foliage height. The simple, starry, 6-petalled flowers are usually red, but garden forms are just as likely to be pink or white. *Schizostylis* multiplies freely and is considered a minor weed in some areas.

Cultivation

In the wild, this genus is usually found along watercourses and seasonally damp areas, but it is equally well at home in normal well-drained garden soil, provided it never becomes completely dry. It combines well with late-flowering perennials, such as goldenrod, Michaelmas daisies, and *Rudbeckia*. Plant in full sun or morning shade and propagate from seed or natural offsets.

Favorites	Flower Color	Blooming Season	Flower Fragrance
Schizostylis coccinea	red to pink or white	autumn	no
Schizostylis coccinea 'Alba'	white	autumn	no
Schizostylis coccinea 'Jennifer'	pale pink	autumn	no
Schizostylis coccinea 'Major'	red	autumn	no
Schizostylis coccinea 'Sunrise'	salmon pink	autumn	no
Schizostylis coccinea 'Viscountess Byng'	pale pink	autumn	no

Above *The spectacular scarlet red flowers of* Schizostylis coccinea *'Major' add great autumn color to a sunny border or a bed along a concrete path.*

Top Tip

Schizostylis plants provide excellent cut flowers. They can be grown in containers and should be divided regularly to maintain vigor. Divide the plants in spring.

Left Schizostylis coccinea *blooms steadily from autumn until temperatures fall. In mild climates, it has the potential to be in flower all winter.*

Plant Height	Plant Width	Hardiness Zone	Frost Tolerance
12–24 in (30–60 cm)	12–24 in (30–60 cm)	6–9	yes
12–24 in (30–60 cm)	12–24 in (30–60 cm)	6–9	yes
12–24 in (30–60 cm)	12–24 in (30–60 cm)	6–9	yes
12–24 in (30–60 cm)	12–24 in (30–60 cm)	6–9	yes
12–24 in (30–60 cm)	12–24 in (30–60 cm)	6–9	yes
12–24 in (30–60 cm)	12–24 in (30–60 cm)	6–9	yes

ABOVE Schizostylis coccinea *hybrids are commonly known as kaffir lilies, river lilies, or crimson flag. Each flower spike contains 5 to 20 flowers.*

LEFT Schizostylis coccinea *'Sunrise' bears large salmon pink flowers 2 in (5 cm) across, larger than most other hybrids. It also has a longer blooming period. In bad weather, pick the buds and bring them inside to flower away from the frost.*

SCILLA

A genus of around 90 species of bulbs in the hyacinth (Hyacinthaceae) family, *Scilla* species are found from Europe to South Africa and temperate Asia. The foliage is strap-like or grassy, may be near-evergreen in mild climates, and can be long and lax, making for a rather untidy foliage clump. Commonly known as squills or bluebells, the species vary in flowering time, though most bloom in spring or early summer. While some have open hyacinth-like flowerheads, many have densely packed rounded heads on strong stems. Purple or blue are the predominant flower colors; white, pink, and lavender are less common. *Scilla* extracts are used in herbal medicines but the "squill" often referred to in the literature is a different plant, *Urginea maritima*.

CULTIVATION

Scilla species are mostly hardy and easily grown in sun or part-shade with moist, humus-rich, well-drained soil. Propagation is usually by division in winter when dormant or from seed, which sometimes self-sows.

ABOVE Scilla hyacinthoides *is found throughout the Mediterranean region. From mid-spring its tall stems are filled with numerous starry violet-blue flowers.*

BELOW *Native to France and Spain, and known as the Pyrenean squill,* Scilla liliohyacinthus *has glossy strap-like leaves. The pale violet flowers are borne on sturdy stems.*

BELOW Scilla peruviana *is a wondrous sight when in bloom, as its tall stems rise above the glossy leaves bearing their clusters of starry blue flowers.*

RIGHT *With grassy leaves and violet-blue flowers,* Scilla ramburei *is a lovely subject for borders and bedding and is well suited to coastal environments.*

Scilla flower spikes are naturals for cut flowers. Those left on the plant should be trimmed back to near ground level once the flowers are spent.

Favorites	Flower Color	Blooming Season	Flower Fragrance	Plant Height	Plant Width	Hardiness Zone	Frost Tolerance
Scilla hyacinthoides	violet-blue	mid-spring	no	36 in (90 cm)	12 in (30 cm)	8–11	yes
Scilla liliohyacinthus	pale violet	mid- to late spring	no	4 in (10 cm)	4 in (10 cm)	6–8	yes
Scilla peruviana	indigo blue	mid-spring to early summer	no	12 in (30 cm)	18 in (45 cm)	8–11	yes
Scilla ramburei	violet-blue	spring	no	6 in (15 cm)	4 in (10 cm)	7–10	yes
Scilla siberica	bright blue	early spring	no	6 in (15 cm)	3 in (8 cm)	2–8	yes
Scilla tubergeniana	white, pale blue	early spring	no	5 in (12 cm)	4 in (10 cm)	5–7	yes

TRILLIUM

Primarily North American, with a few temperate Asian representatives, this group of 30 species of perennials forms the type genus for the wake-robin (Trilliaceae) family. The most visible parts of the plants are grouped in 3s: each stem has 3 leaves and the flowers have 3 petals and 3 sepals. While completely dormant in winter, with the arrival of spring the plants develop quickly, first producing their often mottled foliage and then the flowers, which form at the intersection of the 3 leaves. The petals may be white, soft yellow, pink, or maroon-red; the sepals are often green but can be the same color as the petals. Native North Americans used the roots medicinally.

CULTIVATION

While some of the smaller species thrive in rockeries, most trilliums are woodland plants that prefer deep, fertile, humus-rich, moist soil and dappled shade, ideally beneath an airy canopy of deciduous trees. Propagation is usually by division or from seed.

Favorites	Flower Color	Blooming Season	Flower Fragrance
Trillium chloropetalum	white, yellow, pink, maroon	spring	yes
Trillium cuneatum	burgundy to yellow-green	early spring	yes
Trillium erectum	red-and-green	spring	no
Trillium grandiflorum	white, fading to pink	late spring to early summer	no
Trillium luteum	yellow to yellow-green	early spring	yes
Trillium rivale	white	early spring	no

Top Tip

Trillium species will do best in shady spots. If sited in a favorable position, there is little maintenance required other than to remove dead foliage in autumn.

LEFT *With mottled foliage that has the appearance of toad skin, it is easy to understand how* Trillium cuneatum *earned its common name of toad shade.*

Plant Height	Plant Width	Hardiness Zone	Frost Tolerance
8–20 in (20–50 cm)	8–20 in (20–50 cm)	6–9	yes
24 in (60 cm)	16 in (40 cm)	6–9	yes
8–20 in (20–50 cm)	12–20 in (30–50 cm)	4–9	yes
10–18 in (25–45 cm)	12–20 in (30–50 cm)	3–9	yes
18 in (45 cm)	18 in (45 cm)	5–9	yes
4 in (10 cm)	6 in (15 cm)	5–9	yes

ABOVE *The yellow wake robin—*Trillium luteum*—bursts into bloom in early spring. The yellow to yellow-green petals are held erect above the mottled foliage.*

ABOVE *A charming woodland species from California,* Trillium chloropetalum *features large, often mottled leaves and fragrant, white, yellow, or maroon flowers.*

RIGHT *Visually beautiful,* Trillium erectum *has bright green leaves coupled with red-and-green flowers. The plant, however, carries an unpleasant scent.*

TULIPA

Widespread in the northern temperate zones but based around Central Asia, this spring-flowering genus belonging to the lily (Liliaceae) family includes around 100 species of bulbs, some of which have been cultivated for centuries. Most tulips have just a few stemless, broad, blue-green leaves and most often just one 6-petalled flower, though some have up to 6 flowers per bulb. The flowers occur in all colors except true blue. The genus is divided into 15 groups based on flower type and parentage. When the Dutch "tulipomania" of the 1630s subsided, some of those who lost fortunes found out through necessity what tribespeople of Central Asia had long known: tulip bulbs are edible.

ABOVE *The Single Early Group, such as* Tulipa *'Apricot Beauty' seen here, are among the first tulips to bloom, bringing a flush of color to the spring garden.*

CULTIVATION

Tulips do best in temperate areas with distinct seasons and relatively cool summers. Cold weather is necessary for proper dormancy and hot weather can split the bulbs. Plant bulbs in autumn at a depth of about 6 in (15 cm) in a sunny position with fertile well-drained soil. Propagation is usually from natural offsets, though of course they may also be raised from seed.

RIGHT Tulipa *'African Queen' is a splendid example of the Triumph Group tulips, with tall blooms of deep purple-red, each petal featuring a fine feathered edge of white.*

ABOVE Tulipa *'Primavera', one of the Single Late Group, features fiery orange-red petals that shade to yellow at the base and to almost white at the edges.*
LEFT *An impressive edging of gold adorns the brilliant orange-red petals of* Tulipa *'Ad Rem', one of the Darwin Hybrid Group, sometimes called cottage tulips.*

Favorites	Flower Color	Blooming Season	Flower Fragrance	Plant Height	Plant Width	Hardiness Zone	Frost Tolerance
Tulipa clusiana	red; white interior	mid- to late spring	no	8–12 in (20–30 cm)	2–4 in (5–10 cm)	3–8	yes
Tulipa tarda	cream to yellow	spring	yes	4–6 in (10–15 cm)	6–8 in (15–20 cm)	5–9	yes
Tulipa, **Darwin Hybrid Group**	yellow, orange, red, pink	spring	no	20–27 in (50–70 cm)	6 in (15 cm)	5–9	yes
Tulipa, **Double Early Group**	yellow, pink, red, purple	spring	no	12–16 in (30–40 cm)	4–12 in (10–30 cm)	5–9	yes
Tulipa, **Fringed Group**	white, yellow, pink to purple	late spring	no	18–26 in (45–65 cm)	4–12 in (10–30 cm)	5–9	yes
Tulipa, **Greigii Group**	yellow to red	early to mid-spring	no	6–12 in (15–30 cm)	8 in (20 cm)	5–9	yes
Tulipa, **Lily-flowered Group**	various	late spring	no	15–26 in (38–65 cm)	6 in (15 cm)	5–9	yes
Tulipa, **Parrot Group**	various	late spring	no	18–26 in (45–65 cm)	6 in (15 cm)	5–9	yes
Tulipa, **Single Early Group**	white to deep purple	early to mid-spring	no	6–18 in (15–45 cm)	6 in (15 cm)	5–9	yes
Tulipa, **Single Late Group**	various	late spring	no	18–30 in (45–75 cm)	6 in (15 cm)	5–9	yes
Tulipa, **Triumph Group**	various	mid- to late spring	no	15–24 in (38–60 cm)	6 in (15 cm)	5–9	yes
Tulipa, **Viridiflora Group**	various	late spring	no	12–22 in (30–55 cm)	6 in (15 cm)	5–9	yes

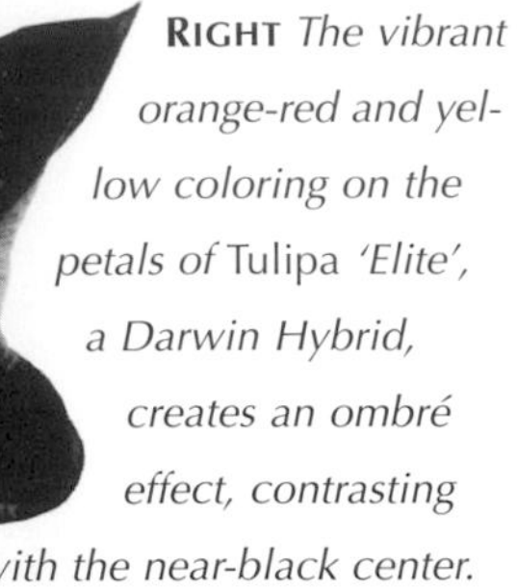

Right *The vibrant orange-red and yellow coloring on the petals of* Tulipa *'Elite', a Darwin Hybrid, creates an ombré effect, contrasting with the near-black center.*

Above *The Greigii Group tulips, such as the magnificently colored* Tulipa *'Plaisir' seen here, are small in stature and are sometimes known as rock or rockery tulips.*
Right *Crystalline fringed edges identify the Fringed Group of tulips.* Tulipa *'Maja' features goblet-shaped blooms of bright yellow, with the signature edging.*

Right *Pink and red colors predominate on the ruffled petals of* Tulipa *'Salmon Parrot', a Parrot Group tulip, highlighted with shades of yellow and cream.*

Left *With superb red coloring and gold edging on the ruffled petals,* Tulipa *'Karel Doorman' is a fine example of the Parrot Group tulips, known for their unusual showy blooms.*

ABOVE *The colors and patterning of* Tulipa *'Color Spectacle' are sure to gain attention, with scarlet stripes emblazoned on the golden yellow petals.*

RIGHT *A Single Late tulip,* Tulipa *'Ile de France' features classic styling with glamorous flowers of bold red.*

Above *The Double Early tulips resemble peonies and flower in early spring.* Tulipa *'Peach Blossom' has large deep pink blooms flecked with white and shading to golden yellow at the center.*

Top Tip

Give potted tulips for a lasting gift. When they have finished flowering indoors the bulbs can be transferred to the garden at the appropriate time.

Above *Classic simplicity of form and elegant ivory flowers are the hallmark of* Tulipa *'Maureen', a member of the Single Late Group.*

Right *Lifting their heads skyward, the fragrant starry flowers of* Tulipa tarda *have green to maroon shading on the petal reverse, and a cream to yellow interior.* **Far right** *With a tailored cut to the pointed petals, the flowers of* Tulipa *'China Pink', a member of the Lily-flowered Group, are a vision in pink.*

RIGHT *Fine fringing adds the finishing touch to the lustrous purple-red blooms of* Tulipa *'Burgundy Lace', a Fringed Group member. It blooms in late spring.*
BELOW *The Single Early Group are heralds of spring, bringing color back to the garden.* Tulipa *'Christmas Marvel' enlivens the landscape with pink-red blooms.*

BELOW *The exquisite blooms of* Tulipa *'Negrita', a Triumph Group tulip, are a sumptuous rich purple, shaded white at the center, and marked with violet-blue.*

Top Tip

The sculptured lines and textural qualities of arum lilies offer decorative possibilities indoors or out. Remove spent flower stems to keep them looking good.

ZANTEDESCHIA

Related to but not of the same genus as the true arums (*Arum* species) and callas (*Calla* species), this genus of 6 species, commonly known as arum lilies or calla lilies, occurs naturally from South Africa to Malawi. Members of the arum (Araceae) family, they form clumps of sturdy stems with large arrowhead- to heart-shaped leaves that are often mottled with small translucent spots. The long-stemmed flowerheads open through the warmer months. They have a cup-like spathe that encircles a fairly short spadix. While the species have white, pale pink, or yellow spathes, garden hybrids and cultivars are available in many colors. The genus name honors Giovanni Zantedeschi (1773–1846), who was an Italian botanist.

CULTIVATION

While *Zantedeschia aethiopica* will grow in fairly wet conditions and is often planted around pond margins, other species and the cut-flower hybrids prefer normal garden conditions and thrive in sun or part-shade with moist, humus-rich, well-drained soil. Watch for snail and slug damage, particularly on young leaves. Propagate the species from seed or by division, the hybrids by division only.

ABOVE *With flowers arising like orange beacons above the large, spotted, dark green leaves,* Zantedeschia *'Flame' adds a tropical element to the garden.*
LEFT *The stately bright red spathes of* Zantedeschia *'Scarlet Pimpernel' are borne among the white-speckled dark green leaves.*

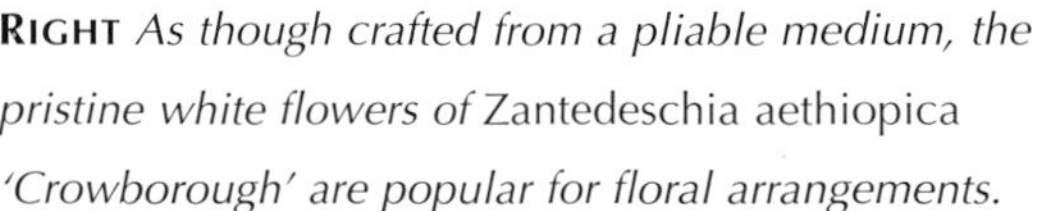

RIGHT *As though crafted from a pliable medium, the pristine white flowers of* Zantedeschia aethiopica *'Crowborough' are popular for floral arrangements.*

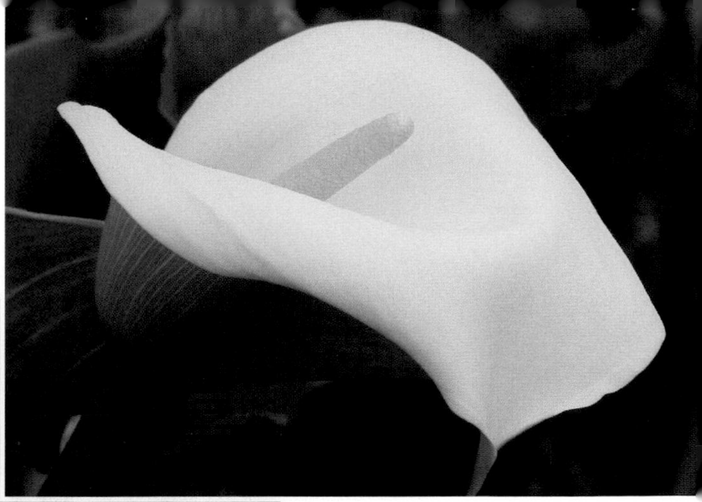

BELOW *While the bright green spathes of* Zantedeschia aethiopica *'Green Goddess' are appealing, this plant has the potential to become invasive.*

Favorites	Flower Color	Blooming Season	Flower Fragrance	Plant Height	Plant Width	Hardiness Zone	Frost Tolerance
Zantedeschia aethiopica	white	spring to autumn	no	3–6 ft (0.9–1.8 m)	2–5 ft (0.6–1.5 m)	8–11	yes
***Zantedeschia aethiopica* 'Childsiana'**	white; pink tinted	spring to autumn	no	12 in (30 cm)	2–5 ft (0.6–1.5 m)	8–11	yes
Zantedeschia elliottiana	deep yellow	summer	no	12–18 in (30–45 cm)	12–18 in (30–45 cm)	9–11	yes
***Zantedeschia* 'Flame'**	yellow-orange, flecked red	summer	no	18–24 in (45–60 cm)	12 in (30 cm)	9–11	yes
Zantedeschia pentlandii	golden yellow	summer	no	12–36 in (30–90 cm)	8–16 in (20–40 cm)	9–11	yes
***Zantedeschia* 'Scarlet Pimpernel'**	red-orange	spring to summer	no	18–36 in (45–90 cm)	12–24 in (30–60 cm)	9–11	yes

Cacti and Succulents

Ranging from tiny cliff-hugging ground covers to immense tree-like specimens, succulents—which include cacti—feature a vast array of forms and occupy habitats from frosty plains to seashores to the canopy of tropical rainforests. By growing slowly, evading competition, and using a variety of physiological adaptations, succulents are able to make maximum use of limited available water. Succulents have been used since ancient times for purposes including medicine, religious ceremonies, shelter and fabric construction, food, and drink. *Aloe vera* is perhaps the best-known succulent of all; mentioned on Sumerian clay tablets nearly 4,000 years ago, it is still used today for medicinal purposes.

Above *The succulent leaves of* Crassula pseudohemisphaerica *are arranged in tightly spiraled rosettes that bear spikes of tubular flowers in spring.*

Left Kalanchoe tomentosa *has unusual heavily felted leaves with brown markings. Like many succulents, it makes an ornamental indoor plant in cooler climates.*

THE CAMELS OF THE GARDEN

The term "succulent" describes a plant that stores water in its leaves, stems, or roots for use during periods when water is unavailable. Most succulents employ a variety of methods to prevent water loss. The characteristic round or barrel shape of most cacti and many other succulents is designed to minimize the surface area exposed to the drying sun. Ribs, thorns, and furry hairs allow any available nightly dew to condense, run down the side of the plant, and be collected by the roots.

In the species classified as leaf succulents, virtually the whole leaf is devoted to water storage tissue. Leaf succulents have very short stems, and different species have evolved various methods to reduce water loss. Crassulas have a waxy skin to prevent water loss, while aloes have compacted leaves providing protection from the sun. Those that store water in their leaves include some of the most common and readily available succulents, such as the popular jade plant *(Crassula ovata),* as well as agaves and aloes, with their fleshy pointed leaves.

Succulents that store water in their stems have few or no leaves. The stems are responsible for water collection and transpiration. Stem succulents have varied forms and can range from small mounds to elongated plants with multiple stems. Cacti, a group of New World plants, are a type of stem succulent and possess a number of distinctive features including a modified axillary bud from which spines, branches, and flowers arise. Containing some 2,500 species (about a quarter of all succulent plants), all members of the cactus (Cactaceae) family are succulents—but not all succulents are cacti. Examples include the genera *Echinocereus, Mammillaria, Opuntia,* and *Rebutia.*

Root succulents survive dry conditions by storing water and nutrients in tuberous or swollen roots. Belowground storage prevents moisture loss and protects the roots from both fire and grazing animals. Many such root succulents are deciduous, losing their leaves during dormancy. Some of the strangest and most interesting root succulents are caudiciforms, named for the swollen aboveground root or stem base called a caudex. These plants can have small, globular, aboveground caudexes or massive ones such as the famous African baobab tree *(Adansonia digitata),* capable of developing a trunk 35 ft (10 m) in diameter. Many other genera

RIGHT *The striking variegated leaves of this* Yucca filamentosa *cultivar make an eye-catching feature. This is one of the hardier succulent plants.*
BELOW *Known as the beaver tail cactus,* Opuntia basilaris *stores water in thick fleshy stem segments, and needs very little care once established.*

RIGHT Mammillaria spinosissima *bears rosettes of bright flowers in spring.* Mammillaria *is one of the most popular cactus genera.*
BELOW Rebutia perplexa *is a clump-forming cactus species mainly grown for its tall funnel-shaped flowers. These plants are very easy to grow.*

more suitable to garden cultivation, such as *Crassula* and *Sedum,* have caudiciform members.

Being adapted to periodic drought, most succulents are best grown in gritty well-drained or sandy soil. In most cases, full sun is preferred. But as the habitats from which they come vary, so too do their requirements for light, warmth, water, and nutrients.

Succulents look gorgeous planted in gravel and near stone, materials that often surround them in their native habitats. They make fine container plants and often thrive in the excellent drainage afforded by terracotta pots. Particularly fine in pots or massed in warm-climate borders are *Echeveria* species, with exquisitely ruffled, tinted, and hued leaves in smoky blue-greens, lavenders, and pinks. Planted in dry gardens, succulents of all sorts are complemented by other drought-tolerant plants such as rock roses (*Cistus* species), beardtongues (*Penstemon* species), sages (*Salvia* species), and treasure flowers (*Gazania* species). Ground-cover succulents such as *Delosperma* species, with their brilliantly colored starry blossoms, look wonderful planted on rock walls and hot dry banks. Taller spiky types such as aloes and yuccas can be grown as specimens or used to lend architectural presence and stature to perennial beds.

In cool climates, many succulents take well to indoor culture, enjoying a bright spot inside during the winter and a summer vacation on a porch or patio when possible. During the winter, growth generally slows and watering should be likewise minimized. In the summer, succulents in containers appreciate plenty of water, although they need to dry out between waterings. If kept indoors for the summer, they should receive bright but indirect sun to avoid burning.

Many succulents are surprisingly hardy: Adam's needle *(Yucca filamentosa)*, banana yucca *(Y. baccata)*, and soapweed *(Y. glauca)* tolerate freezing temperatures. Frost-tolerant cacti include claret cup cactus *(Echinocereus triglochidiatus)* and *E. reichenbachii*. The genus *Opuntia* also contains some cold-hardy species. And sedums are among the most popular of perennials and are grown in temperate climates around the world. For their diversity, adaptability, and sheer beauty, there is a place for succulents in every garden.

Favorites	Flower Color	Blooming Season	Flower Fragrance
Agave americana	yellow	spring	no
Agave attenuata	pale yellow	spring	no
Agave colorata	bright yellow to orange	spring	no
Agave filifera	greenish with purple tinge	spring	no
Agave parryi	yellow, tinged red	spring	no
Agave victoriae-reginae	green to cream	varies	no

ABOVE Agave americana *is a highly variable species from northeastern Mexico. The variegated 'Mediopicta Alba' has a white mid-stripe distinguishing its leaves.*

AGAVE

The type genus for the agave (Agavaceae) family is a group of some 225 species of fleshy-leafed perennials found from southern USA through the Caribbean and Central America to Venezuela and Colombia. Forming rosettes of large leaves, they often have fiercely toothed edges and long spines at the tips. The cream to chrome yellow flowers are borne in clusters on tall branching stems. While flower stems can be spectacular both in size and color, agave rosettes are often monocarpic (dying after flowering), and those species with only a few very large rosettes, such as *Agave americana*, are grown mainly for their foliage and form. The alcoholic drink tequila is made from the pith of the foliage of *Agave tequilana*.

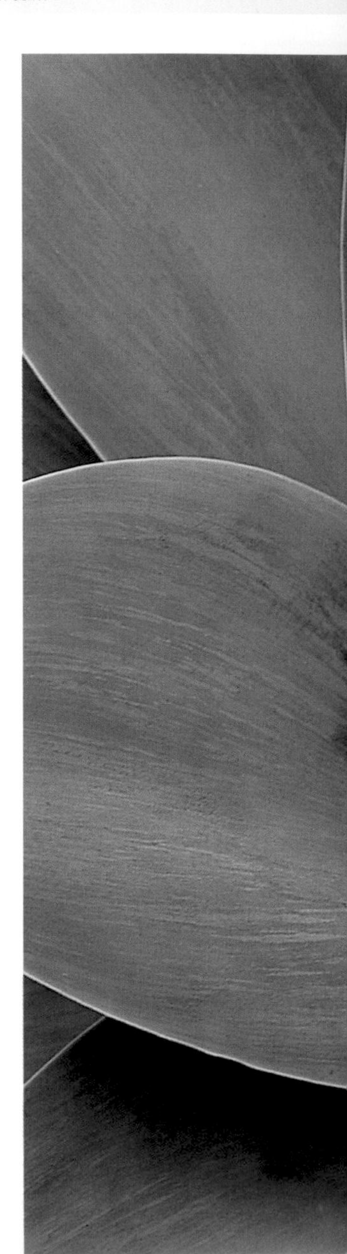

BELOW Agave colorata *is an attractive small plant from Sonora, Mexico. Gray-blue wavy-edged leaves grow to 24 in (60 cm) long, and flower spikes can reach 7–10 ft (2–3 m) in length.*

CULTIVATION

Hardiness varies and some species are very tender. Plant in full sun with very free-draining, rather gritty soil. While agaves appreciate reliable moisture during the growing season, they can survive without it and may suffer in prolonged wet conditions, especially in winter.

Plant Height	Plant Width	Hardiness Zone	Frost Tolerance
17–50 ft	7–15 ft (5–15 m)	8–11 (2–4.5 m)	yes
3–7 ft (0.9–2 m)	2–5 ft (0.6–1.5 m)	9–11	no
7–10 ft (2–3 m)	4–6 ft (1.2–1.8 m)	9–11	no
7–8 ft (2–2.4 m)	27 in (70 cm)	8–11	yes
12–20 ft (3.5–6 m)	20–27 in (50–70 cm)	8–11	yes
10–15 ft (3–4.5 m)	20–27 in (50–70 cm)	9–11	no

ABOVE *The distinctive* Agave victoriae-reginae *'Variegata' has recently been renamed as 'Golden Princess'. Its creamy yellow leaf margins stand out best in part-shade.* **LEFT** Agave attenuata *has brittle, almost flat, rounded, lime green to bluish green leaves, lacking teeth and a terminal spike, and is from just a few Mexican habitats.*

Top Tip

The common name for the agave is the century plant, and the right conditions will see them outlive their owners. Remember to allow enough room for them to expand.

LEFT *From South Africa,* Aloe claviflora *has upright gray-green leaves edged by widely spaced teeth, and pink-red to orange inflorescences that reach 24 in (60 cm) in length.*

ALOE

Formerly listed in the lily (Liliaceae) family but now considered the type genus for the aloe (Aloaceae) family, this group of over 300 species of fleshy-leafed, rosette-forming, sometimes tree-like succulents is found from the Arabian Peninsula and down through Africa to Madagascar. Their long leaves taper to a fine point and are often edged with sharp teeth. Flowers are tubular, usually in warm shades such as yellow, orange, or red, and are borne in spikes at the tips of long, sometimes branching inflorescences. The pithy jelly from the leaves of one species, *Aloe vera*, is so widely used around the world medicinally, as well as cosmetically, that it is often known as the "medicine plant."

BELOW *Forming rosettes of light-spotted, narrow, fleshy, green leaves, and valued for the medicinal properties of its sap,* Aloe vera *is perhaps the best known of all aloes.*

CULTIVATION

A few species will tolerate light frosts but many are tender and all prefer warm dry conditions. Plant in full sun with light, very free-draining soil. Water when actively growing and flowering, but otherwise keep dry. Numerous species adapt to greenhouse or container conditions quite well. Propagation is from offsets, stem cuttings, or seed.

Top Tip

Aloes should not be grown outside if there is any risk at all of freezing, but they will make very good house plants with enough light, doing even better if summered outside.

Favorites	Flower Color	Blooming Season	Flower Fragrance	Plant Height	Plant Width	Hardiness Zone	Frost Tolerance
Aloe arborescens	orange to red	winter	no	10 ft (3 m)	6 ft (1.8 m)	9–11	no
Aloe brevifolia	red with green tips	early summer	no	20 in (50 cm)	20–32 in (50–80 cm)	9–11	no
Aloe chabaudii	red-brown	winter	no	2–5 ft (0.6–1.5 m)	3–5 ft (0.9–1.5 m)	9–11	no
Aloe claviflora	pinkish red to orange	spring to summer	no	5 ft (1.5 m)	3–7 ft (0.9–2 m)	9–11	no
Aloe dorotheae	yellow to red with green tips	winter	no	20–32 in (50–80 cm)	3–7 ft (0.9–2 m)	10–11	no
Aloe ferox	orange-red and golden yellow	late winter	no	7–17 ft (2–5 m)	5–10 ft (1.5–3 m)	9–11	no
Aloe plicatilis	red	winter	no	15 ft (4.5 m)	7 ft (2 m)	9–11	no
Aloe polyphylla	red to orange-pink	spring	no	30 in (75 cm)	16–32 in (40–80 cm)	8–10	yes
Aloe* × *spinosissima	orange-red	winter	no	40 in (100 cm)	24–48 in (60–120 cm)	9–11	no
Aloe striata	dull to bright red	winter	no	3 ft (0.9 m)	4–7 ft (1.2–2 m)	9–11	no
Aloe vera	yellow	summer	no	32 in (80 cm)	24–48 in (60–120 cm)	9–12	no
Aloe virens	red	spring to summer	no	20 in (50 cm)	20–32 in (50–80 cm)	10–11	no

LEFT Aloe chabaudii *is found from South Africa to Zambia. It has rosettes of thick fleshy leaves with red-brown toothed edges. The flowers are also red-brown.*
BELOW *From Lesotho,* Aloe polyphylla *has short-stemmed rosettes with spirals of light-toothed gray-green leaves, and red to orange-pink flowers.*

LEFT *From southern Africa's bush and open forest,* Aloe arborescens *has blue-green toothed leaves, curved and tapering, and spikes of red to orange flowers in winter.*

RIGHT Aloe × spinosissima, *a hybrid of* A. arborescens and A. humilis, *has clumps of short-stemmed or stemless rosettes with upright inflorescences in winter.*

BELOW *From Tanzania,* Aloe dorotheae *has loose rosettes of narrow, fiercely toothed, red-brown leaves and green-tipped yellow to red flowers that appear in winter.*

ABOVE Aloe striata *has broad, flat, toothless, blue-gray leaves, with faint longitudinal stripes and reddish edges. Red flowers appear from winter.*

LEFT *From South Africa's Cape region,* Aloe plicatilis *grows into a shrub to 15 ft (4.5 m) tall, with leaves of rounded tips and tiny teeth, and red flowers in winter.*

LEFT *With a species name that literally means "short leaf,"* Aloe brevifolia *grows to only 20 in (50 cm) tall, with a similar width, and makes an ideal pot plant.*

RIGHT Aloe virens *is from South Africa and has clumps of stemless rosettes of fleshy dark green leaves with fierce teeth. Red flowers are borne on branching inflorescences.*

Top Tip

When growing in pots use a cactus compost, and in areas of frost grow under glass. Liquid fertilizer, applied each month from spring to autumn, can improve results.

CRASSULA

Crassula contains some 300 species, many of them spreading perennials or bushy, woody-stemmed succulents. The type genus for the stonecrop (Crassulaceae) family, species of it occur naturally from Asia to South Africa. The leaves are usually short and stemless, and are often closely spaced, opposite, and spiraled around the stems. Many species have a gray powdery bloom on their foliage, and heads of small, sometimes vividly colored, flowers open generally in spring or after rain. The name *Crassula* comes from the Latin *crassus* meaning "thick," and refers to the thickened leaves.

RIGHT Crassula *'Buddha's Temple' has thin, upward-curved, gray-green leaves tiered like a pagoda roof, and pale cream flowers.*

CULTIVATION

Often cultivated as house plants, these are equally at home outdoors in mild, near frost-free areas in full or half-sun. Plant in light, gritty, well-drained soil, watering them when actively growing and flowering, but otherwise keeping dry. Deadhead to keep compact and encourage new growth. Propagation is usually from leaf cuttings or small stem cuttings; seeds germinate freely, but seedlings are slow to develop.

Favorites	Flower Color	Blooming Season	Flower Fragrance	Plant Height	Plant Width	Hardiness Zone	Frost Tolerance
Crassula anomala	cream to pale pink	spring	no	12 in (30 cm)	12 in (30 cm)	9–11	no
***Crassula* 'Buddha's Temple'**	pale cream	spring	no	2–8 in (5–20 cm)	2–10 in (5–25 cm)	9–11	no
***Crassula* 'Morgan's Beauty'**	soft pink ageing to red	spring	no	2–8 in (5–20 cm)	2–10 in (5–25 cm)	9–11	no
Crassula ovata	pink-tinted white	autumn to spring	no	18 in (45 cm)	24–48 in (60–120 cm)	10–11	no
Crassula perfoliata	white through pink to red	summer	no	60 in (150 cm)	24–40 in (60–100 cm)	9–11	no
Crassula rupestris	red-tinted white	summer	no	8–20 in (20–50 cm)	6–12 in (15–30 cm)	9–11	no

LEFT *Native to South Africa,* Crassula ovata *is an upright branching shrub with fleshy rounded leaves, usually a shiny green with red or paler green edges.*

BELOW Crassula perfoliata *has thickened gray-green leaves, which can be almost flat. Leafy thick-stemmed flowerheads bear blooms of white through pink to red.*

ABOVE Crassula *'Morgan's Beauty' has mounding rosettes of fleshy, flat, gray-green leaves to 2 in (5 cm) long, and showy soft pink flowers that open from pink buds and age red.*

DELOSPERMA

This showy-flowered genus, a member of the iceplant (Aizoaceae) family, is made up of 150 species of low and often widely spreading annuals, biennials, and perennials mainly native to southern Africa but also found northward through East Africa to the Arabian Peninsula. Their foliage is cylindrical, keeled, and fleshy, and is sometimes reduced to small knob-like protrusions. In spring in the temperate zones or after rain in the dry subtropics, they burst into a profusion of brightly colored daisy-like flowers. Colors include the most vivid shades of pink, magenta, and orange, and a few subtle tones such as pale yellow. Although the flowering is often very brief, it is quite spectacular.

RIGHT Delosperma cooperi *is a densely branched South African perennial that will spread quickly, and which may become shrubby. It has pink to magenta flowers.*

ABOVE *The small spreading* Delosperma aberdeenense *is a slightly mounding and densely branched plant. It makes an ideal covering for dry banks and rock walls.*

CULTIVATION

Mostly intolerant of hard or repeated frosts and lengthy cold wet conditions, they are otherwise easily grown in any light well-drained soil in full or half-sun. They thrive in coastal gardens and can help to bind sandy soil. Propagate from cuttings, layers, or seed.

RIGHT Delosperma crassuloides *is a mat-forming plant with densely crowded, oblong, green leaves and scattered pink flowers.*

Top Tip

Delospermas are drought tolerant, making excellent ground covers in hot dry climates. Water occasionally during hot weather; free-draining soil will prevent rotting.

RIGHT Delosperma brunnthaleri *is a multi-branched small shrub with cylindrical leaves and yellow or pink flowers. Native to South Africa, it does best in sandy well-drained soil.*

Favorites

	Flower Color	Blooming Season	Flower Fragrance	Plant Height	Plant Width	Hardiness Zone	Frost Tolerance
Delosperma aberdeenense	pale pink to magenta	spring	no	4–8 in (10–20 cm)	20 in (50 cm)	7–10	yes
Delosperma brunnthaleri	pink or yellow	spring	no	12–16 in (30–40 cm)	20 in (50 cm)	8–10	yes
Delosperma cooperi	pink to magenta	late spring to summer	no	2–20 in (5–50 cm)	18–32 in (45–80 cm)	8–11	no
Delosperma crassuloides	pink	spring	no	2 in (5 cm)	24 in (60 cm)	9–11	no
Delosperma nubigenum	bright yellow to orange-red	late spring to summer	no	2–4 in (5–10 cm)	20–36 in (50–90 cm)	7–11	yes
***Delosperma* 'Ruby Star'**	magenta	spring	no	2–4 in (5–10 cm)	18–36 in (45–90 cm)	9–11	no

Echeveria

This genus of 150 species of mainly small, rosette-forming succulents of the stonecrop (Crassulaceae) family is found principally in Mexico, but a few species range down to Central America. Often the rosettes are densely clustered and may form a small mound. Short-stemmed, small, yellow, orange, pink, or red blooms develop from late spring, but the plants are grown more often for the unusual blue-green foliage, sometimes with a powdery coating, which may develop red tints at the tips and edges. *Echeveria* is named after Atanasio Echeverria Codoy, an eighteenth-century Spanish botanical artist who illustrated a monograph on the genus.

Above Echeveria *'Morning Light' is characterized by clusters of small blue-green rosettes edged in dark pink. It grows to 24 in (60 cm) high, and has pink flowers.*

Cultivation

Hardiness varies but few will tolerate cold wet winters and repeated frosts. Plant in full or half-sun with light, gritty, very free-draining soil. Water occasionally when in active growth, otherwise keep dry, especially in winter. Propagate from stem or leaf cuttings or from seed, which germinates freely but can be prone to damping off.

Top Tip

Indoor pot plants will enjoy summers spent outdoors. Water plants from below; avoid water on the leaves as it will pool into the rosette center and can lead to rotting.

Below Echeveria pallida *has broad, spoon-shaped, light-textured, pale green leaves, which form loose, open rosettes, and has pink flowers during winter.*

Above Echeveria *'Dondo', a hybrid of* E. dehrenbergii and E. setosa, *has rosettes of gray-blue leaves with scalloped and pointed tips, and pretty golden yellow flowers.*

Favorites	Flower Color	Blooming Season	Flower Fragrance	Plant Height	Plant Width	Hardiness Zone	Frost Tolerance
Echeveria agavoides	orange-pink, yellow inside	spring to early summer	no	6–8 in (15–20 cm)	8–12 in (20–30 cm)	9–11	no
***Echeveria* 'Dondo'**	golden yellow	spring to early summer	no	6–24 in (15–60 cm)	4–18 in (10–45 cm)	9–11	no
Echeveria elegans	deep pink, gold center	spring to early summer	no	6–8 in (15–20 cm)	12–16 in (30–40 cm)	9–11	no
***Echeveria* 'Fire Light'**	orange-yellow to pink-red	spring to early summer	no	6–24 in (15–60 cm)	4–18 in (10–45 cm)	9–11	no
Echeveria gigantea	deep pink-red	winter	no	5–7 ft (1.5–2 m)	20 in (50 cm)	10–12	no
Echeveria leucotricha	orange with red edges	spring to early summer	no	24 in (60 cm)	20–40 in (50–100 cm)	9–11	no
***Echeveria* 'Morning Light'**	bright pink	spring to early summer	no	6–24 in (15–60 cm)	4–18 in (10–45 cm)	9–11	no
Echeveria pallida	pink	winter	no	24–40 in (60–100 cm)	16–24 in (40–60 cm)	9–11	no
Echeveria peacockii	soft orange to pinkish red	spring to early summer	no	12 in (30 cm)	12–24 in (30–60 cm)	9–11	no
***Echeveria* 'Princess Lace'**	orange-yellow to pink-red	spring to early summer	no	6–24 in (15–60 cm)	4–18 in (10–45 cm)	9–11	no
***Echeveria* 'Violet Queen'**	orange-yellow to pink-red	spring to early summer	no	6–24 in (15–60 cm)	4–18 in (10–45 cm)	9–11	no
***Echeveria*, Galaxy Series**	orange-red, yellow petal tips	spring to early summer	no	6–24 in (15–60 cm)	4–18 in (10–45 cm)	9–11	no

ABOVE Echeveria *'Violet Queen' is an award-winning hybrid cultivar with clusters of 6 in (15 cm) wide, pink-edged, pale blue-green rosettes. It is hardy, with a clumping habit.*

RIGHT Echeveria gigantea *is a winter-flowering species that has loose open rosettes. This cultivar, 'Dee', has broad blue-green leaves that age red in the sun.*
BELOW Echeveria *'Princess Lace' has pale green rosettes, to 12 in (30 cm) across, with edges that are heavily crimped, and which age to a shade of red.*

BELOW *The slightly branched inflorescences of* Echeveria leucotricha *grow to 16 in (40 cm) tall, bearing up to 15 red-edged orange flowers opening from red buds.*

LEFT Echeveria elegans *has clusters of densely foliaged short-stemmed rosettes, 4 in (10 cm) across, with pale gray-green leaves that are coated with a white powder.*

LEFT Echeveria peacockii *has powdery pale blue-gray rosettes, up to 6 in (15 cm) across, and inflorescences with up to 20 soft orange to pinkish red flowers.*

BELOW *Like 'Apollo', seen here, plants in the Galaxy Series of* Echeveria *bear flowers in a range of brilliant orange-reds with varying amounts of yellow on the petal tips.*

LEFT Echeveria *'Fire Light' is an award-winning cultivar with broad-leafed rosettes of frilled edges that, while starting off blue-green, rapidly age to a deep glossy red.*

LEFT Echinocereus viereckii *is a low alpine species from Mexico with clusters of deep green branching stems that are upright then spreading and have tiny tubercles.*

RIGHT *Native to the western USA–Mexico border region,* Echinocereus triglochidiatus *var.* melanacanthus *has red flowers and the descriptive common name claret cup.*

ECHINOCEREUS

A small globose or cylindrically stemmed genus, it belongs to the cacti (Cactaceae) family and is native to Mexico and southern USA. Including about 120 species, the genus now incorporates many of the species previously in *Lobivia* and *Trichocereus*. The stems are usually many-ribbed and have conspicuous areoles on tubercles or on the ribs themselves. Spines, often large in comparison to the plant size, may be curved or hooked, and flowers, in shades of cream, pink, orange and red, appear from spring to midsummer. These blooms are tubular, long, and often spectacular. *Echinocereus* means "hedgehog cactus," and as much care should be exercised when tending this cactus as when handling its spiny namesake.

CULTIVATION

Plant in full sun with light, gritty, very well-drained soil. Water occasionally when young or in periods of extreme drought, but otherwise leave to survive on natural rainfall. The seed germinates well but seedlings are slow to develop and inclined to rot at the base. Offsets are easier to establish and are often numerous.

BELOW *From Mexico, the solitary or few stems of* Echinocereus subinermis *have up to 11 well-defined ribs bearing starry clusters of usually short stout spines.*

Top Tip

Grow *Echinocereus* plants in a shallow soil—without organic matter—that is fast draining and in full sun. The soil should be allowed to dry out between summer waterings.

ABOVE *From the western USA–Mexico border region,* Echinocereus stramineus *forms dense colonies of up to several hundred narrow cylindrical stems in the wild.*

Favorites	Flower Color	Blooming Season	Flower Fragrance	Plant Height	Plant Width	Hardiness Zone	Frost Tolerance
Echinocereus coccineus	scarlet, yellow at center	spring to summer	no	3 in (8 cm)	4 in (10 cm)	6–11	yes
Echinocereus engelmannii	lavender to purple-red	summer	no	10–20 in (25–50 cm)	10–24 in (25–60 cm)	8–11	yes
Echinocereus stramineus	bright magenta	mid-summer	no	12–18 in (30–45 cm)	16–84 in (40–200 cm)	8–11	yes
Echinocereus subinermis	yellow	summer	no	8–10 in (20–25 cm)	6–12 in (15–30 cm)	9–11	no
Echinocereus triglochidiatus	scarlet	spring to summer	no	6–16 in (15–40 cm)	8–36 in (20–90 cm)	8–11	yes
Echinocereus viereckii	purple, mauve	spring to autumn	no	12 in (30 cm)	12–24 in (30–60 cm)	9–11	no

Kalanchoe

A member of the stonecrop (Crassulaceae) family, this genus has around 125 species of mostly bushy succulents found mainly in eastern and southern Africa, with a few species in Asia. They are a variable group, often with rather large, powder-coated or felted, silver-gray leaves that have notched edges. Some species produce tiny plantlets along the leaf margins. The small, starry, 4-petalled flowers are clustered in heads. They open at varying times depending on the species and may be very brightly colored, often in yellow, orange, or red shades. *Kalanchoe beharensis* is among the largest-leafed succulents, with foliage to 12 in (30 cm) long.

Cultivation

Smaller species and cultivars are often grown as house plants. Outdoors, most require frost-free conditions; full sun for those with silver leaves; light, gritty, free-draining soil; and some water during the growing season. Propagate from stem cuttings, leaf cuttings, or seed, or by removing plantlets.

Above *An upright spreading succulent,* Kalanchoe fedtschenkoi *makes an attractive ground cover. The flowers can vary in color.*

Left *A mature* Kalanchoe beharensis *'Oak Leaf' plant has many small, tubular, yellowish flowers and large, felted, oak-shaped leaves.*

Top Tip

Whether grown for their ornamental foliage or tightly packed long-lasting flower clusters, *Kalanchoe* make low-maintenance indoor plants for a bright position.

ABOVE RIGHT *The colorful flowers of* Kalanchoe pumila *contrast strongly with the white-frosted leaves. These plants need full sun for the foliage to be at its best.*

RIGHT *Hybrids of* Kalanchoe blossfeldiana *are grown for their showy display of bright orange, yellow, pink, red, white, or purple flowers and interesting fleshy leaves.*

Favorites	Flower Color	Blooming Season	Flower Fragrance	Plant Height	Plant Width	Hardiness Zone	Frost Tolerance
Kalanchoe beharensis	yellow	late winter	no	10 ft (3 m)	3 ft (0.9 m)	10–11	no
Kalanchoe blossfeldiana	deep red	early spring	no	15 in (38 cm)	15 in (38 cm)	10–12	no
Kalanchoe fedtschenkoi	orange to red	spring	no	20 in (50 cm)	12 in (30 cm)	11–12	no
Kalanchoe pumila	pink with purple markings	spring	no	8 in (20 cm)	18 in (45 cm)	11–12	no
Kalanchoe thyrsiflora	yellow	spring	yes	24 in (60 cm)	12 in (30 cm)	11–12	no
Kalanchoe tomentosa	purple-tinged yellow-green	early spring	no	15–36 in (38–90 cm)	8 in (20 cm)	10–12	no

MAMMILLARIA

Hailing from southwestern USA, Mexico, Central America, and northern South America, this genus, commonly known as pincushion cactus, is a member of the family Cactaceae and contains more than 150 species. These solitary or clustering cacti have round to cylindrical, spiny, green stems. The spines appear from the pimple-like openings (tubercles) of the raised segments (areoles) on the stems. Funnel-shaped flowers, in colors ranging from white to yellow, green, or pink to purple, encircle the crowns of the stems thoughout spring and summer. The attractive flowers are followed by round berry-like seed pods.

ABOVE *A clustered mound-forming cactus,* Mammillaria geminispina *usually has short cylindrical stems. This mutated "crest" form has an interesting twisted growth habit.*

CULTIVATION

These plants do well in well-drained soils in an open sunny position. Reduce watering in winter. Propagate most species by division of offsets, or from seed in spring and summer.

LEFT Mammillaria compressa f. cristata *is an unusual form in which growth occurs in a line, not from a single growth tip, giving a fan-like or crested appearance.*

ABOVE *The bright pink flowers of* Mammillaria melanocentra *are carried at the top of its single undivided stem. They are followed by pinkish red fruits.*

LEFT Mammillaria canelensis *begins as a single-stemmed plant but later develops more stems. The flowers add a touch of color when they open during the day.*

Top Tip

Mammillaria species are often grown for their flowers. Water and fertilize regularly throughout the growing season to encourage flower production.

Favorites	Flower Color	Blooming Season	Flower Fragrance	Plant Height	Plant Width	Hardiness Zone	Frost Tolerance
Mammillaria bocasana	creamy white, rose pink	spring to summer	no	4–8 in (10–20 cm)	12–24 in (30–60 cm)	9–11	no
Mammillaria canelensis	pink to red, yellow	summer	no	6–8 in (15–20 cm)	3–4 in (8–10 cm)	9–11	no
Mammillaria carmenae	pink- or cream-tinged white	spring	no	2–3 in (5–8 cm)	2–3 in (5–8 cm)	9–11	no
Mammillaria compressa	purplish pink	spring	no	1½–2½ in (3.5–6 cm)	6 in (15 cm)	9–11	no
Mammillaria geminispina	deep pink to red	spring to autumn	no	6–10 in (15–25 cm)	6–20 in (15–50 cm)	9–11	no
Mammillaria klissingiana	pink, ageing to red	summer	no	4–6 in (10–15 cm)	2½–4 in (6–10 cm)	9–11	no
Mammillaria laui	purplish pink	spring	no	1–1½ in (2.5–3.5 cm)	1½–2 in (3.5–5 cm)	9–11	no
Mammillaria longimamma	bright yellow	summer	no	3–5 in (8–12 cm)	3–5 in (8–12 cm)	9–11	no
Mammillaria melanocentra	pink	spring	no	3–5 in (8–12 cm)	4–6 in (10–15 cm)	9–11	no
Mammillaria parkinsonii	brown- or pink-tinged yellow	spring	no	4–6 in (10–15 cm)	3–6 in (8–15 cm)	9–11	no
Mammillaria tayloriorum	reddish pink	spring	no	3–6 in (8–15 cm)	2½–3 in (6–8 cm)	9–11	no
Mammillaria winterae	yellow and white	summer	no	8–12 in (20–30 cm)	8–12 in (20–30 cm)	9–11	no

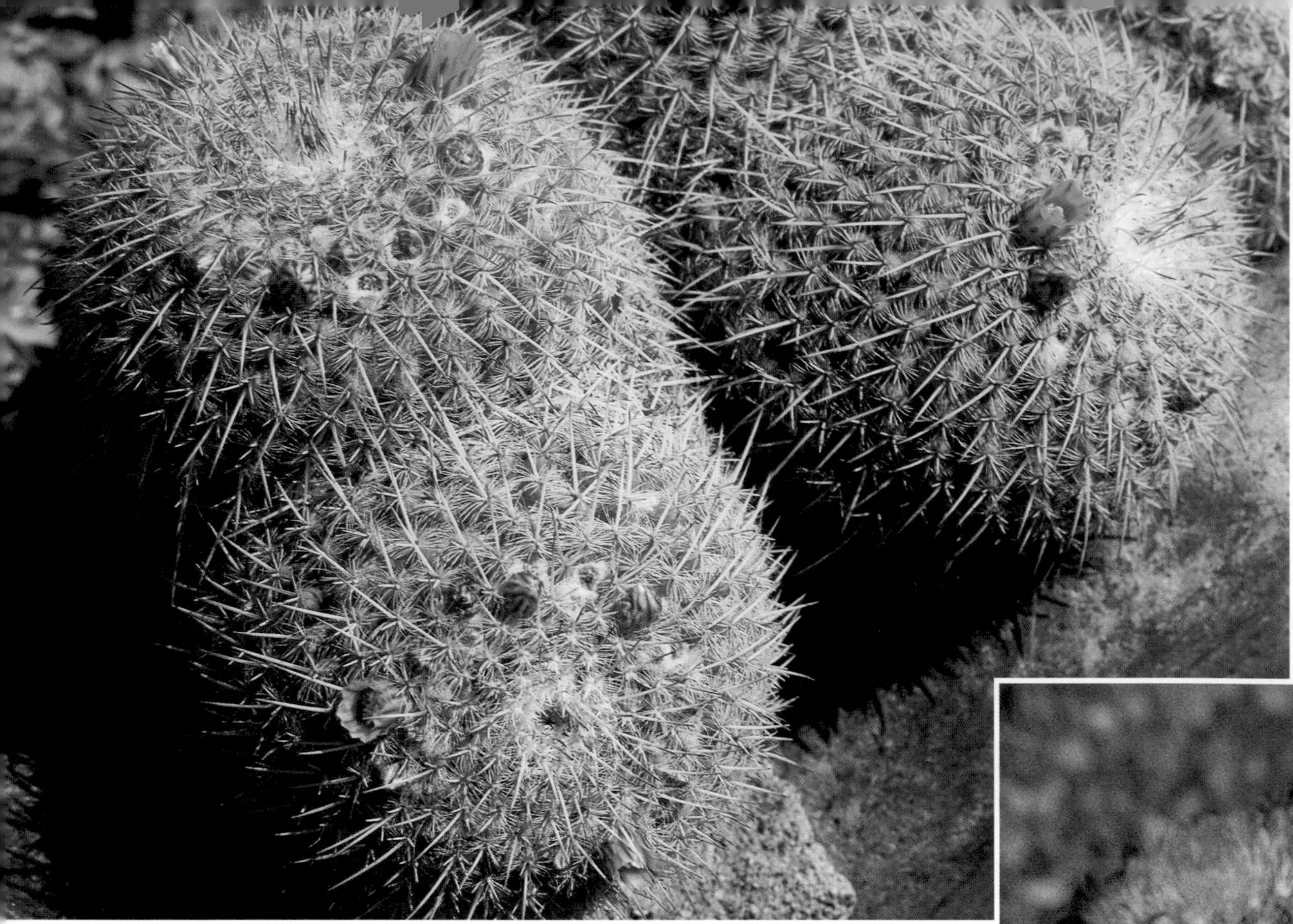

ABOVE *Also known as owl's eye cactus,* Mammillaria parkinsonii *has a spherical body at first, later branching to eventually form a large mound.*

RIGHT *Like most members of this genus,* Mammillaria klissingiana *has relatively small flowers occurring in a ring around the top of the plant. The pink flowers age to red.*

FAR RIGHT *Much more brightly colored than the species, the intense pink flowers of* Mammillaria carmenae *'Jewel' make an eye-catching display.*

RIGHT Mammillaria longimamma, *also known as finger cactus, has big bright yellow flowers about 2½ in (6 cm) in diameter. The large protruding tubercles are the reason for the common name.*

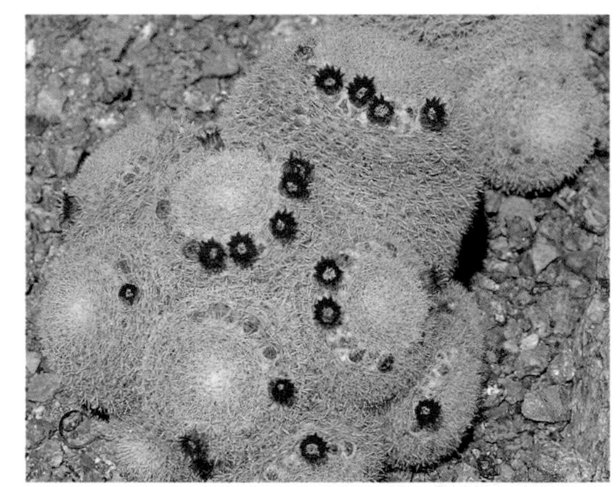

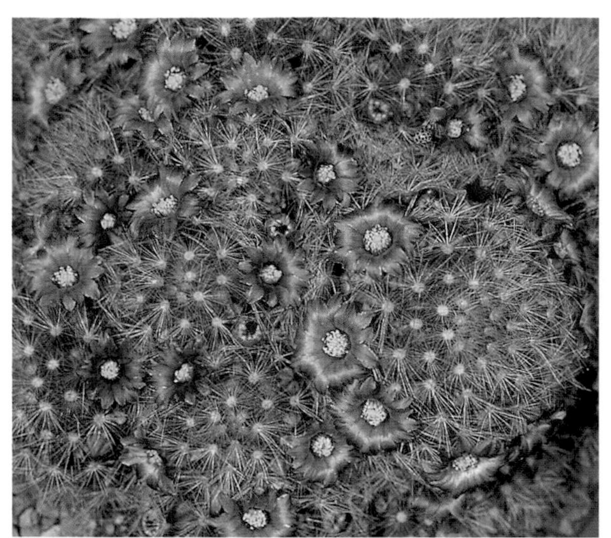

LEFT *The shiny vividly colored flowers of* Mammillaria laui var. rubens *are borne in spring. Most* Mammillaria *species will produce a second flush of blooms during the year.*

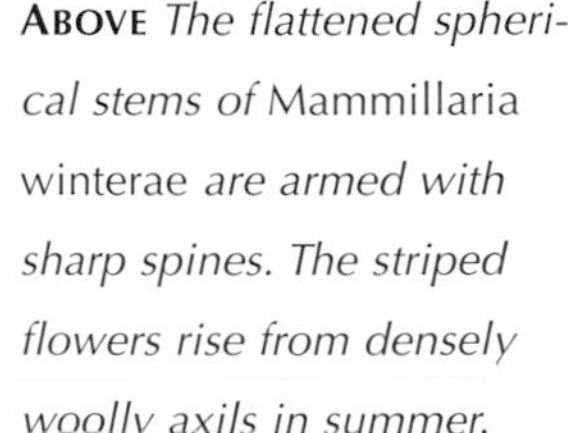

ABOVE *The flattened spherical stems of* Mammillaria winterae *are armed with sharp spines. The striped flowers rise from densely woolly axils in summer.*

ABOVE *In spring, the spherical stems of* Mammillaria tayloriorum *are topped with a "halo" of attractive reddish pink flowers, each about $\frac{1}{2}$ in (12 mm) in diameter.*

OPUNTIA

This genus in the cactus (Cactaceae) family is made up of around 180 species, some of them tree-like, that are widespread in the Americas and include some of the hardiest cacti, found as far north as southern Canada. The best-known forms have flat, paddle-shaped, areole-studded stem segments, that develop yellow, orange, or red flowers along the margins. The flowers are followed by soft, rounded, red or yellow fruits called prickly pears. Not all species follow this pattern; some have cylindrical stems, a few are ground covers, and some have insignificant fruits. *Opuntia stricta* was introduced to Australia in the 1830s to provide hedging material in arid regions. It quickly covered vast areas, but in an early example of natural management was brought under control by introduced insects.

CULTIVATION

These cacti are very adaptable and well able to survive outside what would be considered "normal" cactus conditions. Plant in full or half-sun with gritty, very free-draining soil and water only when absolutely necessary. Propagate from stem cuttings or by division.

Favorites	Flower Color	Blooming Season	Flower Fragrance
Opuntia aciculata	yellow, red	spring to summer	no
Opuntia aoracantha	white to yellow, pinkish	spring to summer	no
Opuntia basilaris	purplish red	summer	no
Opuntia macrocentra	bright yellow, orange-red at base	spring	no
Opuntia microdasys	red-tinged yellow	spring to summer	no
Opuntia strigil	creamy white	spring to summer	no

ABOVE Opuntia strigil *has fleshy red fruits that follow the creamy white flowers. This prickly pear species can grow as an upright or sprawling shrub.*

LEFT *The bright flowers of* Opuntia macrocentra *are about $2\frac{1}{2}$ in (6 cm) wide. They will only last one day out in the sun, but will last for 2–3 days if taken inside.*

Top Tip

Most *Opuntia* species are easy to grow and make excellent house plants. They do best in full sun, and flower production will fall if conditions are too dark.

Plant Height	Plant Width	Hardiness Zone	Frost Tolerance
3–5 ft (0.9–1.5 m)	3–5 ft (0.9–1.5 m)	9–11	no
12–24 in (30–60 cm)	12–24 in (30–60 cm)	9–11	no
2–3 ft (0.6–0.9 m)	4 ft (1.2 m)	9–11	no
4 ft (1.2 m)	4 ft (1.2 m)	9–11	no
18–24 in (45–60 cm)	18–24 in (45–60 cm)	8–11	no
2–3 ft (0.6–0.9 m)	4–7 ft (1.2–2 m)	9–11	no

Below Opuntia aciculata *has flattened stem segments dotted with tufts of spines and bristles. Protuberant flowers appear on the stem segment edge.*

Above *The colorful flowers of* Opuntia aoracantha *have thick stems called pericarpels. This is a small species, often branching at ground level.*

REBUTIA

Found in the Bolivian Andes and neighboring parts of Argentina, *Rebutia* is a genus in the cactus (Cactaceae) family of around 40 small, almost spherical- or cylindrical-stemmed species. Their clustered stems are densely studded with spine-bearing tubercles, and the spines themselves are often very fine and bristle-like, though still sharp. Brightly colored funnel-shaped flowers develop around the tops of the stems and can be abundant. The flowers close at night. The botanist Karl Schumann classified the genus in 1895, naming it after a French cactus grower and vigneron with whom he corresponded, Monsieur P. Rebut.

Top Tip

It is good to re-pot rebutias regularly, particularly when they are young. This will increase the number and size of the stems and the number of flowers produced.

CULTIVATION

Although tolerant of occasional very light frosts, *Rebutia* species usually perform best with mild winter conditions. Plant in full or half-sun with gritty, very free draining soil. Water during the growing season but otherwise keep dry. These cacti are very easily propagated from the numerous offsets.

ABOVE *The pretty funnel-shaped flowers of* Rebutia neocumingii *bloom during the day. They are yellow to orange in color and grow to 1 in (25 mm) long.*
LEFT Rebutia marsoneri *typically flowers a bright and vibrant yellow. However, there are varieties that have red flowers.*

LEFT Rebutia fiebrigii, *native to the mountainous regions of Bolivia and northwestern Argentina, is a hardy specimen with bristly but soft white spines.*

BELOW *Usually a spherical solitary species,* Rebutia flavistyla *can be grown from seed. It bears long-tubed, vivid orange flowers from spring.*

Favorites	Flower Color	Blooming Season	Flower Fragrance	Plant Height	Plant Width	Hardiness Zone	Frost Tolerance
Rebutia fiebrigii	orange to red	summer	no	1¼–2 in (3–5 cm)	1¼–3 in (3–8 cm)	9–12	no
Rebutia flavistyla	orange	spring	no	2–4 in (5–10 cm)	2–6 in (5–15 cm)	10–12	no
Rebutia heliosa	dark pink to orange-pink	summer	no	¾–2 in (18–50 mm)	½–4 in (12–100 mm)	9–12	no
Rebutia marsoneri	yellow, red, or orange-yellow	summer	no	1¼–4 in (3–10 cm)	1½–8 in (3.5–20 cm)	9–12	no
Rebutia neocumingii	yellow to orange	summer	no	4–8 in (10–20 cm)	3–4 in (8–10 cm)	9–10	no
Rebutia perplexa	lilac-pink	summer	no	½–1 in (12–25 mm)	1–3 in (25–80 mm)	9–12	no

Left *The attractive smooth-textured foliage of* Sedum rubrotinctum *is blunt-tipped and most commonly mid-green in color, but turns red in sunlight.*

Sedum

This genus of 300 species of mainly low spreading succulents is found over much of the Northern Hemisphere. It is part of the stonecrop (Crassulaceae) family. Their leaves are usually short, very fleshy, and often develop bright red or bronze tones in the sun. Dense sprays of tiny, light to golden yellow or pink flowers develop at the stem tips, most often during the warmer months. Many of the larger autumn-flowering species are now classified under *Hylotelephium* and *Rhodiola*. The name *Sedum* is from the Latin *sedere*, to sit, referring to the low spreading habit.

Cultivation

Of varying hardiness, they are otherwise easily grown in any sunny or partly shaded position with light well-drained soil. The hardier species are often quite at home in everyday garden conditions, but those from arid areas should be kept dry during winter. Remove spent flower-heads as they dry. Propagation is from short stem cuttings, leaf cuttings, or seed. Many species will self-layer.

RIGHT *Plant this species,* Sedum kamtschaticum, *in a well-drained border. It will also grow well in cracks and crevices in walls and pavements.*

LEFT *The foliage of* Sedum spathulifolium *'Purpureum' turns purplish red in the sun. The yellow flowers appear in spring and early summer.*

BELOW LEFT Sedum spectabile, *known as ice plant and showy sedum, can survive drought conditions but does best with regular watering.*

Top Tip

Sedum species transplant readily from cuttings, often rooting from broken foliage. Clumps may be divided and replanted at any time during the growing season.

Favorites	Flower Color	Blooming Season	Flower Fragrance	Plant Height	Plant Width	Hardiness Zone	Frost Tolerance
Sedum album	white	summer	no	2–6 in (5–15 cm)	2–24 in (30–60 cm)	6–10	yes
Sedum kamtschaticum	golden yellow	summer	no	4–12 in (10–30 cm)	10–24 in (25–60 cm)	7–10	yes
Sedum rubrotinctum	pale yellow	spring	no	10 in (25 cm)	12–24 in (30–60 cm)	9–11	no
Sedum sieboldii	pale pink	autumn	no	4 in (10 cm)	12–20 in (30–50 cm)	7–10	yes
Sedum spathulifolium	yellow	late spring to early summer	no	4–6 in (10–15 cm)	24 in (60 cm)	7–10	yes
Sedum spectabile	pink to red	late summer to autumn	no	18–27 in (45–70 cm)	16–32 in (40–80 cm)	7–10	yes

YUCCA

Found mainly in USA and Mexico, this genus in the agave (Agavaceae) family is made up of around 40 species of stiffly foliaged perennials, shrubs, and small trees. They have large heads of narrow, blue-green, sword-shaped leaves that are sometimes tipped with spines. Some species branch and bush out at ground level, some develop a single short trunk, and others have branching trunks. Tall flower spikes develop quickly in spring or from late summer into autumn. They carry pendulous greenish-cream flowers, sometimes pink-tinted, that may be slightly scented. Several *Yucca* species are under threat in the wild because the moths that pollinate them have become endangered.

ABOVE *The bell-shaped flowers of* Yucca baccata *are sometimes tinged with purple. Its leaves are green with yellow or blue tints.*

CULTIVATION

All *Yuccas* will tolerate light frost and several species are very hardy. They thrive in a bright sunny position with light well-drained soil. Although very drought tolerant, they will usually accept normal garden watering. Propagate from suckers, root cuttings, or seed.

Favorites	Flower Color	Blooming Season	Flower Fragrance	Plant Height	Plant Width	Hardiness Zone	Frost Tolerance
Yucca baccata	cream	spring	no	5 ft (1.5 m)	4 ft (1.2 m)	9–11	no
Yucca elephantipes	white or cream	summer to autumn	no	30 ft (9 m)	10 ft (3 m)	10–12	no
Yucca filamentosa	white or cream	summer	no	3–12 ft (0.9–3.5 m)	5–8 ft (1.5–2.4 m)	6–10	yes
Yucca glauca	white	summer	no	2 ft (0.6 m)	3 ft (0.9 m)	4–9	yes
Yucca recurvifolia	cream	late summer to autumn	no	4–8 ft (1.2–2.4 m)	4–8 ft (1.2–2.4 m)	8–11	yes
Yucca whipplei	white	late summer to early autumn	no	3–12 ft (0.9–3.5 m)	3–6 ft (0.9–1.8 m)	8–11	yes

LEFT Yucca filamentosa *'Bright Edge' looks great in a garden all year round. The creamy flowers are borne in summer, but the green and yellow foliage adds color in winter.*

BELOW Yucca recurvifolia *is a robust plant with bluish to deep green leaves that can be recurved and drooping in some forms, but are usually straight and erect.*

LEFT *The leaves of* Yucca whipplei *have very sharp tips and fine-toothed edges. Because of this, this species should not be planted along a path.*

Top Tip

Yucca species must have at least half a day of full sun each day to flower well. Plants in shady or partially shady locations will produce less flowers.

Vegetables and Herbs

Vegetables and herbs are some of the most prized and practical plants in the garden. Even those who claim not to care about plants will often grow (or aspire to grow) a tomato plant and a few herbs. The flavor of home-grown vegetables is incomparable to store-bought: even the best vegetable stands and farmers' markets cannot offer vegetables that have spent less than an hour between the garden and the plate. Still warm from the sun and at the peak of ripeness, freshly harvested vegetables and herbs seem to distill the essence of all that is good about gardening—and eating.

Above *Tomatoes* (Lycopersicon esculentum) *are among the most common plants in the home vegetable garden, perhaps because freshly picked perfectly ripe tomatoes taste so good.*
Left *A herb and vegetable garden can range in size from a small pot to quite a large area. Whatever the size, the rewards will be high, in flavor and sense of achievement.*

GROW YOUR OWN DELICIOUS FOOD

Vegetables and herbs encompass a vast range of mostly herbaceous annual, biennial, and perennial plants with many uses in the kitchen, in medicine, and in arts and crafts. Edible or useful parts include roots, tubers, stems, leaves, flowers, seeds, or fruits.

LEFT *Widely used in salads, lettuce is now available in a variety of forms and colors.* Lactuca sativa *'Cosmic' is an award-winning cos-type lettuce.*

Root crops include beets, carrots, garlic, onions, artichokes, parsnips, potatoes, and turnips. These plants store water and nutrients in their plump rootstocks. Some, such as potatoes and Jerusalem artichokes, are actually tubers.

Many vegetables are primarily leaf crops. Some are typically cooked; others are eaten raw. Leaf crops include kales and cabbages, spinach, leeks, Asian greens, and the many salad crops including lettuce, radicchio (chicory), arugula (rocket), and corn salad (mache). Brussels sprouts are composed of tiny leaf buds produced directly from the plant's main stem.

A number of vegetable plants are grown for their stems. These include the popular celery and asparagus, a perennial plant with spears that are best eaten when young and tender in early spring.

The bulk of garden vegetables are grown for their edible fruits, seeds, or flowers. These include the legumes (peas and beans), eggplants (aubergines), peppers (capsicums), cucumbers, melons, sweet corn, pumpkins, squash (marrows), and tomatoes. Broccoli and cauliflower are grown for their immature flower buds.

Many vegetables spring from the same basic plant, and have been cultivated over the centuries to create diverse forms. For example, the brassicas (family Brassicaceae) include the non-heading kales (*Brassica oleracea,* Acephala Group), broccoli and cauliflower (*B. o.,* Botrytis Group), cabbages (*B. o.,* Capitata Group), Brussels sprouts (*B. o.,* Gemmifera Group), kohlrabi (*B. o.,* Gongylodes Group), and

ABOVE Capsicum annuum, *Grossum Group, contains sweet bell peppers in various colors. 'Blushing Beauty' ripens to apricot-flushed yellow.*

LEFT *Broccoli is an easy-to-grow cool-season vegetable. Award-winning 'Shogun' belongs to the Botrytis Group within* Brassica oleracea.

sprouting broccoli (*B. o.,* Italica Group). Other edible brassicas include turnip (*B. rapa,* Rapifera Group) and bok choy (*B. rapa,* Chinensis Group). Mustards such as brown mustard, Chinese mustard, and mustard greens are all derived from *Brassica juncea*. Rutabagas (swedes) and a number of other important brassicas are derived from *Brassica napus*.

Vegetables can be grown from seed or purchased as young starts. Vegetable packets typically indicate how many weeks ahead of the last frost date each type needs to be started. When selecting which plant to grow, consider flavor, color, fruit or plant size, ripening time, storage quality, and resistance to insects or diseases. Heirloom varieties may take up more space, produce later, or be more prone to certain diseases—but their flavor is usually better. New varieties are bred as much for compact size and fruit production as for flavor.

ABOVE *The purple-red leaves of* Ocimum basilicum *'Red Rubin' basil are a decorative and flavorful addition to the herb garden.*

LEFT Mentha suaveolens *is known as apple mint. Mint plants can be invasive and are often grown in pots.*

Additionally, many vegetables are better suited to particular climates than others. A tomato variety that ripens well in Sydney, Australia, might not suit the climate of London, England. Local information about suitable varieties is essential.

Although there are many kinds of vegetables, the best vegetables are produced when plants are grown in full sun in reasonably rich soil and supplied with consistent moisture during the growing season. Since many vegetables are annuals or tender biennials or perennials growing for only one season, it is essential that plants receive everything they need to reach maturity quickly. For instance, mulching warms the soil, conserves moisture, and increases the level of organic matter. Crop rotation prevents nutrient depletion and minimizes disease.

Broadly defined, herbs are plants that are used to flavor foods and beverages, dye cloth, repel insects, scent toiletries, and prevent or treat ailments. Encompassing annuals, biennials, and perennials, the plants range in size from prostrate species to large evergreen trees. Herbs are generally ornamental and their flowers are often nectar-rich and sought after by butterflies, bees, and hummingbirds. Many herbs do well in pots, are suitable as low hedges, or can be integrated into perennial beds.

Most herbs are aromatic to some degree. Sunny dry climates increase the taste, fragrance, and potency of many of the aromatic Mediterranean herbs such as lavender, oregano, rosemary, thyme, and sage, most of which grow in rather dry poor soil in their native habitats. While most Mediterranean herbs thrive in full sun, there are many that tolerate shade, such as mint (*Mentha* species). Herbs such as basil, parsley, and dill prefer more moisture and nutrients, as they are prone to bolting (going to seed) when stressed.

Vegetables and herbs are easy to work into almost any garden, requiring only some initial attention to available soil, moisture, and light. Whether grown for culinary or ornamental purposes, they are easy to grow and can provide access to fresh organic food that tastes more delicious than almost anything purchased commercially. While the flavor of fresh vegetables and herbs is enough in itself to inspire one to tend a produce garden, the sense of achievement derived is also a great impetus.

ASPARAGUS

This asparagus (Asparagaceae) family genus is composed of about 300 species of tuberous or rhizome-rooted perennial herbs, shrubs, and climbers that are widespread outside the Americas. The species most often grown for its succulent young stems is *Asparagus officinalis*, which develops a dense crown of rhizomes and produces a large head of feathery foliage with small white flowers and red berries. Plants are not only long lived (they can be expected to produce for up to 25 years), but are also versatile—in herbal medicine *Asparagus* is considered to have a cleansing effect on both the liver and kidneys.

CULTIVATION

The fresh new shoots are the edible part and it takes several seasons for new crowns (roots) to become fully productive. Before planting, work in plenty of compost, enough to raise the bed. If necessary, add coarse sand or fine gravel to improve the drainage. Harvest the young spears by cutting them off near ground level with a sharp knife. Do not harvest any spears until the crowns are at least 2 years old. Propagate by dividing the crowns. Plants can be raised from seed but only male plants produce an edible crop.

RIGHT Asparagus officinalis *is the species people generally mean when referring to asparagus. Widely grown as a foodcrop, it has erect multi-branched stems.*

ABOVE Asparagus officinalis *'Larac' is a French variety noted for its wide adaptability. Like the species, it has rich green feathery foliage, but its spears are white.*

ABOVE *Known as the foxtail fern or cat-tail asparagus, for self-apparent reasons,* Asparagus densiflorus *'Myersii' has needle-like branchlets on upright stems.*
LEFT Asparagus macowanii *is a robust shrub with many long-lived stems springing from a raised root mass. Profuse pure white flowers are borne in mid-summer.*

Favorites

	Common Name	Produce Season	Plant Height	Plant Width	Hardiness Zone	Frost Tolerance
Asparagus asparagoides	florists' smilax	spring	5–6 ft (1.5–1.8 m)	3 ft (0.9 m)	7–10	yes
Asparagus densiflorus	emerald fern	spring	30–36 in (75–90 cm)	36 in (90 cm)	7–9	yes
***Asparagus densiflorus* 'Myersii'**	foxtail fern	spring	30–36 in (75–90 cm)	36 in (90 cm)	7–9	yes
Asparagus macowanii	—	spring	6 ft (1.8 m)	8 ft (2.4 m)	9–11	no
Asparagus officinalis	asparagus	spring	3–5 ft (0.9–1.5 m)	3–5 ft (0.9–1.5 m)	4–8	yes
Asparagus setaceus	plumosa fern lily	spring	12–48 in (30–120 cm)	24 in (60 cm)	7–11	yes

Top Tip

Growing from seed will mean a 3-year wait for first harvest, so it is best to use crowns (roots) purchased from a nursery when planting out the crop.

BETA

The sole species in this genus of the goosefoot (Chenopiaceae) family is a Eurasian biennial that occurs in 2 main forms. One is grown for its edible swollen roots (beets), the other for its iron-rich deep green to purple-red foliage (chards). The leaves of both forms are edible, the leaves of chards being heavily puckered with a thick and often contrastingly colored midrib. With beets, the top of the root often emerges from the soil as it matures. Roots were used as a food source from the sixteenth century. In times past beet juice was considered a virtual cure-all, able to alleviate everything from ringing in the ears to toothache.

ABOVE *The Conditiva Group includes vegetables such as sugar beet and beetroot.* Beta vulgaris, *Conditiva Group, 'Bull's Blood' has red leaves and striped roots.*

RIGHT *The Cicla Group includes spinach and silver beet.* Beta vulgaris, *Cicla Group, 'Bright Lights' has stems in shades of orange, red, yellow, pink, or white.*

CULTIVATION

Although generally raised from seed sown from spring through to mid-summer, in mild areas autumn sowings may also be successful. Beets favor light well-drained soil, provided it is not too rich. Chards prefer rich, moist, well-drained soil. Both need to be planted in full sun. Any nutrient deficiencies, usually of manganese, show up in chards as yellowing leaves and poorly formed roots. Very heavy soil also has a tendency to lead to poorly formed or stunted roots.

RIGHT Beta vulgaris, *Cicla Group, 'Rhubarb Chard' has crimson stalks and dark green crinkly leaves. Its midribs can be used as a celery or asparagus substitute.*

Top Tip

Beets are slightly tolerant to drought, but keep chards moist. Water both before the soil entirely dries out. Beet roots will crack if moisture varies too much.

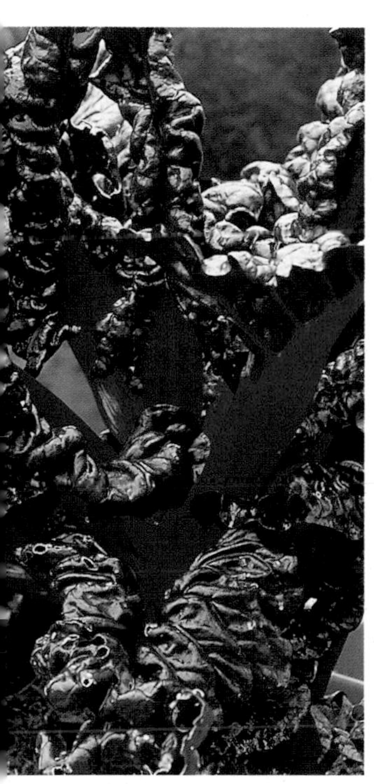

Favorites

	Common Name	Produce Season	Plant Height	Plant Width	Hardiness Zone	Frost Tolerance
Beta vulgaris	beet	spring to early summer	27 in (70 cm)	27 in (70 cm)	8–11	yes
***Beta vulgaris*, Cicla Group**	spinach, chard, silver beet	spring to early summer	27 in (70 cm)	27 in (70 cm)	8–11	yes
***Beta vulgaris*, Cicla Group, 'Bright Lights'**	Swiss chard	spring to early summer	24 in (60 cm)	12 in (30 cm)	8–11	yes
***Beta vulgaris*, Cicla Group, 'Rhubarb Chard'**	ruby chard	spring to early summer	27 in (70 cm)	27 in (70 cm)	8–11	yes
***Beta vulgaris* Conditiva Group**	beet	spring to early summer	27 in (70 cm)	27 in (70 cm)	8–11	yes
***Beta vulgaris*, Conditiva Group, 'Forono'**	beetroot	spring to early summer	27 in (70 cm)	27 in (70 cm)	8–11	yes

Above Beta vulgaris, *Cicla Group, 'Bright Yellow' is a Swiss chard whose green crinkly leaves can be used as a spinach substitute. Its golden stalks are a colorful addition to any vegetable garden and can be steamed, or eaten raw when young.*

Left Brassica oleracea, *Botrytis Group, 'Perfection' is a mini cauliflower with a cream-colored head that grows to about 4 in (10 cm) in diameter in 2 months.*

Right Brassica oleracea, *Capitata Group, 'Dynamo' is a cabbage developed in Germany, which has a small head, a mild flavor, and is not prone to splitting.*

Brassica

With a history of use spanning thousands of years, the cabbage and its relatives feature in many of the world's cuisines. There are few species but many subspecies, groups, and cultivars, treated as annuals, biennials, and perennials, depending on climate. Originally from temperate coastal regions of Europe and North Africa, the versatile brassicas are grown for their leaves (cabbages, kale, Asian greens), their flowering parts (broccoli, cauliflower, Brussels sprouts), their seed (rape/canola), or their roots (turnip, swede). As a rule, the leaves are large and waxy with a whitish bloom, and flowers are usually yellow, but are sometimes white. Flowering times will be dictated by the climatic region and the age of the plant.

Cultivation

These easy-to-grow adaptable plants do best in well-drained moist soil that has been enriched with well-rotted manure. Propagate from seed throughout the year, depending on the variety.

Above Brassica rapa, *Rapifera Group, 'Atlantic' is a purple-topped turnip that is harvested when it reaches the size of a golf ball. Its leaves can be used in salads.*

Below Brassica oleracea, *Capitata Group, 'Primavoy' is a good storage cabbage cultivar, with compact flattened heads and dark blue-green puckered leaves.*

Favorites

Favorites	Common Name	Produce Season	Plant Height	Plant Width	Hardiness Zone	Frost Tolerance
Brassica juncea	mustard	summer	8–40 in (20–100 cm)	8–40 in (20–100 cm)	9–11	no
Brassica napus	swede	summer	8–16 in (20–40 cm)	8–16 in (20–40 cm)	8–11	yes
Brassica oleracea	wild cabbage	summer	16 in (40 cm)	12 in (30 cm)	8–11	yes
***Brassica oleracea,* Botrytis Group**	cauliflower and broccoli	early summer	16 in (40 cm)	12 in (30 cm)	8–11	yes
***Brassica oleracea,* Capitata Group**	cabbage	summer	16 in (40 cm)	12 in (30 cm)	8–11	yes
Brassica rapa	turnip	spring to autumn	12–20 in (30–50 cm)	12–20 in (30–50 cm)	9–11	no

Top Tip

Rotate *Brassica* plants in vegetable gardens to prevent soil-borne diseases. Use a different site each year for 3 years, starting again in the fourth year.

CAPSICUM

A nightshade (Solanaceae) family genus of 10 species of annuals and short-lived perennials, peppers have been cultivated for thousands of years and are derived from several species, mainly *Capsicum annuum*. The 2 primary groups they fall into are sweet or bell peppers, which are mild, and chillies, which can be spicy to extremely hot. Typically small bushes with dark green ovate leaves, they have small white flowers that appear at the leaf axils and develop into variably shaped and colored fruits. The heat of chillies can be measured on the Scoville dilution scale. The super-hot 'Habanero' pepper is still detectable when diluted to 1/300,000th of its original strength and the molten 'Tezpur' is reputedly stronger still.

LEFT Capsicum annuum, *Longum Group, 'Sweet Banana' grows to 20 in (50 cm) tall, and has pale yellowish fruits that mature to red, crisp, sweet flesh.*

CULTIVATION

Peppers need long warm summers to mature well. Plant in full sun with moist well-drained soil and feed well when young, but reduce feeding as the bulk of the fruits set. Fruits may be harvested before color develops, provided they have reached full size. Propagation is from seed.

Top Tip

To avoid carryover diseases, don't plant peppers where any other nightshade family members—such as tomatoes, potatoes, eggplants, or other peppers—have grown before.

Favorites	Common Name	Produce Season	Plant Height	Plant Width	Hardiness Zone	Frost Tolerance
Capsicum annuum	bell pepper, chilli pepper	summer	8–60 in (20–150 cm)	8–20 in (20–50 cm)	6–12	yes
***Capsicum annuum*, Cerasiforme Group**	bell pepper	summer	8–60 in (20–150 cm)	8–20 in (20–50 cm)	6–12	yes
***Capsicum annuum*, Conioides Group**	chilli pepper	summer	8–60 in (20–150 cm)	8–20 in (20–50 cm)	6–12	yes
***Capsicum annuum*, Grossum Group**	sweet bell pepper	summer	8–60 in (20–150 cm)	8–20 in (20–50 cm)	6–12	yes
***Capsicum annuum*, Longum Group**	chilli pepper	summer	8–60 in (20–150 cm)	8–20 in (20–50 cm)	6–12	yes
Capsicum frutescens	chilli pepper, goat pepper	summer	8–60 in (20–150 cm)	8–20 in (20–50 cm)	6–12	yes

LEFT Capsicum annuum, *Cerasiforme Group cultivars have spherical, aromatic, small fruits. 'Guantanamo' has smooth green skin and walls of medium thickness.*

BELOW Capsicum annuum, *Longum Group members have hot fruits. This cultivar, 'Cayenne', has long, thin, slightly curved fruits, dried to make cayenne pepper.*

LEFT Capsicum annuum, *Conioides Group, 'Jalapeño' is a Mexican variety, known commonly as hot pepper or chilli. Dark green-black fruits ripen to a hot red hue.*

CUCUMIS

ABOVE Cucumis sativus *'Muncher' is a cucumber with thin smooth skin, which is easily digestible. It is tasty both when young and when mature.*

BELOW Cucumis sativus *'Spacemaster' has disease-resistant, compact, dark green fruits that are good for pickling when small and for slicing when mature.*

This genus of about 25 species of trailing or climbing annuals originating from warm to tropical areas of Africa and Asia belongs to the pumpkin (Cucurbitaceae) family. Probably better known as cucumbers and melons, these plants are now grown worldwide for their fruits, which are generally green and either long and narrow or round, with smooth, bumpy, spiny, or ridged skin. Both male and female flowers —usually yellow or orange—are borne on the same plant. Cultivated since 3000 B.C., the use of melons was recorded by the Persians, and cucumbers are now thought to have left India by around 1000 B.C., spreading to Greece and Italy, where they were a favorite of the Romans, and then on to China.

CULTIVATION

Cucumbers appreciate a rich soil with lots of organic matter and a constant supply of moisture during a lengthy warm growing period. Melons are less demanding. Both are suitable for greenhouse culture where summers are short. Propagate from seed.

Top Tip

Natural climbers, cucumbers love trellises. Better air circulation means less disease, and the healthier fruits are more uniform—as well as 2–3 times more plentiful!

ABOVE Cucumis sativus *'Bush Champion' is a compact bush-type cucumber, which is good for slicing. Bright green straight fruits grow to around 10 in (25 cm) long, and are produced over a long season.*

ABOVE Cucumis sativus *'Sunsweet' has fruits that are shaped like lemons. The cream-colored young fruits are sweet and can be eaten raw; the yellowy orange mature fruits have a sharper taste and are best cooked.*

Favorites	Common Name	Produce Season	Plant Height	Plant Width	Hardiness Zone	Frost Tolerance
Cucumis anguria	cucumber, gherkin	summer	20 in (50 cm)	7–10 ft (2–3 m)	9–12	no
Cucumis melo	cantaloupe, honeydew melon	summer	16–27 in (40–70 cm)	7–10 ft (2–3 m)	9–12	no
***Cucumis melo*, Cantalupensis Group**	sweet fragrant melons	summer	16–27 in (40–70 cm)	7–10 ft (2–3 m)	9–12	no
***Cucumis melo*, Reticulatus Group**	netted melons	summer	16–27 in (40–70 cm)	7–10 ft (2–3 m)	9–12	no
Cucumis sativus	cucumber, gherkin	summer	8–20 in (20–50 cm)	3–10 ft (0.9–3 m)	9–11	no
***Cucumis sativus*, Alpha Group**	Lebanese cucumber	summer	8–20 in (20–50 cm)	3–10 ft (0.9–3 m)	9–11	no

CUCURBITA

A pumpkin (Cucurbitaceae) family genus, it has 27 species of annual or perennial ground covers and vines found in the Americas. Their stems and large lobed leaves are bristly or prickly, and spiraled clinging tendrils are often present at the leaf axils. Yellow or orange trumpet shaped flowers develop into variably sized, shaped, marked, and colored fruits. The title of the world's largest fruit is currently held by a 1,337 lb (607 kg) pumpkin grown in Manchester, New Hampshire, USA in 2002.

RIGHT Cucurbita pepo *'Gold Rush' has rich golden yellow zucchini-type fruits. It is easy to harvest and its color can add variety and interest to summer meals.*

BELOW *Dark green-striped* Cucurbita pepo *'Delicata' is a sweet potato squash, with very orange flesh, that is excellent for stuffing and baking. It is a good keeper.*

CULTIVATION

Pumpkins and squashes are very rapid-growing plants, which are best grown in a well-drained humus-enriched soil in full sun with a long and warm growing season. A popular method for the raising of pumpkins is to sow the seed in a patch of warm compost, but starting in pots is often more convenient. Only when all danger of frost has passed should they be planted. Feed plants regularly with a liquid fertilizer and make sure that fruits are not sitting on wet soil. Mildew and botrytis can occur in humid areas. Some cultivars are better keepers than others, but this makes no difference to their growth requirements.

Favorites

	Common Name	Produce Season	Plant Height	Plant Width	Hardiness Zone	Frost Tolerance
Cucurbita ficifolia	gourd	winter	12–20 in (30–50 cm)	3–10 ft (0.9–3 m)	8–11	yes
Cucurbita maxima	squash	winter	12–20 in (30–50 cm)	3–10 ft (0.9–3 m)	8–11	yes
Cucurbita moschata	pumpkin	winter	12–20 in (30–50 cm)	3–10 ft (0.9–3 m)	8–11	yes
***Cucurbita moschata* 'Butternut'**	pumpkin	winter	12–20 in (30–50 cm)	3–10 ft (0.9–3 m)	8–11	yes
Cucurbita pepo	zucchini	summer	12–20 in (30–50 cm)	3–10 ft (0.9–3 m)	8–11	yes
***Cucurbita pepo* 'Gold Rush'**	zucchini	summer	12–20 in (30–50 cm)	3–10 ft (0.9–3 m)	8–11	yes

Top Tip

Only harvest pumpkins when the shell is completely hardened. Leave the stems on; this helps thwart bacteria entry, and prevents early spoilage. Do not store in the sun.

ABOVE Cucurbita maxima *'Autumn Cup' is a butternut-type hybrid. It produces a dark green squash with fine orange flesh that tastes good steamed, boiled, or baked.*

RIGHT Cucurbita maxima *'Atlantic Giant' is the largest of the pumpkins and the biggest fruit in the world—specimens over 1,000 lb (450 kg) are not uncommon.*

LEFT Cucurbita pepo *'Table King' is a winter squash and has dark gray-green fruits with yellow-orange, moist and slightly crunchy, flesh with an excellent flavor.*

BELOW *A very productive, fast-maturing, Lebanese-type squash is* Cucurbita pepo *'Clarimore', which is light green, speckled, tapered, and has a sweet nutty flavor.*

BELOW Cucurbita pepo *'Black Beauty' has long, straight, smooth, dark green fruits, best eaten when 6–8 in (15–20 cm) long. Greenish white flesh is delicately flavored.*

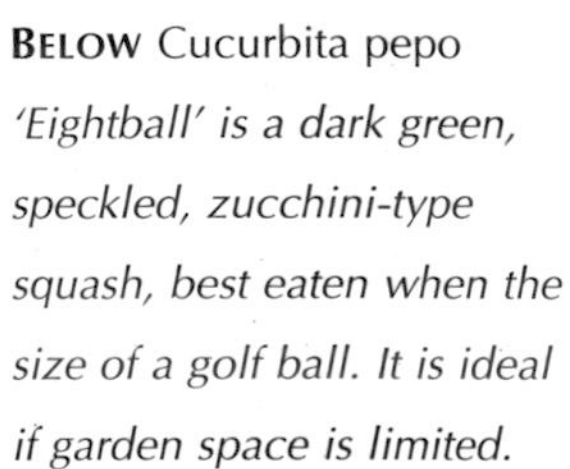

BELOW Cucurbita pepo *'Eightball' is a dark green, speckled, zucchini-type squash, best eaten when the size of a golf ball. It is ideal if garden space is limited.*

DAUCUS

This widely distributed carrot (Apiaceae) family genus is made up of 22 species of annuals and biennials of which one, *Daucus carota,* is widely cultivated for its long, orange, edible taproot. Carrots have bright green ferny foliage, which is relished by grazing animals, and long flower stems with sprays of small white flowers, though the roots are harvested in the first year, before flowerheads develop. The longest carrot on record was over 17 ft (5 m), the heaviest was over 15 lbs (6.8 kg).

CULTIVATION

Carrots require careful cultivation to give their best. Sow the seed in a soil that has been worked to a fine tilth. Heavy soil will result in poor root development. The seed usually germinates well, unless the soil surface becomes caked hard. In many areas carrot fly, the larvae of which tunnels into the root, can be a major problem. Late sowing lessens the problem, or soil insecticides can be applied at sowing time. Carrots take about 80 days to reach full maturity but they can be used from a younger age.

ABOVE *The word carrot is a Celtic one, and means "red of color."* Daucus carota *subsp.* sativus *'Corrie', seen here, typifies the rich hues that gave the plant its name.*
LEFT Daucus carota *subsp.* sativus *'Vita-Treat'. A case of "green shoulders," where the sun hits the top of the root; this will turn it green and also make it taste bitter.*

Favorites

Favorites	Common Name	Produce Season	Plant Height	Plant Width	Hardiness Zone	Frost Tolerance
Daucus carota	wild carrot	autumn to spring	40 in (100 cm)	20 in (50 cm)	3–9	yes
Daucus carota* subsp. *sativus	carrot	autumn to spring	40 in (100 cm)	20 in (50 cm)	3–9	yes
***Daucus carota* subsp. *sativus* 'Canada'**	carrot	autumn to spring	40 in (100 cm)	20 in (50 cm)	3–9	yes
***Daucus carota* subsp. *sativus* 'Red Intermediate'**	carrot	autumn to spring	40 in (100 cm)	20 in (50 cm)	3–9	yes
***Daucus carota* subsp. *sativus* 'Topweight'**	carrot	autumn to spring	40 in (100 cm)	20 in (50 cm)	3–9	yes
***Daucus carota* subsp. *sativus* 'Vita-Treat'**	carrot	autumn to spring	40 in (100 cm)	20 in (50 cm)	3–9	yes

Top Tip

Carrots prefer an even soil moisture. Mulching can help retain dampness, as well as preventing "green shoulders" where carrot tops are sun-exposed.

LACTUCA

Although this Northern Hemisphere daisy (Asteraceae) family genus contains about 75 species of annuals and perennials, only one species, *Lactuca sativa*, is widely cultivated. It is of course grown for its foliage rather than for its flowers, which are small white, yellow, or soft blue daisies that are borne on a tall stem. The cultivated varieties show a large range of foliage texture and color and also vary in flavor. The milky sap of some lettuce leaves is used in herbal medicines.

BELOW *A winter lettuce for growing in unheated greenhouses or outdoors,* Lactuca sativa *'Valdor' is resistant to botrytis. Sow seed in autumn for a spring harvest.*

CULTIVATION

In many areas lettuces may be planted year-round. The two main types are heart-forming (romaine) and non-heart-forming (cos). Heart-forming lettuces are usually cut whole when mature, while non-hearting lettuces can be used as they grow, a few leaves picked as required. Lettuces need well-drained soil and a steady supply of moisture and nutrients. Compost should be added before planting and liquid feed while growing. Slugs and snails often damage the foliage and birds will destroy young plants that are not covered with netting or other protection. Aphids can be another potential problem. Raise from seed.

BELOW *Bred in the UK, the award-winner* Lactuca sativa *'Bubbles' is a compact green lettuce, which has notably blistered leaves and a fairly firm sweet head.*

Top Tip

With planning, lettuces can be grown all year-round. If aiming at a midsummer harvest, however, grow in part-shade as the summer sun will trigger bolting.

ABOVE Lactuca sativa *'Cocarde' is a red oak-leaf type with large arrow-shaped leaves, which are tinged red and tender. Pick lettuces before they go to seed to avoid bitterness.*

ABOVE Lactuca sativa *'Red Salad Bowl' is a red-tinged form of 'Oak Leaf', which is a loose-leaf variety with deeply divided leaves like those of an oak, first listed in France in the 1770s.*

Favorites

Favorites	Common Name	Produce Season	Plant Height	Plant Width	Hardiness Zone	Frost Tolerance
Lactuca sativa	lettuce	spring to winter	4–12 in (10–30 cm)	4–12 in (10–30 cm)	6–11	yes
***Lactuca sativa* 'Bubbles'**	lettuce	spring to winter	4–12 in (10–30 cm)	4–12 in (10–30 cm)	6–11	yes
***Lactuca sativa* 'Cocarde'**	lettuce	spring to winter	4–12 in (10–30 cm)	4–12 in (10–30 cm)	6–11	yes
***Lactuca sativa* 'Iceberg'**	lettuce	spring to winter	4–12 in (10–30 cm)	4–12 in (10–30 cm)	6–11	yes
***Lactuca sativa* 'Little Gem'**	lettuce	spring to winter	4–12 in (10–30 cm)	4–12 in (10–30 cm)	6–11	yes
***Lactuca sativa* 'Valdor'**	lettuce	spring to winter	4–12 in (10–30 cm)	4–12 in (10–30 cm)	6–11	yes

LEFT Lycopersicon *'Green Zebra' is a vigorous high-yielding hybrid cultivar. As the tomatoes ripen they become more yellow, but the green stripes are still visible.*

LYCOPERSICON

This genus of 7 species of aromatic herbs in the nightshade (Solanaceae) family is best known for *Lycopersicon esculentum*—the tomato. Annuals or short-lived perennials with an erect or sprawling habit, they originate from western South America and the Galapagos Islands, and were reputedly introduced to Western civilization following the Spanish conquest of South and Central America. They have hair-covered stems and aromatic toothed leaves. The starry yellow flowers feature a 5-lobed calyx, and are followed by fleshy berries that have 2 or more seed-filled chambers. While the fruits of wild species are usually small, the fruits of the cultivars vary considerably in size, from as small as a grape to massive fruit weighing 4 lbs (1.8 kg).

CULTIVATION

In areas with a long warm growing season, plant in fertile well-drained soil in an open sunny position. In cooler areas seedlings may need to be protected from late frosts. Propagation is from seed.

Top Tip

Use stakes to provide support for taller plants, or grow them against a fence or trellis, securing taller stems as they grow. Keep branches off the ground.

ABOVE *Dark red when ripe,* Lycopersicon esculentum *'Abraham Lincoln' tomatoes are of medium size, with a mild flavor and solid texture. They are ideal for slicing.*

RIGHT *The grape-type fruits of* Lycopersicon esculentum *'Juliette' are produced in clusters on a large plant. They ripen to red, and are good salad tomatoes.*

Favorites

Favorites	Common Name	Produce Season	Plant Height	Plant Width	Hardiness Zone	Frost Tolerance
Lycopersicon esculentum	tomato	summer to autumn	6 ft (1.8 m)	1–2 ft (0.3–0.6 m)	8–12	no
***Lycopersicon esculentum* 'Gardener's Delight'**	cherry tomato	summer to autumn	4–6 ft (1.2–1.8 m)	1–2 ft (0.3–0.6 m)	8–12	no
***Lycopersicon esculentum* 'Moneymaker'**	tomato	summer to autumn	4 ft (1.2 m)	1–2 ft (0.3–0.6 m)	8–12	no
***Lycopersicon esculentum* 'Yellow Boy'**	tomato	summer to autumn	4–5 ft (1.2–1.5 m)	1–2 ft (0.3–0.6 m)	8–12	no
***Lycopersicon* 'Green Zebra'**	tomato	summer to autumn	6–8 ft (1.8–2.4 m)	1–2 ft (0.3–0.6 m)	8–12	no
***Lycopersicon* 'Sungold'**	cherry tomato	summer to autumn	4–6 ft (1.2–1.8 m)	1–2 ft (0.3–0.6 m)	8–12	no

BELOW Lycopersicon *'Sungold' produces an excellent crop of very sweet tangerine-colored cherry tomatoes. This outstanding hybrid makes a neat bush.*

MENTHA

The type genus for the mint (Lamiaceae) family, *Mentha* is made up of 25 species of aromatic perennial herbs found from Europe to North Africa and Asia. Commonly known as mint, they have angled upright stems with soft, often heavily veined leaves that may have wavy or scalloped edges. All parts are aromatic, especially when crushed. The species have a variety of flavors, such as apple, pineapple, and spearmint. Corsican mint *(Mentha requienii)* is a small-leafed ground cover with a strong crème de menthe scent. In addition to their culinary uses, mints are widely used as medicinal herbs and for fragrance.

ABOVE *The leaves of curly spearmint,* Mentha spicata *'Crispa', can be used in cooking, and the decorative pale mauve-pink flowers will attract butterflies to the garden.*

CULTIVATION

Mint is probably the best-known culinary herb and flavoring, but has a bad reputation for being attacked by a rust disease, though rust-resistant types are available. It is best grown in moist soil in light shade. Propagate from half-hardened cuttings, self-layered stems, or suckers. Mint spreads by underground runners and can be very invasive, so plant where it can be contained.

BELOW Mentha × piperita *'Variegata' has unusually colored small leaves on spreading stems. The peppermint flavor is not as strong in this cultivar as it is in other forms.*

Top Tip

Most mint species reproduce from shallow, creeping, long stems. Stop the plant taking over the garden by burying a large container almost to the top and placing the plant within it.

Favorites

	Plant Height	Plant Width	Hardiness Zone	Frost Tolerance
Mentha × *piperita*	2–3 ft (0.6–0.9 m)	3 ft (0.9 m)	3–7	yes
Mentha pulegium	8–12 in (20–30 cm)	20 in (50 cm)	7–9	yes
Mentha requienii	$\frac{3}{4}$ in (1.8 cm)	27 in (70 cm)	7–10	yes
Mentha spicata	4 ft (1.2 m)	3–6 ft (0.9–1.8 m)	3–7	yes
Mentha suaveolens	3 ft (0.9 m)	3 ft (0.9 m)	6–9	yes
Mentha × *villosa*	3 ft (0.9 m)	5 ft (1.5 m)	5–8	yes

LEFT *Held on purple stems, the bright green leaves of* Mentha × piperita *f.* citrata *'Chocolate' have a delicate chocolate scent. This is an excellent tea mint.*

BELOW Mentha × piperita *is better known as peppermint. Its leaves have an intense minty flavor and aroma. The mauve-pink flowers appear in summer.*

OCIMUM

A genus of 35 species of aromatic annuals and perennials of the mint (Lamiaceae) family, the plants occur naturally in the tropics and subtropics of Africa and Asia. They develop quickly into small soft-stemmed bushes with oval to elliptical leaves that often have toothed or lobed edges. Erect spikes of flowers develop at the stem tips but these are usually removed to encourage continued foliage production. The genus is commonly known as basil, and its leaves are used as a flavoring in cooking. Sweet basil *(Ocimum basilicum)* also has a long history of medicinal use, and yields an oil used in fragrances and aromatherapy.

ABOVE LEFT Ocimum basilicum *'Genova' is a spicy Italian cultivar with a strong scent. It is very productive over a particularly long growing season.*

ABOVE Ocimum basilicum *'Purple Ruffles' is a striking addition to the herb garden. Its large, purple, glossy leaves with serrated edges are very aromatic.*

CULTIVATION

Basil is a very popular culinary herb and some species have cultivars in several sizes and with colored foliaged forms. Basil is very sensitive to cold when young and should be planted in moist well-drained soil in a position sheltered from drafts. When young, pinch out the tips to encourage bushy growth. Raise the annuals from seed, the perennials from seed or cuttings.

Favorites	Plant Height	Plant Width	Hardiness Zone	Frost Tolerance
Ocimum basilicum	12–24 in (30–60 cm)	12 in (30 cm)	10–12	no
Ocimum basilicum var. *minimum*	10–12 in (25–30 cm)	6–10 in (15–25 cm)	10–12	no
Ocimum basilicum 'Genova'	24 in (60 cm)	18 in (45 cm)	10–12	no
Ocimum basilicum 'Green Ruffles'	18–24 in (45–60 cm)	18–24 in (45–60 cm)	10–12	no
Ocimum basilicum 'Red Rubin'	18–24 in (45–60 cm)	12–15 in (30–38 cm)	10–12	no
Ocimum tenuiflorum	12–36 in (30–90 cm)	6–12 in (15–30 cm)	9–10	yes

BELOW *The curly and frilly leaf edges of* Ocimum basilicum *'Green Ruffles' make this cultivar a decorative as well as flavorful choice for use in a salad or as a fresh garnish.*

Top Tip

Pinch back the top of basil plants regularly and remove flower spikes to encourage foliage growth and better leaf flavor. The taste is not as good after flowers appear.

BELOW Ocimum basilicum *'Siam Queen' is a compact bush with fragrant licorice-flavored leaves and rosy purple flowers. It is very suitable for Thai cooking.*

ORIGANUM

A member of the mint (Lamiaceae) family, this genus includes some 20 species of aromatic perennials and subshrubs found from the Mediterranean to East Asia. Most are low spreading bushes with simple, small, rounded leaves in shades from yellow-green to deep green. The ornamental forms often have their flowers enclosed within large colorful bracts, but those grown as herbs usually have simple starry pink flowers, though often in abundance. The various species of *Origanum* are popular pot herbs right around the Mediterranean, especially in Italy, where oregano *(Origanum vulgare)* adds its distinctive flavor to many dishes. Several species yield oils used in perfumery and flavorings.

CULTIVATION

Hardiness varies, though few will tolerate hard frosts or prolonged wet cold winters. Grow in light well-drained soil in a sunny position. Propagate the species from seed, the hybrids from half-hardened cuttings or layers.

ABOVE *With attractively variegated leaves,* Origanum vulgare *'Gold Tip' is a popular cultivar. It looks even better in summer when the pink flowers appear.*

ABOVE LEFT Origanum *'Kent Beauty' is among the best ornamental hybrids. Ideal for the rockery or border, it produces tubular flowers with deep rose pink bracts in summer.*

RIGHT Origanum vulgare *var.* humile *makes a useful flowering ground cover. It is quite drought tolerant, and the tasty leaves can be used in cooking.*

Top Tip

The flavor of the leaves is directly proportional to the amount of sun they receive. The more intense the light, the stronger the flavor.

Favorites	Plant Height	Plant Width	Hardiness Zone	Frost Tolerance
Origanum amanum	2–4 in (5–10 cm)	6 in (15 cm)	8–10	yes
Origanum 'Kent Beauty'	8–10 in (20–25 cm)	12–18 in (30–45 cm)	6–9	yes
Origanum laevigatum	12–24 in (30–60 cm)	18–24 in (45–60 cm)	8–10	yes
Origanum majorana	24 in (60 cm)	18 in (45 cm)	7–10	yes
Origanum rotundifolium	12 in (30 cm)	12 in (30 cm)	8–10	yes
Origanum vulgare	12–18 in (30–45 cm)	12 in (30 cm)	5–9	yes

LEFT Origanum vulgare *is the best-known species in this genus. It is a popular culinary herb with very aromatic foliage that can be used fresh from the garden or dried for later use.*

Top Tip

Parsley grows well indoors in a pot. Harvest the outer leaves of the plant as needed. Parsley will provide usable leaves for garnish for 6 to 9 months.

LEFT Petroselinum crispum *is the typical curly-leafed parsley often seen. It has many cultivars. Its edible leaves are dark to bright green and aromatic.*

PETROSELINUM

Probably best known in its triple-curled form, which is a very popular garnish, this Eurasian genus in the carrot (Apiaceae) family is made up of just 3 species of annuals and biennials but it is cultivated in a wide variety of forms. The finely divided, broadly triangular leaves are a bright or deep green and often rolled and curled at the edges of the leaflets. Parsley is usually spent and bitter once the sprays of tiny white flowers appear. In some forms, such as *Petroselinum crispum* var. *tuberosum*, the taproot is enlarged and can be used like a small parsnip. Parsley also has numerous uses in herbal medicine and provides an oil used as a fragrance fixative in men's toiletries.

CULTIVATION

Parsley prefers to grow in cool moist soil in light shade. Water it well or the foliage may become stringy and bitter. Cutting the foliage promotes fresh growth. Raise from fresh seed sown in spring, or autumn in frost-free areas.

ABOVE RIGHT Petroselinum crispum *'Forest Green' is a strongly flavored variety. Such varieties are good to dry for later use, however parsley retains more flavor if it is frozen fresh.*

ABOVE Petroselinum crispum *'Krausa' has triple-curled leaves which keep their crisp texture and bright green color very well in the garden and after harvest.* **LEFT** *Parsley has a higher vitamin C content than an orange and is a natural breath freshener.* Petroselinum crispum *'Bravour' is a winter-hardy parsley and has a mild flavor.*

Favorites	Plant Height	Plant Width	Hardiness Zone	Frost Tolerance
Petroselinum crispum	12–36 in (30–90 cm)	8–36 in (20–90 cm)	7–9	yes
Petroselinum crispum* var. *neopolitanum	12–36 in (30–90 cm)	8–36 in (20–90 cm)	7–9	yes
Petroselinum crispum* var. *tuberosum	12–36 in (30–90 cm)	8–36 in (20–90 cm)	7–9	yes
***Petroselinum crispum* 'Bravour'**	12–36 in (30–90 cm)	8–36 in (20–90 cm)	7–9	yes
***Petroselinum crispum* 'Forest Green'**	12–36 in (30–90 cm)	8–36 in (20–90 cm)	7–9	yes
***Petroselinum crispum* 'Krausa'**	12–36 in (30–90 cm)	8–36 in (20–90 cm)	7–9	yes

LEFT Phaseolus vulgaris *'Ferrari' is an award-winning dwarf cultivar. It gives a good supply of stringless beans.*

BELOW Phaseolus vulgaris *is the most popular bean species. Although green beans are the norm, decorative cultivars like 'Purple Speckled' are also available.*

PHASEOLUS

A member of the pea-flower subfamily of the legume (Fabaceae) family, this genus of around 20 species of annuals and perennials, often climbing, is grown for its edible seed pods or for the beans held within. Found from southwestern USA to northern South America, most have thin, often downy, heart-shaped leaves and a twining habit. Short racemes of white, pale yellow, mauve, or orange-red flowers develop into flat pods that vary in size with the species. Kidney beans yield a reddish dye.

CULTIVATION

The common types of bean are the bushy dwarf beans or French beans, lima beans and kidney beans, and climbing runner beans. Plant in humus-enriched well-drained soil in full sun and keep the soil moist or the beans will age prematurely. Plants are often raised from fresh seed each year but runner beans will reshoot from the base and can be left in the ground for several years.

RIGHT *The attractive and colorful flowers of* Phaseolus coccineus *'Painted Lady' look and taste good in salads. The beans that follow are delicious, too.*

RIGHT *One of the large-seeded pole-type of lima beans,* Phaseolus lunatus *'King of the Garden' is easy to grow.*

Favorites

Favorites	Common Name	Produce Season	Plant Height	Plant Width	Hardiness Zone	Frost Tolerance
Phaseolus acutifolius	tepary bean	summer to autumn	18–40 in (45–100 cm)	12–24 in (30–60 cm)	8–10	no
Phaseolus coccineus	scarlet runner bean	summer to autumn	6–12 ft (1.8–3.5 m)	2 ft (0.6 m)	8–10	no
***Phaseolus coccineus* 'Painted Lady'**	scarlet runner bean	summer to autumn	6–10 ft (1.8–3 m)	2 ft (0.6 m)	8–10	no
Phaseolus lunatus	lima bean	summer to autumn	24–36 in (60–90 cm)	8–12 in (20–30 cm)	8–10	no
Phaseolus vulgaris	French/string/ snap bean	summer	3–10 ft (0.9–3 m)	6–10 in (15–25 cm)	8–11	no
***Phaseolus vulgaris* 'Goldmarie'**	French/string/ snap bean	summer	8 ft (2.4 m)	1 ft (0.3 m)	8–11	no

Top Tip

When grown for the pods, beans should be picked before the pods become stringy; otherwise, allow the beans to develop before picking.

LEFT *A free-flowering, aromatic, evergreen shrub,* Rosmarinus officinalis *'Tuscan Blue' responds well to pruning and can be shaped into an attractive hedge or screen.*

Top Tip

The upright forms of *Rosmarinus* make good subjects for topiary. The prostrate types look great cascading over pots and in rock gardens.

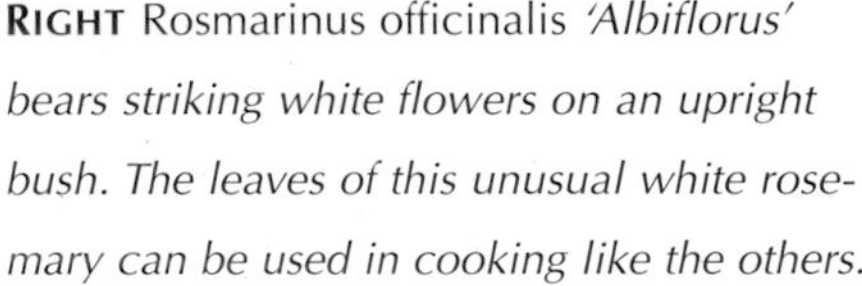

RIGHT Rosmarinus officinalis *'Albiflorus' bears striking white flowers on an upright bush. The leaves of this unusual white rosemary can be used in cooking like the others.*

RIGHT *Award-winning* Rosmarinus officinalis *'Benenden Blue' (syn. 'Balsam') makes a good container plant. Its strongly pine-scented leaves can be used in potpourri.*

ROSMARINUS

Just 2 species of evergreen aromatic shrubs from southern Europe and North Africa make up this genus in the mint (Lamiaceae) family. Grown for both ornament and function, rosemary has stiff woody stems that are densely covered with short, narrow, dark green to bronze-green leaves. From winter's end, small mauve-blue to purple flowers appear in the leaf axils and are followed by small seed pods. The foliage is very pungent and distinctively flavored, and is among the most widely used herbs in Western cooking. Rosemary is also dried and used in potpourri, and the oil can be found in many perfumes and cosmetics.

CULTIVATION

Surprisingly hardy, rosemary grows best in a bright sunny position with moist well-drained soil. It is drought tolerant once established and prefers to stay fairly dry in winter. Most of the plants in gardens are cultivars propagated from half-hardened cuttings or layers; the species may be raised from seed.

Favorites	Flower Color	Blooming Season	Flower Fragrance	Plant Height	Plant Width	Hardiness Zone	Frost Tolerance
Rosmarinus officinalis	pale blue to purple-blue	spring to autumn	no	3–7 ft (0.9–2 m)	5–6 ft (1.5–1.8 m)	6–11	yes
***Rosmarinus officinalis* 'Benenden Blue'**	blue	spring to autumn	no	5 ft (1.5 m)	3 ft (0.9 m)	6–11	yes
***Rosmarinus officinalis* 'Joyce DeBaggio'**	blue	spring to autumn	no	3 ft (0.9 m)	5 ft (1.5 m)	6–11	yes
***Rosmarinus officinalis* 'Majorca Pink'**	lilac-pink	spring to autumn	no	3 ft (0.9 m)	5 ft (1.5 m)	6–11	yes
***Rosmarinus officinalis* 'Sissinghurst Blue'**	blue	spring to autumn	no	5 ft (1.5 m)	6 ft (1.8 m)	6–11	yes
***Rosmarinus officinalis* 'Tuscan Blue'**	blue	spring to autumn	no	5 ft (1.5 m)	5 ft (1.5 m)	6–11	yes

LEFT *The lilac-pink flowers of* Rosmarinus officinalis *'Majorca Pink' are borne on long, densely leafed, arching branches. This is one of the best of the pink-flowered cultivars.*

SOLANUM

BELOW *The attractive purple flowers of* Solanum ellipticum *are about 1 in (25 mm) across. They are followed by nutritious fruits known as bush tomatoes.*

A member of the nightshade (Solanaceae) family, this widespread genus has around 1,400 species, most of which occur in South and Central America. Foliage varies with the species. It is often pinnate, with large leaflets, but may be simple, lobed, and downy. The flowers, usually purple or creamy white, have 5 fused petals and are followed by berry-like fruits of varying sizes and colors. Some species are grown for their decorative flowers or fruit. Several species have edible parts. In the case of the eggplant *(Solanum melongena),* tamarillo *(Solanum betaceum),* and pepino *(Solanum muricatum)* it is the fruit, but the most famous member of the genus, the potato *(Solanum tuberosum),* is cultivated for its edible tubers, which are an absolute staple of modern life. Although the potato has tropical origins, it occurs at high altitudes and grows well in temperate gardens.

CULTIVATION

Among vegetable gardeners no topic provokes such earnest debate as "Which is the best potato?" Whatever your choice: large, small, yellow, white, purple, or red, there's a potato for everyone. They take up a significant amount of room, but are a crop that is certain to be used and appreciated.

The soil should be fertile, humus enriched, and well drained. Potatoes can be raised from the true seed but are generally grown by planting small "seed" tubers, which are sprouted from late winter in a well-lit, airy, frost-free position. Time the planting so that the tops do not emerge above soil level until any frost danger has passed. Plant in a 4–6 in (10–15 cm) deep furrow and backfill to create a mound.

Some varieties, known as main crop potatoes, keep better than others. They are usually left until fully mature (when the tops have died back) before harvesting. New or early potatoes are harvested and used as soon as they are ready. Potatoes are subject to fungal diseases known as "blight" and are also likely to rot if the soil remains wet after heavy rain.

Eggplants and other species grown for their fruits prefer warm conditions, and in areas with cool summers they are greenhouse plants. They grow quickly and easily, and other than an occasional aphid, the main problem is pollination. Outdoors, natural pollination is usually adequate; indoors it may be necessary to hand-pollinate with a small brush.

Favorites	Flower Color	Blooming Season	Produce Season	Plant Height	Plant Width	Hardiness Zone	Frost Tolerance
Solanum aviculare	purple	spring to summer	summer	3–12 ft (0.9–3.5 m)	3–12 ft (0.9–3.5 m)	9–11	no
Solanum betaceum	pale pink	spring to summer	early autumn	7 ft (2 m)	10 ft (3 m)	9–11	no
Solanum crispum	lilac-blue	summer	autumn (inedible)	10–20 ft (3–6 m)	8 ft (2.4 m)	8–11	yes
Solanum ellipticum	purple, blue	spring to summer	summer	3–7 ft (0.9–2 m)	3–7 ft (0.9–2 m)	9–11	no
Solanum hispidum	white, mauve-blue	summer	late summer to autumn	10 ft (3 m)	6–8 ft (1.8–2.4 m)	10–12	no
Solanum jasminoides	blue-tinged white	summer	autumn (inedible)	10–20 ft (3–6 m)	8–15 ft (2.4–4.5 m)	9–12	no
Solanum melongena	violet to light blue	spring to summer	summer	3 ft (0.9 m)	2 ft (0.6 m)	9–12	no
Solanum pseudocapsicum	white	summer	autumn (inedible)	3–6 ft (0.9–1.8 m)	4 ft (1.2 m)	9–11	no
Solanum pyracanthum	bluish violet	summer	autumn (inedible)	3–6 ft (0.9–1.8 m)	2–3 ft (0.6–0.9 m)	10–12	no
Solanum rantonnetii	violet-blue	spring to autumn	summer (inedible)	4–8 ft (1.2–2.4 m)	3–7 ft (0.9–2 m)	9–11	no
Solanum tuberosum	white to pale violet	summer	spring to autumn	18–24 in (45–60 cm)	18 in (45 cm)	7–11	yes
Solanum wendlandii	lilac-blue	summer	late summer to autumn	8–20 ft (2.4–6 m)	5–10 ft (1.5–3 m)	10–12	no

LEFT *The unusual leaves of* Solanum pyracanthum *carry eye-catching long orange spines on the midrib to protect the plant from grazing animals in its native Africa.*

ABOVE *The fruits of* Solanum aviculare *can only be eaten when perfectly ripe—otherwise they will burn the throat. Use this plant as a fast-growing screen.*

BELOW *The showy fruits of* Solanum pseudocapsicum *(the Jerusalem cherry) can be eaten by birds but not by humans. This plant can be grown indoors.*

ABOVE *A scrambling shrub or semi-climber,* Solanum rantonnetii *'Royal Robe' carries its decorative purple flowers all through the warmer weather.*

RIGHT *The pale flowers of* Solanum melongena *'Black Beauty' are followed by nearly black oval fruits. This is one of the most popular eggplant cultivars.*

Top Tip

Potatoes will grow in most areas. They can be grown almost all year in warm climates, but in cold climates must be fully grown before the onset of severe frosts.

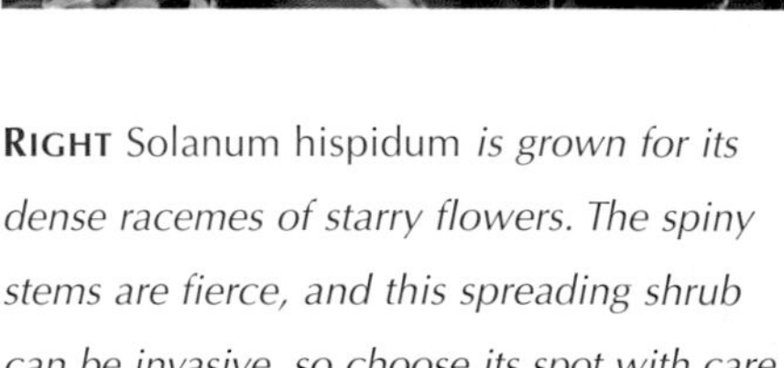

RIGHT Solanum hispidum *is grown for its dense racemes of starry flowers. The spiny stems are fierce, and this spreading shrub can be invasive, so choose its spot with care.*

RIGHT *Potato cultivars offer tubers of varying textures, flavors, skin colors, and maturing times.* Solanum tuberosum *'Mimi' produces small reddish brown-skinned tubers.*

RIGHT Solanum melongena *'Bonica' is an early-maturing eggplant cultivar. Its purplish black fruits make a striking display against the foliage.*

BELOW *The fruits of the Japanese eggplant cultivars are smaller and more elongated in shape than the others.* Solanum melongena *'Ping Tung' bears well.*

THYMUS

Thyme is a genus of around 350 species of low spreading perennials and subshrubs in the mint (Lamiaceae) family. Although mostly found around the Mediterranean, they are also grown from western Europe to North Africa, and eastward to Japan. They have very fine wiry stems and minute, often hairy leaves that form a dense mat. Heads of tiny flowers in all shades of pink and purple, or white, appear mainly in summer and can be very showy. Commonly grown for ornamental reasons, as a culinary herb, and for thyme oil, which is used in fragrances and disinfectants, thyme is also popular with herbalists because the oil contains thymol, a phenol with important pharmacological properties.

CULTIVATION

Thyme prefers to grow in full or half-sun with moist well-drained soil. Shear off the old dry flowerheads to encourage fresh growth. The species may be raised from seed, but selected forms must be propagated vegetatively, usually from small cuttings or self-layered pieces.

Top Tip

Thyme grows well in containers. Pot in loose fertile soil. If you are growing thyme indoors, place the plant in a well-lit position, perhaps on the kitchen windowsill.

LEFT *The leaves of* Thymus serpyllum *'Snow Drift' have a faint scent, and its white flowers form over a spreading mat. This species is known as creeping thyme.*

ABOVE Thymus pulegioides *is a European species. It is popular as a ground cover, bears aromatic leaves, and blooms a colorful pink-purple in spring–summer.*

LEFT *An ideal plant to sprawl over small rocks or ledges in a rock garden,* Thymus polytrichus *subsp.* britannicus *also looks brilliant on dry slopes.*

BELOW Thymus praecox *'Albiflorus' is a cultivar that produces white flowers on dark green foliage. Most species of* T. praecox *produce mauve-purple blooms.*

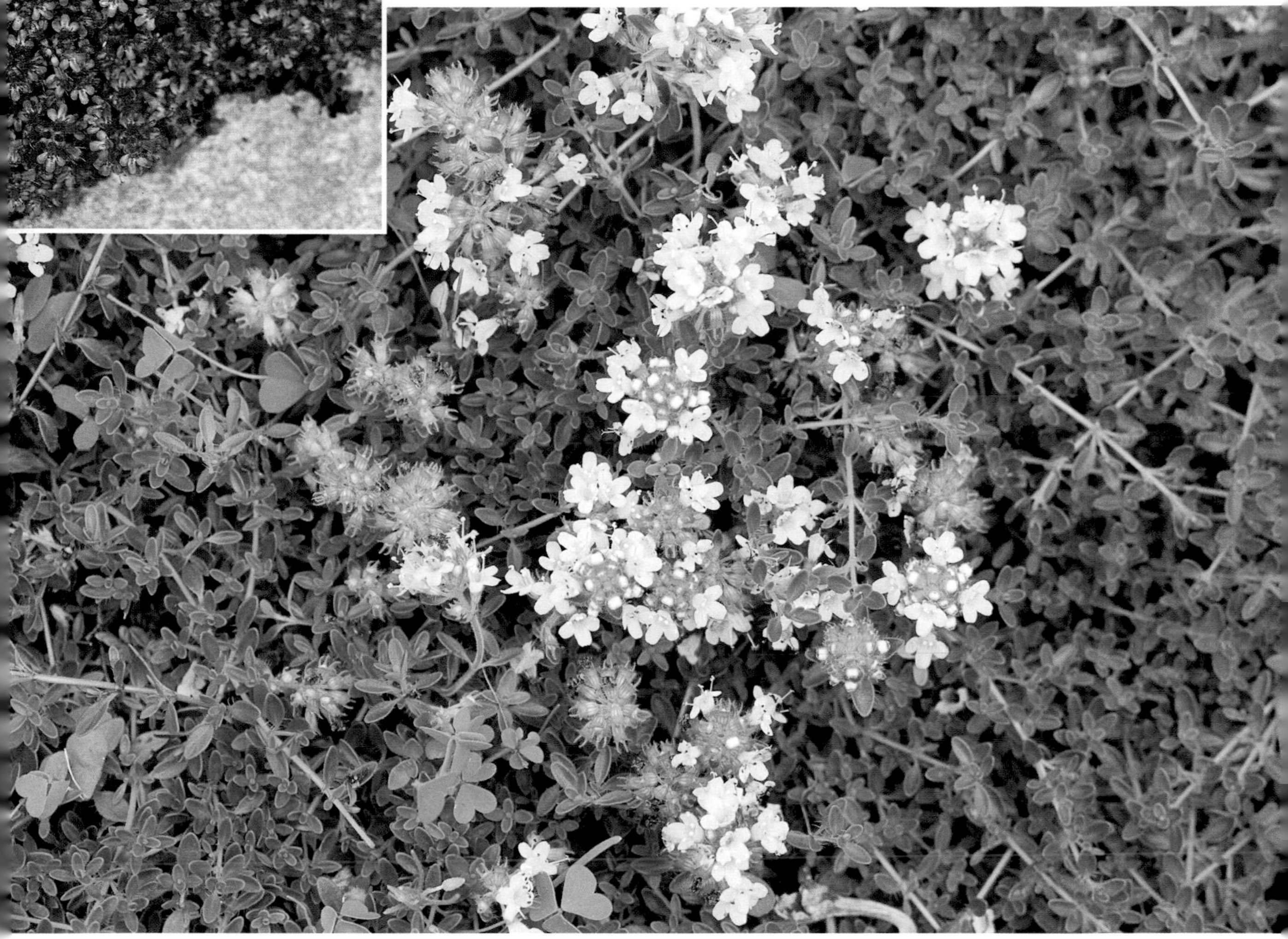

Favorites	Flower Color	Blooming Season	Flower Fragrance	Plant Height	Plant Width	Hardiness Zone	Frost Tolerance
Thymus* × *citriodorus	lavender-pink	summer	yes	6–12 in (15–30 cm)	24 in (60 cm)	5–10	yes
Thymus polytrichus	pale to deep purple with white blotches	summer	yes	2 in (5 cm)	24 in (60 cm)	5–9	yes
Thymus praecox	mauve, purple, or white	summer	yes	2–4 in (5–10 cm)	24 in (60 cm)	4–9	yes
Thymus pulegioides	pink and purple	spring to summer	yes	10 in (25 cm)	12 in (30 cm)	4–9	yes
Thymus serpyllum	lavender-purple	early summer	yes	1–4 in (2.5–10 cm)	36 in (90 cm)	4–9	yes
Thymus vulgaris	white to pinkish purple	summer to autumn	yes	12 in (30 cm)	10 in (25 cm)	7–10	yes

RIGHT *Corn usually requires a long warm season to ripen the cob.* Zea mays *'Earlivee' is a sweet corn. It is compact, with an early maturing yellow form.*

ZEA

This is a genus of 4 species of large grasses. Native to Central America, they are grown for their edible seeds which are massed in elongated heads around a core and more commonly known as corn cobs or ears of corn. They have erect cane-like stems and long, broad, drooping leaves. Heads of male flowers appear at the top of the plant and shed pollen on the female flowers in the leaf axils, which then develop into the cobs. Until the 1930s, the British considered maize fit only for animals. This practice was revised after observing American soldiers eating corn during World War II.

CULTIVATION

Sweet corn or maize is the only cereal crop commonly grown in domestic gardens. Plants are raised from seed, which is sown in spring once the soil has warmed to around 60°F (15°C), or germinated indoors and then planted out once all danger of frost has passed. Plant in humus-enriched soil in full sun with very good drainage. To lessen wind damage and enhance pollination it is best to plant corn in blocks or at least double rows. The cobs are ripe once the flower tassels have withered.

Favorites

Favorites	Common Name	Produce Season	Plant Height	Plant Width	Hardiness Zone	Frost Tolerance
Zea mays	corn, maize, sweet corn	late summer to autumn	7–15 ft (2–4.5 m)	20–40 in (50–100 cm)	8–10	no
***Zea mays* 'Blue Jade'**	corn, maize, sweet corn	late summer to autumn	24 in (60 cm)	20–40 in (50–100 cm)	8–10	no
***Zea mays* 'Cuties Pops'**	corn, maize, sweet corn	late summer to autumn	7–15 ft (2–4.5 m)	20–40 in (50–100 cm)	8–10	no
***Zea mays* 'Earlivee'**	corn, maize, sweet corn	summer to autumn	4 ft (1.2 m)	20–40 in (50–100 cm)	8–10	no
***Zea mays* 'Indian Summer'**	corn, maize, sweet corn	late summer to autumn	7–15 ft (2–4.5 m)	20–40 in (50–100 cm)	8–10	no
***Zea mays* 'New Excellence'**	corn, maize, sweet corn	late summer to autumn	7–15 ft (2–4.5 m)	20–40 in (50–100 cm)	8–10	no

LEFT *The white, yellow, red, and purple kernels of Zea mays 'Indian Summer' will develop a stronger color as the cob matures.*

BELOW Zea mays *'Cuties Pops' is an ornamental variety. Its foliage is striped with purple and the kernels on the cob are also multi-colored.*

BELOW Zea mays *'New Excellence' is a cultivar that produces cobs with sweet yellow kernels. It is grown almost wholly for human consumption.*

Top Tip

Set out corn plants about 12 in (30 cm) apart. If they are too far apart the plants will produce fewer cobs and the stalks will grow weak and spindly.

CLIMBERS AND CREEPERS

Featuring some of the garden's most versatile plants, climbers and creepers are equally at home festooning an arbor with bright flowers or modestly cloaking a bare patch on the ground. They offer all sorts of enticing creative possibilities, with their seemingly endless array of leaf and flower colors, sizes, and textures. Their upward or spreading growth habit means they are among the easiest plants to weave into any garden, taking advantage as they do of some of the most underutilized outdoor space. These useful plants lend height and dimension to the garden, whether winding up arbors or trellises, clambering walls, scaling trees, or weaving through shrubs.

ABOVE *Like many climbers,* Clematis, *Patens Group, 'Doctor Ruppel' produces stunning blooms. Some flowering climbers enliven the garden with a year-round floral display.*
LEFT *Climbers are useful for disguising and covering bare or unsightly surfaces. Ivies, such as* Hedera helix *'Amberwaves', are classic climbers valued for their attractive foliage.*

Divine Vines for the Garden

Broadly encompassing any plants that climb, clamber, scramble, or otherwise ascend, vines achieve height through various methods including coiling stems, tendrils, hook-like thorns, and aerial rootlets. Many, such as *Allamanda, Bougainvillea,* and *Thunbergia* species, add a touch of tropical color to the garden, while others are more famous for their wonderfully scented flowers (*Jasminum* and *Trachelospermum* species).

Twining species that coil or wrap themselves around supports include wisteria, jasmine, mandevilla, and wax flower (*Hoya* species). Some form thick tree-like trunks, as in the case of wisteria, and it is best to provide sturdy, relatively permanent supports for these heavier vines. Vines such as poet's jasmine *(Jasminum officinale)* and Chilean jasmine *(Mandevilla laxa)* also coil somewhat, although their smaller size and looser twining habit make them less likely to overwhelm their supports than wisteria.

Other vines use various sorts of tendrils, shoots, or leaves to grasp their hosts and ascend. Vines such as clematis use their twisting leaf stalks to clamber, while some such as passionflowers (*Passiflora* species) have tightly curling tendrils that encircle small twigs, wires, or other supports.

Using either aerial roots or tiny adhesive grips, self-clinging vines attach themselves to tree trunks, stone, masonry, wood fences, or other rough structures. Trumpet vines (*Campsis* species) and English ivy *(Hedera helix)* are examples of aerial-rooting vines. The tender wax flower *(Hoya carnosa),* known for its heavy clusters of chocolate-scented pink to white flowers, employs aerial rootlets, although it also twines. Boston and Virginia creepers (*Parthenocissus* species) are tendril climbers that use adhesive pads to cling. Either way, the result is the same: self-clinging vines do not need assistance to climb, except perhaps during their first season as they establish a firm grip.

Some shrubs employ long supple shoots armed with stiff downward-facing thorns to scale to great heights. Bougainvilleas and rambling roses have such hefty thorns, both for climbing and also as a defense against browsing beasts. Designed to hook and tangle their way up large trees and through brush in order to reach the sun, these shrubs produce frothy swags of blossoms and can reach the tops

Above left *Using tendrils to attach to structures is a method employed by many climbers, including the beautiful* Passiflora *'Debby' pictured here.*
Left *Twining climbers, such as* Hoya carnosa, *need a support that offers surfaces to coil around, rather than a solid vertical surface.*

Right *Using thorns to hold fast to their climbing surface, bougainvilleas, such as* Bougainvillea 'Alexandra', *will quickly blanket surfaces with vibrant color.*
Below *Many climbers offer the added bonus of intoxicating fragrance. Traditional favorites like* Jasminum sambac *will provide year-round fragrant blooms.*

of trees or completely cover an enormous arbor. Though pruning of climbers can be challenging, annual removal of the oldest wood can keep them in check if they are grown on smaller structures.

There are a number of so-called vines that are actually scandent shrubs. Producing long supple stems that sometimes root at the tips, these plants can be grown as mounded shrubs if left freestanding, or be trained up a wall or through a trellis. Scandent shrubs include winter jasmine *(Jasminum nudiflorum)*, whose bare green stems are clothed in acid yellow flowers in late winter.

Many vines make marvelous ground covers. The most vigorous, such as English ivy, can cover a considerable area, mounding over small plants, walls, or other obstacles. (The rampant growth of English ivy has made it a noxious invasive weed in some places.) Other vines, such as the evergreen star jasmine (*Trachelospermum* species), are often used as a tidy formal ground cover. And smaller hybrid clematis plants can work as ground covers at the front of a border, weaving their way through and between other plants.

Evergreen vines such as jasmine, star jasmine (*Trachelospermum* species), and evergreen clematis *(Clematis armandii)*, are ideal where year-round coverage is desired. Alternatively, deciduous vines can shade the sunny side of a house in summer, yet allow winter light to penetrate.

Although some 90 percent of vines come from only 10 botanical families, they are nevertheless a very diverse group of plants, with correspondingly different cultural needs. Most appreciate sun, but some, such as Dutchman's pipe (*Aristolochia* species), *Cissus* species, *Parthenocissus* species, and *Clematis* species, tolerate shade—even requiring some shade in hot climates, particularly at their roots. Some need plenty of water when in growth, while others, such as English ivy, are drought tolerant. Most appreciate well-drained soil that is rich in organic matter, although bougainvilleas prefer lean soil.

Climbers and creepers are marvelous for covering fences and arbors, screening or framing views, creating shade, visually softening bare walls, and reducing noise. They work beautifully in virtually any garden and should be used far more often.

ALLAMANDA

Hailing from tropical America, the genus *Allamanda* contains 12 species of evergreen shrubs, including both semi-climbing and upright types. Members of the dogbane (Apocynaceae) family, these luxuriant and exotic plants are the epitome of a tropical shrub. The large, glossy, deep green leaves and usually deep golden yellow flowers strike the perfect partnership. Appearing mainly in summer and autumn, the dramatic trumpet-shaped flowers feature a widely flared throat of 5 large overlapping petals. Popular for ornamental use in climates similar to their native habitat, these plants can also be grown in sheltered areas or conservatories in cooler climates. The genus is named for an eighteenth-century Swiss botanist—Frédéric Allamand.

ABOVE Allamanda cathartica *is a vigorous climber, variously known as the climbing allamanda or the golden trumpet. It has given rise to a number of cultivars.*

Top Tip

Wear gloves when taking cuttings of *Allamanda* species, or when pruning. A milky sap exudes when they are cut, which can sometimes cause itchy skin irritations.

CULTIVATION

As a rule, allamandas are frost-tender plants, best suited to a moist subtropical to tropical climate. The combination of rich well-drained soil and plenty of summer moisture will promote a prolific flower display over a long flowering season. Allamandas are most often propagated from half-hardened cuttings.

LEFT *The dusky pink flowers of* Allamanda blanchetii *distinguish it from its fellow species. It bears the typical glossy leaves and is ideal for training on a trellis.*

Favorites	Flower Color	Blooming Season	Flower Fragrance	Plant Height	Plant Width	Hardiness Zone	Frost Tolerance
Allamanda blanchetii	pink to purple	summer to autumn	no	6–8 ft (1.8–2.4 m)	6–8 ft (1.8–2.4 m)	11–12	no
Allamanda cathartica	bright yellow	summer	no	17 ft (5 m)	10 ft (3 m)	10–12	no
Allamanda schottii	golden yellow	summer to autumn	no	6 ft (1.8 m)	6 ft (1.8 m)	11–12	no

ARISTOLOCHIA

Commonly known as Dutchman's pipe or birthwort, and the type genus for the birthwort (Aristolochiaceae) family, *Aristolochia* contains around 300 species. Found throughout tropical and temperate regions, the genus includes vigorous climbers and perennials, both deciduous and evergreen. Often heart-shaped, the attractive leaves can be smooth-edged or lobed. The brown, purple, pink, and creamy white flowers often have eye-catching mottling. The unusual flower shape, somewhat tubular in structure with a swollen bladder-like base—often coupled with an offensive smell—is designed to attract pollinating insects. The genus name is derived from Greek—*aristos*, meaning excellent, and *lochia*, meaning birth, referring perhaps to the fetal shape of the flowers, or to the herbal properties of the plant, once used as an aid in childbirth.

BELOW *Often concealed by the lush bright green leaves, the maroon-brown blooms of* Aristolochia littoralis *are detailed with a fine network of ivory markings.*

Top Tip

Aristolochia species are undemanding plants, requiring little attention from the gardener. They may need a little routine pruning to keep them manageable.

BELOW Aristolochia californica *will quickly climb vertical surfaces, draping them with attractive foliage. The curiously shaped flowers are borne in summer.*

CULTIVATION

In favorable conditions, these plants can be grown outdoors in sun or half-sun in a rich well-drained soil. In areas where temperatures fall below 23°F (–5°C), they are better suited to greenhouse cultivation. Provide support for climbing species and carry out any necessary pruning in late winter. Propagate from softwood cuttings or seed or by division.

Favorites	Flower Color	Blooming Season	Flower Fragrance	Plant Height	Plant Width	Hardiness Zone	Frost Tolerance
Aristolochia californica	dull purple-red interior	summer	no	15 ft (4.5 m)	10 ft (3 m)	8–10	yes
Aristolochia littoralis	brown, purple, ivory	summer	no	20 ft (6 m)	15 ft (4.5 m)	9–11	yes
Aristolochia macrophylla	green; brown, pink, ivory mottling	summer	no	30 ft (9 m)	20 ft (6 m)	6–9	yes

BOUGAINVILLEA

Top Tip

Though best known for their climbing and covering abilities, colorful bougainvilleas can be kept low and shrub-like with regular pruning.

Like the Papua New Guinean island that honors the same man, this genus is named for the famous French explorer Louis Antoine de Bougainville (1729–1811). Members of the four-o-clock (Nyctaginaceae) family, the 14 species in this genus are scrambling shrubs that can become vigorous climbers in favorable conditions resembling the climate of their native habitat—warm-temperate to tropical South America. If unsupported, these plants will remain compact or behave as ground covers, while if given support they will climb vigorously, using their sharp thorns as a means of attachment. While the thin-textured, downy, tapering leaves and small, tubular, ivory to yellow flowers play a role in the overall attractive appearance of these plants, it is the brilliantly colored petal-like bracts that create its dramatic impact.

BELOW *The tiny, tubular, white flowers of* Bougainvillea *'Elizabeth Doxey' are surrounded by white bracts that sometimes bear tinges of soft green.*

CULTIVATION

For best results, plant bougainvilleas in a light well-drained soil in a sunny spot. They appreciate regular watering during summer. These plants will not tolerate heavy or repeated frosts. Propagate from cuttings taken in summer.

RIGHT *Bougainvilleas—such as the mauve-pink-bracted 'Zakiriana' seen here—can be used as screening plants, providing a curtain of color when in bloom.*

Below *A Brazilian species, commonly known as paper flower,* Bougainvillea glabra *bears white or magenta bracts that almost obscure the dark green foliage.*

Right *A tall climber reaching up to 15 ft (4.5 m) high,* Bougainvillea × buttiana *'Enid Lancaster' features bracts of soft yellow that slowly age to gold.*

Favorites	Flower Color	Blooming Season	Flower Fragrance	Plant Height	Plant Width	Hardiness Zone	Frost Tolerance
Bougainvillea* × *buttiana	orange-pink to red bracts	spring to autumn	no	17–40 ft (5–12 m)	10–20 ft (3–6 m)	9–12	no
***Bougainvillea* × *buttiana* 'Raspberry Ice'**	magenta bracts	summer to autumn	no	3–4 ft (0.9–1.2 m)	3–4 ft (0.9–1.2 m)	9–12	no
***Bougainvillea* 'Elizabeth Doxey'**	white bracts	summer to autumn	no	12–15 ft (3.5–4.5 m)	5–20 ft (1.5–6 m)	9–12	no
Bougainvillea glabra	white to magenta bracts	spring to autumn	no	10–30 ft (3–9 m)	10–20 ft (3–6 m)	10–12	no
Bougainvillea spectabilis	pink to purple bracts	spring	no	12 ft (3.5 m)	15 ft (4.5 m)	10–12	no
***Bougainvillea* 'Zakiriana'**	mauve-pink bracts	summer to autumn	no	2–20 ft (0.6–6 m)	5–20 ft (1.5–6 m)	9–12	no

CAMPSIS

Belonging to the bignonia (Bignoniaceae) family, and commonly known as trumpet creeper, this genus contains just 2 species of impressive climbing plants. Their origins vary, one coming from China and Japan, the other being a North American native, where it is considered a weed in some places. Ideal for growing over walls or fences, these vigorous deciduous climbers use their aerial roots to cling to their support. Lance-shaped toothed-edged leaflets are arranged in pairs giving the long leaves a feathery appearance. Throughout summer and autumn widely flared trumpet-shaped flowers can have a dramatic impact in the garden—not only through the gorgeous orange or red hues that add a colorful splash to their setting, but also through the birdlife that is attracted by the nectar-rich blooms.

CULTIVATION

Plant in a well-drained soil in full sun. In cool climates, place them in a warm sheltered spot to encourage greater flowering. Plants that produce few aerial roots need to be attached to their support. To keep plants manageable, prune back hard in late winter/early spring. Propagate from cuttings, layers, or seed.

ABOVE Campsis grandiflora *has orange to red trumpet-shaped flowers that are 3–4 in (8–10 cm) wide, borne on 20 in (50 cm) panicles from summer.*
LEFT Campsis × tagliabuana *'Madame Galen' is a robust vine that climbs with aerial roots. It has loose panicles of large flaring flowers in rich salmon orange shades.*

Top Tip

Keep *Campsis* vines well pruned as they mature. Left alone, the top becomes too heavy and the vine can collapse. Once established, cut many of the plant stems back.

Favorites	Flower Color	Blooming Season	Flower Fragrance	Plant Height	Plant Width	Hardiness Zone	Frost Tolerance
Campsis grandiflora	scarlet to orange	late summer to autumn	no	10–30 ft (3–9 m)	8–15 ft (2.4–4.5 m)	7–11	yes
Campsis radicans	orange to red	late summer to autumn	no	15–35 ft (4.5–10 m)	8–15 ft (2.4–4.5 m)	4–10	yes
Campsis* × *tagliabuana	orange to red	summer	no	8–20 ft (2.4–6 m)	8–15 ft (2.4–4.5 m)	6–10	yes

CISSUS

This genus of around 200 species, found throughout tropical and subtropical parts of the world, belongs to the grape (Vitaceae) family, and is commonly known as grape ivy. Though mostly vines, some are shrublets and some have succulent or herbaceous stems. Most climb by tendrils, though some have adhesive discs. The leaves, located opposite the tendrils, are usually simple, sometimes palmately lobed. Candelabra-like cymes carry the hermaphroditic flowers, which feature a cup-shaped calyx, 4 free petals, 4 stamens, a round style, and a tiny stigma. The single-seeded, spherical to egg-shaped berries that follow the flowers are usually inedible.

Top Tip

Though undemanding and adaptable, *Cissus* species need regular pruning to contain growth and reduce congested stems. Tip pruning will encourage thicker foliage.

CULTIVATION

Cissus species are grown for their glossy foliage or succulent stems. They make fine garden subjects in warmer areas or shade-tolerant house plants in cooler regions. Provide support for climbing species; they may also need tying to the support. Propagate from stem cuttings, or seed for the succulent species.

TOP Cissus quadrangularis *acquires its specific epithet for its 4-angled stems. Heart-shaped or lobed leaves appear fleetingly on the stems before dropping.*

ABOVE Cissus hypoglauca *is commonly known as native grape or jungle vine. This stealthy climber from Australia has glossy leaves and tiny yellow summer flowers.*

Favorites	Flower Color	Blooming Season	Flower Fragrance	Plant Height	Plant Width	Hardiness Zone	Frost Tolerance
Cissus hypoglauca	yellow	early summer	no	17–35 ft (5–10 m)	20 ft (6 m)	10–11	no
Cissus quadrangularis	green	early summer	no	60 in (150 cm)	32 in (80 cm)	10–12	no
Cissus rhombifolia	greenish white	summer	no	10 ft (3 m)	6 ft (1.8 m)	10–11	no

CLEMATIS

Found in temperate zones around the world, and at higher altitudes in the tropics, *Clematis* is a genus of over 200 evergreen and deciduous species in the buttercup (Ranunculaceae) family. Incorporating a wide diversity of plants, they are known around the world by various common names including leather vine, traveler's joy, vase flower, and Virgin's bower. Within the genus, climbing or scrambling types dominate—using tendrils to attach to their support—however, there are also shrubby or perennial types. The leaves are simple or pinnate and the usually showy flowers, with 4 to 8 petal-like sepals, come in a variety of colors. Fluffy seed heads follow the spectacular blooms.

ABOVE *Bred in America,* Clematis *'Perrin's Pride' is a Viticella Group hybrid. A colorful addition to the garden, this vigorous climber bears stunning purple flowers.*

CULTIVATION

While these plants usually need to be in a sunny spot, the roots require cool moist conditions. Adding plenty of humus-rich compost before planting will pay dividends. *Clematis* wilt disease is a problem in many areas. Propagate species and cultivars from cuttings or layers; species may be raised from seed.

RIGHT *Though small, the scented, 4-petalled, white flowers of* Clematis montana *var.* wilsonii *are borne in abundance in spring.*

ABOVE *Belonging to the Lanuginosa Group,* Clematis *'Hybrida Sieboldii' bears its lovely, large, pale lavender flowers throughout summer and autumn.*

LEFT *Producing its stunning rich red flowers over a long flowering season,* Clematis *'Niobe' is a member of the Jackmanii Group, and an extremely popular plant.*

Favorites	Flower Color	Blooming Season	Flower Fragrance	Plant Height	Plant Width	Hardiness Zone	Frost Tolerance
Clematis alpina	blue to mauve	spring	no	8–10 ft (2.4–3 m)	5 ft (1.5 m)	5–9	yes
Clematis armandii	white	spring	yes	10–30 ft (3–9 m)	6–10 ft (1.8–3 m)	5–10	yes
Clematis cirrhosa	cream	late winter to early spring	no	8–15 ft (2.4–4.5 m)	5–6 ft (1.5–1.8 m)	7–10	yes
Clematis montana	white to pale pink	spring	no	15–25 ft (4.5–8 m)	10–20 ft (3–6 m)	6–9	yes
***Clematis*, Diversifolia Group**	blue-violet, rose pink	summer to early autumn	no	3–12 ft (0.9–3.5 m)	3–5 ft (0.9–1.5 m)	5–9	yes
***Clematis*, Florida Group**	white to purple	late spring to summer	no	8–12 ft (2.4–3.5 m)	5–8 ft (1.5–2.4 m)	5–9	yes
***Clematis*, Forsteri Group**	white to greenish yellow	mid-spring to early summer	no	8–12 ft (2.4–3.5 m)	10 ft (3 m)	5–9	yes
***Clematis*, Jackmanii Group**	pink, red, blue to purple	summer to autumn	no	7–20 ft (2–6 m)	5–10 ft (1.5–3 m)	5–9	yes
***Clematis*, Lanuginosa Group**	white to red to violet	summer to autumn	no	8–15 ft (2.4–4.5 m)	5–8 ft (1.5–2.4 m)	5–9	yes
***Clematis*, Patens Group**	white, blue, red, purple	late spring to summer	no	6–12 ft (1.8–3.5 m)	5–8 ft (1.5–2.4 m)	5–9	yes
***Clematis*, Texensis Group**	pink, red	summer to mid-autumn	no	6–12 ft (1.8–3.5 m)	3–6 ft (0.9–1.8 m)	5–9	yes
***Clematis*, Viticella Group**	white to red to purple	summer to early autumn	no	8–20 ft (2.4–6 m)	5–8 ft (1.5–2.4 m)	5–9	yes

Top Tip

A layer of mulch around the plant base will keep *Clematis* roots cool. Alternatively, plant ground-cover or low-growing shade plants around the base of the plant.

RIGHT *A mid-stripe of rich red runs through each of the purple-red sepals of* Clematis *'Beth Currie'. A compact climber, this beautiful plant belongs to the Patens Group.*

BELOW *An evergreen hybrid belonging to the Forsteri Group,* Clematis *'Moonbeam' puts on a splendid display with its masses of starry flowers of creamy white.*

BELOW *Wavy-edged rich pink sepals surround the tuft of dark reddish stamens of* Clematis *'Helen Cropper'. This hybrid is a member of the Patens Group.*

BELOW *The single large blooms of* Clematis *'Pink Fantasy', a Jackmanii Group hybrid, feature soft pink pointed sepals with a mid-stripe of darker pink.*

BOTTOM *Impressive fully double blooms of silvery mauve are the trademark characteristic of* Clematis *'Belle of Woking', a Florida Group hybrid.*

BELOW *Flowering in summer,* Clematis *'Beauty of Worcester', a Lanuginosa Group member, bears stunning large flowers of violet-blue, highlighted with creamy white stamens.*

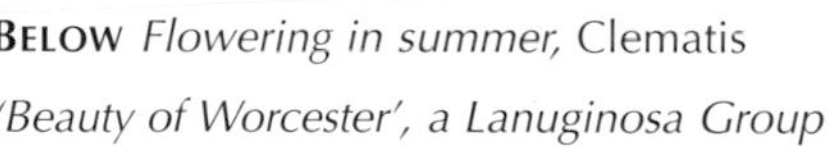

LEFT *Unlobed, as ivies can be when exposed to full sun, the leaves of* Hedera helix *'Variegata' are glossy green with a border of cream to yellowish green.*

BELOW *The lush leaves of* Hedera helix *'Green Ripple' have long tapering lobes and highly polished surfaces that are lined with paler veining.*

HEDERA

Better known by its common name, ivy, this genus contains 11 evergreen species from Europe, Asia, and northern Africa, and is a member of the family Araliaceae. Accomplished climbers, they can tackle almost any surface using their aerial roots to cling on as they make their ascent. Not only can they be used to cover vertical surfaces and grow up trees, they also make efficient ground covers. The foliage usually takes on its adult shape when it can no longer grow any taller. Borne in clusters, the flowers are small, and of little interest to all but their fly pollinators. The berries that follow are usually black.

CULTIVATION

As a rule, ivies are not fussy about climate or soil type, however, they can become quite weedy outside their native habitats. They also make excellent indoor pot plants. Propagate from cuttings, which strike easily at almost any time of the year.

Favorites

	Plant Height	Plant Width	Hardiness Zone	Frost Tolerance
Hedera canariensis	15–20 ft (4.5–6 m)	20–60 ft (6–18 m)	8–10	yes
Hedera colchica	20–35 ft (6–10 m)	20–60 ft (6–18 m)	6–10	yes
Hedera helix	35–50 ft (10–15 m)	20–60 ft (6–18 m)	5–10	yes
***Hedera helix* 'Green Ripple'**	35–50 ft (10–15 m)	20–60 ft (6–18 m)	5–10	yes
Hedera hibernica	25–35 ft (8–10 m)	20–60 ft (6–18 m)	6–10	yes
Hedera nepalensis	10–17 ft (3–5 m)	20–60 ft (6–18 m)	6–10	yes

ABOVE Hedera colchica *bears the largest leaves of all the species in the genus, but the bright green leaves of its cultivar 'Dentata', seen here, are even larger.* **TOP LEFT** *The rounded, 3- to 5-lobed dark green leaves of* Hedera helix *'Cockle Shell' are slightly cupped, resembling their namesake—the cockle shell.*

Top Tip

Ivies can provide quick coverage of unsightly walls and surfaces, but they need to be pruned and controlled or they have the potential to become invasive.

Right Hoya carnosa *is a climber native to India and southeastern China widely grown as a house plant. It has white to palest pink flowers with a red center.*

Hoya

Popularly known as wax flowers, the 200 species in this genus, a member of the milkweed (Asclepiadaceae) family, are mainly climbing, sometimes shrubby or succulent, evergreen plants. Originating in Asia, Polynesia, and Australia, they are woody-stemmed plants, which in the wild can reach 20 ft (6 m) tall or more. The glossy dark green foliage provides a backdrop for the exquisite waxy flowers that resemble fine porcelain. The dainty fragrant blooms are arranged in a star-upon-star configuration—a "star" of thick petals, usually white or in pale shades of pink, studded at the center with a contrasting starry corona.

Cultivation

In suitably warm climates grow outdoors in semi-shade in a moist, rich, free-draining soil. Elsewhere wax flowers are popular house plants often grown in hanging baskets. Grow them in bright filtered light in a well-drained potting mix. Feed and water regularly, ensuring a high level of humidity is maintained. Propagate from cuttings.

Top Tip

Hoya plants prefer it if their soil is left to dry out somewhat between waterings. Be careful where the plants are positioned, particularly if hanging, as they drip a sticky nectar.

Favorites	Flower Color	Blooming Season	Flower Fragrance	Plant Height	Plant Width	Hardiness Zone	Frost Tolerance
Hoya australis	white to pale pink	summer	yes	12–30 ft (3.5–9 m)	10 ft (3 m)	10–12	no
Hoya carnosa	white to pale pink	summer	yes	10–20 ft (3–6 m)	10 ft (3 m)	10–12	no
***Hoya carnosa* 'Exotica'**	white to pale pink	summer	yes	10 ft (3 m)	3 ft (0.9 m)	10–12	no
***Hoya carnosa* 'Krinkle Kurl'**	white to pale pink	summer	yes	10 ft (3 m)	3 ft (0.9 m)	10–12	no
***Hoya carnosa* 'Rubra'**	white to pale pink	summer	yes	10 ft (3 m)	3 ft (0.9 m)	10–12	no
***Hoya carnosa* 'Variegata'**	white to pale pink	summer	yes	10 ft (3 m)	3 ft (0.9 m)	10–12	no

ABOVE Hoya australis *is an Australian climber that has thick, shiny, dark green leaves and umbels of small, starry, scented, white to pale pink flowers, with reddish purple coronas.* **LEFT** Hoya carnosa *'Exotica' has flowers that are similar in appearance to the species, but differs in that it has showy variegated leaves, which are yellow and pink with green margins.*

IPOMOEA

A member of the bindweed (Convolvulaceae) family, this large variable genus acquired its botanical name from the Greek word for a type of worm, a reference to its many species of twining climbers, though it is probably better known to most by its common name—morning glory. With around 500 species in total, the genus also encompasses annual or perennial herbs, shrubs, and small trees. Easily grown in tropical to warm-temperate areas, these plants will reward with showy tubular to bell-shaped flowers and stealthy growth, and are ideal subjects for growing over fences, trellises, and walls. Some, such as the sweet potato *(Ipomoea batatas)*, have tuberous roots that are used as food.

CULTIVATION

Though adaptable to most conditions, morning glories prefer full sun and plenty of water in the growing season. These plants need plenty of room, and should be cut back after flowering. Given the right conditions, they can become invasive. Propagate annuals from seed, other types from softwood or half-hardened cuttings taken in summer.

Favorites	Flower Color	Blooming Season	Flower Fragrance
Ipomoea batatas	white to pale purple	summer	no
Ipomoea horsfalliae	red to maroon	summer to winter	no
Ipomoea indica	dark blue to purple, white	throughout the year	no
Ipomoea mauritiana	pink to maroon	summer	no
Ipomoea* × *multifida	red with white center	summer to autumn	no
Ipomoea tricolor	sky blue to purple	summer to early autumn	no

ABOVE Ipomoea × multifida *is an annual climber, known as the cardinal flower for its white-centered red blooms. The interesting leaves are deeply divided and somewhat fan-like in appearance.*

RIGHT *A stalwart climber from tropical regions of the world,* Ipomoea mauritiana *has large leaves with up to 9 lobes, and pink to maroon blooms that intensify in color toward the center.*

Plant Height	Plant Width	Hardiness Zone	Frost Tolerance
1–10 ft (0.3–3 m)	10 ft (3 m)	9–12	no
10–25 ft (3–8 m)	3–10 ft (0.9–3 m)	9–12	no
10–30 ft (3–9 m)	10–30 ft (3–9 m)	10–12	no
15 ft (4.5 m)	6 ft (1.8 m)	9–12	no
15 ft (4.5 m)	6 ft (1.8 m)	9–12	no
10 ft (3 m)	5–8 ft (1.5–2.4 m)	8–12	no

BELOW Ipomoea indica, *the blue dawn flower, is an agile climber with dark green heart-shaped leaves and colorful flowers that fade in intensity as the day draws to a close.*

ABOVE *A West Indian perennial, commonly known as cardinal creeper,* Ipomoea horsfalliae *bears lovely rich red to maroon blooms over a long flowering season.*

Top Tip

Ipomoea plants are great climbers and are regarded as weeds in some warmer areas. To overcome this problem and still enjoy their beauty, plant in containers.

JASMINUM

Jasmine is a traditional favorite with gardeners—its powerful evocative scent wafts through gardens, often signaling the onset of warmer weather. With a range of natural distribution from Africa to Asia, and a solitary American representative, the genus *Jasminum* contains some 200 or so species of deciduous, semi-deciduous, and evergreen shrubs and woody-stemmed climbers that are members of the olive (Oleaceae) family. The variable leaves encompass a range of textures and colors. Appearing in clusters at the branch tips and leaf axils, the usually white, white flushed pink, or yellow tubular flowers have 5 widely flared lobes. Though jasmine is synonymous with beautiful fragrance, there are a number of species that have little or no perfume.

CULTIVATION

Growing requirements for *Jasminum* species vary, though most will not tolerate repeated severe frosts or drought. They do best in moist, humus-rich, well-drained soil in full sun or part-shade. Given the right conditions most jasmines grow rapidly and can become invasive. Propagate from seed, cuttings, or layers, which with some low-growing species may form naturally.

LEFT Jasminum nudiflorum *is commonly known as winter jasmine. This yellow-flowered species will provide a welcome splash of color in the often somber winter garden.*

Favorites	Flower Color	Blooming Season	Flower Fragrance
Jasminum azoricum	white	late summer	yes
Jasminum humile	bright yellow	spring to autumn	yes
Jasminum nudiflorum	bright yellow	late winter to early spring	no
Jasminum officinale	white or pale pink	summer to early autumn	yes
Jasminum polyanthum	white	spring	yes
Jasminum × stephanense	pale pink	summer to autumn	yes

FAR LEFT *Known as Azores jasmine for its native habitat,* Jasminum azoricum *is an evergreen climber. It has dark green leaves and highly scented white flowers.*

LEFT *The dainty pink buds of* Jasminum polyanthum *begin to appear from late winter. They open in late spring to reveal highly perfumed white flowers.*

Top Tip

Although the climbing jasmines are generally vigorous and adaptable, they may need supplemental water during extended dry periods to perform well.

Plant Height	Plant Width	Hardiness Zone	Frost Tolerance
20 ft (6 m)	20 ft (6 m)	10–11	no
8–12 ft (2.4–3.5 m)	10–12 ft (3–3.5 m)	8–10	yes
5–10 ft (1.5–3 m)	10 ft (3 m)	6–9	yes
8–30 ft (2.4–9 m)	8–15 ft (2.4–4.5 m)	6–10	yes
10–17 ft (3–5 m)	25 ft (8 m)	7–9	yes
3–17 ft (0.9–5 m)	5–10 ft (1.5–3 m)	7–11	yes

ABOVE *When in bloom during late spring and into summer, the starry golden flowers of* Jasminum humile *'Revolutum' are a perfect foil for the lush dark green leaves.*

MANDEVILLA

Comprising around 120 species of mainly tuberous perennials, subshrubs, and twining vines, *Mandevilla* is a Central and South American genus belonging to the dogbane (Apocynaceae) family. It is the beautiful vines that are most often seen in cultivation, their vigorous growth quickly transforming a bare surface into a visually appealing frieze of foliage and flowers. Large deep green leaves with prominent elongated tips provide a backdrop for the impressive, often large, trumpet-shaped flowers that appear throughout the warmer months. These showy blooms occur in white, cream, and pink, and can be fragrant.

CULTIVATION

Mandevilla species are mostly frost tender and prefer a mild to warm climate, dappled sunlight, and moist, humus-rich, well-drained soil. Water well during the growing and flowering seasons. Take care if trimming back as all parts exude a sometimes irritant milky latex when cut. They can be propagated from half-hardened stems in summer, or from cuttings.

ABOVE *The lush dark green, sometimes bronze-tinted foliage and heavily scented white flowers of* Mandevilla laxa *provide perfect camouflage for bare walls.*

LEFT Mandevilla × amabilis *'Alice du Pont' features lustrous deep green foliage, accompanied by large deep pink flowers that provide a long summer show.*

Favorites

	Flower Color	Blooming Season	Flower Fragrance	Plant Height	Plant Width	Hardiness Zone	Frost Tolerance
Mandevilla* × *amabilis	pink, darker at center	mid- to late spring	no	12–15 ft (3.5–4.5 m)	6–15 ft (1.8–4.5 m)	10–12	no
Mandevilla boliviensis	white with yellow throat	mid- to late summer	no	12–15 ft (3.5–4.5 m)	4–10 ft (1.2–3 m)	10–12	no
Mandevilla laxa	white, creamy white	summer	yes	15 ft (4.5 m)	17 ft (5 m)	9–11	no
Mandevilla sanderi	rose pink	spring	no	3–17 ft (0.9–5 m)	17 ft (5 m)	10–12	no
Mandevilla splendens	pink with yellow throat	late spring to early summer	no	10–20 ft (3–6 m)	6 ft (1.8 m)	10–12	no
***Mandevilla* 'White Delight'**	white with yellow throat	spring to summer	no	10–15 ft (3–4.5 m)	4–10 ft (1.2–3 m)	10–12	no

BELOW *The pale pink buds of* Mandevilla *'White Delight' unfurl to reveal impressive trumpet-shaped flowers of white, often pink-flushed, with golden yellow coloring at the throat.*

Top Tip

In cooler climates plant mandevillas in containers. The plants can then be enjoyed in a garden setting before being moved indoors when temperatures fall.

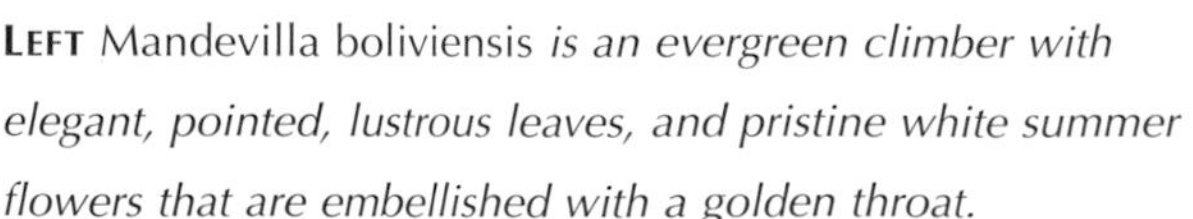

LEFT Mandevilla boliviensis *is an evergreen climber with elegant, pointed, lustrous leaves, and pristine white summer flowers that are embellished with a golden throat.*

PARTHENOCISSUS

Perhaps better known by its common names—Virginia creeper or Boston ivy—*Parthenocissus* is a member of the grape (Vitaceae) family. The genus comprises 10 species of deciduous tendril-producing climbers from East Asia and North America. They are grown for their attractive foliage and, in most species, their clinging ability, which makes them ideal to clothe walls and fences. Most species feature adhesive discs on the tendrils, which they use to hold fast to their climbing surface. The leaves are either divided into leaflets or maple-like, and usually take on fiery autumn coloring before they fall. Tiny and green, the flowers are somewhat insignificant, with little ornamental value. Small black berries follow the flowers.

Top Tip

Virginia creepers grown over pergolas and similar structures will provide leafy shade in summer and allow in welcome winter sun when the leaves fall.

CULTIVATION

Undemanding plants, Virginia creepers will grow in any moderately fertile soil in sun or part-shade. They can be propagated from cuttings at almost any time or by removing rooted layers. Alternatively, raise from seed.

LEFT *Interspersed among the leaves as they develop their spectacular autumn coloring are the small black berries of* Parthenocissus tricuspidata *'Veitchii'.*

ABOVE LEFT *Found from eastern USA down to Mexico,* Parthenocissus quinquefolia *has somewhat shiny dark green leaves that turn glowing red in autumn before falling.*

Favorites

Favorites	Plant Height	Plant Width	Hardiness Zone	Frost Tolerance
Parthenocissus henryana	30–35 ft (9–10 m)	20 ft (6 m)	7–10	yes
Parthenocissus inserta	30–35 ft (9–10 m)	30 ft (9 m)	3–10	yes
Parthenocissus quinquefolia	40–50 ft (12–15 m)	30 ft (9 m)	3–10	yes
Parthenocissus tricuspidata	50–70 ft (15–21 m)	20 ft (6 m)	4–10	yes
***Parthenocissus tricuspidata* 'Lowii'**	10–20 ft (3–6 m)	10–20 ft (3–6 m)	4–10	yes
***Parthenocissus tricuspidata* 'Veitchii'**	40–60 ft (12–18 m)	20 ft (6 m)	4–10	yes

LEFT *Ablaze with a "traffic light" coloring of green, orange, and red, the autumn leaves of* Parthenocissus tricuspidata *overlap to form a blanket of color.*

BELOW *The white veining on the mid-green leaves of* Parthenocissus henryana *becomes more pronounced when the plant is grown in shade.*

PASSIFLORA

Taking its botanical name from a transliteration of Latin, *Passiflora* is the type genus for its family, the Passifloraceae. Comprising 500-odd species of mainly evergreen tendril-climbing vines, the genus also includes a few shrubby species. Commonly known as passionflowers or passionfruit, they mostly come from tropical America, though the range does extend to Asia and the Pacific Islands. Grown mainly for their beautiful flowers and subsequent pulpy fruit, passionflowers are vigorous growers that clamber and cover surfaces quickly. Unusual in structure, the flowers feature a tubular calyx around 5 conspicuous sepals and usually 5 petals, which are overlaid with an often decorative crown of anthers, and 3 styles emerging from the flower center. Many parts of the flower are regarded as symbolic of the crucifixion of Christ.

ABOVE *A native of Ecuador,* Passiflora reflexiflora *has pink to magenta flowers with long petals that gradually become reflexed, and distinctive 3-pointed leaves.*

RIGHT *An agile climber from the Amazon region of Brazil and Peru,* Passiflora alata *bears fragrant rich red flowers that feature a ring of purple and white filaments.*

CULTIVATION

Many of these climbers are frost tender; they prefer a warm climate in full or half-sun with deep, moist, humus-rich, well-drained soil. Keep well watered during the warmer months. Trim to shape in spring. Propagate from seed or cuttings, or by layering.

RIGHT *The yellow-green to bright yellow flowers of* Passiflora citrina *are small compared with many of its relatives, but they produce a colorful display throughout the year.*

BELOW *The unusual hairy buds of* Passiflora foetida*—commonly known as love-in-a-mist or running pop—open in summer to reveal the mauve-pink flowers.*

Top Tip

With their rapid growth, handsome foliage, and impressive flowers, *Passiflora* species are ideal for fast coverage of bare vertical surfaces.

Favorites	Flower Color	Blooming Season	Flower Fragrance	Plant Height	Plant Width	Hardiness Zone	Frost Tolerance
Passiflora alata	red	summer	yes	20 ft (6 m)	8–20 ft (2.4–6 m)	10–12	no
Passiflora citrina	yellow-green to bright yellow	throughout the year	no	15 ft (4.5 m)	15 ft (4.5 m)	10–12	no
***Passiflora* 'Debby'**	white	summer to autumn	no	6–12 ft (1.8–3.5 m)	6–15 ft (1.8–4.5 m)	8–12	yes
Passiflora edulis	white	summer	no	15 ft (4.5 m)	8–15 ft (2.4–4.5 m)	10–12	no
Passiflora foetida	mauve-pink	summer to autumn	no	6–10 ft (1.8–3 m)	3–6 ft (0.9–1.8 m)	10–12	no
Passiflora reflexiflora	deep pink to magenta	summer	no	6–10 ft (1.8–3 m)	4–8 ft (1.2–2.4 m)	10–12	no

THUNBERGIA

Belonging to the acanthus (Acanthaceae) family, the genus *Thunbergia* contains some 100 species of annuals, perennials, and shrubs. Natives of tropical Africa and Asia, and also found in Madagascar and South Africa, there are many twining climbers, as well as some shrubby types in this variable genus. They are admired for their attractive foliage and flowers, and the vigorous climbers are a popular choice when quick coverage is a requirement. The leaves usually range from pointed oval to heart-shaped and can be lobed or smooth-edged. The long-tubed trumpet-flowers occur in many colors, but are most often yellow, orange, and purple-blue shades. The genus was named for Carl Peter Thunberg (1743–1828), a Swedish physician and botanist.

CULTIVATION

At best, these plants are tolerant only of the very lightest of frosts. They do best in a warm sheltered position in moist, humus-rich, well-drained soil, benefiting from frequent watering and feeding. Any essential pruning should be carried out in early spring. Propagate from cuttings or seed, rarely by division.

ABOVE *Dangling in long racemes, the maroon buds of* Thunbergia mysorensis *open to reveal the deep red and yellow flowers. They are produced throughout the year, peaking in spring.*
LEFT *Hailing from tropical Africa,* Thunbergia gregorii *is commonly known as orange clock vine. This perennial climber is often grown as an annual in cooler climates.*
FAR RIGHT *The stunning summer blooms of* Thunbergia togoensis *are richly colored. Glowing yellow at the throat, the large lobes are imperial purple.*
RIGHT *With its long summer display of abundant golden flowers, the black-eyed Susan vine,* Thunbergia alata, *is an ideal candidate for growing in hanging baskets.*

Favorites	Flower Color	Blooming Season	Flower Fragrance	Plant Height	Plant Width	Hardiness Zone	Frost Tolerance
Thunbergia alata	gold with black center	summer to autumn	no	5–10 ft (1.5–3 m)	10 ft (3 m)	9–12	no
Thunbergia erecta	creamy yellow; purple lobes	summer	no	4–8 ft (1.2–2.4 m)	2–7 ft (0.6–2 m)	10–12	no
Thunbergia grandiflora	sky blue to dark blue	summer	no	15–30 ft (4.5–9 m)	10–15 ft (3–4.5 m)	10–12	no
Thunbergia gregorii	orange	summer	no	6 ft (1.8 m)	6 ft (1.8 m)	9–12	no
Thunbergia mysorensis	yellow and deep red	spring	no	10–20 ft (3–6 m)	10–20 ft (3–6 m)	10–12	no
Thunbergia togoensis	violet-blue; yellow center	summer	no	10–20 ft (3–6 m)	6–20 ft (1.8–6 m)	10–12	no

Top Tip

Though they generally require tropical conditions, some *Thunbergia* species can be grown as annuals in cooler climates. Many are quick to establish and bloom.

TRACHELOSPERMUM

Found in woodland areas from Japan to India, the 20 species in this genus are evergreen climbing and twining plants belonging to the dogbane (Apocynaceae) family. Commonly known as confederate jasmine or star jasmine, they feature attractive, glossy, oval leaves that are pointed at both ends, and—as the common names suggest—fragrant, white, starry, jasmine-like flowers, in summer. These versatile plants are very effective when used to cover fences and pergolas or to clamber up tree trunks, as they cling readily to hard surfaces and clamber over supports with ease. They are also useful for softening the appearance of outdoor walls, will absorb heat in urban landscapes, and are suitable as ground covers and container plants. Their versatility extends to the indoors, as they make great house plants or greenhouse specimens.

ABOVE *Colored cream or pink when young, the leaves of* Trachelospermum jasminoides *'Tricolor' age to green, with some mottling. It is a slow-growing cultivar.*

CULTIVATION

While these plants prefer well-drained situations with some organic matter, they are not fussy as to soil type or aspect. They require average amounts of water initially, but are somewhat drought tolerant once established. Propagate from half-hardened cuttings in summer.

RIGHT Trachelospermum jasminoides *'Variegatum' has white-marked green leaves. This award-winning cultivar is one of the most popular of this species.*

Favorites

	Flower Color	Blooming Season	Flower Fragrance	Plant Height	Plant Width	Hardiness Zone	Frost Tolerance
Trachelospermum asiaticum	white	summer	yes	20 ft (6 m)	10–17 ft (3–5 m)	8–10	yes
Trachelospermum jasminoides	white	summer to mid-autumn	yes	30 ft (9 m)	17–25 ft (5–8 m)	9–10	yes
***Trachelospermum jasminoides* 'Variegatum'**	white	summer to mid-autumn	yes	15 ft (4.5 m)	8–12 ft (2.4–3.5 m)	9–10	yes

LEFT Trachelospermum jasminoides *is a fast-growing climber that is covered with masses of very fragrant clusters of white flowers during the warmer months.*

BELOW *The glossy leaves of* Trachelospermum asiaticum *can grow up to 2 in (5 cm) long. 'Bronze Beauty' has bronze new growth which matures to rich green.*

Top Tip

These plants will climb if support is provided, otherwise they make fragrant ground covers or spreading bushes. Prune as required to keep them under control.

WISTERIA

The 10 species of twining vines in this genus are members of the pea-flower subfamily of the legume (Fabaceae) family, and are natives of China, Japan, and eastern USA. These hardy, heavy-wooded, vigorous, deciduous vines are invaluable for screening and for draping over verandahs and porches, with the dense foliage providing cool shade during the warmer months, then as the weather cools and the leaves fall, the winter sun is allowed to penetrate. Initially soft bronze-green, the young leaves mature to light green. Wisterias are a magnificent sight when in bloom, with abundant, long, pendent racemes of usually mauve flowers that are often highly scented. The limited color range of the species is extended in the cultivated forms to include white and a range of pink to purple tones.

CULTIVATION

Wisterias like to grow in a sunny spot, but the roots must be kept cool—moist, humus-rich, well-drained soil is the preferred growing medium. Routine trimming is required to contain the spread of these nimble climbers. They can be propagated from cuttings or seed, or by layering or grafting.

Top Tip

While wisterias are best known for their climbing ability, the cascades of flowers can be displayed to full advantage when the plants are espaliered.

LEFT *From late spring, the profuse violet flowers of* Wisteria × formosa, *enhanced by their heady perfume, will become a focal point in the garden.*

Left *Cascading among the the foliage, there can be up to 100 white flowers on each of the 24 in (60 cm) long racemes of* Wisteria floribunda *'Alba'.*

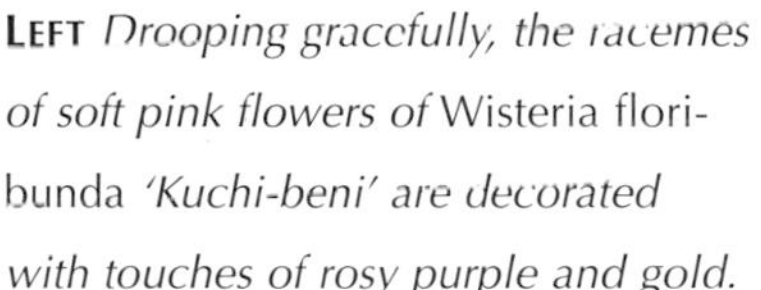

Left *Drooping gracefully, the racemes of soft pink flowers of* Wisteria floribunda *'Kuchi-beni' are decorated with touches of rosy purple and gold.*

Above Wisteria brachybotrys *'Shiro-kapitan' has leaves with a fine covering of silky hairs and highly fragrant white, sometimes pink-tinged, flowers.*

Favorites	Flower Color	Blooming Season	Flower Fragrance	Plant Height	Plant Width	Hardiness Zone	Frost Tolerance
Wisteria brachybotrys	white	late spring to early summer	yes	30 ft (9 m)	30 ft (9 m)	6–10	yes
Wisteria floribunda	white, pink, violet, magenta-red	late spring to early summer	yes	15–30 ft (4.5–9 m)	10–30 ft (3–9 m)	5–10	yes
***Wisteria floribunda* 'Rosea'**	rose pink	late spring to early summer	yes	15–30 ft (4.5–9 m)	10–30 ft (3–9 m)	5–10	yes
Wisteria* × *formosa	pale violet	late spring to early summer	yes	15–30 ft (4.5–9 m)	10–30 ft (3–9 m)	5–10	yes
Wisteria sinensis	lavender, purple-blue	mid-spring to early summer	yes	15–35 ft (4.5–10 m)	10–35 ft (3–10 m)	5–10	yes
***Wisteria sinensis* 'Caroline'**	grayish purple	spring	yes	15–35 ft (4.5–10 m)	10–30 ft (3–9 m)	5–10	yes

ORCHIDS

Without a doubt, orchids rank among the most beautiful and coveted plants on earth. Individual orchid flowers can range from almost microscopic to some 8 in (20 cm) across, while the plants themselves range from less than 2 in (5 cm) high to 70 ft (21 m) tall. Flowers can be flat or nearly tubular, and arranged in racemes, spikes, or clusters of one to dozens of blooms that can be deliciously scented, lacking scent, or even fetid (to humans). The color spectrum is amazing: whether single-toned or elaborately patterned, flowers range from brown, green, yellow, blue, and nearly black to torrid shades of purple, red, and pink.

ABOVE *Though exotic and tropical in appearance, there are orchids suited to a wide variety of climates.* Paphiopedilum insigne *is a cool-growing orchid that bears winter flowers.*
LEFT *Orchids are popular with gardeners around the world, and with glamorous examples such as* Cymbidium *Highland Advent, the attraction and fascination is understandable.*

NATURE'S MOST UNIQUE FLOWERS

LEFT *Cattleyas are among the most popular orchids in cultivation, and have given rise to thousands of beautiful hybrids, such as the striking* Cattleya *(Browniae ×* loddigesii*) seen here.* **BELOW** *With long-lived blooms in a vast range of colors, vandas, such as* Vanda *Reverend Masao Yamada, are epiphytic warm-growing orchids that are highly valued as cut flowers.*

Orchids comprise the largest plant family—Orchidaceae—in the world of flowering plants. Containing over 20,000 species within 900 genera, and found on every continent except Antarctica, they are both widespread and diverse. However different they may look, all orchids have several traits in common: 3 sepals (the outer sheath of the bud) and 3 petals, of which one is usually lower than the others and is called the labellum, or lip. The lip is usually larger and more brightly colored than the other segments and can be marked with speckles or stripes. In some orchids, the labellum is modified to form a pouch, as with slipper orchids such as *Paphiopedilum* plants.

Another distinctive feature in orchids is the column, a fleshy structure integral to the unique pollination strategies of orchids that combines the reproductive organs of stamen, style, and stigma. The reproductive techniques of orchids are some of the most fascinating, if not bizarre, in the plant kingdom and have preoccupied botanists for centuries. Orchids attract their pollinators with a variety of tricks such as insect mimicry, tantalizing odors, and slippery ramps that cause insects to be dunked in nectar then doused with pollen. Some are pollinated by only one species of insect, snail, or bat, without which the orchid cannot reproduce.

Once pollinated, orchids produce millions of microscopic seeds that are wind-dispersed, sometimes traveling long distances. Lacking food reserves, the seeds depend on specific fungi, without which they will not germinate. While the necessary nutrients can now be supplied in laboratories, permitting the orchid seeds to germinate without the fungi, those plants growing in the wild depend on a complex but fragile ecological web.

Orchid plants vary greatly in their growth forms. Three main types are recognized: saprophytic, terrestrial, and epiphytic. Saprophytes mainly grow underground and, lacking chlorophyll, absorb nutrients from decaying matter in the soil.

Temperate terrestrial orchids such as marsh orchids (*Dactylorhiza* plants) are perennial herbs that obtain nutrients from the soil, like other herbaceous plants. Most terrestrial orchids have fleshy roots or tubers for water storage and are dormant for a while, either in winter or summer. *Pleione,* a warm-temperate climate orchid, is almost entirely terrestrial but has a plump pseudobulb, unlike most terrestrial orchids.

Over half of all orchids are epiphytes, including most of the cattleyas, dendrobiums, and cymbidiums commonly seen in florists' bouquets and sold in shops. In their native habitats, epiphytic orchids are found suspended to trees, shrubs, and sometimes rocks, secured by tenacious roots. Epiphytes gather moisture from rain, fog, and dew. Nutrients mainly come from rotting organic matter. Epiphytic orchids that grow on rocks are called lithophytes.

Mostly found in the tropics and subtropics, epiphytic orchids often come from climates that dry out seasonally, with only nighttime dew for moisture. The plump pseudobulbs, or thickened stems, of many orchids are designed to store moisture and nutrients during these dry periods. Although pseudobulbs vary in size and shape, each is adapted to the vagaries of its native environment. The epiphytic moth orchids (*Phalaenopsis* plants), on the other hand, cling to trees or occasionally rocks in damp shady areas of the tropics where temperatures, rainfall, and ambient moisture are uniform.

In general, orchids are not difficult to grow, provided their basic needs are met. They require appropriate light, temperature, air circulation, moisture (watering and humidity), and nutrients. Since temperature is usually the most challenging and expensive variable to control, it is best to begin with species suited to the temperatures at hand. Vandas generally require a great deal of warmth and light and are best grown in tropical climates. On the other hand, many cymbidiums require cool night temperatures to flower. In cool- to warm-temperate climates, they perform well in bright unheated rooms where minimum winter temperatures stay above 50°F (10°C) at night. Subtropical and warm-temperate climates can support a range of warm- and cool-growing orchids, although few of the lusciously flowered orchids will tolerate any measure of frost.

While there are a few transitional orchids with exotic flowers that are nearly frost tolerant, such as *Epidendrum ibaguense* and *Cymbidium tracyanum,* most cool- to warm-temperate gardeners must rely on the rich and varied hardy terrestrial orchids outdoors and protect the more exotic types indoors in winter. Greenhouses, sunrooms, and windowsills where overnight temperatures can be maintained above 50–70°F (10–21°C) can house a variety of exquisite orchids and provide immense satisfaction.

ABOVE *Many orchids are embellished with decorative markings or spots, as seen here in* Phalaenopsis *Night Shine.* **RIGHT** *A vital component of the cut flower industry,* Dendrobium *includes such lovely hybrids as Colorado Springs.*

CATTLEYA

A member of the family Orchidaceae, *Cattleya* is a tropical American genus of about 50 species, most of which are epiphytes or lithophytes. Their sprays of large, colorful, and often fragrant flowers develop from conspicuous pseudobulbs that have 1 or 2 thick leathery leaves. They occur in a range of flower colors. The sepals and petals are similarly colored, but the lip (labellum) may be contrasting. As well as being a popular genus in its own right, *Cattleya* has been extensively hybridized with other genera.

CULTIVATION

Spectacular and reasonably tough plants, *Cattleya* are easy for beginners and often represent the next step after *Cymbidium*. They like bright, lightly shaded conditions and those with 2 leaves per pseudobulb will withstand a little winter cold. The large pseudobulbs endow them with reasonable drought tolerance, and they prefer to dry out between waterings. They may be divided when dormant into clusters of 4 or more pseudobulbs.

ABOVE *The large flowers of* Cattleya Earl *'Imperialis' are pristine white, with a bold shot of gold at the throat. The petals feature attractive ruffling along the edges.*

LEFT *Stunning cyclamen pink flowers, accented with a white labellum that is tinged with pink and gold, are the hallmark characteristics of* Cattleya loddigesii *'Impassionata'.*

RIGHT Cattleya intermedia *is a dainty orchid from Brazil. While the flowers can vary in size, shape, and color, they all carry a distinctive heady perfume.*

Favorites	Flower Color	Blooming Season	Flower Fragrance	Plant Height	Plant Width	Hardiness Zone	Frost Tolerance
Cattleya bicolor	green to greenish brown	autumn	yes	8–48 in (20–120 cm)	8–24 in (20–60 cm)	10–12	no
***Cattleya* Earl 'Imperialis'**	white	autumn to spring	yes	8–32 in (20–80 cm)	8–24 in (20–60 cm)	10–12	no
***Cattleya* Frasquita**	golden brown	autumn to spring	yes	8–32 in (20–80 cm)	8–24 in (20–60 cm)	10–12	no
Cattleya intermedia	white to deep purple	spring	yes	6–16 in (15–40 cm)	4–12 in (10–30 cm)	10–12	no
Cattleya loddigesii	white, pale pink to purple	autumn	yes	6–24 in (15–60 cm)	4–18 in (10–45 cm)	10–12	no
***Cattleya* Penny Kuroda 'Spots'**	pink; darker spotting	autumn to spring	yes	8–32 in (20–80 cm)	8–24 in (20–60 cm)	10–12	no

ABOVE *The striking combination of lustrous blooms of golden brown coupled with a hot pink labellum make* Cattleya *Frasquita an eye-catching orchid.*

Top Tip

Cattleyas grow well in plastic or terra-cotta pots. Plant in a bark-based medium, ensuring both the medium and pot allow for excellent drainage.

CYMBIDIUM

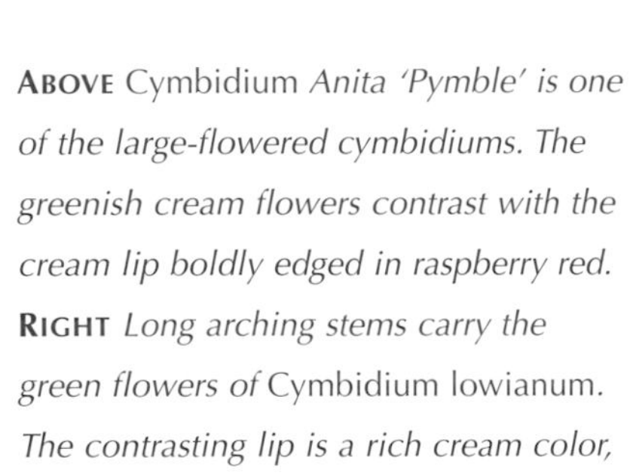

With a long history of cultivation in China and Japan, *Cymbidium* is an enormously popular genus in the family Orchidaceae. It contains around 50 species that are found from subtropical and tropical East Asia to northern Australia. Lowland species tend to be epiphytic, while those from higher altitudes are terrestrial. The pseudobulbs, which can form large clumps, each have many long strappy leaves. Borne on long stems, the flowers occur in an enormous range of colors and patterns, and most often open from winter to late spring. *Cymbidium* is one of the most important orchids for the cut-flower trade.

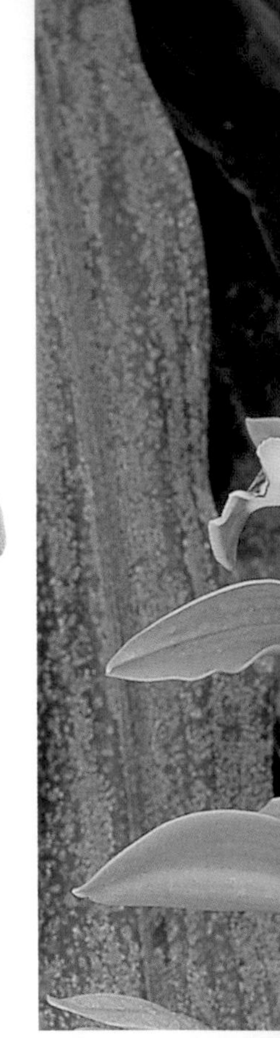

ABOVE Cymbidium *Anita 'Pymble' is one of the large-flowered cymbidiums. The greenish cream flowers contrast with the cream lip boldly edged in raspberry red.*
RIGHT *Long arching stems carry the green flowers of* Cymbidium lowianum. *The contrasting lip is a rich cream color, and features strong red markings.*

CULTIVATION

Cymbidium is the ideal choice of orchid for the beginner. Adaptable, tough, drought tolerant, and able to survive extended periods with overnight temperatures of 40°F (4°C), it is very hard to kill a *Cymbidium* but they do so much better when looked after. In winter, allow the soil to dry out before watering, but keep the plants moist when in active growth and feed regularly. Propagate by dividing the clumps down as far as single pseudobulbs.

RIGHT Cymbidium *Bolton Grange produces lovely creamy white blooms streaked with purple-red veins, while the lip is heavily edged in maroon.*

BELOW *Pure white flowers, pink tinged at the base, and a dusty pink lip spotted with maroon are the eye-catching features of* Cymbidium Baldoyle 'Melbury'*.*

Favorites	Flower Color	Blooming Season	Flower Fragrance	Plant Height	Plant Width	Hardiness Zone	Frost Tolerance
***Cymbidium* Anita 'Pymble'**	greenish cream; lip with red markings	winter to spring	no	12–48 in (30–120 cm)	8–36 in (20–90 cm)	7–11	yes
***Cymbidium* Astronaut 'Raja'**	yellow; lip with dark spotting	winter to spring	no	12–48 in (30–120 cm)	8–36 in (20–90 cm)	7–11	yes
***Cymbidium* Baldoyle 'Melbury'**	white; pink lip spotted maroon	winter to spring	no	12–48 in (30–120 cm)	8–36 in (20–90 cm)	7–11	yes
***Cymbidium* Bolton Grange**	creamy white; lip with maroon markings	winter to spring	no	12–48 in (30–120 cm)	8–36 in (20–90 cm)	7–11	yes
***Cymbidium* Bulbarrow 'Friar Tuck'**	cream; lip with maroon markings	winter to spring	no	12–48 in (30–120 cm)	8–36 in (20–90 cm)	7–11	yes
Cymbidium ensifolium	pale yellow to green	summer	yes	12–27 in (30–70 cm)	12 in (30 cm)	9–12	no
Cymbidium erythrostylum	white; yellow lip with red veining	spring to summer	no	12–27 in (30–70 cm)	8–24 in (20–60 cm)	8–10	yes
***Cymbidium* Fanfare 'Spring'**	green; cream lip with maroon markings	winter to spring	no	12–48 in (30–120 cm)	8–36 in (20–90 cm)	7–11	yes
***Cymbidium* Little Big Horn 'Prairie'**	green; cream lip with maroon spotting	winter to spring	no	12–18 in (30–45 cm)	8–36 in (20–90 cm)	7–11	yes
Cymbidium lowianum	green; cream lip with red markings	spring	no	12–48 in (30–120 cm)	8–36 in (20–90 cm)	7–11	yes
***Cymbidium* Mavourneen 'Jester'**	green with maroon markings	winter to spring	no	12–48 in (30–120 cm)	8–36 in (20–90 cm)	7–11	yes
***Cymbidium* Sumatra 'Astrid'**	dark pink; yellow lip with maroon markings	winter to spring	no	12–48 in (30–120 cm)	8–36 in (20–90 cm)	7–11	yes

BELOW *The soft green petals of* Cymbidium *Mavourneen 'Jester' mirror the lip, displaying similar pink-red "ink-blot" markings.*

ABOVE *The apple green flowers of* Cymbidium *Little Big Horn 'Prairie' are 2½–3½ in (6–9 cm) wide. The contrasting lip is cream with rich red markings.*

Top Tip

Cymbidiums are the most widely grown orchids around the world. Whether growing them inside or out, they prefer a spot with medium to high light levels.

LEFT *Sunny yellow blooms, burnished with bronze highlights, and a heavily dappled lip are the outstanding characteristics of* Cymbidium *Astronaut 'Raja'.*

Above *The cream blooms of* Cymbidium *Sumatra 'Astrid' are overlaid with dusky pink. The contrasting pale yellow lip is marked with maroon and pink.*

Below *Verdant green petals combine with a maroon-spotted cream lip to make* Cymbidium *Fanfare 'Spring' an impressive sight in any garden or home.*

Above *Simple yet stunning sums up the blooms of* Cymbidium erythrostylum. *The golden lip is marked with red-orange and is surrounded by the pristine white petals.*

DACTYLORHIZA

Commonly known as the marsh orchid, the genus *Dactylorhiza* comprises around 35 species of deciduous, tuberous, spring- to summer-flowering, terrestrial orchids. Belonging to the family Orchidaceae, they are widespread in the northern temperate zones, where they are usually found growing in moist grasslands. They form a clump of broad, often maroon-spotted basal leaves that taper to a point. Upright stems with shorter narrower leaves bear conical spikes with flowers ranging from palest pink to deep purple-red in color, usually with darker spotting. The 2-pronged tubers are quite edible and yield an extract called salep, which is reputedly very nutritious and also has some medicinal uses.

CULTIVATION

Most marsh orchids are frost hardy and easily grown in moist humus-rich soil with a position in dappled sunlight. Propagate by breaking up established clumps when dormant.

Top Tip

Marsh orchids are popular plants for cool rockeries and also do well in containers. Keep well watered in summer. Plants must be kept drier in winter.

RIGHT Dactylorhiza fuchsii, *the common spotted orchid, has maroon-spotted green leaves and abundant mauve-spotted white flowers.*

BELOW *Known as the early marsh orchid,* Dactylorhiza incarnata *is found throughout Europe. In spring and summer it produces small pink to purple-pink flowers.*

BELOW *The white blooms and bright green leaves of* Dactylorhiza fuchsii *'Rachel' will brighten the garden in summer. It makes an attractive subject for waterside planting.*

BELOW *Commonly known as the Madeiran orchid,* Dactylorhiza foliosa *bears pink to purple flowers. It has unspotted leaves, unlike many of the species in the genus.*

Favorites	Flower Color	Blooming Season	Flower Fragrance	Plant Height	Plant Width	Hardiness Zone	Frost Tolerance
Dactylorhiza foliosa	pink to purple	spring to summer	no	12–27 in (30–70 cm)	4–10 in (10–25 cm)	6–9	yes
Dactylorhiza fuchsii	pink, white, mauve	summer	no	8–24 in (20–60 cm)	4–10 in (10–25 cm)	6–9	yes
Dactylorhiza incarnata	purple-pink	spring to summer	no	8–24 in (20–60 cm)	4–10 in (10–25 cm)	6–9	yes
Dactylorhiza praetermissa	red-purple	summer	no	8–27 in (20–70 cm)	4–10 in (10–25 cm)	6–9	yes
Dactylorhiza purpurella	purple-red	summer	no	12–16 in (30–40 cm)	4–10 in (10–25 cm)	6–9	yes
Dactylorhiza urvilleana	lilac to purple	spring to summer	no	10–32 in (25–80 cm)	4–10 in (10–25 cm)	6–9	yes

DENDROBIUM

An enormously diverse genus of both hardy and tender orchids, *Dendrobium* contains up to 1,400 mainly epiphytic and lithophytic species. Members of the family Orchidaceae, they are found from China and Japan through Indonesia and the Pacific Islands to Australia and New Zealand. Some have long cane-like stems with leaves along the stems, others develop conspicuous leafy pseudobulbs and most produce their flowers on long canes. The flowers are usually quite small but abundant, varying widely in shape. Some have very narrow sepals and petals, others are broader and more rounded. The lip may be almost absent or enlarged and frilly, and the color range is huge. Few orchid genera cover as wide a latitude range as *Dendrobium:* from 45°N to 45°S.

CULTIVATION

The hardy *Dendrobium* species are seldom cultivated outside their natural range. Most interest is in the tropical species and their many hybrids, which require reasonably warm night temperatures preferably not falling below 54°F (12°C) in winter. The stems of species that produce aerial roots may be used as cuttings; those with pseudobulbs may be divided.

Favorites	Flower Color	Blooming Season	Flower Fragrance	Plant Height	Plant Width	Hardiness Zone	Frost Tolerance
Dendrobium bigibbum	white, mauve to magenta, pink	autumn to winter	no	8–36 in (20–90 cm)	8–24 in (20–60 cm)	11–12	no
Dendrobium bigibbum* subsp. *compactum	pink	autumn to winter	no	5 in (12 cm)	8–24 in (20–60 cm)	11–12	no
Dendrobium cuthbertsonii	various	spring	no	1–3 in (2.5–8 cm)	2–8 in (5–20 cm)	10–11	no
Dendrobium fimbriatum	yellow to orange	late spring	no	1–7 ft (0.3–2 m)	1–4 ft (0.3–1.2 m)	10–12	no
Dendrobium kingianum	pink, red, mauve, purple, white	late winter to spring	yes	2–36 in (5–90 cm)	4–48 in (10–120 cm)	9–11	no
Dendrobium nobile	deep purple to white	spring	yes	8–24 in (20–60 cm)	8–24 in (20–60 cm)	9–12	no
Dendrobium speciosum	white to yellow	late winter to spring	yes	4–48 in (10–120 cm)	1–10 ft (0.3–3 m)	9–11	no
Dendrobium victoriae-reginae	lilac to deep purplish blue	year-round	no	8–24 in (20–60 cm)	8–20 in (20–50 cm)	9–11	no
***Dendrobium,* Australian Hybrids**	various	winter to spring	yes	4–24 in (10–60 cm)	8–30 in (20–75 cm)	9–11	no
***Dendrobium,* "Hardcane" Hybrids**	various	year-round	no	8–40 in (20–100 cm)	8–32 in (20–80 cm)	11–12	no
***Dendrobium,* "Nigrohirsute" Hybrids**	white to cream	spring to summer	no	8–16 in (20–40 cm)	8–16 in (20–40 cm)	10–12	no
***Dendrobium,* "Softcane" Hybrids**	various	spring	no	8–24 in (20–60 cm)	6–16 in (15–40 cm)	9–11	no

LEFT Dendrobium victoriae-reginae *does best in cool moist conditions. Blooming year-round, up to a dozen cream and purple flowers are carried on each raceme.*

ABOVE *The many-flowered racemes of* Dendrobium *White Fairy—a "Hardcane" Hybrid—carry pure white flowers accented with an ivory to lemon-green lip.*
LEFT *Mauve-pink tipped blooms of pure white and a lemony yellow center are the appeal of* Dendrobium *Sailor Boy, a "Softcane" Hybrid.*
BELOW *Qualities such as compact habit, pleasant fragrance, and a color range from white to purple make* Dendrobium kingianum *a popular orchid.*

LEFT *The* Dendrobium *"Softcane" Hybrids, such as Sailor Boy 'Pinkie' pictured here, produce abundant blooms along the length of each stem.*

RIGHT *A favorite of orchid lovers,* Dendrobium *Hilda Poxon is an Australian Hybrid. This spectacular orchid bears wispy yellow-green blooms.*

BELOW RIGHT *Occurring in a range of bright colors,* Dendrobium cuthbertsonii *produces lovely large flowers that are extremely long lasting.*

BELOW Dendrobium *Sedona, one of the frost-tender "Hardcane" Hybrids, produces beautiful ivory blooms with a contrasting magenta lip.*

Top Tip

When choosing *Dendrobium* species for the garden or greenhouse, select those for which the conditions of the native habitat can be most closely matched.

LEFT *Often seen as a cut flower,* Dendrobium *Thai Pinky is one of the "Hardcane" Hybrids, which are derived from lowland tropical species.*
BELOW *An eye of darkest purple marks the otherwise pristine white blooms of* Dendrobium *Yukidaruma 'King', a member of the "Softcane" Hybrids.*

ABOVE Dendrobium *"Nigrohirsute" Hybrids are distinguished by black hairs on the pseudobulbs. Frosty Dawn bears long-lasting ivory flowers with an orange lip.*

EPIDENDRUM

There are up to 1,000 members of this orchid genus from South and Central America. A member of the family Orchidaceae, the genus contains epiphytes, lithophytes, and terrestrial species. The common "crucifix" orchids, such as *Epidendrum ibaguense*, are terrestrial species with reed-like stems and many aerial roots, but others, especially the epiphytes, often have much shorter stems. The flowers range from minute to large and are starry, with the petals and sepals held flat. A few species have very elongated, almost filament-like sepals and petals. The lip is usually long-tubed and projects from the center of the flower.

ABOVE *An unusual species from Ecuador,* Epidendrum ilense *was thought to be extinct in its native habitat, until the recent discovery of a very small population.*

CULTIVATION

Some *Epidendrum* species can tolerate very light frosts, but most require at least frost-free conditions, preferably with winter minimums above 50°F (10°C). Plant in a bright position and water and feed well while actively growing and flowering. Some species do not have a dormant period. The reed-stemmed species are propagated by removing pieces with aerial roots and growing them on, while the smaller species are divided.

Top Tip

Ideal for the orchid novice, epidendrums are easy-to-grow reliable bloomers. Plant in full sun as they tend to wane with insufficient light.

RIGHT *Bright yellow starry blooms and a delicately fringed labellum are the drawcards of* Epidendrum *Pele 'Pretty Princess'.*

BELOW RIGHT *Whether in a sunny spot in the garden or in a container,* Epidendrum *Hokulea 'Santa Barbara' will provide year-round color with its scarlet blooms.*

FAR RIGHT Epidendrum parkinsonianum *features fleshy leaves that are tinged with purple, and spidery spring blooms of greenish yellow accented with a crisp white labellum.*

Favorites

Favorites	Flower Color	Blooming Season	Flower Fragrance	Plant Height	Plant Width	Hardiness Zone	Frost Tolerance
Epidendrum ciliare	green; white lip	summer to autumn	yes	8–24 in (20–60 cm)	8–36 in (20–90 cm)	10–12	no
***Epidendrum* Hokulea 'Santa Barbara'**	scarlet	year-round	no	8–24 in (20–60 cm)	8–48 in (20–120 cm)	9–12	no
Epidendrum ibaguense	red to orange	year-round	no	8–48 in (20–120 cm)	8–48 in (20–120 cm)	9–12	no
Epidendrum ilense	pinkish green; white lip	year-round	no	8–48 in (20–120 cm)	8–24 in (20–60 cm)	11–12	no
Epidendrum parkinsonianum	green to yellow-green; white lip	spring	no	1–7 ft (0.3–2 m)	8–24 in (20–60 cm)	10–12	no
***Epidendrum* Pele 'Pretty Princess'**	yellow	year-round	no	8–48 in (20–120 cm)	8–48 in (20–120 cm)	9–12	no

BELOW *A Central American species,* Oncidium sphacelatum *needs a bright spot to produce its pendulous sprays of yellow and brown blooms in abundance.*

ONCIDIUM

Hailing from tropical America, the genus *Oncidium* belongs to the family Orchidaceae and is commonly known as the dancing lady orchid. The 650-odd species of epiphytic, lithophytic, and terrestrial multi-stemmed orchids in the genus have clustered pseudobulbs that range from hard-to-find to large and conspicuous, each with one or a few blunt-tipped strappy leaves. Most species have small yellow and brown flowers, some a little reminiscent of pansies, massed on wiry branching stems. Sometimes the sepals and petals are very much reduced, making the lip—which usually has large lobes and may be multi-colored—the main feature.

CULTIVATION

This very complex genus is allied with other genera, such as *Miltonia* and *Brassia,* and intergeneric forms are common. *Oncidium* species and hybrids require bright conditions and winter lows of not less than 50°F (10°C). Plant in a bright but shaded position with coarse, very free-draining mix and allow to dry before watering. Propagation is by division.

Top Tip

In favorable conditions, mount *Oncidium* plants on cork slabs to allow the roots freedom to develop. Smaller species often make good candidates for pot culture.

Favorites	Flower Color	Blooming Season	Flower Fragrance	Plant Height	Plant Width	Hardiness Zone	Frost Tolerance
Oncidium cebolleta	golden yellow and brown	summer	no	8–48 in (20–120 cm)	4–16 in (10–40 cm)	11–12	no
Oncidium croesus	yellow and brown	spring	no	4–8 in (10–20 cm)	4–12 in (10–30 cm)	10–12	no
Oncidium flexuosum	bright yellow	mid-summer	no	8–60 in (20–150 cm)	8–36 in (20–90 cm)	10–12	no
***Oncidium* Sharry Baby 'Sweet Fragrance'**	reddish pink, brown, and white	throughout the year	yes	8–48 in (20–120 cm)	8–36 in (20–90 cm)	10–12	no
Oncidium sphacelatum	yellow and brown	spring	no	8–60 in (20–150 cm)	8–36 in (20–90 cm)	10–12	no
***Oncidium* Sweet Sugar**	bright yellow; tan markings	throughout the year	no	8–48 in (20–120 cm)	8–36 in (20–90 cm)	10–12	no

LEFT Oncidium cebolleta *bears summer sprays of yellow and brown flowers. It is often known as a "rat's tail" oncidium—referring to its long cylindrical leaves.*

LEFT *Oncidiums are known as dancing lady orchids for their resemblance to a full-skirted dancer, as is seen in the bright yellow and tan blooms of* Oncidium Sweet Sugar.

BELOW *A miniature species from Brazil,* Oncidium croesus *produces attractive pansy-like blooms of brown and yellow in spring.*

PAPHIOPEDILUM

Commonly known as slipper orchids for the large slipper-shaped lip common to most species, this genus of around 80 species of terrestrial, lithophytic, and epiphytic orchids belongs to the family Orchidaceae. Firm favorites with orchid growers, they have long, strappy, often mottled leaves and are found from India to the Philippines and the Solomon Islands. The flowers are very distinctive, with a large erect sepal, 2 lateral petals that sometimes arch downward, and the slipper-like lip. The color range is huge and the flowers are often intricately marked. *Paphiopedilum* or paphs, as they are known, are popular buttonhole orchids, though perhaps not the near-black forms known as "macabres."

Top Tip

Slipper orchids are well suited to pot culture. Do not use too large a pot—the roots should be comfortably contained, in order to remain moist but not wet.

LEFT *In conjunction with several other species,* Paphiopedilum insigne *has played a role in the development of many of the "complex hybrids."*

RIGHT *With checkered leaves and gleaming single blooms of green and pink,* Paphiopedilum hainanense *is a beautiful species from China's Hainan Island.*

CULTIVATION

Slipper orchids are easily grown, except that meeting their temperature requirements can present difficulties. Most require warm winter nights with temperatures above 60°F (15°C). Daytime temperatures should be below 77°F (25°C) year-round. They prefer low to medium light levels and should be kept moist throughout the year, with routine feeding during the growing season. Propagate by division.

RIGHT *A popular species,* Paphiopedilum villosum *features narrow strap-like leaves and lustrous flowers in shades of green with red to maroon markings.*

Left *The green leaves of* Paphiopedilum victoria-regina *are often flushed with purple on the undersides. The exotic blooms, in shades of green, pink, and maroon, often appear throughout the year.*

Favorites	Flower Color	Blooming Season	Flower Fragrance	Plant Height	Plant Width	Hardiness Zone	Frost Tolerance
Paphiopedilum hainanense	green and pink-purple	late winter to spring	no	6–20 in (15–50 cm)	8–12 in (20–30 cm)	10–12	no
Paphiopedilum insigne	yellow-green and reddish brown	autumn to spring	no	4–18 in (10–45 cm)	8–18 in (20–45 cm)	9–11	no
Paphiopedilum rothschildianum	green and maroon	spring to summer	no	8–36 in (20–90 cm)	8–32 in (20–80 cm)	10–12	no
Paphiopedilum spicerianum	olive green and white	autumn	no	4–16 in (10–40 cm)	8–12 in (20–30 cm)	9–11	no
Paphiopedilum victoria-regina	green, maroon, and pink	throughout the year	no	4–27 in (10–70 cm)	8–24 in (20–60 cm)	10–12	no
Paphiopedilum villosum	green, brown; maroon markings	winter to spring	no	4–16 in (10–40 cm)	8–12 in (20–30 cm)	9–11	no

PHALAENOPSIS

Found from subtropical East Asia to north-eastern Australia, the genus *Phalaenopsis* contains about 60 species of epiphytic orchids in the family Orchidaceae. They form a cluster of short leathery leaves from which emerge stems with flowers that have 2 large, wing-like, horizontal petals; 3 smaller and narrower sepals; and a conspicuous, usually lobed lip. The wings are the origin of the common name—the moth orchid—though in the fancier hybrids the sepals are often almost as large, creating a rather round flower. The color range is enormous, especially in pink and gold shades. Moth orchids are popular buttonhole orchids, as any wedding guest will confirm.

BELOW *Show-stopping blooms of bright magenta-pink, with the merest hint of orange at the lip, are the hallmark of* Phalaenopsis *Queen Beer.*

RIGHT *The classic white* Phalaenopsis *hybrids are enduringly popular. Cottonwood is no exception, with its elegant form and muted colors at the lip.*

CULTIVATION

Moth orchids require winter temperatures above 54°F (12°C) and prefer comfortable day-time temperatures. Most prefer low to medium light and moderate humidity, and they need plenty of air at the roots and are consequently best grown in baskets in a very coarse mix. Small pieces with aerial roots can sometimes be taken for growing on, otherwise plants are usually bought from tissue culture specialists.

ABOVE *White petals and sepals with deep pink veining, overlaid with rose pink, frame the pink-red lip of* Phalaenopsis *Taisuco Pixie.*
RIGHT *The yellow blooms of* Phalaenopsis *Brother Golden Wish are finely spattered with deep red across their lustrous surface.*

Favorites	Flower Color	Blooming Season	Flower Fragrance	Plant Height	Plant Width	Hardiness Zone	Frost Tolerance
Phalaenopsis amabilis	white	spring to summer	yes	12–36 in (30–90 cm)	8–20 in (20–50 cm)	11–12	no
Phalaenopsis aphrodite* subsp. *formosana	cream to white	spring to summer	yes	12–36 in (30–90 cm)	8–16 in (20–40 cm)	11–12	no
***Phalaenopsis* Brother Golden Wish**	yellow-bronze	throughout the year	no	8–36 in (20–90 cm)	5–24 in (12–60 cm)	11–12	no
***Phalaenopsis* City Girl**	white; rose red lip	throughout the year	no	8–36 in (20–90 cm)	5–24 in (12–60 cm)	11–12	no
***Phalaenopsis* Cottonwood**	white	throughout the year	no	8–36 in (20–90 cm)	5–24 in (12–60 cm)	11–12	no
Phalaenopsis equestris	pink to rose purple	autumn to winter	no	4–12 in (10–30 cm)	5–12 in (12–30 cm)	11–12	no
***Phalaenopsis* Hsinying Facia**	rose pink with magenta markings	throughout the year	no	8–36 in (20–90 cm)	5–24 in (12–60 cm)	11–12	no
***Phalaenopsis* Oregon Delight**	white	throughout the year	no	8–36 in (20–90 cm)	5–24 in (12–60 cm)	11–12	no
***Phalaenopsis* Pumpkin Patch**	yellow; red-orange spotted	throughout the year	no	8–36 in (20–90 cm)	5–24 in (12–60 cm)	11–12	no
***Phalaenopsis* Queen Beer**	magenta	throughout the year	no	8–36 in (20–90 cm)	5–24 in (12–60 cm)	11–12	no
***Phalaenopsis* Quilted Beauty**	white with magenta markings	throughout the year	no	8–36 in (20–90 cm)	5–24 in (12–60 cm)	11–12	no
***Phalaenopsis* Taisuco Pixie**	white with rose pink markings	throughout the year	no	8–36 in (20–90 cm)	5–24 in (12–60 cm)	11–12	no

RIGHT *A combination of magenta stripes and tiny dots covers the white blooms of* Phalaenopsis *Quilted Beauty, complemented by a crimson and gold lip.*

Top Tip

To promote vigorous new growth, cut back stems of *Phalaenopsis* plants. This should be done only after flowering potential is exhausted and the stem has died off.

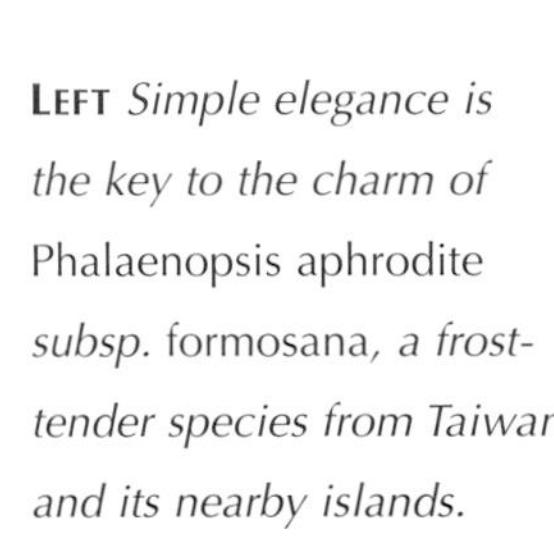

LEFT *Simple elegance is the key to the charm of* Phalaenopsis aphrodite *subsp.* formosana, *a frost-tender species from Taiwan and its nearby islands.*

ABOVE *The glistening white blooms of* Phalaenopsis *City Girl are somewhat rounded in appearance, and embellished with a lip of deepest rose red.*

LEFT *There are numerous white* Phalaenopsis *hybrids, such as Oregon Delight, and they are traditional favorites for incorporating in wedding bouquets.*

Above *The glossy golden yellow blooms of* Phalaenopsis *Pumpkin Patch are blanketed with red-orange spotting that intensifies toward the center of the flower.*

Above *The rose pink petals and sepals of* Phalaenopsis *Hsinying Facia are netted with magenta veining. The lip continues the pink theme with hints of white and gold.*

Right *The large fragrant blooms of* Phalaenopsis amabilis *are carried in pendulous sprays. Many of the white-flowered hybrids are derived from this species.*

Top Tip

Repotting pleiones in late winter each year allows for the removal of spent pseudobulbs and time for new shoots to settle in before the main growth season begins.

PLEIONE

Known for the very high prices that superior forms fetch, *Pleione* is a genus of about 20 terrestrial and epiphytic orchids. These natives of Nepal and China are members of the family Orchidaceae. Forming small clumps of narrow leaves, these unassuming crocus-like plants produce a dazzling display of orchids. The flowers are large in comparison to the plant size and have narrow petals and sepals, with a large frilly-edged lip that is often contrastingly colored. The genus name comes from Greek mythology: Pleione was the wife of Atlas and the mother of Pleiades.

CULTIVATION

Pleione species and hybrids are mostly quite hardy and easily grown with average indoor conditions on a bright but lightly shaded windowsill. They are usually grown in shallow pans and are not fussy about soil type as long as it is gritty and well-drained. Water and feed well when in active growth, but keep dry until spring once the foliage has fallen. Propagate by division.

ABOVE *The large starry blooms of* Pleione *El Pico are a vibrant hot purple-pink. The heavily fringed lip is decorated with impressive rich red spotting.*

ABOVE *As elegant as the palace name it bears,* Pleione *Versailles is a stunning hybrid with narrow petals and sepals of rich pink, adorned with a tan-spotted fringed lip.*

Favorites	Flower Color	Blooming Season	Flower Fragrance	Plant Height	Plant Width	Hardiness Zone	Frost Tolerance
Pleione **El Pico**	purple-pink	early spring	no	8–16 in (20–40 cm)	8–16 in (20–40 cm)	8–10	yes
Pleione formosana	pink	early spring	no	16 in (40 cm)	16 in (40 cm)	8–10	yes
Pleione **Shantung**	peach and cream to pink and lilac	early spring	no	8–16 in (20–40 cm)	8–16 in (20–40 cm)	8–10	yes
Pleione **Soufrière**	pink	early spring	no	8–16 in (20–40 cm)	8–16 in (20–40 cm)	8–10	yes
Pleione **Tolima**	purple	early spring	no	8–16 in (20–40 cm)	8–16 in (20–40 cm)	8–10	yes
Pleione **Versailles**	pink to purple	early spring	no	8–16 in (20–40 cm)	8–16 in (20–40 cm)	8–10	yes

BELOW Pleione *Shantung* *bears gorgeous blooms that can vary from cream hues to mauve. Pleiones generally bear large flowers relative to overall plant size.*

BOTTOM *The delicate pink coloring on the petals and sepals of* Pleione *Soufrière* *contrasts with the white labellum that is boldly spotted with bronze-red.*

VANDA

Favorites	Flower Color	Blooming Season	Flower Fragrance
Vanda coerulea	lilac-blue	spring to summer	no
***Vanda* (Gold Spots × *insignis*)**	mustard; brown spotting	throughout the year	no
***Vanda* Marlie Dolera**	deep rose and cerise	throughout the year	no
***Vanda* Miss Joaquim**	pink	throughout the year	no
***Vanda* Rothschildiana**	violet-blue; dark veins	throughout the year	no
Vanda sanderiana	pink to reddish brown	throughout the year	no

Vanda is a genus of about 50 species of epiphytic orchids in the family Orchidaceae, that are found from Himalayan India to northeastern Australia. Often tall and usually single-stemmed, each stem has 2 rows of deeply channeled, fairly short, strappy leaves and they often develop many aerial roots near the base. The flowers occur in several distinct forms, some with a much-reduced lip. Some are in solid colors, many others are mottled or spotted, and some have a large lobed lip. Those with particularly long-lasting blooms are grown as cut flowers.

CULTIVATION

Some *Vanda* species will tolerate winter lows down to 46°F (8°C), but most are more tender. They prefer bright light and plenty of summer moisture, but they should be allowed to dry over winter. High humidity is preferable. Lengths of stems with aerial roots may be removed and grown on as new plants.

ABOVE Vanda *Rothschildiana is an immensely popular hybrid, famed for its rounded purple to blue flowers, qualities inherited from the parent species* V. coerulea *and* V. sanderiana.

LEFT *Liberally dappled with brown spotting, the mustard yellow blooms of* Vanda *(Gold Spots ×* insignis*) will add a sunny glow to their surroundings.*

Plant Height	Plant Width	Hardiness Zone	Frost Tolerance
6–36 in (15–90 cm)	4–10 in (10–25 cm)	9–11	yes
8–48 in (20–120 cm)	8–20 in (20–50 cm)	11–12	no
8–48 in (20–120 cm)	8–20 in (20–50 cm)	11–12	no
8–48 in (20–120 cm)	8–20 in (20–50 cm)	11–12	no
8–24 in (20–60 cm)	8–12 in (20–30 cm)	11–12	no
8–48 in (20–120 cm)	8–20 in (20–50 cm)	11–12	no

ABOVE *Singapore was the first country to honor a hybrid as its national flower when* Vanda *Miss Joaquim was selected as its floral emblem in 1981.*

LEFT *Though it demands ideal conditions to perform well,* Vanda *Marlie Dolera will reward with beautiful cerise blooms that are centered with a deep red lip.*

Top Tip

Plant *Vanda* species in baskets or pots and place them in a well-lit spot that is out of direct sunlight. It may be necessary to stake some of the taller varieties.

ZYGOPETALUM

Native to South America, *Zygopetalum* is a genus of 16 terrestrial and epiphytic orchids in the family Orchidaceae. Most species have conspicuous pale green pseudobulbs and long narrow leaves. The flowers are the main attraction, with the maroon-mottled green sepals and petals contrasting with the large lip, which is usually white with purple-pink markings or solid pink. The small hood may be a different color. Interesting tetraploid forms have been created by treating plants with colchicine.

CULTIVATION

Zygopetalum species and hybrids will tolerate brief periods of cool conditions in winter, but prefer minimum temperatures above 55°F (12°C). They should be planted in deep pots with coarse, very free-draining potting mix and kept in a bright position, out of direct sunlight. Plants should be kept moist year-round but fed only during the growing season. Propagation is by division.

LEFT *Glossy strap-like leaves form a clump from which the erect stems emerge carrying the fragrant and eye-catching blooms of* Zygopetalum crinitum.

Favorites	Flower Color	Blooming Season	Flower Fragrance	Plant Height	Plant Width	Hardiness Zone	Frost Tolerance
***Zygopetalum* Alan Greatwood**	maroon-brown and green	autumn to winter	yes	4–16 in (10–40 cm)	4–16 in (10–40 cm)	9–11	no
Zygopetalum crinitum	yellow-green with maroon markings	winter to spring	yes	8–24 in (20–60 cm)	4–16 in (10–40 cm)	9–11	no
Zygopetalum intermedium	green with maroon-purple markings	autumn to winter	yes	4–16 in (10–40 cm)	4–16 in (10–40 cm)	9–11	no
***Zygopetalum* Kiwi Dust**	green with maroon markings	autumn to winter	yes	4–16 in (10–40 cm)	4–16 in (10–40 cm)	9–11	no
Zygopetalum mackayi	green with maroon-purple markings	autumn to winter	yes	4–16 in (10–40 cm)	4–16 in (10–40 cm)	9–11	no
***Zygopetalum* Titanic**	green with maroon markings	autumn to winter	yes	4–16 in (10–40 cm)	4–16 in (10–40 cm)	9–11	no

Above Zygopetalum intermedium *bears striking green blooms that are heavily marked with maroon. The impressive lip is white with extensive purple veining.*

Below *The maroon-brown blooms of* Zygopetalum Alan Greatwood *are edged with green. The dark coloring contrasts well with the purple-veined white lip.*

Above *A Brazilian species,* Zygopetalum mackayi *has maroon-spotted green petals and similarly colored shorter sepals, with a large white lip speckled with purple.*

Top Tip

Situate zygopetalums in a well-ventilated spot with high humidity to prevent foliage from becoming disfigured under adverse conditions.

Ferns, Palms, and Cycads

Botanically, ferns, palms, and cycads are completely different, but they are all used to add lush tropical greenery to the garden. Ferns are an extremely diverse group, but their main contribution is one of charm and grace. Palms and cycads are arguably the landscape plants with the strongest presence and form in the garden. Commanding attention with their solid trunks, stiffly arching leaves, and sometimes formidable size, they suggest grandeur and opulence like few other plants do. Cycads, although unrelated to palms, are often mistaken for them, having a central trunk from which rosettes of leaves emerge.

Above Adiantum reniforme *is an unusual maidenhair fern, because each frond has just a single, thick, leathery blade. This is a small creeping fern with short rhizomes.*

Left *Palms have leaves varying from less than 12 in (30 cm) to 70 ft (21 m) long. The cliff date palm* (Phoenix rupicola) *has arching fronds that can grow up to 10 ft (3 m) long.*

ANCIENT PLANTS FOR MODERN GARDENS

Ferns belong to a primitive group of plants known as pteridophytes. Rather than flowering and producing seeds or fruits, ferns reproduce by spores—reproductive cells that, once shed by the parent plant, grow directly into a new plant.

While their forms and sizes vary, all ferns consist of a leaf (or frond), a rhizome or stem, and roots. There are terrestrial, epiphytic, and even aquatic ferns, and their sizes vary from diminutive creepers to towering tree ferns reaching up to 50 ft (15 m) high. Contrary to popular belief, ferns are widespread in habitat, from the Arctic to the tropics. Not all ferns require moisture: there are desert ferns as well as swamp-dwellers.

While this means that there is a fern for virtually any garden, it also means that care varies greatly. However, most ferns appreciate filtered light; moist, rich, well-drained soil; and a reasonable degree of humidity. Ferns make beautiful potted specimens, often growing in lower-light areas of the house or outdoors. The Boston fern (*Nephrolepis exaltata* 'Bostoniensis') was popular during the Victorian era for its tolerance of stuffy, dimly lit parlors, and is still a popular cool-climate house plant. Suitable choices for a temperate garden include Himalayan maidenhair fern *(Adiantum venustum)*, with lacy fronds atop wiry black stems, and the Japanese painted fern *(Athyrium niponicum* var. *pictum)*, whose new fronds emerge a metallic gray suffused with pink.

Indigenous to every continent except Antarctica, palms occur as far north as southern Europe and as far south as New Zealand's North Island, with the majority occurring in equatorial climates. Their habitats range from dry bluffs and desert oases to coastal mangrove areas and freshwater swamps—even to fully aquatic environments.

BELOW LEFT *The common maidenhair fern* (Adiantum capillus-veneris) *is found worldwide in warm-temperate to tropical climates. It is a robust wiry fern, despite its dainty lacy appearance.*
BELOW *The sword ferns are generally easy to grow, and make excellent house plants. A graceful small-growing species,* Nephrolepis lauterbachii *is from the highlands of New Guinea.*

Palms are diverse in size and form—not surprising, given that there are around 2,300 species within some 190 genera. There are shrubby, tree-like, and even vining forms of palms. They range from 6 in (15 cm) to over 150 ft (45 m) in height. Foliage can be palm-shaped, ferny, or bamboo-like. The solitary or clumping trunks can be smooth, textured with the marks of former leaves, or feature rings of spines. Some species develop a "petticoat" of dried leaves. Palms are flowering plants and, while individual blossoms are small, their flower clusters and resulting fruits can be immense, sprouting from various points on the trunk or leaves. Some palms produce edible fruits, such as the date palm *(Phoenix dactylifera)*.

Most palms appreciate full sun, steady moisture, and neutral to slightly acidic soil, but some accept varying degrees of drought, shade, alkaline soil, salt spray, and frost. Perhaps the most cold-tolerant palm is the Chinese windmill palm *(Trachycarpus* fortunei), which can tolerate temperatures below 10°F (–12°C). Quite a few palms from arid grasslands and deserts can survive a fair amount of drought.

Cycads resemble palms, but are not related. Consisting of some 250 species within 11 genera, they come from warm-temperate to tropical regions and range in size from almost trunkless ground-huggers like *Zamia pygmaea* to the Kwango giant cycad *(Encephalartos laurentianus),* reaching some 50–60 ft (15–18 m) in height. While both cycads and palms produce similar rosettes of leaves at the top of a woody trunk, cycad leaves are much tougher, stiffer, and often shorter.

Cycads are known to have lived over 200 million years ago, and these ancient plants are botanically closer to conifers than to palms. Cycad plants are dioecious (they have male and female reproductive structures borne on separate plants). Both male and female cycads produce a rosette of leaves emerging from a central point at the top of a single trunk or several trunks. At the center emerges a cone that, on female plants, bears red or orange seeds.

Several species of cycad are grown in gardens. Particularly popular is the sago cycad *(Cycas revoluta),* often cultivated in warm-climate gardens or in pots in cooler climates. The sago cycad is known for its tidy elegant appearance and for its relative cold hardiness to 15°F (–9°C). Also seen is guayiga *(Zamia pumila).* Both species, along with a number of others, make superb and long-lived container specimens as well as distinguished subjects for beds and borders in warm climates. Requiring only good drainage (many species grow in sand or poor soils) and plenty of light, most cycads do best when watered and lightly fertilized, but are nevertheless quite tolerant of drought conditions.

ABOVE Cycas revoluta *has male and female plants. The female flowerhead looks like an array of feathers. These extremely slow-growing plants are the most widely grown cycads.*
BELOW LEFT *Date palms* (Phoenix dactylifera) *have been grown for thousands of years. They make good landscaping plants.*

ADIANTUM

Commonly known as maidenhair fern, this cosmopolitan genus of about 200 terrestrial fern species in the brake (Pteridaceae) family includes some popular indoor plants. They feature a wide range of frond colors: new growths are often pink and red, maturing to shades of green, and are sometimes variegated. The black or brown stems are thin and shiny, with oblong or fan-shaped leaflets. Spores are produced around the edge of the leaflets. The genus name comes from the Greek *adiantos*, meaning dry, unmoistened, or unwettable, because the leaflets appear to be waterproof.

CULTIVATION

Adiantum species require organically rich loams, which should be kept just moist. Surface mulching should be provided in humid semi-shaded situations. Soil pH requirements vary with the species. These plants need plenty of light, but should be protected from direct sun and wind. They can be propagated from spores or by division.

Favorites	Plant Height	Plant Width	Hardiness Zone	Frost Tolerance
Adiantum excisum	12–20 in (30–50 cm)	12–20 in (30–50 cm)	9–12	no
***Adiantum excisum* 'Rubrum'**	12–20 in (30–50 cm)	12–20 in (30–50 cm)	9–12	no
Adiantum hispidulum	12–20 in (30–50 cm)	12–20 in (30–50 cm)	9–12	no
Adiantum pedatum	12–24 in (30–60 cm)	12–24 in (30–60 cm)	4–9	yes
Adiantum peruvianum	32–40 in (80–100 cm)	32–40 in (80–100 cm)	10–12	no
Adiantum raddianum	18–24 in (45–60 cm)	18–24 in (45–60 cm)	11–12	no

ABOVE Adiantum raddianum *is a popular fern that features fronds with delicate lacy leaflets. It has given rise to many cultivars, such as 'Waltonii' seen here.*

BELOW Adiantum hispidulum *is commonly known as rosy maidenhair—a reference to its bronzy pink new growth. The fronds gradually mature to dark green.*

Top Tip

Maidenhair ferns are very popular indoor plants. They need a well-ventilated spot with a humid atmosphere—bathrooms often offer the ideal environment.

ARCHONTOPHOENIX

An eastern Australian genus, *Archontophoenix* contains 6 species of slender-trunked feather palms in the family Arecaceae. They have rather open foliage heads and the slightly twisted fronds are of moderate length, sometimes with rather drooping leaflets. The trunks are prominently ringed and often bulge slightly near the base. Flower stems emerge at the base of the crownshaft, bearing many small mauve-pink flowers that develop into red fruits. The central bud mass or "cabbage" is edible but would be a survival food only.

BELOW LEFT *Commonly known as the bangalow or piccabeen palm,* Archontophoenix cunninghamiana *has a crown of drooping mid-green fronds.*

BELOW RIGHT *Found in a small region of Far North Queensland, Australia, the fronds of* Archontophoenix purpurea *emerge from a purplish gray crownshaft.*

Top Tip

Fast-growing *Archontophoenix* species will bring an exotic tropical element to the garden, but when young these palms should be grown in light shade.

CULTIVATION

Most *Archontophoenix* species are able to tolerate occasional very light frosts but are best grown in mild areas in sun or half-shade with moist, well-drained, humus-rich soil. These palms are very popular because of their predictable growth and tidiness: they don't constantly shed fronds or debris. They are also widely cultivated as container plants. Propagate from fresh seed.

Favorites	Plant Height	Plant Width	Hardiness Zone	Frost Tolerance
Archontophoenix alexandrae	50 ft (15 m)	15 ft (4.5 m)	10–12	no
Archontophoenix cunninghamiana	60 ft (18 m)	15 ft (4.5 m)	10–11	no
Archontophoenix purpurea	80 ft (24 m)	15 ft (4.5 m)	9–12	no

ASPLENIUM

Common throughout the tropics and subtropics and extending into the temperate zones, *Asplenium* is a grouping of around 600 species of mostly terrestrial evergreen ferns. It is the type genus for the spleenwort (Aspleniaceae) family. These ferns spread by scaly rhizomes and rarely develop a trunk. The fronds are variable and may be feathery and finely divided, pinnate, or long, leathery, and undivided. Fertile and sterile fronds have the same shape. Some species are used in modern herbal medicines, and the genus takes its name from the Greek *a* (not) and *spleen* (spleen), in reference to its medicinal properties.

BOTTOM *Slender stems, up to 6 in (15 cm) long, hold the dark green fronds of* Asplenium sagittatum, *an Australian species often known as mule's fern.*

ABOVE *The lustrous bright green fronds of* Asplenium scolopendrium *'Crispum Speciosum' have a pleated appearance, and sometimes feature yellow striping.*

CULTIVATION

Hardiness varies, and many *Asplenium* species are frost tender. Plant in a cool shaded position with ample humus, moisture, and humidity. Several of the species are cultivated as indoor plants because they can tolerate low light and cool drafts. Propagate by division, from spores, or by removing and growing on the plantlets that form on the fronds of some species.

Favorites

Favorites	Plant Height	Plant Width	Hardiness Zone	Frost Tolerance
Asplenium bulbiferum	24–48 in (60–120 cm)	24–48 in (60–120 cm)	9–11	no
Asplenium nidus	18–60 in (45–150 cm)	18–60 in (45–150 cm)	10–12	no
Asplenium sagittatum	4–6 in (10–15 cm)	4–6 in (10–15 cm)	8–10	yes
Asplenium scolopendrium	8–24 in (20–60 cm)	8–24 in (20–60 cm)	4–10	yes
Asplenium scolopendrium 'Kaye's Lacerated'	8–24 in (20–60 cm)	8–24 in (20–60 cm)	4–10	yes
Asplenium trichomanes	3–16 in (8–40 cm)	3–16 in (8–40 cm)	2–6	yes

Top Tip

Though diverse in appearance, all *Asplenium* species will appreciate occasional feeding—this will ensure the production of lush dark green foliage.

ATHYRIUM

Athyrium is a genus of about 100 species of evergreen and deciduous terrestrial ferns that are widespread in the temperate and tropical zones. Members of the shield-fern (Dryopteridaceae) family, they have short scaly rhizomes and spread to form small clumps. The sometimes brittle fronds are usually bipinnate and may be very finely divided but are seldom very long. The common lady fern *(Athyrium filix-femina)* often produces interestingly mutated fronds and it was a particular favorite with nineteenth-century collectors—so much so that it was, for a brief time, endangered in the wild.

CULTIVATION

Hardiness of these ferns varies with the native range of the species. Plant in moist humus-rich soil in shade or dappled sunlight. Propagate by division or from spores. Some of the species produce plantlets that can be removed and grown on.

Favorites	Plant Height	Plant Width	Hardiness Zone	Frost Tolerance
Athyrium filix-femina	2–5 ft (0.6–1.5 m)	3–7 ft (0.9–2 m)	3–6	yes
***Athyrium filix-femina* 'Vernoniae'**	2–5 ft (0.6–1.5 m)	3–7 ft (0.9–2 m)	3–6	yes
Athyrium niponicum	12–15 in (30–38 cm)	20–24 in (50–60 cm)	3–6	yes
Athyrium niponicum* var. *pictum	12–15 in (30–38 cm)	20–24 in (50–60 cm)	3–6	yes
Athyrium otophorum	12–18 in (30–45 cm)	15–24 in (38–60 cm)	4–8	yes
Athyrium otophorum* var. *okanum	12–18 in (30–45 cm)	15–24 in (38–60 cm)	4–8	yes

Top Tip

Athyrium species need to be kept well watered during summer. Mist leaves to provide additional moisture. Protect young fronds from slugs and snails.

ABOVE RIGHT Athyrium filix-femina *has feathery bright green fronds that can be spreading or arching. This species has given rise to hundreds of cultivars.*

RIGHT Athyrium niponicum var. pictum *is known as the Japanese painted fern—so-named for the new fronds that are metallic gray tinged with red or blue.*

CHAMAEDOREA

A Central American genus containing around 100 species of feather palms, *Chamaedorea* belongs to the family Arecaceae. Most of the species do not form a single trunk but instead develop into a cluster of cane-like stems, which better suits their natural role as understory plants. The fronds are not always divided and may remain until maturity in the "fishtail" form often seen in juvenile *Chamaedorea*. The sprays of yellow-green to orange flowers can appear at any time of year. The male and female flowers are borne on separate plants, and female flowers develop into fruits. The unopened inflorescences of some species are eaten by local peoples.

CULTIVATION

Chamaedorea species are very frost tender but surprisingly tolerant of cool conditions, which along with their compact growth has made them popular as indoor plants. Plant in part- or full shade with moist humus-rich soil, preferably in a warm humid area. They are mostly propagated from seed, though it is occasionally possible to remove a rooted sucker.

TOP RIGHT *In stark contrast to the matt green fronds of* Chamaedorea microspadix, *the small single-seeded berries that follow the green female flowers are colored vivid scarlet.*

RIGHT Chamaedorea elegans, *commonly known as the parlor palm, is an extremely popular indoor plant, beloved for its attractive appearance, slow growth, and easy-care nature.*

Top Tip

Limited space can often restrict plant choice. Potted *Chamaedorea* palms can add tropical ambience and can be placed indoors or out.

Favorites	Plant Height	Plant Width	Hardiness Zone	Frost Tolerance
Chamaedorea elegans	6 ft (1.8 m)	3 ft (0.9 m)	10–12	no
***Chamaedorea elegans* 'Bella'**	6 ft (1.8 m)	1 ft (0.3 m)	10–12	no
Chamaedorea geonomiformis	5–7 ft (1.5–2 m)	4 ft (1.2 m)	10–12	no
Chamaedorea microspadix	8 ft (2.4 m)	10 ft (3 m)	10–12	no
Chamaedorea plumosa	10–12 ft (3–3.5 m)	5–8 ft (1.5–2.4 m)	9–12	no
Chamaedorea stolonifera	3–5 ft (0.9–1.5 m)	3–5 ft (0.9–1.5 m)	9–11	no

CYCAS

The 60-odd species in this genus are ancient plants, and have been traced back to prehistoric times. Members of the cycad (Cycadaceae) family, these slow-growing woody-stemmed plants are palm-like in appearance, and are mostly natives of tropical and subtropical habitats. A crown of bright green glossy foliage emerges from the top of the sturdy trunk. The male and female cones develop on separate plants. Several species can be garden grown, though they do best in climates similar to their native environment. In cooler climates, some of the forest dwellers have adapted to indoor conditions.

CULTIVATION

Though they can tolerate periods of drought, *Cycas* species perform best when planted in well-drained soil in full sun. They can be propagated from seed or by removing and rooting dormant buds which can be taken from the mature plants' trunks.

Favorites	Plant Height	Plant Width	Hardiness Zone	Frost Tolerance
Cycas angulata	25–40 ft (8–12 m)	6–12 ft (1.8–3.5 m)	9–11	no
Cycas circinalis	15 ft (4.5 m)	15 ft (4.5 m)	10–12	no
Cycas media	15 ft (4.5 m)	10 ft (3 m)	10–12	no
Cycas revoluta	10 ft (3 m)	6 ft (1.8 m)	9–12	no
Cycas rumphii	20–30 ft (6–9 m)	10–12 ft (3–3.5 m)	9–11	no
Cycas taitungensis	10–15 ft (3–4.5 m)	5–10 ft (1.5–3 m)	8–10	no

Top Tip

Cycas species are stunning plants, but are extremely slow growing. For more immediate results mature plants can be purchased, but these can be costly.

TOP *The sago palm,* Cycas circinalis, *often forms several trunks, with a dense crown of lustrous green arching fronds topping each gray-brown trunk.*

LEFT Cycas media *is native to northern Australia. When its stiff, glossy, dark green fronds eventually fall, they leave a hatched pattern of scars on the stout trunk.*

NEPHROLEPIS

Widespread in the tropics, *Nephrolepis* is a genus of around 40 species of terrestrial and epiphytic ferns in the family Oleandraceae. They have short rhizomes and spread by fine wiry runners that can often be seen cascading from plants growing in trees or in pots. The fronds, which are often held erect and can be long, are usually simply divided with opposite pairs of leaflets of similar length. Fertile fronds may differ slightly, having narrower leaflets. The genus as a whole has become known as Boston fern because of the enormous popularity of *Nephrolepis exaltata* 'Bostoniensis', a nineteenth-century cultivar discovered in Boston, Massachusetts, USA.

BELOW LEFT *The long yellow-green to dark green fronds of* Nephrolepis cordifolia *carry many leathery leaflets. Frost tender, it is otherwise adaptable and easy to grow.*

ABOVE *Impressive in hanging baskets, where the leaflets can flutter in the breeze,* Nephrolepis exaltata *is more commonly seen in the form of its many cultivars.*

CULTIVATION

Boston ferns are frost tender but are easily grown in mild areas in full or part-shade with moist humus-rich soil and steady high humidity. Some species are rapid colonizers and are considered serious weeds in several countries. They can be propagated by division or from spores.

Favorites	Plant Height	Plant Width	Hardiness Zone	Frost Tolerance
Nephrolepis cordifolia	12–48 in (30–120 cm)	12–48 in (30–120 cm)	11–12	no
***Nephrolepis cordifolia* 'Duffii'**	18–24 in (45–60 cm)	18–24 in (45–60 cm)	11–12	no
Nephrolepis exaltata	36 in (90 cm)	36 in (90 cm)	11–12	no
***Nephrolepis exaltata* 'Bostoniensis'**	36 in (90 cm)	36 in (90 cm)	11–12	no
***Nephrolepis exaltata* 'Childsii'**	6–12 in (15–30 cm)	6–12 in (15–30 cm)	11–12	no
Nephrolepis falcata	8 ft (2.4 m)	5 ft (1.5 m)	9–11	no

Top Tip

Boston ferns are widely cultivated as indoor plants. In cooler climates, if they are grown in heated indoor situations, ensure they receive plenty of bright filtered light and ample water.

PHOENIX

This feather palm genus in the family Arecaceae is made up of around 7 species found from the Canary Islands through the Mediterranean and Arabia to East Asia. Most have strong trunks ringed with old leaf bases and long, gracefully arching fronds. Large golden-stemmed sprays of yellow flowers are followed by soft, single-seeded, orange to near-black fruits. *Phoenix* species yield many products, including the dates of commerce, other fruits, sugar syrup from the sap, and an edible central "cabbage." Also, the fronds have been used as temporary thatching material.

CULTIVATION

Hardiness varies, as does the summer heat requirement. The Canary Island date palm *(Phoenix canariensis)* is the least demanding species and will tolerate moderate frosts and cool summers. Others, such as the date palm *(Phoenix dactylifera)*, need hot summers and some need subtropical conditions. Plant in sun or half-shade with light well-drained soil. They are propagated mainly from seed but will grow from suckers.

Top Tip

Phoenix species are adaptable to a range of soil types, but will do best in fertile soil. Keep the plants well watered, particularly while establishing.

Favorites	Plant Height	Plant Width	Hardiness Zone	Frost Tolerance
Phoenix canariensis	70 ft (21 m)	30 ft (9 m)	9–11	yes
Phoenix dactylifera	70 ft (21 m)	30 ft (9 m)	9–12	no
Phoenix loureiroi	6–15 ft (1.8–4.5 m)	12 ft (3.5 m)	10–12	no
Phoenix reclinata	40 ft (12 m)	25 ft (8 m)	9–11	no
Phoenix roebelenii	10 ft (3 m)	8 ft (2.4 m)	10–12	no
Phoenix rupicola	25 ft (8 m)	15 ft (4.5 m)	10–12	no

ABOVE RIGHT *The lush bright green fronds of* Phoenix rupicola *sprout fountain-like from the crown of the slender trunk.*

TOP RIGHT Phoenix canariensis *features a crown of long arching fronds atop a stout trunk. Cream to yellow flowers are followed by orange fruits.*

POLYSTICHUM

A cosmopolitan genus in the shield-fern (Dryopteridaceae) family, *Polystichum* is composed of around 175 species of evergreen and deciduous terrestrial ferns. They have strong, woody, scaly rhizomes that may be spreading or erect, sometimes developing into a short stocky trunk. The fronds are often stiff and bristly, leathery, very dark green, and long, sometimes with scaly undersides. The fronds are usually bipinnate and may be very finely divided. The fertile fronds appear similar. The soft shield fern *(Polystichum setiferum)* often produces cristate or otherwise mutated fronds, and unusual forms are popular with collectors.

RIGHT *Distinguished by the rough dry scales that coat the fronds,* Polystichum polyblepharum *var.* fibrilloso-paleaceum *otherwise resembles the species.*

CULTIVATION

Many *Polystichum* species are very hardy and are among the toughest ferns. They appreciate cool, moist, humus-rich soil in shade or dappled sunlight, but can survive in drier brighter locations. While not overly invasive, the strong rhizomes are difficult to remove and some species are local weeds. Propagate by division in spring or from spores in summer.

ABOVE *An attractive evergreen fern native to 2 very different regions—eastern North America and the Portuguese island of Madeira—* Polystichum falcinellum *has bright green sword-shaped fronds.*

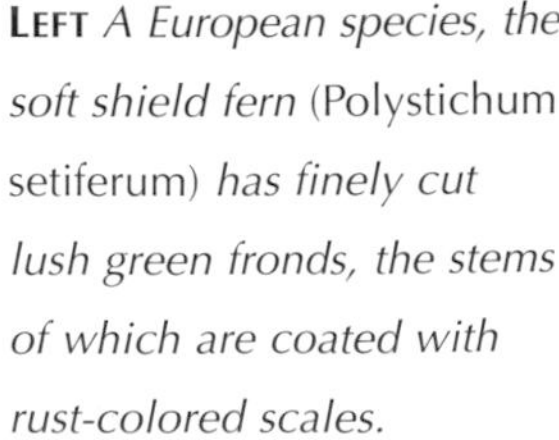

LEFT *A European species, the soft shield fern* (Polystichum setiferum) *has finely cut lush green fronds, the stems of which are coated with rust-colored scales.*

ABOVE Polystichum setiferum, *Divisilobum Group, 'Herrenhausen' is an attractive dwarf cultivar that forms a dense clump of arching, dark green, leathery fronds with finely cut leaflets. This easily grown fern is an excellent subject for container planting.*

Favorites	Plant Height	Plant Width	Hardiness Zone	Frost Tolerance
Polystichum acrostichoides	18–24 in (45–60 cm)	18–24 in (45–60 cm)	3–9	yes
Polystichum aculeatum	18–24 in (45–60 cm)	18–24 in (45–60 cm)	4–8	yes
Polystichum andersonii	24–30 in (60–75 cm)	24–30 in (60–75 cm)	4–8	yes
Polystichum braunii	24–36 in (60–90 cm)	24–36 in (60–90 cm)	4–8	yes
Polystichum californicum	20–30 in (50–75 cm)	20–30 in (50–75 cm)	7–9	yes
Polystichum falcinellum	18–24 in (45–60 cm)	18–24 in (45–60 cm)	5–8	yes
Polystichum munitum	36–48 in (90–120 cm)	36–48 in (90–120 cm)	4–6	yes
Polystichum polyblepharum	48 in (120 cm)	48 in (120 cm)	5–9	yes
Polystichum setiferum	18–24 in (45–60 cm)	18–24 in (45–60 cm)	5–7	yes
***Polystichum setiferum* 'Divisilobum'**	18–36 in (45–90 cm)	18–36 in (45–90 cm)	5–7	yes
Polystichum* × *setigerum	18–24 in (45–60 cm)	18–24 in (45–60 cm)	3–6	yes
Polystichum tsussimense	6–18 in (15–45 cm)	12–16 in (30–40 cm)	6–9	yes

LEFT Polystichum andersonii *is a North American fern commonly known as Alaskan holly fern or Anderson's sword fern. Numerous leaflets are packed along each of the sword-shaped fronds.*
BELOW LEFT *Braun's holly fern* (Polystichum braunii) *features silvery new growth that ages to dark green. The leaf undersides and stalks are coated with scales.*

Top Tip

Delicate in appearance but fairly robust in nature, *Polystichum* species are ideal for shady borders and rock gardens, and also make great container plants.

LEFT *The fine fronds of* Polystichum setiferum 'Divisilobum Densum' *bunch together to create a lush bright green burst of foliage.*

BELOW *Held on stems covered with orange to brown scales, the large sword-shaped fronds of* Polystichum setiferum 'Divisilobum' *are finely cut.*

ABOVE Polystichum polyblepharum, *a species from Japan and South Korea, is commonly known as the tassel fern. The lacy fronds droop down as they unfurl, creating a tassel-like effect.*
LEFT *The yellowish green new growth of* Polystichum aculeatum *matures to shiny dark green. This robust plant is known as hard shield fern or prickly shield fern.*

SABAL

Favorites	Plant Height	Plant Width	Hardiness Zone	Frost Tolerance
Sabal bermudana	40 ft (12 m)	10 ft (3 m)	10–11	no
Sabal causiarum	50 ft (15 m)	20 ft (6 m)	9–12	no
Sabal mexicana	60 ft (18 m)	12 ft (3.5 m)	9–12	no
Sabal minor	10 ft (3 m)	12 ft (3.5 m)	8–11	yes
Sabal palmetto	80 ft (24 m)	15 ft (4.5 m)	8–12	yes
Sabal uresana	25 ft (8 m)	10 ft (3 m)	8–12	yes

Commonly known as palmetto, *Sabal* comprises around 16 species found from southern USA to northern South America and the Caribbean. Belonging to the family Arecaceae, some are low and clumping, while others have tall sturdy trunks. The fronds are often blue-tinted, sometimes quite large and the leaflets are usually narrow and sometimes sharp-tipped. Sprays of small cream flowers open from late spring and are followed by small black fruits. The central "cabbage" is edible, though harvesting it destroys the plant. Native Americans used the fronds in basketry and other weaving.

CULTIVATION

The hardier *Sabal* species are among some of the tougher palms and will survive reasonably hard winters provided the summers are warm enough and long enough to encourage steady growth. Plant in full sun or half-sun with light well-drained yet moisture-retentive soil. Water well when young and during active growth. Propagation is usually from seed, although rooted suckers can occasionally be removed.

LEFT *An elegant palm perfect for tropical gardens,* Sabal bermudana*—commonly known as the Bermuda palmetto—has a single stem with a crown of fan-shaped fronds.*

BELOW *Commonly known as the Puerto Rico hat palm,* Sabal causiarum *is a single-stemmed palm with fan-shaped fronds of bright green to blue-green.*

ABOVE *Found from Texas to Mexico,* Sabal mexicana *is a single-trunked palm that displays a crown of light green to bright green deeply divided fronds.*

LEFT *A native of southeastern USA,* Sabal palmetto *is the state tree of both South Carolina and Florida. The single stem bears fan-shaped fronds of blue-green.*

Top Tip

When in active growth, palmettos will benefit from routine feeding. A neat and tidy appearance will be maintained if dead fronds are cut back.

TRACHYCARPUS

A member of the family Arecaceae, *Trachycarpus* contains 6 species of palms found in southern China and the Himalayan region. They are tall and have medium-sized bright green fronds with fairly narrow leaflets and sometimes spiny leaf stalks. The most distinguishing feature is the thick thatch of hairy fibers that cover the trunk. The large sprays of soft yellow flowers are followed by small grape-like fruits that ripen to steel blue or black. The unopened inflorescences of some species are eaten raw or cooked by local peoples, and extracts of the roots are used medicinally. The fiber from the trunks has been used to make ropes and coarse cloth.

CULTIVATION

Hardy for palms, *Trachycarpus* species are easily cultivated in temperate to subtropical regions and will grow in sun or light shade. Give them moist, well-drained, humus-rich soil to ensure lush foliage. Propagate these palms from fresh seed in spring.

Favorites	Plant Height	Plant Width	Hardiness Zone	Frost Tolerance
Trachycarpus fortunei	35 ft (10 m)	12 ft (3.5 m)	8–11	yes
Trachycarpus martianus	50 ft (15 m)	10 ft (3 m)	9–11	yes
Trachycarpus wagnerianus	10–20 ft (3–6 m)	8 ft (2.4 m)	9–10	yes

Top Tip

Although they are reasonably hardy, *Trachycarpus* species are easily damaged by wind, and should be planted in a sheltered position.

ABOVE *The single trunk of* Trachycarpus fortunei *bears old leaf bases and a dense covering of fibers. The fan-shaped fronds are deep green.*

LEFT *Many palms are impractical for smaller gardens, but smaller palms such as* Trachycarpus wagnerianus *can provide a tropical element in a limited space.*

WASHINGTONIA

A genus of just 2 species of tall fan palms found in southwestern USA and northwestern Mexico, *Washingtonia* is a member of the family Arecaceae. They have strongly erect, very narrow trunks, a feature that has made them popular avenue trees. The fronds make a dense head at the top of the trunk and often form a thick thatch or "skirt" of dead fronds around the crownshaft. Fiercely hooked teeth edge the frond stalks and small fibrous hairs hang from the fronds. The clusters of cream to soft pink flowers develop into small edible fruits. The foliage has been used for weaving and thatching. These days, though, *Washingtonia* is best known as the symbol of the palm-lined boulevards of Los Angeles.

CULTIVATION

Both species tolerate moderate frost and are quite adaptable. They prefer to be slightly shaded when young, and although drought tolerant they grow best with moist well-drained soil. They are propagated from seed, which germinates freely and remains viable for a long period of time.

Favorites	Plant Height	Plant Width	Hardiness Zone	Frost Tolerance
Washingtonia filifera	50 ft (15 m)	25 ft (8 m)	9–11	yes
Washingtonia robusta	80 ft (24 m)	25 ft (8 m)	9–11	yes

Top Tip

The characteristic "skirt" of old fronds that is typical of *Washingtonia* species can pose a fire hazard. Where possible, old fronds should be removed to reduce fire risk.

RIGHT *Sometimes known as the petticoat palm for its "petticoat" of persistent old fronds,* Washingtonia filifera *has a stout gray trunk and gray-green fronds.*

RIGHT Washingtonia robusta *is a tall-growing palm with a slender trunk. Reaching a height of up to 80 ft (24 m), this palm is best suited to parks and larger gardens.*

ZAMIA

The type-genus of the family Zamiaceae, *Zamia* is made up of around 55 species of cycads from the American tropics and subtropics. The tuber-like stem is usually subterranean but may be partly emergent, forming a short trunk. The pinnate fern- or palm-like leaves often emerge directly from the soil and have thick leathery leaflets. Male and female cones are borne on separate plants and some species may drop some of their foliage as the cones mature. The seeds within the cones are often very toxic. The starchy stems, however, were used by local peoples to make a type of bread.

Favorites	Plant Height	Plant Width	Hardiness Zone	Frost Tolerance
Zamia fairchildiana	8 ft (2.4 m)	5 ft (1.5 m)	11–12	no
Zamia furfuracea	3 ft (0.9 m)	7 ft (2 m)	11–12	no
Zamia loddigesii	5 ft (1.5 m)	5–6 ft (1.5–1.8 m)	9–12	no
Zamia pumila	5 ft (1.5 m)	6 ft (1.8 m)	10–12	no
Zamia splendens	5 ft (1.5 m)	4–10 ft (1.2–3 m)	10–12	no
Zamia vazquezii	5 ft (1.5 m)	4–10 ft (1.2–3 m)	9–12	no

CULTIVATION

Most *Zamia* species are intolerant of frost. To thrive they require lightly shaded, warm, humid conditions with moist, humus-rich, well-drained soil. Keep well watered during active growth. Propagate from fresh seed.

ABOVE Zamia furfuracea, *a native of Mexico, is commonly known as the cardboard palm. The spiny stalks carry pairs of stiff olive green leaflets that can be toothed.*
LEFT *Appearing among the often dense foliage, the cylindrical pink to brown male and female cones of* Zamia furfuracea *are borne on separate plants.*

Top Tip

Though best suited to tropical or subtropical climates, *Zamia* species make excellent container plants for cooler regions and may be kept outdoors in summer.

Glossary

Achene A small, dry, single-seeded fruit resulting from fertilization of a single carpel of a flower.
Acid (of soils) Having a pH below about 6. The more strongly acid soils are mostly high in organic materials such as peat; lime (calcium carbonate) is completely absent from them. Acid soils dominate in regions of higher rainfall. See also ALKALINE.
Aerial (of plant parts) Arising anywhere above the ground.
Air layering A technique of propagation whereby a branch is stimulated to root by cutting the bark and then wrapping a moisture-retentive medium such as sphagnum moss around the wound; the medium is then wrapped in air-tight plastic. When roots form, the branch is cut off and planted in soil.
Alkaline (of soils) Having a pH above about 8. Alkaline soils usually contain lime in the form of calcium carbonate or calcium hydroxide. They occur naturally in regions of lower rainfall. See also ACID.
Alpine (of plants) Those adapted to high mountain environments where they are usually blanketed in snow during winter; they may be damaged by very severe frosts if not protected by snow, and in cold climates are therefore grown in "alpine houses" under glass. Alpine vegetation is the low herbs and shrubs growing above the treeline on high mountains.
Alternate (of the arrangement of leaves on a stem) Arising one from each node in a staggered formation.
Anemone-form (of a cultivar) Having a double flower with an outer circle of relatively flat petals around a dome of crowded inner petals or staminodes.
Angiosperms The flowering plants, now classified as division Magnoliophyta, defined by possession of true flowers and seeds fully enclosed in fruit. The vast majority of the world's larger land plant species are angiosperms, the main exceptions being the conifers, cycads, and ferns.
Annual A plant species or variety with a life span of one year or less, within which time it flowers and fruits. Annuals depend entirely on seeds for reproduction.
Anther The pollen-containing part of a stamen, the other part being the filament (stalk).
Aquatic A plant species that grows in water for at least the greater part of its life cycle. Aquatics are divided into submerged, emergent, and floating.
Arctic (of climates) Those of lands above the Arctic Circle (latitude 66 deg 30 min North).
Areole Characteristic organ of the cacti (Cactaceae) family situated at each stem node: a small area or point from which emerge spines, bristles, and hairs, also leaves (often tiny or short lived) and potentially flowers.
Aromatic (of plant smells) Those of a spicy, resinous, or musky character, and often associated with foliage or fruit, whereas sweet-smelling flowers are normally described as "fragrant."
Aspect The way a slope faces, which determines how much sunshine it receives, and at what time of day; or more generally the outlook of a part of a house or garden especially in relation to sunlight.
Axil The inner angle between an organ such as a leaf and the organ that supports it, usually a stem.
Axillary (of buds, flowers, inflorescences) Arising from a leaf axil.
Bamboo Member of the bamboo subfamily of the grass (Poaceae) family, plants with long-lived aboveground stems, usually hollow, with thick strong walls and grassy leaves.
Bark Outer layer of stem containing protective corky and fibrous tissues as well as the phloem which conducts sugary sap downward. Bark is best developed in trees, often becoming very thick with age.
Basal At or near the base of a plant's trunk, stem, leaf, etc.
Bean Pod or plant of legume genera, used as vegetables or pulses, or applied more loosely to various leguminous (or even non-leguminous) plants with bean-like fruits.
Bedding plants Mostly compact colorful plants used for ornamental effect when mass-planted in display beds; traditionally annuals, short-lived perennials, or bulbs, but more recently frost-tender foliage plants, shrubs, and grasses have become widely used for summer bedding.
Berry In botanical usage, a fleshy fruit in which seeds are embedded without being surrounded by a hard or fibrous layer (as in a drupe). Blueberries and tomatoes are examples. In popular usage, berries include such fruits as blackberries and mulberries which are quite different in structure.
Biennial A plant that completes its life cycle within two years and then dies. It may flower and fruit in each of the two years, or only in the second year.
Bipinnate (of compound leaves) Divided pinnately into leaflets (pinnae) that are themselves further divided into smaller leaflets (pinnules). Examples include *Gleditsia* and *Jacaranda*.

Bisexual (of plants) Having flowers or cones of both sexes on the one plant; (of flowers) having both functional male and functional female organs present.
Blade The flat part of a leaf, as opposed to the stalk.
Bloom General term for a flower or flower-like inflorescence such as a daisy; or, on leaf or fruit surfaces, a thin, delicate, white or bluish film of wax, as on grapes or plums.
Blossom A flower, or flowers in mass as on orchard trees, or used to designate the part of a fruit bearing floral remains, as in the "blossom end" of a pumpkin or marrow *(Cucurbita)* as opposed to the "stalk end."
Bole The trunk of a tree below the first branch.
Bolting (of leaf vegetables) Progressing too early from production of edible leaves or shoots to elongation of inflorescence, flowering, and seeding; a response to planting too late in the season or to interruptions in watering or fertilizing.
Botrytis Botanically, a genus of microscopic fungi that cause rots in some flowers and fruits, perhaps best known for producing "noble rot" of wine grapes left too long on the vine, which when finally picked produce sweet wines of a remarkable flavor.
Bract A modified leaf associated with a flower or inflorescence; not to be confused with a sepal, though in some plants bracts may mimic sepals.
Bristle A stiff outgrowth of a plant organ such as a stem, leaf, sepal, or fruit; intermediate between a prickle and a hair, as is seen on the stems of some rose species.
Bud The early stage of a flower or group of flowers, or of a leafy shoot (vegetative bud), before expanding or elongating.
Budding A propagation technique similar to grafting, except that the scion is no more than a single vegetative bud sliced off with a sliver of bark, inserted in contact with the rootstock's cambium through a slit in its bark and bound securely until the tissues unite.
Bulb Storage organ of herbaceous perennials consisting of expanded fleshy leaf bases arranged in concentric layers. A bulb is known as tunicate if the leaf bases are all encircling, as in an onion, or referred to as scaly if they are narrower with overlapping edges, as in a lilium.
Bulbil, bulblet Small bulb or bulb-like shoot developing from the base of a parent bulb or from various other parts of a plant, e.g. from the leaf axils in some *Lilium* species, or from the inflorescence in some onions; readily used for propagation.
Cactus (plural cacti) Any member of the large American plant family, Cactaceae, consisting mainly of spiny, leafless, succulent plants. There are many other succulents that are not cacti, although the name is often carelessly applied to them.
Calyx (plural calyces) The lowest or outermost of the layers attached to the receptacle of a flower. The calyx consists of sepals, that may be separate or partly or fully fused and which are commonly green, contrasting with the more colorful petals.
Cambium Layer of continuously dividing cells forming the boundary between wood and bark in the stems of dicotyledons and conifers. The dividing cells lay down tissues on either side, wood on the inner and bark on the outer, resulting in the stem increasing in diameter as long as growth continues.
Campanulate Bell-shaped, as in many campanulas.
Cane (in gardening) A long straight branch produced by one season's growth, as in raspberries. The cane of commerce comes from bamboos or climbing palms (rattans).
Canopy (of a tree) The whole of the foliage and outer parts of branches, being the part of the tree that shades the ground; (of a forest) the uppermost layer of tree crowns.
Capsule A non-fleshy fruit derived from an ovary of two or more carpels that opens to release its seeds.
Carpel The fundamental unit of a flower's gynoecium (female organ), usually differentiated into an ovary, and a narrower style which receives pollen. Carpels may be single or multiple in one flower, and multiple carpels are often fused together.
Catkin A type of spike, often pendulous, found mostly in wind-pollinated plants, with small flowers of reduced structure and usually of one sex only.
Caudex A more or less fleshy, long-lived, usually unbranched stem supporting a crown of fronds, as seen in cycads, or smaller branches and foliage in some desert plants.
Central spines In cacti, the spines that stick straight out (more or less) from an areole, in contrast to the radial spines that radiate in a plane tangential to the plant body. Number, size, and other features of central and radial spines are often diagnostic for a cactus species.
Cephalium In cacti, an area of stem, often at or near its apex but sometimes lower on the stem, from which flowers emerge each year from a mass of bristles and/or woolly hairs.
Cereal The edible grain harvested in quantity from certain grasses grown as crops, including wheat, barley, oats, rye, maize, and millet.
Chlorophyll The green pigment in plants, mainly in leaves, that with the aid of light energy combines carbon dioxide from the air and water from the soil to create the sap sugars that are the building blocks of plant cell-wall materials such as cellulose and lignin. The process is known as photosynthesis.

Claw In flowers, any basal narrowing of an organ such as a petal into a slender stalk-like portion (as in the petals of *Lagerstroemia*), in which case the petal is said to be "clawed."

Clay Mineral substance forming the finest particles in most soils, swelling and becoming sticky when wetted. Clays consist primarily of hydrous aluminium silicates with smaller amounts of other minerals that are of major importance to plant nutrition.

Climber A plant species or variety able to climb to heights that its own stem could not support, allowing it to reach sunlight that might otherwise be blocked by competing plants. A variety of mechanisms enable climbers to support themselves on other plants, including tendrils, spirally twining stems, clinging roots, hooked thorns, or even leaves with reflexed stalks.

Clone A group of plants that are genetically identical, usually resulting from propagation using cuttings, grafts, layers, division, or tissue culture. Most tree and shrub cultivars are single clones and repeated propagation can spread one clone around the world, e.g. *Rosa* 'Iceberg'.

Column (in orchids) The fleshy structure in the flower's center consisting of fused style, stigma, and stamens. Similar structures are found in some other plant families.

Columnar (of growth habit) More or less resembling a column or cylinder in shape.

Common name Name of a plant species that is not its botanical or scientific name and has no scientific status. Common names are generally in the language of the country where the plant is growing. A species may have many common names, or if obscure may never have acquired any.

Compost Decayed or decaying organic matter used in gardening to improve soil or as a mulch. Any plant material can be converted to compost by heaping it and keeping it moist, encouraging breakdown by fungi, bacteria, worms, and microfauna. Addition of animal manure or nitrogenous fertilizer will hasten the process. Other animal products such as meat or fish scraps can also be added, though with the disadvantage of bad smell or attraction of vermin. Good compost management and container design will promote spontaneous heating, which should kill weed seeds or bulbs as well as shortening composting time.

Cone Reproductive organ of gymnosperms (conifers and cycads), consisting of scales arranged around a central axis; pollen cones have scales bearing tiny pollen sacs, while seed cones have scales with seeds attached to the surface.

Conifer Member of the largest group of gymnosperms, the conifers, now classified as division Pinophyta; mostly trees with seeds and pollen borne in separate cones and leaves mostly needle-like or scale-like, containing resin. Largest conifer genera are *Pinus, Abies,* and *Picea.*

Conservatory An attachment to a house, glass-roofed or at least with glass external walls, in which tender plants may be grown.

Container Any item in which a plant may be grown out of the ground, such as pots, tubes, hanging baskets, and tubs. In the nursery industry container-grown plants are the major alternative to bare-rooted plants at point of sale.

Cool-temperate (of climatic regions) Those in the cooler half of the temperate zone, where winter frosts and snow are of regular occurrence; lands at sea level that lie approximately 40 to 60 degrees latitude.

Cordate (of leaves) Heart-shaped, with an indentation where the leaf stalk joins at the base; also used to describe the leaf base only, irrespective of the overall shape.

Corm A swollen stem modified for the purpose of food storage and annual renewal, with a new corm or section of corm added above each growing season and an old one withering below.

Corolla A collective term for the petals of a flower, which may be separate or wholly or partly fused into a tube, bell, or disc; the tubular part is then termed the corolla tube and the flared part the corolla limb, which may consist of corolla lobes (the free ends of the petals).

Corona A crown-like part of a flower, consisting of a ring of fused outgrowths from either the petals (as in *Narcissus* species) or stamens.

Corymb An inflorescence, usually a modified raceme, in which the stalks of the lower flowers are elongated to bring them to the same level as the upper flowers.

Cotyledon The first leaf produced by a germinating seed.

Creeper A plant species or variety that can rapidly spread horizontally over the soil surface to cover an area of ground (when alternatively called a prostrate or groundcover plant), or vertically to cover a wall or tree trunk, usually clinging by aerial roots or adhesive pads (as in *Parthenocissus* species). A vertical creeper may also be called a climber, but there are many climbers that are not creepers.

Crest (of irises) Ridge-like projection along the center-line of each of the fall (lower) petals near the petal base; (in cacti and other succulents) a plant of any species with a growth aberration resulting in the growing point extending sideways into a line, which may become wavy or convoluted. Sometimes termed CRISTATE.

Cristate Adjective for any plant organ of crest-like form. For cacti and succulents, see CREST.

Crop A planting of a single species or cultivar covering a large area and most often numbering thousands of plants, usually of annuals or biennials, and usually of edible plants. Common crop plants are cereal grains, pulses, and broad-acre vegetables such as potatoes or cabbages.
Cross A less formal term for hybrid, also applicable to plants resulting from cross-pollination of different races or cultivars within a species.
Cross-pollination The transmission of pollen from one plant to another plant that is not part of the same clone or cultivar, with resulting fertilization of its flowers.
Crown The part of a tree held up by the trunk, consisting of limbs, smaller branches, twigs, and foliage.
Crownshaft Part of some palms, formed by the sheathing frond bases wrapped around one another to form a smooth, usually green cylinder that forms an apparent continuation of the trunk.
Culm The erect stem, usually hollow, of grasses including bamboos and some other monocots such as sedges and rushes, as contrasted to the rhizome from which it arises. In most such plants it terminates in the inflorescence but in bamboos the culms may hardly ever bear flowers.
Culinary herb A herb (in the popular not the botanical sense) that is grown for use in cooking, or more doubtfully in salads, rather than for its medicinal properties.
Cultivar A cultivated variety that has been given a distinguishing name. A cultivar is assumed to be constant in its horticultural qualities and able to be propagated with those qualities unaltered. Tree and shrub cultivars are nearly always single clones, selected either from the variation within a species or from hybrid seedlings between two or more species. Modern cultivars must be given names of non-Latin form. Their names are enclosed in single quotes and are capitalized, e.g. 'Golden Delicious'.
Cultivar group A group of cultivars sharing a common character or origin, e.g. *Prunus* Sato-zakura Group.
Cultivated (of a plant species) Established in cultivation with its requirements known to gardeners.
Cutting A piece of plant stem (more rarely of leaf, root, or rhizome) cut off the plant for purposes of propagation; its lower end is inserted in soil or a sterile medium until roots form and a new plant is obtained.
Cycad Member of the second largest group of gymnosperms after the conifers, now classified as division Cycadophyta; plants with palm-like fronds and very large cones, the pollen and seed cones on separate plants. The largest genera are *Cycas, Encephalartos, Macrozamia,* and *Zamia.*
Cyme Inflorescence in which each branch is terminated by a solitary flower, with new flowering branches emerging laterally below the flower. If lateral branches are paired it is known as a dichasial cyme; if single, a monochasial cyme.
Daisy Flowerhead of family Asteraceae, more specifically those types with conspicuous ray florets radiating from the central mass of disc florets, e.g. shasta and ox-eye daisies, though the original English daisy is *Bellis perennis*. Also used as a collective term for the entire family, although many of its genera do not have the daisy type of flowerhead.
Deadhead To remove spent or dead flowers on a regular, often daily basis, both for reasons of tidiness and to prolong flowering season by preventing the plant's food resources going into fruit and seed development.
Deciduous (of a plant species) Losing all leaves at a certain season of the year. This usually occurs in winter in the case of cool-climate species, and most often in the dry season in the case of tropical species.
Dehiscent (of fruits) Splitting open at maturity to release seeds.
Dentate (of leaf margins) With a row of more or less triangular teeth.
Dicotyledon (or dicot) The larger of the two great classes into which the flowering plants (angiosperms) are divided—the other being the monocotyledons. As the name implies, dicotyledons have two seed leaves and additionally they mostly have net-veined leaves, flower parts in multiples of four or five, and a cambium layer in the stems.
Digitate (palmate) Type of compound leaf in which the leaflets are all attached to the apex of a common stalk, their individual stalks radiating out like the spokes of an umbrella. Also used to describe a pattern of lobing in which the lobes appear to radiate out from a central point, as in *Acer palmatum*.
Dioecious (of a plant species) With male and female flowers borne on different plants, so that plants of both sexes need to be present for pollination and fruit set. Flowers can be termed dioecious if of different sexes though borne on the same plant.
Disease Any kind of ill health or disfigurement of a plant caused by micro-organisms such as bacteria, viruses, fungi, or nematodes, or by deficiency or excess of a particular nutrient element.
Disc floret One of the individual small flowers that make up the central disc of a daisy flower (family Asteraceae), especially when these differ from the outer circle of longer-petalled ray florets, as in a sunflower.
Dispersal The natural spread of a plant to new sites, usually by seed but sometimes by bulbs, pieces of stem, or even detached leaves. A species' dispersal mechanism is

the way it ensures this spread, e.g. by wind-carried seed, fruits eaten by birds which pass the seed, or by fruits that hook onto animal fur or human clothing.

Dissected (of leaves, bracts, petals, etc.) Deeply divided into many small or narrow segments.

Diurnal (of a species' flowering habit) Opening its flowers during the daytime, generally in the morning.

Division The most simple means of propagation of most clump-forming perennials, usually achieved by lifting the entire plant out of the soil or its container, and cutting through the root-crown or rhizomes with a sharp blade or, for some plants, just pulling apart, into two or more pieces, which are then replanted. Also one of the higher levels of plant classification (see also CLASS); the flowering plants are now treated as the division Magnoliophyta.

Dormant In a state of suspended growth of a plant, usually during winter or other adverse season, and usually in a leafless state.

Double (of garden flowers) Having more than the regular number of petals occurring in the wild form.

Drainage (of soils or growing media) The means by which excess water is enabled to flow away by gravity, so opening up air spaces needed by the roots of most plants for absorption of gases, principally oxygen. In gardens, good drainage is ensured by raising of beds, improving soil texture, or inserting special drainage pipes and/or gravel beds beneath the soil. In container-grown plants drainage is achieved by adequate number and size of holes in the base, and sometimes by the addition of a layer of coarse rot-resistant material below the growing medium, which itself should be open and free-draining.

Drupe A fleshy fruit in which the seeds are separated from the outer flesh by a hard inner layer of bony, woody, or fibrous tissue, such as in plums or olives.

Elliptic (of leaves, petals, etc.) In the shape of an ellipse but commonly with both ends more or less pointed, with the widest part at the mid-point of the length.

Endemic (of a species, genus, etc.) Occurring in the wild only in one readily defined geographical region, e.g. *Kalmia latifolia* is endemic to North America; *Eucalyptus tetraptera* is endemic to Western Australia.

Entire (of margins of leaves, leaflets, petals, etc.) Smooth, without indentations or projections such as teeth or lobes.

Epiphyte (of a plant species) One that habitually grows in the wild on the branches or trunk of a tree, well above the ground. Epiphytes do not feed on living tissues of their host but on dead bark, leaf litter, and dust, often using a symbiotic fungus to extract nutrients from these. Most cultivated orchids are epiphytes.

Erect Directed vertically upward or almost so.

Escape (or garden escape) A plant that has dispersed from where it was planted to nearby places, most often by seed (see DISPERSAL) or sometimes from dumped garden waste, but which may not have become fully naturalized.

Espalier A tree or shrub trained into a single vertical plane along a trellis or against a wall.

Essential oil Highly aromatic oil present in various parts of certain plants, often in minute cavities (oil glands), in leaves, petals, or fruit (e.g. in lemon rind), or mixed with resins as a surface exudation (e.g. in pelargoniums). In many plants the oil is a mixture of several pure oils such as peppermint oil (piperitol), lemon oil (citral), or oil of thyme (thymol) in varying proportions. Originally termed "essential" oils because each was considered the essence of a particular perfume.

Everlasting Mostly species of the daisy (Asteraceae) family with flowerheads surrounded by dry, colored, often translucent bracts that resemble ray florets; often the bracts do not deteriorate as the flowerhead ages and dies, making the bloom "everlasting" and suitable for dried arrangements. All species of *Helichrysum, Rhodanthe, Xerochrysum,* and *Xeranthemum* are classed as everlastings.

Evergreen (of a plant species) Maintaining its foliage through all seasons, although old leaves may be shed in larger numbers in certain seasons.

Eurasia Term used for the combined continent of Europe and Asia, usually including their major islands such as the British Isles and Japan.

Exotic (of a plant species) One that is not native to the country or region in question.

Family The next major category above genus in plant classification. A family may contain a single genus (e.g. Cercidiphyllaceae) or many genera (e.g. Fabaceae with approximately 650 genera). In modern systems all family names end in -aceae though the *International Code of Botanical Nomenclature* allows some traditional alternatives including Leguminosae (for Fabaceae) and Compositae (for Asteraceae). A family name is grammatically a plural.

Fan palm One of the two major types of palm in terms of frond structure, with a fan-shaped frond (leaf) in which segments radiate from the end of the frond stalk. See also FEATHER PALM.

Fancy Used for classes of cultivars of certain genera, mostly with multi-colored foliage (as in *Pelargonium*, Zonal Hybrids, Fancy-leaf) or bi- or multi-colored flowers (as in *Dianthus*, Garden Pinks, Fancy).

Feather palm One of the two major types of palm (see also FAN PALM) in which frond segments or leaflets are arranged along either side of a midrib, giving the whole frond a feather-like appearance.
Female (of flowers) Possessing no functional male organs, only female; (of plants) producing only female flowers or cones.
Fern Member of the largest living group of pteridophytes, the Filicopsida, characterized by fronds bearing wind-carried spores which germinate to produce small, delicate, sexual plantlets (gametophytes) with male and female organs. These rely on water droplets for fertilization, producing a new spore-bearing plant.
Fertile (of soil) Having adequate amounts of the major and minor mineral nutrients for plant growth; (of plants or flowers) bearing viable sexual organs.
Fertilize (in gardening and agriculture) To add nutrients to soil; (in botany) to bring pollen to a stigma and effectively pollinate it so that the pollen nucleus combines with the egg nucleus in the ovule.
Fertilizer Any material added to the soil to provide nutrients for plants, including compost, manure, manufactured chemicals such as urea, potassium sulfate, or superphosphate, and liquid extracts such as fish emulsion.
Filament The stalk of a stamen, bearing the anther at its tip.
Fimbriate Fringed with hairs or very narrow fine lobes.
Floret Any one of the small flowers that make up a dense inflorescence.
Flower The reproductive organ of all members of the flowering plants (angiosperms) consisting typically of a perianth that is often differentiated into calyx and corolla, a group of stamens that release pollen, and one or more carpels containing ovules that on fertilization develop into seeds. Many flowers are reduced in structure with some of these parts missing.
Flowerhead Any dense cluster of flowers of more or less regular size, including a head (capitulum) in the strict botanical sense.
Foliage Leaves and twigs in mass, a term used only in the singular.
Follicle A fruit derived from a single carpel that splits open along one side or across its apex in order to release the seeds.
Forma A level in botanical classification below species, subspecies, and variety, normally applied to a variation in a single character that may recur in wild stands. Thus *Gleditsia triacanthos* forma *inermis* differs from typical *Gleditsia triacanthos* only in being thornless. Abbreviated as f., and referred to as "form" in English.
Frond Any large, much-divided or compound leaf that to a non-botanist might appear to consist of many leaves. The leaves of palms and tree ferns are usually referred to as fronds.
Frost The condition of air temperature falling below the freezing point of water (32°F or 0°C), resulting in formation of ice crystals if the air contains moisture. Because cold air sinks, frost may occur at soil level when temperature at the standard meteorological measuring height (5 ft or 1.5 m) is several degrees above freezing. In dry air there may be no ice crystals (hoar frost) formed but plant foliage may be killed; such an event is known as a black frost.
Frost hardy (of plant species, varieties, or cultivars) Able to withstand exposure to frost without damage to foliage, stems, or whatever parts normally persist through winter. Frost hardiness is entirely relative to climate, e.g. *Abutilon megapotamicum* survives the light frosts in the hills of southeastern Australia (Zone 8) but will not survive outdoors in the interior of Britain (Zone 7); and while *Araucaria araucana* tolerates winters in most parts of Britain, it is killed outright by winter frost in northeastern USA (Zone 5).
Fruit (in the botanical sense) The seed-containing organ of any of the flowering plants, whether fleshy or dry. Usually one fruit is developed from one flower.
Genus (plural genera) The next level of botanical classification above species. The genus name can stand by itself, e.g. *Quercus* (the oak genus) but it also forms the first part of a species name, e.g. *Quercus rubra* (the red oak).
Germination The emergence of a new plant from a seed, mostly requiring absorption of water by the seed and certain temperature and light levels.
Glabrous (of plant parts) Lacking any covering of hairs or scales.
Glaucous (of leaves, stems, fruits) Having a bluish cast due to a surface film of wax or a wax-impregnated cuticle, and so modifying the green color from the chlorophyll in the underlying tissues.
Globose Roughly spherical in form.
Graft The joining of two different plants, one termed the stock (or rootstock) with lower stem and roots, the other termed the scion cut from a branch, so that their tissues fuse at the junction. The aim of grafting is to "borrow" vigor or disease resistance from the rootstock for the more desirable scion, or to enable vegetative propagation of a cultivar that is difficult to raise from cuttings. The stock must be compatible for grafting to succeed, belonging to a closely related cultivar, species, or genus—for example Hybrid Tea roses grafted onto *Rosa multiflora* stock. There are many different techniques of grafting. See also BUDDING.

Grain The small dry fruit of any grass, though more popularly used for the cereals and grasses grown as food crops.

Grass In the botanical sense, any member of the very large monocot family Poaceae (alternative name Gramineae), though in common use the taller members of the bamboo subfamily (Bambusoideae) are not generally called grasses. Most grasses are annuals or herbaceous perennials with linear leaves; they have greatly reduced flowers borne in specialized inflorescence units called spikelets. They include the major crop plants wheat, oats, barley, rye, maize, millet, and sorghum.

Greenhouse An enclosed structure with roof of transparent or translucent material, traditionally glass but nowadays usually plastic, in which plants are grown, its purpose being to raise the temperature of their environment and so protect them from winter frost and/or promote faster growth even in summer in cool climates. Greenhouses may be heated artificially or unheated, relying on their capacity to absorb and trap solar radiation. In normal use a greenhouse is a high-roofed structure distinguished from a frame, cloche, tunnel, or "igloo." The term greenhouse is now preferred over both glasshouse and hothouse.

Grex All the progeny of a cross between two species or two other grexes (or a species and a grex), regardless of when and where the crossing occurred; a concept applied in practice in only in a few groups of plants, notably orchid and rhododendron hybrids. A grex name is similar in form to a cultivar name but without quotation marks, and may precede a cultivar name, e.g. *Rhododendron* Avalanche 'Alpine Glow'. A single grex may include many named cultivars.

Ground cover Any plant that can spread to effectively blanket an area of ground in a garden. Most ground covers used in landscaping are longer-lived prostrate plants, but creepers and many stoloniferous or rhizomatous plants (e.g. *Fragaria*) are often used as well.

Growing season The season in which growth of a plant takes place. In cool-temperate climates this is nearly always between spring and the end of summer, in drier tropical climates growth usually takes place during the wet season.

Growth habit The overall form or shape of a plant.

Gymnosperm That large class of plants that reproduce from seeds but bear them more or less exposed on the scales of a cone, rather than fully enclosed in a fruit (as in the flowering plants or angiosperms). Gymnosperms lack true flowers. They are now considered a stage of evolution rather than a natural group derived from a single common ancestor. The two major gymnosperm groups are conifers and cycads. There are also four evolutionary "dead ends" with a single genus each, namely *Ginkgo, Ephedra, Gnetum,* and *Welwitschia.*

Habitat (of a species) The sum of geographical location, topography, soil, and vegetation type in which a species is normally found wild.

Hair Any fine hair-like outgrowth from the surface of a plant part. A hair that is noticeably flattened is usually termed a scale.

Half-hardened Used of cuttings to distinguish those taken from close to the tips of actively growing shoots, though not so close that they are still very soft and tender. An alternative term is "semi-ripened."

Half-hardy (of plant species) Able to survive occasional light frosts, of down to around 25°F (–4°C), especially when in a state of dormancy.

Hardwood (of tree species) Having a hard timber, though more traditionally signifying any dicotyledonous (broadleaf) tree as opposed to a softwood or conifer, regardless of relative hardness or density of timber; (of cuttings) taken from stems that are mature and more or less woody, whether from the last season's or the current season's growth.

Hardy (of a species or cultivar) Able to survive and thrive in a hostile environment; but gardeners in colder climates have generally narrowed its meaning to frost hardy.

Heath Vegetation type dominated by low wiry shrubs, usually treeless, occurring on boggy, acid, infertile soils. Also shrubs of the genus *Erica,* or more generally any small-leafed shrub of family Ericaceae or its Australasian counterpart Epacridaceae.

Hemisphere One half of the earth's surface, most commonly the Northern or Southern Hemisphere, divided by the equator, although historically Eastern and Western Hemispheres were just as important, the latter centered on the Americas.

Herb (in botany) A plant with non-woody stems; (in gardening and cookery) an edible plant that adds flavor rather than bulk to both cooked dishes or salads; (in medicine) a plant that is believed to have healing or health-giving properties and is used in various medicinal preparations.

Herbaceous (in botany) The adjectival form of herb; (in gardening) usually taken to refer to perennials that die back each winter to a rootstock, rhizome, or tuber.

Herbal (adjective) Indicating origin from herbs in the third sense above, i.e., used for medicinal purposes; (noun) a book, usually first published several centuries ago, describing all plants used medicinally and detailing their uses.

Herbicide Any poison used to kill plants, or more specifically weeds; nowadays nearly all being chemicals that have very low toxicity to humans. A selective herbicide is one that, at a prescribed dilution, kills one class of plants without harming another, e.g. broad-leafed weeds growing among lawn grasses.

Hermaphrodite (of flowers) Having fully functional male and female organs present in the same flower.

Hip (or hep) The fruit of roses *(Rosa)*, comprising a fleshy hollowed-out receptacle that develops from the flower's receptacle, to the inner surface of which are attached the dry "seeds" (achenes or nutlets), each derived from a single carpel.

Horticulture The practice of growing plants, and other aspects of gardening. Commercial horticulture (as opposed to agriculture) embraces the growing of fruit, nuts, and cut-flowers, as well as the nursery and landscape industries.

House plant Any plant grown full-time for ornament inside a house, generally being a species or cultivar able to tolerate low light levels and other adverse environmental factors associated with house interiors.

Humus The organic matter in soil, derived in nature from leaf and twig litter, dead roots, and decayed tree trunks; in gardens it can be added in the form of compost, manure, or peat. Humus greatly improves soil by retaining moisture and mineral nutrients and keeping the soil open and well aerated.

Hybrid The progeny resulting from fertilization of a species, variety, or cultivar by a different species, variety, or cultivar, combining the genetic makeup of both. The progeny of hybrids continue to be hybrids. Botanical names of hybrids between two species are indicated by the multiplication sign "×" inserted in one of two positions, namely: (a) where no hybrid name has been published—between the names of the two parent species, e.g. *Freesia alba* × *F. leichtlinii*; (b) where a hybrid name has been published for a hybrid between two species—before the epithet, e.g. *Magnolia* × *soulangeana* [*M. denudata* × *M. liliiflora*]; where three or more species are involved in a hybrid, the "×" sign is not used; the resulting hybrid may be given a grex name, as in rhododendrons, or a cultivar name is used directly following the genus name, as in modern roses.

Hybrid cultivar A cultivar selected and named from the progeny of a cross. The variation found in hybrid progeny is greater than within wild species, thus giving more scope for selection of cultivars. In the case of a cultivar derived from a named cross between two species, the cultivar name may follow the epithet, e.g. *Magnolia* × *soulangeana* 'Burgundy'. If originating from three or more species and/or earlier hybrids, the cultivar name may follow directly after the genus name, e.g. *Rhododendron* 'Markeeta's Prize', or sometimes after a grex name, if one has been registered.

Imbricate (of leaves, petals) Overlapping the adjacent leaves or petals, like shingles on a roof.

Incised (of leaf or petal margins) With an edging of deep, narrow, finely pointed teeth.

Incurved (of leaves, etc.) With margins curved upward and inward, as opposed to recurved.

Indehiscent (of fruit types) Not splitting open at maturity to release their seed, as opposed to dehiscent. Most fleshy fruits are indehiscent.

Indigenous (of plant species or subspecies) Forming part of the original natural flora of a country or region (though not necessarily endemic).

Indoor In horticulture, general term for any enclosed growing environment, whether in a house, conservatory, or greenhouse.

Inflorescence Specialized flower-bearing branch of a plant, together with the flowers on it.

Informal (of garden flowers, mainly "double" cultivars) Having the petals (and sometimes also the stamens and staminodes) loosely and irregularly arranged.

Insecticide A substance, nowadays usually of synthetic chemical origin, used to kill insect pests (see also PESTICIDE). Modern insecticides are mostly designed to target biochemical processes specific to insects or even particular types of insects, and to have low toxicity to humans and other vertebrate animals.

Internode The interval between two successive nodes in a plant stem or twig.

Introduced (of plant species) Not native (indigenous) to the country or region in question; usually implying deliberate introduction by humans.

Invasive (of a species or cultivar) Tending to spread well beyond the place where it was planted in the garden, whether by seeds, rhizomes, etc., and thereby becoming a nuisance.

Involucre A ring or cup of bracts beneath a flower or group of flowers, as in most members of the daisy (Asteraceae) family.

Irregular (of flowers) Not having the petals, sepals, and/or stamens arranged like the spokes of a wheel and of equal shape and size in the one whorl. Zygomorphic flowers are irregular, e.g. *Salvia*, but so are flowers with no symmetry.

Juvenile (of leaves or leafy shoots) Showing the characteristics of seedling leaves; e.g. in mulberries juvenile leaves are deeply lobed. The first shoots from lopped branches often revert to the juvenile type.

Keel (in flowers of the pea subfamily of the legume (Fabaceae) family) The two fused lower petals which usually project forward and enclose the stamens; (of leaves) having the midrib projecting like the keel of a boat or forming a sharp "V" in cross-section.
Labellum In an orchid flower, the usually large and distinctively shaped petal that commonly juts forward from the flower's center; it is technically the upper of the three petals (or inner perianth segments), but because most orchid flowers have stalks twisted through 180 degrees, it may appear to be the lower. The various protuberances and color patterns on an orchid labellum are nearly always adaptations to attract and guide pollinating agents, principally insects.
Laciniate (of leaf or petal margins) Divided into very deep, narrow, finely pointed lobes.
Lateral On the sides of a plant part, such as a branch or leaf, as opposed to its apex or base.
Lax With a loose, open, or floppy habit, as seen in the branches of many trailing plants.
Layering Propagation method by which branches are encouraged to produce roots and are then detached to be grown as new plants. Most basically it is simply the mounding of soil or damp sand around bases of multiple stems or sucker growths; or lower branches are bent down and pegged against the ground, often cut halfway through, until they take root. When a plant's lower branches spontaneously root where they touch the ground, it is said to be "self-layering." See also AIR LAYERING.
Leaf The plant organ primarily responsible for photosynthesis.
Leaflet One of the leaf-like parts that make up a compound leaf.
Legume Any member of the large plant family Fabaceae (alternative name Leguminosae), characterized by their fruits like peas or beans. Most have root nodules containing bacteria that can convert the air's nitrogen into a form that the plant can utilize. This large family is divided into three subfamilies, with the largest subfamily containing all the pea-flowered legumes, another subfamily containing mimosas and acacias, and the third subfamily containing bauhinias and cassias (among many other genera). In botany the term "legume" has also been used to describe the fruit type.
Limb (of trees) The larger branches that spring directly from the trunk, as opposed to smaller branches and twigs; (of flowers) the part of an elongated corolla that spreads outward, in contrast to the corolla tube.
Lime Mineral component of or additive to soil, always a form of the element calcium. Quick lime is calcium oxide, slaked or hydrated lime calcium hydroxide, crushed limestone calcium carbonate—all are alkaline or at least neutralize acidity in soils, making certain nutrients more available to plants, others less so.
Linear (of leaves) Narrow in relation to length, used for leaves that are more than about eight times longer than their width.
Lip An upper or lower lobe, or group of several lobes, of the usually tubular corolla of a flower with a single vertical plane of symmetry (zygomorphic). Most such flowers are 2-lipped, e.g. *Salvia*.
Lithophyte A plant species that habitually grows on rocks, virtually in the absence of soil. Many epiphytes are also capable of growing as lithophytes.
Loam A soil in which the proportions of clay, sand, and silt are fairly evenly balanced and the humus content is adequate. A clay loam is one with higher clay content, a sandy loam is one with more sand.
Lobe (of leaves) A large projection of the margin, generally one that measures at least a third of the distance from the leaf's midrib to its outer edge.
Male (of flowers or cones) Having only pollen-bearing organs, though in some male flowers non-functional (vestigial) female organs may also be present; (of plants) producing only male flowers or cones.
Manure Any organic material used as fertilizer, though nowadays generally understood as the excreta of animals, in particular domestic herbivores such as cattle, horses, sheep.
Margin (of a leaf) The edge.
Mediterranean (of countries) Those bordering the Mediterranean Sea; (of climates) those of warm-temperate regions with hot dry summers and rainfall concentrated in the winter months—they occur on the west-facing coasts of the continents and include California, Chile, southwestern South Africa, and southwestern and southern Australia, as well as the Mediterranean itself.
Microclimate The climate of any small area as modified by local topography, vegetation, structures, or activities, in contrast to the regional climate. For example, the shelter of trees or masonry walls may create a frost-free microclimate in an otherwise frosty climate. Microclimates are an important part of plant habitats, both in gardens and in the wild.
Midrib A leaf's main central vein, usually thickened and slightly projecting on at least one surface.
Mist In meteorological terms, the slow falling of tiny water droplets that are light enough to be blown around by wind; (in plant propagation and indoor growing) the use of fine nozzles that give a mist-like spray of water, achieving saturation of the air and gentle wetting of foliage (also called fogging).

Monocotyledon (or monocot) A plant belonging to the smaller of the two great classes into which the flowering plants (angiosperms) are divided, the larger being the dicotyledons. As the name implies, monocotyledons have only one seed leaf and additionally they mostly have parallel-veined leaves, flower parts in multiples of three, and no cambium layer in the stems. Only a minority of monocotyledons are trees or shrubs, e.g. palms, aloes, and yuccas.
Mulch (in gardening) Any material that can be spread over the soil surface for the purposes of preventing water loss, insulating from cold or heat, and suppressing weed growth.
Native (of a species) Forming part of the original wild flora of the country or region under consideration. See also INDIGENOUS.
Naturalized (of a species) Not originally native to the country or region under consideration but now established, reproducing itself freely and spreading into new areas without human aid. In gardening, naturalizing sometimes means letting a particular plant multiply and spread over successive seasons, with no need for cultivation.
Nectar Sugary liquid exuded by plants, mainly from nectar glands (nectaries) of flowers, being a food reward for insects or birds (sometimes even mammals) that in return carry away pollen to another flower.
Nectary (or nectar gland) A specialized area of surface tissue that exudes nectar, usually in flowers and located at bases of petals, stamens, ovaries; taking many forms including a tiny pit, a knob, or colored band; or an extrafloral nectary may be located on a stem, leaf, or leaf stalk.
Needle A leaf modified into needle-like form, as in the true pines *(Pinus).*
Neutral (of soils) Having a pH of 7 or very close to 7 (on a scale of 0–14).
Node The region of a stem to which a leaf or leaves are attached. If leaves are alternate in their arrangement then there is only one leaf per node, but if opposite then there are two, and if whorled, three or more. Nodes alternate with internodes on a stem.
Noxious (of weeds) Any weed identified as a major threat to agriculture, horticulture, or natural environments and listed as such by government agencies responsible for weed control, usually with a range of legal requirements.
Nut Botanically, a fruit that is not fleshy but does not split open when ripe; in popular usage an edible seed, larger than a grain, that can be eaten raw or with minimal roasting.
Nutrient (of plants) The mineral elements that the plant absorbs from the soil or growing medium through its roots, in the form of salts dissolved in the water taken up. They are divided into the major or essential elements nitrogen, phosphorus, potassium, sulfur, calcium, and magnesium; and the minor or trace elements iron, manganese, copper, zinc, boron, and molybdenum. Plant nutrients do not themselves form the bulk of the plant, which is built essentially from air and water, but they are key components of molecules essential to plant metabolism.
Oblong Having more or less parallel margins and with length about two to eight times the width; the base and apex may be rounded or obtuse, not necessarily squared-off.
Offset Any small basal shoot of a plant that can be detached and used for propagation.
Opposite (of leaves) Attached to the stem in pairs, on opposite sides of a node.
Orchid Any member of the very large monocot family Orchidaceae, exceeded in number of species only by the dicot family Asteraceae (composites or daisies), occurring in most of the world's lands but most diverse in the tropics, where the great majority grow as epiphytes. Orchids have zygomorphic flowers of elaborate structure, capsular fruits containing vast numbers of minute seeds with no food reserves, and roots that contain symbiotic fungal mycorrhiza, essential for the orchid's nutrition. They are little used by humans except as ornaments.
Organic (of substances) Being composed of molecules that originated in living things. Organic chemistry concerns itself with compounds in which carbon and hydrogen predominate; (in horticulture and agriculture) any plants and produce grown without the use of manufactured chemical fertilizers or pesticides (except simple inorganic chemicals), based on the belief that such chemicals are harmful to the soil and to humans and animals who consume the produce.
Ornamental A plant grown chiefly for ornament, as opposed to food, timber, fiber, drugs, and the like.
Ovary (in flowers) The swollen part of the female organ that contains the ovules.
Ovate (of leaves, bracts, petals, etc.) Approximately egg-shaped in outline with the widest part toward the stalk end; it refers to the overall outline and the base or apex may be acute, obtuse, or rounded.
Ovule The future seed but before fertilization; in flowering plants enclosed in the ovary but in cycads and conifers borne on the scale of a cone.
Palm Any member of the large monocot family Arecaceae or Palmae, palms are mostly tropical plants with large fronds (actually leaves) that are usually divided into many leaflets or segments folded along their midribs. Palm trunks may be tall and apparently woody but they do not have a cambium layer.

Panicle In the looser sense, any inflorescence that is repeatedly branched, though more strictly it is a branched raceme.

Pea-flower The type of flower characteristic of the largest subfamily (Faboideae) of the legume family (Fabaceae, alternative name Leguminosae); the flowers are zygomorphic, with a broad upper petal known as the standard, two forward-pointing outer petals known as the "wings," and two partially fused lower petals that form the keel: held within these are a slender group of 10 stamens and a single carpel.

Pedicel The stalk of an individual flower.

Peduncle The common stalk of a group of flowers or of a whole inflorescence.

Perennial (of species) In botanical usage, a plant that has an indefinite life span, or at least three years' life span. By this criterion all trees and shrubs are perennials, but gardeners tend to use the term to mean an herbaceous perennial.

Perianth The parts of a flower that enclose the sexual organs in bud, usually the combined petals (corolla) and sepals (calyx). Used mainly for flowers where petals are not clearly distinguishable from sepals, e.g. palms, lilies, in which case they are all termed perianth-segments.

Persistent Lasting beyond one season on a plant, or into a different phase of reproduction, e.g. the sepals of a flower persistent on the fruit.

Pest (in gardening) Mostly insects or other small fauna that feed on plants, either weakening them or disfiguring them. Contrast with DISEASE.

Pesticide General term for chemicals used to kill undesirable organisms, whether weeds, fungi, insects, snails, etc.—though the more precise terms are herbicide, fungicide, insecticide, molluscicide, etc.

Petal One of the inner layer of the two layers of organs that surround the sexual organs of a flower, the outer being the sepals. Petals are often thin and brightly colored or white. The petals of one flower are collectively termed the corolla. They may be fused into a tube, bell, or funnel, or may be absent.

pH (in chemistry) The scale by which acidity and alkalinity are measured. It runs from 0 (extreme acidity) to 14 (extreme alkalinity) with the midpoint 7.0 regarded as neutral. Most soils fall within a pH range of between 4 and 9.

Phloem The conducting tissue found mainly in bark (except in monocots), responsible for conducting synthesized products to various parts of the plant.

Photosynthesis The process that takes place in green leaves of plants. With the aid of the pigment chlorophyll and the sun's energy, water from the soil and carbon dioxide from the air are combined to produce carbohydrates (initially sugars) essential to the formation of new tissues.

Picotee Pattern of flower coloring in some groups of cultivars, principally in *Dianthus*, characterized by petals having a narrow marginal zone of contrasting color.

Pinnate (of compound leaves) Having the leaflets attached in two rows to either side of a center stalk, in the manner of a feather.

Pod Any fruit that is hollow inside and eventually splits open to reveal its seeds or, in a narrower sense, the elongated fruit of legumes (family Fabaceae or Leguminosae) that splits along its top and bottom sides (or top only) to reveal a row of seeds.

Pollen The dust-like material produced by the male organs of both flowering plants and gymnosperms, each tiny grain containing a male nucleus that combines with a female nucleus in an ovule to create a seed. In flowering plants a pollen grain is received on the stigma and "germinates," producing an extremely fine tube that grows down through the style and into an ovule, the nucleus descending through this tube.

Pollination The mechanism by which pollen is transferred from stamens to stigma (or male cones to female cones in the conifers), whether in the same flower or different flowers, or on different plants. Agents of pollination include wind, insects, and birds; pollen can be deliberately transferred by humans.

Pome The characteristic fruit type of that subfamily of the rose family that includes apples, pears, hawthorns, cotoneasters, and related genera. The "flesh" of a pome derives from the floral receptacle; the true fruit containing several seeds is fused to the inner wall of the floral receptacle, with only its apex exposed in a small pit at the top.

Pot A container for growing a plant in, in common usage being one of small to medium size (under about 12 in or 30 cm in diameter) and usually tapering slightly from top to bottom, with a drainage hole or holes in the base.

Potpourri A mixture of dried aromatic and fragrant plants, usually flowers.

Prickle In botany, a sharp-pointed, broad-based outgrowth of a stem, as in roses *(Rosa)* and blackberries *(Rubus fruticosus)*, as opposed to a thorn or a spine.

Procumbent (of a plant's growth habit) With branches tending to lie flat on the ground but with growing tips more upward-pointing, rather than horizontally as for prostrate.

Propagation The practice of multiplying plants artificially, whether by seed, cuttings, layering, grafts, division, or tissue culture.

Prostrate (of plants) With branches lying flat on the ground.

Prune To improve or maintain the shape of a plant, most commonly a shrub (e.g. rose bush) or woody climber (e.g. grape vine), by carefully cutting off some branches at the base and shortening others, often with the aim of increasing quantity or size of flowers or fruit.

Pseudobulb A bulb-like storage organ that is not a bulb, i.e., does not consist of concentrically arranged leaves modified for food storage. Used almost exclusively for the stems of some orchid genera, based on their bulb-like form, e.g. *Cymbidium,* but among orchid growers its use has extended to some much more elongated or slender stems.

Pubescence Any coating of hairs on plant parts such as leaf, stem, fruit.

Pungent Very sharp-pointed, e.g. like the spines of a cactus. This is the literal meaning of pungent still used by botanists, though in popular use it has come to mean sharp-smelling.

Raceme An unbranched inflorescence consisting of an elongated stem bearing a succession of stalked flowers, the youngest at the tip.

Radial spines In cacti, the spines that radiate from an areole in a plane tangential to the plant body. Contrast with CENTRAL SPINES.

Rainforest Luxuriant forest with a completely closed canopy developed in areas of high rainfall. Tropical rainforest is characterized by a great diversity of tree species and abundance of lianes and epiphytes, while temperate rainforest may have only three to six tree species.

Ray (medullary ray) In wood, the bands of tissue that run across the grain from the inner core of a tree trunk to the outer boundary of the wood. Each ray runs along a radius in a cross-section of the trunk. They vary greatly in size from large and conspicuous as in oak timber, to fine and hardly visible as in pine.

Ray floret (in members of the daisy family, Asteraceae or Compositae) The outer ring of florets in a head, when these are distinct from the inner ones or disc florets. They usually have longer petals that are fused together side by side to form a flat strap; such florets are termed ligulate.

Recurved (of leaves, flower stalks, petals, or sepals) Curved downward; (of a leaf margin) curved gently downward but not rolled.

Reed Name used loosely for a number of grasses, sedges, or rushes, generally with well-developed flat leaves and found growing in marshy areas or along stream banks. The genus *Typha,* which has a cosmopolitan distribution, is commonly known in some regions as reed mace.

Reflexed Like recurved but more sharply bent rather than curved.

Rhizomatous (of a plant species) Having rhizomes as its form of food storage or mode of spread.

Rhizome A stem that runs horizontally along or below the soil surface, putting out roots along its length and sending up erect shoots at intervals; it may be swollen and behave as a storage or overwintering organ.

Rock garden A style of garden incorporating natural rocks, often large and carefully placed to produce a more or less natural effect, the aims of its design being both aesthetic and to provide appropriate rooting conditions and microclimates for the selected plants, which usually originate from similar rocky wild habitats.

Rockery Like a rock garden but usually on a smaller scale and more humble in its aesthetic ambitions.

Root The organ of absorption of water and nutrients, as well as of anchorage to the soil, in the higher plants. Differs from underground stems in anatomical structure.

Rootstock The base of a stem, from which the roots emerge. The underground overwintering stem bases of many herbaceous perennials are termed rootstocks. In grafting, the rootstock is the stem, usually grown from a seedling, onto which the scion is grafted.

Rosette Any group of plant organs, such as leaves, that radiate out from a central point on a stem, e.g. the "stemless" yuccas or the short shoots of *Cedrus.*

Runner Any horizontally spreading stem, usually fairly slender and fast-growing, capable of rooting where it touches the soil and sending up more erect shoots at intervals. Much the same as a STOLON.

Rush In the narrower sense, a member of the large genus *Juncus,* consisting of plants from boggy and marshy habitats, mostly with tufts of slender terete leaves and culms, and rather insignificant flowers.

Samara A dry fruit that retains its seed (does not split open) and is extended at the apex or on one side into a wing.

Sand The coarsest component of most soils, defined as having particles greater than 0.5 mm but less than 2 mm in diameter (larger particles are classed as gravel). Sands are composed of hard minerals, in most cases predominantly quartz that is almost pure silica and is extremely hard and virtually insoluble in water; however, beach sands may also contain shell grit, which is chemically similar to limestone.

Scale Minute organ found on leaves and other plant surfaces, like a hair but flattened and thin. Some closely appressed scales, e.g. on olive leaves, are attached by a stalk at their center and are termed peltate scales. Also that part of the cone in conifers and cycads to which the seeds or pollen sacs are attached.

Scale leaves Leaves that are reduced to a small size and pressed against the twig, usually overlapping one another, as found in most species of *Juniperus*.

Scion That part of a graft that is the subject of propagation, usually a cut piece of branch or twig of the desired cultivar, which is grafted onto the rootstock.

Sedge Any member of the large cosmopolitan family Cyperaceae, and in particular members of its two largest genera, *Carex* and *Cyperus*. Sedges have grass-like leaves and spikelets of tiny but numerous flowers concealed among dry bracts that are often reddish to blackish; most grow in marshy ground. See also RUSH.

Seed Organ of reproduction and dispersal of flowering plants and gymnosperms (collectively called the seed plants), developing enclosed in the fruit of the former or on scales of female cones of the latter. A seed consists of a plant embryo, food storage tissue, and a protective seed coat. A seed may remain dormant for a long period before its germination is initiated by moisture and warmth.

Seed head Any fruiting inflorescence of compact form.

Segment One of the lobes of a deeply lobed leaf, or any similar structure.

Self-seeding Used of any plant that sheds its seed and grows in the garden without aid from the gardener; a term usually applied to desired plants.

Semi-double (of cultivars) Having flowers with more than the normal number of petals of the wild species, and usually forming more than one row, but with stamens still visible in the flower's center.

Sepal One segment of the calyx of a flower. Sepals are usually green in contrast to the colored petals; they may be fused to one another, at least toward their bases.

Series (of cultivars) A group of cultivars with a common ancestry and often sold under the one name but with mixed colors, most usually encountered in annuals; (in botanical classification) a named group of closely similar species; series is lowest of the ranks between genus and species, the next higher being section and then subgenus.

Sheath (of leaves) A leaf stalk or base of a sessile leaf that is expanded and wraps around the stem.

Shoot A leafy branch or stem that is in the process of growing and elongating.

Shrub A plant with permanent, woody, aboveground stems from which new growths arise, and that is too small to be classed as a tree.

Simple (of leaves) Individual leaves without discrete leaflets.

Single (of cultivars) Having flowers with much the same number of petals as the wild species of the genus, or at least having the petals forming a single row.

Soil The thin mantle of material covering most of the earth's lands, derived mainly from the chemical breakdown of bedrock over many centuries. It is composed of mineral particles of various sizes as well as particles of dead organic matter from plant roots, leaves, and fallen logs, this organic matter often mixed into the soil by earthworms. Soil contains the moisture and mineral nutrients that plants need for growth.

Softwood (of tree species) Having a soft timber—more traditionally signifying any conifer—as opposed to a hardwood (flowering plant), regardless of relative hardness or density of timber; (of cuttings) taken from stems at or near their growing tips of the current year's growth, where tissues have not fully hardened.

Solitary (of flowers) Borne singly, not grouped in an inflorescence. A flower may be solitary and terminal, borne at the tip of a branch, or solitary and axillary, borne in a leaf axil; (of palms) consisting of only a single trunk.

Spadix A spike or dense panicle of flowers. A somewhat obsolete term except for its use for the specialized inflorescence of the arum family.

Spathe A large bract that encloses a whole inflorescence in bud. Most commonly used for the inflorescence of the arum family.

Species (abbreviation sp., plural spp.) The basic unit of plant classification, usually consisting of a population of individuals that are fairly uniform in character and breed freely with one another over many generations without obvious change in their progeny. A species is normally unable to breed with another species or if it does, the resulting progeny do not remain constant or do not produce viable seed. The scientific name of a species consists of the name of the genus to which it belongs, followed by a name referred to as the specific epithet, somewhat like a person's given name—e.g. *Pinus contorta*.

Spike (in botany) An unbranched inflorescence in which the flowers lack individual stalks.

Spine In botany, a sharp needle-like organ that is a modification of an organ such as a leaf or sepal, though not of a branch, as that is a thorn.

Spore Minute reproductive bodies of ferns, carried by wind and germinating in moist shady places to produce the sexual plantlets (gametophytes) with male and female organs that on fertilization produce another spore-bearing plant.

Spur A backward projection from a petal or sepal in the shape of a spur or horn, usually hollow and containing nectar. A spur shoot is one of the short lateral branches of trees such as apples that bear the flower clusters.

Stalk The part of a leaf (technically the petiole) that attaches to the plant stem, at least when it is distinct from the leaf blade; likewise the organ (technically the pedicel) that supports an individual flower, or that supports a whole inflorescence (technically the peduncle).

Stamen The male reproductive organ in a flower, consisting typically of a slender stalk (filament) and a pollen-sac (anther), which opens by a slit or pore to release pollen. The stamens form the third row of organs from the outside of a flower, inside the sepals and petals.

Standard (in gardening) Usually a shrub (sometimes a tree) trained to have a long bare stem topped by a compact crown of foliage; or often a grafted plant with a tall unbranched rootstock; (of irises) a term used for each of the three outer perianth segments that in many species and cultivars stand erect, alternating with the three outer ones, the "falls," which are bent downward; (of pea-flowers) the upper and usually largest petal of the flower, usually standing erect and to the rear of the other petals, often marked with a basal blotch of contrasting color or with radiating lines.

Stem The organ of a plant that supports leaves and flowers, and to which the roots attach; in the broadest sense, any shoot, trunk, branch, or twig is a stem. Distinguished from a STALK.

Sterile (of flowers) Lacking functional reproductive organs; (of stamens) not containing pollen.

Stigma That part of a carpel, or of two or more fused carpels, that is receptive to pollen, often separated from the ovary by a slender style.

Stolon A slender horizontal stem that extends from a parent stem and forms a new plantlet at the end. This takes root and the process is often repeated. Much the same as RUNNER.

Stoloniferous (of a species) Spreading by stolons.

Stone fruit All those edible fruits produced by members of the genus *Prunus*. They all bear drupes with a single seed enclosed in a very hard ridged "stone."

Stratification Treatment of seeds to promote germination by breaking dormancy, usually by refrigerating for 2 to 4 months in a slightly moist medium. Traditionally achieved by layering in a medium in an outdoor location that experiences frosts and receives little sun. In nature the seeds lie in moist leaf litter over winter.

Striate (of stems, leaves, seeds, etc.) Marked with fine longitudinal furrows, or fine stripes of a darker color.

Style The slender portion of a carpel, or of several fused carpels, between the ovary and the stigma.

Subarctic (of climates) Those characteristic of lands just outside the Arctic Circle.

Subfamily In the hierarchy of botanical classification, a major subdivision of a plant family, higher in rank than tribe. Subfamily rank is indicated by the termination -oideae, and there will always be a "type" subfamily that takes the name of its family except for this change in ending. In the classifications of some smaller and even some larger families no subfamilies are recognized, only tribes, but in others there are subfamilies of significance to gardeners, e.g. the bamboo subfamily (Bambusoideae) of the grass (Poaceae) family.

Subshrub A low shrub that is not very woody at the base, and hence is somewhat intermediate between a shrub and a herbaceous perennial.

Subspecies A major division of a species, ranking above variety and forma, though used by some botanists instead of variety. A subspecies may be thought of as a species still in the process of evolving but not yet reproductively isolated from related subspecies except by geography; there are usually intermediate plants where subspecies adjoin. The "type" subspecies takes the same epithet as the species, thus *Acer saccharum* is divided into around six subspecies including subsp. *saccharum* and subsp. *grandidentatum*, with each subspecies from a different region of North America. Abbreviated to "subsp." or "ssp."

Subtropical (of climates) Those characteristic of lands just outside the tropical zones, generally warm and frost free, at least in coastal regions.

Succulent (of a species, or its leaves or stems) Swollen and consisting of fleshy tissue with a very high water content, as opposed to fibers and wood cells. Succulent plants occur in semi-arid regions mainly in Africa and the Americas; they include most of the cacti and many euphorbias.

Sucker A vigorous erect shoot arising from the base of a shrub or the trunk or limb of a tree; also known as a stool or water shoot.

Synonym Any name referring to the same species or genus as another name, though usually taken to mean a name that is currently not accepted. When a genus has been merged with or split from another genus, the synonym is never the larger or older genus: e.g. *Fortunella* is a synonym of *Citrus*, but *Citrus* is not a synonym of *Fortunella*.

Taproot A thick central root that goes vertically down into the soil; a carrot is an extreme example.

Temperate (of climates) Those of lands lying between the Tropic of Cancer and the Arctic Circle, or between the Tropic of Capricorn and the Antarctic Circle—but climates close to the tropics (within about 10 degrees of latitude) are generally termed subtropical, and those close to the Arctic Circle are termed subarctic. Temperate climates may also be found at high altitudes in the tropics. See also COOL-TEMPERATE and WARM-TEMPERATE.

Tendril A modified branch, leaf, stipule, or inflorescence that coils around twigs, wires, or other such objects to enable a plant to climb.

Tepal Alternative term for perianth-segment in flowers where petals and sepals are not strongly differentiated.

Terete (of leaves or stems) Circular in cross-section.

Terminal (of flowers) Positioned at the apex of a stem or inflorescence branch and terminating its growth.

Terrestrial (of a species) Normally found in the ground and on dry land, as opposed to epiphytic or aquatic.

Tessellated (of tree bark) Marked into small squares or angular shapes.

Thorn In botany, a branch or twig that terminates in a sharp point, as in hawthorns. Not to be confused with a prickle or spine.

Throat (of flowers) The inside of the tube of a trumpet-shaped or funnel-shaped flower.

Topiary The art of trimming densely-foliaged plants into geometric or fanciful shapes and maintaining the plants in those shapes indefinitely.

Trailing (of a plant's growth habit) With stems lying on the ground and spilling down slopes or over banks.

Tree A woody plant, usually at least 15 ft (4.5 m) high, though shorter plants may be regarded as trees if they have a single thick trunk.

Tree fern A fern with a long-lived vertical stem and a single crown of fronds. Tree ferns are restricted to the tropics and warm-temperate regions where rainfall is high.

Trifoliate (of compound leaves) Having three leaflets—this can be a minimal case of either a pinnate or digitate (palmate) leaf. Trifoliolate is the more pedantic term.

Tropical (of climates, species) Occurring in the tropics, that is, in lands between the Tropic of Cancer and Tropic of Capricorn.

Trunk The central stem of a tree that supports the crown; it may continue well above the lowest branches though where the trunk stops and the upper limbs start is a subjective judgment.

Tuber A stem modified into a storage organ, either underground or at the soil surface. A potato is the archetypal tuber.

Tubercle Any small projection from a plant surface that is more or less bulbous in shape, the surface being then termed tuberculate.

Tuberous root A root that is swollen so as to resemble a tuber (which is a swollen stem). Dahlias have tuberous roots, not true tubers.

Tunic In bulbs and corms, the tough or membranous outer "skin" (a modified leaf base), as in an onion. It may be shredded into fibers or form a net in some plants.

Twig The ultimate branches of a tree or shrub's canopy, usually weak and slender.

Twiner A climber that gains its support from other plants by its stems twining spirally around their stems. Any one species of twiner will (with few exceptions) spiral either in a clockwise or an anticlockwise direction (viewed from above).

Umbel An inflorescence in which the individual flower stalks (pedicels) radiate from the end of the common stalk (peduncle). It may be derived from either a raceme or a cyme, when internodes of the inflorescence are reduced to zero length.

Unisexual (of a species) Dioecious, having only male or female flowers; (of flowers) having only male or female organs.

Variegated (of leaves) Streaked, mottled, edged, or striped with colors (mostly white to yellow) other than the normal green of wild plants.

Variety (in plant classification) A subdivision of a species, of lower rank than subspecies but higher than forma, though used by some botanists instead of subspecies. In a looser sense "variety" may refer to a cultivar.

Vegetative Pertaining to those parts of a plant not associated with flowers or fruits.

Vein A visible strand of conducting tissue in a leaf or a petal.

Vine A climbing plant; in the original sense, the wine-grape plant *(Vitis vinifera)*.

Warm-temperate (of climates) Those of lands in the warmer halves of the temperate zones, at latitudes between about 25 and 40 degrees.

Weed A plant that is not wanted in a garden but multiplies nonetheless, robbing cultivated plants of light, moisture, and nutrients and appearing unsightly.

Whorled (of leaves) Arranged in groups of three or more at the one node, distributed equally around the node.

Winged (of stems or leaf stalks) Having one or more longitudinal thin flanges projecting; (of fruits or seeds) having a flat papery extension from one or more edges.

Wood The main conducting and supporting tissue in trees and shrubs, found only in dicotyledons, formed by the cambium layer on its inner side and known as xylem in plant anatomy.

Woody (of plant species) Those developing wood in their stems and branches.

Zygomorphic (of flowers) Having only one, vertical plane of symmetry, e.g. as in snapdragons and nearly all orchids. Contrasted with "actinomorphic," in which a plane of symmetry passes through each petal and sepal.

KEYS

The following lists are keys to the Seasonal Calendars and Cultivation Guidelines that follow. The Seasonal Calendars are divided into summer, autumn, winter, and spring; the page numbers given under the main plant group headings in these keys will take you to the first entry for that plant group in each particular season.

The Cultivation Guidelines are easy to follow. If, for example, you wish to find out how to propagate *Impatiens balsamina,* you simply locate it in the keys below (Annuals, medium-growing, summer-flowering), find that group in the Cultivation Guidelines, then move across the columns until you reach the one headed "Propagation."

For ease of reference, each of the plants listed here is also listed in the Index to Plants, with page numbers referring to where it occurs in the text and where it occurs in these keys.

TREES

Summer page 608 **Autumn page 622**
Winter page 638 **Spring page 650**

Choosing the right tree for a location requires careful consideration—the tiny seedling tree you admire in a pot may grow to overwhelm a small garden or cause major problems to building foundations and underground pipes. Always check the mature height of a tree before purchase and allow plenty of room for it to fully develop. Visit a botanic garden or arboretum to see trees growing at their best when choosing one for your own garden.

At planting time dig a hole at least 3 times the root volume and add compost and a complete fertilizer. To help the tree get off to a good start, cut off any coiled or damaged roots, then plant firmly, leaving a slight depression around the main stem to allow rainwater to collect. Although many trees are drought-tolerant, they still require a good supply of water for growth. As the tree grows, avoid root disturbance at all times and remove any crossing or rubbing branches. Fertilize to the dripline of trees during rainy weather.

When pruning mature trees always cut flush to a branch or trunk, leaving no stubs—these look unsightly and give insect pests and diseases an easy entry into the tree. Seasonal checks for insect pests may be necessary. Small holes or sawdust on the trunk can indicate the presence of borers.

Evergreen

Acacia baileyana
Acacia crassa
Acacia dealbata
Acacia pravissima
Acacia retinoides
Acacia stenophylla
Arbutus andrachne
Arbutus × andrachnoides
Arbutus glandulosa
Arbutus 'Marina'
Arbutus menziesii
Arbutus unedo
Jacaranda caerulea
Nothofagus cunninghamii
Nothofagus dombeyi
Quercus glauca
Quercus phillyreoides
Quercus virginiana

Deciduous, taller than 35 ft (10 m)

Acer griseum
Acer saccharum
Aesculus flava
Aesculus hippocastanum
Aesculus indica
Aesculus × neglecta
Betula albosinensis
Betula alleghaniensis
Betula alnoides
Betula mandschurica
Betula pendula
Catalpa bignonioides
Catalpa × erubescens
Catalpa fargesii
Catalpa speciosa
Cercidiphyllum japonicum
Cercidiphyllum japonicum var. *sinense*
Cercidiphyllum japonicum 'Rotfuchs'
Cornus nuttallii
Fagus grandifolia
Fagus orientalis
Fagus sylvatica
Fagus sylvatica 'Purpurea'
Fagus sylvatica 'Riversii'
Gleditsia caspica
Gleditsia japonica
Gleditsia triacanthos

Gleditsia triacanthos f. *inermis*
Gleditsia triacanthos f. *inermis* 'Rubylace'
Gleditsia triacanthos f. *inermis* 'Sunburst'
Jacaranda cuspidifolia
Jacaranda mimosifolia
Jacaranda mimosifolia 'Variegata'
Jacaranda mimosifolia 'White Christmas'
Liquidambar formosana
Liquidambar styraciflua 'Lane Roberts'
Liriodendron tulipifera
Liriodendron tulipifera 'Aureomarginatum'
Liriodendron tulipifera 'Fastigiatum'
Magnolia grandiflora
Nothofagus alessandrii
Nothofagus antarctica
Nothofagus obliqua
Nothofagus pumilio
Platanus × *hispanica*
Platanus × *hispanica* 'Bloodgood'
Platanus occidentalis
Platanus orientalis
Platanus orientalis var. *insularis*
Platanus racemosa
Quercus robur
Quercus rubra
Quercus texana
Robinia × *ambigua*
Robinia pseudoacacia
Sorbus alnifolia
Sorbus aria
Tilia americana
Tilia cordata
Tilia × *euchlora*
Tilia × *europaea*
Tilia platyphyllos
Tilia tomentosa
Ulmus glabra
Ulmus × *hollandica*
Ulmus parvifolia
Ulmus procera
Ulmus 'Sapporo Autumn Gold'

Deciduous, 35 ft (10 m) or shorter

Acer campestre
Acer japonicum
Acer palmatum
Acer palmatum 'Sango-kaku'
Aesculus × *carnea*
Aesculus pavia
Betula nigra
Catalpa bungei
Catalpa ovata
Cercidiphyllum japonicum f. *pendulum*
Cercidiphyllum magnificum
Cercidiphyllum magnificum 'Pendulum'
Cercis canadensis
Cercis canadensis 'Flame'
Cercis chinensis
Cercis griffithii
Cercis occidentalis
Cercis siliquastrum
Chionanthus retusus
Chionanthus virginicus
Chionanthus virginicus 'Angustifolius'
Cornus alba
Cornus alternifolia
Cornus florida
Cornus kousa
Cornus sericea
Fagus crenata
Jacaranda jasminoides
Lagerstroemia fauriei
Lagerstroemia indica
Lagerstroemia limii
Lagerstroemia 'Tuscarora'
Liquidambar orientalis
Liquidambar styraciflua
Liquidambar styraciflua 'Rotundiloba'
Liquidambar styraciflua 'Worplesdon'
Magnolia 'Elizabeth'
Magnolia × *loebneri*
Magnolia sieboldii
Magnolia × *soulangeana*
Magnolia virginiana
Nyssa sinensis
Nyssa sylvatica
Nyssa sylvatica 'Wisley Bonfire'
Robinia fertilis
Robinia hispida
Robinia × *slavinii*
Robinia viscosa
Sorbus americana
Sorbus hupehensis
Sorbus randaiensis
Sorbus sargentiana
Styrax japonicus
Styrax obassia
Styrax officinalis
Ulmus glabra 'Camperdownii'

Conifers

Abies alba
Abies concolor
Abies koreana
Abies nordmanniana
Abies nordmanniana 'Golden Spreader'
Abies religiosa
Cedrus atlantica
Cedrus atlantica 'Glauca Pendula'
Cedrus deodara
Cedrus deodara 'Aurea'
Cedrus libani
Cedrus libani 'Sargentii'
Chamaecyparis lawsoniana
Chamaecyparis lawsoniana 'Ellwoodii'
Chamaecyparis nootkatensis
Chamaecyparis obtusa
Chamaecyparis pisifera
Chamaecyparis thyoides
Ginkgo biloba
Ginkgo biloba 'Autumn Gold'
Ginkgo biloba 'Tremonia'
Juniperus chinensis
Juniperus communis
Juniperus communis 'Depressa Aurea'
Juniperus recurva
Juniperus virginiana
Juniperus virginiana 'Burkii'
Picea abies
Picea breweriana
Picea glauca
Picea omorika
Picea orientalis
Picea pungens
Pinus densiflora
Pinus mugo

Pinus nigra
Pinus radiata
Pinus strobus
Pinus sylvestris

Ornamental, blossom and/or fruit

Malus 'Christmas Holly'
Malus coronaria
Malus ioensis
Malus × pumila
Malus × pumila 'Fuji'
Malus × purpurea

Tropical and subtropical

Lagerstroemia floribunda
Lagerstroemia speciosa

Eucalyptus

Eucalyptus cinerea
Eucalyptus erythrocorys
Eucalyptus gunnii
Eucalyptus scoparia
Eucalyptus tetraptera
Eucalyptus torquata

SHRUBS

Summer page 608 **Autumn page 624**
Winter page 638 **Spring page 652**

The cultivation of shrubs will only be successful if they are correctly located. A sun-loving shrub will never flower brilliantly if it has been planted in a dark damp corner; instead, it will sulk for years and produce only a few flowers if any at all.

Always provide adequate water for shrubs during dry spells as water stress often leaves them vulnerable to insect attack. Using plenty of mulch around plants will help to conserve water. Conversely, planting in water-logged soils may result in shrubs suffering root rot or fungal diseases, so an even balance needs to be found.

Regular controlled pruning after flowering will result in well-formed healthy shrubs. Deciduous shrubs should not be cut back when the leaves drop off as the next season's flowers may be inadvertently removed as well. If you don't have the time for regular pruning, plant the same shrub in groups of 3 or 5, as this will look much better than a single straggly individual. Also, lightly fertilize every few months rather than in one big hit; avoid heaping animal manure up around plants' main stems.

Wander through a botanic garden to see shrubs growing well. At the same time you can discover which shrubs might be suitable for your garden.

Low-growing, frost-hardy, evergreen

Abelia engleriana
Abelia schumannii
Abutilon megapotamicum 'Variegatum'
Aucuba japonica 'Rozannie'
Berberis × bristolensis
Berberis × gladwynensis
Calluna vulgaris
Calluna vulgaris 'Blazeaway'
Calluna vulgaris 'Gold Haze'
Calluna vulgaris 'Kinlochruel'
Calluna vulgaris 'Robert Chapman'
Calluna vulgaris 'Silver Queen'
Ceanothus gloriosus
Daphne × burkwoodii
Daphne cneorum
Daphne cneorum 'Eximia'
Daphne laureola
Daphne × odora
Hypericum calycinum
Hypericum 'Hidcote'
Kalmia angustifolia
Kalmia polifolia
Nandina domestica 'Firepower'
Nandina domestica 'Harbor Dwarf'
Nandina domestica 'Richmond'
Nandina Plum Passion/'Monum'

Low-growing, frost-hardy, deciduous

Berberis thunbergii
Deutzia × elegantissima
Deutzia × elegantissima 'Rosealind'
Deutzia × kalmiiflora
Forsythia 'Arnold Dwarf'
Forsythia 'Happy Centennial'
Forsythia Maree d'Or/'Courtasol'
Forsythia 'New Hampshire Gold'
Hypericum androsaemum
Hypericum frondosum
Hypericum olympicum
Hypericum 'Rowallane'
Paeonia lutea
Paeonia 'Souvenir de Maxime Cornu'

Medium- to tall-growing, frost-hardy, evergreen

Abelia chinensis
Abelia × grandiflora
Abutilon × hybridum
Abutilon megapotamicum
Aucuba japonica
Aucuba japonica 'Crotonifolia'
Aucuba japonica 'Gold Dust'
Aucuba japonica 'Golden King'
Aucuba japonica 'Variegata'
Berberis darwinii
Berberis julianae
Berberis × stenophylla
Ceanothus arboreus
Ceanothus griseus
Ceanothus 'Julia Phelps'
Ceanothus 'Pin Cushion'
Ceanothus thyrsiflorus
Daphne bholua
Elaeagnus × ebbingei
Elaeagnus pungens
Ilex aquifolium
Ilex aquifolium 'Silver Queen'
Ilex cornuta
Ilex crenata
Ilex vomitoria
Kalmia latifolia
Kalmia latifolia 'Olympic Fire'
Kalmia latifolia 'Ostbo Red'
Kalmia 'Pink Charm'
Nandina domestica

Nandina 'San Gabriel'
Taxus baccata
Taxus baccata 'Aurea'
Taxus chinensis
Taxus cuspidata
Taxus × *media*
Taxus × *media* 'Hicksii'

Medium- to tall-growing, frost-tender, evergreen

Abelia floribunda

Medium- to tall-growing, frost-hardy, deciduous

Abelia biflora
Abutilon ochsenii
Abutilon × *suntense*
Abutilon vitifolium
Clethra acuminata
Clethra alnifolia
Clethra alnifolia 'Paniculata'
Clethra alnifolia 'Rosea'
Clethra arborea
Clethra barbinervis
Corylopsis glabrescens
Corylopsis pauciflora
Corylopsis sinensis
Corylopsis sinensis var. *clavescens* f. *veitchiana*
Corylopsis sinensis 'Spring Purple'
Corylopsis spicata
Deutzia compacta
Deutzia longifolia
Deutzia setchuenensis
Elaeagnus angustifolia
Elaeagnus commutata
Elaeagnus 'Quicksilver'
Elaeagnus umbellata
Forsythia × *intermedia*
Forsythia suspensa
Hamamelis 'Brevipetala'
Hamamelis × *intermedia*
Hamamelis × *intermedia* 'Arnold Promise'
Hamamelis japonica
Hamamelis mollis
Hamamelis virginiana
Ilex verticillata
Lonicera chaetocarpa
Lonicera etrusca
Lonicera japonica
Lonicera korolkowii
Lonicera maackii
Lonicera xylosteum
Paeonia delavayi
Paeonia × *lemoinei*
Paeonia rockii
Paeonia suffruticosa

Banksia

Banksia coccinea
Banksia ericifolia
Banksia 'Giant Candles'
Banksia prionotes
Banksia serrata
Banksia speciosa

Buddleja

Buddleja alternifolia
Buddleja davidii
Buddleja globosa
Buddleja lindleyana
Buddleja 'Lochinch'
Buddleja × *weyeriana*

Callistemon

Callistemon citrinus
Callistemon 'Harkness'
Callistemon 'Little John'
Callistemon salignus
Callistemon viminalis
Callistemon 'Violaceus'

Camellia

Camellia 'Freedom Bell'
Camellia hiemalis
Camellia 'Inspiration'
Camellia japonica
Camellia japonica 'Doctor Burnside'
Camellia japonica 'Mrs Tingley'
Camellia japonica 'Yours Truly'
Camellia oleifera
Camellia pitardii
Camellia reticulata
Camellia sasanqua
Camellia sasanqua 'Crimson King'
Camellia sasanqua 'Jean May'
Camellia sinensis
Camellia × *williamsii*
Camellia × *williamsii* 'Anticipation'
Camellia × *williamsii* 'Brigadoon'
Camellia × *williamsii* 'E. G. Waterhouse'

Cistus

Cistus creticus
Cistus ladanifer
Cistus × *pulverulentus*
Cistus × *purpureus*
Cistus × *skanbergii*
Cistus 'Victor Reiter'

Erica

Erica bauera
Erica carnea
Erica cinerea
Erica erigena
Erica lusitanica
Erica ventricosa

Fuchsia

Fuchsia boliviana
Fuchsia 'Isis'
Fuchsia magellanica
Fuchsia 'Marcus Graham'
Fuchsia procumbens
Fuchsia thymifolia

Gardenia

Gardenia augusta
Gardenia augusta 'Chuck Hayes'
Gardenia augusta 'Florida'
Gardenia augusta 'Kleim's Hardy'
Gardenia augusta 'Radicans'
Gardenia thunbergia

Grevillea

Grevillea alpina
Grevillea juncifolia
Grevillea juniperina
Grevillea lanigera
Grevillea 'Robyn Gordon'
Grevillea victoriae

Hebe

Hebe albicans
Hebe × *andersonii*
Hebe macrocarpa

Hebe 'Margret'
Hebe 'Midsummer Beauty'
Hebe odora

Hibiscus

Hibiscus arnottianus
Hibiscus brackenridgei
Hibiscus moscheutos
Hibiscus rosa-sinensis
Hibiscus rosa-sinensis 'Agnes Galt'
Hibiscus syriacus

Hydrangea

Hydrangea arborescens
Hydrangea aspera
Hydrangea aspera subsp. *sargentiana*
Hydrangea heteromalla
Hydrangea macrophylla
Hydrangea quercifolia

Lavandula

Lavandula angustifolia
Lavandula × intermedia
Lavandula lanata
Lavandula latifolia
Lavandula stoechas
Lavandula stoechas 'Otto Quast'

Nerium

Nerium oleander
Nerium oleander 'Album'
Nerium oleander 'Hardy Pink'
Nerium oleander 'Hardy Yellow'
Nerium oleander 'Petite Salmon'
Nerium oleander 'Splendens Variegatum'

Philadelphus

Philadelphus 'Belle Etoile'
Philadelphus coronarius
Philadelphus inodorus
Philadelphus mexicanus
Philadelphus 'Schneesturm'
Philadelphus subcanus

Rhododendron

Rhododendron augustinii
Rhododendron impeditum
Rhododendron schlippenbachii
Rhododendron, Azaleodendron Hybrids
Rhododendron, Ghent Azalea Hybrids
Rhododendron, Hardy Medium Hybrids
Rhododendron, Hardy Small Hybrids
Rhododendron, Hardy Tall Hybrids
Rhododendron, Indica Azalea Hybrids
Rhododendron, Knap Hill and Exbury Azalea Hybrids
Rhododendron, Kurume Azalea Hybrids
Rhododendron, Mollis Hybrids
Rhododendron, Occidentale Azalea Hybrids
Rhododendron, Rustica Flore Pleno Azalea Hybrids
Rhododendron, Satsuki Azalea Hybrids
Rhododendron, Tender Hybrids
Rhododendron, Vireya Hybrids
Rhododendron, Yak Hybrids

Rosa

Rosa glauca
Rosa moyesii
Rosa rugosa
Rosa, Modern, Cluster-flowered (Floribunda)
Rosa, Modern, Hybrid Rugosa
Rosa, Modern, Large-flowered (Hybrid Tea)
Rosa, Modern, Miniature
Rosa, Modern, Modern Shrub
Rosa, Modern, Patio (Dwarf Cluster-flowered)
Rosa, Modern, Polyantha
Rosa, Old, Alba
Rosa, Old, Bourbon
Rosa, Old, China
Rosa, Old, Damask
Rosa, Old, Gallica
Rosa, Old, Hybrid Perpetual
Rosa, Old, Moss
Rosa, Old, Tea

Spiraea

Spiraea japonica
Spiraea mollifolia
Spiraea nipponica
Spiraea thunbergii
Spiraea trichocarpa
Spiraea trilobata

Syringa

Syringa laciniata
Syringa meyeri
Syringa pubescens
Syringa vulgaris
Syringa vulgaris 'Charles Joly'
Syringa vulgaris 'Sensation'

Viburnum

Viburnum bitchiuense
Viburnum × burkwoodii
Viburnum plicatum
Viburnum setigerum
Viburnum tinus
Viburnum tinus 'Variegatum'

ANNUALS AND PERENNIALS

Summer page 612 Autumn page 628
Winter page 642 Spring page 656

The cultivation of annual and perennial plants is rewarding, as a large variety of flowering plants can be grown to bloom throughout the year. To grow the more unusual annual flowers from seed requires patience, as germination can be erratic, and constant attention, as seedlings must never be allowed to dry out. In other words, giving seedlings their best chance of healthy development requires daily care.

Perennials, on the other hand, are not called hardy for nothing. Different perennials can be found for cold mountainous climates, for salt-sprayed coastal gardens, and for excessively dry, wet, or shady positions. Simple maintenance practices such as removing spent flowers, checking under leaves for pests, and tidying up during winter are all they need. Regular mulching and fertilizing during the growing and flowering seasons helps maintain their vigor, and before long there will be excess plants to give away to friends.

Annuals, low-growing, summer–autumn-flowering

Petunia × *hybrida*
Petunia × *hybrida*, Fantasy Series
Petunia × *hybrida*, Mirage Series
Petunia × *hybrida*, Storm Series
Petunia × *hybrida*, Surfinia Series
Phlox drummondii
Tagetes 'Naughty Marietta'
Tagetes, Antigua Series
Tagetes, Little Hero Series
Tagetes, Safari Series
Tropaeolum majus, Alaska Series
Zinnia angustifolia

Annuals, low-growing, spring–summer-flowering

Dianthus, Annual Pinks
Lobelia erinus
Papaver rhoeas
Tropaeolum majus, Jewel Series

Annuals, medium-growing, summer-flowering

Impatiens balsamina
Impatiens walleriana
Papaver somniferum
Petunia integrifolia
Tagetes tenuifolia
Tropaeolum majus
Zinnia elegans
Zinnia elegans, Ruffles Series
Zinnia haageana
Zinnia peruviana

Annuals, medium-growing, spring–summer-flowering

Calendula arvensis
Calendula officinalis
Calendula officinalis, Bon Bon Series
Calendula officinalis, Fiesta Gitana Group
Calendula officinalis 'Orange Salad'
Calendula officinalis, Pacific Beauty Series
Tagetes 'Jolly Jester'

Annuals, tall-growing, spring–summer-flowering

Lathyrus odoratus
Lathyrus odoratus 'Anniversary'
Lathyrus odoratus 'Jilly'

Annuals, tall-growing, summer-flowering

Cosmos bipinnatus
Cosmos bipinnatus 'Picotee'
Cosmos bipinnatus, Sensation Series
Cosmos bipinnatus, Sonata Series
Cosmos sulphureus
Digitalis purpurea
Helianthus annuus
Helianthus debilis

Perennials, spring–early summer-flowering

Achillea 'Coronation Gold'
Anemone blanda
Anemone coronaria
Anemone nemorosa
Anemone pavonina
Anemone sylvestris
Coreopsis gigantea
Coreopsis grandiflora
Coreopsis lanceolata
Coreopsis 'Sunray'
Dianthus, Malmaison Carnations
Dianthus, Perpetual-Flowering Carnations
Dianthus, Pinks
Digitalis × *fulva*
Digitalis × *mertonensis*
Euphorbia polychroma
Geranium phaeum
Lathyrus cyaneus
Penstemon pinifolius
Phlox carolina
Phlox divaricata
Phlox douglasii
Salvia indica
Viola cornuta

Perennials, spring–early summer-flowering, short-lived

Aquilegia chrysantha
Aquilegia olympica
Aquilegia vulgaris
Aquilegia, Butterfly Series
Dianthus arenarius
Dianthus, Border Carnations
Digitalis lanata
Papaver nudicaule
Viola 'Banner Violet with Blotch'
Viola 'Crystal Bowl True Blue'
Viola 'Joker Poker Face'
Viola 'Ultima Baron Red'

Perennials, summer-flowering, sun

Achillea filipendulina
Achillea 'King Edward'
Achillea ptarmica
Alstroemeria 'Friendship'
Alstroemeria 'Fuego'
Alstroemeria psittacina
Alstroemeria psittacina 'Royal Star'
Aquilegia flabellata
Aster sedifolius
Delphinium × *belladonna*
Delphinium 'Clifford Pink'
Delphinium 'Loch Leven'
Diascia barberae
Diascia barberae 'Blackthorn Apricot'
Diascia Coral Belle/'Hecbel'
Diascia Redstart/'Hecstart'
Digitalis grandiflora
Digitalis parviflora
Euphorbia griffithii
Euphorbia griffithii 'Dixter'
Gentiana makinoi
Geranium palmatum
Helianthus giganteus
Hemerocallis 'Corky'
Hemerocallis 'Many Happy Returns'

Hemerocallis 'Red Precious'
Hemerocallis 'Stafford'
Hemerocallis 'Stella d'Oro'
Hemerocallis 'Stoke Poges'
Kniphofia northiae
Lathyrus latifolius
Lobelia aberdarica
Lobelia × *gerardii*
Monarda 'Beauty of Cobham'
Monarda 'Croftway Pink'
Monarda didyma
Monarda 'Fire Beacon'
Monarda 'Ruby Glow'
Papaver orientale
Papaver orientale 'Cedric Morris'
Penstemon 'Blackbird'
Penstemon eatonii
Penstemon heterophyllus
Penstemon 'Maurice Gibbs'
Penstemon 'Rich Ruby'

Perennials, summer-flowering, shade to part-shade

Aquilegia alpina
Astilbe × *arendsii*
Astilbe chinensis
Astilbe chinensis 'Pumila'
Astilbe × *crispa*
Astilbe japonica
Astilbe koreana
Begonia gracilis
Campanula punctata
Geranium renardii
Hosta 'Frances Williams'
Hosta 'Krossa Regal'
Hosta 'Shade Fanfare'
Impatiens pseudoviola
Tricyrtis macropoda
Tropaeolum ciliatum

Perennials, winter–early summer-flowering

Begonia crassicaulis
Helleborus argutifolius
Helleborus cyclophyllus
Helleborus foetidus
Helleborus lividus
Helleborus niger
Helleborus orientalis
Lathyrus vernus

Perennials, summer–autumn-flowering

Achillea millefolium
Agapanthus africanus
Agapanthus 'Ellamae'
Agapanthus inapertus
Agapanthus Midnight Blue/ 'Monmid'
Agapanthus orientalis
Agapanthus 'Storm Cloud'
Alstroemeria, Little Miss Series
Alstroemeria, Princess Series
Anemone × *hybrida*
Aster ericoides
Aster × *frikartii*
Aster novae-angliae
Aster novae-angliae 'Andenken an Alma Pötschke'
Aster novi-belgii
Begonia aconitifolia
Begonia grandis
Begonia grandis var. *evansiana*
Begonia, Shrub-like Group
Canna 'Gran Canaria'
Canna 'Lucifer'
Canna 'Orange Punch'
Canna 'Pink Sunburst'
Canna 'Rosever'
Canna 'Strawberry'
Chrysanthemum weyrichii
Chrysanthemum zawadskii
Chrysanthemum, Anemone-centered
Chrysanthemum, Incurved
Chrysanthemum, Pompon
Chrysanthemum, Quill-shaped
Chrysanthemum, Reflexed
Chrysanthemum, Single
Chrysanthemum, Spider-form
Chrysanthemum, Spoon-shaped
Chrysanthemum, Spray
Coreopsis tinctoria
Coreopsis verticillata
Cosmos atrosanguineus
Dahlia coccinea
Dahlia imperialis
Dahlia tenuicaulis
Dahlia, Anemone-flowered
Dahlia, Ball
Dahlia, Cactus
Dahlia, Collarette
Dahlia, Decorative
Dahlia, Pompon
Dahlia, Semi-cactus
Dahlia, Single
Dahlia, Waterlily
Delphinium, Elatum Group
Delphinium, Elatum Group, Magic Fountain Series
Delphinium, Elatum Group, 'Sandpiper'
Dianthus plumarius
Dianthus plumarius 'Essex Witch'
Diascia fetcaniensis
Diascia vigilis
Euphorbia schillingii
Gentiana asclepiadea
Gentiana × *macaulayi*
Gentiana sino-ornata
Geranium 'Ann Folkard'
Geranium 'Johnson's Blue'
Helianthus × *multiflorus*
Helianthus 'Sunny'
Helianthus tuberosus
Heuchera × *brizoides*
Heuchera 'Chocolate Ruffles'
Heuchera 'Fireglow'
Heuchera 'Mint Frost'
Heuchera 'Petite Marble Burgundy'
Heuchera 'Wendy'
Hosta plantaginea
Hosta sieboldiana
Hosta ventricosa
Impatiens omeiana
Kniphofia caulescens
Kniphofia ensifolia
Kniphofia linearifolia
Kniphofia pumila
Kniphofia triangularis
Lobelia × *speciosa*
Monarda 'Cambridge Scarlet'
Phlox paniculata
Salvia buchananii
Tricyrtis affinis
Tricyrtis formosana
Tricyrtis hirta
Tricyrtis ohsumiensis
Tricyrtis 'Tojen'
Verbena bonariensis
Verbena 'Homestead Purple'

Perennials, ground covers and rock plants, mild climate

Achillea × *kellereri*
Chrysanthemum yezoense
Gazania 'Bronze Gnome'
Gazania 'Burgundy'
Gazania linearis
Gazania rigens
Gazania 'Tiger Mixture'
Gazania, Chansonette Series
Geranium harveyi
Tropaeolum polyphyllum
Tropaeolum tricolor
Verbena rigida
Verbena 'Sissinghurst'
Verbena 'Temari Bright Pink'
Verbena tenuisecta

Perennials, alpines, ground covers, and rock plants, cool climate

Campanula betulifolia
Campanula chamissonis
Campanula portenschlagiana
Dianthus deltoides
Dianthus gratianopolitanus
Dianthus gratianopolitanus 'Tiny Rubies'
Dianthus pavonius
Gentiana acaulis
Gentiana septemfida
Papaver rhaeticum
Phlox subulata
Viola pedata

Perennials, subshrubs, sun

Campanula poscharskyana
Campanula poscharskyana 'Multiplicity'
Euphorbia characias
Lobelia laxiflora
Salvia elegans
Salvia guaranitica
Salvia microphylla
Salvia officinalis
Solenostemon scutellarioides
Solenostemon scutellarioides 'Black Dragon'
Solenostemon scutellarioides 'Crimson Ruffles'
Solenostemon scutellarioides 'Display'
Solenostemon scutellarioides 'Walter Turner'
Solenostemon scutellarioides 'Winsley Tapestry'
Zinnia grandiflora

Perennials, subshrubs, shade to part-shade

Lobelia tupa
Phygelius aequalis
Phygelius aequalis 'Yellow Trumpet'
Phygelius capensis
Phygelius × *rectus*
Phygelius × *rectus* 'African Queen'
Phygelius × *rectus* 'Devil's Tears'

Perennials, for tropical effect

Impatiens, New Guinea Group
Impatiens, New Guinea Group, 'Tango'

Perennials, irises

Iris ensata
Iris laevigata
Iris pallida
Iris sibirica
Iris, Arilbred Hybrids
Iris, Californian Hybrids
Iris, Dutch Hybrids
Iris, Dwarf Bearded
Iris, Intermediate Bearded
Iris, Louisiana Hybrids
Iris, Spuria Hybrids
Iris, Tall Bearded

Perennials, pelargoniums

Pelargonium cordifolium
Pelargonium fruticosum
Pelargonium, Angel
Pelargonium, Dwarf
Pelargonium, Ivy-leafed
Pelargonium, Miniature
Pelargonium, Regal
Pelargonium, Regal, 'Rembrandt'
Pelargonium, Scented-leafed
Pelargonium, Stellar
Pelargonium, Unique
Pelargonium, Zonal

Perennials, primulas

Primula auricula
Primula denticulata
Primula forrestii
Primula 'Inverewe'
Primula sieboldii
Primula, Pruhonicensis Hybrids

GRASSES, SEDGES, AND BAMBOOS

Summer page 616 **Autumn page 632**
Winter page 646 **Spring page 660**

Cultivating the perfect lawn is the aim of every gardener; it can even develop into an obsession. The key to success is a fine, even, well-drained ground surface that is free from weeds.

The chosen grass or ground cover must be suitable for the climate and able to withstand its intended use. Softer grasses and ground covers are suitable for occasional foot traffic, while tough grasses are more able to withstand sport, children, and dogs. Pests and diseases will take hold in lawns if the chosen type is unsuitable for the usage it receives.

Regular watering is essential to keep a nice green surface, but is quite wasteful of a valuable resource. A brown lawn will quickly recover after adequate rain. Light frequent applications of fertilizer during the growing season will provide the best results.

Always weed and mow on a regular basis, never mowing the lawn to lower than ¾–1¼ in (18–30 mm) in height. Ground-cover lawns may just need the occasional once-over with hedge shears.

Ornamental grasses, sedges, and bamboos grow best in garden conditions that are not overly fertile. Add some moisture-retaining compost to the soil, and give these plants plenty of space to develop.

However, some form of barrier may be necessary to stop the spread of the more vigorous species. Few pests worry them.

Propagation is from seed or by division of clumps in spring. When dividing clumps or cultivating soil near them, be sure to wear protective clothing as the sharp leaf blades and fine hairs of some species can irritate the skin.

Lawns and ground covers

Pennisetum setaceum
Pennisetum setaceum 'Atrosanguineum'

Ornamental grasses, sedges, and bamboos

Bambusa multiplex
Bambusa multiplex 'Alphonse Karr'
Bambusa multiplex 'Fernleaf'
Bambusa oldhamii
Bambusa vulgaris
Bambusa vulgaris 'Striata'
Calamagrostis × *acutiflora*
Calamagrostis × *acutiflora* 'Karl Foerster'
Calamagrostis × *acutiflora* 'Overdam'
Calamagrostis brachytricha
Calamagrostis foliosa
Calamagrostis foliosa 'Zebrina'
Carex buchananii
Carex comans
Carex elata
Carex grayi
Carex oshimensis
Carex pendula
Cyperus albostriatus
Cyperus involucratus
Cyperus involucratus 'Variegatus'
Cyperus longus
Cyperus papyrus
Cyperus papyrus 'Nanus'
Deschampsia cespitosa
Deschampsia cespitosa Golden Dew/ 'Goldtau'
Deschampsia flexuosa
Festuca californica
Festuca californica 'Serpentine Blue'
Festuca glauca
Festuca glauca 'Blaufuchs'
Festuca valesiaca
Festuca varia
Glyceria maxima
Glyceria maxima var. *variegata*
Glyceria striata
Lomandra banksii
Lomandra glauca
Lomandra longifolia
Miscanthus oligostachyus
Miscanthus sacchariflorus
Miscanthus sinensis
Miscanthus sinensis 'Gracillimus'
Miscanthus sinensis 'Morning Light'
Miscanthus transmorrisonensis
Muhlenbergia capillaris
Muhlenbergia emersleyi
Muhlenbergia japonica
Muhlenbergia japonica 'Cream Delight'
Muhlenbergia lindheimeri
Muhlenbergia rigens
Pennisetum alopecuroides
Pennisetum alopecuroides 'Little Bunny'
Pennisetum orientale
Pennisetum villosum
Phyllostachys aurea
Phyllostachys aureosulcata
Phyllostachys bambusoides
Phyllostachys edulis
Phyllostachys flexuosa
Phyllostachys nigra
Pleioblastus auricomus
Pleioblastus chino
Pleioblastus gramineus
Pleioblastus humilis
Pleioblastus pygmaeus
Pleioblastus variegatus
Sasa kurilensis
Sasa palmata
Sasa palmata 'Nebulosa'
Sasa tsuboiana
Sasa veitchii
Sasa veitchii f. *minor*
Typha angustifolia
Typha latifolia
Typha latifolia 'Variegata'
Typha minima
Typha orientalis
Typha shuttleworthii

FRUIT TREES, NUT TREES, AND OTHER FRUITS

Summer page 616 **Autumn page 632**
Winter page 646 **Spring page 660**

The basic requirement for fruit trees is a good, deep, fertile soil that is well-drained. Have your soil tested in a laboratory to see if it is deficient in certain elements; this will save a lot of problems later on after planting. As well, check with a reputable dealer for varieties suitable for your area and for the pollination requirements of these plants.

Remember to always choose virus-free or organically grown fruit trees. Prune to allow light and air into the tree and to encourage continuous cropping. To achieve the best results, keep the area around trees free of weeds, and mulch and fertilize regularly.

Pest and disease problems may be numerous, so always seek expert advice on the safest way of dealing with them. Plant companion plants that are beneficial for insect control and fruit production. Do not attempt to grow cool-temperate fruits in warm climates. If you follow these simple procedures you will soon be able to enjoy the "fruits" of your labor.

Tropical to subtropical

Mangifera caesia
Mangifera indica
Mangifera indica 'Campeche'
Mangifera indica 'Edward'
Mangifera indica 'Kensington Pride'
Mangifera indica 'Kent'

Cool-temperate

Actinidia arguta
Actinidia arguta 'Issai'
Actinidia kolomikta
Corylus americana
Corylus avellana
Corylus cornuta
Corylus maxima
Corylus maxima 'Purpurea'
Fragaria × *ananassa*
Fragaria × *ananassa* 'Benton'
Fragaria × *ananassa* 'Fort Laramie'
Fragaria × *ananassa* 'Rainier'
Fragaria chiloensis
Fragaria 'Rosie'
Juglans ailanthifolia
Juglans cathayensis
Juglans cinerea
Juglans nigra
Juglans regia
Pyrus calleryana
Pyrus communis
Pyrus communis 'Doyenné du Comice'
Pyrus pyrifolia
Pyrus pyrifolia 'Nijisseiki'
Pyrus salicifolia
Ribes nigrum
Ribes uva-crispa
Ribes uva-crispa 'Leveller'
Rubus idaeus
Rubus idaeus 'Autumn Bliss'
Rubus idaeus 'Tulameen'
Rubus parviflorus
Rubus spectabilis
Rubus 'Tayberry'
Vaccinium corymbosum
Vaccinium corymbosum 'Bluecrop'
Vaccinium corymbosum 'Patriot'
Vaccinium nummularia
Vaccinium vitis-idaea

Warm-temperate

Actinidia chinensis
Actinidia deliciosa
Actinidia deliciosa Zespri Green/'Hayward'
Corylus colurna
Juglans major
Ribes aureum
Ribes malvaceum
Ribes rubrum
Vaccinium 'Sharpeblue'
Vitis 'Concord'
Vitis vinifera
Vitis vinifera 'Cabernet Sauvignon'
Vitis vinifera 'Chardonnay'
Vitis vinifera 'Pinot Gris'
Vitis vinifera 'Thompson Seedless'

Citrus

Citrus × *aurantiifolia*
Citrus × *aurantium*
Citrus japonica
Citrus maxima
Citrus × *meyeri* 'Meyer'
Citrus × *microcarpa*

Prunus

Prunus × *domestica*
Prunus maackii
Prunus mume
Prunus × *persica*
Prunus salicina
Prunus salicina 'Satsuma'
Prunus serrula
Prunus × *subhirtella*
Prunus × *subhirtella* 'Autumnalis'
Prunus tomentosa
Prunus triloba
Prunus, Sato-zakura Group

BULBS, CORMS, AND TUBERS

Summer page 618 **Autumn page 632**
Winter page 646 **Spring page 662**

Bulbs are one of the easiest groups of plants to grow, as they are adaptable to a wide range of climates and growing conditions.

Select firm healthy bulbs when buying and check around the surface or under the outer papery casing for any sign of insects or grubs. Soft damp spots or gray mold may indicate damage from a fungus. Many popular bulbs are now available ready-planted in pots already in flower or very close to their flowering time.

If you live in a warm climate and wish to grow cold-climate bulbs, you may have to give the bulbs an artificial winter in the refrigerator crisper for around 6 weeks before planting. In a cold climate, lift frost-tender bulbs over winter, grow them in pots, and plant them out in spring when the danger of frost has passed.

Certain bulbs are known as "garden escapees." In spring, many of these bulbs in lawns or on roadsides look very attractive and cause no problems, however, other bulbs appearing in prime country pasture can cause heartache for farmers. Check with a reputable dealer if in doubt about the suitability of any bulb.

Summer-flowering, sun

Crocosmia 'Citronella'
Crocosmia × *crocosmiiflora*
Crocosmia × *crocosmiiflora* 'Solfaterre'
Crocosmia 'Lucifer'
Crocosmia masoniorum
Crocosmia pottsii
Muscari armeniacum
Muscari aucheri
Muscari azureum
Muscari botryoides
Muscari latifolium

Summer-flowering, part-shade

Cyclamen purpurascens
Hippeastrum reticulatum
Zantedeschia elliottiana
Zantedeschia 'Flame'
Zantedeschia pentlandii

Autumn-flowering

Colchicum agrippinum
Colchicum cilicium

Colchicum parnassicum
Colchicum 'Rosy Dawn'
Colchicum speciosum
Colchicum 'Waterlily'
Crocus sativus
Crocus serotinus
Cyclamen africanum
Cyclamen cilicium
Cyclamen hederifolium
Nerine bowdenii
Nerine bowdenii 'Marnie Rogerson'
Nerine filifolia
Nerine masoniorum
Nerine sarniensis
Nerine undulata
Schizostylis coccinea
Schizostylis coccinea 'Alba'
Schizostylis coccinea 'Jennifer'
Schizostylis coccinea 'Major'
Schizostylis coccinea 'Sunrise'
Schizostylis coccinea 'Viscountess Byng'

Winter-flowering

Cyclamen persicum

Winter–spring-flowering

Crocus tommasinianus
Cyclamen coum
Hippeastrum papilio

Spring-flowering, sun

Crocus chrysanthus
Muscari macrocarpum
Scilla hyacinthoides
Scilla liliohyacinthus
Scilla ramburei
Scilla siberica
Scilla tubergeniana

Spring-flowering, shade to part-shade

Crocus 'Jeanne d'Arc'
Erythronium californicum
Erythronium helenae
Erythronium 'Pagoda'
Erythronium revolutum
Erythronium tuolumnense
Hyacinthus orientalis
Hyacinthus orientalis 'Bismarck'
Hyacinthus orientalis 'Carnegie'
Hyacinthus orientalis 'King of the Blues'
Hyacinthus orientalis 'Multiflora Blue'
Hyacinthus orientalis 'Violet Pearl'
Trillium chloropetalum
Trillium cuneatum
Trillium erectum
Trillium luteum
Trillium rivale
Zantedeschia 'Scarlet Pimpernel'

Spring–summer-flowering, sun

Crocus sieberi
Hippeastrum 'Flamingo'
Hippeastrum 'Las Vegas'
Hippeastrum 'Pamela'
Hippeastrum 'Royal Velvet'
Scilla peruviana

Spring–summer-flowering, shade

Erythronium dens-canis
Ranunculus asiaticus
Ranunculus asiaticus, Bloomingdale Series
Ranunculus asiaticus 'Cappucino'
Ranunculus asiaticus 'Double Mixed'
Ranunculus asiaticus, Tecolote Hybrids
Ranunculus asiaticus, Victoria Series
Trillium grandiflorum
Zantedeschia aethiopica
Zantedeschia aethiopica 'Childsiana'

Allium

Allium howellii
Allium moly
Allium paradoxum
Allium rosenbachianum
Allium schoenoprasum
Allium tuberosum

Fritillaria

Fritillaria biflora
Fritillaria camschatcensis
Fritillaria glauca
Fritillaria meleagris
Fritillaria olivieri
Fritillaria tuntasia

Gladiolus

Gladiolus callianthus
Gladiolus communis
Gladiolus tristis
Gladiolus viridiflorus
Gladiolus, Grandiflorus Group
Gladiolus, Primulinus Group

Lilium

Lilium candidum
Lilium martagon
Lilium nepalense
Lilium pumilum
Lilium, American Hybrids
Lilium, Asiatic Hybrids
Lilium, Candidum Hybrids
Lilium, LA Hybrids
Lilium, Longiflorum Hybrids
Lilium, Martagon Hybrids
Lilium, Oriental Hybrids
Lilium, Trumpet and Aurelian Hybrids

Narcissus

Narcissus bulbocodium
Narcissus pseudonarcissus
Narcissus, Cyclamineus
Narcissus, Double-flowered
Narcissus, Jonquilla
Narcissus, Large-cupped
Narcissus, Poeticus
Narcissus, Small-cupped
Narcissus, Split-corona
Narcissus, Tazetta
Narcissus, Triandrus
Narcissus, Trumpet

Tulipa

Tulipa clusiana
Tulipa tarda
Tulipa, Darwin Hybrid Group
Tulipa, Double Early Group
Tulipa, Fringed Group
Tulipa, Greigii Group
Tulipa, Lily-flowered Group

Tulipa, Parrot Group
Tulipa, Single Early Group
Tulipa, Single Late Group
Tulipa, Triumph Group
Tulipa, Viridiflora Group

CACTI AND SUCCULENTS

Summer page 620 **Autumn page 636**
Winter page 648 **Spring page 664**

Most of these weirdly decorative and fascinating plants are native to arid regions of the world, and their cultivation requirements are fairly simple: a warm dry atmosphere and protection from too much moisture. The misconception arising from this, unfortunately, is that they should all be planted in the hottest, most desolate site in a garden or be allowed to languish in pots without any attention. This simply is not true, and plants that are treated in this manner will not flourish.

Species such as *Kalanchoe* prefer shade and more fertile soil, and they will tolerate humidity. As a general rule, water well only during the growing or flowering periods, then give them a rest.

Propagation is from seed or cuttings in spring and summer. The stored moisture inside leaves and stems is mucilaginous, or jelly-like, and should be allowed to dry out slightly before propagation.

Wear thick gloves when handling cacti with sharp spines and protect your eyes. Watch for pests such as scale insects, mealy bugs, and aphids, which tend to hide between cacti spines or in the closely packed rosette leaves of succulent plants.

Cacti and succulents are fun to collect, so join a cacti and succulent society to obtain the more unusual species and cultivars or visit a specialist nursery.

Agave americana
Agave attenuata
Agave colorata
Agave filifera
Agave parryi
Agave victoriae-reginae
Aloe arborescens
Aloe brevifolia
Aloe chabaudii
Aloe claviflora
Aloe dorotheae
Aloe ferox
Aloe plicatilis
Aloe polyphylla
Aloe × spinosissima
Aloe striata
Aloe vera
Aloe virens
Crassula anomala
Crassula 'Buddha's Temple'
Crassula 'Morgan's Beauty'
Crassula ovata
Crassula perfoliata
Crassula rupestris
Delosperma aberdeenense
Delosperma brunnthaleri
Delosperma cooperi
Delosperma crassuloides
Delosperma nubigenum
Delosperma 'Ruby Star'
Echeveria agavoides
Echeveria 'Dondo'
Echeveria elegans
Echeveria 'Fire Light'
Echeveria gigantea
Echeveria leucotricha
Echeveria 'Morning Light'
Echeveria pallida
Echeveria peacockii
Echeveria 'Princess Lace'
Echeveria 'Violet Queen'
Echeveria, Galaxy Series
Echinocereus coccineus
Echinocereus engelmannii
Echinocereus stramineus
Echinocereus subinermis
Echinocereus triglochidiatus
Echinocereus viereckii
Kalanchoe beharensis
Kalanchoe blossfeldiana
Kalanchoe fedtschenkoi
Kalanchoe pumila
Kalanchoe thyrsiflora
Kalanchoe tomentosa
Mammillaria bocasana
Mammillaria canelensis
Mammillaria carmenae
Mammillaria compressa
Mammillaria geminispina
Mammillaria klissingiana
Mammillaria laui
Mammillaria longimamma
Mammillaria melanocentra
Mammillaria parkinsonii
Mammillaria tayloriorum
Mammillaria winterae
Opuntia aciculata
Opuntia aoracantha
Opuntia basilaris
Opuntia macrocentra
Opuntia microdasys
Opuntia strigil
Rebutia fiebrigii
Rebutia flavistyla
Rebutia heliosa
Rebutia marsoneri
Rebutia neocumingii
Rebutia perplexa
Sedum album
Sedum kamtschaticum
Sedum rubrotinctum
Sedum sieboldii
Sedum spathulifolium
Sedum spectabile
Yucca baccata
Yucca elephantipes
Yucca filamentosa
Yucca glauca
Yucca recurvifolia
Yucca whipplei

VEGETABLES AND HERBS

Summer page 620 **Autumn page 636**
Winter page 650 **Spring page 664**

It was not practicable to include vegetables in the Seasonal Calendars and Cultivation Guidelines in this book. For detailed information on their cultivation and propagation refer to books specifically dealing with vegetables.

Herbs are ideally suited to cultivation in cool-temperate climates where summers may be hot but not humid. They can tolerate a range of growing conditions within a garden, from dry, gravelly, limy positions in full sun to cool, moist, partly shaded positions.

Herbs don't need a special garden of their own, although this is often more convenient. Prepare the garden bed by adding plenty of compost and a light application of fertilizer, or else grow in pots with a good-quality potting mix and some slow-release fertilizer.

Annual herbs grown from seed need to be sown regularly to ensure a constant supply for the kitchen. They tend to bolt to seed when fluctuations of temperature occur. Perennial herbs should be tip pruned regularly for compact growth, checked occasionally for invasions of leaf-eating insects or snails, and tidied up in late winter before spring growth starts.

Cuttings strike readily during spring and summer, or herbs can be divided during the cooler months. Frost-tender herbs may need to be moved to a sheltered position during winter in cold climates. Otherwise, their demands are few.

Herbs make good companion plants and they mix happily with flowers, vegetables, and fruits, or they can be used as ground covers among shrubs.

Herbs

Mentha × *piperita*
Mentha pulegium
Mentha requienii
Mentha spicata
Mentha suaveolens
Mentha × *villosa*
Ocimum basilicum
Ocimum basilicum var. *minimum*
Ocimum basilicum 'Genova'
Ocimum basilicum 'Green Ruffles'
Ocimum basilicum 'Red Rubin'
Ocimum tenuiflorum
Origanum amanum
Origanum 'Kent Beauty'
Origanum laevigatum
Origanum majorana
Origanum rotundifolium
Origanum vulgare
Petroselinum crispum
Petroselinum crispum var. *neopolitanum*
Petroselinum crispum var. *tuberosum*
Petroselinum crispum 'Bravour'
Petroselinum crispum 'Forest Green'
Petroselinum crispum 'Krausa'
Rosmarinus officinalis
Rosmarinus officinalis 'Benenden Blue'
Rosmarinus officinalis 'Joyce DeBaggio'
Rosmarinus officinalis 'Majorca Pink'
Rosmarinus officinalis 'Sissinghurst Blue'
Rosmarinus officinalis 'Tuscan Blue'
Thymus × *citriodorus*
Thymus polytrichus
Thymus praecox
Thymus pulegioides
Thymus serpyllum
Thymus vulgaris

CLIMBERS AND CREEPERS

Summer page 622 **Autumn page 636**
Winter page 650 **Spring page 664**

Both climbers and creepers are quite adaptable to a wide range of climates, and even exotic-looking subtropical ones may adapt to cold frosty areas. They will look ragged, tattered, or even leafless over winter, but will spring back into growth once the weather warms up.

Be prepared to work hard to look after climbing and creeping plants, pruning, training, and tying them up to shape them the way you want; even self-clinging types will wander if they are not strictly controlled. Be careful not to leave training for too long, as brittle stems will break.

Before planting climbers and creepers, carefully prepare the soil by digging in plenty of compost and a complete fertilizer to ensure healthy results. Adequate watering during the growing season and mulching are also essential practices. Check the Cultivation Guidelines table for information on propagation plus pest and disease problems that may occur.

Warm-temperate to cool-temperate

Aristolochia californica
Aristolochia macrophylla
Campsis grandiflora
Campsis radicans
Campsis × *tagliabuana*
Clematis alpina
Clematis armandii
Clematis cirrhosa
Clematis montana
Clematis, Diversifolia Group
Clematis, Florida Group
Clematis, Forsteri Group
Clematis, Jackmanii Group
Clematis, Lanuginosa Group
Clematis, Patens Group
Clematis, Texensis Group
Clematis, Viticella Group
Hedera canariensis
Hedera colchica
Hedera helix
Hedera helix 'Green Ripple'
Hedera hibernica
Hedera nepalensis
Hoya australis
Hoya carnosa
Hoya carnosa 'Exotica'
Hoya carnosa 'Krinkle Kurl'

Hoya carnosa 'Rubra'
Hoya carnosa 'Variegata'
Jasminum humile
Jasminum nudiflorum
Jasminum officinale
Jasminum polyanthum
Jasminum × *stephanense*
Mandevilla laxa
Mandevilla splendens
Parthenocissus henryana
Parthenocissus inserta
Parthenocissus quinquefolia
Parthenocissus tricuspidata
Parthenocissus tricuspidata 'Lowii'
Parthenocissus tricuspidata 'Veitchii'
Trachelospermum asiaticum
Trachelospermum jasminoides
Trachelospermum jasminoides 'Variegatum'
Wisteria brachybotrys
Wisteria floribunda
Wisteria floribunda 'Rosea'
Wisteria × *formosa*
Wisteria sinensis
Wisteria sinensis 'Caroline'

Tropical to subtropical

Allamanda blanchetii
Allamanda cathartica
Allamanda schottii
Aristolochia littoralis
Bougainvillea × *buttiana*
Bougainvillea × *buttiana* 'Raspberry Ice'
Bougainvillea 'Elizabeth Doxey'
Bougainvillea glabra
Bougainvillea spectabilis
Bougainvillea 'Zakiriana'
Cissus hypoglauca
Cissus quadrangularis
Cissus rhombifolia
Ipomoea batatas
Ipomoea horsfalliae
Ipomoea indica
Ipomoea mauritiana
Ipomoea × *multifida*
Ipomoea tricolor
Jasminum azoricum
Mandevilla × *amabilis*
Mandevilla boliviensis
Mandevilla sanderi
Mandevilla 'White Delight'
Passiflora alata
Passiflora citrina
Passiflora 'Debby'
Passiflora edulis
Passiflora foetida
Passiflora reflexiflora
Thunbergia alata
Thunbergia erecta
Thunbergia grandiflora
Thunbergia gregorii
Thunbergia mysorensis
Thunbergia togoensis

ORCHIDS

Summer page 622 **Autumn page 636**
Winter page 650 **Spring page 666**

There is a large selection of orchids for warm-temperate climates, or cooler climates if extra protection is given over winter. You don't need a special greenhouse to cultivate orchids as they can be successfully grown outdoors in pots, in garden beds, or on the trunks and branches of trees.

There is no great mystery to growing orchids, as their requirements are similar to other groups of plants. Although the correct temperature is the most important factor, lighting, atmosphere, water supply, and food should also be taken into consideration. Propagation is usually carried out in spring by division of well-established clumps. The method of division depends on the species.

Terrestrial orchids grown in gardens or pots need good drainage and plenty of leaf mold and well-rotted cow manure at planting time. Epiphytes can be grown in pots or on trees; if planting on a tree make sure it is one with rough, fibrous bark that does not shed. Pests and diseases will be kept to a minimum if plants are well fertilized, well watered, and there is good air circulation around them. Look out for the dendrobium beetle, though, as it is well known for causing havoc.

If you want to include orchids in your garden, try just a few different types first before considering a large and expensive collection.

Cattleya bicolor
Cattleya Earl 'Imperialis'
Cattleya Frasquita
Cattleya intermedia
Cattleya loddigesii
Cattleya Penny Kuroda 'Spots'
Cymbidium Anita 'Pymble'
Cymbidium Astronaut 'Raja'
Cymbidium Baldoyle 'Melbury'
Cymbidium Bolton Grange
Cymbidium Bulbarrow 'Friar Tuck'
Cymbidium ensifolium
Cymbidium erythrostylum
Cymbidium Fanfare 'Spring'
Cymbidium Little Big Horn 'Prairie'
Cymbidium lowianum
Cymbidium Mavourneen 'Jester'
Cymbidium Sumatra 'Astrid'
Dactylorhiza foliosa
Dactylorhiza fuchsii
Dactylorhiza incarnata
Dactylorhiza praetermissa
Dactylorhiza purpurella
Dactylorhiza urvilleana
Dendrobium bigibbum
Dendrobium bigibbum subsp. *compactum*
Dendrobium cuthbertsonii
Dendrobium fimbriatum
Dendrobium kingianum
Dendrobium nobile
Dendrobium speciosum
Dendrobium victoriae-reginae
Dendrobium, Australian Hybrids
Dendrobium, "Hardcane" Hybrids
Dendrobium, "Nigrohirsute" Hybrids
Dendrobium, "Softcane" Hybrids
Epidendrum ciliare

Epidendrum Hokulea 'Santa Barbara'
Epidendrum ibaguense
Epidendrum ilense
Epidendrum parkinsonianum
Epidendrum Pele 'Pretty Princess'
Oncidium cebolleta
Oncidium croesus
Oncidium flexuosum
Oncidium Sharry Baby 'Sweet Fragrance'
Oncidium sphacelatum
Oncidium Sweet Sugar
Paphiopedilum hainanense
Paphiopedilum insigne
Paphiopedilum rothschildianum
Paphiopedilum spicerianum
Paphiopedilum victoria-regina
Paphiopedilum villosum
Phalaenopsis amabilis
Phalaenopsis aphrodite subsp. *formosana*
Phalaenopsis Brother Golden Wish
Phalaenopsis City Girl
Phalaenopsis Cottonwood
Phalaenopsis equestris
Phalaenopsis Hsinying Facia
Phalaenopsis Oregon Delight
Phalaenopsis Pumpkin Patch
Phalaenopsis Queen Beer
Phalaenopsis Quilted Beauty
Phalaenopsis Taisuco Pixie
Pleione El Pico
Pleione formosana
Pleione Shantung
Pleione Soufrière
Pleione Tolima
Pleione Versailles
Vanda coerulea
Vanda (Gold Spots × *insignis*)
Vanda Marlie Dolera
Vanda Miss Joaquim
Vanda Rothschildiana
Vanda sanderiana
Zygopetalum Alan Greatwood
Zygopetalum crinitum
Zygopetalum intermedium
Zygopetalum Kiwi Dust
Zygopetalum mackayi
Zygopetalum Titanic

FERNS, PALMS, AND CYCADS

Summer page 622 Autumn page 636
Winter page 650 Spring page 666

Ferns thrive in quite unusual places and often appear on moist rock ledges or among rotting tree trunks where no soil seems to be present, which should give an indication of how best to grow them. They need fairly moist conditions, and plenty of leaf humus compost should be added to the soil before planting. Apply a weak solution of liquid fertilizer in the warmer months. During dry spells ferns may brown off or disappear completely, only to reappear after rain. Inspect new fronds for any signs of pests such as caterpillars, aphids, or snails, which may congregate around the fresh young foliage and distort their growth before they unravel.

Palm trees promote the image of carefree days on tropical islands. On a practical level, palms are ideal for growing close to swimming pools and structures as their root systems are not extensive or destructive. Add plenty of compost and a slow-release fertilizer at planting time. Mature palms are heavy feeders and enjoy frequent applications of nitrogenous fertilizer along with an adequate water supply. Pest and disease problems are more likely to occur on dry underfed palms. Certain caterpillars and grasshoppers can sew the leaves of palms together, resulting in a ragged appearance. Control caterpillars with a bacterial pesticide, and grasshoppers with a strong insecticide.

To propagate ferns, collect mature spores by placing older fronds in a paper bag until dry, or carefully divide older plants in spring. Propagation of palms is from seed, although this can be slow and erratic. Prune off old or dead fronds of both ferns and palms regularly to create a neat appearance, although many palms are "self-cleaning."

Frost can cause considerable damage in cold districts, even to mature specimens, and will cause the fronds of ferns to blacken. In these areas choose hardy specimens and plant out in sheltered sites protected from wind.

Ferns

Adiantum excisum
Adiantum excisum 'Rubrum'
Adiantum hispidulum
Adiantum pedatum
Adiantum peruvianum
Adiantum raddianum
Asplenium bulbiferum
Asplenium nidus
Asplenium sagittatum
Asplenium scolopendrium
Asplenium scolopendrium 'Kaye's Lacerated'
Asplenium trichomanes
Athyrium filix-femina
Athyrium filix-femina 'Vernoniae'
Athyrium niponicum
Athyrium niponicum var. *pictum*
Athyrium otophorum
Athyrium otophorum var. *okanum*
Nephrolepis cordifolia
Nephrolepis cordifolia 'Duffii'
Nephrolepis exaltata
Nephrolepis exaltata 'Bostoniensis'
Nephrolepis exaltata 'Childsii'
Nephrolepis falcata
Polystichum acrostichoides
Polystichum aculeatum
Polystichum andersonii
Polystichum braunii
Polystichum californicum
Polystichum falcinellum
Polystichum munitum
Polystichum polyblepharum
Polystichum setiferum

Polystichum setiferum 'Divisilobum'
Polystichum × *setigerum*
Polystichum tsussimense

Palms and cycads

Archontophoenix alexandrae
Archontophoenix cunninghamiana
Archontophoenix purpurea
Chamaedorea elegans
Chamaedorea elegans 'Bella'
Chamaedorea geonomiformis
Chamaedorea microspadix
Chamaedorea plumosa
Chamaedorea stolonifera
Cycas angulata
Cycas circinalis
Cycas media
Cycas revoluta
Cycas rumphii
Cycas taitungensis
Phoenix canariensis
Phoenix dactylifera
Phoenix loureiroi
Phoenix reclinata
Phoenix roebelenii
Phoenix rupicola
Sabal bermudana
Sabal causiarum
Sabal mexicana
Sabal minor
Sabal palmetto
Sabal uresana
Trachycarpus fortunei
Trachycarpus martianus
Trachycarpus wagnerianus
Washingtonia filifera
Washingtonia robusta
Zamia fairchildiana
Zamia furfuracea
Zamia loddigesii
Zamia pumila
Zamia splendens
Zamia vazquezii

INDOOR PLANTS

Cultivation of indoor plants is simple if they are given positions with reasonable light and warmth, are kept evenly moist (but slightly drier during the winter months), and have regular weak doses of liquid fertilizer.

Check regularly for pests such as mealy bugs, scale insects, and mites on the stems and undersides of leaves, as these bugs thrive in warm enclosed conditions. Also, take plants outside occasionally to wash the dust from the leaves, never allowing them to sit in the sun as they will quickly burn.

If you live in a warm climate, don't be tempted to plant indoor plants in the garden if they have become too big for the house—they may grow even bigger outside and cause real problems.

Propagation is fairly easy, particularly from stem or leaf cuttings during the warmer months. Clump-forming types can be divided once they have outgrown their pots. Seasonal flowering plants such as cyclamen are best discarded after they flower, as they rarely perform as well the next year.

Indoor flowering and foliage plants

Anthurium andraeanum
Anthurium × *ferrierense*
Anthurium scandens
Anthurium scherzerianum
Anthurium upalaense
Anthurium warocqueanum
Euphorbia pulcherrima

Seasonal Calendars

PLANT	EARLY SUMMER
TREES	
Evergreen	Take half-hardened cuttings
Deciduous, all heights	Mulch and lightly fertilize
Conifers	Ensure adequate water during dry spells • Check stems for scale insect damage
Ornamental, blossom and/or fruit	Provide cool moist conditions over summer • Mulch and fertilize
Tropical and subtropical	Prune young trees to shape • Mulch
Eucalyptus	Provide adequate water during dry spells
SHRUBS	
Low-growing, frost-hardy, evergreen	Provide adequate water during dry spells • Prune after flowering • Mulch and fertilize
Low-growing, frost-hardy, deciduous	Take softwood cuttings • Mulch and fertilize • Check for summer insect pests
Medium- to tall-growing, frost-hardy, evergreen	Provide adequate water during dry spells • Prune after flowering • Mulch and fertilize
Medium- to tall-growing, frost-tender, evergreen	Check for summer pests • Provide adequate water during dry spells
Medium- to tall-growing, frost-hardy, deciduous	Take softwood cuttings • Mulch and fertilize • Check for summer insect pests
Banksia	Apply a leaf mulch of gum leaves

Mid-Summer	Late Summer
Watch for summer insect pests	Watch for summer insect pests
Watch for summer insect pests	Watch for summer insect pests
Thrips may cause brown or dead foliage in patches • Check *Picea* for mite damage in warm climates	Thrips may cause brown or dead foliage in patches • Check *Picea* for mite damage in warm climates
Prune back suckers near ground level • Watch for insect pests during warm weather	Watch for insect pests during warm weather
Mulch to conserve water	Watch for summer insect pests
Watch for summer insect pests • Prune young trees of unwanted branches	Watch for summer insect pests • Ensure soil is well-drained or root rot diseases may occur
Take half-hardened cuttings • Tip prune regularly	Check for insect pests • Prune after flowering • Mulch and fertilize
Provide adequate water during dry spells • Mulch	Prune after flowering • Mulch and fertilize
Take half-hardened cuttings • Tip prune regularly	Check for insect pests • Prune after flowering • Mulch and fertilize
Mulch • Fertilize	Ensure good drainage in hot humid weather
Ensure adequate water during dry spells • Mulch	Prune after flowering • Mulch and fertilize
Ensure adequate water during dry spells	Plants may suffer root rot disease in very humid weather

PLANT	EARLY SUMMER
SHRUBS *(cont.)*	
Buddleja	*B. globosa* in flower
Callistemon	Take cuttings of half-hardened wood • Apply mulch around plants • Fertilize lightly with complete or slow-release plant food
Camellia	Sunburn may cause brown patches on leaves; move plant to cooler location
Cistus	Apply gravel mulch to imitate natural habitat
Erica	*E. cinerea* in flower • Lightly prune after flowering
Fuchsia	Liquid fertilize regularly to promote continuous flowering
Gardenia	If growth is stunted, dig up plants and check roots for nematode infestation; treat soil with a nematicide or plant marigolds
Grevillea	Check leaves for caterpillar larvae, especially on tip growth • Spray with pyrethrum • Tip prune regularly
Hebe	Ensure adequate water during dry spells, although most are drought-tolerant
Hibiscus	Check for insect pests but spray only when necessary
Hydrangea	Protect from hot dry winds, as foliage and flowers may burn
Lavandula	Take half-hardened cuttings • Provide gravel mulch

Mid-Summer	Late Summer
Prune spent flowers regularly to encourage continuous blooming	Ensure adequate water during dry spells, although all are drought-tolerant
Ensure adequate water during dry spells • Mulch well • Tip bug may cause wilting and death of young shoots	Check for pests; sawfly larvae may defoliate shrubs, thrip damage may cause deformed leaves
Check for aphids, thrips, and mealy bugs • Cut out variegated leaves	Check for aphids, thrips, and mealy bugs • Cut out variegated leaves
Ensure adequate water during dry spells, although *Cistus* is drought-tolerant	*Cistus* resents humid weather • Ensure soil is well-drained • Allow free air movement around plants
Take half-hardened cuttings	Take half-hardened cuttings
Provide adequate water during dry spells	Cuttings may be taken • Check leaves for spider mite damage
Ensure adequate water during dry spells or buds may drop • Check for scale insects and mealy bugs on leaves and stems	Some leaves will turn yellow and drop off • If foliage is yellow or pale green, add iron or magnesium
Check plants for scale insects; spray with white oil • Take cuttings of half-hardened wood	*G.* 'Robyn Gordon' may develop leaf spot disease in humid weather
Check for damage by scale insects or leaf miner	Downy mildew may occur in humid weather; spray with a fungicide
Hibiscus spray will control aphids, caterpillars	Do not apply mulch around stem or collar rot may occur
Provide adequate water and mulch well • Two-spotted mite may cause silvery leaves	Powdery mildew may occur in humid weather; spray with a fungicide • Take cuttings
Ensure good drainage and air flow around plants • Fertilize lightly	Stems may blacken and die in humid weather • Prune out dead wood

PLANT	EARLY SUMMER
***SHRUBS** (cont.)*	
Nerium	Take half-hardened cuttings • Striped orange caterpillars may be present; leave to watch turn into butterflies
Philadelphus	Take softwood cuttings
Rhododendron	Apply compost or leaf litter around plants • Supply adequate water • Do not dig around plants as root system may be damaged
Rosa	Soak plants heavily once a week • Spray scale insects on stems with white oil plus an insecticide
Spiraea	Provide adequate water during dry spells • Take softwood cuttings
Syringa	Mulch around plants and keep moist during dry spells
Viburnum	Take softwood cuttings of deciduous plants • Take half-hardened cuttings of evergreens • Prune old flower stems • Mulch and fertilize
ANNUALS AND PERENNIALS	
Annuals, low-growing, summer–autumn-flowering	Mulch plants to conserve water • Peak flowering time
Annuals, low-growing, spring–summer-flowering	Add spent plants to compost • Practice crop rotation
Annuals, medium-growing, summer-flowering	Water and liquid fertilize regularly • Compost to conserve water, suppress weeds, and keep roots cool

Mid-Summer	Late Summer
Nerium plants are drought-tolerant, but provide them with adequate water for good flowering	Prune as flowers fade • Spray wax or brown scale on stems with white oil
Provide some shade in warm districts	Ensure adequate water • Mulch • Lightly fertilize
Protect plants from hot afternoon sun • Propagation may be carried out by layering	Remove unsprayed plants that have been badly damaged by insect attack • Check for mildew during humid weather; spray with a fungicide
Spray rust spores with sulfur; remove affected leaves • Prune back sucker growth from base rootstocks • Propagate by budding	Mildew may be a problem • Spray black spot at 2-week intervals • Allow good air movement
Provide adequate water during dry spells • Take softwood cuttings	Provide adequate water during dry spells • Take softwood cuttings
Take softwood cuttings or buy grafted specimens for greater hardiness	Lightly prune to shape
Ensure adequate water during dry spells • Mulch and fertilize	Two-spotted mite may cause silvering on leaves of *V. tinus*; control may be difficult
Compost spent flowers • Watch for aphids, white fly; spray with pyrethrum • Peak flowering time • Store saved seed in dry place	Check for nematodes • Cut back straggly growth or replant with fresh seedlings • Spray powdery mildew with a fungicide or wettable sulfur
Add spent plants to compost • Practice crop rotation	Add spent plants to compost • Practice crop rotation
Remove spent flowers regularly to prolong flowering • Pick *Zinnia* flowers regularly to prolong flowering • Protect *Impatiens* from afternoon sun	Spray powdery mildew with a fungicide

PLANT	EARLY SUMMER
ANNUALS AND PERENNIALS *(cont.)*	
Annuals, medium-growing, spring–summer-flowering	*Calendula officinalis* and hybrids in flower • Deadhead to increase flower production
Annuals, tall-growing, spring–summer-flowering	Remove spent flowers • Spray rust and powdery mildew with a fungicide or wettable sulfur • Break down organic matter with liquid fertilizer
Annuals, tall-growing, summer-flowering	Mulch garden • Liquid fertilize • Spray black aphids with pyrethrum • Spray leaf spot with a fungicide
Perennials, spring–early summer-flowering	Prune dead flower stems and liquid fertilize
Perennials, spring–early summer-flowering, short-lived	Plants can be allowed to seed—scatter seed to produce new plants
Perennials, summer-flowering, sun	Flowering begins • Liquid fertilize regularly
Perennials, summer-flowering, shade to part-shade	Protect plants from hot drying winds • Ensure plentiful supply of water • Pick flowering stems to encourage more blooms
Perennials, winter–early summer-flowering	Ensure adequate water • Provide a leaf compost and light dressing of blood and bone fertilizer • Protect plants from hot winds
Perennials, summer–autumn-flowering	Mulch around plants to conserve water and suppress weeds • Watch for snails and slugs
Perennials, ground covers and rock plants, mild climate	Mulch plants with compost; side dress with blood and bone fertilizer • Remove spent flowers • Cut back plants that overgrow others
Perennials, alpines, ground covers, and rock plants, cool climate	Cut back spring-flowering plants

MID-SUMMER	LATE SUMMER
Calendula officinalis and hybrids in flower • Deadhead to increase flower production	Sow seed • As seedlings emerge, drench soil with a fungicide to prevent damping off
Remove spent plants and add to compost heap • Practice crop rotation	Sow seed in seed-raising mix • Protect seedlings from damping off using a fungicide
Add spent blooms to compost heap • Spray mildew with a fungicide or wettable sulfur • Ensure adequate water for optimum flowering	Cut back overgrown plants to continue flowering • Store saved seed in dry location • Add summer weeds to compost before seed sets
Water well during hot dry periods to prolong flowering period	Water sparingly in humid weather to prevent root rot • Collar rot may occur in *Dianthus* • Gravel mulch
Provide a mulch of compost but keep away from plant stems	Provide gravel mulch for those plants that need sharp drainage
Remove spent flowers and add to compost • Ensure adequate water	Tidy up plants, removing old foliage • Liquid fertilize to encourage continuous blooming
Liquid fertilize regularly • Check plants for snail or slug damage	Remove old flowers
Ensure adequate water • Provide a leaf compost and light dressing of blood and bone fertilizer • Protect plants from hot winds	Ensure adequate water • Provide a leaf compost and light dressing of blood and bone fertilizer • Protect plants from hot winds
Liquid fertilize regularly • Flowering stems appear	Flowering • Provide stakes for tall flower stems
Ensure adequate water for plants	Provide gravel mulch in humid conditions to prevent root rot diseases of *Gazania* • Take half-hardened cuttings
Take half-hardened cuttings • Provide shade and extra water if required • Remove dead sections from rosette plants	Take half-hardened cuttings • Provide shade and extra water if required • Remove dead sections from rosette plants

PLANT	EARLY SUMMER
***ANNUALS AND PERENNIALS** (cont.)*	
Perennials, subshrubs, sun	Mulch plants with compost; side dress with blood and bone • Cuttings may be planted out
Perennials, subshrubs, shade to part-shade	Flowering season • Ensure adequate water during summer • Apply liquid fertilizer regularly
Perennials, for tropical effect	Mulch with compost and ensure adequate water for summer flowering
Perennials, irises	Fertilize and mulch
Perennials, pelargoniums	Mulch around plants to conserve water • Water only during very dry spells
Perennials, primulas	Liquid fertilize regularly • Remove old leaves from around base of plants
GRASSES, SEDGES, AND BAMBOOS	
Lawns and ground covers	Mow on a regular basis and never lower than ¾–1¼ (18–30 mm)
Ornamental grasses, sedges, and bamboos	Cut out dead or overcrowded stems • Cut back vigorous creeping grasses
FRUIT TREES, NUT TREES, AND OTHER FRUITS	
Tropical to subtropical	Establish plants during or after good summer rain • Add plenty of compost and complete fertilizer to soil
Cool-temperate	Practice fruit thinning so that branches are able to support crop • Mulch well to inhibit summer weeds

MID-SUMMER	LATE SUMMER
Spray leaf miner with an insecticide • Ensure adequate water in dry weather	Pinch out *Solenostemon* flower spikes to keep foliage lush
Flowering season • Ensure adequate water during summer • Apply liquid fertilizer regularly	*Lobelia tupa* begins flowering; flower stems may need staking
Shade *Impatiens* from the hottest sun	Shade *Impatiens* from the hottest sun
Divide and replant bearded irises	Divide and replant bearded irises
Spray bud caterpillars on flowers with an insecticide • Water early morning to discourage black stem rot • Treat soil with a fungicide	Spray rust on plants with a fungicide or wettable sulfur
Keep plants moist during summer • Shelter from hot winds	Remove plants after 3 years if flowering diminishes • Spray two-spotted mite with insecticide
Insect pests active	Fungal diseases common during humid weather
If planting out, restrict growth around bamboos by using a barrier	If planting out, restrict growth around bamboos by using a barrier • Sow annual grasses
Fertilize established plants • Buy virus-free stock, or from an organic grower	Check for seasonal pests • Identify common problems and treat with safe methods
Use trickle irrigation in dry spells • Summer prune where appropriate to encourage fruit • Bud graft tree fruits onto suitable rootstocks	Bud graft tree fruits onto suitable rootstocks • Check for branches rubbing against stakes

PLANT	EARLY SUMMER
FRUIT TREES, NUT TREES, AND OTHER FRUITS *(cont.)*	
Warm-temperate	Use netting to protect developing fruits from birds • Mulch well with compost to inhibit summer weeds
Citrus	Check for pests • If leaves are discolored, check for signs of deficiency in soil
Prunus	Provide adequate water during dry spells
BULBS, CORMS, AND TUBERS	
Summer-flowering, sun	Provide adequate water during summer months while plants are in active growth and producing flowers
Summer-flowering, part-shade	Flowering
Autumn-flowering	Allow summer sun to bake bulbs in the ground
Winter-flowering	—
Winter–spring-flowering	Dormancy
Spring-flowering, sun	Dry off over summer • Bulbs may be lifted and stored in a cool dry place or left to naturalize
Spring-flowering, shade to part-shade	—

MID-SUMMER	LATE SUMMER
Fertilize regularly with appropriate fertilizer • Water well during dry spells • Summer prune where appropriate to encourage regular crops of high yields	Check for pests and diseases weekly • Allow good air circulation to discourage mildew in humid weather
Leaf miner a common problem; cut off damaged section or spray weekly with an insecticide in cool of day	Mulch and fertilize
Clear summer weeds away from trees	Clear summer weeds away from trees
Flowering • Provide adequate water	Flowering • Provide adequate water
Flowering	Allow *Cyclamen purpurascens* plants to dry out
Plant bulbs • Prepare soil with plenty of compost and slow-release fertilizer for bulbs • Select *Colchicum* for a cool climate	Foliage dies down • Reduce watering • Plant bulbs just below ground in hot districts or with neck exposed in cool districts
—	Order bulbs from a reputable grower • Sow seed of *Cyclamen persicum* in compost seed-raising mix • Pot on when large enough
Plant out *Hippeastrum papilio* with top at ground level in humus-rich soil	Dig in plenty of compost and well-rotted cow manure • Make sure soil is well-drained or bulbs may rot • Order bulbs
Dry off (bake) bulbs in ground	Add light dressing of lime/dolomite compost and blood and bone fertilizer to soil
—	Add compost, leaf mold, and a low-nitrogen fertilizer to soil

PLANT	EARLY SUMMER
***BULBS, CORMS, AND TUBERS** (cont.)*	
Spring–summer-flowering, sun	Allow bulbs to dry off during summer • A hot dry summer will help bulbs mature
Spring–summer-flowering, shade	Ensure plenty of shade so foliage and flowers do not burn or wilt
Allium	*A. moly* in flower through summer
Fritillaria	Store bulbs in a cool dry place
Gladiolus	Leave 3 or 4 leaves when flowers are cut
Lilium	Mulch with compost and fertilizer • Cut flower stems for decoration • Remove seed capsules as flowers fade
Narcissus	Cut down yellow foliage • Lift bulbs and store in cool dry place in warm climates
Tulipa	Check stored bulbs for any insect damage • Keep only large healthy bulbs • Use insecticide granules to control insect attack
CACTI AND SUCCULENTS	Check for pests on spines or under leaves
HERBS	Harvest and dry leaf herbs • Place paper bag over annual herbs to collect seed

MID-SUMMER	LATE SUMMER
Allow bulbs to dry off during summer • A hot dry summer will help bulbs mature	Allow bulbs to dry off during summer • A hot dry summer will help bulbs mature
Ensure plenty of shade so foliage and flowers do not burn or wilt	Add plenty of compost and fertilizer to soil
Leave foliage to die down • Pick flowers for indoor decoration	*A. tuberosum* begins to flower
Store bulbs in a cool dry place	In cold climates prepare part-shaded moist sites with compost, cocopeat, and leaf mold • *Fritillaria* plants tolerate slightly limy soil
Lift when foliage starts to fade • Cut off stems when dry	Add compost and complete fertilizer • Dig sandy loam into heavy soils • *G. callianthus* in flower
L., Longiflorum Hybrids reliable in warm climates • Take scales from flowering plants for propagation	Plant bulbs in a sunny spot in well-drained, rich, neutral soil • Allow plants to die down naturally after flowering
Order bulbs from catalog of reputable grower	Planting may start in cool districts • Lightly dress soil with dolomite/lime and/or add compost, well-rotted manure, and small amount of complete fertilizer
Order bulbs from reputable grower • Plan a garden display keeping same variety together for mass planting	In warm climates store bulbs in refrigerator before planting • Lightly dress soil with dolomite/lime and/or add compost and well-rotted manure
Protect tender specimens from really hot sun	Root rot diseases occur in humid weather • Top up gravel mulch and ensure good drainage
Mulch garden to conserve water	Take cuttings of all perennial herbs

PLANT	EARLY SUMMER
CLIMBERS AND CREEPERS	
Warm-temperate to cool-temperate	Mulch around climbers as weather heats up • Ensure adequate water during dry spells • Frequent wilting indicates dryness
Tropical to subtropical	Plant evergreen climbers during or after rain periods • Check foliage for damage by caterpillars; spray with a pesticide
ORCHIDS	Mist spray daily • Water daily as required in late afternoon • Fertilize weekly with weak solution of orchid food
FERNS, PALMS, AND CYCADS	
Ferns	Provide cool misty water during dry spells • Mulch around plants with leaf litter • Lightly apply liquid fertilizer
Palms and cycads	Transplant palms during rainy weather • Clean up old fronds

PLANT	EARLY AUTUMN
TREES	
Evergreen	Plant new trees in areas of autumn rains • Lightly fertilize established trees
Deciduous, all heights	Prepare planting site 2 months ahead if planting bare-rooted young trees
Conifers	Prepare soil for planting by digging in compost and complete fertilizer

Mid-Summer	Late Summer
Cut overgrowth back drastically • Fertilize, mulch, and water well and growth should recommence • Spray caterpillars on large-leafed climbers with a pesticide	Prune back early summer-flowering climbers • Lightly apply complete fertilizer • If soil is badly drained, root rot diseases may occur
Mulch around plants	Prune back excess or rampant growth regularly
Control pests and diseases as noticed • Allow air circulation around pots • Fertilize weekly with weak solution of orchid food	Ensure plants are dry before watering • Check for fungal diseases in humid weather
Protect fronds from hot dry winds • Check under leaf hairs for insect pests; use weak-strength insecticides or remove by hand	Aphids may cause deformed fronds • Check stems for scale insects
Ensure adequate water during dry spells	Ensure adequate water during dry spells

Mid-Autumn	Late Autumn
Plant new trees in areas of autumn rains • Lightly fertilize established trees	Plant new trees in areas of autumn rains • Lightly fertilize established trees
Dig in plenty of compost and complete fertilizer	Transplant established trees
Water new plants until established	Take hardwood cuttings from young plants

PLANT	EARLY AUTUMN
***TREES** (cont.)*	
Ornamental, blossom and/or fruit	Prepare planting site 2 months ahead for bare-rooted trees
Tropical and subtropical	Mulch and lightly fertilize
Eucalyptus	Plant if autumn rains occur
SHRUBS	
Low-growing, frost-hardy, evergreen	Choose right shrub for right location • Prepare planting site with compost and complete fertilizer
Low-growing, frost-hardy, deciduous	Mulch • Lightly fertilize for winter hardiness
Medium- to tall-growing, frost-hardy, evergreen	Choose right shrub for right location • Prepare planting site with compost and complete fertilizer
Medium- to tall-growing, frost-tender, evergreen	Mulch • Lightly prune • Lightly fertilize
Medium- to tall-growing, frost-hardy, deciduous	Mulch • Lightly fertilize for winter hardiness
Banksia	Ensure soil is well-drained before planting
Buddleja	Prune old flowers • Apply compost around plants
Callistemon	Sow seed collected from previous season; keep moist until germination • Lightly fertilize with blood and bone
Camellia	Lightly fertilize; water well before and after • Apply compost mulch around plants; keep away from main stem
Cistus	Prune lightly • Tip prune

Mid-Autumn	Late Autumn
Dig in plenty of compost and complete fertilizer	Ornamental fruits appear on *Malus* • Leave on tree for winter or until fallen
Prune out dead or diseased limbs • Plant new trees during rainy weather	Prune out dead or diseased limbs • Plant new trees during rainy weather
Plant if autumn rains occur	Plant if autumn rains occur
Water well until established • Mulch	Water well until established
Autumn color on some plants	Autumn color on some plants
Water well until established • Mulch	Water well until established
Add compost and complete fertilizer at planting time	Add compost and complete fertilizer at planting time
Autumn color on some plants	Autumn color on some plants
Use a low-phosphorus plant food for banksias	Flowers appear on *B. ericifolia*
Prune lightly	Prune lightly
Mulch well and check again for insect pests	Watch for web worm in dry districts
Debud large flowering varieties to encourage better size and color • *C. sasanqua* in flower • Established plants may be moved	Debud
Cistus tolerates coastal conditions	*Cistus* tolerates coastal conditions

PLANT	EARLY AUTUMN
***SHRUBS** (cont.)*	
Erica	Provide well-drained soil for planting • Check soil pH
Fuchsia	Plant in sites sheltered from strong wind • Apply compost and complete fertilizer before planting • Lightly fertilize established plants
Gardenia	Tip prune regularly • Lightly fertilize with blood and bone
Grevillea	Top up mulch after summer and lightly fertilize
Hebe	Mulch • Lightly fertilize with complete fertilizer
Hibiscus	Select a warm location for planting • Ensure good drainage • Dig in compost • Fertilize once established
Hydrangea	Flowering
Lavandula	Some species still flowering
Nerium	Prune old or faded flowers
Philadelphus	—
Rhododendron	Apply light application of fertilizer, and water in well • Take cuttings of half-hardened wood • Pot on layer-grown plants
Rosa	Lightly dress soil with dolomite/lime and/or dig in compost or well-rotted manure, especially in sandy soil • Improve drainage in heavy soil
Spiraea	Prune lightly to shape

Mid-Autumn	Late Autumn
Cut old flowering stems and lightly prune to shape	—
Flowering continues in warm districts	Flowering may continue in warm districts
Second flush of flowers may occur	Second flush of flowers may occur
Flowering most of the year • Lightly prune regularly	Flowering most of the year • Lightly prune regularly
Some species flowering	Some species flowering
Flowering continues	Flowering continues
Remove spent flowerheads	Remove spent flowers • Prune out dead wood
Some species still flowering	Prune off dead flowers to encourage continuous blooming of *L. angustifolia*
—	—
—	Some species may be deciduous over winter
Apply mulch of compost or well-rotted animal manure	Spot flowering occurs
Pick rose hip stems for decoration • Check rose catalogs for varieties suitable for your area	Do not prune old-fashioned roses • Clip annually; shorten back flowering canes • Take cuttings
In cold districts autumn leaf color may occur	In cold districts autumn leaf color may occur

PLANT	EARLY AUTUMN
***SHRUBS** (cont.)*	
Syringa	Mulch around established plants with compost
Viburnum	Mulch and fertilize lightly
ANNUALS AND PERENNIALS	
Annuals, low-growing, summer–autumn-flowering	Apply liquid fertilizer at 2-week intervals • Peak flowering time • Watch out for snails and caterpillars
Annuals, low-growing, spring–summer-flowering	Sow seed • Mix seed with sand for even coverage • Dress soil with dolomite/lime and/or add compost and complete or slow-release fertilizer
Annuals, medium-growing, summer-flowering	End of flowering period for *Zinnia haageana* and *Z. peruviana*
Annuals, medium-growing, spring–summer-flowering	Plant seedlings • Mildew can be a problem with *Calendula* plants
Annuals, tall-growing, spring–summer-flowering	Sow seed • Protect from damping off using a fungicide • Lightly apply dolomite/lime to soil and/or add compost and slow-release fertilizer
Annuals, tall-growing, summer-flowering	Add compost or waste from worm farm • Store saved seeds in dry location
Perennials, spring–early summer-flowering	Take cuttings of *Dianthus*
Perennials, spring–early summer-flowering, short-lived	Cut back old foliage of *Aquilegia* and mulch with compost • Liquid fertilize to encourage new growth

MID-AUTUMN	LATE AUTUMN
Mulch around established plants with compost	Prepare soil for planting with light application of dolomite/lime and/or compost • Ensure good drainage
Autumn leaf color may occur in deciduous species • Berries may remain on some species	Autumn leaf color may occur in deciduous species
Add spent flowers to compost • Peak flowering time • Store saved seed in dry place	Practice crop rotation • Use green manure crops • Wear safety equipment if you plan to spray
Sow large seed direct	Protect seedlings from transplant shock by drenching soil with liquid fertilizer
Add spent annuals to compost heap	Sow seed • Keep sheltered • For hard-to-get seeds contact a reputable seed supply company
Plant seedlings • Mildew can be a problem with *Calendula* plants	Thin seedlings to avoid overcrowding and diseases • Plant seedlings • Mildew can be a problem with *Calendula* plants
Plant seedlings • Give weak solution of liquid fertilizer once established • Protect from snails	Plant seedlings • Give weak solution of liquid fertilizer once established
Add spent plants to compost heap • Practice crop rotation • Remove autumn weeds as they appear	Investigate companion planting to reduce spraying with chemicals
Plants begin winter dormancy • Plants may be divided now	Add both compost and complete fertilizer to the soil • Apply low-phosphorus fertilizer to native plants
Prepare a cool site for *Aquilegia;* apply compost and a complete fertilizer	Prepare a cool site for *Aquilegia;* apply compost and a complete fertilizer

PLANT	EARLY AUTUMN
***ANNUALS AND PERENNIALS** (cont.)*	
Perennials, summer-flowering, sun	Collect seed from flower stems and store in cool dry place
Perennials, summer-flowering, shade to part-shade	Prepare soil with generous amount of compost, leaf mold, cocopeat • Order new plants • Collect seed and store in cool dry place
Perennials, winter–early summer-flowering	—
Perennials, summer–autumn-flowering	Peak flowering • Cut flower stems for indoor decoration
Perennials, ground covers and rock plants, mild climate	Take cuttings of gazanias and place in peat/sand mix in warm position • Second flush of flowers as weather cools
Perennials, alpines, ground covers, and rock plants, cool climate	Take cuttings now • Sow seed and keep moist until germination
Perennials, subshrubs, sun	Plant seed collected during summer; keep moist until germination • Light pruning of plants
Perennials, subshrubs, shade to part-shade	Some plants still producing flowers in warmer areas
Perennials, for tropical effect	Add plenty of manure and compost to soil • Establish plants in pots then plant in spring
Perennials, irises	Sow seed and keep moist until germination
Perennials, pelargoniums	Take cuttings from overgrown summer growth; strike in sand • Keep cuttings in warm dry location

Mid-Autumn	Late Autumn
Order new plants for summer flowering • Check heights and spreads • Organize a color scheme	Cut down old flower stems to ground level • Plants may be divided now • Prepare soil as for early spring
Divide established plants	Tidy up plants of old flowering stems • Allow leaves from deciduous trees to gently cover established plants
Divide plants • Prepare soil with good quantity of compost and complete fertilizer	Prune any old remaining leaves from deciduous *Helleborus* plants when the flower buds appear
Peak flowering	Flowering may continue until frosts • Cut down spent flower stems to ground level • Divide established plants
Plants may be divided • Liquid fertilize plants in warm districts	Reset stones in rock gardens to protect plants during winter
Divide mat- and clump-forming plants	Protect plants from winter wet if necessary • Plan a raised bed to display alpine plants
Spot flowering occurs on some plants	Spot flowering occurs on some plants
Plants may be divided now	Allow leaves from deciduous trees to protect plants over winter
Tidy up plants	Tidy up plants
Divide overcrowded clumps • Do not damage rhizomes when digging up • Cut foliage down before replanting	Divide overcrowded clumps • Do not damage rhizomes when digging up • Cut foliage down before replanting
Remove spent flowers	Remove old foliage and tidy up plants

Plant	Early Autumn
***ANNUALS AND PERENNIALS** (cont.)*	
Perennials, primulas	Apply blood and bone to existing plants • Remove plants that flower poorly
GRASSES, SEDGES, AND BAMBOOS	
Lawns and ground covers	Lightly fertilize in warm districts or prepare site for planting
Ornamental grasses, sedges, and bamboos	If planting out, restrict growth around bamboos by using a barrier • Sow annual grasses
FRUIT TREES, NUT TREES, AND OTHER FRUITS	
Tropical to subtropical	Prune to allow light into tree, or shape for good fruiting
Cool-temperate	Prepare ground for planting bare-rooted trees and soft-fruit canes • Dig in compost or well-rotted manure • Check soil pH; the ideal level is 6–6.5
Warm-temperate	Prepare ground for planting container-grown specimens • Dig in compost or well-rotted manure • Avoid over-rich soil • Check pollination requirements
Citrus	Mulch and fertilize
Prunus	Prepare planting site for new trees several months in advance
BULBS, CORMS, AND TUBERS	
Summer-flowering, sun	In warm climates, plant bulbs just below soil surface

MID-AUTUMN	LATE AUTUMN
Prepare garden site with compost and old manure • Select site with heavy or clay soil	Set out new plants • Divide old plants; trim old roots and excess foliage
Lightly fertilize in warm districts or prepare site for planting	Lightly fertilize in warm districts or prepare site for planting
Remove flowerheads if grass presents a weed problem	Collect seed when fully ripe for sowing
Mulch • Fertilize lightly	Mulch • Fertilize lightly
Check pollination requirements of new plants • Provide stakes or trellis support where appropriate • Take hardwood cuttings from established plants	Check pollination requirements of new plants • Take hardwood cuttings from established plants
Provide sturdy trellis or stake where necessary • Take hardwood cuttings from established plants • Remove spent annual summer fruit plants and add to compost	Check pollination requirements • Take hardwood cuttings from established plants • Remove spent annual summer fruit plants and add to compost
Ensure adequate water at all times	Ensure adequate water at all times
Dig in compost and a complete fertilizer • Ensure soil is well drained	Check with a reputable dealer for trees suitable for your area • Spray bacterial canker with a fungicide at leaf fall
In warm climates, plant bulbs just below soil surface	In frost-prone regions, lift *Crocosmia* bulbs and store dry over winter

PLANT	EARLY AUTUMN
BULBS, CORMS, AND TUBERS *(cont.)*	
Summer-flowering, part-shade	Do not divide bulbs
Autumn-flowering	Flowering • Top dress areas of naturalized bulbs with compost • Liquid fertilize regularly
Winter-flowering	Select a cool, moist, part-shaded site under deciduous trees or shrubs • Add compost, leaf mold, and slow-release fertilizer • Plant bulbs 2 in (5 cm) deep
Winter–spring-flowering	Plant *Crocus* under deciduous trees in cold climates • In warm areas plant in pots of bulb fiber
Spring-flowering, sun	Bulb planting time • Keep moist during growing season
Spring-flowering, shade to part-shade	Choose a cool moist spot for these bulbs • Remove dead foliage of *Trillium* species
Spring–summer-flowering, sun	Sow bulb seed in seed-raising mix
Spring–summer-flowering, shade	Plan a woodland garden in a part-shaded site with plenty of leaf compost
Allium	Plant all seed varieties; sow in seed-raising mix and pot when ready • Top dress with blood and bone as flowering dies down
Fritillaria	In cold climates only, plant *Fritillaria* 4 in (10 cm) deep, 8 in (20 cm) apart • Choose *F. tuntasia* for warmer climates
Gladiolus	Start planting spring-flowering plants; plant below freezing depth

Mid-Autumn	Late Autumn
Propagate *Cyclamen purpurascens* from seed	Mulch planting area with compost or allow leaves from deciduous trees to gently cover bulbs
Flowering • Divide established clumps • Replant healthiest bulbs • Plant *Nerine filifolia* in a rock garden	Flowering • Fertilize bulbs as foliage begins to die down • *Nerine* foliage appears after flowering
Select a cool, moist, part-shaded site under deciduous trees or shrubs • Add compost, leaf mold, and slow-release fertilizer • Plant bulbs 2 in (5 cm) deep	—
Crocus tommasinianus in flower	*Crocus tommasinianus* in flower
Bulb planting time	Bulb planting time
Plants left in ground may be divided • Remove dead foliage of *Trillium* species	Allow deciduous leaves to fall over bulb planting area • Remove dead foliage of *Trillium* species
Lightly apply compost, but average soil is tolerated	—
Main bulb planting time	Main bulb planting time
Plant bulbs of all varieties when available	Plant bulbs of all varieties when available
—	—
Plant spring-flowering corms below freezing depth	Corms can be planted in subtropical or warm climates • Plant at intervals to flower over a long period

PLANT	EARLY AUTUMN
***BULBS, CORMS, AND TUBERS** (cont.)*	
Lilium	Sow seed in seed-raising mix mulched with organic matter • Raise in pots • Divide and plant new bulbs in conditioned soil
Narcissus	Plant *N.*, Cyclamineus hybrid cultivars in rock gardens or pots 2 in (5 cm) deep, 1¼ in (3 cm) apart • Plant others 3 in (8 cm) deep, 4 in (10 cm) apart
Tulipa	Planting time • Overplant with viola • Add slow-release bulb fertilizer
CACTI AND SUCCULENTS	Root rot diseases occur in humid weather • Ensure perfect drainage
HERBS	Continue to take cuttings • Harvest ripening seed
CLIMBERS AND CREEPERS	
Warm-temperate to cool-temperate	Check undersides of leaves for snails • Spray scale insects with white oil • Ants climbing up stems indicates presence of scale insects
Tropical to subtropical	Summer-flowering species continue to flower in warm districts
ORCHIDS	Provide a well-lit position but not direct sunlight
FERNS, PALMS, AND CYCADS	
Ferns	Check for caterpillars on young fronds • Lightly fertilize
Palms and cycads	Mulch and fertilize

Mid-Autumn	Late Autumn
Plant bulbs immediately; do not store	Avoid using garden forks as bulbs damage easily • Greenhouse-grown plants available in flower • After flowering, plant out in spring
Lightly fertilize bulbs with blood and bone if naturalized in garden position	Overwatering bulbs may cause bulb rot • Watch for aphids when buds form • Otherwise few problems
Planting time	Planting time
Remove old dry leaves around succulents • Repot crowded specimens	Tidy up plants and move to a sunny location • Give weak solution of liquid fertilizer for those with flower buds
Harvest and dry last of summer herbs • Remove spent annual herbs and add to compost heap	Cut back overgrown plants • Shelter over winter
Deciduous climbers show autumn color • Prune after all leaves have dropped or growth may recommence while weather is still warm	Dig plenty of compost and a complete fertilizer into soil • Allow adequate space and strong support • Ensure soil is well-drained
Second flush of flowers for spring-flowering species	Mulch well around plants and ensure adequate water during dry spells
Protect flower spikes from insect damage	Reduce watering in deciduous species
Remove old fronds • Tidy up plants	Reduce watering during cooler weather
Check leaf tips of potted specimens—they turn brown if humidity is low • Spray foliage	If trying palms in cold districts, protect well when young • Move potted specimens to warm sheltered location

Plant	Early Winter
TREES	
Evergreen	Mulch around young trees with gravel to protect from frost, or cover with hessian overnight
Deciduous, all heights	Protect young trees with gravel mulch in frosty areas
Conifers	Frost damage may occur on young *Abies* and *Picea* plants
Ornamental, blossom and/or fruit	Purchase bare-rooted trees • Do not let roots turn up when planting • Prune branches lightly after planting
Tropical and subtropical	Protect trees from cold wind if growing in cooler climates
Eucalyptus	Protect young trees with gravel mulch in frosty areas
SHRUBS	
Low-growing, frost-hardy, evergreen	Protect young plants in frosty areas
Low-growing, frost-hardy, deciduous	Take hardwood cuttings
Medium- to tall-growing, frost-hardy, evergreen	Protect young plants in frosty areas
Medium- to tall-growing, frost-tender, evergreen	Provide some winter protection if growing in cold districts
Medium- to tall-growing, frost-hardy, deciduous	Take hardwood cuttings
Banksia	Provide a gravel mulch around plants in very cold districts
Buddleja	Plants may be deciduous in very cold districts

Mid-Winter	Late Winter
Mulch around young trees with gravel to protect from frost, or cover with hessian overnight	Mulch around young trees with gravel to protect from frost, or cover with hessian overnight
Take hardwood cuttings	Remove old or dead branches • Shape trees if not flowering species
Take hardwood cuttings	Take hardwood cuttings
Water well until established, but not excessively	Water well until established, but not excessively
Protect trees from cold wind if growing in cooler climates	Protect trees from cold wind if growing in cooler climates
Protect young trees with gravel mulch in frosty areas	Protect young trees with gravel mulch in frosty areas
Protect young plants in frosty areas	Protect young plants in frosty areas
Flowering may begin in warm districts	Flowering may begin
Protect young plants in frosty areas	Protect young plants in frosty areas
Provide some winter protection if growing in cold districts	Prune after flowering in warm districts • Mulch and fertilize
Remove dead wood • Flowering may begin in warm districts	Flowering may begin
Provide a gravel mulch around plants in very cold districts	Provide a gravel mulch around plants in very cold districts
Plants may be deciduous in very cold districts	Cut out old or woody stems

PLANT	EARLY WINTER
***SHRUBS** (cont.)*	
Callistemon	Watch for web worm in dry districts
Camellia	Select camellias while in flower • Sun may damage flowers in the morning if they are wet with dew
Cistus	Protect from very cold winds
Erica	—
Fuchsia	Provide some shelter from cold winter winds
Gardenia	Provide shelter from cold winds • Move plants in pots to warm location in frosty areas
Grevillea	Protect young plants in frosty areas • Provide gravel mulch and hessian cover at night
Hebe	Some species flowering
Hibiscus	In warm districts cut back by half deciduous hibiscus • After pruning, mulch and fertilize with complete fertilizer
Hydrangea	Frost may cause some damage in cold districts; wait until spring to prune
Lavandula	Some lavender plants are quite tender, so protect from frost
Nerium	Give protection to young plants in frosty areas
Philadelphus	Protect *P. mexicanus* from frost; grow in pot and move to sheltered location
Rhododendron	Protect young plants in frosty areas • Move vireyas into warm sheltered position if in pots

MID-WINTER	LATE WINTER
—	—
Prepare planting site • Dig in plenty of compost • Add cocopeat • Ensure soil is well drained to deter root rot	Prune while blooming to remove dead, diseased, or straggling branches
Protect from very cold winds	Protect from very cold winds
E. carnea in flower • Tolerates a position with some lime	—
Frost may damage some stems but growth will recommence in spring	Frost may damage some stems but growth will recommence in spring
Provide shelter from cold winds • Move plants in pots to warm location in frosty areas	Provide shelter from cold winds • Move plants in pots to warm location in frosty areas
Protect young plants in frosty areas • Provide gravel mulch and hessian cover at night	Protect young plants in frosty areas • Provide gravel mulch and hessian cover at night
Some species flowering	Some species flowering
As for early winter in cooler districts • Use prunings for cutting material	—
Prune *H. macrophylla* in warm climates; prune to flowering buds	Prune *H. macrophylla* in warm climates; prune to flowering buds
Some lavender plants are quite tender, so protect from frost	Some lavender plants are quite tender, so protect from frost
Give protection to young plants in frosty areas	Give protection to young plants in frosty areas
Protect *P. mexicanus* from frost; grow in pot and move to sheltered location	Some species may be deciduous
Ensure adequate water if cold dry winds occur	Flowering in warm districts

PLANT	EARLY WINTER
***SHRUBS** (cont.)*	
Rosa	Main pruning time for Large-flowered (Hybrid Tea) and Cluster-flowered (Floribunda) roses • Prune back dead, weak, or spindly growth • Prune to outward pointing bud
Spiraea	—
Syringa	Select grafted, bare-rooted, healthy specimens for planting
Viburnum	*V. tinus* flowering
ANNUALS AND PERENNIALS	
Annuals, low-growing, summer–autumn-flowering	Sow seed in hot districts • Sharpen and oil garden tools
Annuals, low-growing, spring–summer-flowering	In frosty areas protect plants with loose straw or sow seed in protected position then plant when frost is over
Annuals, medium-growing, summer-flowering	Protect plants in frosty areas
Annuals, medium-growing, spring–summer-flowering	Use loose straw to protect against frost, or plant seedlings in spring • Sow seed in hot districts • Protect seedlings from wind
Annuals, tall-growing, spring–summer-flowering	Protect seedlings from frost in cold districts or plant out when danger of frost is over
Annuals, tall-growing, summer-flowering	Look for seed suppliers in garden magazines • Sow seed in hot districts
Perennials, spring–early summer-flowering	Protect plants over winter with loose straw

Mid-Winter	Late Winter
Pruning continues • Bare-rooted roses may be purchased • Water well after planting • When planting, do not allow roots to be bent	Spray scale insects with a white oil and water mix • To exhibit roses, join a horticultural society
—	—
Prune out dead or weak shoots on established plants	Some species may flower again
V. tinus flowering	*V. tinus* flowering
Join a garden club to discuss your success with others	Sow seed • Lightly apply dolomite/lime to soil and/or add compost and apply fertilizer • In shaded positions add extra cocopeat
In frosty areas protect plants with loose straw or sow seed in protected position then plant when frost is over	In frosty areas protect plants with loose straw or sow seed in protected position then plant when frost is over
Sow seed in warm districts • Plant a children's summer garden • Do not use sprays in gardens where children play	Sow seed in warm districts • Plant a children's summer garden • Do not use sprays in gardens where children play
Use loose straw to protect against frost, or plant seedlings in spring • Sow seed in hot districts • Protect seedlings from wind	Use loose straw to protect against frost, or plant seedlings in spring • Sow seed in hot districts • Protect seedlings from wind
Apply loose straw around plants to help protect from cold	Protect plants from cold winds • Give weak solution of liquid fertilizer
Start a worm farm for valuable humus and summer fishing	Sow seed ensuring good light and even moisture • Lightly apply dolomite/lime to soil and/or add compost and fertilizer
Protect plants over winter with loose straw	Protect plants over winter with loose straw

PLANT	EARLY WINTER
***ANNUALS AND PERENNIALS** (cont.)*	
Perennials, spring–early summer-flowering, short-lived	Protect frost-tender plants from early frost with a layer of loose straw
Perennials, summer-flowering, sun	Protect plants with loose straw in frosty areas
Perennials, summer-flowering, shade to part-shade	Winter dormancy
Perennials, winter–early summer-flowering	Some plants develop red-tinted foliage
Perennials, summer–autumn-flowering	Winter dormancy
Perennials, ground covers and rock plants, mild climate	Protect plants with loose straw in frosty areas • Provide minimum water over winter
Perennials, alpines, ground covers, and rock plants, cool climate	Protect plants from winter wet if necessary • Plan a raised bed to display alpine plants
Perennials, subshrubs, sun	Protect plants in areas of severe frost
Perennials, subshrubs, shade to part-shade	Allow leaves from deciduous trees to protect plants over winter
Perennials, for tropical effect	Reduce watering and allow plants to rest
Perennials, irises	Divide overcrowded clumps, if necessary
Perennials, pelargoniums	Protect plants in frosty areas • Move to warm location over winter
Perennials, primulas	Take root cuttings of *P. denticulata* in 2 in (5 cm) pieces; propagate in sharp sand

Mid-Winter	Late Winter
Protect plants in frosty areas with loose straw	Protect plants in frosty areas with loose straw
Take cuttings of *Delphinium, Diascia, Monarda, Penstemon*	Take cuttings of *Delphinium, Diascia, Monarda, Penstemon*
Winter dormancy	Winter dormancy
New foliage begins to appear • *Helleborus* in flower	New foliage begins to appear • Some plants may start to flower • Apply a weak solution of liquid fertilizer
Winter dormancy	Protect emerging foliage from snail damage
Protect plants with loose straw in frosty areas • Provide minimum water over winter	Prepare soil for spring planting with compost and general-purpose fertilizer • Prepare heavy soil with gypsum and drainage material
Apply loamy soil, cocopeat, and sharp sand • Provide extra cocopeat for acid-loving plants such as *Gentiana*	Apply loamy soil, cocopeat, and sharp sand • Provide extra cocopeat for acid-loving plants such as *Gentiana*
Protect plants in areas of severe frost	Protect plants in areas of severe frost
Allow leaves from deciduous trees to protect plants over winter	Allow leaves from deciduous trees to protect plants over winter
Supply a well-drained position	Supply a well-drained position
Divide overcrowded clumps, if necessary	Divide overcrowded clumps, if necessary
Prepare soil for summer display • Dig in compost and complete fertilizer • Ensure good drainage	Protect plants from strong winds
Propagate dormant plants by dividing established clumps	Move plants outdoors as weather warms up

PLANT	EARLY WINTER
GRASSES, SEDGES, AND BAMBOOS	
Lawns and ground covers	Warm-climate grasses may lose green color in cool winters • Oversow with cool-climate grass
Ornamental grasses, sedges, and bamboos	Leave flowers for winter decoration in cold districts
FRUIT TREES, NUT TREES, AND OTHER FRUITS	
Tropical to subtropical	Protect plants from cold winds if growing in warm-temperate climates
Cool-temperate	Soak bare-rooted plants well, before planting out; do not plant below graft level • Protect young plants from severe frost with hessian tent • Prune established plants to maintain high yields
Warm-temperate	Prune young trees to shape, selecting 3 main branches to form a framework • Cut back current season's fruited shoots
Citrus	Choose citrus species by cold tolerance; some are frost tender
Prunus	Buy virus-free stock from an organic grower
BULBS, CORMS, AND TUBERS	
Summer-flowering, sun	Give some protection in areas of severe frost with mulch of loose straw or dry leaves
Summer-flowering, part-shade	Keep in pots over winter
Autumn-flowering	Flowers die down • Allow leaves from deciduous trees to cover areas of naturalized bulbs

MID-WINTER	LATE WINTER
Warm-climate grasses may lose green color in cool winters • Oversow with cool-climate grass	Warm-climate grasses may lose green color in cool winters • Oversow with cool-climate grass
Leave flowers for winter decoration in cold districts	Leave flowers for winter decoration in cold districts
Protect plants from cold winds if growing in warm-temperate climates	Protect plants from cold winds if growing in warm-temperate climates
Protect young plants from severe frost with hessian tent • Prune established plants to maintain high yields • Prune to open structure and allow light to reach ripening fruit	Protect young plants from severe frost with hessian tent • Prune established plants to maintain high yields • Prune to open structure and allow light to reach ripening fruit
Cut back current season's fruited shoots • Remove crossing or rubbing branches or dead wood • Protect young plants from cold winds or frosty spells	Remove crossing or rubbing branches or dead wood • Protect young plants from cold winds or frosty spells
Cold winds and frost can cause foliage to curl up	Fertilize and mulch
Buy virus-free stock from an organic grower	Water young plants well until established, but not excessively • Check for blossom diseases on established trees
Give some protection in areas of severe frost with mulch of loose straw or dry leaves	Give some protection in areas of severe frost with mulch of loose straw or dry leaves
Keep in pots over winter	Keep in pots over winter
Protect bulbs with loose straw in areas of severe frost	Protect bulbs with loose straw in areas of severe frost

PLANT	EARLY WINTER
BULBS, CORMS, AND TUBERS *(cont.)*	
Winter-flowering	Main flowering period
Winter–spring-flowering	Protect *Hippeastrum papilio* bulbs in frosty areas with mulch of loose straw • Bulb flowering time from now until mid-spring
Spring-flowering, sun	Provide shelter from cold winds • Protect bulbs in frosty areas with mulch of loose straw or dry leaves
Spring-flowering, shade to part-shade	Protect bulbs in frosty areas with mulch of loose straw
Spring–summer-flowering, sun	In frost-prone areas grow potted bulbs in sheltered positions; plant out in spring • If left in ground, protect with straw
Spring–summer-flowering, shade	Protect plants from frost in cold districts; keep in a dry sheltered position
Allium	—
Fritillaria	Watch for winter weeds
Gladiolus	Lift bulbs in cold areas or wet areas • Dust bulbs with sulfur fungicide and store in a cool dry place
Lilium	Do not water bulbs over winter
Narcissus	Protect plants from strong wind • A few odd flowers of *N.*, Jonquilla may appear in warm climates
Tulipa	Watch for winter weeds
CACTI AND SUCCULENTS	Some are frost-hardy but most will require protection over winter • Move pots to sheltered location

Mid-Winter	Late Winter
Main flowering period • Do not allow to seed as plants may escape to areas of native vegetation	Leave bulbs to naturalize
Protect *Hippeastrum papilio* bulbs in frosty areas with mulch of loose straw	Protect *Hippeastrum papilio* flower buds from snails • Liquid fertilize regularly • Plant in pots for indoor decoration
Provide shelter from cold winds • Protect bulbs in frosty areas with mulch of loose straw or dry leaves	Flowering may start in warm climates • Pick naturalized flowers from roadsides and areas of native vegetation
Do not water bulbs unless it is an extremely dry winter	Ensure adequate moisture if cold dry winds occur
In frost-prone areas grow potted bulbs in sheltered positions; plant out in spring • If left in ground, protect with straw	In frost-prone areas grow potted bulbs in sheltered positions; plant out in spring • If left in ground, protect with straw
Protect plants from frost in cold districts; keep in a dry sheltered position	Liquid fertilize as buds start to develop in late winter and early spring
—	—
Watch for winter weeds	Watch for winter weeds
Store bulbs in a cool dry place	Store bulbs in a cool dry place
Frost-hardy over winter	Frost-hardy over winter
Liquid fertilize as flower stems appear • *N.*, Tazetta in flower	*N.*, Cyclamineus and *N.*, Jonquilla may start to flower
Watch for winter weeds	—
Reduce watering for all except those in flower	Bring potted specimens indoors for brief periods and place in a well-lit location

PLANT	EARLY WINTER
HERBS	Mulch plants with loose straw over winter
CLIMBERS AND CREEPERS	
Warm-temperate to cool-temperate	Add gypsum to badly drained heavy soil or use gravel at bottom of planting hole • Protect frost-tender species with hessian
Tropical to subtropical	Mulch well around plants and ensure adequate water during dry spells • Protect with hessian blanket if growing in cold districts
ORCHIDS	Maintain warmth during winter months where appropriate • Reduce watering
FERNS, PALMS, AND CYCADS	
Ferns	Protect ferns in very cold districts • Fronds may blacken when damaged by frost
Palms and cycads	Check for appearance of scale insects • Use very weak solution of white oil or an insecticide

PLANT	EARLY SPRING
TREES	
Evergreen	Sow tree seed and keep moist until germination
Deciduous, all heights	Plant container specimens

MID-WINTER	LATE WINTER
Mulch plants with loose straw over winter	Sow annual seeds either under glass or in a well-protected position • Lightly apply dolomite/lime to soil and/or dig in compost and complete fertilizer
Planting time for deciduous climbers • Prune *Wisteria* to flowering buds	Wait until all frost danger has passed before cutting back damaged climbers
Frost may kill tropical species or damage subtropical ones • Growth may recommence from base in spring	In warm districts, prune back stems that have been damaged by cold weather or wind • Side dress established plants with blood and bone or complete fertilizer
Maintain warmth during winter months where appropriate • Reduce watering	Maintain warmth during winter months where appropriate • Reduce watering
Protect from cold dry winds in all districts	Protect from cold dry winds in all districts
Water container plants sparingly	Water container plants sparingly

MID-SPRING	LATE SPRING
Mulch well as weather warms up • Fertilize during periods of good rain	Mulch well as weather warms up • Fertilize during periods of good rain
Prune blossom trees after flowering • Mulch and fertilize	Ensure adequate water during dry spells

PLANT	EARLY SPRING
***TREES** (cont.)*	
Conifers	Prune new growth (not old wood) to shape • Sow seed after giving cold treatment if necessary
Ornamental, blossom and/or fruit	Cut flowering branches for indoor decoration
Tropical and subtropical	Mulch and fertilize • Plant seed and keep moist until germination
Eucalyptus	Prepare ground for planting; dig large hole and incorporate suitable compost and fertilizer.
SHRUBS	
Low-growing, frost-hardy, evergreen	Prune after flowering
Low-growing, frost-hardy, deciduous	Flowering
Medium- to tall-growing, frost-hardy, evergreen	Prune after flowering • Mulch and fertilize
Medium- to tall-growing, frost-tender, evergreen	Fertilize established shrubs • Add compost and complete fertilizer at planting time
Medium- to tall-growing, frost-hardy, deciduous	Flowering
Banksia	Flowering
Buddleja	Cut back plants • Add compost and complete fertilizer
Callistemon	Flowering period
Camellia	Test soil pH if growth is unsatisfactory

Mid-Spring	Late Spring
Mulch and fertilize	Mulch and fertilize
Mulch and fertilize well	Prune after flowering; shorten interior branches only
Prune established trees after flowering • Take cuttings	Prepare planting site if good rains have fallen • Dig in compost and complete fertilizer
Planting continues if rain is present	Fertilize young trees with slow-release fertilizer • Mulch
Sow seed and keep moist until germination	Take half-hardened cuttings • Mulch • Lightly fertilize
Prune after flowering • Mulch and fertilize	Prune after flowering • Mulch and fertilize
Prune after flowering • Mulch and fertilize • Sow seed and keep moist until germination	Take half-hardened cuttings • Mulch • Lightly fertilize
Add compost and complete fertilizer at planting time	Mulch • Take half-hardened cuttings
Prune after flowering • Mulch and fertilize	Prune after flowering • Mulch and fertilize
Apply iron chelate for banksias with yellow leaf tips and margins	Treat seed cones with heat to release seed • Lightly prune to shape
Give plenty of space when planting	*B. davidii* begins to flower
Flowering period	Prune off all spent flowers; retain some for seed collection
Prune long or straggly growth • Lightly fertilize with azalea/camellia food	Mulch around plants as weather warms up • Spray scale insect attack with white oil

PLANT	EARLY SPRING
***SHRUBS** (cont.)*	
Cistus	Ensure perfect drainage when planting • Dig in compost and slow-release fertilizer
Erica	Dig in plenty of compost and complete fertilizer before planting
Fuchsia	Prune • Fertilize with complete fertilizer
Gardenia	Dig in plenty of compost and complete or slow-release fertilizer • Check soil pH; it should be slightly acid
Grevillea	Prepare planting site with compost and slow-release low-phosphorus fertilizer • Ensure excellent drainage
Hebe	Some species flowering
Hibiscus	In warm districts prune *H. rosa-sinensis* • Prune by a third; use for cuttings • Mulch and fertilize after pruning
Hydrangea	Prune *H. quercifolia* by a half • Mulch and fertilize well
Lavandula	When planting, add light application of dolomite/lime to soil and/or compost and complete fertilizer
Nerium	Leaves and flowers are poisonous • Sow seed; keep moist until germination • Prune to shape • Mulch and fertilize
Philadelphus	Prepare planting site • Dig in compost and complete fertilizer

Mid-Spring	Late Spring
Flowering • Prune lightly after flowering	Take cuttings • Apply light application of fertilizer
Sow seed; keep moist until germination	Fertilize and mulch
Tip prune young plants for good shape	Mulch around plants with compost
Prune old or woody plants hard • Fertilize and mulch	Remove spent flowers regularly
Tip prune regularly or pick bunches of flowers • Fertilize established plants • Sow seed; keep moist until germination	Mulch plants with gum leaf mulch
Prune back old flowering stems • Fertilize and water well	Mulch around plants • Take half-hardened cuttings
In warm districts prune *H. rosa-sinensis* • Prune by a third; use for cuttings • Mulch and fertilize after pruning	Flowering season late spring to late autumn • Fertilize regularly with a high-potassium fertilizer • Mulch well but keep away from stem
Select a cool moist location for planting • Dig in plenty of compost and complete fertilizer • Take cuttings	Liquid fertilize as buds develop • Take cuttings
Tip prune young plants to ensure compact habit	Prune lightly after or during flowering
Tip prune young plants to promote compact growth or train as a standard	Old plants may be cut back hard
Provide part-shade in hot districts	Prune after flowering, especially older shoots • Mulch and fertilize

PLANT	EARLY SPRING
***SHRUBS** (cont.)*	
Rhododendron	Main flowering period • Apply compost or well-rotted animal manure and a complete plant food for rhododendrons • Water well before planting
Rosa	Protect new foliage from wind damage • In warmer districts some roses begin to flower • Choose roses by perfume
Spiraea	Cut out old or dead wood
Syringa	—
Viburnum	Prepare planting site • Dig in plenty of compost and complete fertilizer
ANNUALS AND PERENNIALS	
Annuals, low-growing, summer–autumn-flowering	Sow seed or plant seedlings • Water regularly • Protect from snails • Apply liquid fertilizer to increase humus level and prevent transplant shock
Annuals, low-growing, spring–summer-flowering	Pinch out growing tips to encourage bushy growth • Liquid fertilize • Spray leaf spot with a fungicide • Plant seedlings in cool districts
Annuals, medium-growing, summer-flowering	Plant seed in cold areas after frost has passed • Cultivate soil for direct sowing and add sand
Annuals, medium-growing, spring–summer-flowering	Sow seed in cold districts
Annuals, tall-growing, spring–summer-flowering	Provide support for flower stems using lightweight stakes • Liquid fertilize regularly • Plant seedlings in cold districts

Mid-Spring	Late Spring
Main flowering period • Do not water directly onto flowers • Spray petal blight with a fungicide • Take cuttings 6 weeks after flowering	Prune lightly after flowering • If growth is poor, check soil pH • Use a systemic insecticide regularly to combat insect damage on leaves
Use commercial preparations on insect pests and diseases, or plant garlic or onion chives and encourage birds • Prune after flowering	Mulch thickly with straw or old cow manure; keep mulch away from plant stems • Lightly apply fertilizer every 6 weeks
Prune after flowering • Cut out old or dead wood	Fertilize and mulch well
Fertilize young plants with complete fertilizer once established	Prune old flowers; prune to shape after flowering
Ensure adequate water as flower buds develop	Prune out any old or dead wood • Pick flowering branches for indoor decoration
Thin seedlings if too close • Plant seedlings in cold districts • Protect seedlings from damping off with a fungicide	Collect rainwater to water garden • Tip prune • Liquid fertilize buds at 2-week intervals
Spray caterpillars with a pesticide • Check undersides of leaves	Flowering continues • If growth is poor, check soil for nematode activity
Protect young seedlings from snails and slugs • Practice crop rotation	As flower buds form, liquid fertilize at 2-week intervals
As buds appear, liquid fertilize at 2-week intervals	Spray rust on foliage underside with a fungicide • Spray budworm with an insecticide • Pick flowers for indoor decoration
Spray pests with pyrethrum or use biological control • Liquid fertilize to promote flowering	Remove spent flowers • Spray rust and powdery mildew with a fungicide or wettable sulfur • Mulch • Break down organic matter with liquid fertilizer

PLANT	EARLY SPRING
***ANNUALS AND PERENNIALS** (cont.)*	
Annuals, tall-growing, summer-flowering	Sow seed direct or plant out seedlings when frost is over • Protect from snails • Apply liquid fertilizer when transplanting seedlings
Perennials, spring–early summer-flowering	Main flowering season begins
Perennials, spring–early summer-flowering, short-lived	Main flowering period • Deadhead flowers to encourage continuous blooming • Fresh seed may be sown
Perennials, summer-flowering, sun	Take stem cuttings • Divide plants • Lightly dress soil with lime; dig in compost, complete fertilizer, or slow-release fertilizer especially for perennials
Perennials, summer-flowering, shade to part-shade	Plant seed and keep moist until germination in warm sheltered place
Perennials, winter–early summer-flowering	Plants in flower
Perennials, summer–autumn-flowering	Divide plants
Perennials, ground covers and rock plants, mild climate	Flowering • Take stem cuttings
Perennials, alpines, ground covers, and rock plants, cool climate	Plant out rock-garden plants • Fertilize lightly with complete plant food or slow-release fertilizer
Perennials, subshrubs, sun	Liquid fertilize as plants come into bud • For planting out choose a sunny, well-drained, light soil
Perennials, subshrubs, shade to part-shade	Divide overgrown clumps • Replant with addition of compost

Mid-Spring	Late Spring
Thin out seedlings and support with stakes or tripods • Spray caterpillars with an insecticide • Liquid fertilize regularly	Spray cutworms with an insecticide • Control weeds to reduce cutworm population • Sow extra seed to fill in gaps of planting
Spray budworm on *Dianthus* with an insecticide	Collect seed as it matures
Main flowering period • Deadhead flowers to encourage continuous blooming • Fresh seed may be sown	Cut back plants after flowering • Use for cuttings
Protect new foliage from snails and slugs • Take stem cuttings from established plants	Mulch around plants to conserve water and suppress weeds • Add water-storing granules in dry arcas • Side dress plants with blood and bone
Side dress with blood and bone as weather warms up	Mulch garden and compost around plants
Collect and sow seed as it ripens • Stake tall-flowering stems	Pot on self-sown seedlings
Add compost around plants • Side dress established plants with blood and bone	Side dress plants with blood and bone
Flowering • Remove spent blooms regularly	Flowering • Plants may be divided or cut back after flowering • Liquid fertilize regularly to prolong flowering into summer
Plants begin to flower and continue into summer • Plants may be divided now	Flowering continues • Plants may be divided
Main flowering period through to late summer • Take cuttings and strike in sand/peat mix	Flowering • Prune after flowering to maintain good shape
Place flat rocks near plants to keep roots cool and for plants to grow over	Mulch around plants with leaf mold compost; side dress with blood and bone

PLANT	EARLY SPRING
ANNUALS AND PERENNIALS *(cont.)*	
Perennials, for tropical effect	—
Perennials, irises	Fertilize and mulch
Perennials, pelargoniums	Flowering • Remove dead flowers
Perennials, primulas	Sow seed in seed-raising mix • *P. denticulata* in flower
GRASSES, SEDGES, AND BAMBOOS	
Lawns and ground covers	Lightly fertilize • Ensure adequate water
Ornamental grasses, sedges, and bamboos	Clumps may be divided and planted out • Sow annual grasses
FRUIT TREES, NUT TREES, AND OTHER FRUITS	
Tropical to subtropical	Provide adequate water during dry spells • Mulch well
Cool-temperate	Plant out container-grown fruits; choose healthy sturdy plants, less than 2 years old • Spread a balanced fertilizer just beyond where branches grow • Check weekly for signs of pest or disease problems
Warm-temperate	Plant out annual fruits of *Cucumis* • Fertilize established plants to encourage fruits • Mulch heavily with compost or manure as weather warms up

Mid-Spring	Late Spring
—	Liquid fertilize *Impatiens* to produce good flowers
Visit a specialist grower to choose correct iris for your garden • Apply generous compost • Check soil pH before planting	Check plants for any sign of pests and disease, especially discolored or streaked foliage • Iris may suffer from fungus disease
Tip prune regularly • Plant *P.*, Scented-leafed hybrid cultivars near a path so they release fragrance when brushed against	Liquid fertilize regularly to encourage flowers
Treat gray mold botrytis with a fungicide	Mulch around plants • Remove spent flowers
Prepare planting site • Ensure good drainage • Cultivate to fine tilth and even surface • Water well until established	Top dress with sandy loam • Lightly fertilize • Check for appearance of summer weeds
Cut out dead or overcrowded stems • Cut back vigorous creeping grasses	Cut out dead or overcrowded stems • Cut back vigorous creeping grasses
Ensure good pollination of flowers	Apply mulch • Suppress weeds • Plant companion plants
Mulch established plants with compost and manure • Check for leaf discoloration as a nutrient deficiency may be present • Protect buds and developing fruits from birds	Spread a balanced fertilizer just beyond where branches grow • Check weekly for signs of pest or disease problems • Protect buds and developing fruits from birds
Fertilize established plants to encourage fruits • Take softwood cuttings where appropriate	Check for any sign of aphids or scale insects and take necessary action • Take softwood cuttings where appropriate

PLANT	EARLY SPRING
***FRUIT TREES, NUT TREES, AND OTHER FRUITS** (cont.)*	
Citrus	Choose a sheltered position for planting • Prepare site with compost and a complete fertilizer • Ensure good drainage
Prunus	Check for blossom diseases on established trees
BULBS, CORMS, AND TUBERS	
Summer-flowering, sun	Plant bulbs just below soil surface • Add compost and blood and bone fertilizer
Summer-flowering, part-shade	Liquid fertilize as weather warms up and plants emerge or grow
Autumn-flowering	Divide bulbs if overcrowded • Sow seed from previous autumn flowering
Winter-flowering	Allow bulbs to dry off after flowering • Mulch area with compost • Bulbs may be divided
Winter–spring-flowering	Water well while in flower
Spring-flowering, sun	Main flowering period • Pick flowers regularly for indoor decoration
Spring-flowering, shade to part-shade	Bulbs in full flower • Pick flowers for indoor decoration
Spring–summer-flowering, sun	Water bulbs well during the growing and flowering season
Spring–summer-flowering, shade	Flowering time begins and continues to early summer
Allium	Some alliums begin to flower

MID-SPRING	LATE SPRING
Mulch and fertilize • Keep mulch away from main trunk	Keep trunk free from weeds
Check for blossom diseases on established trees	Mulch and fertilize
Protect plants from snails and slugs	Mulch bulbs with compost and use liquid fertilize regularly • Give plants plenty of room to grow
Liquid fertilize as weather warms up and plants emerge or grow	Keep soil evenly moist over summer
Plant fresh bulbs	Provide adequate water while foliage is growing; reduce watering once foliage has died down
—	—
Sprinkle blood and bone fertilizer over bulbs as they die down	Dormancy
Main flowering period	Cut off flower stems after flowering • Collect seed for autumn sowing • Destroy surplus bulbs if growing close to areas of native vegetation
Flowering continues	Leave bulbs in ground to die off • Mulch with compost
Main flowering period begins • Water bulbs well during the growing and flowering season	Water bulbs well during the growing and flowering season
Pick flowers regularly for indoor decoration	Pick flowers regularly for indoor decoration
Divide clumps of *A. moly*	Give summer-flowering species adequate water

PLANT	EARLY SPRING
***BULBS, CORMS, AND TUBERS** (cont.)*	
Fritillaria	Flowering in cold climates
Gladiolus	Plant bulbs in cool climates • Add compost and lightly apply blood and bone fertilizer • Discard insect-damaged bulbs
Lilium	Avoid overwatering as bulbs may rot • Mulch soil with compost and water infrequently • Apply a liquid fertilizer once growth starts
Narcissus	*N. bulbocodium* in flower • Pick flower stems just before they open
Tulipa	Save seed of species tulips for sowing
CACTI AND SUCCULENTS	Sow seed or take cuttings • In garden, build up soil to allow good drainage; add sand, gravel, and slow-release fertilizer
HERBS	Lightly apply dolomite/lime and/or dig in compost and fertilize with complete or slow-release fertilizer • Prune dead wood • Sow seed of annuals in seed-raising mix
CLIMBERS AND CREEPERS	
Warm-temperate to cool-temperate	Prepare evergreen climbers; planting position as for late autumn • Spring climbers in flower • Cut back frost-damaged shoots and leaves on tender plants

Mid-Spring	Late Spring
Flowering	Lift bulbs from areas with high summer rain or bulbs may rot • Store in cool dry place
Gladiolus hybrids flowering in warm climates • *G. tristis* in flower	Thrips may cause silver streaks on leaves and deformed flowers • Spray with an insecticide • Stake flowering stems in windy sites
Protect flower stems from snail damage • Stake tall flower stems	*L.,* Longiflorum Hybrids in flower • Cucumber mosaic virus may cause reflexing and streaking of leaves; destroy affected plants immediately before virus spreads
Main flowering period for hybrids	Liquid fertilize as bulbs die down • Tie up untidy foliage • Divide bulbs every 2 to 3 years • Reduce watering
Spray any aphid infestation with an insecticide • Spray tulip fire botrytis with a fungicide • Do not water tulip plants from overhead • Practice crop rotation	Remove spent flowers and let bulbs die down naturally • Lift bulbs and store in cool dry place
Divide established clumps and repot or replant • Give weak solution of liquid fertilizer	Cut off old flowering stems • Watch for snails—they enjoy the fleshy leaves
Plant out established plants in pots • Harvest young fresh leaves • Apply a weak solution of liquid fertilizer	Tip prune plants regularly to ensure compact growth
Plant evergreen climbers • Prune established climbers after flowering • Side dress with blood and bone • Sow fresh climber seed in seed-raising mix	Tie new growth into growing position • Spray aphids with pyrethrum • Take half-hardened cuttings from vigorous plants • Strike in coarse sand/peat mix 3:1

PLANT	EARLY SPRING
***CLIMBERS AND CREEPERS** (cont.)*	
Tropical to subtropical	Sow fresh seed in seed-raising mix • Prune summer–autumn-flowering climbers • Apply blood and bone or complete fertilizer
ORCHIDS	Repot overcrowded specimens • Trim dead or damaged roots from plants if repotting
FERNS, PALMS, AND CYCADS	
Ferns	Prepare planting site with plenty of compost and leaf litter • Use slow-release fertilizer at planting time
Palms and cycads	Mulch well • Fertilize

MID-SPRING	LATE SPRING
Dig plenty of compost and a complete fertilizer into soil • Ensure strong support for holding growth • Tip prune regularly	Take half-hardened cuttings from vigorous young plants • Train climbers where you want them to grow • Tie up with soft material
Water regularly during growing period • Fertilize regularly • Divide established plants	Apply extra leaf mold and well-rotted cow manure on garden specimens
Propagate spores from mature fronds under moist conditions • Side dress establshed plants with blood and bone • Divide established ferns with rhizomes	Remove dead fronds • Cut them up and use as mulch around ferns • Lightly apply liquid fertilizer
Collect fresh seed when ripe and sow • For successful germination, high temperatures and high humidity are required	Mulch well and apply nitrogenous fertilizer • Dig in plenty of compost and a slow-release fertilizer when planting new palms

CULTIVATION GUIDELINES

PLANT	ORIGIN	LIGHT	SOIL PREPARATION
TREES			
Evergreen	Subtropical to cool-temperate	Sun to part-shade	Well-drained, humus-rich, fertile soil
Deciduous, taller than 35 ft (10 m)	Temperate	Sun to part-shade	Well-drained, humus-rich, fertile soil
Deciduous, 35 ft (10 m) or shorter	Temperate	Sun to part-shade	Well-drained, humus-rich, fertile soil
Conifers	Temperate	Sun	Well-drained humus-rich soil
Ornamental, blossom and/or fruit	Temperate	Sun	Well-drained, humus-rich, deep soil
Tropical and subtropical	Tropical to subtropical	Sun to part-shade	Well-drained, humus-rich, fertile soil
Eucalyptus	Warm-temperate to cool-temperate	Sun	Well-drained, humus-rich, fertile to average soil
SHRUBS			
Low-growing, frost-hardy, evergreen	Warm-temperate to cool-temperate	Sun or part-shade	Well-drained humus-rich soil, pH adjustment likely
Low-growing, frost-hardy, deciduous	Cool-temperate	Sun or part-shade	Well-drained, fertile, humus-rich soil
Medium- to tall-growing, frost-hardy, evergreen	Warm-temperate to cool-temperate	Sun, part-shade, or shade	Well-drained, fertile, humus-rich soil

MAINTENANCE	PLANT PROTECTION	PROPAGATION
Regular pruning when young to shape • Mulch • Fertilize on drip line	Seasonal insect pests, root rot diseases on poorly drained soils	Seed, cuttings, grafting
Regular pruning when young to shape • Mulch • Fertilize on drip line	Seasonal insect pests, root rot diseases on poorly drained soils	Seed, cuttings, grafting
Regular pruning when young to shape • Mulch • Fertilize on drip line	Seasonal insect pests, root rot diseases on poorly drained soils	Seed, cuttings, grafting
Prune to shape if necessary • Mulch • Fertilizer	Thrips, two-spotted mites, beetles	Seed, cuttings, grafting
Prune after flowering to shape • Mulch • Fertilizer	Shot hole, rust, leaf curl, pear and cherry slugs, aphids	Cuttings, grafting
Regular pruning when young to shape • Mulch • Fertilize on drip line	Seasonal insect pests, root rot diseases on poorly drained soils	Seed, cuttings
Prune to shape when young • Gum-leaf mulch	Various insect pests, root rot diseases	Seed
Mulch regularly • Prune regularly • Some protection for young specimens in very cold conditions	Occasional insect damage; less in fertile well-drained soils	Seed, cuttings, layering
Mulch regularly • Prune regularly	Occasional insect damage; less in fertile soils	Seed, cuttings
Mulch regularly • Prune regularly • Some are able to withstand dry periods	Occasional insect damage; less in fertile soils	Seed, cuttings

PLANT	ORIGIN	LIGHT	SOIL PREPARATION
***SHRUBS** (cont.)*			
Medium- to tall-growing, frost-tender, evergreen	Subtropical to warm-temperate	Sun or part-shade	Average, fertile, humus-rich soil
Medium- to tall-growing, frost-hardy, deciduous	Temperate	Sun or part-shade	Compost • Complete fertilizer • Well-drained soil
Banksia	Cool-temperate to warm-temperate	Sun or part-shade	Well-drained soil, low pH
Buddleja	Temperate	Sun	Average soil
Callistemon	Temperate	Sun	Compost • Complete fertilizer • Moisture-retaining soil
Camellia	Temperate	Sun or part-shade	Moist, well-drained, humus-rich soil
Cistus	Warm-temperate	Sun	Well-drained light soil
Erica	Temperate	Sun	Acid well-drained soil
Fuchsia	Temperate	Part-shade	Moist, well-drained, humus-rich soil
Gardenia	Warm-temperate	Sun or part-shade	Moist, well-drained, humus-rich soil, acid pH
Grevillea	Warm-temperate to subtropical	Sun	Acid well-drained soil, low pH
Hebe	Temperate	Sun	Average soil

MAINTENANCE	PLANT PROTECTION	PROPAGATION
Prune to shape or after flowering • Mulch	Occasional insect damage; less in fertile well-drained soils	Seed, cuttings
Prune regularly • Mulch	Occasional pest damage; less in fertile soils	Cuttings, grafting
Fertilize with low-phosphorus fertilizer • Leaf mulch	Phytophthora root rot	Seed
Prune	Few problems	Cuttings
Prune after flowering	Sawflies, tip bugs, thrips, borers	Seed, cuttings
Provide shelter from weather extremes • Debud	Scale insects, mites	Cuttings
Prune after flowering	Few problems	Cuttings
Prune after flowering	Few problems	Cuttings
Protect from strong winds	Thrips, mites, mealy bugs	Cuttings
Prune and fertilize regularly • Correct iron or magnesium deficiency	Mealy bugs, scale insects, nematodes	Cuttings
Tip prune	Borer, caterpillars, plant bugs	Cuttings
Prune regularly	Scale insects, leaf miners, downy mildew	Cuttings

PLANT	ORIGIN	LIGHT	SOIL PREPARATION
SHRUBS *(cont.)*			
Hibiscus	Warm-temperate to subtropical	Sun	Well-drained fertile soil
Hydrangea	Temperate	Part-shade	Cool, moist, humus-rich soil
Lavandula	Temperate	Sun	Well-drained fertile soil
Nerium	Warm-temperate	Sun	Average soil
Philadelphus	Temperate	Sun or part-shade	Moist humus-rich soil
Rhododendron	Temperate	Sun, part-shade, or shade	Well-drained humus-rich soil, acid pH
Rosa	Temperate	Sun	Well-drained, organic, humus-rich soil
Spiraea	Temperate	Sun	Average soil
Syringa	Cool-temperate	Sun	Alkaline, rich, cool soil
Viburnum	Temperate	Sun or part-shade	Fertile humus-rich soil
ANNUALS AND PERENNIALS			
Annuals, low-growing, summer–autumn-flowering	Warm to cool-temperate	Sun or part-shade in all districts	Light application of dolomite/lime and/or add compost and fertilizer

MAINTENANCE	PLANT PROTECTION	PROPAGATION
Prune regularly	Aphids, scale insects, mealy bugs, hibiscus beetles, collar rot	Cuttings
Prune regularly	Mildew, two-spotted mites	Cuttings
Tip prune regularly	Few problems	Cuttings
Prune after flowering	Scale insects	Cuttings
Prune hard after spring flowering	Few problems	Cuttings
Water regularly • Mulch	Two-spotted mites, lace bugs, thrips, caterpillars, leaf miners, petal blight, mildew	Layering, cuttings
Water regularly • Lightly apply fertilizer • Remove dead or unproductive branches • Mulch with straw or old animal manure • Allow good air circulation	Thrips, aphids, scale insects, mildew, rust, blackspot, caterpillars	Buds, cuttings
Prune straggly growth to shape	Few problems	Cuttings
Remove sucker growth	Keep under cool conditions	Graft on *Privet* rootstock
Prune after flowering	Two-spotted mites, thrips	Cuttings
Water by trickle irrigation • Tip prune to encourage compact habit • Liquid fertilize to prolong flowering	Snails, slugs, mildew, nematodes, aphids, white flies	Seed, seedlings

PLANT	ORIGIN	LIGHT	SOIL PREPARATION
***ANNUALS AND PERENNIALS** (cont.)*			
Annuals, low-growing, spring–summer-flowering	Temperate	Sun; part-shade in hot districts	Dolomite/lime and/or compost and fertilizer
Annuals, medium-growing, summer-flowering	Cool to warm-temperate	Sun or part-shade	Light application of dolomite/lime and/or compost and fertilizer
Annuals, medium-growing, spring–summer-flowering	Cool-temperate to warm-temperate	Sun; part-shade in hot districts	Light application of dolomite/lime and/or compost and fertilizer
Annuals, tall-growing, spring–summer-flowering	Temperate	Sun; part-shade in hot districts	Light application of dolomite/lime and/or compost and fertilizer
Annuals, tall-growing, summer-flowering	Cool-temperate to warm-temperate	Sun or part-shade in all districts	Light application of dolomite/lime and/or compost and fertilizer
Perennials, spring–early summer-flowering	Temperate	Sun	Compost • Fertilizer • Drainage material
Perennials, spring–early summer-flowering, short-lived	Warm-temperate	Part-shade	Compost • Fertilizer • Sharp sand or grit for drainage
Perennials, summer-flowering, sun	Temperate	Sun; part-shade in hot districts	Dolomite/lime and/or compost and complete fertilizer • Well-drained soil
Perennials, summer-flowering, shade to part-shade	Cool-temperate	Part-shade to shade in all districts	Moist humus-rich soil
Perennials, winter–early summer-flowering	Temperate	Part-shade to shade	Moist humus-rich soil

MAINTENANCE	PLANT PROTECTION	PROPAGATION
Pick flowers to encourage more blooms • Liquid fertilize regularly • Mulch	Aphids, caterpillars, snails, slugs, damping off, leaf spot, root rot	Seed, seedlings
Pick flowers to encourage continuous blooming • Liquid fertilize regularly • Mulch	Snails, mildew, caterpillars, aphids	Seed, seedlings
Shelter from strong winds • Pick flowers regularly to encourage continuous flowering • Liquid fertilize regularly • Mulch	Rust, aphids, snails, mites, budworms, leaf miners	Seed, seedlings
Provide tripods if necessary or stakes • Remove spent flowers • Liquid fertilize at regular intervals • Mulch	Rust, mildew, aphids, snails, two-spotted mites	Seed, seedlings
Provide tripods if necessary • Shelter from wind • Remove spent flowers • Liquid fertilize regularly • Mulch	Mildew, aphids, leaf-eating insects, snails, cutworms, leaf spot	Seed, seedlings
Remove spent flowers	Few problems	Division, seed, cuttings
Remove plants after several seasons or allow to self-seed	Root rot diseases	Cuttings, seed, root cuttings
Stake tall-flowering plants • Deadhead old flowers	Snails, slugs, few problems	Division, seed, root cuttings, stem cuttings
Divide every few years	Snails, slugs	Division, seed, stem cuttings
Divide every few years	Snails, slugs, wilt disease	Division, seed, root cuttings

PLANT	ORIGIN	LIGHT	SOIL PREPARATION
ANNUALS AND PERENNIALS *(cont.)*			
Perennials, summer–autumn-flowering	Temperate	Sun or part-shade	Compost • Fertilizer
Perennials, ground covers and rock plants, mild climate	Cool-temperate to warm-temperate	Sun	Tolerant of average well-drained soil conditions
Perennials, alpines, ground covers, and rock plants, cool climate	Cold-temperate	Sun or part-shade	Use a quality garden loam that has a little compost and sharp sand in a 3:2:1 ratio • Fertilizer
Perennials, subshrubs, sun	Cool-temperate to warm-temperate	Sun	Average garden soil is suitable if it is enriched with compost and a complete fertilizer
Perennials, subshrubs, shade to part-shade	Temperate	Part-shade to shade	Humus-rich, cool, moist soil
Perennials, for tropical effect	Tropical to subtropical	Sun or part-shade	Moist humus-rich soil
Perennials, irises	Cool-temperate	Sun, part-shade, or shade	Soil requirements as specified in genus entry
Perennials, pelargoniums	Warm-temperate	Sun or part-shade	Average garden soil is suitable if it is enriched with compost and a complete fertilizer
Perennials, primulas	Temperate	Part-shade	Moisture-retaining humus-rich soil

MAINTENANCE	PLANT PROTECTION	PROPAGATION
Remove spent flowers • Divide every few years	Snails, slugs, few problems	Division, seed, root cuttings
Prune overgrown plants	Few problems	Cuttings, division
Winter protection from wet	Few problems	Seed, cuttings
Remove spent flowers • Prune to shape	Few problems	Cuttings, seed
Cut back overgrown plants	Mildew, root rot	Division, cuttings
Remove spent flower stems	Stem borers, snails	Division, cuttings, seed
Remove spent flowers • Divide when overcrowded	Mosaic virus, rust, collar rot	Division in autumn to spring, seed in autumn
Regular pruning	Caterpillars, rust, stem rot	Cuttings, seed
Frequent liquid fertilizer • Cool site required • Mulch	Snails, mold, mites	Division, seed, root cuttings for some species

Plant	Origin	Light	Soil Preparation
GRASSES, SEDGES, AND BAMBOOS			
Lawns and ground covers	Warm-temperate to cool-temperate	Sun or part-shade	Drainage material • Fine tilth; even surface
Ornamental grasses, sedges, and bamboos	Cool-temperate to warm-temperate	Sun to part-shade	Dry to poorly drained soil plus compost, depending on species
FRUIT TREES, NUT TREES, AND OTHER FRUITS			
Tropical to subtropical	Tropical to subtropical	Full sun	Topsoil at least 24 in (60 cm) deep • Compost • Fertilizer
Cool-temperate and warm-temperate	Temperate	Sun	Well-drained humus-rich soil
Citrus	Warm-temperate to cool-temperate	Sun	Humus-rich well-drained soil
Prunus	Warm-temperate to cool-temperate	Sun	Humus-rich well-drained soil
BULBS, CORMS, AND TUBERS			
Summer-flowering, sun	Warm-temperate to cool-temperate	Sun or part-shade	Rich, organic, well-drained soil
Summer-flowering, part-shade	Cool-temperate	Part-shade	Cool, moist, humus-rich soil

MAINTENANCE	PLANT PROTECTION	PROPAGATION
Mowing • Fertilizing • Spraying • Rolling • Aerating	Insect and fungal diseases	Runners, seed, turf
Remove seed heads before dispersal • Restrict spread of bamboos using a barrier	Few problems	Seed, division
Training • Pruning • Fertilizing • Shelter	Seasonal pest problems, root rot diseases	Seed, cuttings, grafting
Regular pruning for maximum fruit production • Mulch • Fertilizer • Weed control • Check pollination requirements	Root rot diseases, insects, various bacteria canker	Grafting, budding, cuttings
Regular fertilizer • Mulch • Prune	Scale insects, leaf miners, aphids, caterpillars	Grafting, *trifoliata* or *citronelle* root stocks
Correct pruning for maximum fruit production • Check pollination requirements • Weed control • Mulch	Leaf curl, silver leaf, brown rot, rust, bacterial canker, various insects	Grafting
Provide adequate water during growing season • Protect plants with loose straw in frosty areas	Few problems	Seed, division, offsets
Mulch with compost once or twice a year	Few problems	Seed, division

PLANT	ORIGIN	LIGHT	SOIL PREPARATION
***BULBS, CORMS, AND TUBERS** (cont.)*			
Autumn-flowering	Temperate	Sun or part-shade	Well-drained humus-rich soil • Add compost, fertilizer, or bulb food
Winter-flowering	Temperate	Sun or part-shade	Humus-rich soil with compost
Winter–spring-flowering	Cool-temperate	Sun or part-shade in warm districts	Prepare soil with compost and complete fertilizer • Soil should be well-drained
Spring-flowering, sun	Warm-temperate	Sun	Average well-drained soil • Add compost before planting and complete fertilizer or bulb food
Spring-flowering, shade to part-shade	Temperate to cool-temperate	Part-shade to shade	Moist humus-rich soil • Add compost and complete fertilizer or bulb food
Spring–summer-flowering, sun	Warm-temperate to cool-temperate	Sun or part-shade in all districts	Average well-drained soil enriched with compost or bulb food
Spring–summer-flowering, shade	Temperate	Sun, but most prefer cool shade	Well-drained fertile soil enriched with compost and bulb food
Allium	Temperate	Sun	Well-drained fertile soil
Fritillaria	Cold-temperate	Sun or part-shade	Lime/dolomite • Deep, rich, well-drained soil
Gladiolus	Warm-temperate	Sun	Well-drained, light, sandy loam

MAINTENANCE	PLANT PROTECTION	PROPAGATION
Leave to naturalize or lift and store when dormant	Aphids, snails, bacterial rot	Seed, division
Leave to naturalize	Few problems	Division
Remove spent flowers • Lift and divide every 3 to 5 years	Snails	Seed in autumn, or offsets; divide clumps
Keep moist during growing season; dry off in summer • Protect with loose straw in frosty areas	Few problems	Seed, division, offsets
Annual compost	Few problems	Seed, division
Protect bulbs with straw in frosty areas • Lift and store in areas with wet humid summers	Few problems	Seed, offsets
Naturalize or replant each year • Protect bulbs with loose straw in frosty areas	Few problems	Seed, bulbs, tuber-claw
Remove spent flowers	Few problems	Seed, division
Summer moisture	Bulb rot	Seed, offsets
Lift and divide every few years	Thrips	Corms, cormlets

PLANT	ORIGIN	LIGHT	SOIL PREPARATION
BULBS, CORMS, AND TUBERS *(cont.)*			
Lilium	Temperate	Sun or, preferably, part-shade	Well-drained fertile soil; neutral pH
Narcissus	Temperate	Sun or part-shade	Well-drained soil • Dolomite/lime and/or compost and low-nitrogen fertilizer
Tulipa	Temperate	Sun	Well-drained • Lightly apply dolomite/lime and/or add compost and blood and bone fertilizer • Add coarse sand in heavy soils
CACTI AND SUCCULENTS	Tropical to subtropical	Sun or part-shade	Light gritty soil • Sharp drainage essential
HERBS	Warm-temperate to cool-temperate	Sun or part-shade	Dolomite/lime and/or compost and fertilizer
CLIMBERS AND CREEPERS			
Warm-temperate to cool-temperate	Warm-temperate to cool-temperate	Sun or part-shade	Compost • Complete fertilizer
Tropical to subtropical	Tropical to subtropical	Sun or part-shade	Compost • Complete fertilizer
ORCHIDS	Tropical to subtropical, temperate	Part-shade	Open free-draining soil containing bark/leaf litter/charcoal/peatmoss mixture for epiphytes and terrestrials

Maintenance	Plant Protection	Propagation
Minimal disturbance of established plants • Mulch in spring/summer • Allow stems to die down before removal	Bulb rot, cucumber mosaic virus	Seed, offsets, bulb scales
Provide shelter from strong winds • Lift and divide in warm climates	Bulb rot, aphids	Offsets
Disease control in spring	Tulip fire botrytis, mosaic virus, aphids	Seed, division
Water during flowering, then rest	Root rot diseases, mealy bugs, scale insects, aphids	Seed, cuttings
Tip prune regularly • Harvest spring and summer	Few problems	Cuttings, seed, division
Regular pruning • Mulch	Few problems	Seed, cuttings
Regular pruning • Mulch	Few problems	Seed, cuttings
Regular fertilizer when not in flower • Maintain high humidity where appropriate • Good air circulation	Aphids, scale insects, mealy bugs, beetles, bulb rot	Seed, seedlings, division

PLANT	ORIGIN	LIGHT	SOIL PREPARATION
FERNS, PALMS, AND CYCADS			
Ferns	Subtropical to cool-temperate	Sun or part-shade	Well-drained, humus-rich, moist soil
Palms and cycads	Tropical to warm-temperate	Sun or part-shade	Compost • Humus-rich, moist, well-drained soil • Complete or slow-release fertilizer
INDOOR PLANTS			
Indoor flowering and foliage plants	Subtropical to warm-temperate	Good light to part-shade	Humus-rich soil

MAINTENANCE	PLANT PROTECTION	PROPAGATION
Cut back old fronds • Leaf litter mulch • Regular application of weak solution of liquid fertilizer	Aphids, mealy bugs, scale insects, snails, staghorns, fern beetles	Spores, cuttings, division
Some wind protection when young • Nitrogenous fertilizer • Mulch • Prune old fronds	Mealy bugs, mites, palm dart caterpillars, scale insects, grasshoppers	Seed
Keep soil evenly moist • Dry in winter • Warm conditions • Remove dead flowers/foliage	Mealy bugs, mites, scale insects	Seed, cuttings

INDEX TO PLANTS

Bold page numbers indicate genus entry. *Italicized* page numbers indicate reference in caption. Plain page numbers indicate reference in text, table, or keys.

A

D

E

F

G

H

I

Photography

Chris Bell, Rob Blakers, Lorraine Blyth, Ken Brass, Geoff Bryant, Derek Butcher, Claver Carroll, Leigh Clapp, Grant Dixon, e-garden Ltd, Katie Fallows, Richard Francis, Gil Hanly, Bill Grant, Denise Greig, Barry Grossman, Ivy Hansen, Dennis Harding, Jack Hobbs, Neil Holmes, Paul Huntley, Richard I'Anson, David Keith Jones, Ionas Kaltenbach, Willie Kempen, Robert M. Knight, Carol Knoll, Albert Kuhnigk, Mike Langford, Gary Lewis, Geoff Longford, Stirling Macoboy, John McCann, David McGonigal, Richard McKenna, Ron Moon, Eberhard Morell, Connall Oosterbrock, Larry Pitt, Craig Potton, Janet Price, Geof Prigge, Nick Rains, Howard Rice, Jamie Robertson, Tony Rodd, Rolf Ulrich Roesler, Don Skirrow, Raoul Slater, Peter Solness, Ken Stepnell, Oliver Strewe, J. Peter Thoeming, David Titmuss, Wayne Turville, Sharyn Vanderhorst, Vic Widman, Brent Wilson, Grant Young, James Young

Produced by Global Book Publishing Pty Ltd
1/181 High Street, Willoughby, NSW Australia 2068
Phone 61 2 9967 3100   Fax 61 2 9967 5891
Email rightsmanager@globalpub.com.au

Photographers

Global Book Publishing would be pleased to hear from photographers interested in supplying photographs.